List of Chapt[...]

M000218331

DB2 for z/OS and OS/390 Developme[...]

DB2 for z/OS and OS/390 Development for Performance Volume 2

Acknowledgments

This book has over 15,000 contributors since 1984 from attendees of seminars and courses upon which it is based.

Special gratitude goes to the leading professionals in the world of DB2 who graciously reviewed and significantly contributed to some or all chapters of the book.

- **Lou Agosta, Ph.D.,** Independent Consultant, North Sheridan Rd 8C, Chicago, IL 60660, phone: 773-784-7978, email: lagosta@ibm.net
- **Peter Backlund,** DB2 Consultant, Sweden, email: pbacklu@ibm.net
- **Marilyn Bohl,** VP Engineering, Work Process Systems, Inc., email: marilyn_bohl@hotmail.com
- **Richard Bolesta,** PLATINUM technology, inc., bolesta@platinum.com
- **Willie Favero,** BMC Software, Inc., wfavero@ibm.net
- **Michael Hannan,** DB2 Applications Design, SQL & Performance Tuning Specialist, Melbourne, Australia, phone: + 66 419 356 145, email: mhannan@C031.aone.net.au
- **Frank J. Ingrassia,** I M S I, 4720 Little John Trail, Sarasota, FL, 34232 USA, phone: 941-371-1930, email: FrankJIngrassia@prodigy.net
- **Robert W. Lyle**
- **Blaine Lucyk,** DB2 Specialist, 43 Compton Road, Regina, SK, Canada S4S 2Y2, phone: 306-761-0164, email: blucyk@stones.com
- **Jaydeep Ghosh,** Progressive Insurance, phone: 330-920-9397 email: bluish99@hotmail.com

The review process requires a great deal of work. The reviewers took their valuable time from their busy schedule to provide outstanding comments that have been incorporated in the book. The book is greatly improved as a result of the excellent input of these reviewers. It is the reader that benefits the most from their dedication to DB2 and contributing their knowledge to the book.

This book is dedicated to Fleurette Ann Wiorkowski, the greatest achievement of my life, and to John J. Wiorkowski and Iva Ann Johnson who made me what I am.

Gabrielle & Associates   Web site: http://www.GabrielleDB2.com
9922 Lincolnshire Court   Email: Gabrielle@GabrielleDB2.com
Rockwall, TX 75087   Telephone: 972-412-8866
USA   FAX: 972-412-8867

PREFACE

DB2 for z/OS and OS/390 Development for Performance in its fourth edition includes the features and facilities of V7 integrated into the book. It is the oldest and newest book on DB2. It is the oldest in that the original material was developed during ESP of V1.1 in 1983 and rewritten in each of the author's previous six books. It is the newest in that it is constantly updated for each release/version (plus current PTFs and APARs), has incorporated the input of over 16,000 course attendees in 27 countries on 6 continents, and has grown with DB2 to 1,417 pages. This edition even has V7, V6, or V5 APAR number noted with the first occurrence of a feature specific to the version or APAR. In addition, the index has an entry for each item as generated by a word processor so you can easily find features of V7, V6, and V5 APARs. The web site http://techsupport.services.ibm.com/server/390.CAPARdb provides for locating a detailed description of an APAR by key word or APAR ID.

The book is organized to follow the life cycle of an application system, beginning with the creation of objects and the design of indexes to lay the foundation for high performing systems. Programmer/analyst must develop high performing SQL to process data efficiently and have the knowledge base to tune SQL when required to meet response time requirements with minimal I/O and CPU time usage to minimize costs. The book concludes with the use of the new utilities for efficient maintenance of the data.

It provides indepth coverage of the design and development of application systems for performance using DB2. Many examples of high performing SQL are given including actual timings to indicate the order of magnitude improvements that can be achieved by following the guidelines discussed. Alternatives are presented and discussed along with the pros and cons so that you can make the proper decisions for your application system. The author provides many practical examples, hints, tips, and guidelines for the design and development of application systems.

This book is an excellent resource for experienced DB2 professionals and provides a concise and easy-to-read guide for those new to DB2. The following list of chapters give you an idea of the content.

Table of Contents

Concepts and Components

Creating Stogroups, Databases, & Buffer Pools

Creating Tablespaces

Creating Tables and Views

Index Usage for Performance

Index Design for Performance

The Basics of SQL Data Manipulation

Concurrency Control

Program Development

Batch Processing

Triggering Actions in DB2

Stored Procedures

User Defined Functions

Program Preparation and Execution

Join Performance

Subselects and Nested Table Expressions

Parallel Processing

Programming for Performance

The Optimizer

Explain the Access Path Chosen by the Optimizer

Load and Check Data Utilities

Runstats and Reorganization

Copy, Quiesce, Report, Recover, & Rebuild

INDEX

Concepts and Components

CO.1 INTRODUCTION

DB2 is based on the relational model which was invented and first published by Dr. E. F. Codd in 1970. Prior to Dr. Codd's invention at IBM, database management systems (DBMS) had no theoretical foundation. Rather, they were developed heuristically as needed. For example, hierarchical DBMS are based on bill of material processing to meet the requirements of the space program for building spacecraft. Network DBMS are based on a model for communications networks.

The invention of the relational model started a great deal of research into DBMS, both in the academic world and in industry. Thousands of articles were published on the relational model and how it can be used in industry during the 1970s, 1980s, and 1990s. Chris Date gives comprehensive coverage of the relational model, System R, and DB2 in several of his many books. System R was the first major prototype developed during 1974 to 1979. Portions of the prototype were used in the DB2 and SQL/DS products. IBM researchers turned their attention to R* research during 1980 to 1982 which grew into distributed capability among multiple DB2 subsystems on mainframes. The next step that Starburst research dealt with distributed capability for DBMS on mainframes, work stations and personal computers (PCs). Research into extensions for DB2 continues at the IBM Database Technology Institute.

DB2 was first announced as a product by IBM in June of 1983. There have been numerous versions and releases since the original announcement as summarized below. More are expected in the future:

- ◆   V1.1   June 1983
- ◆   V1.2   Feb. 1986
- ◆   V1.3   May 1987
- ◆   V2.1   April 1988
- ◆   V2.2   October 1988
- ◆   V2.3   September 1990
- ◆   V3.1   March 1993

◆   V4.1   September 1994
◆   V5.1   April 1996
◆   V6.1   May 1998
◆   V7.1   April 2000

The DB2 for z/OS and OS/390 home page on the World Wide Web (WWW) provides for the latest information, useful software that can be downloaded at no cost, and access to the DB2 manuals. The address is http://www.software.ibm.com/data/db2/os390/.

CO.2 DB2 USAGE ARCHITECTURE

All usage of data in DB2 is through the structured query language (SQL).

SQL consists of data definition, data manipulation, and data control components as shown in Figure CO.1. We will briefly describe each of these components in this section and indicate where details on the components can be found in the book.

Figure CO.1. DB2 usage architecture

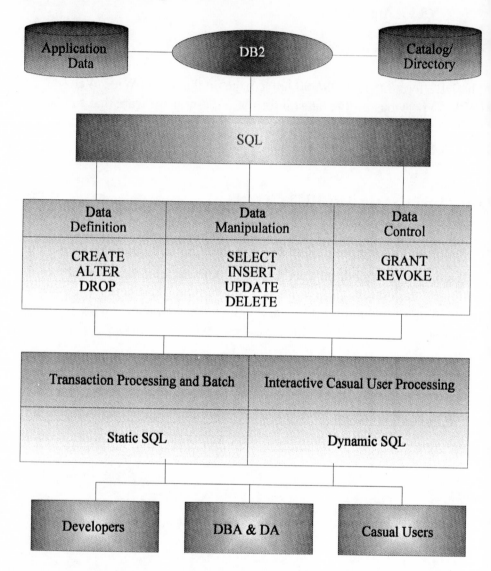

SQL Data Definition

The data definition language (DDL) component of SQL provides for creating, altering, and dropping objects including storage groups, databases, tablespaces, tables, indexes, views, aliases, and synonyms as discussed in Chapters CD, TS, CT, and ID. DB2 automatically records information about objects that you create and alter in one or more catalog tables. When objects are dropped, DB2 deletes the rows describing the objects. The three basic data definition statements are CREATE, ALTER, and DROP.

A storage group consisting of one or more DASD devices to house tables and indexes is one of the first objects to be created. If a storage group is not created before creating a table, a tablespace is automatically created in the default SYSDEFLT storage group in the default DSNDB04 database. You will want to create a storage group, database, and tablespace before creating a table rather than taking the defaults in most cases.

Most parameters that are specified to control the creation of objects can be changed with the ALTER statements. The DROP statement provides for deleting objects that have been created and removing their definitions from the catalog tables.

SQL Data Manipulation

The data manipulation language (DML) component of SQL provides for selecting, inserting, updating, and deleting rows of a table. Typically when a person uses the term *SQL* they are referring to the DML portion of the language.

The four basic data manipulation statements are SELECT, INSERT, UPDATE, and DELETE. The SELECT statement provides for retrieving one or more rows from one or more tables. The INSERT statement provides for inserting one row into one table. An INSERT with a subselect allows for INSERTING many rows into a table as selected from another table. An UPDATE statement provides for changing one or more columns in one or more rows of a table. The DELETE statement provides for deleting one or more rows from a table. The use of these statements is described in Chapters SL and PD. Developing and tuning SQL statements for performance are discussed in Chapters JP, ST, PP and throughout the book.

DML, DDL, and DCL statements can be executed interactively or embedded in programs written in COBOL, PL/1, C, REXX, Java, FORTRAN, and Assembler. Typically, DDL and DCL statements are executed interactively. DML statements are executed interactively and embedded in host programs.

Binding SQL DML into a Plan or Package

All static SQL DML statements are bound into a plan or package. The bind process takes one or more SQL DML statements and compiles them into a usable control structure for execution. The result of the bind is an application plan or package. Static SQL means the SQL DML statements in a host program are bound into a plan or package and stored in the directory. The plan or package does not have to be bound again when executed if you are using the default bind parameters. Dynamic SQL means that bind processing is required for each SQL statement each time it is executed if you are using the default bind parameters. This is a major distinction between static and dynamic SQL DML. However, this distinction is blurred for static SQL when using reoptimization as discussed in Chapter OP and for dynamic SQL when using the dynamic cache and the KEEPDYNAMIC YES bind parameter as discussed in Chapters PD and PE. Plans, packages, and the bind process are described in Chapter PE.

SQL statements executed using SQL processing using file input (SPUFI) or an interactive product such as IBM's Query Management Facility (QMF) are executed dynamically. Most CASE tools and fourth generation languages provide the option to execute the SQL statements statically or dynamically. REXX is an interpretative language. Therefore, SQL is executed dynamically from a REXX program. The use of Open Database Connectivity (ODBC) results in the use of dynamic SQL. Some application systems products that can be purchased from software companies and application programs developed in-house at user companies use dynamic SQL in their host programs.

If objects that a plan or package depends on are dropped (an index, table, view, etc.), a primary or foreign key is added, or privileges are revoked, the plan or package is marked as invalid. An automatic rebind occurs when the plan or package is next executed. It will be successful if required objects and privileges exist. Otherwise, an error will be issued.

The Optimizer

Part of the bind process is optimization. The optimizer determines a good access path for each data manipulation statement based on statistics in the catalog tables describing the data and indexes. This avoids developers and business professionals having to know how the data is stored and navigate through the database as is required with older non-relational DBMS. Chapter OP covers the optimization process in detail. You can determine the access path chosen by the optimizer using EXPLAIN. EXPLAIN causes rows to be inserted into PLAN_TABLE describing the access path chosen to locate data as described in Chapter EX.

SQL Data Control

The data control language (DCL) component of SQL provides for granting privileges to technical and business professional that allow them to perform various operations including the definition and manipulation of objects. Privileges given using the GRANT statement can be removed using the REVOKE statement. The DB2 SQL Reference and DB2 Command Reference provides details on the privileges required for each operation.

Authorization IDs: A person is identified to DB2 using an authorization identifier (AUTHID). The primary AUTHID is required and usually is an individual's TSO user identifier (ID), CICS ID, or IMS ID. Optionally, each person can also have up to and including 245 secondary AUTHIDs that are assigned through connection or signon exits. This is usually done in conjunction with security software products like RACF, ACF2, or TOP SECRET.

Project team members can be assigned a secondary AUTHID of say POSYSTEM. Privileges can be granted to POSYSTEM rather than to each team member's primary AUTHID which eases the management of security. Composite privileges are all primary and secondary AUTHID privileges. The current SQLID is any of the composite IDs as set by the connection and signon exits or the SET statement executed interactively or from a host program. A person can set their current SQLID to POSYSTEM by executing:

```
SET CURRENT SQLID = 'POSYSTEM'
```

Authority to perform actions: No one can take any action on any DB2 object or resources until the person is granted privileges. An exception is the person who installs the DB2 subsystem. That person has install system administration (SYSADM) privileges.

Explicit and implicit privileges: Explicit privileges are granted using the DCL GRANT statement. Implicit privileges are received automatically by virtue of the person taking some action. For example, a person can explicitly be granted privileges to create a table. The person has implicit privileges to execute SQL DML, load data into the table, and explicitly grant privileges on the table to others.

Single and grouped capabilities: An individual privilege can be granted to an AUTHID to create a table or select from an existing table, for example. A grouped privilege can be granted to an AUTHID. For example, the database administration (DBADM) privilege allows a person to create tablespaces, tables, views, indexes and manipulate these objects using DML statements and control the usage of the objects by granting and revoking privileges to AUTHIDs using DCL statements. Figure CO.2 shows the individual privileges that can be granted as well as the privileges within boxes which can be granted as a group.

Figure CO.2. Single and grouped privileges

SYSADM (SYSCTRL)	DBADM	DBCTRL	DBMAINT
CREATEDBA CREATEDBC CREATSG PACKADM BIND BINDADD BINDAGENT CREATE IN STOSPACE ARCHIVE BSDS CREATE ALIAS MONITOR 1 MONITOR 2	SELECT INSERT UPDATE DELETE INDEX ALTER	DROP LOAD RECOVERDB REORG REPAIR	CREATETAB, DISPLAYDB CREATETS, STARTDB IMAGCOPY, STOPDB STATS
	SYSOPR DISPLAY RECOVER START DATABASE STOPALL TRACE		

SQLCODE and SQLSTATE

The SQLCODE and SQLSTATE provide information on the status of executing an SQL statement. These codes are reported after the execution of every SQL statement for both static and dynamic SQL. The codes are returned after the execution of SQL interactively and are returned in the SQL communications area (SQLCA) when the SQL statements are embedded in a host program as discussed in Chapter PD.

An SQLCODE of 0 means that the statement executed successfully. If the code has a value of +100, no rows qualified for the SQL statement or no more rows qualify when selecting a number of rows. A three-digit positive integer is an informative or warning message. A three-digit negative integer indicates an error condition. A brief message accompanies the SQLCODE and SQLSTATE when executing SQL interactively and some information is provided in the SQLCA for embedded SQL. More detail is available from the *Messages and Codes* manual or by calling a sample program as discussed in Chapter PD.

The SQLSTATE reports similar information as the SQLCODE. The SQLSTATE conforms to the American National Standards Institute (ANSI) standard. The same value is reported for all relational DBMS that comply with the standard. This means that programs receive the same status as to the result of executing a statement on different relational DBMS. The SQLSTATE is a five-digit character standard code with a range of '00000' to '65535'. The first two digits indicate the error class. The last three digits indicate the specific error. For example, a values of '00000' means successful execution and '02000' means that no rows qualify or no more rows qualify.

SQL99 Standard

The SQL99 standard consists of the following five volumes. They are available from the web site http://webstore.ansi.org/ at a cost of $20.00 per volume.

◆   ANSI/ISO/IEC 9075-1-1999 Information Technology - Database Language - SQL Part 1: Framework (SQL/Framework)
◆   ANSI/ISO/IEC 9075-2-1999 Information Technology - Database languages - SQL - Part 2: Foundation (SQL/Foundation)
◆   ANSI/ISO/IEC 9075-3-1999 Information Technology - Database Languages - SQL - Part 3: Call-level Interface (SQL/CLI)
◆   ANSI/ISO/IEC 9075-4-1999 Information Technology - Database languages - SQL - Part 4: Persistent Stored Modules (SQL/PSM)
◆   ANSI/ISO/IEC 9075-5-1999 Information Technology - Database Languages - SQL - Part 5: Host Language Bindings (SQL/Bindings)

Utilities

A number of utilities are provide for the management and maintenance of databases, tablespaces, tables, and indexes in DB2. Some of the utilities are part of the base product including CATMAINT, DIAGNOSE, LISTDEF, OPTIONS, QUIESCE, REPAIR, REPORT, TEMPLATE, and all standalone utilities. All DB2 utilities that operate on the catalog, directory and sample objects, require no additional products. Additional utilities can be purchased in one or more of the following products.

1. DB2 Diagnostic and Recovery Utilities (5655-E62) includes CHECK DATA, CHECK INDEX, CHECK LOB, COPY COPYTOCOPY, MERGECOPY, MODIFY STATISTICS, REBUILD INDEX, and RECOVER .

2. DB2 Operational Utilities (5655-E63) includes COPY, EXEC SQL, LOAD, REBUILD INDEX. RECOVER, REORG INDEX, REORG TABLESPACE, RUNSTATS, STOSPACE, and UNLOAD.

3. DB2 Utilities Suite (5697-E98) all products in the first two products.

Most of the utilities are covered in detail in Chapters LC, RR, and CR.

Catalog Tables

DB2 inserts rows into the catalog tables describing all objects created, including storage groups, databases, tablespaces, tables, indexes, views, aliases and synonyms. It changes the rows when the objects are altered and deletes the rows when the objects are dropped. DB2 records information about all privileges that are granted. It records information about all plans and packages that are bound. Statistics determined by the RUNSTATS and STOSPACE utilities are recorded in the catalog tables. Indeed, the execution of most of the utilities updates the catalog tables, particularly the SYSIBM.SYSCOPY table. We will see in Chapter CT how the COMMENT ON and LABEL ON statements can be used to describe tables and columns.

You can insert, update, and delete data used by the optimizer as discussed in Chapter RR and OP. The most common direct manipulation of the catalog tables is to report on information placed there by DB2. We will see a number of examples of doing this throughout the book. All catalog tables have a qualifier of SYSIBM. For example, the full name of a local catalog table is SYSIBM.SYSCOPY. Typically, the SYSIBM qualifier is not used in discussion of the catalog tables. However, it must be used when selecting from them as will be seen in the following example.

If you are given an assignment to work on the POSYSTEM and tables in the application system are created with the authorization ID of POSYSTEM, you can determine the table layout of the tables in the application system with the statement:

```
SELECT NAME, COLTYPE, LENGTH, SCALE,
       NULLS, FOREIGNKEY, COLNO
FROM   SYSIBM.SYSCOLUMNS
WHERE  TBCREATOR = 'POSYSTEM'
ORDER BY TBNAME, COLNO;
```

You may want to determine information on indexes created on the S table. This can be accomplished with the statement:

```
SELECT I.TBCREATOR, I.TBNAME, I.CREATOR,
       I.NAME, I.UNIQUERULE, I.CLUSTERING,
       K.ORDERING, K.COLNAME, K.COLSEQ,
       K.COLNO
FROM   SYSIBM.SYSKEYS    K,
       SYSIBM.SYSINDEXES I
WHERE  I.TBCREATOR = 'POSYSTEM'
AND    I.TBNAME    = 'S'
AND    I.CREATOR   = K.IXCREATOR
AND    I.NAME      = K.IXNAME
ORDER BY I.NAME, K.COLSEQ;
```

Control Center

The Control Center provides a graphical user interface for the management of DB2 for z/OS and OS/390 objects from a PC/workstation. One of the many options available is to get information from the catalog table as indicated by the arrow in Figure CO.3. The Control Center itself runs on DB2 for non-z/OS and OS/390 platforms which includes DB2 Connect for the PC/workstation. There are several prerequisites that must be installed to allow for the use of the Control Center including the enablement of stored procedures using Work Load Manager (WLM) in goal or compatibility mode. Goal or compatibility mode is acceptable whenever WLM is required in most cases.

Figure CO.3. Control Center panel

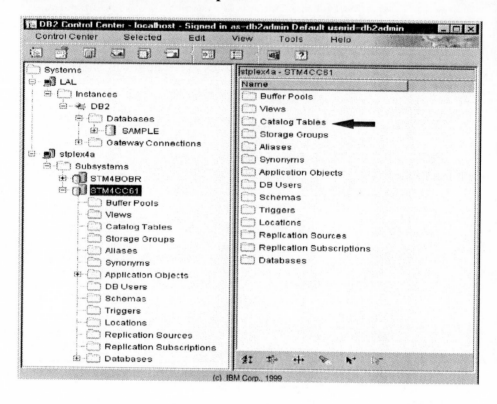

The Directory

The directory tables like the catalog tables are maintained by DB2 when you take certain actions. However, you cannot select directly from the directory tables like the catalog tables. There are methods for getting information on most of the five tables and tablespaces in the directory database DSNDB01.

1) The database descriptors DBD) describing objects in a database are maintained in the DBD01 tablespace and accessed by DB2 using a hashing algorithm. You can get information on objects in a database using the DISPLAY DATABASE command like:

```
-DISPLAY DATABASE(DASPJDB)
```

2) DB2 maintains the start and stop relative byte addresses of log records in

the SYSLGRNX table in the SYSLGRNX tablespace. (An overview of logging is in Section CO.4 and the details are in Chapter CR.) This information is used by DB2 to locate updates in the log to apply to a copy during a recovery. The information is accessed by DB2 using the DSNLLX01 and DSNLLX02 indexes. You can get information from SYSLGRNX using the REPORT utility.

3) DB2 tracks the progress and status of utilities that have been submitted but not successfully completed in the SYSUTILX tablespace. It accesses the information using the DSNLUX01 and DSNLUX02 indexes. You can get information about the progress and status of a utility by naming it in the DISPLAY UTILITY command like:

```
-DISPLAY UTILITY(RUNSPJ)
```

4) Application plans that result from a bind are stored by DB2 in the SCTR table in the SCT02 tablespace. The DSNSCT02 index is used by DB2 to locate the required plan when it is executed. Similarly, application packages that result from a bind are stored in the SPTR table in the SPT01 tablespace. The DSNSPT02 index is used to locate the required package when it is executed.

How Many Bytes?

The number of bytes of central, expanded, and DASD storage used in a computer complex has been growing by leaps and bounds since mainframes first became widely used in the 1960s. The abbreviations and the number of bytes they represent are summarized in Figure CO.4.

Figure CO.4. Number of byte units

Ab.	Desc.	Number of Bytes Base 2	Number of Bytes Base 10
KB	Kilobytes	1,024	1,000
MB	Megabytes	1,048,576	1,000,000
GB	Gigabytes	1,073,741,824	1,000,000,000
TB	Terabytes	1,099,511,627,776	1,000,000,000,000
PT	Petabytes	1,125,899,906,842,624	1,000,000,000,000,000

Ab.	Desc.	Number of Bytes Base 2	Number of Bytes Base 10
EX	Exabytes	1,152,921,504,606,847,500	1,000,000,000,000,000,000

CO.3 DB2 INTERACTIVE

DB2 interactive (DB2I) is a menu-driven tool for executing dynamic SQL using SPUFI, generating data structures from the catalog tables for inclusion in host programs, program preparation and execution of DB2 commands and utilities. These options are shown in Figure CO.5.

Figure CO.5. DB2I primary option menu

```
DSNEPRI                  DB2I PRIMARY OPTION MENU              SSID: DSN
COMMAND ===> _

Select one of the following DB2 functions and press ENTER.

 1   SPUFI              (Process SQL statements)
 2   DCLGEN             (Generate SQL and source language declarations)
 3   PROGRAM PREPARATION (Prepare a DB2 application program to run)
 4   PRECOMPILE         (Invoke DB2 precompiler)
 5   BIND/REBIND/FREE   (BIND, REBIND, or FREE plans or packages)
 6   RUN                (RUN an SQL program)
 7   DB2 COMMANDS       (Issue DB2 commands)
 8   UTILITIES          (Invoke DB2 utilities)
 D   DB2I DEFAULTS      (Set global parameters)
 X   EXIT               (Leave  DB2I)

PRESS:   END to exit                       HELP for more information
```

SQL Processing Using File Input (SPUFI)

SPUFI is useful for executing multiple SQL statements as keyed into a member of a partitioned data set (PDS) or sequential file that you have created before using SPUFI. Do replace "AUTHID.SPUFI.IN(MEMBER)" in option 1 of the SPUFI Panel as shown in Figure CO.6 with the name of a PDS that already exists and specify a member name to identify SQL statements that you want to retain. A PDS member is used to key and edit SQL statements. "AUTHID.SPUFI.OUT" in option 4 should be replaced with the name of a sequential data set into which you want the results of the execution to be written. DB2 creates this data set automatically and reuses it for each execution of SQL from a member of the "AUTHID.SPUFI.IN" PDS in the example. Options 5 through 9 are described well on the SPUFI panel. You will probably want to use the indicated defaults except for option 5 after the first execution. You can place an "N" for option 5 after you have changed the defaults that are reviewed in the next paragraph to avoid having the CURRENT SPUFI DEFAULTS panel displayed each time that you use SPUFI.

Figure CO.6. SPUFI panel

```
DSNESP01                      SPUFI                    SSID: DSN
===>
Enter the input data set name: (Can be sequential or partitioned)
  1 DATA SET NAME..... ===> 'AUTHID.SPUFI.IN(MEMBER)'
  2 VOLUME SERIAL..... ===>          (Enter if not cataloged)
  3 DATA SET PASSWORD. ===>          (Enter if password protected)

Enter the output data set name:    (Must be a sequential data set)
  4 DATA SET NAME..... ===> 'AUTHID.SPUFI.OUT'

Specify processing options:
  5 CHANGE DEFAULTS... ===> Y (Y/N - Display SPUFI defaults panel?)
  6 EDIT INPUT........ ===> Y (Y/N - Enter SQL statements?)
  7 EXECUTE........... ===> Y (Y/N - Execute SQL statements?)
  8 AUTOCOMMIT........ ===> Y (Y/N - Commit after successful run?)
  9 BROWSE OUTPUT..... ===> Y (Y/N - Browse output data set?)

For remote SQL processing:
 10 CONNECT LOCATION   ===>

PRESS: ENTER to process      END to exit      HELP for more info.
```

Most of the default values on the SPUFI defaults panel in Figure CO.7 are good. You will want to change option 1 from RR to CS to minimize lock contention as discussed in Chapter CC. Do be cautious with option 2 which allows you to specify the maximum number of lines that are returned in the output file regardless of the number that qualifies. The default value of 250 is a reasonable starting point. However, if you need to review or search the results of more than 250 lines, do increase this value.

Figure CO.7. SPUFI defaults

```
DSNESP02              CURRENT SPUFI DEFAULTS              SSID: DSN
===>
Enter the following to control your SPUFI session:
 1 SQL TERMINATOR .. ===> ;   (SQL Statement Terminator)
 2 ISOLATION LEVEL . ===> RR (RR=Repeatable Read, CS=Cursor Stability)
 3 MAX SELECT LINES  ===> 250 (Maximum number of lines to be
                                 returned from a SELECT)
Output data set characteristics:
 4 RECORD LENGTH ... ===> 4092 (LRECL= logical record length)
 5 BLOCKSIZE ....... ===> 4096 (Size of one block)
 6 RECORD FORMAT.... ===> VB (RECFM= F, FB, FBA, V, VB, or VB)
 7 DEVICE TYPE...... ===> SYSDA (Must be a DASD unit name)

Output format characteristics:
 8 MAX NUMERIC FIELD ===> 33 (Maximum width for numeric field)
 9 MAX CHAR FIELD .. ===> 80 (Maximum width for character field)
10 COLUMN HEADING .. ===> NAMES (NAMES, LABELS, ANY, or BOTH)

PRESS: ENTER to process     END to exit      HELP for more info.
```

A brief war story will demonstrate why the value specified for option 3 can be very important. A person was testing a batch update program and wanted to verify that the rows were being changed correctly. The person selected the rows from the table updated by the batch program and found that changed rows did not appear in the SPUFI output. The person spent a good deal of time trying to debug the batch program thinking that it was in error. After a good deal of time and frustration debugging a program that was working correctly, it was discovered that the real problems was that the changed rows appeared correctly beyond the first 250 rows displayed by SPUFI.

After you have made any changes to the defaults, press the ENTER key before pressing F3 to exit to ensure the changes take effect.

You are presented with an interactive system productivity facility (ISPF) panel for keying and editing SQL statements that you want to execute as indicated in Figure CO.8. If there is more than one SQL statement in the input file, each statement must be terminated with a semicolon (";"). The use of the semicolon for terminating SQL statements when using the QMF product is optional.

Figure CO.8. ISPF panel for keying and editing SQL statements

```
EDIT ----------'AUTHID.SPUFI.IN(MEMBER)'------------ COLUMNS 001 072
COMMAND INPUT ===> ;;;                              SCROLL ===> PAGE
************************* TOP OF DATA *****************************
000100 SELECT SN, PN, JN, QTY
000200 FROM    SPJ
000300 WHERE   SN = 'S4';
000400
000500 -- 2 hyphens can be used followed by comments
000600
000700 SELECT JN, JNAME, CITY
000800 FROM    J
000900 WHERE   JN = 'J2';
*********************** BOTTOM OF DATA ****************************
```

When you are ready to execute the SQL statements, key three semicolons (";;;") on the command input line, then press F3 like:

```
COMMAND INPUT ===>  ;;;
```

The three semicolon are not required. However, they do save having to pass through several panels and pressing F3 to go past the panels to get into ISPF browse mode to review the results of executing the SQL statements. You do need to press F3 with or without the three semicolons.

The SQL statements that you keyed and their results are displayed in ISPF browse mode as shown in Figure CO.9. You can return to the ISPF editor by keying three semicolons (";;;") on the command line and pressing F3. Again using the three semicolons avoids going thru intermediate panels. If you prefer to return to the SPUFI panel, simply press F3 without entering the three semicolons.

Figure CO.9. Results in browse mode

```
   Menu   Utilities  Compilers  Help

 ------------------------------------------------------------------------
 BROWSE     RDAGXW.SPUFI.OUT                    Line 00000000 Col 001 080
 ****************************** Top of Data ******************************
 ---------+---------+---------+---------+---------+---------+---------+------

 SELECT  SN, PN, JN, QTY
 FROM    SPJ
 WHERE   SN = 'S4';


 ---------+---------+---------+---------+---------+---------+---------+------
 SN      PN      JN               QTY
 ---------+---------+---------+---------+---------+---------+---------+------
 S4      P6      J3               300
 S4      P6      J7               300

 DSNE610I NUMBER OF ROWS DISPLAYED IS 2
 DSNE616I STATEMENT EXECUTION WAS SUCCESSFUL, SQLCODE IS 100
 ---------+---------+---------+---------+---------+---------+---------+------

 -- 2 hyphens can be used followed by comments

 Command ===>
 F1=Help    F3=Exit    F5=Rfind  F12=Cancel            Scroll ===> PAGE

   Menu   Utilities  Compilers  Help

 ------------------------------------------------------------------------
 BROWSE     RDAGXW.SPUFI.OUT                    Line 00000019 Col 001 080

 SELECT  JN, JNAME, CITY
 FROM    J
 WHERE   JN = 'J2';
 ---------+---------+---------+---------+---------+---------+---------+------
 JN      JNAME                    CITY
 ---------+---------+---------+---------+---------+---------+---------+------
 J2      Punch                    Rome

 DSNE610I NUMBER OF ROWS DISPLAYED IS 1
 DSNE616I STATEMENT EXECUTION WAS SUCCESSFUL, SQLCODE IS 100
 ---------+---------+---------+---------+---------+---------+---------+------
 ---------+---------+---------+---------+---------+---------+---------+------
 DSNE617I COMMIT PERFORMED, SQLCODE IS 0
 DSNE616I STATEMENT EXECUTION WAS SUCCESSFUL, SQLCODE IS 0
 ---------+---------+---------+---------+---------+---------+---------+------
 DSNE601I SQL STATEMENTS ASSUMED TO BE BETWEEN COLUMNS 1 AND 72
 DSNE620I NUMBER OF SQL STATEMENTS PROCESSED IS 2
 DSNE621I NUMBER OF INPUT RECORDS READ IS 13
 DSNE622I NUMBER OF OUTPUT RECORDS WRITTEN IS 37
 ****************************** Bottom of Data ***************************
 Command ===>                                          Scroll ===> PAGE
 F1=Help    F3=Exit    F5=Rfind  F12=Cancel
```

Schema Definition in Batch

Often DB2 objects discussed in Chapters CD, TS, and CT are created using
SPUFI. Optionally, objects can be created with a schema processor executed
in batch (cannot be executed interactively nor within a host program).

Schema definitions are provided for conformance to ISO/ANSI standards. A schema name is an option to a qualifier name for objects that require a qualifier including tables, indexes, aliases, and views as discussed in Chapters CT and ID. A schema can also include a collection of distinct types, functions, stored procedures, and triggers as discussed in Chapters CT, TR, UD, and SP. These objects can use the schema name as the qualifier or the user SQLID of the creator of the objects.

Here is an example of what can be placed in a file and used as input to the schema processor. The schema processor is executed using the batch program DSNHSP with JCL from prefix.SDSNSAMP(DSNTEJ1S). The input is read from the SYSIN data set and the output written to SYSPRINT. The schema processor sets the current SQLID to the value of the specified schema AUTHID (POSYS in the example) before executing any of the statements in the schema definition.

```
CREATE SCHEMA AUTHORIZATION POSYS;

CREATE TABLE S
   (SN      CHAR(6)  NOT NULL PRIMARY KEY,
    SNAME   CHAR(20) NOT NULL WITH DEFAULT,
    STATUS  SMALLINT NOT NULL WITH DEFAULT,
    CITY    CHAR(15) NOT NULL WITH DEFAULT);

GRANT SELECT ON S TO PUBLIC;

CREATE VIEW AMSTERDAM S AS
   SELECT SN, SNAME, STATUS, CITY
   FROM    S
   WHERE   CITY = 'Amsterdam';
```

There are some differences in processing statement using the schema processor and SPUFI. All statements are executed even if one or more statements results in a negative SQL code unlike SPUFI which terminates when the first error is encountered. All statements executed by the schema processor are rolled back and must be resubmitted for successful execution as with SPUFI. The schema processor allows for performing actions on an object that does not yet exist when statements are executed in sequence. For example, you can grant privileges on a table that is created later in the schema definition as in the previous example. This is not true for SPUFI. The creation of a table with a column defined as a PRIMARY KEY or UNIQUE results in automatic creation of a unique index. This also applies when conforming to the SQL92 standard.

Only one schema definition is accepted by the schema processor in a single job.

CO.4 DB2 SUBSYSTEM ARCHITECTURE

The DB2 subsystem consists of three required address spaces and two or more optional address spaces as shown in Figure CO.10. The three required address spaces are the Systems Services, Database Services, and Internal Resource Lock Manager address spaces. The fourth Distributed Data Facility address space is optional but highly advisable if distributed processing is required. The fifth Stored Procedure address space is optional and also highly advisable in a distributed environment. Indeed, there can be multiple stored procedure address spaces managed dynamically by the z/OS and OS/390 operating system. The maximum size of each address space, with 32 bit minus 1 parity bit, 31 bit addressing (2^{31}) prior to zSeries computers is 2 GB. zSeries computers provide for the maximum size 64 GB for each address space with 64 bit addressability minus 1 parity bit, 63 bit addressing (2^{63}).

Figure CO.10. DB2 subsystem architecture

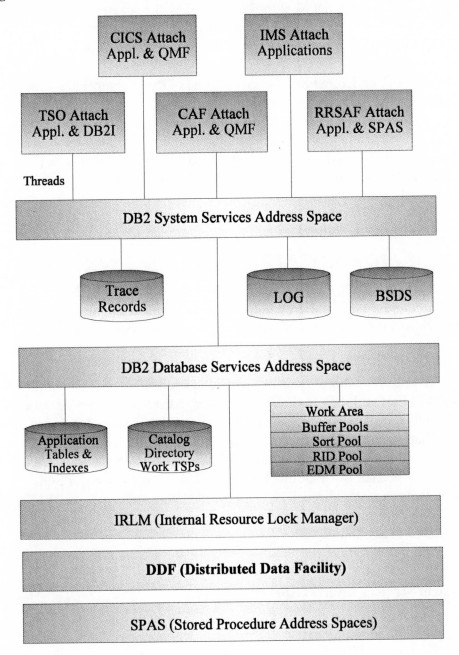

Attaches and Threads

Access to the DB2 subsystem is through the Customer Information Control

System (CICS), Information Management System (IMS), Time Sharing Option (TSO) Terminal Monitor Program (TMP), Call Attachment Facility (CAF), Recoverable Resource Manager Services Attachment Facility(RRSAF), or the DSNU attachment facility for utilities.

The System Services address space uses one of the attachment facilities to establish a thread of communication with the DB2 subsystem when the first SQL statement is executed in a plan or package. A thread is a task control block (TCB) that is used to describe an application's connection existence, trace its progress, and provides the ability to perform processing in DB2. A thread is deallocated upon completion of processing or can be canceled with the cancel thread command like:

```
-CANCEL THREAD (414)
```

The value of 414 in the example is a token used to identify the thread. It can be determined using the DISPLAY THREAD command. -CANCEL THREAD (414) NOBACKOUT (V7) avoids a rollback which can be lengthy. However, it is necessary to recover effected objects for data integrity.

Thread reuse is available when using CICS, and IMS wait for input (WFI) and IMS Fast Path (IFP). Thread reuse means that a thread can be reused by a defined transaction rather than allocating and deallocating the thread each time that a transaction is executed. This has performance advantages if the transaction is executed one or more times every 30 to 45 seconds. A savings of 5 to 20 percent of CPU time for transactions with 10 or fewer SQL statements can be realized. The work avoided with the use of and the activities performed when a thread is created, used and deallocated are described in Section CO.10.

System Services Address Space

The System Services Address Space is also known as DSN1MSTR. This address space is responsible for a number of activities in DB2. It is responsible for starting and stopping the DB2 subsystem when the START and STOP commands are executed. Indeed, it is responsible for all command processing including starting and stopping traces, starting and stopping a database, and displaying information about threads and databases.

System Services collects statistics, accounting, performance, audit, global, and monitor trace records when the appropriate trace is started. This information is available from performance monitor products which use the instrumentation facility interface to access the trace records.

Logging and Recovery Management

System Services is responsible for logging and recovery management. It writes a before and after image of all updated rows to the log buffer in central storage as shown in Figure CO.11. Each log record is assigned a relative byte address (RBA) when it is written to the log. An RBA is an offset from beginning of the log where log records can be found. It can be thought of a log record sequence number. The RBA is 6 bytes (48 bits) in length with a maximum value of 2^{48}. It is used to locate log records to be applied to an image copy during a recovery.

Figure CO.11. Logging and recovery

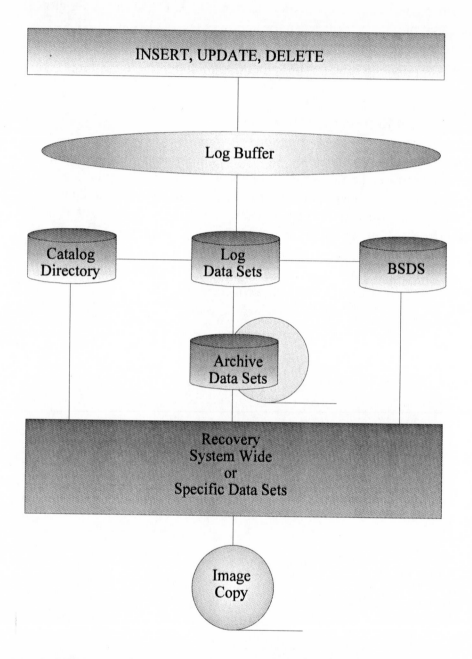

The OUTPUT BUFFER in central storage is used to log before and after images of updated data. The buffer is 4,000 KB by default (can be 40 to 400,000 KB in V6). The goal is to size the output buffer to minimize a force write of the buffer to active log. The size can be specified in DSNZPARM DSN6LOGP OUTBUFF or the DSNTIPB installation panel. You can change a copy of DSNZPARM macros in prefix.SDSNSAMP(DSNTIJUZ) and executing it. The "prefix" portion of the PDS name is specified by the person who installs DB2 on the DSNTIPA1 installation panel. The value DSN710 is the default for Version 7. The 7 portion of the name indicates the version and the 10 portion indicates the release of DB2.

The WRITE THRESHOLD is the number of contiguous 4 KB output buffer pages that are allowed to fill before data is written to the active log data set. It can be 1 to 256 with a default of 20. A value within the range of 32 to 128 is reasonable. A high value is good for SQL statements that update and delete a large number of rows. The value can be specified in DSNZPARM DSN6LOGP WRTHRSH or on the DSNTIPB installation panel. Regardless of the value specified the log buffer is written to the active log on DASD when a commit is issued by any program to ensure that no committed data is lost. Commit processing is discussed in Chapter CC.

The NUMBER OF LOGS is the number of data sets per active log copy. You can have from 2 to 31 active log data sets with a default of 3. The default is a good starting point. If you need more active log data sets, the number can be specified on the DSNTIPB installation panel.

The ARCHIVE LOG FREQ is the interval in hours at which the active log is offloaded to the archive log. You can specify a value of 1 to 200 with a default of 24 hours. The default is a good starting point and can be changed on the DSNTIPB installation panel. An image copy of critical tablespaces taken every 24 hours is a good choice to decrease the likelihood that the archive log will be required for a recovery. Recovery from the active log improves recovery time significantly over having to use the archive log.

The UPDATE RATE is an estimate of the number of inserts, updates, and deletes expected per hour. The DSNTINST CLIST assumes that 400 bytes of data are logged for each insert, update, and delete when it calculates this value. For example, 10 GB of data can be logged per hour for processing millions of updates and inserts. The value can be specified on the DSNTIPB installation panel.

The ARCHIVE LOG FREQ and UPDATE RATE can be used to determine the size of the active logs.

LOGLOAD determines when checkpoints are taken for DB2 subsystem restart. DB2 takes periodic checkpoints to ensure that all committed units of recovery are written to the tablespaces and all uncommitted units of recovery are rolled back to reduce recovery time. The information written during a checkpoint is used for recovery of one or more tablespaces when the RECOVER utility is executed and when DB2 is started after an abend due to a power failure for example. If LOGLOAD is too large, restart of DB2 time is increased. A checkpoint is taken when 50,000 log records have been written by default (can specify 0 or 200 to 16,000,000).

LOGLOAD can be dynamically changed until DB2 is restarted with a command like (V6):

```
-SET LOG LOGLOAD(150000)
```

The new value takes affect following the next system checkpoint. Indeed, you can initiate a system checkpoint like:

```
-SET LOG LOGLOAD(0)
```

If the checkpoint frequency is be changed permanently, change DSNZPARM DSN6SYSP or use the DSNTIPB installation panel. A good goal is to take a checkpoint every 15 to 20 minutes. The LOGLOAD values can be calculated based on a formula invented by Joel Goldstein: Take the DB2PM "Write-NoWait" value and divide it by the statistics interval which is typically 15 or 30 minutes and multiply by 20 minutes. A checkpoint is also taken when switching from one active log data set to another, at the end of a successful restart, and at normal termination of DB2. The active log should be sized to contain data for about 10 checkpoints.

You can specify a time interval between checkpoints in V7 in terms of wall clock time. A checkpoint is taken every 20 if the following command is executed.

```
-SET LOG CHKTIME(20)
```

The checkpoint frequency can be determined with the command:

```
-DISPLAY LOG
```

Tracking Recovery Information

BSDS: System Services manages the boot strap data set (BSDS) which contains the beginning and ending RBA of the active and archive log data sets. This is a wrap around inventory of checkpoints. Dual active and archive logs, and the BSDS are managed by Systems Services by default. The log data set pairs can be written to DASD. It is important to spread data sets across multiple DASD devices, channels, and control units to minimize I/O contention. Data Facility Storage Management Subsystem data facility product (DFSMSdfp, frequently referred to simply as SMS) can be used to write archive logs to tape units. Optionally, one set of logs can be written to DASD and one to tape units.

Recovery Information in the Catalog and Directory: The catalog table SYSCOPY contains a record of all copies. The most recent copy is written to the tablespace by the recovery utility for a recovery. The directory table SYSLGRNX contains the start and stop RBA for each tablespace and index to locate updates in the log to apply to a copy during a recovery.

INPUT BUFFER is used for reading the active and archive log data sets. It is 60 KB with no option to change the size (V6). Each RECOVER utility job has an input buffer.

Fast Log Apply (V6)

The log can be read with up to and including 100 parallel prefetch tasks. Log records are sorted with a single pass of the log. This enables multiple log records to be applied to a page or series of pages with fast log apply. Multiple log apply tasks are used to apply log records in parallel. This avoids having to repeatedly read a single page for each log record that applies to the page. Fast log apply is not the default. It must be enabled with the LOG APPLY STORAGE field on the DSNTIPL installation panel.

Monitor Statistics for Resizing Log

The log buffer and active log data set should be sized so that a recovery can be done without access to the archive log to minimize unavailability of the data during a recovery. If the archive log must be accessed, the log buffer and/or active log data set sizes should be increased in size. Figure CO.12 contains partial log statistics from the DB2 PM Statistics Report. If READS SATISFIED FROM ARCHIVE LOG A is high, consider increasing the size of the active log.

Figure CO.12. Partial log statistics from the DB2 PM Statistics Report

LOG ACTIVITY		QUANTITY
READS SATISFIED-OUTPUT BUFF		269.00
READS SATISFIED-OUTP.BUF(%)		98.18
READS SATISFIED-ACTIVE LOG		5.00
READS SATISFIED-ACTV.LOG(%)		1.82
READS SATISFIED-ARCHIVE LOG	A	0.00
READS SATISFIED-ARCH.LOG(%)		0.00
TAPE VOLUME CONTENTION WAIT		0.00
WRITE-NOWAIT		298.9K
WRITE OUTPUT LOG BUFFERS		19200.00
BSDS ACCESS REQUESTS		377.00
UNAVAILABLE OUTPUT LOG BUFF	B	0.00
CONTR.INTERV.CREATED-ACTIVE		6980.00
ARCHIVE LOG READ ALLOCATION		0.00
ARCHIVE LOG WRITE ALLOCAT.		0.00
CONTR.INTERV.OFFLOADED-ARCH		0.00
READ DELAYED-UNAVAIL.RESOUR		0.00
READ DELAYED-ARCH.ALLOC.LIM		N/A
LOOK-AHEAD MOUNT ATTEMPTED		0.00
LOOK-AHEAD MOUNT SUCCESSFUL		0.00

It should be possible to write the log buffer to the active log without a wait. If write request to the active log must wait, do increase the output buffer size. An alternative is to adjust the write threshold if you believe that the size of the write threshold might be too close to the size of the output buffer. A high value for UNAVAILABLE OUTPUT LOG BUFF B in Figure CO.12 indicates that adjustments are needed.

Chapter CR contains a detailed description of logging, making copies, and recovery.

Instrumentation Facility Interface

The Instrumentation Facility Interface (IFI) in the System Services Address Space writes records describing the work done by all of the DB2 subsystem address spaces depending on the trace that has been started. Records can be written by AUTHID, plan, class, and instrumentation facility component ID (IFCID) to GTF, SMF, etc. data sets. The IFCID is an identifier of records written as described in the sample library prefix.SDSNSAMP(DSNWMSGS).

The accounting trace can be started like:

```
-START TRACE(ACCTG) PLAN(SUPDATE) AUTHID(FLEUR)
    CLASS(1,2,3,7,8) IFCID(...) DEST(GTF)
```

One or more plan names and AUTHIDs can be specified using the PLAN and AUTHID parameters. The CLASS parameter provides for specifying groups of IFCID records to be collected. The IFCID parameter provides for specifying that only specific records are to be collected. The accounting trace records are also identified as storage management facility (SMF) record ID of 101.

The requested accounting trace records are written each time an application thread is created and used, and when a distributed data facility thread changes from an active to inactive state. Accounting records include:

- CPU and elapsed time
- Number of synchronous I/Os
- Number of latches, locks taken/released, timeouts, deadlocks, and lock avoidance
- Number of SQL statements executed by type
- Text of SQL

Following is an estimate of the additional CPU cost by class when the trace is turned on:

Class	Increase in CPU Costs
1	< 5 %
2	1-10 %, higher value if fetch intensive environment because fetch costs are low relative to the cost of writing the trace records
3	< 1 %
7 & 8	< 1 %

The statistics trace can be started like:

```
-START TRACE(STAT) PLAN(SUPDATE) AUTHID(FLEUR)
   CLASS(1,2,3) DEST(GTF)
```

The records are written when DB2 is started and stopped, at specified intervals, when there is a switch to another active log data set, and when a distributed data facility thread changes from an active to inactive state. The statistics trace collects information on overall DB2 subsystem usage including:

♦ Total threads created, commits, and commands issued
♦ Log manager statistics
♦ Total number of SQL statements executed by type
♦ Total number of binds
♦ Number of locks taken/released, timeouts, and deadlocks
♦ Buffer pool usage
♦ Record ID pool usage
♦ Environmental Descriptor Manager pool usage
♦ Distributed data facility statistics

The activation of the statistics trace is low cost. It simply enables the use of the statistics. These statistics are always collected regardless of whether the trace has been turned on.

The statistics trace records are also identified as SMF record ID of 100.

The performance trace can be started like:

```
-START TRACE(PERFM) PLAN(SUPDATE) AUTHID(FLEUR)
   CLASS(4) IFCID(6) DEST(GTF)
```

The performance trace can collect information for all or specific DB2 operations depending on the trace classes started. It can trace operations done for one or more of resource managers, including storage management, data manager, and relational database services. The performance trace is resource intensive. If only the default classes of 1, 2, and 3 are turned on, the increase in CPU costs can be 5 to 30 percent. The performance trace is best used only when necessary, and the records collected should be limited as much as possible using the PLAN, AUTHID, CLASS, and IFCID parameters particularly when more than the default classes are activated.

The performance trace records are also identified as SMF record ID of 102.

The global trace is used for servicing DB2. The increase in CPU costs can be 10 to 150 percent while the trace is turned on.

The audit trace records information if auditing is specified when a table is created, and security related classes can be turned on.

The monitor trace records information for online monitoring and user-written programs.

Monitoring products are usually used to analyze the trace records in real time and through batch reports. Some monitors insert data into tables for analysis with SQL. DB2 performance monitor (DB2PM) is the monitoring product sold by IBM.

Recommendation: Do execute the DISPLAY TRACE command periodically to determine if unnecessary traces are turned on. Traces could have been turned on for an analysis and not turned off after the analysis. Also beware of the use of DSNTRACE DD DUMMY.

Database Services Address Space

The Database Services address space is also known as DSN1DBM1. This address space is responsible for managing most application work when SQL statements and utilities are executed as well as the catalog and directory tables. It consists of two major components: data manager and the relational data system.

Data manager (DM) interfaces with the buffer manager for getpage and release page (relpage) of data and index pages, and sets write pending indicating that a page must be written to the tablespace. It also interfaces with buffer manager for latch processing and with the Internal Resource Lock Manager for locks. DM interfaces with log manager for writing log records. It services utilities with data access and manipulation. It manages the directory tables. DM does all referential integrity and table constraint checking. It performs Enterprise System Architecture (ESA) compression and decompression of data. DM is best known for applying stage 1 predicates on pages in the buffer. (A predicate is a condition specified in the WHERE clause of SQL statements that must be met for the row to qualify for processing.) The use of stage 1 predicates reduces CPU costs as discussed in Chapter PP and throughout the book. DM passes qualifying rows one column at a time to the relational data system for further processing.

Relational Data System (RDS) applies stage 2 predicates on columns passed from DM. It does join processing and a good deal of subselect processing. It does internal sorts of rows as required by SQL statements and sorts record IDs if list prefetch is chosen as part of the access path by the optimizer. RDS interfaces with the environmental data manager for access to plans, packages, and DBDs. It manages the catalog tables, VSAM control blocks, and working storage.

CO.5 BUFFER POOLS

DB2 manages a number of shared pools in the Database Services address space including the buffer pools, sort pool, record ID pool, environmental descriptor pool, and working storage. These pools can be used by all SQL statements as they are executed. The pools are in central storage and can be paged to expanded storage by z/OS and OS/390.

The primary goal of the buffer pools is to reduce I/O wait time. Indeed, this is true for all of the pools. If we assume a "typical" online transaction with 0.5 second response time, about 68 percent of the time is spent waiting for pages to be read from DASD as shown in Figure CO.13.

Figure CO.13. Resources required by a "Typical" transaction.

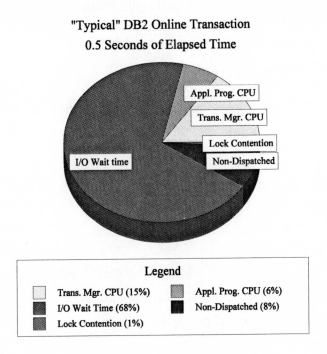

"Typical" DB2 Online Transaction
0.5 Seconds of Elapsed Time

Buffer manager keeps frequently referenced tablespace and index pages in the buffer pools to minimize I/O to DASD. DM issues getpages for the pages that it needs to do its work. Buffer manager searches the buffer pool to determine if the page is already in the pool as a result of having read the page for another user. If the page is present, DM can work on the page without a physical I/O to DASD. If the page is not present in the buffer pool, buffer manager passes a read request to Data Facility Product (DFP) manager. It is the DFP media manager that issues the physical I/O. A read of a single page at random with a single I/O is called a *synchronous* I/O. It is performed under the user Task Control Block (TCB) priority. The CPU time for issuing the I/O appears in the accounting trace records and can be used to bill users for their usage of the resources. Sequential I/O is used to read up to and including 32 pages with a single I/O. This is referred to as *asynchronous* I/O. It is performed under the DB2 Service Request Block (SRB). This means that the CPU time used to issue the I/O does not appear in accounting records for bill back, monitoring, and tuning. The number of I/O issued is collected for all types I/O.

Buffer manager is responsible for a number of activities in addition to keeping frequently processed pages in up to 50 4 KB pages, 10 8 KB, 10 16

KB, and 10 32 KB page buffer pools as indicated in Figure CO.14. How these 80 buffer pools can be managed is discussed in Chapter CD.

Figure CO.14. Buffer manager responsibilities

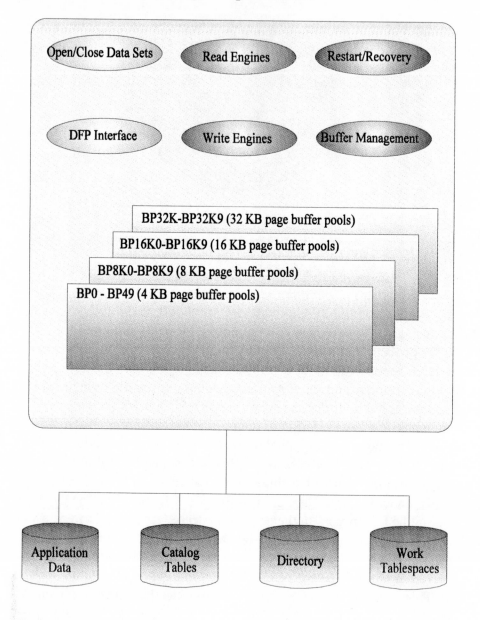

When Data Sets are Opened

Before I/O can be issued, the underlying data sets for the tablespaces and indexes must be opened by buffer manager if they are not already open as a result of earlier processing. The acquire and release parameters specified when SQL statements are bound determines when the data sets are opened and closed. (These parameters are best known for determining when table and tablespace locks are acquired and released and are discussed in Chapters CC and PE.) If acquire of use is specified, the data sets are opened when an SQL statement is executed that requires the tablespace or index is executed. If acquire of allocate is specified, all data sets used by the thread are opened when the thread is allocated. Buffer manager maintains a counter for each open data set. The counter is incremented by one for each user of the data set. The counter is decremented by one when a commit is issued if the plan or package was bound with release of commit. If release of deallocate was specified, the counter is decremented when the thread is deallocated.

Read Engines

The component of buffer manager responsible for reading multiple pages with a single I/O is called the *read engines*. Buffer manager can allocate a number of read engines, each of which can read pages from a data set. The read engines perform read ahead processing with asynchronous I/O. This means that buffer manager attempts to have the required pages in the buffer pool when DM issues a getpage. One of three types of prefetch is used to read up to and including 32 4 KB pages with a single I/O assuming that the buffer pool being used contains 1,000 or more pages. (BP0 has 2,000 pages by default.)

1) Asynchronous sequential prefetch always reads 32 data or index pages with a single I/O. The optimizer determines whether sequential prefetch should be used. It is frequently used for tablespace and index space scans. The details of the use of sequential prefetch are given in Chapters BP and OP.

2) Asynchronous dynamic prefetch is similar to sequential prefetch. The difference is that if the optimizer does not choose to use sequential prefetch but prefetch appears to be beneficial during the process of reading pages, dynamic prefetch is activated based on a sequential detection algorithm covered in Chapter BP.

All types of prefetch read pages forward. In addition, dynamic prefetch can read data and index pages backward (V7) with and without the use of a cursor. This will be particularly useful when dynamic scrollable cursors are available in the future. A loop where data is read backward as the result of values provided in the predicate of an SQL statement can benefit significantly from backward dynamic prefetch.

3) Asynchronous list prefetch can read up to and including 32 data pages as identified from the index pages. The optimizer determines whether list prefetch should be used. Index processing is required prior to the use of list prefetch as discussed in Chapter PP.

Prefetch of 32 4 KB pages means reading 128 KB of data. The same principle applies to 8, 16, and 32 KB pages. The prefetch quantity is 128 KB of data (16 8 KB pages, 8 16 KB pages, and 4 32 KB pages).

Write Engines

Write engines perform write behind processing. Write engines are basically the opposite of read engines in that they are used to write up to and including 32 pages rather than read them. SQL statements need not wait while updated pages are being written to DASD in the great majority of cases. Up to 10 percent of updated pages for a single data set are written using asynchronous deferred write in 1 to 32 page groups by default. The page IDs are sorted and the pages are written in sequence as they appear on DASD to minimize seek time. Pages can be read and updated by many users without physical reads and writes as discussed in Chapter CD.

Asynchronous deferred writes are triggered by thresholds and specific activities. If more than 10 percent of the pool or 64 pages (whichever is larger) are occupied by updated pages for a single data set, deferred write is initiated. The 64 page limit is used to determine when pages updated by the load, reorganization, and recover utility are written. If less than or equal to 50 percent (default) of the pool is stealable, the updated pages are written to DASD. If there is a shortage of space in the buffer pool and a page slot must be reused, updated pages at the beginning of the least recently used chain are written to DASD. A DB2 checkpoint causes all updated pages to be written to DASD. If you execute the QUIESCE utility with write of yes, stop the database, tablespace, or index space, or stop the DB2 subsystem. These options cause the updated pages to be written to DASD. A switch to read-only processing or a close of a data set also causes the updated pages to be written to DASD.

Once deferred write is started, write processing continues until 60 percent (default) of the pages are available for use in a buffer pool.

CO.6 SORT POOLS

There are three types of sorts used with DB2: the utilities use an external sort (DFSORT for example), sort of record IDs, and sort of rows as required by SQL statements. This section describes how DB2 sorts rows as required by SQL statements.

DM issues getpages for the required pages and buffer manager locates the pages in the buffer pool or initiates physical I/O to read the pages from DASD as shown in Figure CO.15. DM applies the stage 1 predicates and passes only the qualifying rows one column at a time to RDS. RDS applies the stage 2 predicates to further minimize the number of rows that must be processed further. This processing in the database services address space occurs with or without a sort.

Figure CO.15. Sort processing

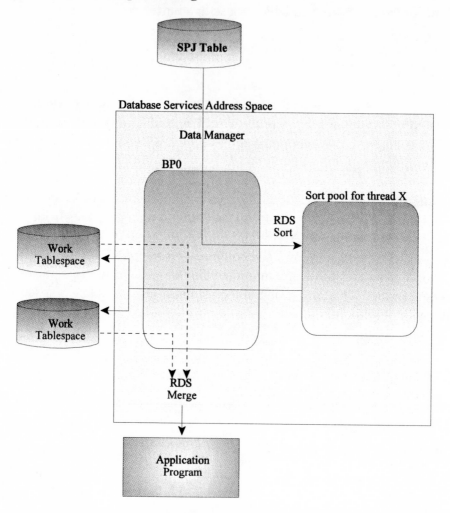

If a sort is required, RDS sorts the rows in a sort pool using a tournament sort. The default size of a sort pool is 1,000 KB. The size can be changed in the SORT POOL SIZE field of the installation panel DSNTIPC or DSNZPARM DSN6SRPM SRTPOOL.

A sort pool is allocated in working storage for each thread that requires a sort. A SELECT statement can require multiple sorts if it has a UNION and ORDER BY clause, for example. The maximum number of nodes in a tournament sort tree is 16,000. The optimal sort pool size for a single sort, assuming hardware sort is available, can be calculated as:

```
16,000 (maximum nodes in a sort tree) *
(16 bytes of control information + sort key
```

```
length + sort data length) * the number of
sorts
```

For example, assume a statement selects four 10 byte columns--SN, PN, JN, QTY--and the statement does a UNION *and* an ORDER BY on one of the 10 byte columns. The multiplier of 2 in the following example of estimating the space to sort the data is for the two sorts, one sort for the UNION and one sort for the ORDER BY.

```
16,000 * (16 + 10 + 40) * 2 = 2,112,000 bytes
```

Notice that the more columns selected and sorted the more space is required. (You can compute averages from QW0096KL (key length) and QW0096DL (data length) from IFCID 96 sort trace. This suggests that only the columns that are required be selected and sorted for the best performance. If columns in the ORDER BY clause are not in the SELECT clause, they need to be included in the sort data length. If the sort cannot be done in the sort pool, as many rows as possible are sorted and written to logical work files on work tablespaces in the DSNDB07 database. Each batch of sorted rows is considered a run. Each run is written to a work tablespace via the buffer pool assigned to DSNDB07, read from work tablespaces via buffer pool assigned to DSNDB07, sorted runs must be merged before rows can be returned to the user.

The number of logical work files containing sorted rows can be minimized with a sort pool of 2 MB in the example and for similar statements that require sorts. Minimizing the number of work files written to DASD and merging them reduces the costs of a sort significantly. It is a challenge to estimate the sort pool size for the many SQL statements that require a sort. Do identify a few SELECT statements that require a sort and for which you want to maximize performance. Use the formula to calculate the sort pool size in central storage so that the sort can be done with minimal use of the work files. Of course, you must work within the constraints that you have on the use of central storage. However, you can probably justify more central storage to save CPU and elapsed time required for sorts.

The buffer pool (BP0 by default) assigned to DSNDB07 is used for writing the runs to DASD and merging them. Buffer manager places limits on the amount of a buffer pool that can be used. If 20 percent of the buffer pool assigned to DSNDB07 is stealable, up to 10 percent of the sum of the four buffer pools used to determine the default sort pool can be used for I/O to the work tablespaces and merging. Do have sufficient space in the buffer pool for this processing to avoid degrading performance of the sorts.

Create and Size Work File Tablespaces for the Workload: The system administrator must be sure there are enough work file tablespaces and that the work file tablespaces are large enough to support sorts required by many SQL statements and other processing. This means creating perhaps five to seven work file tablespaces in most cases rather than using the two provided by default at installation time. Less than or equal 16,000 node runs are written to logical work files in DSNDB07 work tablespaces via BP0 (default). Logical work files (LWF) are allocated in physical work tablespaces (PWT). If 2 PWT are allocated, LWFs are allocated like:

♦   LWF1 placed on PWT1
♦   LWF2 placed on PWT2
♦   LWF3 placed on PWT1
♦   LWF4 placed on PWT2
♦   LWF5 placed on PWT1

> **1 LWF per PWT has performance advantages.**

Space is freed with a commit (not using CURSOR WITH HOLD) or rollback.

The number and size of work file tablespaces is highly dependent on the size and frequency of sorts on the DB2 subsystem. One possible approach is to create each of five to seven work file tablespaces with 500-1,000 cylinders of primary quantity (PRIQTY) each and 25-50 cylinders of secondary quantity (SECQTY). Then monitor the space usage.

Indicators for Sizing DSNDB07 Tablespaces: Consider creating the number of work tablespaces to be the average to near maximum logical work files required from IFCID 96 sort trace records. An indication of insufficient work tablespaces is long I/O time (over 200 milliseconds, for example). A less accurate indication of whether there is insufficient work space is to determine if the work tablespaces have gone into secondary extents. An indicator of too small of a work tablespace is an extent failure or the sort will abend when there is no more space available, after running for perhaps a long period of time, if there is insufficient space with a message of DSN4Kxx full. This indicates the work tablespace is too small for the workload. However, an exceptionally large sort requiring many extents diminishes the usefulness of this technique.

If real-time statistics are recorded (discussed in Chapter RR),

SYSIBM.TABLESPACESTATS contains space information for DSNDB07 and TEMP tablespaces in the columns NACTIVE, SPACE, EXTENTS. It is not possible to analyze space using the catalog tables, because RUNSTATS does not collect statistics on DSNDB07.

Once you have determined the number and PRIQTY of work tablespace, consider setting the SECQTY to 0 on all but the last work tablespace. It is not necessary to stop DSNDB07 to add, delete, and change work tablespaces and start it for further use (V7). The work tablespaces should be spread across multiple DASD devices, channels, and control units. This minimizes seek time and I/O contention. It allows for parallel I/O for merging the logical work files.

Chuck Hoover did extensive research to determine the breakeven point between DB2 V5 sort and DFSORT. He found it to be 2.2 million 225 byte rows which were sorted in about 3.4 minutes. DB2 sort costs increase rapidly beyond this point. DFSORT sort costs increase much more slowly. This suggests the use of DFSORT when sorting more data.

DSNDB07 is used for trigger processing, data for global temporary tables (not declare global temporary tables), materialization of nested table expression and views, correlated and noncorrelated subselect processing, star join processing, referential integrity checking for self-referencing tables, and more in addition to sort processing.

A tag sort is used if the row of qualifying columns plus overhead is greater than 4 KB. This means that the required columns are sorted and a tag (pointer) is used to locate columns in the row that are not sorted. This increases sort costs significantly which is one of many reasons for selecting only the required columns especially when a sort is required.

CO.7 RID POOL

Four byte record IDs (RIDs) follow indexed values in leaf pages and reference rows on data pages. RIDs and the use of list prefetch are discussed in detail in Chapters IU and PP. If the optimizer chooses list prefetch as part of the access path, DM retrieves the qualifying RIDs from the index leaf pages and places them in the RID pool. In most cases, the RIDs are sorted and duplicate page identifiers are eliminated before list prefetch I/Os are issued. This allows for retrieving the pages in the sequence in which they appear on DASD, thus minimizing seek time. The elimination of duplicate page identifiers avoids DM having to issue multiple getpages for multiple rows on a page. DM can get the page once and process all of the qualifying rows on the page.

The RID pool is an area of central storage used to store and sort RID lists. No DASD work files are used to sort RIDs. The maximum RID pool size is the minimum of the value specified as RID POOL SIZE on install panel DSNTIPC (or DSNZPARM DSN6SPRM MAXRBLK). The RID pool can be specified as 16 KB to 1 GB or 0 with the default being 4 GB. The RID pool size can be specified as RID POOL SIZE on installation panel DSNTIPC or DSNZPARM DSN6SPRM MAXRBLK.

Each SQL statement is allowed a minimum of one RID block of 4,096 RIDs (4,096 RIDs * 4 byte RID = 16 KB). Even if there is a shortage of space in the RID pool, an SQL statement can process 4,096 RIDs before DB2 changes to a tablespace scan. This reduces the likelihood that transactions will vary in response time when the RID pool space becomes scarce during peak periods of activity. The additional space is allocated in the general working storage of the database services address space up to the equivalent RID pool size. If the number of RIDs is less than 4,096 for an SQL statement, online transactions benefit from list prefetch in most cases.

If the RID pool size is set to 0, list prefetch is disabled as is multiple index access and hybrid joins. Be careful about disabling list prefetch, especially after plans and packages have already been bound. If the optimizer chooses list prefetch for an SQL statement when it is bound and there is not enough space in the RID pool, a tablespace scan is used at execution time.

Monitoring RID Pool Processing: It is best to monitor the use of list prefetch rather than disabling it. List prefetch is usually a very good technique for processing the data. Indeed, if the RID list is beyond a 150 page boundary, other I/O requests are serviced to avoid one SQL statement causing delays for other statements.

DB2 collects statistics on the use of the RID pool in accounting trace records. A performance monitor (DB2PM for example) can be used to report on these statistics. The DB2PM "Instrumentation Accounting Data" panel shows a count of the number of times that the RID pool was used successfully, list prefetch was not used as requested by the optimizer because insufficient space was available for RID processing, and the number of times RID processing was terminated because a threshold limit was exceeded. The DB2PM "Statistic Trace - Long" panel shows a count of the number of times that more than 25 percent of table RIDs qualify, more than 50 percent of the RID pool is required for one statement, and when space for 4,096 RIDs (default) cannot be allocated as "Failed-RDS limit exceeded". The "Failed-DM limit exceeded" shows the number of times that one SQL statement required more than 16 million RIDs. The "Process limit exceeded" shows the number of times that no more space is available for processing the RIDs.

CO.8 EDM POOL

Environmental Descriptor Manager (EDM) pool contains plans, packages, and DBDs required for execution of SQL. Buffer manager reads these objects from the directory into the EDM pool via BP0. The EDM pool is analogous to a buffer pool in that the goal is to keep frequently used objects in the pool and minimize I/O to DASD.

Skeleton cursor table (SKCT) and skeleton package table (SKPT) are basically master copies of a plan and package. SKCT and SKPT sections are loaded as SQL statements are executed. Each section contains code structures for one or more SQL statements and is 4 KB in size. A complex SQL statement can span multiple sections. Only those sections required as the program runs must be in the EDM pool for execution. The sections for a SKCT or SKPT are chained in non-contiguous space in the EDM pool. SKCT and SKPT allocation occurs when the first SQL statement is executed in a program at thread allocation time. The Cursor Table (CT) and Package Table (PT) are copies of the SKCT and SKPT sections. Each active user has an individual copy. Each section is allocated as needed during execution. The EDM manager attempts to keep a copy of the SKCT and SKPT in the pool in order to make a copy for a new user who executes the plan or package to avoid I/O to the directory for each user execution. When a BIND REPLACE, REBIND, FREE, or DROP is issued, the SKCT and SKPT are read from the directory.

Figure CO.16. EDM Pool

```
                    High storage
┌─────────────────────────────────────────┐
│ SKCT Directory for SUPDATE                │
├─────────────────────────────────────────┤
│ SKCT Header      for SUPDATE              │
├─────────────────────────────────────────┤
│ Authorization cache for SUPDATE           │
├─────────────────────────────────────────┤
│ SKCT Section 1 for SUPDATE                │
├─────────────────────────────────────────┤
│                                           │
│          DBD for DASPJDB                  │
│                                           │
├─────────────────────────────────────────┤
│ SKCT Section 2 for SUPDATE                │
├─────────────────────────────────────────┤
│ SKCT Directory for PORDER                 │
├─────────────────────────────────────────┤
│ SKCT Header      for PORDER               │
├─────────────────────────────────────────┤
│ Authorization cache for PORDER            │
├─────────────────────────────────────────┤
│ SKCT Section 1 for PORDER                 │
├─────────────────────────────────────────┤
│ SKCT Section 3 for SUPDATE                │
├─────────────────────────────────────────┤
│ SKCT Section 2 for PORDER                 │
├─────────────────────────────────────────┤
│                                           │
│          DBD for DAPOSDB                  │
│                                           │
├─────────────────────────────────────────┤
│                                           │
│            Unused space                   │
│                                           │
├─────────────────────────────────────────┤
│ CT Section 2 for PORDER   - Adam          │
├─────────────────────────────────────────┤
│ CT Section 3 for SUPDATE - Fleur          │
├─────────────────────────────────────────┤
│ CT Section 1 for PORDER   - Adam          │
├─────────────────────────────────────────┤
│ CT Header      for PORDER   - Adam        │
├─────────────────────────────────────────┤
│ CT Section 2 for SUPDATE - Fleur          │
├─────────────────────────────────────────┤
│ CT Section 1 for SUPDATE - Eric           │
├─────────────────────────────────────────┤
│ CT Header      for SUPDATE - Eric         │
├─────────────────────────────────────────┤
│ CT Section 1 for SUPDATE - Fleur          │
├─────────────────────────────────────────┤
│ CT Header      for SUPDATE - Fleur        │
└─────────────────────────────────────────┘
                    Low storage
```

An example of how the EDM pool is used will be given with reference to Figure CO.16. Assume that Fleur is the first person that executes the SUPDATE plan. The SKCT directory, header, and section 1 for the plan are read from the SCTR table in tablespace SCT02 and a copy is made and allocated in low storage as a CT. The SKCT directory, header, authorization cache, and section 1 are placed in high storage for use by additional users who execute the plan. Next Eric executes the same SUPDATE program, and the EDM manager makes a copy of the SKCT information that was already read from the directory for Fleur. We will assume that Fleur continues executing statements in the program and requires another section, section 2. It is read from the directory, a copy is made in low storage, and the SKCT for the section is placed in high storage. When Eric executes an SQL statement in section 2, a copy is made for him in low storage based on the SKCT and header in high storage read, and processed for Fleur. This processing continues as Fleur and others execute the plan.

Next, assume that Adam executes the PORDER plan. The SKCT directory, header, and first required section are read from the directory. The CT copy is made and placed in low storage where it is executed. The SKCT objects are placed in high storage for use as a master copy for others to execute the PORDER plan. As Adams executes more SQL statements in the PORDER plan, more sections are processed as described.

If a plan or package is bound or deleted, the EDM manager must read the new SKCT or SKPT from the directory or issue an error message if the plan has been deleted.

The DBD for the database being processed, DASPJDB in the example, would have been read from the directory tablespace DBD01 and placed in the EDM pool prior to plan allocation.

The cursor table database block (CTDB) is a portion of the header with information on objects manipulated. There is one CTDB for each DBD used by the plan and package. The cursor block (CUB) is a linked child of the CTDB for each cursor. The CUB contains control information on the position in a table and on a leaf page if an index is used, information needed for CURSOR WITH HOLD, index lookaside, and sequential detection. (These topics are discussed in Chapters PD, IU, and BP.)

If acquire of allocate is specified, a static CUB is built in the header at bind time which improves performance but requires more space in the EDM pool. The PLSIZE column in the catalog table SYSPLAN has the header size. If acquire of use is specified, a dynamic CUB is built in working storage at execution time.

The release parameter specified with a bind also effects the use of the EDM pool and deallocation of resources. Release of deallocate has performance advantages over release of commit as can be seen in the comparison of processing required using the two options in Figure CO.17.

Figure CO.17. Release parameter effect on the EDM pool

Release of Commit	Release of Deallocate
CUB counters are reset with a commit work. Index lookaside and sequential detection must be re-initialized.	CUB counters are not reset with a commit work which increases the benefits of index lookaside and sequential detection and reduces costs.
CT and PT space is reusable after a commit work.	CT and PT space is not reusable until thread deallocation which avoids having to recreate the CT/PT.
RDS portion of the header counters decremented by 1 at commit (unless CURSOR WITH HOLD is used). Space for the DM portion is held.	RDS portion of the header counters are not decremented by 1 until thread deallocation. Sections, DM, and RDS portions of the header are held until thread deallocation which minimizes the resources required.

Release of Commit	Release of Deallocate
If header counter is 0, SKCT and SKPT section space is reusable.	If header counter is 0, SKCT and SKPT section space is not reusable until thread deallocation which decreases the chances of rereading the directory.
DBD counter of users decremented by 1 for DBDs at commit (unless CURSOR WITH HOLD is used).	DBD counter of users is not decremented by 1 until thread deallocation which decreases the chances of having to reread the DBD.
Data set counter of users decremented by 1 at commit.	Data set counter of users is not decremented by 1 until thread deallocation.
Global temporary table logical work file space is released with a commit.	Many uses of the same temporary table do not cause repeated allocation and deallocation of the logical work files. Beware of holding onto space for a long period of time if you do not plan to use it.

Recommendation: Acquire of allocate and release of deallocate have performance advantages. The use of these parameters does require more space in the EDM pool. Usually, the use of more storage is a positive trade-off to decrease I/O and CPU usage, and improves performance. The exception is when more than 2 GB of space is required in DSN1DBM1 using 32 bit addressing (64 bit addressing is expected in the future which can allow 9 exabytes of addressable space). The parameters are particularly important to maximize the benefits of thread reuse. Indeed, thread reuse has minimal benefits without the use of the parameters. About the only disadvantage is that a plan or package cannot be rebound until it is deallocated. This can be a long time if the plan or package is frequently executed. It is necessary to find a time in a production environment where the plan or package can be deallocated for a rebind.

Acquire of allocate and release of deallocate do not increase the likelihood of lock contention in most cases as discussed in Chapter CC.

Authorization and the EDM Pool

An authorization cache in the EDM pool can be used to minimize I/O to determine if the user AUTHID has authority to execute a plan. The authority of an AUTHID is checked once in the SYSPLANAUTH and SYSPACKAUTH catalog tables and stored in the plan or package cache if the user is authorized for execution. This avoids checking the AUTHID each time it is used. Use of the cache requires that a plan be bound with a cache size of 256 to 4,096 bytes. The default of 1024 bytes allows for storing 124 AUTHIDs with a base portion of 32 bytes. If more than 124 AUTHIDs attempt to execute a plan, the space is reused, and it is necessary to verify privileges the next time that the reused AUTHID slot attempts to execute the plan. This suggests that the cache size be made larger or that privileges be granted to the public as will be discussed below.

The package cache is 32 KB which allows for about 400 AUTHIDs by default. (The size can be changed in DSNZPARM or PACKAGE AUTH CACHE field of DSNTIPP installation panel.) The package cache is a global cache for all packages. It is necessary to GRANT EXECUTE ON collid.* TO AUTHIDS for use of the package cache. There is a plan cache for each plan by default.

A good alternative to using plan and package caches is to grant execution privileges to the public. This causes a bit to be turned on in the SKCT or SKPT and to avoid further authorization checks as long as the bit remains in the EDM pool. A security software product can be used to control who can execute which plans and packages. If you choose this option, do specify CACHESIZE of 0 for each applicable plan and use 0 as the global package cache to avoid wasting space in the EDM pool. The default of 1024 for a plan cache can be changed to 0 on the installation panel DSNTIPP to avoid having to specify CACHESIZE of 0 each time a plan is bound.

DBDs in the EDM Pool

The DBD contains descriptor blocks for each object in a database including each tablespace, table, index, etc. as discussed in Chapter CD. Figure CO.18 summarizes the space required for each object in a DBD.

Figure CO.18. Space for each object in a DBD

Bytes	Each Object in a DBD
160	Tablespace
104	Tablespace partition
64	Table in segmented tablespace
90	Table in nonsegmented tablespace
10	Column in each table
158	Index
100	Index partition
10	Index column in each index
24	Referential integrity relationship

DBDs are shared resources. One copy is used for all SQL referencing objects in the database. DBD can be broken into 32 KB chunks to avoid allocating contiguous space in EDM pool (V6) as shown in Figure CO.16. This minimizes EDM pool fragmentation where sufficient space is available, but it is not contiguous. However, it is advisable not to create too many objects in a database which results in a large DBD, because it is necessary to log the entire DBD when objects in the DBD are created, dropped, or altered.

If space fragmentation is a problem and the pool cannot be increased in size, consider executing the DISPLAY DATABASE command and name frequently used databases after starting the DB2 subsystem like:

```
-DISPLAY DATABASE (DASPJDB, DAEMPDB)
```

This results in loading DBDs in contiguous space. It also avoids transactions from waiting for initial loading of DBDs as objects in the database are referenced.

If there is insufficient space to load a DBD, a -904 SQLCODE is issued indicating that resources unavailable. No SQL statement referencing objects in the database can be executed until space is available to load the DBD from the directory.

EDM Pool Size

The EDM pool should be sized to retain frequently used plans, packages, and DBDs. If DYNAMIC SQL YES is specified on installation panel DSNTIP4, more space is required for skeletons of dynamic SQL. Data spaces can be used for the EDM pool as discussed in Chapter PD when using the dynamic cache. The default size is 14,812 KB. Sizing the EDM pool for the workload is second only in importance to sizing the buffer pools for the workload to achieve good performance of application systems. Both the EDM and buffer pools can be sized based on a hit ratio. That is, the required pages should be found in central storage 80 to 90 percent of the time. The hit ratio for the EDM pool can be calculated as:

```
1 - (number of loads from directory / number
of requests)
```

For example, if the number of loads from the directory is 20 and the number of requests is 100, the hit ratio is 0.80. That is, the required SKCT or SKPT sections are found in the EDM pool 80 percent of the time based on:

```
0.80 = 1 - (20 / 100)
```

A good hit ratio not only reduces I/O to the directory but also reduces the costs of allocation and deallocation of CTs, PTs, SKCTs, SKPTs, and DBDs. In addition, it reduces the costs of re-initializing counters and controls information if release of deallocate is used.

The least recently used (LRU) algorithm is used to reuse space in the EDM pool when it is full. The CTs and PTs space is reused before SKCT and SKPT space. If there is insufficient space in EDM pool, a -904 SQLCODE is received with reason code 00C90089 indicating that resources are not available to allocate a plan, package, or DBD.

Locating Plans and Packages

The precompiler reads the host program with embedded SQL, comments out the SQL statements, and writes a copy of the statements to the database request modules (DBRM) library. The DBRM name, section number, and consistency token are written to the modified host program by the precompiler. This processing is detailed in Chapter PE.

DB2 uses an index on the plan name and section to locate the plan in the directory based on the information placed in the modified host program by the precompiler. It uses an index on the location.collection.name.contoken.rds#.seq# to locate the package in the directory. Information about the location and collection can be determined from the plan depending on a number of factors to be discussed. This information must be determined to allow for a matching index scan to locate the required package. (There is also an index on version.location.collection.name.contoken to guarantee uniqueness.)

Locating package information: The package name is in the modified host program similar to the plan name. However, in order for DB2 to do a matching index scan to locate a specific package, it must determine the location and collection since they are the two leading columns of the composite index. The location is in the current server special register if SET CURRENT SERVER has been used to set it. If the current server special register is blank, the local server is assumed. The collection ID is in the current package set special register if SET CURRENT PACKAGE SET has been used to set it. If the current package set special register is blank, DB2 uses the first collection entry in the plan header for a matching index scan on the location.collection.name.contoken.rds#.seq# composite index. If the package is not found in the first collection, the second, third, etc., collection entry is used in a matching index scan. If the package is not found in the last collection, a -805 SQLCODE is received or -812 SQLCODE if last entry is "*" at execution time.

Recommendation: The search algorithm suggests that the most frequently used collection should be named first in the PKLIST when the plan is bound. The PKLIST and relationship between plans and packages are discussed in Chapter PE.

Space for Plans and Packages

If many DBRMs are bound to a plan, the plan header and directory portions are large which can result in EDM pool fragmentation and unavailable space at execution time. This is because the plan header and directory must be in contiguous space. If there is insufficient contiguous space in the EDM pool to load a large header and directory, a -904 SQLCODE is received with the reason code of 00C90089.

The EDM manager attempts to minimize fragmentation of space by tracking the number of sections previously allocated for plans and packages. Based on this information, the EDM manager attempts to allocate a block of space to contain the number of frequently used sections when next executed.

One of the many advantages of packages over binding many DBRMs into a plan, as discussed in Chapter PE, is that packages reduce the size of the plan header and directory, compared to a plan with many DBRMs. The plan does not have a listing of SQL sections in its packages. Packages also avoid redundant SKCT sections in the EDM pool for a DBRM bound into multiple plans.

One of the few disadvantages of packages, and a rather minor one assuming that you do not have an extreme shortage of EDM space, compared to binding many DBRMs into a plan, is that a package like a plan must be on a 4 KB boundary, and has a header and a directory. This means that 10 packages may use 40 KB compared to 10 DBRMs bound to a plan that may use only 20 KB, for example.

Compiled Assignment Procedures

Compiled column assignment procedures are used to move columns to host variable output areas to reduce CPU time. There are three procedures IPROC, UPROC, and SPROC for inserts, updates, and selects. These procedures increase the plan/package size in the EDM pool and directory. If the procedure exceeds 4 KB, it is not stored in the directory with the plan/package. Rather the procedures are compiled at run time if more than three rows are processed and savings are achieved after processing more than 5 rows. The systems administrator can disable or modify the 4 KB and greater than three row threshold with the hidden DSNZPARM parameter SPRMSPS.

If the compiled assignment procedures are generated at run time after processing three rows, the procedures are lost with a commit if the release of commit is specified with a bind. It is best to use release of deallocate so that the procedures are retained across commits. This is one of the many advantages of using release of deallocate as discussed in Chapter CC.

CO.9 WORKING STORAGE

Working storage is a general central storage work area that can be paged to DASD by z/OS and OS/390. It is 5,960 KB in size by default. DB2 has a variety of uses for this work area. The bind and rebind process uses some space in working storage. There is 24 KB used, per thread, that also uses static SQL in addition to the plan and package in the EDM pool. There is 76 KB of working storage used per thread that uses dynamic SQL in addition to a miniplan and space for SKCT if the dynamic cache is used in the EDM pool. A compression directory for each compressed tablespace is kept in working storage, when the tablespace is processed. Control blocks for open data sets are kept in working storage. Space is used for in-memory tables, in-memory indexes, etc., to improve performance of SQL statements as discussed in Chapter ST.

CO.10 THREAD CREATION, USE, AND TERMINATION

A thread is created when the first SQL statement in a program is executed which requires about 50,000 instructions. This thread allocation, execution of SQL, commit processing, and termination of the thread requires a number of activities as summarized in Figure CO.19. Also a brief summary of how to minimize the resources required for the activities is shown. More detail on the activities are discussed throughout the book. The activities marked with an asterisk (*) are those that are not required for a transaction that is using thread reuse. That is, the transaction is using a protected thread and the thread is reused by the transaction every 30 to 45 seconds in most cases. Clearly, thread reuse has significant performance advantages for frequently executed transactions.

Figure CO.19. Activities required for thread creation, use, and termination

Activity	Minimize Resources Required
Create thread	
Sign on	Verify authority to connect
*Write account record	One record for all trans. with thread reuse
Load SKCT header	Minimize number of DBRMs bound to a plan
Create CT header	Minimize number of DBRMs bound to a plan
*Check exec authority	Use authorization cache or grant to public
Acquire all TSP locks	Use acquire allocate if most SQL executed
Increment claim count	Use acquire allocate if most SQL executed
Load all DBDs	Use acquire allocate if most SQL executed
Log.open all datasets	If acquire allocate
Each SQL executed	
*Load SKCT section	Size EDM pool to hold frequently used SKCT
*Create CT copy	Release deallocate avoids space reuse
*Load SKPT hdr/dir/sec	If package, load SKPT now (not with plan)
*Create PT copy	Release deallocate avoids space reuse
*Acquire TSP locks	Use acquire allocate if most SQL executed
*Load DBDs	Use acquire allocate if most SQL executed
*Log. open data sets	Use acquire allocate if most SQL executed
Process SQL	Use efficient SQL & programming techniques
Commit processing	
Write log records	Commit every 10 updates for transactions
Release page locks	Above & use lock table for batch
*Release TSP locks	Use release deallocate
*Free CT/PT sections	Release deallocate avoids space reuse
Decrement claim count	Use release deallocate

Activity	Minimize Resources Required
Log. close data sets	Use release deallocate
Terminate thread	(Not done if thread reused)
*Write account record	One record for all trans. with thread reuse
*Release TSP locks	Not released if thread reuse
*Free CT/PT space	Not freed if thread reuse
*Free working storage	Not freed if thread reuse
*Log. close data sets	If release deallocate

*Thread reuse minimizes or eliminates resources required.
SK represents SKCT and SKPT sections.

The cost of commit processing is reduced with thread reuse since table or tablespace intent locks need not be released and CT sections are not freed. Notice that many of the items marked with an asterisk, indicating that the work need not be repeated with thread reuse, are influenced by the acquire and release parameters specified at bind time. Indeed, thread reuse saves few resources without specifying ACQUIRE(ALLOCATE) and RELEASE(DEALLOCATE) at bind time. The ACQUIRE and RELEASE parameters are discussed in Chapter CC.

CO.11 IRLM ADDRESS SPACE

The Internal Resource Lock Manager (IRLM) address space is used to take and release locks when data is selected or updated. It is also known as the IRLMPROC. Its size is 335,000 KB by default. It is advisable to retain the default PC value of N so that the extended common service area (ECSA) is used and about 5 percent savings in CPU time can be realized. If PC of Y is specified, cross memory services is used for lock requests.

The primary goal of the IRLM is to avoid one person's updates being written over by another person's updates. It basically serializes updates. The IRLM also provides for synchronizing several updates in conjunction with a unit of recovery.

Chapter CC is devoted to the work done by the IRLM.

CO.12 DISTRIBUTED DATA FACILITY

Distributed Data Facility (DDF) is an optional fourth address space that manages a distributed environment. It is also known as DSN1DIST. DDF is responsible for establishing and managing a connection with one or more remote DBMSs. The BSDS contains the DB2 location name and password. Virtual telecommunications access method (VTAM) is used for remote site communications as shown in Figure CO.20.

Figure CO.20. Distributed data facility

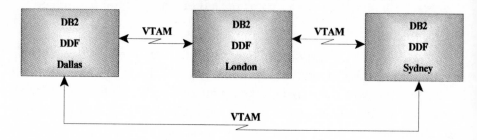

Multi–Site Update

DDF provides for updating data on multiple remote DBMSs, within a remote unit of recovery, when using the CICS, IMS, IMS batch, TSO, CAF, and RRSAF attaches. Coordinated recovery is supported among all relational DBMSs that conform to distributed relational database architecture (DRDA), support multi-site updates, and two-phase commit processing. DB2 Universal Database (UDB) has this support on a number of platforms including z/OS, OS/390, Windows 2000, ME, 98, 95, Linux, Unix, AIX, HP-UX, Solaris, UNMA-Q, OS/2, and OS/400. Optionally, Linux can run on z/OS and OS/390. This provides for running DB2 UDB for Linux under z/OS and OS/390. This book concentrates on DB2 UDB for z/OS and OS/390.

Most DBMS software companies support or plan to support DRDA.

DB2 for z/OS and OS/390 supports DRDA application directed distributed facilities and system directed distributed facilities, which is an earlier implementation.

Application directed distributed facilities provides for selecting, inserting, updating, and deleting rows from multiple sites using multiple

DBMSs. The remote site can be designated with the CONNECT statement or the entire three part name of the table including the location which must be used before executing static or dynamic SQL at a remote site prior to V6. Location independence is available thru the use of three part names without the use of a CONNECT statement in V6. Three part names of objects are discussed in Chapter CT.

System directed distributed facilities uses the DB2 private protocol (not DRDA). This means that only DB2 for z/OS and OS/390 can be used as a client or server (not other DBMSs). This is an older distributed facility for which support is expected to be discontinued in the future. It has only one primary advantage over application directed distributed facilities prior to V6. It has location independence which means that a developer need not be concerned with the location of the data. Rather, the database administrator (DBA) creates aliases for tables that indicate their locations and defines the distributed environment in the communications database. Developers name the aliases without specifying the locations in their SQL statements. DB2 determines the location based on information in the catalog table SYSTABLES placed there as a result of creating the alias. This can be done in with DRDA in V6.

There are a number of disadvantages to the older system directed distributed facilities. Even though SQL statements are embedded in the host program as static SQL, the text of the statements is transmitted to the remote site and executed dynamically. There is a good deal of overhead when transmitting data. Five bytes of overhead are required per column value transmitted. In contrast, DRDA does not have column overhead. Plans and packages that use the private protocol can be identified from the catalog tables SYSSTMT and SYSPACKSTMT with an 'A' in the STATUS column.

Distributed Request in DataJoiner

DataJoiner provides for a distributed request. This means that one SQL statement can reference tables in multiple DBMSs at multiple sites. Two phase commit processing is supported as with application and system directed distributed facilities. A global catalog provides for location transparency.

DataJoiner includes global optimization which determines where most of the processing should be done based on the size of the answer set at each site, the MIPS (million of instructions per second) rating of computers at each site, and the communications links and their speed between the sites.

DB2 Connect can be used to communicate with DataJoiner. It provides for read-only access to IMS and VSAM data including joins with relational tables.

Detailed information about DataJoiner and related products is available on the world wide web using the address http://www.software.ibm.com/data/datajoiner/aboutdj.html.

CO.13 STORED PROCEDURE ADDRESS SPACES

Stored procedures are subroutines or main programs that are callable from a remote or local site. A primary goal of stored procedures is to reduce the interchange of messages in a client/server environment. The calling program can call multiple stored procedures at multiple sites with two phase commit processing.

The stored procedure address spaces are allied address spaces. DB2 manages the DSN1SPAS address space. It can start, stop, and display information about the address space. Multiple address spaces can be managed by the WLM component of z/OS and OS/390 using compatibility or goal mode based on the work load and assigned priorities. There are several advantages to multiple address spaces. You can dedicate high priority threads to an address space. A single stored procedure or group of procedures can be dedicated to an address space. You can isolate stored procedures so that one does not abend and cause another to abend.

The many advantages of stored procedures and their uses are discussed in Chapter SP which is dedicated to the subject.

CO.14 CHANGING DSNZPARM PARAMETERS

Many DSNZPARM parameter (over 60 at present) can be changed without stopping and starting DB2 (V7) and more are expected in the future. You can load a specified subsystem parameter load module provided SYSADM,

SYSOPR, or SYSCTRL authority is held with the command:

```
-SET SYSPARM LOAD (load-module-name)
```

The RELOAD parameter reloads the last named subsystem parameter load module. The STARTUP resets initially loaded (startup) parameters. The sample program DSNTEJ6Z can be used to report on current parameter settings.

CO.15 SUMMARY

The same language, namely SQL, is used by DBAs, developers, and business professionals to create, manipulate, and control information in DB2. This offers a good deal of flexibility and facilitates communication on the usage of DB2. The catalog tables provide accurate and up to the second information on all objects in DB2.

The systems services address space is used to manage the overall DB2 subsystem. The database services address space is used to manage application data and indexes as well as the catalog tables and the directory tables.

The buffer pools, EDM pool, sort pool, RID pool, and working storage are used to achieve and maintain good performance. The buffer pool and EDM pool are particularly important in minimizing I/O.

The use of DDF and stored procedures positions DB2 for z/OS and OS/390 as the super server in a distributed environment.

EXERCISES

1. Is static or dynamic SQL used when using SPUFI and QMF? Is static or dynamic SQL usually used when embedding SQL in a host program?

2. Is a plan or package is produced and stored in the DB2 directory as a result of binding static or dynamic SQL?

3. What is the purpose of SQLCODEs and SQLSTATEs?

4. What is the purpose of the optimizer?

5. How are you known to DB2?

6. How are the catalog tables used by DB2? How can you use the catalog tables?

7. How can you access information in the directory?

8. When is a thread allocated for a COBOL program?

9. Trace statistics are collected by which address space on which address spaces?

10. How do you read and analyze trace statistics in most cases?

11. DM and RDS are executed from which address space?

12. The buffer pools, EDM pool, sort pools, RID pool, and general working storage are part of which address space?

13. Which of the pools are not shared among multiple programs executing concurrently?

14. The tuning of which two components affects performance more than any other tuning of the DB2 subsystem?

15. Why is it important to size the EDM pool to achieve an 80 percent hit ratio or better?

16. What is the purpose of read engines?

17. What is the purpose of write engines?

18. What are the SKCT and SKPT and where are they kept during execution?

ANSWERS

1. Dynamic SQL is used when using SPUFI and QMF. Static SQL is usually used when embedding SQL in a host program.

2. A plan or package is produced and stored in the DB2 directory as a result of binding static SQL. Dynamic SQL is bound at run time and is not stored in the directory.

3. SQLCODEs and SQLSTATEs give a description of whether an SQL statement is executed successfully, the statement was executed but resulted in a warning, or the statement was not successfully executed because of an error condition.

4. The purpose of the optimizer is to choose a good access path for retrieving or changing data without the person writing the SQL having to know how the data is stored other than knowing the table and column names.

5. You are known to DB2 through your authorization ID. This can be your TSO user ID, CICS ID, IMS ID, or a secondary authorization ID.

6. DB2 records information on all objects created, plans and packages that are bound, privileges granted, and utilities execution in the catalog tables. You can select from the catalog tables to get information on objects that have been created, plans and packages that have been bound, privileges granted, and the status of objects after executing utilities if you have authority to select from the catalog tables.

7. You can access most information in the directory but not with SELECT statements. The DISPLAY DATABASE command can be used to get information on databases. The REPORT utility can be used to get information on the resources required for a recovery. The DISPLAY UTILITY command can be used to get information on utilities that have been submitted and have not completed successful execution. Information on the plans and packages in the directory cannot be accessed. Information is available from several catalog tables on plans and packages.

8. A thread is allocated for a host program (including one written in COBOL) when the first SQL statement is executed in the program. A thread is not allocated when the program initially executes COBOL statements before it executes SQL.

9. Trace statistics are collected by the systems services address space on all of the address spaces including systems services, database services, IRLM, DDF, and stored procedures address spaces.

10. Typically trace statistics are read and analyzed using a performance monitor product.

11. DM and RDS are executed from the database services address space.

12. The buffer pools, EDM pool, sort pools, RID pool, and general working storage are part of the database services address space.

13. The sort pool is not shared among multiple programs executing concurrently. A sort pool is allocated and used for a single program.

14. The tuning of the buffer pools and EDM pool affects performance more than any other tuning of the DB2 subsystem.

15. Is it important to size the EDM pool to achieve an 80 percent hit ratio to minimize I/O and resources to read and allocate the plan, package, and DBD each time a program is executed.

16. Read engines are used by buffer manager to read up to and including 32 pages with a single I/O for sequential prefetch, dynamic prefetch, and list prefetch.

17. Write engines are used by buffer manager to write up to and including 32 pages with a single I/O for deferred write.

18. The SKCT and SKPT are basically master copies of the plans and packages kept in the EDM pool during execution.

FIGURES

Creating STOGROUPs, Databases, and Buffer Pools

CD.1 INTRODUCTION

A database is a collection of tablespaces, tables, and indexes in DB2. These are physical objects that occupy space on DASD. Before physical objects are created it is necessary to provide space on DASD using storage groups or user defined data sets. Figure CD.1 shows the use of a storage group with two volumes of DASD. A database is created referencing the storage group. Tablespaces and indexes are created referencing the database and optionally referencing other storage groups as discussed in Chapter TS. A tablespace can contain one or multiple tables, and one or multiple indexes can be created on a table. A view unlike physical objects does not occupy space on DASD. A view is a way of looking at some or all columns and rows in one or more tables as discussed in Chapter CT.

Figure CD.1. DB2 objects

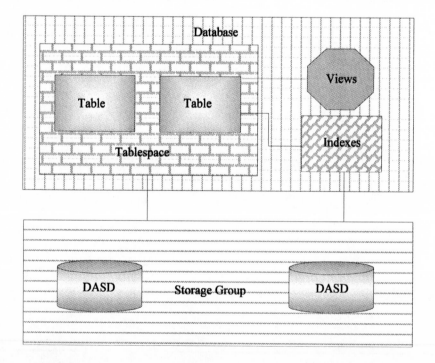

The creation of databases is straightforward but there are a number of guidelines that should be considered in sizing the database. The data must be brought into central storage for processing. We will discuss the many options that you have available in designing buffer pools to contain the data depending on how it is processed.

CD.2 SPACE FOR TABLESPACES AND INDEX SPACES

Tablespaces and indexes reside in virtual storage access method (VSAM) data sets. DB2 creates a VSAM linear data set (LDS) when you create a tablespace or index if you are using storage groups. If more than one data set is required to house a large tablespace, DB2 creates them. Multiple data sets used for a tablespace or index are referred to as a page set. Optionally, you can create a LDS or entry sequence data set (ESDS). We will first look at how to create storage groups and user defined data sets, and then at the pros and cons of these alternatives as well as data set placement on DASD.

Create a Storage Group

Here is an example for creating the storage group DASPJSTG consisting of two volumes.

```
CREATE STOGROUP DASPJSTG
    VOLUMES (VOL1, VOL4)
    VCAT VCATID;
```

The VOLUMES parameter is used to give the volume serial identifiers of DASD for the storage group. Volumes are used by DB2 in the order in which they are listed in the VOLUMES parameter. Once the first volume is filled, DB2 uses the volume listed second, third, etc. Optionally, you can use VOLUMES ('*') to have Data Facility Storage Management Subsystem data facility product (DFSMSdfp) control placement of tablespaces and indexes across volumes. The DFSMSdfp product is often referred to simply as SMS as is done in this book. The VCAT parameter is used to specify the integrated catalog facility (ICF) high level qualifier of the catalog name (or alias if the name is more than 8 bytes), VCATID is used in the example.

If there is more than one DB2 subsystem on a processor and you are not using sysplex data sharing, do create a separate ICF catalog for each DB2 subsystem. Otherwise, more than one tablespace can be created with the same VSAM data set name and the tablespaces will use the same VSAM data set. Obviously, this can result in data integrity problems.

A volume assigned to a storage group is not dedicated to it. Non-DB2 data sets can be allocated on the volume and a volume can be assigned to more than one storage group. The maximum number of volumes in a storage group is 133. The volumes must be of the same device type. The maximum number of volumes per data set is 59.

Typically, the systems administrator creates storage groups. Indeed, the person who creates storage groups must have SYSADM, SYSCTRL, or CREATESG privileges.

Alter a Storage Group

Volumes can be added and removed from a storage group like:

```
ALTER STOGROUP DASPJSTG
   ADD     VOLUMES(VOL6)
   REMOVE VOLUMES(VOL4);
```

There is no loss of data when removing a volume. Once a volume is removed, no more objects will be placed on the volume. The execution of the reorganization, load replace, or recover utilities result in the object being placed on another volume in the storage group. If all volumes are removed from a storage group, objects must be altered to place them in another storage group. Otherwise, the utilities will have no space to place the data.

The DROP STOGROUP DASPJSTG statement can be used to remove a storage group. If any page sets refer to the storage group, a -616 SQLCODE is issued and the storage group is not dropped. It is necessary to first alter tablespaces and indexes to reside in another storage group after stopping the objects.

User Defined Data Sets

An alternative to using storage groups is to create VSAM data sets using the

IDCAMS program to execute access method services (AMS) commands to create, alter, and delete data sets. Some VSAM parameters can be tailored, other must have specific values, and some are ignored by DB2.

Some parameters can be tailored to specific requirements, for example, LDS or ESDS, STAGE and NODESTAGEWAIT for 3850 MSS and TO or FOR can be used to prevent deletion for a specified period of time.

Some parameters must have specific values when using ESDS data sets, for example, NONINDEXED, RECORDSIZE of 4089, CONTROLINTERVALSIZE of 4096, and SHAREOPTIONS (3,3) or SHAREOPTIONS (1,3) for shared databases.

Some parameters will not be used by DB2, for example, SPANNED, EXCEPTIONEXIT, SPEED, BUFFERSPACE, and WRITECHECK.

A strict naming convention must be used when creating the VSAM data sets for use by DB2. The naming convention follows the form c.s.d.p.i.t, for example:

Tablespaces are named like:

```
ICFNAME.DSNDBD.DASPJDB.PTSP.I0001.A001
```

Indexes are named like:

```
ICFNAME.DSNDBD.DASPJDB.PTSPX.I0001.A001
```

Here is a brief description of each node of the data set name:

c = ICFNAME (ICF catalog name or alias) to be specified in USING VCAT clause on the CREATE TABLESPACE statement

s = DSNDBD for VSAM data
    DSNDBC for VSAM cluster

d = Database name into which the tablespace or index is to be created

p = Tablespace name to be used in the CREATE TABLESPACE statement or index name to be used in CREATE INDEX statement

I = The literal I0001 or J0001 when using online reorganization as discussed in Chapter RR. Do not use T0001 because it is used when renaming data sets if FASTSWITCH NO is used.

t = The literal "A" followed by a 4-digit data set number (0001, for example). This node of the tablespace is incremented by 1 for each data set.

Comparison of Storage Groups and User Defined Data Sets

DB2 professionals responsible for creating tablespaces and indexes need not be knowledgeable in creating and maintaining VSAM data sets when using storage groups. DB2 creates, alters, and deletes the necessary VSAM data sets for tablespaces and index spaces. Even if the developer is knowledgeable of VSAM, it is certainly a time consuming task to create 450 data sets for 150 tables each of which has two indexes on average, for example.

If a tablespace exceeds the maximum number of bytes allowed for a VSAM data set, DB2 will automatically create additional data sets as needed to allow for up to 64 GB of data for a tablespace or 16 TB (V6) of data for large partitioned tablespaces when using storage groups as discussed in Chapter TS. If user defined data sets are used, you must know when the additional data sets are required and create and maintain them. It is necessary to delete the underlying data sets after dropping a tablespace or index for the space to be reusable when using user defined data. In contrast, DB2 automatically deletes the data sets when objects are dropped when using storage groups.

The ALTER statement can be used to change the space allocation for tablespaces and indexes when using storage groups. In contrast, when using user defined data sets, you must make the changes using IDCAMS commands typically after unloading the data and before reloading the data as discussed in Chapter RR. In addition, the selects from the catalog tables described in Chapter RR cannot be used for space management because the space allocations for user defined data sets are not in the catalog tables. One technique used by some developers is to alter to use storage groups, execute the STOSPACE utility, and alter back to use VCAT.

User defined data sets are used by some developers to control the placement of data sets on DASD and to comply with storage management policies of the organization.

Data Set Placement on DASD

Small to medium (a few cylinders, for example) tablespaces and indexes can be placed on contiguous DASD space. This is advisable because minimal seek time will be required to access the indexes followed by the tablespace.

It is important to spread large tablespaces and indexes across multiple volumes, channels, and control units. This will spread I/O activity across the devices and also provide for efficient DB2 parallelism. Figure CD.2 shows the separation of tablespaces from their associated indexes on DASD. This is a good strategy. It avoids having to seek to the tablespace after having located reference to rows using indexes. Work can be done on the tablespace and indexes in parallel with minimal seek time.

Figure CD.2. Separation of tablespaces and indexes

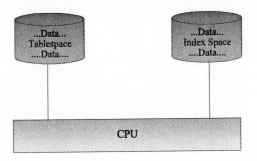

You do have direct control over placement of data sets on DASD when using user defined data sets. However, this is a manual and time consuming process. Some DASD placement control can be achieved, when using storage groups, by creating a storage group for tablespaces and a separate storage group for indexes. If you need to favor some frequently processed tablespaces or indexes, they can be placed in a storage group along with infrequently processed data to minimize seek time. You need to create and manage storage groups for data set placement. A technique used by some developers is to assign only one or a few DASD volumes to a storage group and create or alter tablespaces and indexes to achieve the required volume separation. You can create a storage group for specific tablespaces and another one for specific indexes.

SMS is a good product for managing DASD. However, special considerations are required for data set placement. You can assign data sets to specific storage classes based on an established naming convention to achieve separation. For example, if the index names begin with X, VCAT.*.*.X* can be used for the assignment of indexes. The guarantee space option of SMS can be used to specify the volume ID where the data sets are to be placed. Of course, for the named data set, the advantages of using SMS for space management is lost. Other alternatives are to use separate SMS storage groups or an exit can be used to determine placement of data sets.

Dr. Lou Agosta clarifies the use of GUARANTEED SPACE = YES in that it tells SMS three things. First, do not execute the Automated Class Selection (ACS) routines to determine volume placement of the data set based on its name, storage class, performance characteristics, or other data set attributes. Second, place the data set on the user-specified device. Third, space is not guaranteed in that if there is no space available where the data set is supposed to be placed, no space is allocated. Lou cautions that "GUARANTEED SPACE" does not really guarantee anything, much less space. Rather the DBA (or responsible person) has to guarantee that space is available on the specified volume. Space is "guaranteed" by the DBA, not by SMS or DB2.

Recommendation: Consider using a naming convention to control placement of data sets.

CD.3 CREATING A DATABASE

The CREATE DATABASE statement causes the initial creation of a Database Descriptor (DBD). Descriptive information about objects and object IDs are placed in the DBD by DB2 as the objects are created. Object IDs are two-byte small integers assigned by DB2 to objects when they are created. They are used internally by DB2 to manage objects. DBDs reside in the Environmental Descriptor Manager (EDM) pool along with plans and packages in central storage when SQL data manipulation statements are executed that reference objects in the database. The DBD is divided into 32 KB chunks to minimize fragmentation of space in the EDM pool. The maximum number of databases that can be created on a DB2 subsystem is 65,279. Here is an example of creating the DASPJDB database.

```
CREATE DATABASE DASPJDB
   STOGROUP DASPJSTG
   CCSID EBCDIC
   BUFFERPOOL BP1
   INDEXBP BP2;
```

The maximum length of a database, storage group, or tablespace name is eight alphanumeric characters. The STOGROUP, and INDEXBP (V6) parameters establish a default storage group, buffer pool for tablespaces, and buffer pool for indexes for objects created in the database. The defaults can be overridden when creating tablespaces and indexes in the database. If the buffer pools for tablespace and indexes are not specified, the installation default of BP0 is used. The installation default can be changed from BP0 to another buffer pool for application tablespaces and yet another buffer pool for application indexes on installation panel DSNTIP1 or DSNZPARM DSN6SYSP TBSBPOOL and IDXBPOOL (V6). The STOGROUP, BUFFERPOOL, and INDEXBP parameters can be altered as shown in the following statement. We will discuss the CCSID parameter later in this section.

```
ALTER DATABASE DASPJDB
   STOGROUP DANEWSTG
   BUFFERPOOL BP3
   INDEXBP BP4;
```

Factors that Affect Placement of Objects in a Database

Creating a database is very straightforward. There are a number of considerations in designing a database. In general, one database is created for an application system. However, this depends to a very large extent on the number of objects that need to be created and managed within an application system or a subject area.

Concurrency and the DBD: An exclusive lock is taken on a DBD when objects are created, altered, or deleted. The bind of static and dynamic SQL requires a share lock on the DBD. Such operations must wait for commit processing to release the exclusive lock required by a data definition statement. Locks are held during the bind and execution of dynamic SQL until commit processing. The utilities take locks on the DBD. These factors suggest that placing too many objects in a database can result in lock contention.

Logging: When objects are created, altered, and dropped, and when segmented tablespaces are reorganized, the entire DBD is replaced and logged. A large DBD increases the resources required for logging and the required size of the logs considerably.

Administration and privileges can be at the database level: Database administration (DBADM) privileges can be granted at the database level. This allows a person with DBADM privileges to create, alter, and delete objects in the database, use utilities on the objects, execute commands on the objects including START and STOP, and DISPLAY database commands. This suggests that objects to be managed by an AUTHID be placed in a database and the AUTHID be given DBADM authority.

Databases for business professionals: If business professionals are given the privilege to create their own personal tables or save data using an interactive tool such as Query Management Facility (QMF), exercise caution as to the number of users that use a given database to avoid lock contention and ease management of the objects in the database. You might consider a database for each department of about 10 users as a rule of thumb.

Location of Objects in Databases: You need not be concerned with the location of objects in various databases when issuing SQL data manipulation statements. DB2 will make this determination at bind time based on information in the catalog and directory tables.

Database Size

The maximum number of objects allowed by DB2 in a database is 10,000. (The theoretical maximum size of a DBD is 2 GB.) However, you do not want too many objects in a database, nor do you want it to be too large for the reasons discussed in the previous subsection, this subsection, and in Chapter CO.

DB2 limits the DBD size to < 25 percent of the EDM pool. A -904 SQLCODE (00C9008F reason code) is received (resource unavailable). This limit is imposed by DB2 at run time and can result in an unpleasant surprise. Be cautious regarding too large of a DBD for the EDM pool and workload. Tablespaces and indexes cannot be altered to use another database. It is necessary to unload the data; drop the tablespace; create the tablespace, table, and indexes; load the data; grant privileges; execute RUNSTATS; and rebind plans and packages (or accept an automatic rebind).

DBD Increases in Size: If tables are created and dropped in a segmented tablespace, the DBD increases in size. This can occur in a test environment, and in a decision support system where users create and drop their own objects, drop and recreate data entry type tables, etc. In order to make the space reusable, it is necessary to perform several steps:

♦   Reorganize the tablespace which places a Relative Byte Address (RBA) in SYSCOPY beyond the dropped table.
♦   Delete old image copies of the tablespace with the MODIFY utility as discussed in Chapter CR. For example, the -MODIFY RECOVERY TABLESPACE DASPJDB.DASPJTSP DELETE DATE(*) command will delete all image copies for the DASPJTSP tablespace in the DASPJDB.
♦   Take 1 to 4 image copies for local and recovery sites with one tablespace scan as described in Chapter CR.

Control information in the DBD is no longer required for recovery, and the object IDs can be reused for future recoverability after the procedure is performed. In one case, a 2.5 MB DBD was reduced to 113 KB by following the procedure.

An alternative is to rebuild the DBD from the catalog tables using the REPAIR utility like:

```
REPAIR DBD REBUILD DATABASE DASPJDB
```

EBCDIC, UNICODE, and ASCII Encoding Schemes

IBM stores data using the Extended Binary Coded Decimal Interchange

Code (EBCDIC) encoding scheme on mainframes data sets in most cases. Tables will contain data in EBCDIC format by default. The default is Coded Character Set Identifier (CCSID) of EBCDIC as shown in the earlier CREATE DATABASE statement. The data can be stored using American Standard Code for Information Interchange (ASCII) encoding scheme by specifying CCSID ASCII. Optionally, the data can be stored in UNICODE which supports multilingual data (V7). (We will probably see a great deal more usage of UNICODE in V7+1.) It supports almost all living languages in the world and conforms to the ISO-10646 standard. UNICODE is a good choice for companies that do business internationally. You can get details from http://www.unicode.org. UNICODE characters require from one to size bytes, depending on the character and type of UNICODE chosen. This is in contrast to EBCDIC and ASCII which require one byte per character (except when using the double byte character set for Asian languages). UNICODE UTF-8 requires one byte for most characters (except n with ~ on top, for example). This is a good choice for most English speaking countries. A sort is done in binary sequence, not necessarily in EBCDIC sequence.

The CCSID of EBCDIC, UNICODE or ASCII can be specified when creating a database or tablespace in which case all tables created in the database or tablespace use the specified encoding scheme. It can also be specified on the installation panel DSNTIPF. Optionally, the CCSID can be specified for specific tables as well as declare and create global temporary tables as they are created. The encoding scheme need not match the format of other tables in the database and tablespace. However, all tables referenced in an SQL statement must be defined with the same encoding scheme and the encoding screen can be specified when binding SQL. Data to be loaded into a table using the LOAD utility can be in EBCDIC, UNICODE, or ASCII format with the default being EBCDIC format.

Most personal computers (PC) and work stations store data using the ASCII encoding scheme. If a table is going to be processed mostly by a client on a PC or work station, storing the data using the ASCII encoding scheme has advantages. It avoids the costs of translating from the EBCDIC to the ASCII encoding scheme before the data is transmitted to a client as well as translation from ASCII to EBCDIC when data is returned to the mainframe. When a table is accessed from an EBCDIC application (3270 terminal users, batch applications, etc.), DB2 translates from UNICODE or ASCII to EBCDIC automatically.

You can ALTER CCSID identifier to include/exclude the Euro symbol for newly created objects. Existing tablespaces can be altered as discussed in Chapter TS.

CD.4 BUFFER POOLS

One or more buffer pools must exist to hold data and index pages in the central storage while they are being processed. A buffer pool consists of a virtual pool which resides in central storage, and optionally, a data space in central storage and a hiperpool (hiper is derived from the first two characters of *high* and the first three characters of *performance*.) which resides in expanded storage. How virtual pools, data spaces, and hiperpools are used and managed is discussed throughout the remainder of this section.

Advantages of Virtual Pools

The primary purpose of buffer pools is to hold frequently referenced data and index pages in storage to minimize the number of I/O to DASD, the I/O transfer time, the CPU time to issue the physical I/O, and I/O contention. Buffer manager uses look-aside buffering to minimize these costs. For example, a user can cause one or more pages to be read into a virtual pool by executing SQL statements. The user can select and update the data while it resides in a virtual pool or data space. Other users can select and update the same pages without incurring I/O to DASD. A user must commit any inserts, updates, and deletes before subsequent users can process the same data. The updated page need not be written to the database immediately after it is committed and before the next user reads or updates the same page. However, the changed data is logged to DASD to avoid any loss of data in case of a power failure, for example. Chapter CC contains a detailed description of the serialization of update activity to ensure data integrity.

Disadvantages of Small Virtual Pools

If a virtual pool is too small for the workload, it is considered a small virtual pool. The hit ratio is the percentage of times that a page is found in the pool and a physical I/O is not required. It is used to determine if the virtual pool is too small for the workload as discussed later in this section.

There are a number of thresholds used for controlling how the buffer pool is used as discussed in Section CD.7. Frequently exceeding these thresholds can adversely affect performance. For example, the optimizer may have requested sequential prefetch, list prefetch, dynamic prefetch, or parallelism at bind time. These efficient techniques cannot be used at run time or are discontinued during execution if there is insufficient space in the virtual pool. In addition, deferred write can be disabled which detracts from the performance of writing updated pages to DASD.

If the virtual pool is too small for the workload, two critical thresholds can be reached. If 95 percent of the pages are marked in-use (data management threshold), an I/O is issued for each row rather than the usual process of reading a page and processing all qualifying rows on the page. If 97.5 percent of pages are marked in-use (immediate write threshold), writes are synchronous to the log and data. This means that the I/O to write an updated page is not issued until after the completion of the I/O to the log. Normally, I/O to the data pages is issued immediately after issuing I/O to the log.

Example of hitting the 95 percent threshold: A batch job at a particular company normally completed using about one minute of CPU time. One evening the operator noticed that the job was still running after using about 30 minutes of CPU time. The operator canceled the job, knowing that there must be a problem. The next day an investigation was done into the cause of the problem. It was discovered that the 95 percent threshold had been reached and over 6 million getpages had been issued compared to the more typical 430,000 getpages for the job. The problem was that a getpage was issued for each row rather than for each page in most cases.

An IBM test was conducted on a 3090-200 computer to get an idea of the effect of buffer pool size on the transaction rate. The transaction rate went from 32 transactions per second with, 2,000 pages in the buffer, to 42 transactions per second with 8,000, pages in the buffer, while maintaining, 0.4 second response time.

Sizing the buffer pool for the workload is the single most important tuning of a DB2 subsystem in achieving good application system performance. It impacts the number of I/O that must be issued, the I/O time, the number of getpages, and CPU time to issue the I/O and getpages.

Page Size Depends on Buffer Pool Assignment

The data page size is determined by your choice of a buffer pool when creating a database, tablespace, or index space. BP0, BP1, BP2, through BP49 house 4 KB pages, BP8K0 thru BP8K9 house 8 KB pages (V6), BP16K0 thru BP16K9 house 16 KB pages (V6), and BP32K, BP32K1, BP32K2, through BP32K9 house 32 KB pages. Do be cautious with the using buffer pool pages greater than 4 KB. An I/O brings in 8, 16, or 32 pages with other buffer pool page sizes.

BP0 is used by the utilities and when reading and writing the work tablespaces in DSNDB07 by default. This can be changed as will be discussed. BP0 is used when DB2 processes the catalog and directory tables. This cannot be changed at present.

4 KB page buffers should be used for most tablespaces and is used for all indexes.

8, 16, and 32 KB page buffers are useful for long rows with a length greater than 2037 (½ of 4 KB less overhead). This is because only one row fits on a 4 KB page and the remainder of the page cannot be used. If the tablespace has rows longer than 4 KB, including the page overhead, it is necessary to use 8, 16, or 32 KB size pages. The goal is to minimize the amount of unusable space on a page.

Large page sizes reduce resources required for serialization, which is particularly important in a sysplex data sharing environment. One-fourth of the resources for page registration and serialization are required when using 16 KB pages, compared to 4 KB pages, assuming page level locking. However, larger page sizes opens the door for increased serialization contention.

If mostly batch processing, where most rows are processed on a page, the number of getpage and relpage are reduced which reduces CPU time.

Larger page sizes require more I/O time and virtual storage usage for most row lengths. A 32 KB page must be brought into the virtual pool to process 1 row of say 100 bytes, for example. Contiguous virtual storage is required for each of the 8, 16, or 32 KB page. This can result in fragmented space where there is space for a number of 4 KB pages but insufficient contiguous space for the larger page sizes, particularly 32 KB pages. The I/O transfer time for 32 KB pages is 8 times that of using 4 KB buffers (8 * 4 KB page = 32 KB page) which is clearly not desirable for average row lengths.

Even if you have no 32 KB page tablespaces, a 32 KB page buffer pool is required in case selecting from multiple tables gives a result row of over 4 KB. In this case, DB2 automatically uses the 32 KB page buffer pool.

Buffer Management

An overview of the work done by the buffer manager was covered in Chapter CO. In this section, we will look at the details of how buffer management locates a required page to satisfy an SQL statement. The buffer manager is a very important component of DB2. It was invented, developed, and remains under the management of Dr. Jim Teng. Indeed, IBM which holds several patents on the buffer manager as a result of his work.

A virtual pool (VP) is created using a GETMAIN instruction when the first data set is opened that references the VP. The VP is deleted when all data sets using a buffer pool are closed to avoid wasting space.

Buffer pages are located using a hash table of anchor points and buffer headers as indicated in Figure CD.3. The page set ID and relative page number within the page set are input to the hashing algorithm. The result is a pointer to an entry in an anchor point table which points to a buffer header. The number of anchor points in the table is MAX(624, 0.2 * number of buffers in the pool). (The anchor point table is dynamically reconfigured when the pool size is changed.)

Figure CD.3. Locating a page in the buffer

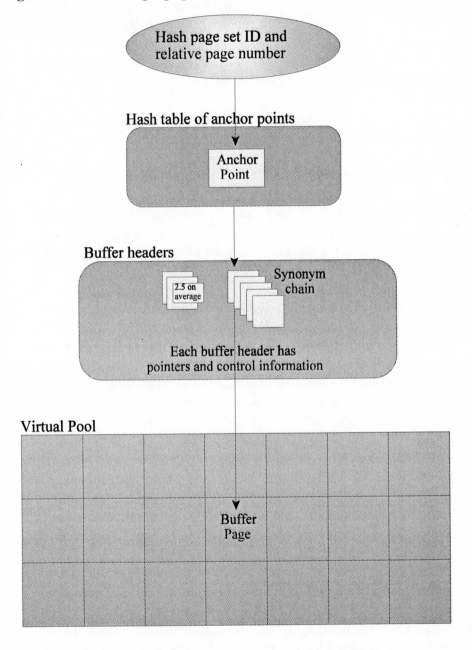

A hashing algorithm always results in producing duplicate values. These duplicate values of synonym pointers are managed in the buffer header. There are a maximum of 5 synonym pointers with an average search of 2.5 based on a Poisson distribution. In addition, the buffer header contains a pointer to a buffer page or a value of 0 indicates that the page is not in buffer. It contains chains of page addresses for reuse of pages, deferred write, etc. There is also control information, counters, flags, etc. in the buffer header. A good deal of information on the operations of buffer manager is from Chuck Hoover's mini books (as he calls them) published by his previous employer, Compuware, Inc.

If the page is not in the virtual pool and a hiperpool exists, similar structures and processing are used to determine if the page is in the hiperpool.

Reuse of Buffer Pages

A buffer pool will be filled with pages read and updated for various processing. The buffer pages are reused based on how they are read, processed, and placed on reuse chains in the buffer headers. The pages are reused in the following order.

1) **Most Recently Used (MRU)** pages are reused first. Pages read for parallel processing (pages from a large table can be placed on the MRU chain and pages from a small table can be placed on the LRU chain) are placed on the MRU chain of pages in the buffer header. Also placed on the chain are pages read for merging of sorted rows and pages read for some utilities. Basically MRU pages are those that are very unlikely to be rereferenced by others.

2) **Sequential Least Recently Used (SLRU)** pages are reused after all the page slots on the MRU chain have been reused. SLRU pages are those that are read with sequential, dynamic, and list prefetch. If a SLRU page is referenced at random, it is placed on the LRU chain to allow others to reference the page for as long as possible. No more than 80 percent of the buffer is used for sequentially read pages by default.

3) **Least Recently Used (LRU)** pages are those that are read at random using a matching index scan, for example. Twenty percent of the buffer is reserved for random reads by default. Randomly read pages can also use the 80 percent of pages used for sequential read pages if the space is not already in use.

There are SLRU and LRU chains for the reuse of hiperpool pages.

4) **A first-in-first-out (FIFO)** algorithm can be used for the reuse of pages.

It is a lower cost method for reuse of pages than LRU as will be discussed.

You can specify LRU or FIFO by buffer pool.

Status of Buffer Pool Pages

Each page in a virtual pool has a status indicating how the page can be used.

A buffer page cannot be used to receive a page from DASD if it is marked as in-use or considered an updated page. An in-use page is one where data manager (DM) has issued a getpage and has not issued a set write pending or released the page (relpage). An updated page is one where DM has set write pending on for the page and buffer manager has placed the page on a deferred write queue for the data set.

A buffer page can be used to receive a page from DASD if the page is available, stealable or empty. An available page is one that has not been used since the virtual pool was first allocated. A stealable page is one where DM has issued a getpage and relpage, and write pending is not active. A page slot is not stealable if the page or row has a S, U, or X lock in most cases. An empty page is one that has been moved to the hiperpool.

All hiperpool pages are stealable.

CD.5 BUFFER POOL HIT RATIOS

As discussed at the beginning of Section CD.4, sizing the buffer pool for the workload is critical to the performance of application systems. A good measure of whether the buffer pool has been sized for the workload and whether more or less space is required is the hit ratio. The hit ratio is the percentage of time that a page is found in the buffer pool when requested by DM and a physical I/O is not required. A good goal is to locate a required page in the buffer pool 80 to 90 percent of the time, assuming that the pages are referenced by one or more users.

The buffer pool hit ratio can be calculated using the formula:

```
(getpages - synchronous reads - asynchronous reads)
/ getpages
```

If your hit ratio is low, do increase the buffer pool size. Take measurements and calculate the hit ratio again. If the hit ratio is still too low, increase the buffer pool size again and calculate the hit ratio. Repeat this process until the hit ratio flattens out as shown in Figure CD.4.

Figure CD.4. Buffer hit ratios

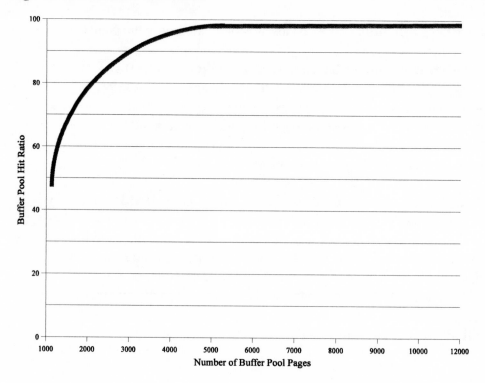

Notice that the hit ratio is less than 50 percent in the example when using a 1,000 page buffer pool. As the number of pages assigned to the buffer pool increases so does the hit ratio until about 5,000 pages have been assigned to the buffer pool. At this point the hit ratio is approaching 98 percent. Adding pages to the buffer pool increases the hit ratio very little. The goal of increasing the hit ratio until it flatten out has been accomplished at about 5,000 pages. If you run out of central storage space to assign to the virtual pool before the required hit ratio is reached, consider using hiperpools.

Initial sizing of a buffer pool can be accomplished using two techniques. Set the number of virtual pool pages equal to number of getpages per second. This yielded a 60 percent hit ratio in one case. An alternative is to size the pool to contain 10 to 20 percent of the tablespaces and indexes pages assigned to a pool. In one case when the virtual pool was sized to contain 10 percent of the data and index pages, a 90 percent hit ratio was achieved.

CD.6 Data Spaces and Hiperpools

Additional storage for buffer pools can be made available though the use of data spaces and hiperpools. This section describes data spaces and hiperpools in terms of what they are, how they can be used, and the advantages and disadvantages of the spaces

Managing within Limits

A word of 4 bytes and 32 bits where 1 bit is used as a parity bit is used for addressability on most computers including mainframes and PCs. This gives an architectural limit of addressable storage of 2 GB, calculated as 2^{31}. Therefore, an address space is limited to 2 GB prior to zSeries computers. Database services resides in an address space in central storage with 0.4 GB of DB2 code, working storage, EDM pool, RID pool, sort pool, and virtual pools. This limits the size of the pools, in particular the virtual pool.

Data space provides for addressing a large number of pages with zSeries computers,
32 GB if using 4 KB pages and 256 GB if using 32 KB pages with 64 bit addressing minus 1 parity bit (2^{63}). You can page fix data space buffers above 2 GB (V7 APAR PQ25914). Virtual pool buffers and log buffers that reside above 2 GB real storage will not be moved when they need to be page fixed for I/O (V7 APAR PQ36933).

A hiperpool (high performance pool) provides for addressing 8 GB calculated as 2 GB per hiperpool times 4 which is the maximum number of hiperpools that an be used with a buffer pool. Hiperpools reside in expanded storage only (ESO) (also known as cache) type hiperspace. SCROLL type hiperspace cannot be accessed in a cross memory environment. Therefore, it cannot be used for hiperpools.

Virtual Pool, Data Spaces, and Hiperpools Comparison

Data spaces and hiperpools both provide relief from the 1.6 GB (2 GB is the current limit per address space less other central storage required by DB2) virtual pool limit if this is an issue at your company. They both reside outside of the database services address space (DBM1). Virtual pools and data spaces reside in central storage as contrasted to hiperpools which reside in expanded storage. The primary benefit of data spaces is their size of 32 GB if 1.6 GB is a constraining factor (not part of 2 GB limit per address space). They are particularly useful with 64 bit addressability.

Virtual pools are byte addressable in contrast to data spaces and hiperpools which are page addressable as used by DB2. This means that a data space and hiperpool page must be moved to central storage for comparisons and extraction of columns and rows. Programs like buffer manager and data manager can manipulate data directly in a virtual pool (unlike a data space and hiperpool). Only the virtual pool can contain common areas, system data, and programs. Buffer management of buffers must be done in the virtual pool. Data spaces pages are copied (MVCL) into a lookaside buffer in DBM1 (1 buffer for each page size of 4, 8, 16 and 32 KB pages) for comparisons and extraction of columns and rows when getpages are issued by data manager. Changed pages are copied to the virtual pool when a relpage is issued. The lookaside buffer is sized and managed by DB2 based on the number of active threads (10 to 40 MB, for example, with an initial size of 1 MB). Architecturally, data spaces are byte addressable. However, they are managed by DB2 at the page level through the use of the lookaside buffer. A data space page requires 128 bytes in the virtual pool. More space is required to manage hiperpools in comparison. The use of data spaces can increase CPU time by from 1 to 10 percent.

All three types of spaces can contain data and index pages. However, updated pages must reside in the virtual pool or data space. Updated pages must be written to DASD before they can be moved to a hiperpool. Pages reside in a virtual pool or hiperpool, not both. An updated page (also known as a *dirty page*) must be written to DASD before being cached in a hiperpool. Pages in a hiperpool are read-only.

z/OS and OS/390 can page out virtual pool and data space pages to expanded storage or DASD. Pages can be read directly into virtual pool and data space. In contrast, pages must goes through virtual pool to be placed in hiperpool. Hiperpool requires a move page (MVPG) hardware instruction. Fast Synchronous Data Mover Facility is used on zSeries computers (V7 APAR PQ38174). Asynchronous data mover facility (ADMF) microcode is used on earlier computers unlike other 2 types of spaces.

Figure CD.5 summarizes the comparison of virtual pool, data spaces, and hiperpools.

Figure CD.5. Virtual pool, data spaces, and hiperpools comparison

Feature	Virtual Pool	Data Space	Hiper-pool
Type of storage	Central	Central	Expanded
Maximum size	1.6 GB	32 GB	8 GB
Outside of database services address space (DBM1)	No	Yes	Yes
Addressability	Byte	Page*	Page
Can contain common areas, system data, & programs	Yes	No	No
Contain updated pages not written to DASD	Yes	Yes	No
Subject to z/OS and OS/390 paging	Yes	Yes	No
Pages can be read directly into space	Yes	Yes	No
Requires MVPG hardware instruction	No	No	Yes

OS/390 MVS Programming: Extended Addressability Guide manual states that data space pages are byte addressable (perhaps the pages will be byte addressable in DB2 in the future as it takes advantages of 64 bit addressability on zSeries processors).

Data Space Specifics

If more than 1.6 GB of central storage is needed for buffers, data spaces can be considered. Data spaces requires less CPU and elapsed time compared with hiperpools using zSeries processors and z/OS or OS/390 2.1. In one test case, data spaces were 30 percent more efficient that hiperpools in terms of CPU and elapsed time with 100 percent hit ratio. The use of data spaces increases CPU usage by about 1 to 10 percent using 32 bit addressability based on preliminary results. The dynamic cache can be placed in a data space to relieves EDM pool space requirements. A data space can support no more than one virtual pool. However, a virtual pool can have one or more data spaces assigned to it.

Hiperpool Specifics

If you decide to use a hiperpool, there is a one-to-one correspondence between a hiperpool and virtual pool. A hiperpool is created when its virtual pool is created. Typically the hiperpool is larger than its corresponding virtual pool although this is not a requirement. Buffer manager moves pages from the virtual pool to the hiperpool and from the hiperpool to the virtual pool. The paging is similar to what is done by the z/OS and OS/390 operating system when it moves pages to and from central storage and DASD. A hiperpool is somewhat like DASD in that it is used to store tablespace and index pages. Also, it is like DASD in that the unit of data transfer is at the 4 KB page level.

Getting a Page from the Hiperpool: Pages are read from DASD into a virtual pool and passed to a hiperpool. For example, a getpage is issued by data manager. This causes buffer manager to look for the page using its hashing algorithm. If the page is in the virtual pool, the getpage is satisfied. If the required page is not in the virtual pool, buffer manager checks the hiperpool using the same hashing algorithm. If the page is found in the hiperpool, the page is moved to the virtual pool and is no longer addressable in the hiperpool. The getpage is satisfied. If the required page is not in the hiperpool, buffer manager initiates a physical I/O to DASD and accepts the page into the virtual pool. The getpage is satisfied. If there is no hiperpool the sequence of events are the same as described except that buffer manager does not look for the page in expanded storage.

A hiperpool is of limited value for sequentially read pages because it is unlikely that the pages will be rereferenced. A hiperpool is most useful for randomly read and processed pages.

Expanded storage for a hiperpool: Do be cautious of defining a hiperpool as being larger than available expanded storage. z/OS and OS/390 informs buffer manager that the data has been discarded due to an expanded storage shortage when buffer manager attempts to move a page from the hiperpool. Buffer manager reads the data from DASD. A count of the number of times that this occurs is maintained and reported as hiperpool read failures to reflect a shortage of expanded storage. Of course, shortages detract from efficient use of hiperpool.

z/OS and OS/390 Paging

If z/OS and OS/390 paging is experienced, reduce the size of the virtual pool, use data spaces with 64 bit addressability, or hiperpools. Hiperpools are favored if expanded storage is less costly than central storage on your computer. They are also well suited to most read-only tablespaces and indexes. This suggests the assignment these objects to a buffer pool with a hiperpool assigned to it.

Do avoid paging of pages in central storage to auxiliary or expanded storage (uses LRU algorithm). It detracts from performance significantly. Page faults result if pages are in auxiliary or expanded storage. The pages must be reread for processing. If PAGE-INS REQUIRED FOR WRITE and PAGE-INS REQUIRED FOR READ statistics are high, insufficient central storage space is available for the buffers. Do seriously consider the use data spaces or hiperpools.

Relative Cost and Speed of Storage Types

The cost of all types of storage has been decreasing in price and increasing in speed since mainframes first became available in the 1960s, and this trend continues. We will use the prices and speeds in Figure CD.5 as relative estimates. You may purchase the storage at lower prices than indicated in the figure. Central and expanded CMOS storage are priced very similarly at present. There is very little cost savings by using hiperpools. However, the relative prices for bipolar computers are similar to those shown. For example, central storage costs about three times that of expanded storage. The speed of central storage is about 1,000 times faster than that of expanded storage at the high end of the speed range. That is, both the sequential and random speeds of central storage are about 100 nanoseconds (ns) compared to expanded storage speeds of 10 to 100 microseconds (μs). Central and expanded storage are both integrated circuitry.

Figure CD.6. Relative cost and speed of storage

Storage	Cost/MB	Sequential Speed	Random Speed
Processor Cache	$100 K	10 ns	10 ns
Central Storage	3 K	100 ns	100 ns
Expanded Storage	1.2 K	10-100 μs	10-100 μs
3990 Cache	1 K	2 ms	2 ms
3390 DASD/Array	10	2 ms	20 ms
Optical Library	3	10 ms	10 sec
Tape Library	1	2 ms	2 min

The most economical direct access storage with a good sequential and random speed of 2 and 20 milliseconds (ms) is DASD. This makes DASD a good choice for storing the bulk of the data and indexes. Certainly, most companies do just that. DASD cache compares favorably with expanded storage but has a dramatically slower random speed at the time of writing. DASD cache is expected to compare more favorably with expanded storage in the future. Central and expanded CMOS storage are priced very similarly at present. Therefore, there is very little cost savings by using hiperpools. You may want to consider the use of hiperpools with CMOS processor if you are constrained by the 1.6 GB limit for a virtual pool. (Hiperpool space is not included in the 1.6 GB limit.) Low update tablespaces and indexes are a good choice for a buffer pool with a hiperpool.

DASD cache on 3990s with cylinder prestaging is used for random I/O by DB2. The cache is not used for sequential prefetch by default. It can be enabled by specifying SEQCACH of SEQ in the DSNZPARM macro DSN6SPRM or on the DSNTIPE installation panel. This is a good choice when using IBM Enterprise Storage Server (ESS) DASD. Further control is available through the use of SPRMPF32 in DSNZPARM. If SEQCACH of BYPASS is used, SPRMPF32 in DSNZPARM can be set to a non-zero value (0 is the default). This results in 3 contiguous prefetch requests before bypassing prefetch. Enabling the use of the cache with sequential prefetch is a good choice for tablespace scans and non-matching index scans which makes it useful for batch and utility processing, and for data warehousing applications provided that the pages are rereferenced. If the pages are rarely rereferenced, the cache does not improve performance. Indeed, the cache can degrade performance for random I/O by as much as 100 to 200 percent depending on the cache controller (does not apply to ESS DASD). Record rather than track caching degrades performance less, depending on how it is used.

If it is appropriate in your environment to enable the cache for sequential prefetch, it should be disabled for the DSNDB07 tablespaces. Otherwise, many concurrent accesses to logical work files on the work tablespaces will overload the cache. The cache can be disabled by specifying the volume IDs that contain work tablespaces. If you are using SMS to manage DB2 data sets, you can disable the cache at the data set level.

CD.7 CUSTOMIZING VIRTUAL POOLS AND HIPERPOOLS

If you are experiencing z/OS or OS/390 paging of the virtual pool, do use data spaces or hiperpools. A primary objective is to avoid paging.

If insufficient central storage is available for data spaces, consider sizing of hiperpools in expanded storage. A reasonable starting point is to have the hiperpool two to four times the size of its virtual pool. If the hiperpool is less than its corresponding virtual pool, or the hiperpool does not improve the hit ratio, the additional CPU time required for moving pages to and from the hiperpool is not justified in most cases.

The sizing of the hiperpool (HP) should be analyzed similar to the sizing of the virtual pool as discussed in Section CD.5. The first formula in Figure CD.7 for calculating the hit ratio is the same one suggested in the earlier section on calculating the hit ratio. The result of using the formula is the percentage of pages found in a pool (with and without a hiperpool). It can be used for both the virtual pool and hiperpool. You will also want to look at the hit ratio for only the virtual pool and for only the hiperpool which are the second and third formula in the figure.

Figure CD.7. Formula for calculating hit ratios

Ratio	Formula
Buffer pool hits (VP and HP if any)	(getpages - sync reads - asynch reads) / getpages
Virtual pool hits (subtract HP reads if any)	(getpages - HP reads - synch reads - asynch reads) / getpages
Hiperpool hits	HP reads / getpages

Size and Thresholds of Pools

The default sizes and thresholds of BP0 are shown in Figure CD.8. The use of a hiperpool is not the default. Information about virtual pools and hiperpools is recorded in the boot strap data set (BSDS) and can be changed dynamically without stopping and starting DB2. The ALTER BUFFERPOOL command can be used to change the size and thresholds of the pools. Indeed it is also used to create and delete virtual pools and hiperpools. Following is an example of the command specifying default thresholds for the virtual pool and hiperpool. The virtual pool size is set as the default and the hiperpool is made twice the size as a starting point. The assigned values remain in effect until the next ALTER BUFFERPOOL command is executed.

```
-ALTER BUFFERPOOL(BP0)
      VPSIZE   (2000)  HPSIZE  (4000)
      VPSEQT   (80)    HPSEQT   (80)
      VPPSEQT  (50)    PGSTEAL (LRU)
      VPXPSEQT (50)    VPTYPE  (PRIMARY)
      DWQT     (50)    CASTOUT (YES)
      VDWQT    (10)
```

Figure CD.8. Virtual pool and hiperpool thresholds

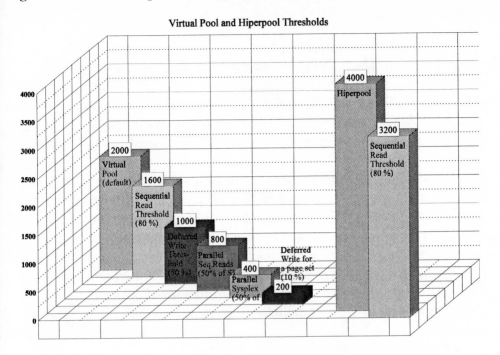

Virtual Pool and Hiperpool Thresholds

The buffer pool name follows the ALTER BUFFERPOOL command in parentheses. Following is a description of each of the parameters and guidelines on the values that should be considered.

VPSIZE is used to specify the number of page buffers in the virtual pool. There can be 0 to 400,000 4 KB pages in a 4 KB virtual pool. The default of 2,000 pages in BP0 should be increased or more virtual pools should be created, assuming medium to heavy usage. This determination can be made based on the hit ratio.

HPSIZE is used to specify the number of buffers in a hiperpool. There can be 0 to 2,097,152 4 KB pages.

VPSEQT limits the number of pages that can be used for sequential reads in the virtual pool. The default is 80 percent and the value can be between 0 and 100 percent. Zero turns off prefetch and sequential data is purged after being read. Consider less than 80 percent for virtual pools used primarily for online transactions with matching index scans. Do be cautious of too low a percentage for the few cases where prefetch is beneficial. Avoid thrashing where pages must be read more than once because the page slots are used by another process before they are used by the process that caused the initial read.

HPSEQT limits the number of pages that can be used for sequential reads in the hiperpool. The default is 80 percent and the value can be between 0 and 100 percent. Pages read with prefetch are not moved to the hiperpool if 0 is specified. This is a good choice if prefetched pages are not reused, for example, tablespace and index spaces used primarily for data warehousing and batch processing. This is the only threshold that applies to a hiperpool.

VPPSEQT limits the number of pages in a virtual pool that can house pages read using I/O and central processor (CP) parallelism as discussed in Chapter PL. VPPSEQT is a percentage of VPSEQT. The default is 50 percent of VPSEQT and can be between 0 and 100 percent. That is parallelism can use 40 percent of pool by default and in the example. The purpose of this threshold is to avoid too many pages being used for I/O and CP parallelism, which can degrade the performance of other processing. Zero turns off all modes of parallelism, which is not advisable in most cases.

VPXPSEQT limits the number of pages that can be used by an assisting DB2 for sysplex parallelism. VPXPSEQT is a percentage of VPPSEQT. The default is 50 percent of VPPSEQT and can be between 0 and 100 percent. That is, an assisting DB2 in sysplex parallelism can use 20 percent of the pool by default and in the example. The purpose of this threshold is to avoid too many pages being used for assisting in sysplex parallelism. Zero disallows a DB2 subsystem from being an assistant for sysplex parallelism and is not advisable in most cases.

DWQT indicates the percentage of in-use pages before deferred write is triggered in the virtual pool. Deferred write continues until in-use pages are 10 percent below the threshold. The default is 50 percent and the value can be between 0 and 90 percent. If 0 is specified, buffer manager uses the MIN(40, 1 percent value) for 4 KB BPs. The write I/O is issued for 32 pages after 40 pages have been updated. This allows for retaining the most recent 8 hot pages including the space map page in the buffer.

VDWQT indicates the percentage of the virtual pool that can contain updated pages from a single page set. Updated pages are written to the table when the threshold is reached. The default is 10 percent and the value can be between 0 and 90 percent. If 0 is specified, buffer manager uses the

MIN(40, 1 percent value) for 4 KB BPs with the DWQT condition. VDWQT should be less than DWQT. VDWQT is overridden by most utilities. Optionally, you can specify a number of updated pages before initiating deferred write for a data set. For example, if VDWQT (0, 250) is used, 0 means not to use a percentage and 250 means to write pages for a page set after 250 pages have been updated. If 0 rather than 250 is specified, this deferred write is not used. A reasonable starting point in estimating the value is to use 150 plus the number of threads currently inserting rows (100 in example). In this example, 128 pages are written with deferred write when the 250 page threshold is reached. The goal is to retain some of the pages in the virtual pool for further processing and avoid having rereading written pages.

DWQT and VDWQT thresholds of 90 percent are a good choice for tablespaces and indexes frequently updated. Regardless of these values, all updated pages are written to DASD at checkpoint, stop database, and stop DB2. Do be cautious of specifying too high a value for DWQT and VDWQT. This can result in delays while writing updated pages to DASD when the thresholds are reached, delays during checkpoint processing, a shortage of write engines, and a delay with stop processing. There are 300 write engines available.

PGSTEAL(LRU) (default) causes pages to be reused on a least recently used basis. It requires maintenance of page chains to determine the least recently used pages. It is a good choice in most cases.

PGSTEAL(FIFO) causes page to be reused on a first-in-first out basis (V6). The algorithm is less costly to maintain than use of the LRU algorithm. It reduces latch contention for buffer pool management. It can be useful for a buffer pool that experiences little or no I/O. For example, a buffer pool sized to page fix pages in memory. Another use of FIFO is for a buffer pool used to house very large tables that are referenced at random with little reuse of pages in the buffer.

Recommendation: Consider assigning object to separate buffer pools when FIFO has advantages. FIFO is a good choice for buffer pools designed to page fix pages in buffer

FIFO is used when VDWQT threshold is reached.

VPTYPE(PRIMARY) means virtual pool resides in the primary address space (database services address space, DBM1). This is the default.

VPTYPE(DATASPACE) means virtual pool resides in a data space.

The VGPTYPE parameters can be specified on DSNTIP1, DSNTIP2, DSNTIP6, installation panels. You can alter the VPTYPE like other parameters. However, altering VPTYPE requires reallocation of the buffer pool. You can reallocate a buffer pool without restarting DB2. The following example changes BP8 VPTYPE to a data space.

```
-ALTER BUFFERPOOL(BP8) VPSIZE(0)
-ALTER BUFFERPOOL(BP8) VPSIZE(10000)
VPTYPE(DATASPACE)
```

The new parameter values takes effect when buffer pool is next allocated.

VPTYPE for BP0 requires restarting DB2 or the following procedure can be used. Issue the ALTER command like:

```
-ALTER BUFFERPOOL(BP8) VPSIZE(0)
```

Use the STOP DATABASE command to stop all tablespaces and indexes that are using BP0. Issue the ALTER command once again like:

```
-ALTER BUFFERPOOL(BP8) VPSIZE(10000)
VPTYPE(DATASPACE)
```

Use START DATABASE command to start all tablespaces and indexes that are using BP0.

The procedure to change BP0 can be used to change any buffer pool without waiting for reallocation of the buffer pool.

CASTOUT(YES) allows z/OS and OS/390 to discard pages in the hiperpool if expanded storage is needed for other processing or usage of pages in the hiperpool is low. This is the default.

If hiperspace is stolen by z/OS and OS/390, buffer manager move page instructions will fail. Pages thought to be in the hiperpool must be read from DASD. Attempts to move pages from the virtual pool to the hiperpool will fail. Of course, performance can be adversely affected. Stolen hiperspace will be returned by z/OS or OS/390 when it is no longer required for use by others.

CASTOUT(NO) does not allow z/OS and OS/390 to steal expanded storage from the hiperpool in most cases. Exceptions are that pages can be stolen if the hiperpool is deleted, hiperspace storage area is explicitly released, z/OS and OS/390 hiperspace maintenance is required, or the address space owning the hiperspace is swapped out (DB2 is not shapable). CASTOUT NO basically pins (page fixes) pages in expanded storage and favors DB2 application systems over other processing on the computer. This can adversely affect other applications on the computer.

Alter of the CASTOUT parameter does not take effect immediately as is the case for all other ALTER BUFFERPOOL parameters.

Creating, Deleting, and Changing Pools

The ALTER BUFFERPOOL command can be used to create, delete, and change the size of a virtual pool and hiperpool. Here is an example of creating BP1 with 4,000 pages, a hiperpool with 8,000 pages, and use of default values for thresholds.

```
-ALTER BUFFERPOOL(BP1)
     VPSIZE(4000)
     HPSIZE(8000);
```

A virtual pool or hiperpool can be deleted by setting the VPSIZE or HPSIZE to 0. This causes all processing in the buffer pool to be quiesced. Here is an example of deleting virtual pool BP5.

```
-ALTER BUFFERPOOL (BP5)
     VPSIZE(0);
```

Any attempted access to an object assigned to BP5 receives a resource unavailable message. It is necessary to ALTER all objects assigned to a BP before deleting it. An exclusive lock is taken on the DBD to alter assignment of an object to a buffer pool. Stop tablespace and index space is an alternative to quiesce plans and packages that hold a share lock on the DBD. However, this does result in unavailability of objects during quiesce processing and execution of ALTER statements.

Here is an example of increasing the size of BP0 to 8,000 pages, its hiperpool to 32,000 pages, and retaining the current thresholds.

```
-ALTER BUFFERPOOL (BP0)
     VPSIZE (8000)
     HPSIZE(32000);
```

Changing the size of the virtual pool or hiperpool causes buffer manager to dynamically reconfigure the hash table for the pools and sets the sizes in the BSDS. The changes remain in effect until the buffer pool is altered again.

Thresholds that Cannot be Altered: There are only two thresholds that cannot be altered. These are the data management threshold (DMTH) and the immediate write threshold (IWTH) which are permanently set at 95 and 97.5 percent. These thresholds are discussed at the beginning of Section CD.4 as reasons for insuring that the virtual pool is well sized for the workload. These thresholds are necessary to slow activity because there is insufficient space available in the virtual pool. Basically, buffer manager has no space to place newly read pages. Hiperpools have no effect on the thresholds.

CD.8 DETERMINING USAGE OF POOLS

The DISPLAY command can be executed to determine the current status and activity of virtual pools and hiperpools like:

```
-DISPLAY BUFFERPOOL(ACTIVE)
     DETAIL(INTERVAL) LIST(ACTIVE) LSTATS
```

BUFFERPOOL(ACTIVE) requests statistics on all active buffer pools and is the default. Optionally, you can specify the name of specific buffer pools (BP0, BP1, BP32K for example) in place of the ACTIVE parameter value. Another choice is to specify BUFFERPOOL(*) which indicates that you want information on all active and inactive buffer pools.

DETAIL(INTERVAL) requests statistics accumulated since the last incremental display and is the default. DETAIL(*) requests accumulated statistics since the buffer pools first became active.

LIST(ACTIVE) requests statistics on all open and in-use tablespaces and indexes and is the default. LIST(*) requests statistics on all open tablespaces and indexes in-use and not in-use.

LSTATS provides information on I/O delays by database, tablespace, and index. The statistics are incremental since the last display.

DBNAME and SPACENAM parameters can be specified along with the name of a database, tablespace or index space when using the LIST and LSTATS parameters. If LIST is not specified, LIST(ACTIVE) is used. A specific name can be given, a range of names separated by a colon, or the wild card of asterisk can be used to take advantage of a naming convention. For example, the following command provides information on all databases beginning with DADB and all tablespaces that begin with DATSP:

```
-DISPLAY BUFFER POOL(ACTIVE)
      DBNAME(DADB*) SPACENAM(DATSP*)
```

Figure CD.9 is an example of a report on all active buffer pools. Notice that the beginning of the report gives the size and thresholds of BP0 as requested in the DISPLAY command. The hiperspace that houses the hiperpool is @001DB2T. The three-digit number is a sequence number of each hiperspace in the hiperpool with a maximum value of 4. The last four bytes are the DB2 subsystem name. The tablespaces currently using the buffer pool are listed along with a count of the number of users. The statistics on each data set are given, including the number of current and changed pages in the VP as well as the maximum. Similar statistics are given for the HP except that the number of changed pages is not given because changed pages must be written to the tablespaces before they are cached in the HP. The synchronous and asynchronous I/O delays including the average and maximum delays, and the total pages are given in the report.

Figure CD.9. Report of displaying BP0 information

```
-DISPLAY BUFFERPOOL(BP0), LIST(ACTIVE), LSTATS
```

```
BUFFER POOL NAME BP0, BUFFER POOL ID 0, USE COUNT 10


VIRTUAL BUFFER POOL SIZE = 2000 BUFFERS
   ALLOCATED                = 2000 TO BE DELETED     = 0
   IN USE/UPDATED           =  400

HIPERPOOL SIZE              = 9000 BUFFERS, CASTOUT  = YES
   ALLOCATED                = 9000 TO BE DELETED     = 0
   BACKED BY ES             = 9000

THRESHOLDS -
   VPSEQENTIAL              = 80   HP SEQUENTIAL     = 80
   DEFERRED WRITE           = 50   VER DEFERRED WR   = 10
   PARALLEL SEQUENTIAL      = 50   ASSISTING PAR SEQT= 50

HIPERSPACE NAMES - @001DB2T

TABLESPACE = DSNDB01.DBD01,    USE COUNT = 2
           = DSNDB06.SYSDBASE, USE COUNT = 1
           = DSNDB06.DSNDLX01, USE COUNT = 4

STATISTICS FOR DATASET 1 -

  VP CACHED PAGES -
     CURRENT       =           12   MAX              =    40
     CHANGED       =            8   MAX              =    20

  HP CACHED PAGES -
     CURRENT       =           40   MAX              =    80

  SYNCHRONOUS I/O DELAYS   -
     AVERAGE DELAY =           22   MAXIMUM DELAY    =    35
     TOTAL PAGES   =           23

  ASYNCHRONOUS I/O DELAYS -
     AVERAGE DELAY =            3   MAXIMUM DELAY    =     5
     TOTAL PAGES   =          640
```

More detail can be gotten by adding the parameter DETAIL to the DISPLAY command as indicated in Figure CD.10. Again the report begins with the size and thresholds of BP0. We have more detail including the number of random and sequential getpages, and synchronous I/O. We are happy to see that the 95 percent DMTH threshold has not been reached since the DISPLAY command was last executed. The number of sequential prefetch requests, prefetch I/Os, and pages read are shown in the report. Similar statistics not shown in the example are reported for list and dynamic prefetch. Prefetch has not been disabled because of no buffers and no read engines. The DWQT and VDWQT thresholds have not been hit as indicated by the zeros for the DWT HIT and VERTICAL DWT HIT field on the report. The number of I/O issued for parallelism is reported as zero. Of course, since parallelism has not been used since the last time the DISPLAY command was executed, parallelism has not been degraded.

Figure CD.10. Report of displaying BP0 detail information

```
-DISPLAY BUFFERPOOL(BP0), DETAIL
```

```
BUFFER POOL NAME BP0, BUFFER POOL ID 0, USE COUNT 10

VIRTUAL BUFFER POOL SIZE = 2000 BUFFERS
    ALLOCATED           = 2000 TO BE DELETED       =    0
    IN USE/UPDATED      =  400

HIPERPOOL SIZE          = 9000 BUFFERS, CASTOUT = YES
    ALLOCATED           = 9000 TO BE DELETED       =    0
    BACKED BY ES        = 9000

THRESHOLDS -
    VPSEQENTIAL         =    80 HP SEQUENTIAL      =   80
    DEFERRED WRITE      =    50 VER DEFERRED WR    =   10

HIPERSPACE NAMES - @001DB2T
INCREMENTAL STATISTICS SINCE 10:14:30 MAR 12, 1993
RANDOM GETPAGES      =  219614 SYN READ I/O (R)  =   7883
SEQ.   GETPAGES      = 7645409 SYN READ I/O (S)  =    521
DM CRITICAL HIT      =       0

SEQUENTIAL PREFETCH -
    REQUESTS         =   72960 PREFETCH I/Os     = 52838
    PAGES READ       = 1627587

Above 3 lines repeated for list and dynamic prefetch

PREFETCH DISABLED -
    NO BUFFER        =       0 NO READ ENGINE    =       0
SYS PAGE UPDATES     =  102335 SYS PAGE WRITTEN  =   17336
ASYNC WRITE I/O      =    1803 SYNC WRITE I/O    =       0
DWT HIT              =       0 VERTICAL DWT HIT  =       0
NO WRITE ENGINE      =       0
HIPERPOOL ACTIVITY (NOT USING ASYNCH. DATA MOVER FACILITY
    SYNC  HP READS   =   14920 SYNC  HP WRITES   =     225
    ASYNC HP READS   =    7928 ASYNC HP WRITES   =    1121
    READ FAILURES    =       0 WRITE FAILURES    =       0
HIPERPOOL ACTIVITY (USING ASYNCH. DATA MOVER FACILITY)
    SYNC HP READS    =  330372 HP WRITES         = 992577
    READ FAILURES    =       0 WRITE FAILURES    =       0
I/O PARALLEL ACTIVITY -
    PARALLEL REQUESTS =      0 DEGRADED PARALLEL =       0
```

The BSDS reports do not show pool sizes even though this information is maintained in the BSDS.

CD.9 GUIDELINES ON THE USE OF MULTIPLE VIRTUAL POOLS

There are a number of guidelines to consider when deciding which tablespaces and indexes to assign to which buffer pools based primarily on the type of data and processing expected. Some of the strategies reviewed below will be good choices for your application system.

A separate virtual pool can be used for data and index pages. This is a particularly good choice for very large tables of, 10 million rows or more, for example. The tablespace virtual pool can be relatively small if random page processing is expected and it is unlikely that the data pages will be rereferenced and remain in the buffer. The index virtual pool should be large to increase the likelihood that the index pages will remain in the buffer. Basically, this configuration assumes that you are willing to accept a physical I/O for most data pages, but seeks to avoid as many I/O to the index as possible, depending on the size of the index and the buffer pool used for the index. One company found that this strategy reduced response time from 3.7 to 0.7 seconds.

If tablespaces and indexes are frequently scanned, consider pinning them in a hiperpool. The goal is to basically make the pages resident in the hiperpool so that they are rarely read from DASD, which reduces I/O time dramatically. One company pinned a 1,655,000 row table on 138,000 pages in a hiperpool. Before the pages were pinned, a tablespace to satisfy a COUNT(*) required 316 elapsed and 8 CPU (TCB, task control block) seconds. After creating a hiperpool to contain the tablespace, the elapsed time dropped to 13 seconds and 8 CPU seconds. The amount of hiperpool space required can be reduced by using data compression as discussed in Chapter TS. If a 50 percent compression ratio is achieved, the hiperpool space required can be reduced by half. The CPU time is expected to increase, particularly for decompression during a tablespace scan.

Place frequently used reference tables in a separate virtual pool sized to basically page fix the pages.

Tablespaces and indexes used by frequently executed transactions can be placed in a separate virtual pool to avoid competition for space with less critical transactions.

Consider placing tablespaces and indexes, used primarily for batch processing, in a separate buffer pool large enough to avoid a degradation in the number of prefetched pages. This avoids batch programs taking space that could be used by online transactions. An alternative is to lower the VPSEQT and HPSEQT thresholds, assuming that batch programs, rather than transactions, are using prefetch.

Frequently updated tablespaces and indexes can be placed in a separate virtual pool with the deferred write thresholds set high (DWQT and VDWQT at 90 percent for example). Do be cautious of hitting the DMTH and IWTH thresholds, delays in writing the pages to DASD when the thresholds are reached, running short of write engines, and delays when the DB2 subsystem is stopped, particularly with a large virtual pool. Consider adjusting the checkpoint frequency to write updated pages to DASD less frequently. Do be cautious about setting the checkpoint frequency because it applies to all virtual pools. This strategy allows pages to be repeatedly updated with minimal writes to DASD. However, do be cautious of a significant performance degradation during checkpoint processing while many updated pages are being written to DASD. Very little other work can be accomplished during this processing. There is no reason to use a hiperpool because dirty pages are not placed in the hiperpool.

Tablespaces and indexes that are not usually rereferenced can be placed in a separate small virtual pool. If a large percentage of pages are read with prefetch and the pages are not referenced, a large virtual pool will not increase the hit ratio. However, the virtual pool should be large enough to enable prefetch of 32 pages (1,000 pages) assuming prefetch is used. Set the deferred write threshold low (11 percent allows for 3 deferred write I/O of 96 pages). This reduces writes of updated pages to DASD at checkpoint time. There is no reason for using a hiperpool if pages are usually not rereferenced.

If application tablespaces, indexes, and work tablespaces are not assigned to BP0 in a production DB2 subsystem, BP0 can be made relatively small for the directory and catalog I/O (minimum of 56 pages). This strategy assumes that the EDM pool is sized to minimize I/O to the directory through BP0, DSNDB07 work tablespaces have been assigned to another buffer pool, the sort pool has been sized for the workload, security checking does not require excessive I/O to the authorization tables, and there is very low usage of reoptimization and dynamic SQL.

Do assign work tablespaces in work database DSNDB07 to a separate virtual pool. This avoids work tablespaces taking buffer pages that would otherwise be used for application data and indexes. This will prevent sort merge pass degradation, work file request rejections, and work file prefetch from being aborted. The VPSEQT threshold can be set at 80 to 90 percent of the virtual pool for sequential reads using this strategy. The use of 100 percent is not advisable because the buffer pool can be accessed at random for some work files including for some subselect and join processing, for example. BP7 is a convenient buffer pool to use for the DSNDB07 database.

Objects used for data warehousing applications can be placed in a separate virtual pool. This prevents space from being taken from transaction usage.

Consider temporarily assigning tablespaces, indexes, and work tablespaces to various virtual pools for analysis of buffer usage. This is useful in determining the size of virtual pools and assignment of objects to them.

It is important to avoid the effect of having pages in buffer pool when testing different formulation of SQL and other testing scenarios. One way of accomplishing this is to alter tablespace and indexes to use a different buffer pool, run tests, alter tablespace and index to use the original buffer pool, and repeat the processing until testing is complete. An alternative is to stop/start tablespaces and indexes used in the tests. This requires that pages be read into the buffer pool when next accessed.

There are many variations on the use of multiple virtual pools and hiperpools. Do not be afraid to experiment and come up with a strategy that works well for your tablespaces and indexes in your environment.

Configuration of your buffer pools and thresholds is a challenge. The workload changes throughout the day. Time and resources are needed to monitor and tune for the workload. If you do not have the time and resources to meet the challenge, consider one buffer pool, particularly if you require 10,000 pages or less. This minimize the possibility of a shortage of space in one buffer pool with sufficient space in another buffer pool regardless of the configuration.

CD.10 ADJUSTING I/O PRIORITY

It is straightforward to assign CPU priority by address space. However, I/O to tablespaces and indexes are issued using the priority of the database services address space. This means that the same priority is given to online transactions using CICS and IMS as are given to batch jobs, utilities, and data warehousing applications. Usually there is a service agreement with the business professionals that online transaction will execute with an agreed upon response time. This response time is difficult to achieve if there are many types of applications executing on a DB2 subsystem.

Your z/OS or OS/390 systems programmer can use work load manager (WLM) to set goals which allows WLM to automatically adjust the I/O priority, CPU usage, and central storage to favor online transactions in certain address spaces and batch programs executing in other address spaces. If WLM is not used in goal mode at your company, an alternative to having all I/O issued under the priority of the database services address space is to manually adjust the I/O priority similar to that shown in Figure CD.11. Your systems programmer should consider giving database services a medium priority and CICS or IMS the highest I/O priority. TSO and data warehousing applications can be given low to medium priority with batch processing having the lowest I/O priority. Your systems programmer can accomplish this adjustment using SYS1.PARMLIB like:

◆   SYS1.PARMLIB(IEAIPSxx), IOQ = PRTY (not FIFO)
◆   SYS1.PARMLIB(IEAIPSxx), PGN = ..., IOP = ...

Figure CD.11. Adjusting I/O priority

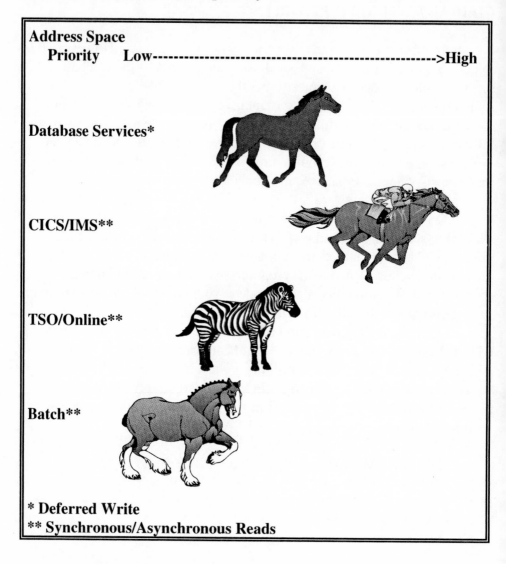

Address Space
Priority   Low--->High

Database Services*

CICS/IMS**

TSO/Online**

Batch**

* Deferred Write
** Synchronous/Asynchronous Reads

Test Results of Adjusting I/O Priority

IBM tested the results of adjusting the I/O priority similar to that shown in
Figure CD.11 using the Relational Transaction Workload (RTW). The tests
were done on a 9121-480 computer with 3390-2 DASD behind one 3990
controller. There were 2,000 pages in BP0 and the sequential read threshold
was set at the default of 80 percent.

Figure CD.12 shows the results of the tests in terms of transactions per second. FIFO means that all I/O was issued under the priority of the database services address space which is the case if the I/O priority is not adjusted and you are not using WLM. IOPQ means that the I/O priority of transactions was set higher than that of tablespace scan processing. There were two tablespace scans on two DASD volumes running continually during the online transaction processing. The tests were done with three think times. The first pair of bars reflect a slow think time where the user needed to look at the screen for awhile to decide the action to be taken. Notice that the transactions per second did not change when using the I/O priorities rather than the default FIFO priority. The second pair of bars reflect medium think times where the user needed to look at the screen for a shorter period of time. In this case the transactions per second again did not change. The third pair of bars reflect a fast think time where the user needed to look at the screen for a short period of time to make a decision as to what action to take. In this case the transactions per second improved from 18 to 27 transactions per second.

Figure CD.12. Transactions per second with and without adjusting I/O priority

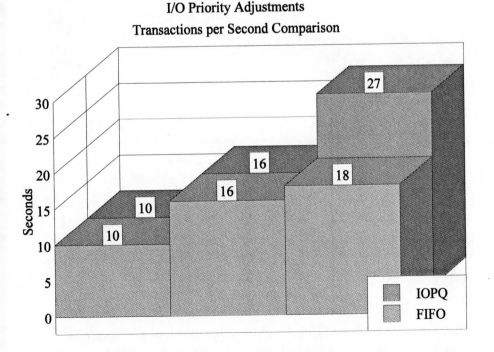

Figure CD.13 shows the results of the tests in terms of response time. The tests were done again with three think times. The first pair of bars for a slow think time shows a little better response time when assigning I/O priorities rather than using the default FIFO priority. The second pair of bars for the medium think time shows the response time improved from 0.67 to 0.42 seconds. The third pair of bars for a fast think time shows the response time improved from 1.5 to 0.85 seconds

Figure CD.13. Response time with and without adjusting I/O priority

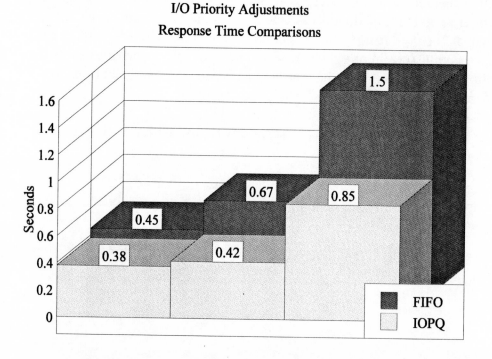

The tests were repeated with the buffer pool increased to 4,000 pages. The sequential read threshold was decreased to 25 percent. This means that only 25 percent rather than 80 percent of the buffer pages can be used for tablespace scans. The online transactions can use 75 percent of the buffer pages without them being stolen by the continually running tablespace scans.

The transactions per second did not change for the slow and medium thinkers. It did increase for the fast thinkers -- from 18 and 27 transactions per second to 25 and 30 transactions per second.

The response time improvements with and without adjusting the I/O priority were greater with the larger buffer pool and more of it dedicated to online transactions as shown in Figure CD.14. The response time for the transactions was improved for all three think times, with the fast thinkers experiencing the greatest improvements. The response time without adjusting the I/O priority remained about the same at 1.49 in the first case and 1.5 seconds with the increased buffer space available to the online transactions. However, the response time went down to 0.85 seconds when adjusting the I/O priority to favor the online transactions with the smaller buffer pool and went down further to 0.44 seconds with the increased number of buffer pages available to the online transactions.

Figure CD.14. Response time with and without adjusting I/O priority using a larger BP

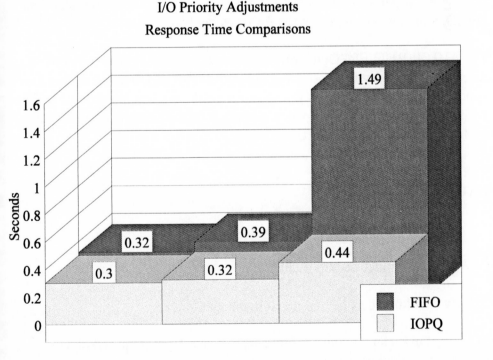

The transactions per second and response time test results give you an idea of whether you should consider running similar tests in your environment and, if justified, adjust the I/O priorities to favor online transactions. An alternative is to use z/OS or OS/390 workload manager.

CD.11 SUMMARY

The use of storage groups allows DB2 to create, delete, and alter VSAM data sets, thus saving you a good deal of time and effort. Do be cautious about using DBDs that are too large for the available space in the EDM pool. Space in the EDM pool is require for the execution of plans and packages.

The buffer pool configuration affects performance more than any other single factor. Do achieve a buffer hit ratio that is suitable for your environment. Consider the use of hiperpools and data spaces for a buffer pool if more than 1.6 GB is required. There are more advantages expected in future for data spaces. If there is insufficient central storage available to achieve a good hit ratio or there are addressability constraints, consider the use of expanded storage. Expanded storage is more costly than DASD storage but significantly less costly than central storage when using bipolar processors. Hiperpool random I/O of 100 µs is over 2,000 times faster than DASD, which makes it very good for moderately read data.

The ALTER BUFFERPOOL command can be used to dynamically create, delete, and change virtual pool and hiperpool sizes and thresholds based on your analysis of the sizes and thresholds required for your environment. The DISPLAY command gives good information on the current configuration of buffer pools and statistics on their usage.

EXERCISES

1. a) What is a general guideline when sizing a DBD?

b) Why is the guideline important?

c) How should objects be organized in databases?

2. a) The DBD can continue to increase in size after all required objects have been created. What causes this to happen?

b) What are two types of processing that result in the DBD increasing in size?

c) What can be done to allow for reuse of DBD space after tables are dropped?

3. Why is it advisable to stop a database before altering objects in the database?

4. a) There are a number of advantages to using storage groups versus using user defined data sets (USING VCAT). What is the disadvantage?

b) How can the disadvantage be minimized? For example, how can you place tablespaces on one volume and indexes on another volume?

c) What is a disadvantage of using SMS for management of DASD and how can it be minimized?

5. What are the disadvantages if a buffer pool is too small for the usage of tablespaces and indexes assigned to it?

6. a) If a page is read and updated by user A, is it necessary to write the changed page to DASD and reread it for user B?

b) How does DB2 avoid losing the updates in central and expanded storage in case of a power failure?

c) How is data integrity maintained?

b) DB2 logs the changed page to DASD in case of a power failure where all data in the buffer pool would be lost.

c) DB2 maintains data integrity using locks and latches to serialize updates so that one user's updates is not overwritten by another user's update.

7. a) What is meant by a buffer page being in-use?

b) What is meant by a buffer page being stealable?

8. a) What is a buffer pool hit ratio?

b) What is a good goal for a hit ratio?

9. If you do not have any 32 KB data pages, is it necessary to have a 32 KB buffer pool? Why?

10. What are the benefits of using 8, 16, or 32 KB pages?

11. What type of storage is used by a virtual pools, data spaces, and hiperpools?

12. What are some advantages of using data spaces compared to hiperpools?

13. a) How are virtual pools, data spaces, and hiperpools created, modified, and deleted?

b) How are their thresholds changed?

14. Which ALTER BUFFERPOOL parameter does not take effect immediately after the ALTER command is executed?

15. How can you determine the number of sequential, dynamic and list prefetch I/O that are used to read pages into BP4?

ANSWERS

1. a) A general guideline when sizing a DBD is that it should not exceed about 5-10 percent of the EDM pool size, or about 250-500 KB, assuming the default EDM size.

b) A DBD that is too large for the EDM pool can result in a resource unavailable message at execution time if there is insufficient space for loading the DBD.

c) The organization of objects in DBDs can be along the lines of subject areas. That is, logical groupings of objects can be placed in a database based on application usage. All objects in a payroll/personnel system can be placed in a database. If this results in a DBD that is too large, the objects relating more to payroll can be placed in one database and the objects relating more to personnel can be placed in another database. Consideration should be given to the administration of database objects so that the appropriate authority can be granted at the database level.

2. a) The DBD increases in size as existing tables are dropped and recreated in a segmented tablespace.

b) 1) A data entry table may have rows inserted for a period of time (for example, daily, weekly, etc.) followed by processing the data, dropping the table, and recreating it. A good alternative is to use the mass delete algorithm. 2) Ad hoc users may create and drop tables for their own personal use in an interactive environment.

c) The DBD space can be made reusable by reorganizing the tablespace, deleting old image copies, and taking an image copy of the tablespace as detailed in Section CD.3.

3. Stopping the database and starting it again after an alter of objects results in the updated DBD being read into the EDM pool. This allows DB2 to recognize the new parameters.

4. a) The disadvantage of using storage groups is that there is less control over placement of tablespaces and index spaces on specific volumes, channels, and control units.

b) If one volume is placed in a storage group for a large tablespace and another volume is assigned to another storage group for indexes, you can achieve separation of the data and indexes by assigning them to the two separate storage groups. This example can be generalized to other types of access and space management. For example a heavily used tablespace and infrequently used data sets can be placed in a storage group with a single volume. In contrast, placing several heavily used tablespaces in a single storage group with one volume will lend to excessive DASD arm movement.

c) SMS does not "know" the difference between tablespaces and index spaces. It is necessary to use separate SMS storage groups and guarantee space on a volume for specific data sets, or an exit can be used to determine placement. A good alternative is to assign data sets to specific storage classes based on an established naming convention to achieve separation. For example, if index names begin with X, VCAT.*.*.X* can be used. However, caution must be exercised as pointed out by Dr. Lou Agosta.

5. If a buffer pool is too small for the usage of tablespaces and indexes assigned to it, the performance of SQL statements that process the tablespaces and indexes is likely to be adversely affected. The number of physical I/O to DASD is likely to be higher than it should be and the I/O wait time will be excessive. This adversely affects the response time of online transactions and the elapsed time of batch and data warehousing

applications. It also increases the CPU time because the CPU is used to issue the physical I/O.

6. If a page is read and updated by user A, it is not necessary to write the changed page to DASD and reread it for user B. User B can reread the page as long as user A has committed the update and the buffer pool has sufficient space to hold the page.

b) DB2 logs the changed page to DASD in case of a power failure where all data in the buffer pool would be lost.

c) DB2 maintains data integrity using locks and latches to serialize updates so that one user's updates are not overwritten by another user's updates.

7. a) An in-use buffer page is one where DM has issued a getpage and has not yet issued a relpage or set write pending.

b) A stealable page is one where DM has issued a getpage and relpage, and write pending is not active.

8. a) A buffer pool hit ratio is the percentage of time that the page is found in the buffer pool when DM issues a getpage and buffer manager does not have to issue a physical I/O.

b) A good goal for a hit ratio is 80 to 90 percent or more assuming that pages are referenced. Keep in mind that if you are using a hiperpool, hit ratios can be calculated for the buffer pool, virtual pool, and hiperpool.

9. It is necessary to have a 32 KB buffer pool even if you do not have any 32 KB data pages. The buffer pool is needed to process result rows of over 4 KB selected from multiple 4 KB page tablespaces.

10. The benefits of using 8, 16, or 32 KB pages have to do with space requirements and the costs of serialization. If the row length is greater than ½ of a 4 KB page size less overhead, the larger page sizes can be used to save space by choosing a page size that fits a multiple of the row length without wasting space. Serialization cost can be reduced by using larger page sizes assuming that you are locking at the page level. This is particularly important in a sysplex data sharing environment. However, be cautious of serialization contention since data is being locked on the larger page sizes.

11. Virtual pools and data spaces reside in central storage. A hiperpool resides in expanded storage. The term *buffer pool* refers to all three types of spaces.

12. Some advantages of using data spaces compared to hiperpools is that data spaces reside in central storage, have a larger maximum size, can contain common areas, system data and programs, updated pages, and pages are read directly into a data space.

13. a) Virtual pools and hiperpools are created, modified, and deleted using the ALTER BUFFERPOOL command. DB2 manages data spaces with no controls available to the system administrator.

b) Virtual pools, and hiperpools are changed using the BUFFERPOOL command.

14. The VPTYPE parameter used to designate private or data space usage does not take effect immediately after issuing the ALTER BUFFERPOOL command. The buffer pool must be deallocated and reallocated for the parameter to take effect.

15. The number of sequential, dynamic and list prefetch I/O that are used to read pages into BP4 can be determined by specifying BUFFERPOOL(BP4) and the DETAIL parameter on the DISPLAY command.

FIGURES

Creating Tablespaces

TS.1 INTRODUCTION

We begin this chapter with a description of the three types of tablespaces. Information is provided upon which to base your decision as to which type of tablespace is best for your data. Many parameters are used to instruct DB2 on how to manage the objects. These parameters are analyzed in detail to assist you in deciding the best design of your tablespaces. The many pros and cons of the parameters are discussed along with real world experiences and test results to give you a basis for your design. Do explicitly specify all of the parameters when creating a tablespace. Otherwise, default values, which may not be appropriate for your application system, are used. The goal is to design tablespaces that can effectively and efficiently store data for your application system. The design provides a basis for ease of access and manipulation of data by online transactions, batch programs, and utilities. The result is high performance with minimal use of I/O, CPU, and elapsed time.

Three Types of Tablespaces

All types of tablespaces resides in a page set of one or more VSAM data sets. The page size can be 4, 8, 16 or 32 KB, depending on your buffer pool choice as discussed in Chapter CD.4. Most often the 4 KB page size is used. The data page format is the same for all types of tablespaces.

A segmented tablespace can house one or more tables (no limit). The tablespace is divided into segments of from 4 to 64 pages, and each segment is dedicated to a table. A table can occupy multiple segments.

A simple tablespace can house one or more tables (no limit) like a segmented tablespace. Rows from multiple tables can be interleaved on a page under the developer's control and maintenance.

A partitioned tablespace can house one table. The tablespace is divided into parts. Each part is housed in a separate VSAM data set.

The term *nonsegmented* tablespace refers to simple and partitioned tablespaces.

TS.2 SEGMENTED AND SIMPLE TABLESPACES

A segmented tablespace is divided into segments as the name suggests. A segment can consist of 4, 8, 16, 32, or 64 pages. You determine the segment size by specifying one of these values with the parameter SEGSIZE. The segment size applies to all of the tables in a tablespace. Each segment is dedicated to a table. The LOAD and REORG (reorganization) utilities leave segments of a table in contiguous space on DASD.

Segment sizes of 32 and 64 pages have advantages, assuming that most tables in the tablespace require 32 or more pages. The benefits of prefetch are maximized. The prefetch quantity is 32 pages, assuming a buffer pool of 1,000 pages or more. A smaller segment size can result in reading pages for another table when there are multiple tables in a tablespace. SEGSIZE of 32 or 64 minimizes the number of space map pages as discussed in Section TS.9. Both values result in about 5,000 data pages following a space map page. SEGSIZE 32 results in 4,800 data pages following each space map page and SEGSIZE 64 has 5,504 data pages following each space map page. The resources required to search for free space are minimized when using a SEGSIZE of 32 or 64. There is an increased likelihood that the space map pages will remain in the buffer pool with the larger SEGSIZE values.

SEGSIZE 32 results in fewer pages being reserved for the 16 page compression and decompression dictionary as discussed in Section TS.8 than for SEGSIZE 64. This fact can serve as a tie breaker for using SEGSIZE of 32 rather than 64 when using compression. If you need to prevent wasting 16 pages of a 32 page segment used for the dictionary, consider SEGSIZE 16.

Small tables should be placed in tablespaces with a small segment size. If you plan to place no more than one table in a tablespace, the SEGSIZE should match the table size. If you plan to place multiple small tables in a tablespace, consider using the average table size in pages as the SEGSIZE.

Advantages of Segmented Tablespaces

A primary advantage of a segmented tablespace over a nonsegmented tablespace is that more detailed information is available on the space map page for the location of free space for maintaining clustering and variable length rows as detailed in Section TS.4. A tablespace scan of a segmented tablespace scans only the segments of the table being processed. This is in contrast to scanning the entire simple tablespace even if only one of multiple tables in the tablespace needs to be processed. The space map pages are used to identify pages that contain active rows of the table being processed in a segmented tablespace. This avoids scanning empty segments and segments containing only deleted data.

The optimizer has a better estimate of the number of pages that contain rows for a table. It uses SYSTABLES.NPAGESF which has the number of pages that contain active rows of a table. This is in contrast to using what is usually a higher value in SYSTABLESPACE.NACTIVEF for simple tablespaces. NACTIVEF contains the number of pages in a tablespace up to the high preformatted page. The COPY utility does not copy empty pages due to a dropped table or the use of the mass delete algorithm when making a full image copy. It uses the space map pages to identify pages that contain active rows. Except if TRACKMOD NO is specified, the space map pages are not used to identify pages that contain active rows. The mass delete algorithm is an efficient method for deleting all of the rows in a table, particularly when there are multiple tables in the tablespace. The details on the use of the algorithm as well as alternatives for effectively deleting all rows in a table are covered in Chapter BP.

Advantages of Multiple Tables in a Tablespace

If you plan to place multiple tables in a tablespace, it should be a segmented tablespace. We will first look at the advantages of multiple tables in a tablespace followed by the pros and cons of using a segmented or simple tablespace to house them.

Related small to medium sized tables can be placed together in a nonpartitioned tablespace. One reason for doing this is that most utilities operate at the tablespace or partition level. Therefore, fewer utilities need to be prepared and executed. This may appear to be a trivial point until you think about the number of tables in your application system and the number of utilities that must be prepared, tested, and executed on a routine basis. An experience at one company will be used to illustrate the point. The developers chose to place one table per tablespace. They had about 300 tables in the application system. They developed and tested 300 RUNSTATS, REORG, COPY, and RECOVER utilities. This is a total of 1200 utility jobs (300 tablespaces * 4 utilities) plus the LOAD utility and a few CHECK DATA, CHECK INDEX, REPAIR, and other utilities. Operations refused to accept the routine scheduling of so many utility jobs. The developers had to go back to the drawing board and combine related tables into fewer tablespaces.

A primary reason for considering multiple tables in a tablespace is to ease the management of referential integrity structures with respect to the utilities. Indeed, one of the reasons for the DB2 developers inventing segmented tablespaces is for the efficient management of multiple tables in a tablespace as detailed in the next section. It is particularly important to synchronize related tables when copying and recovering them as discussed in Chapter CR. If referential integrity is defined to DB2 and all related tablespaces are not recovered to together, they are placed in a check pending state. Check pending must be turned off before you can select and update the related tables.

Fewer VSAM data sets for fewer tablespaces need to be open at any one time. This is particularly important when there are many tablespaces and indexes in many applications system on a DB2 subsystem. Limits on the number of open data sets are discussed in Section TS.6. Deferred write allows many users to update pages for multiple tables and write the updated pages to the tablespace in 32 page chunks as discussed in Chapter CO.

Placing multiple very small reference tables in a single tablespace is a good choice. This avoids a minimum allocation of two tracks for each table and management of a header and space map page for each table.

Multiple Tables in a Simple Versus Segmented Tablespace

There are a number of reasons why, if you decide to have multiple tables in a tablespace, it should be a segmented tablespace. These reasons also point out a number of advantages of segmented tablespaces. As already mentioned, a tablespace scan of a simple tablespace is over all pages, in a tablespace, regardless of whether a page contains a row from the table being processed. For example, scanning the S table requires scanning tables S, P, J, and SPJ if they are in the same tablespace. In addition, empty pages due to deleted rows are processed in a simple tablespace scan. In contrast, a tablespace scan is over only non-empty pages which contain rows of the accessed table when using a segmented tablespace: it is basically a table scan.

An implicit or explicit LOCK TABLE statement locks all tables in a simple tablespace. In contrast, it locks only the referenced table in a segmented tablespace.

The reorganization utility does not recluster data if there is more than one table in a simple tablespace. In contrast, a reorganization reclusters the data for each table regardless of the number of tables in a segmented tablespace.

Reorganization is required to reuse space occupied by a dropped table in a simple tablespace. In contrast, a reorganization is not required to reuse space occupied by dropped tables in a segmented tablespace. This makes segmented tablespaces a particularly good choice for QMF users who frequently create and drop tables explicitly or implicitly. Deleted row space is immediately reusable for all types of tablespaces without a reorganization.

Recommendation: Clearly, segmented tablespaces have significant advantages over nonsegmented tablespaces for multiple tables.

Disadvantages of Multiple Tables in a Tablespace

Although it is clear that if you want multiple tables in a tablespace it should be a segmented tablespace, the next question to be addressed is whether one or multiple tables should be placed in a tablespace. The following issues apply to segmented and simple tablespaces.

As mentioned earlier, most utilities operate at the tablespace or partition level including the REORG, RUNSTATS, COPY and RECOVER utilities. However, you may need different scheduling for each table. In addition, you may need to recover only one table which is not possible with multiple tables in a tablespace.

Reallocation of space is at the tablespace level. However, you may need to reallocate space for a specific table without reorganizing multiple tables.

Different tables may need different tablespace parameter values such as:

PCTFREE, FREEPAGE, SEGSIZE, LOCKSIZE, LOCKMAX, MAXROWS etc. as discussed throughout this chapter.

The compression dictionary for one table may not be the best for another table. The compression dictionary is discussed in Section TS.8.

If a load replace is done of a table, all tables in a tablespace are lost. The reason is that load replace uses the VSAM REUSE parameter which resets the entire tablespace to empty. An alternative method is to use the mass delete algorithm followed by load resume or insertion of rows in a segmented tablespace

Utilities operate at the tablespace or partition level and the pending states apply at these levels, not at the table level. This can result in limited availability if there is more than one table in the tablespace. All tables are unavailable even though only one table needs to be operated on by a utility or caused a pending state to be turned on.

Recommendation: Do not mix frequently and infrequently updated tables in a tablespace. Most of the issues discussed have to do with update activity on a table.

Most companies place one table in one tablespace except for small reference tables. Multiple small reference tables are typically placed in one tablespace.

Simple Tablespaces

There are few advantages of simple tablespaces over segmented tablespace even if you decide to have one table per tablespace. A simple tablespace does have fewer space map pages to be read and updated compared to a segmented tablespace as discussed in Section TS.9. However, there are few space map pages for both types of tablespace. A simple tablespace has a space map page every 10,760 data pages compared to every 4,800 pages using SEGSIZE 32 and 5,504 pages using SEGSIZE 64. A simple tablespace does not have segments; therefore, there is no need to be concerned that segments of a table can become dispersed and fragmented. In addition, you can avoid inserting rows in clustering sequence as discussed in Section TS.7.

A potential advantage of a simple tablespace compared to a segmented tablespace is that rows from multiple tables can be interleaved on a page. For example, a parent row describing a job can be followed by multiple dependent rows from the SPJ table. This would result in fewer I/O when information is needed on both jobs and parts used on the job. However, more I/O are required when processing only the parent or dependent rows. The reason that interleaving of rows is little more than a potential advantage is that DB2 does not support the interleaving. For example, inserted rows are not necessarily interleaved. The reorganization utility does not interleave rows.

If you decide to interleave rows from multiple tables on a single page, you must do a good deal of planning and work. For example, it is necessary to interleave rows on a sequential file before loading multiple tables from a single sequential file. This can be done by sorting on the primary key (PK) and foreign key (FK). (The PK and FK are discussed in Chapter CT.) Creation of the clustering index on the PK and FK encourages maintenance of clustering for inserts. Insertion of PK rows followed by the corresponding FK rows encourages maintenance of the interleaved rows, but does not guarantee it. When doing a reorganization, it is necessary to pause the utility after the unload, then you must sort on the PK and FK, and then restart the utility using the PHASE parameter. A good deal of manual intervention is required for interleaving of rows and is seldom used.

You may find that there are a number of simple tablespaces at your company. This situation frequently exists because the tablespaces were created in the early days of DB2 before segmented tablespaces were supported. There is no option for altering from a simple to a segmented tablespace. It is necessary to unload the data, drop the tablespace, create the tablespace, table, and indexes, load the data, grant privileges, execute RUNSTATS, and rebind plans and packages (or accept an automatic rebind). Many companies do not want to take the time and resources to do the conversion unless there are great benefits. A justification for conversion from simple to segmented tablespaces is if reorganizations are more frequent than desired. The frequency can be reduced by using segmented tablespaces where free space is managed more efficiently as discussed in Section TS.9.

TS.3 ANALYSIS OF TABLESPACE PARAMETERS

The parameters that can be specified when creating a tablespace are included in the following example for the creation of the PTSP tablespace in the DASPJDB database.

```
CREATE TABLESPACE PTSP
  IN DASPJDB
  USING STOGROUP DASPJSTG
    PRIQTY 7200
    SECQTY   720
    ERASE NO
  BUFFERPOOL BP0
  SEGSIZE   32
  PCTFREE   10
  FREEPAGE 31
  LOCKSIZE PAGE
    LOCKMAX 0
  MAXROWS 255
  CLOSE NO
  DEFINE YES
  COMPRESS NO
  TRACKMOD YES;
```

Creation and usage of storage groups, databases, buffer pools, and global buffer pools are described in Chapter CD. The database to house the tablespace is named using the IN clause of the CREATE TABLESPACE statement. The USING STOGROUP clause indicates the storage group to be used for space allocation of the tablespace. The name of the storage group to contain the tablespace need not be the same as that specified when creating the database to contain the tablespace. If you prefer to use a user-defined data set to house the tablespace, you must first create the VSAM data set. You then specify the high level qualifier of the data set in the USING VCAT clause rather than using the USING STOGROUP clause. The buffer pool to be used for processing the data pages is specified using the parameter. If this parameter is not specified, the buffer pool specified when the database was created is used. BP0 is used if a buffer pool is not specified when creating the database.

All parameters specified in the CREATE TABLESPACE statement can be changed with the ALTER statement except for placement of the tablespace in a database, the segment size, and the number of partitions. In order to change these parameters, it is necessary to unload the data and drop the tablespace, which also drops all dependents of the tablespace as discussed in Chapter CT.

Here is an example for altering all non-partitioned tablespace parameters that can be changed with the ALTER statement.

```
ALTER TABLESPACE DASPJDB.PTSP
   USING STOGROUP DATOMSTG
      PRIQTY 14400
      SECQTY    720
   ERASE YES
   PCTFREE 15
   FREEPAGE 7
   MAXROWS 255
   LOCKSIZE ROW
      LOCKMAX 10001
   CLOSE YES
   BUFFERPOOL BP1
   COMPRESS NO
   TRACKMOD NO;
```

You can alter from USING VCAT to USING STOGROUP or vice versa. It is necessary to stop the tablespace to ensure no access to the data can occur during this type of alter. Then start the tablespace after the alter has executed successfully.

You can ALTER CCSID identifier to include/exclude the Euro symbol for newly created objects as discussed in Chapter CD. This also applies to existing tablespaces. However, there are a number of steps that must be followed as described in the *SQL Reference* manual.

Primary and Secondary Space Allocation

The primary and secondary quantities are specified using the PRIQTY and SECQTY parameters. The required space is requested in 1 K byte units. DB2 automatically converts the space allocation to cylinders or tracks. For example, there are 720 KB on a cylinder and 48 KB bytes on a track of a 3390 DASD volume. Both the PRIQTY and SECQTY should be in multiples of cylinders if more than one cylinder is required. If the PRIQTY or SECQTY is less than one cylinder, track allocation is used.

Do use DB2 Estimator to accurately estimate the PRIQTY and allow for growth. Avoid data sets going into secondary allocations because seek time is increased if a data set is spread across DASD in multiple extents. You have heard the saying that on a clear day you can see forever; well, on a cluttered disk you can seek forever. Some DASD devices lessen the importance of multiple extents. However, there is still an overhead in managing multiple extents for most devices including the data set open/close processing, online reorganization switch processing, and an abend occurs if the maximum number of extents (251 with DFP 1.4) is exceeded.

It is not necessary to stop and start the tablespace and indexes to alter PRIQTY and SECQTY in V5 with APAR PQ04053. The new space allocation can be used immediately because DB2 uses space as reflected in the catalog tables. However, LISTCAT will not show the new allocation until after REORG, LOAD REPLACE, RECOVER, or REBUILD INDEX.

It is necessary to stop/start a tablespace and index to alter USING and ERASE parameters.

Space Allocation: Data Facility Product (DFP) media manager allocates space for DB2. If insufficient contiguous space is available to satisfy the PRIQTY on a volume, space can be taken on up to and including 5 extents. If more than five extents are required, the data set is not allocated.

Secondary Space Allocation: If available space in the current extent is less than 10 percent of MIN(half of SECQTY, half of PRIQTY), secondary extension is done by media manager. If the SECQTY is not specified, the default is MAX(10 percent of PRIQTY, 3 times the page size).

The maximum number of extents on multiple volumes is 251 with 4 of the 255 VSAM extents reserved by DB2 (V6).

Preformatting space: Two cylinders or tracks are preformatted at a time for tablespaces and indexes when the objects are created (also formats header and space map pages). Also, preformatting occurs if there is no space on the candidate page and no space formatted at end of data set for an INSERT statement or UPDATE of a row such that it is too long to fit on the original page. Preformatting consists of writing X'00' on the pages. Asynchronous preformatting of space (V7) and having LOAD or REORG preformat space as discussed in Chapters LC and RR improves the performance of preformatting.

LISTCAT shows the preformatted space as the high used RBA and the allocated space as the high allocated RBA. It does not show the altered space until after a reorganization, load replace, or recover. These utilities delete and define the VSAM data sets.

Tablespace Size: The tablespace size is limited by the RID size in the indexes. Four byte RIDs are used for tablespaces less than or equal to 64 GB. The first 3 bytes (24 bits) of a 4 byte RID are used to reference a data page. These 24 bits give the limit of 64 GB for the tablespace, calculated as $2^{24} = 16$ MB * 4 KB page for nonpartitioned tablespaces.

A partitioned tablespace can be up to and including 16 terabytes (TB) (V6). Section TS.7 discusses how to define a tablespace greater than 64 GB. All indexes on these very large tablespaces have 5 byte RIDs. The first 4 bytes (32 bits) of the 5 byte RID are used to reference a data page. The limit of 16 TB is based on $2^{32} = 4$ GB * 4 KB page. The limit in V5 is 1 TB.

ERASE Parameter

The ERASE parameter determines the action to take when a tablespace is dropped. The alter of this parameter requires that the tablespace or index be stopped.

ERASE YES provides added security by filling the data set with zeros when the tablespace is dropped.

ERASE NO means that the tables in a tablespace are not accessible using SQL statement after the tablespace is dropped. However, theoretically, someone can dump the DASD device and still see the data before another data set is written over the space. ERASE NO has performance advantages when dropping a tablespace. This is the default.

TS.4 FREE SPACE FOR UPDATING AND INSERTING ROWS

Free space should be specified for tablespace and indexes that have random insert, update, and delete activity. Free space in the tablespace is important for maintaining rows in sequence, according to the clustering index, and for managing variable length rows. Free space in the index pages minimizes page splitting as discussed in Chapter ID. The amount of free space can be specified using the PCTFREE and FREEPAGE parameters.

The PCTFREE parameter provides for specifying the amount of space to be left free at the bottom of each table and index space page by the LOAD, REORG, RECOVER INDEX, and REBUILD INDEX utilities. The defaults of 5 percent for tablespace pages and 10 percent for index space pages are used unless you specify a value based on the row length in your table as discussed this section.

The FREEPAGE parameter provides for specifying how often an empty page should be interspersed in the tablespace and index space. The default is 0 blank pages with a maximum of 255. Empty pages are brought into the buffer pool when pages are read with sequential and dynamic prefetch. Do specify an appropriate number for your tablespace as discussed in this section.

The LOAD, REORG, RECOVER INDEX, and REBUILD INDEX utilities and build of a newly created index leaves the specified free space as indicated in Figure TS.1.

Figure TS.1. Free space within pages and between pages

Search for Free Space

It is important to understand how DB2 searches for free space, in segmented and non-segmented tablespaces, in order to decide the values to specify for the PCTFREE and FREESPACE parameters. DB2 maintains rows in sequence according to the clustering index as discussed in Chapter ID. The target page for the row is the page with rows having a higher and/or lower value. This is the first choice for INSERTING the row. If there is no free space on the target page to insert the row to maintain the rows in sequence, the space map page, as discussed in Section TS.4, is analyzed to determine if there is any free space within the target segment.

SEGSIZE 32 is used in the CREATE TABLESPACE statement at the beginning of Section TS.3. For this tablespace, the second choice is to insert the row within the 32 page segment based on free space information in the space map page control block for the target segment. If the row is inserted within the target segment, it is considered a near page.

The third choice is to insert the row within the range of pages covered by the space map page. Availability of space is determined by analyzing the remaining control blocks in the space map page to determine if there is sufficient free space to insert the row. If the row can be inserted using this search or the following searches, it is considered a far page.

The fourth choice is to scan the space map pages from the current segment to the end of the tablespace for any available space to determine if the row can be inserted with a maximum of 3 pages being accessed with no free space.

The fifth choice is to allocate a new segment at the end of tablespace. If no more extents can be allocated, the sixth choice is to scan the space map pages from the beginning of the tablespace in an attempt to reuse space previously occupied by deleted rows at the beginning of the tablespace. If still no free space can be found, a -904 SQLCODE indicating resource unavailable is issued.

The search for free space in a nonsegmented tablespace uses a similar algorithm except that the initial search is forward and backward 16 pages within the space map page (less than or equal 3 pages are read). An exception is when using MEMBER CLUSTER parameters as discussed in Section TS.7. Space obtained from the deletion of all rows in a table using the mass delete algorithm and dropping a table is not reusable until after a reorganization.

Free pages used as near pages: FREEPAGE provides for INSERTING a row near the candidate page when the candidate page is full as indicated in Figure TS.2. FREEPAGE 31 provides for a near page within a segment when using a segmented tablespace with a SEGSIZE of 32 pages. FREEPAGE 15 provides for a near page when using a nonsegmented tablespace.

Figure TS.2. Near and far pages

Use of Free Space to Maintain Variable Length Rows

DB2 maintains variable length rows for compressed rows, rows with VARCHAR columns, and when EDITPROC and FIELDPROC are used as discussed in Chapter CT. Also, variable length rows are maintained after a column has been added to a table with the ALTER statement and before a reorganization. Variable length rows can be increased in length with an update. DB2 cannot place a row that is expanded in length in exactly the same position (assuming that there is no free space following the row). LOAD and REORG pack the rows on a page and leave the specified amount of space at the bottom of the page.

If there is insufficient free space on the page to expand a row in length, DB2 will gather all available free space in an attempt to keep the row on its original page. If it cannot get enough free space, it will use its free space search algorithm to locate a near or far page to place the row and leave a pointer in the original location pointing to the new location. If the row is increased in length again in the future with insufficient space on the page, the row is moved again and the first pointer changed to point to the new location. This avoids a chain of pointers that must be followed to locate a moved row. Perhaps of even more significance for improved performance is that the use of a pointer avoids having to update each index referencing the table to point to the new location of the row.

Prefetch I/O time can be adversely affected by moved rows. If there is a pointer to a moved row within the 32 pages prefetched, a synchronous I/O is issued to locate the moved row. The prefetch I/O does not continue until the I/O for the moved row is completed. Although this may sound like a trivial point, one company found that the average time to read a page was 50 ms after many rows had been moved using 3390 DASD. This is in contrast to an average I/O time of 1.7 ms per page after a reorganization which eliminates pointers to moved rows. Obviously, your results will be different. However, the reason for giving company experiences and test results is to provide an order of magnitude difference for your decision making process. In this case, it is an issue of whether variable length rows should be used when the rows are frequently increased in length and insufficient free space has been specified assuming random update activity.

Estimating Free Space for Variable Length Rows

If you have a good deal of update activity that increases variable length rows in length and the update activity is random throughout the tablespace, 10 percent free space is a reasonable starting point. If the update activity is concentrated only in some areas of the tablespace, the free space is of limited value. Free space is left in every page throughout the tablespace but is not used except in the areas where the update activity occurs.

The initial free space that you specify can be adjusted based on the NEARINDREF and FARINDREF columns in SYSTABLEPART. NEARINDREF is the number of rows that have been moved from their original position due to an increase in row length and insufficient free space on the page. FARINDREF is the number of rows that have been moved to a far off position. The distinction between near and far pages is discussed earlier in this section. The RUNSTATS utility must be executed recently for these statistics to accurately reflect the current condition of the tablespace. If (NEARINDREF+FARINDREF)*100/CARDF > 5, consider increasing the PCTFREE and reorganizing the tablespace to eliminate the pointers to moved rows and to provide more free space for future update activity. Another indication that more free space is needed is if the CLUSTERRATIOF in SYSINDEXES falls below 80 percent too quickly after a reorganization.

When you alter a table and add an additional column, do consider a reorganization, depending on the amount of free space that you have on the pages, the length of the added column, and how many rows will be given new values for the newly added column before the next scheduled reorganization. If you believe that free space must be gathered on many pages and that it will be necessary to search for free space often, it is best to do a reorganization so that DB2 can expand all the rows and space on each row to provide for the newly added column.

If you have a good deal of insert activity and are compressing the rows, determine the average row length using DSN1COMP, RUNSTATS (SYSTABLES.AVGROWLEN (V7)), REORG, or LOAD. Estimate free space such that one or more additional compressed rows can fit on a page on average and allow more free space for expanding rows with updates. There is a 50 percent chance that updating a compressed row will increase it in length.

Free Space to Maintain Clustering

Free space should be a multiple of the record length for fixed length rows or the average length for variable length rows. This is particularly important to maintain the rows in clustering sequence. Here is an example for estimating the required free space to insert one row on a page assuming a 100 byte row.

```
0.03 = ceiling ((100 byte row length + 6 byte
row prefix + 2 byte page directory entry) /
4074)
```

Three percent free allows one row to be inserted on a page before DB2 must use its search algorithm to locate free space. If you expect that typically multiple rows will be inserted on a large percentage of the pages at random, multiply the 3 percent by an estimate of the number of rows to be inserted per page between reorganizations.

If the table has been created, the calculation can be done based on statistics in the catalog tables like:

```
SELECT TB.NAME,TB.COLCOUNT, TB.CARDF, TB.NPAGESF,
   TB.RECLENGTH, INTEGER((((TB.RECLENGTH+2.0)/
   4074.0)*100.0)+0.9), TSP.FREEPAGE, TSP.PCTFREE
FROM    SYSIBM.SYSTABLES     TB,
        SYSIBM.SYSTABLEPART TSP
WHERE TB.CREATOR = 'Authid'
AND    TB.TYPE    = 'T'
AND    TB.TSNAME  = TSP.TSNAME
ORDER BY TB.NAME;
```

Add a multiplier to the end of the arithmetic expression with the number of rows expected to be inserted on a page.

Recommendation: Consider checking existing tablespaces to determine if they have an appropriate amount of free space specified. If not, ALTER them to have a percent free that will allow one or more rows to be inserted on a page.

Estimate Free Space Needed between Reorganizations

The reorganization frequency has a significant impact on the amount of free space needed. The REORG utility reallocates the free space specified on the CREATE and ALTER statements. You can base the estimate of free space on the expected percentage or number of rows to be inserted less rows to be deleted over some period of time for which reorganizations are being considered, weekly for example, assuming random insert and delete activity throughout the tablespace.

Estimate based on percentages: If 10 percent of the total number of rows are randomly inserted and 5 percent are deleted on a weekly basis and weekly reorganizations are planned, do calculate free space to allow for 5 percent additional rows. The percentage of rows deleted is subtracted from the percentage of rows to be inserted because deleted row space is immediately reusable. Five percent times 40 rows is 2 rows, assuming a row length of 100 bytes with 40 rows per page. We use the earlier example where 3 percent free space is required to insert 1 row on a page. The 3 percent is multiplied by 2 which is the estimated number of rows to be inserted minus the number of rows to be deleted after applying the percentages to the maximum number of rows that fit on a page. This results in PCTFREE 6 needed to allow for the insertion, deletion, and reorganization estimates.

Estimate based on number of rows: You can base the estimate of free space on the number of rows and pages rather than percentages. Estimate the number of rows to be inserted on a weekly basis less the number of rows to be deleted. Also, estimate the number of data pages. If representative data has been loaded and statistics are collected, SYSTABLES.NPAGESF contains the number of data pages. Divide the estimated number of rows to be inserted after subtracting the number of rows to be deleted (60,000, for example) by the number of pages (30,000, for example). Estimate the average number of rows to be inserted on a page as the number of additional rows to be inserted divided by the number of pages, which gives 2 rows in the example (60,000 rows / 30,000 pages). Multiply the average number of rows to be inserted on a page by the calculated percent free that allows for 1 row. The result is again 6 percent (3 percent free for 1 row * 2 rows).

Avoid Too Much Free Space

Certainly the appropriate use of free space is important. However, there are some tablespaces that do not benefit from free space. Indeed, PCTFREE 0 should be specified on the tablespaces and indexes to avoid using the default free space if the parameter is not specified at all. The use of free space wastes DASD space and more I/O is required to select the same number of rows if a page is only partially filled with rows because of the unnecessary use of free space. This is particularly significant for batch programs that process many rows.

If a tablespace is read-only or has very low insert and update activity, no free space is needed. If rows are always inserted and deleted at the end of the table, only the free space on the last page is used and the free space on all the other pages is wasted. Indeed, this applies to situations where rows are typically inserted, updated, and deleted in only a few specific areas of the tablespace. Free space is best utilized where the insert, update, and delete activity is close to random.

A skewed distribution of insert/delete activity can result in free space on some pages rarely being used. A work around is to load sections with no insert/delete activity and no percent free. Specify a percent free with alter and load resume sections with high insert/delete activity. Index page splitting is another issue to deal with and is discussed in Chapter ID.

Different partitions frequently have different update activity. If this is true for your partitioned tablespaces, do customize the free space by partition. Of course, partitions that contain historical data should have 0 percent free.

PCTFREE 0 and FREEPAGE 0 have advantages. Data pages at the end of the tablespace are filled and written with deferred write using the LOAD utility and INSERT statements. This avoids getpages, synchronous I/O, and lock requests to search for free space to insert rows. Indeed, no I/O is required to read pages upon which to insert the rows. This applies to fixed and variable length rows. The I/O time to use this technique varies with the DASD model used as discussed in Chapter OP. Added benefits are achieved by sorting the input records in clustering sequence as discussed in Chapters BP and LC.

TS.5 PARAMETERS THAT CONTROL LOCKING

The values specified for the LOCKSIZE and LOCKMAX parameters are the first steps in controlling locks taken by DB2. MAXROWS also influences the amount of data that is locked. These parameters are discussed in this section. A detailed description of locks and latches is given in Chapter CC.

Locksize for a Tablespace

The LOCKSIZE parameter is used to indicate the granularity of locking, which can be the row, page, table, or tablespace level.

LOCKSIZE ROW gives the maximum concurrency but can be resource intensive, particularly in a sysplex data sharing environment.

LOCKSIZE PAGE is a good choice in most cases. Escalation to a larger granularity of lock occurs only if repeatable read is used, LOCKMAX 0, and the optimizer chooses a tablespace or non-matching index scan. If these conditions are encountered, a warning is issued at bind time with a +806 SQLCODE, indicating that escalation will occur at run time.

LOCKSIZE ANY is the default and usually results in a page lock. Escalation to a larger granularity of lock occurs if NUMLKTS or LOCKMAX is exceeded as discussed in the next two sections.

LOCKSIZE TABLE can be used for segmented tablespaces.

LOCKSIZE TABLESPACE reduces CPU time (about 5-15 percent over page locks) and virtual storage usage. It is an excellent choice for read-only tables and tables used by only one user in an ad hoc environment, for example. If page or row locking is needed for online transactions but others do not need access to the data during batch processing in the evenings or on weekends, a LOCK TABLE statement can be issued in the batch program as discussed in Chapter BP.

Changing the Lock Size: The lock size can be changed with the ALTER statement. Execution of the statement causes a quiesce of the tablespace and an X lock is taken to ensure that no one is processing the data during the change. It is advisable to execute the ALTER statement during low activity on the tablespace to avoid a timeout. The new LOCKSIZE takes effect immediately after the ALTER is successful. It is not necessary to rebind plans and packages to use the new lock size. You may want to do a rebind if you are changing between a page and row lock size. Additional CPU time is estimated for row locking compared to page locking and can result in a different access path being chosen by DB2.

Maximum Number of Locks

The number of row and page locks any one thread can hold on one table or tablespace are limited including locks taken for referential integrity enforcement. This limit can be set using the LOCKMAX parameter, the NUMLKTS parameter in DSNZPARM, and on the installation panel DSNTIPJ. If the limit is exceeded, the row and page locks are released and the lock is escalated to a share (S) or exclusive (X) lock based on the intent to share (IS) or intent exclusive (IX) held on the table or tablespace. If LOCKPART YES is specified on the CREATE TABLESPACE statement (not the default), only accessed partitions are locked.

No INSERT, UPDATE, and DELETE statements can be issued on the tablespace if the escalation is to an S lock. SELECT statements are denied if the escalation is to an X lock. Sporadic lock contention is usually the symptom of the problem. The cause of the lock escalation is difficult to determine. Unfortunately, no positive or negative SQLCODE is issued to allow for a commit or rollback to release the locks. The number of lock escalations that occurred can be determined from the statistics trace. It is necessary to use the performance trace to determine the programs that caused the escalation.

Control of Lock Limits and Escalation

If LOCKMAX of SYSTEM is specified when the tablespace is created, the NUMLKTS in DSNZPARM is used, which has a default that a maximum of 1,000 locks on the tablespace can be taken before escalation. NUMLKTS can be set to zero to disallow escalations. LOCKMAX can be specified for the lock size of row, page, and any when the tablespace is created along with a value from 0 to 2,147,483,647. Zero means no escalation will occur which is the default when using lock size of page. If LOCKSIZE of ANY is specified and LOCKMAX is not specified, the NUMLKTS value is used. LOCKMAX of SYSTEM is the default when using LOCKSIZE of ANY.

Recommendation: NUMLKTS and LOCKMAX of 0 are good choices in most cases. These parameter values avoid the difficulty of determining what escalations have occurred because escalation cannot occur.

Lock Limit per Thread

There is a second limit that applies to the maximum number of locks that can be held on any number of objects by one thread. This limit can be specified in NUMLKUS of DSNZPARM. The installation panel DSNTIPJ can be used to specify both the NUMLKTS and NUMLKUS limits.

The NUMLKUS lock limit is 10,000 by default. If the limit is exceeded, a -904 SQLCODE is issued and the cursor is automatically closed. If a fetch or close cursor is attempted, a -501 SQLCODE indicates that the cursor is not open for a fetch or close and -507 indicates the same for an update or delete.

The purpose of NUMLKUS is to avoid taking more locks than can be held by the internal resource lock manager (IRLM) based on the space given to the lock manager.

Recommendation: Do not specify a limit of 0 for NUMLKUS because it means that there is no limit. If the IRLM space is filled and a lock request is issued, the IRLM abends, and can cause DB2 to abend as well.

Maximum Number of Rows on a Page

You can specify a value between 1 and 255 to indicate the maximum number of rows on a data page. The maximum number of rows that can be placed on a page is a function of the fact that the last byte of a RID is used to reference a slot in the page directory. (The page directory is discussed in Section TS.4.) Of course, a byte consists of 8 bits. The maximum of 255 rows per data page is calculated as 2^8-1. If the MAXROWS parameter is not specified, the maximum number of rows on a page is 255 by default. This is a good choice if you have very short rows because rows are simply short or they are short due to the use of compression as discussed in Section TS.8.

MAXROWS 1 (or a small number) is a good choice in some cases. It avoids using free space to control the number of rows on a page when heavy random insert activity is expected and row locking is not advisable. This avoids an older technique where 99 percent free is specified to allow 1 row and 1 index value per data and index page. Dummy rows are loaded to match the number of expected pages that will be used. The dummy rows are hidden with a view that excludes a value written in the dummy rows.

MAXROWS 1 (or a small number) has advantages over row locking in a data sharing environment.

TS.6 LOGICAL AND PHYSICAL CLOSE OF DATA SETS

VSAM data sets for tablespaces, partitions, and indexes are opened when first accessed. It can be resource intensive when the required data sets are not open. In one case it required 14 seconds to open 25 tablespaces and 40 indexes. This can detract from performance during prime time. After starting and stopping DB2 or a database, consider opening data sets during non-prime time if it is a problem in your environment. This can be done by executing a program that inserts a row into a table in each tablespace and each partition that is frequently accessed and then issue a rollback.

CLOSE YES (default) or CLOSE NO can be specified to indicate when the data set is to be closed. The close parameter has very little effect unless DSMAX or the z/OS or OS/390 limit of open data sets per address space is reached. An exception is that CLOSE YES allows for removal of inter-DB2 R/W interest and data sets are closed before reaching the limits when using sysplex data sharing.

The default maximum number of open data sets per DB2 subsystem is 2,000. The limit can be changed in DSNZPARM DSN6SPRM DSMAX. The theoretical maximum number of open data sets is 32,767 with OS/390 V2.6 and V5 APAR PQ18543. The practical limit is determined by the space below the 16 MB line. There can be about 15,000 open data sets if OS/390 scheduler work area is below 16 MB line or about 20,000 open data sets if OS/390 Scheduler Work area is above 16 MB line. If either the DB2 or space below the 16 MB line is exceeded, -904 SQLCODE indicating resource unavailable is issued. z/OS with 64 bit addressability provides for close to 100,000 open data sets which is sufficient for the vast majority of companies.

Switch to Read-Only Status

If a tablespace, index, or partition is not updated for 10 minutes or 5 checkpoints or QUIESCE is executed, the data set is switched to read-only processing (also known as a pseudo-close). The specified limits are the default and can be changed in DSNZPARM DSN6SYSP using the PCLOSET and PCLOSEN parameters. The switch to read-only status applies to objects created with CLOSE of YES and NO.

Switch to read-only status consists of a number of actions:

- Changed pages are written to DASD.
- Write RB-RBA (Recovery Based-RBA) to the HPGRBRBA field in the header page. It is used for logonly recovery without an image copy.
- Write RBA of last committed update to SYSLGRNX and close the log range entry. This allows for skipping log records up to the RBA when the data set is next updated to minimize recovery time.
- Information about a read-only data set is not written with a checkpoint. This saves resources at checkpoint time.

Logical Close of Data Sets

A counter is maintained for each data set indicating the number of users actively using the data set. The counter is decremented by one at commit or deallocation time, depending on the release parameter value specified at bind time and discussed in Chapter CC. If a data set no longer has users, that is the counter is zero and no locks are held, the data set is placed at end of a drain queue as indicated in Figure TS.3.

Figure TS.3. Drain queue

Data Set	Drain Queue	FIFO Close
A	Oldest with no active users	1st to close
B	Previous with no active users	2nd to close
C	Most recent with no active users	3rd to close

A logical open occurs when a data set is next referenced. A logical open means that the data set is removed from the logical close drain queue. It is not physically opened by DFP.

Physical Close of Data Sets

Thresholds are used to determine when a data set is physically closed. If 99 percent of DSMAX is reached (includes count of tablespaces created with close of yes and no), there is an asynchronous physical VSAM close of 3 percent of the data sets at the beginning of drain queue on a first-in-first-out (FIFO) basis. If the limit is exceeded, the data sets are closed synchronously.

CLOSE YES data sets are closed first followed by CLOSE NO if 3 percent of the data sets have not been closed. CLOSE YES is a good choice for data sets processed infrequently. CLOSE NO is good for data sets processed frequently. It saves about 0.25 to 1.0 seconds of CPU time to open a data set depending on the processor used.

Data sets are physically closed when the database, tablespace, partition, index, or DB2 is stopped. The physical close of data sets is like switching to read-only processing in that changed pages are written to DASD, the RB-RBA is written to the header page, the RBA of last committed update is written to SYSLGRNX, and the log range is closed.

Limit the Number of Open Data Sets

The objective is to limit the number of data sets that are open at any one time to the number of data sets that are used more than a few times a day. There is no reason to keep data sets open if they are used only weekly or only a few times a day, for example. Working storage in database services address space is required for each open data set. About 1.8 KB is required for each open data set (300 bytes below the 16 MB line or 900 bytes above the 16 MB line, depending on the scheduler work area placement). Although 1.8 KB is not much space, when multiplied by the maximum number of data sets that can be opened for an address space, the space requirement becomes up to 18 MB if 10,000 open data sets is the maximum. This can be significant depending on the availability of central storage.

A rule of thumb on opening data sets is about 0.2 second per data set. About 10 or 20 parallel tasks suggests about 10 minutes to open 10,000 data sets. However, a full restart after an abend of DB2 requires that log records be processed for all open data sets.

Do size DSMAX carefully. It controls the number of open data sets and number of data sets to be closed when the 99 percent threshold is reached. Adjust the DSMAX value based on monitoring the number of open data sets at any one time on your DB2 subsystem.

Definition of VSAM Data Sets

The DEFINE YES (default) means that VSAM data sets are defined when an application tablespace or index is created. DEFINE NO means that VSAM data sets are not defined until rows are placed in the tablespace and referenced in indexes by the LOAD utility or INSERT statements. This is useful to avoid defining all data sets for a purchased application system where not all options are chosen and thus not all data sets are required. It can be useful if you are approaching the limit of open VSAM data sets. It applies only to STOGROUP defined data sets. A 100 SQLCODE is received from a SELECT statement if the data set has not been defined.

TS.7 PARTITIONED TABLESPACES AND INDEXES

A partitioned tablespace is divided into parts. Each part is in a separate VSAM data set. There must be a partitioning index to designate which rows go into which partitions. The partitioning index is itself partitioned into the same number of VSAM data sets as used for the tablespace partitions as shown in Figure TS.4.

Figure TS.4. Partitioned tablespace and index

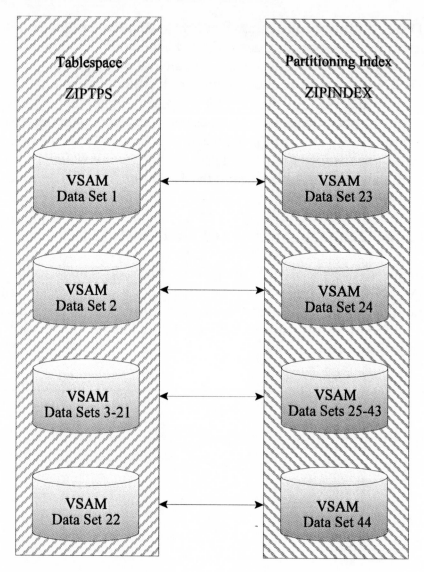

Create a Partitioned Tablespace

All of the tablespace parameters described in this chapter apply to a
partitioned tablespace. The parameters describing space requirements, free
space, and compression can be specified differently for individual partitions.
The NUMPARTS, PART, and LOCKPART parameters apply only to
partitioned tablespaces.

The following CREATE TABLESPACE statement creates a partitioned tablespace with 22 partitions as indicated in the NUMPARTS parameter. The storage group and amount of space required for all partitions can be specified. You can name one or more partitions and specify a different storage group and space allocation for each of them. In the following example, the DAZ00STG group and the indicated space allocation will be used for all partitions except those explicitly named in parentheses with the PART parameter. In most cases, each actively used partition should be placed on a different DASD device on multiple channels and control units to maximize parallel I/O and DB2 parallelism. In the example below, PART 1 uses the DAZ01STG storage group with a different space allocation, free space, and compression. (Data compression is discussed in the next section.) PART 2 uses the DAZ02STG storage group, the same space allocation as PART 1, different free space, and no compression is used.

```
CREATE TABLESPACE ZIPTSP
   IN DAZIPDB
   USING STOGROUP DAZ00STG
      PRIQTY 7200
      SECQTY     0
      ERASE NO
   PCTFREE    0
   FREEPAGE   0
   NUMPARTS 22
   (PART 1 USING STOGROUP DAZ01STG
              PRIQTY 14400
              SECQTY    720
              ERASE NO
           PCTFREE 20
           FREEPAGE 7,
    PART 2 USING STOGROUP DAZ02STG
              PRIQTY 14400
              SECQTY    720
              ERASE NO
           PCTFREE 15
           FREEPAGE 7
           COMPRESS YES)
      LOCKSIZE PAGE
      LOCKMAX 0
   LOCKPART YES
   MEMBER CLUSTER
   BUFFERPOOL BP1
```

```
CLOSE NO;
```

The LOCKSIZE, LOCKMAX, BUFFERPOOL, and CLOSE parameters apply to all parts of a partitioned tablespace and were discussed in the earlier sections of this chapter. The LOCKPART parameter applies only to partitioned tablespaces.

MEMBER CLUSTER is an optional parameter for partitioned and simple tablespaces (V5 APAR PQ02897). The purpose of this parameter is to minimize contention (particularly p-locks) and overhead when INSERTING rows in specific areas of a partition or simple tablespace (not a segmented tablespace at present) including at the end. (This is often referred to as hot spot inserts.) MEMBER CLUSTER causes rows not to be inserted in the data pages in sequence according to the explicitly created clustering index nor the implicit clustering index (usually the first index created) as is usually the case (discussed in Chapters IU and ID). Rather rows are inserted to avoid p-lock contention in a sysplex data sharing environment. Each data sharing member gets its own space page and attempts to insert rows within the range of pages covered by the space map page. Each space map page covers 199 data pages. This is in contrast to the usual case where 10,000 data pages are covered by a space map page for nonsegmented tablespaces. Also, insert processing does not wrap to the first space map page after processing the last space map page.

The duration for holding a page p-lock is extended when using MEMBER CLUSTER. This significantly reduces p-lock negotiation in a sysplex data sharing environment. (P-lock negotiation occurs when another data sharing member requests release of a held p-lock by a data sharing member so it can process the data). The p-lock is held until another agent requests the p-lock unconditionally or the buffer page is stolen.

MEMBER CLUSTER is useful for a partitioned and simple tablespace where multiple concurrent data sharing members have hot spot inserts; row locking is used; rows are inserted at end of a partition based on the clustering index; and records are not sorted in clustering sequence before insertion with a batch program. The disadvantage of using the parameter is that it can require more frequent reorganizations to regain clustering.

You can identify tablespaces created with MEMBER CLUSTER like:

```
SELECT CREATOR, NAME, DBNAME, TYPE
```

```
FROM     SYSIBM.SYSTABLESPACE
WHERE    TYPE IN ('I', 'K');
```

MEMBER CLUSTER is not needed to avoid transaction lock contention for inserts. If the target page is locked, the row is inserted in a near or far page as if there is no free space as discussed in Chapter CC.

LOCKPART YES results in partitions being locked only as they are accessed. This is referred to as selective partition locking. If the default of LOCKPART NO is used, the entire partitioned tablespace is locked. If LOCKSIZE of PAGE, ANY, or ROW is used, the LOCKPART parameter applies to the parent locks of intent to share (IS), intent exclusive (IX), and share with intent exclusive (SIX) discussed in Chapter CC. If lock escalation occurs because the LOCKMAX or NUMLKTS value is exceeded, the escalation is to the partition level (not the tablespace level) as discussed in Section TS.5. The LOCKPART parameter does not apply when using a LOCKSIZE of TABLE and TABLESPACE, if the LOCK TABLE IN EXCLUSIVE MODE statement is executed without the PART parameter, or the plan is bound with ACQUIRE(ALLOCATE).

The maximum size and number of partitions depend on whether the DSSIZE parameter defines partitions as greater than or equal to 8 GB, the LARGE parameter is specified, or more than 64 partitions are defined when the tablespace is created. If any of these conditions are not met, the maximum size of a partitioned tablespace is the same as that for a nonpartitioned tablespace, which is 64 GB. If there are from 1 to 16 partitions, each partition can be 4 GB each. If there are from 17 to 32 partitions, each partition can be 2 GB each. If there are from 33 to 64 partitions, each partition can be 1 GB each. The maximum number of partitions is 64.

If the DSSIZE parameter can be used to define partitions as greater than or equal 8 GB, the LARGE parameter is specified, or more than 64 partitions are defined when creating a partitioned tablespace. The maximum number of partitions is 254 (may be increased to 4,096 in V7+1). Each data partition, index partition, and nonpartitioning index (NPI) can contain 64 GB of data, and a maximum of 16 TB of data in the entire partitioned tablespace (V6). It is advisable to use the DSSIZE parameter rather than the LARGE parameter for upward compatibility. There are several prerequisites to having a data set greater than 4 GB. It is necessary to use SMS managed data sets (DFSMS V1.5) with a SMS data class, ACS (Automatic Class

Section), and extended addressability (EA) must be enabled to allow data sets larger than 4 GB. The DSSIZE clause can be specified on the CREATE TABLESPACE statement with 8GB or more and up to and including 254 partitions.

DSSIZE 8G NUMPARTS 254

In order to change the DSSIZE, it is necessary to drop and recreate the tablespace. It is not possible to alter the DSSIZE.

If DSSIZE is not specified and more than 64 partitions are specified, the maximum data set size is 4 GB and the maximum partitioned tablespace size is 1 TB. This is the limit in V5 in any case.

The Partitioning Index

A partitioning index is required on a partitioned tablespace to designate which rows are to be placed in which partition. The partitioning index must be the CLUSTER index as indicated in the following CREATE statement. The partitioning index is divided into parts corresponding to the parts of the tablespace. Each part is a separate and distinct index referencing rows in its corresponding data partition.

```
CREATE INDEX ZIPINDEX
   ON ZIPTB (ZIPCODE)
   CLUSTER
     (PART 1 VALUES(1000000.)
        USING STOGROUP DAX01STG
           PRIQTY 7200
           SECQTY  720
        PCTFREE  20
        FREEPAGE  7,
      PART 2 VALUES(2000000.)
        USING STOGROUP DAX02STG
           PRIQTY 7200
           SECQTY  720
        PCTFREE  15
        FREEPAGE  7,
      PART 3 VALUES(3000000.)
        USING STOGROUP DAX03STG
           PRIQTY 7200
```

```
                  SECQTY   720,
            PART 4 VALUES(4000000.)
               USING STOGROUP DAX04STG
                  PRIQTY 7200
                  SECQTY   720,
            PART 5 VALUES(5000000.)
               USING STOGROUP DAX05STG
                  PRIQTY 7200
                  SECQTY   720,

                     .

                     .

                     .

            PART 22 VALUES(22000000.)
               USING STOGROUP DAX22STG
                  PRIQTY 14400
                  SECQTY    720)
      PCTFREE   0
      FREEPAGE  0
      BUFFERPOOL BP2
      CLOSE NO;
```

Most of the parameters used when creating the partitioning index have the same meaning as the corresponding parameter used when creating a tablespace. Index usage and design are discussed in Chapters IU and ID. The storage group, space allocation, and free space can be specified differently for each index partition as when creating a partitioned tablespace.

Each partition number must be named along with the limit key value for the columns in the partitioning index. Each limit key value is the maximum value that can be placed in a partition. Indeed, the limit key values are used to determine which row to insert into which partition. In the example, all rows with zip codes less than or equal to 1,000,000 are placed in partition 1 of the index and data pages. All rows with zip codes greater than 1,000,000 and less than or equal 2,000,000 are placed in partition 2 of the index and data pages. This principle applies to partitions 3 through 21.

The limit key specified for the last partition works differently depending on whether the tablespace can contain more than 64 GB of data. If the tablespace cannot contain more than 64 GB of data, all rows with a zip code less than or equal to as well as those greater than 22,000,000 are placed in the last partition of 22. Basically, the limit key is not enforced on the last partition. If the tablespace can contain more than 64 GB, the upper limit is enforced. Rows with a zip code greater than 22,000,000 are not loaded by the LOAD utility. They are written to the discard data set if one is specified as described in Chapter LC. An INSERT statement receives a negative SQLCODE if it attempts to insert a row with a value greater than 22,000,000 in the partitioning index column.

The first 255 bytes of a partitioning index identify the partition number (V6) and 255 bytes is the maximum length of columns in an index. The example assumes that the column used for the upper range values is declared as an integer. If there are any decimal columns described in the upper range values, the values must be specified with a decimal point (1000000. for example). If descending order is specified, values are the lowest rather than the highest values as used in the example.

The partitioning index must be the clustering index. This presents design challenges. You may want to partition on certain columns and have your clustering index on other columns for the performance benefits of clustering as discussed in Chapters IU and ID.

The columns that participate in the partitioning index can be updated (V5 APAR PQ16946) if the partitioned tablespace is created after application of the APAR. This facility is not intended for heavy update activity where the update causes the row to change partitions. If the update causes a row in partition 5 to be moved to partition 10, parts 5 through 10 of the tablespace, partitioning index, and all NPIs are drained. Others cannot access the parts until a commit is issued. This is necessary to avoid a row disappearing from index access temporarily. An alternative is to select the row, save the columns, delete the row, and insert the row after changing the column in the partitioning index. This process requires the update of all indexes on the table as does the use of the UPDATE statement, but minimizes lock contention. Do be cautious if the tablespace is a parent in a referential integrity structure. If the delete cascade or set null rules are in effect, you must manage the dependent tables before deleting rows from the parent partitioned tablespace. Referential integrity is discussed in Chapter CT.

The partitioning index cannot be altered or dropped. It defines the limit key for each partition. That is a row greater than the value specified using the PART and VALUE clause of the create tablespace statement cannot be placed in the specified partition. We will discuss some challenges and alternatives for managing the challenges that result from this rule in the following sections.

Advantages of Partitioning

A partitioning tablespace provides for dividing a large tablespace into smaller more manageable pieces. It improves the availability of data. For example, you can execute a utility or program on one partition and execute another utility or program on other partitions concurrently.

You can spread partitions on multiple DASD devices, channels, and control units. This improves performance by reducing I/O time for online transactions accessing the data at random and batch programs accessing data in different partitions.

Partitioning provides for DB2 parallelism on multiple partitions which is particularly useful in reducing the elapsed time required to process many rows. It also allows for scanning a few partitions rather than the entire tablespace in a limited partition scan. These techniques are discussed in Chapter BP.

Tablespace and index parameters can be specified and altered on individual partitions.

SMS can archive infrequently used partitions and automatically recall them when next accessed to save DASD space.

Partitioning is Not a Panacea

A primary cost of partitioning is maintaining NPIs. An NPI is one index that references rows in all data partitions. All indexes on a table in a partitioned tablespace other than the partitioning index are NPIs. NPI are divided into logical parts which can be processed independently like the physical parts of the partitioning index. This provides for partition independence as discussed in Chapter LC and a sophisticated access path discussed in Chapter IU. PIECESIZE provides for placing NPI in separate data sets and spreading them on different DASD to reduce I/O contention as discussed in Chapter ID.

Reorganization of a single data partition of a tablespace with NPIs can approach but not exceed reorganization of the entire tablespace. The RIDs of NPIs are updated in place only if the RID has changed, to reduce costs. However, load replace of a partition requires that NPI RIDs pointing to replaced rows be deleted and RIDs pointing to new rows be inserted. The load of the second through last partition uses insert mode on the NPIs, which are similar to that when using an INSERT statement.

The load and reorganization of all partitions at once requires fewer resources than processing each partition individually, particularly if there are NPIs. However, processing one or a few partitions leaves all other partitions available for use by others.

Estimating the Number of Partitions

A number of factors must be considered in determining the number of partitions that are best. Business requirements may well determine the number of partitions. For example, it may be necessary to partition by month so that a history of monthly data can be maintained. Processing requirements are a major consideration. It may be necessary to do batch processing in a particular sequence which requires that the clustering index be on the columns that determine the sequence of batch processing as discussed in Chapter BP. Also, the clustering index is valuable in avoiding searches, joins, sorts, and other processing discussed in Chapters IU and ID. The clustering and partitioning index are one and the same.

The number of partitions best for DB2 parallelism depends on whether SQL statements are I/O and/or CPU intensive, and the number of processors, DASD devices, control units, and channels available.

I/O Intensive: If "other read I/O time" (time that DB2 is waiting for pages to be read into a buffer pool) from DB2PM is close to the total elapsed time (accounting trace class 3), the SQL is I/O intensive. You can estimate the number of partitions as the elapsed time divided by the processor time multiplied by the number of processors that can be used. If a representative SQL statement requires 60 elapsed minutes and 30 processor minutes, and there are 10 processors available, 20 partitions is a good goal assuming sufficient I/O paths are available based on:

```
20 = 60 elapsed minutes / 30 processor minutes
   * 10 processors
```

Processor Intensive: If the processor time is about 70 percent or more of the elapsed time (accounting trace class 2), the SQL is processor intensive. This suggests that the number of partitions should be greater than or equal to the number of processors not dedicated to other higher priority work.

Do avoid one or more partitions that are considerably larger than other partitions. This limits the maximum degree of parallelism as discussed in Chapter PL.

Small tablespaces can be partitioned to encourage join parallelism. The small partitioned tablespace is likely to be the outer table of a join. The number of partitions in the outer table determines the maximum degree of parallelism as discussed in Chapter PL.

Maximum Number of Partitions: The number of partitions and your choice of the partitioning index are very important and cannot be changed with an ALTER statement. It is necessary to unload the data, drop the tablespace, create the tablespace, table, and indexes, load data, grant privileges, execute RUNSTATS, and rebind plans and packages (or accept an automatic rebind). Do consider defining the maximum number of partitions allowed. If the tablespace will not exceed 64 GB, 64 partitions can be defined and four byte RIDs are used for all indexes on the table in the tablespace. If the tablespace is greater than 64 GB and less than 16 TB, 254 partitions can be defined and five byte RIDs are used for all indexes on the table in the tablespace.

Limit Key for Each Partition

Once you have determined the number of partitions required, the next question is what limit key values need to be specified to get about the same number of rows in each partition. The following SELECT statement gives the limit key value for each of four partitions on a million row table assuming a partitioning index on SN, PN, and JN. There can be more rows in one partition than there are in others, depending on the cardinality of the column. The limit key value is the value that occurs about every 250,000 rows. This is the reason for the values of 250000, 500000,750000, and 1000000 in each of the outer SELECTS for each UNION ALL block.

```
SELECT 'Part 1 limit key = ',
   MAX(SN CONCAT PN CONCAT JN)
```

```
FROM    SPJ AS SPJ1
WHERE 250000 >
   (SELECT COUNT(*)
    FROM    SPJ AS SPJ2
    WHERE   SPJ2.SN < SPJ1.SN
    OR      (SPJ2.SN = SPJ1.SN
    AND     SPJ2.PN < SPJ1.PN)
    OR      (SPJ2.SN = SPJ1.SN
    AND     SPJ2.PN = SPJ1.PN
    AND     SPJ2.JN < SPJ1.JN))
UNION ALL
SELECT 'Part 2 limit key = ',
   MAX(SN CONCAT PN CONCAT JN)
FROM SPJ AS SPJ1
WHERE 500000 >
   (SELECT COUNT(*)
    FROM    SPJ AS SPJ2
    WHERE   SPJ2.SN < SPJ1.SN
    OR      (SPJ2.SN = SPJ1.SN
    AND     SPJ2.PN < SPJ1.PN)
    OR      (SPJ2.SN = SPJ1.SN
    AND     SPJ2.PN = SPJ1.PN
    AND     SPJ2.JN < SPJ1.JN))
UNION ALL
SELECT 'Part 3 limit key = ',
   MAX(SN CONCAT PN CONCAT JN)
FROM    SPJ AS SPJ1
WHERE 750000 >
   (SELECT COUNT(*)
    FROM    SPJ AS SPJ2
    WHERE   SPJ2.SN < SPJ1.SN
    OR      (SPJ2.SN = SPJ1.SN
    AND     SPJ2.PN < SPJ1.PN)
    OR      (SPJ2.SN = SPJ1.SN
    AND     SPJ2.PN = SPJ1.PN
    AND     SPJ2.JN < SPJ1.JN))
UNION ALL
SELECT 'Part 4 limit key = ',
   MAX(SN CONCAT PN CONCAT JN)
FROM    SPJ AS SPJ1
WHERE 1000000 >
   (SELECT COUNT(*)
    FROM    SPJ AS SPJ2
    WHERE   SPJ2.SN < SPJ1.SN
    OR      (SPJ2.SN = SPJ1.SN
```

```
AND      SPJ2.PN < SPJ1.PN)
OR      (SPJ2.SN = SPJ1.SN
AND      SPJ2.PN = SPJ1.PN
AND      SPJ2.JN < SPJ1.JN))
GROUP BY 1, 2
ORDER BY 1 ASC, 2 DESC;
```

The statement is very resource intensive. It requires a great deal of CPU and I/O time because it is a correlated subselect. Do execute it when the resources are available. Hopefully the statement will have to be executed only once or a few times to provide information on the limit key values needed for partitioning.

An alternative is to sort rows and report on the upper range value every 250,000 rows as determined by host language code using a cursor on:

```
SELECT SN, PN, JN
FROM    SPJ
ORDER BY SN, PN, JN
```

Although this technique may be considered brute force, it is likely to perform better than the correlated subselect.

Partitioning Index Alternatives

We will consider a number of alternatives for designing the partitioning index along with the pros and cons of the alternatives. Hopefully, these alternatives will be useful for the design of your partitioned tablespaces and indexes.

Use of a pseudo random number has some advantages. It provides for spreading insert activity throughout the tablespace and provides for approximately equal partition sizes. It avoids hot spot insert activity which is useful in a data sharing environment and is an alternative to MEMBER CLUSTER.

The disadvantages of partitioning on a pseudo random number should be considered carefully. A random number is not useful for avoiding sorts for ORDER BY, GROUP BY, DISTINCT, and joins in most cases. The usefulness of sorting input, in sequence for batch match/merge processing, is unlikely (good batch technique discussed in Chapter BP.) Partitioning on a random number does not allow for the clustering partition index on a column with a business meaning for searches, joins, and sort avoidance. It does not allow for partitioning according to business requirements (by month, order ID, invoice ID, etc.) either. If high insert activity is expected, a large number of random I/O can detract from performance. The use of a partition scan is unlikely. In most cases, it is necessary to create one or more NPI to provide index access to columns with a business meaning. Additional space is required for each row (19 bytes per row if a ROWID column is used, 2 byte length field and 17 bytes value used as limit key) and for an index that is rarely used to satisfy a user request. Typically, partitioned tablespaces have a larger number of rows making the additional space required for data and the partitioning index significant.

Restrictions on Use of ROWID Column as Partitioning Index: ROWID data type column containing pseudo random numbers can be created as described in Chapter CT and used as described in Chapters IU and PD. It is not possible to use the LOAD utility to load at the partition level (must load entire tablespace). It is necessary to specify upper range value in hexadecimal like:

```
CREATE INDEX SPJX ON SPJ(SPJ_ROWID)
   CLUSTER  (PART 1 VALUES(X'3FFF'),
   CLUSTER   PART 2 VALUES(X'7FFF'),
   CLUSTER   PART 3 VALUES(X'BFFF'),
   CLUSTER   PART 4 VALUES(X'FFFF'))
```

If the restrictions present a problem, an alternative is to determine the maximum required number of partitions, 64 or 254, for example. Define a partitioning index on a partitioning column containing a generated random number between 1 and 64 or 1 and 254.

Partitioning on the PK: The PK is a good choice if you have frequent batch processing in PK sequence and the index can be used for searches, joins, and to avoid sorts. However, there is a disadvantage of this technique if the partitioning tablespace is a parent table with dependent tables defined and the columns constituting the partitioning index are frequently updated as discussed in the above subsection "The Partitioning Index".

Partitioning on a Sequential Value: Partitioning on a sequential value has advantages. For example the partitioning index can be on an ascending date, order number, or invoice number. The maximum number of partitions in a large tablespace (254) can be defined for sequentially inserted rows. This allows for 21 years and 2 months of monthly data before it is necessary to drop and recreate the tablespace. If you are partitioning by a sequential order or invoice number over a 20 year period, for instance, specify a limit key value for each of the 254 partitions to accommodate the orders or invoices. You have a good deal of flexibility in specifying the limit key value for the unused partitions because the limit key can be altered followed by a reorganization as discussed in the following subsection (V6).

Partitioning on a sequential value has additional advantages. You can load or load resume the most current partition while all other partitions are available for other processing. There is no need to continue to reorganize and collect statistics on earlier partitions once the data in partitions has stabilized. You can use 0 PCTFREE and 0 FREEPAGE on all partitions to reduce space requirements.

If you use this technique, do use the ALTER statement to make the unused partitions very small and purge an obsolete partition with load replace of 0 records or use a dummy input file to minimize space requirements.

Partitioning Index Control Table: Each row can be assigned a value of 1, 2, 3, etc. as a partition number in a column defined for this purpose. Rows with a value of 1 are placed in partition 1, rows with a value of 2 are placed in partition 2, etc. The partition number column has advantages when used with a control table. The control table can be used to associate a partition number with a time period or range of order numbers, for example. The control table allows for placing the clustering index on a column that will benefit from clustering. It also provides for the reuse of partition numbers when rolling months or ranges of order numbers. Only the oldest partition is unavailable while executing a load replace of the partition with new data.

We will use an example to demonstrate the use of a control table, assuming that the requirement is to partition by month and retain a two year history. The control table contains the partition number as well as the first and last day of a month. The Reuse Begin and Reuse End columns contain the date range that replaces the oldest partitions date ranges as indicated in Figure TS.5.

Figure TS.5. CONTROL table for partitioning by month

PART_NO	MONTH_BEGIN	MONTH_END	Reuse Begin	Reuse End
1	~~1992-01-01~~	~~1992-01-31~~	1994-01-01	1994-01-31
2	~~1992-02-01~~	~~1992-02-29~~	1994-02-01	1994-02-28
3	1992-03-01	1992-03-31		
. . .	. . .	. . .		
24	1993-12-01	1993-12-31		

The control table is used to determine the partition number before selecting from the target HISTORY table. If the user requests information on rows with a date between 1992-03-15 and 1992-03-20, the following SELECT statement can be used to determine the partition number of the partition that contains the rows required.

```
SELECT  PART_NO
FROM    CONTROL
WHERE   MONTH_BEGIN <= '1992-03-15' --Dates
AND     MONTH_END   >= '1992-03-20';--requested
```

Assume that the HISTORY table has a composite partitioning index on the partition number (PART_NO) and order date (ORDER_DATE). A matching index scan can be used on the partitioning index based on the PART_NO determined from the CONTROL table and order dates required by the user like:

```
SELECT  ACCOUNT_NO, AMOUNT
FROM    HISTORY
WHERE   PART_NO = 3
AND ORDER_DATE BETWEEN '1992-03-15'
                   AND '1992-03-20';
```

If you do not want developers and business professionals who access the data directly to be aware of the CONTROL table, a view can be used to "hide" the CONTROL table. The disadvantage of the technique is that the CONTROL table is an additional reference table to be accessed and must be maintained.

This technique can be used for partitioning by order number, invoice number, or any column values. It is one of the most popular techniques used for managing partitions.

Altering the Limit Key

One or more partition limit keys can be altered (V6) which has a number of advantages. It is useful to accommodate changing business requirements. It may be necessary to alter the limit key of partitions that have grown larger than expected and beyond the limit of a partition size. This allows for moving rows from one partition to another. It also allows for activating more partitions in the future which are not required at the present. You can activate additional partitions that have been previously defined for new time periods and deactivate old partitions that are no longer required. Partitions can be resized so that each partition is approximately equal in size. This improves parallel processing performance as discussed in Chapter PL. In addition, the size of partitions is important in maximizing the availability of critical data during utility and batch processing.

The altered partitions are placed in REORG pending (REORP) status. Rows cannot be selected, inserted, updated, or deleted from the altered partitions while the partitions are in this pending status. It is also necessary to reorganize the altered partitions plus the next partition, the entire tablespace, load replace the tablespace, or drop the tablespace. An exception is that the last partition is not placed in REORG pending if tablespace does not allow for more than 64 GB of data. All plans and packages that reference the partitioned tablespace are marked as invalidate. The first access of a plan or a package causes all of them to be rebound. The rebinds are successful if altered partitioned have been reorganized successfully. Otherwise, a -904 SQLCODE is received when an attempt is made to run a plan or package that accesses the tablespace.

Example of Altering Limit Keys: Assume that about one-half a million calls are estimated per month and it has been decided to specify a limit key of the last day of each month in 1999. However, let's assume November and December have over 1 million calls per month as shown in Figure TS.6.

Figure TS.6. Number of rows in each of 12 partitions

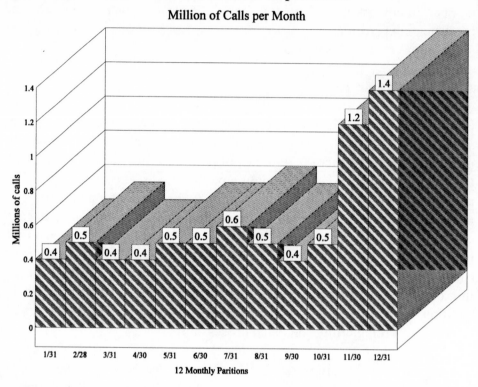

It is decided to alter the two large partitions for November and December to make them more consistent in size with the other partitions at about one-half million rows in each partition. Also the limit key for an unused partition to allow for calls in January of 2000 is specified to activate partition 15.

```
ALTER INDEX MONTH_LIMIT
    PART 11 VALUES ('1999-11-15'),
    PART 12 VALUES ('1999-11-30'),
    PART 13 VALUES ('1999-12-15'),
    PART 14 VALUES ('1999-12-31'),
    PART 15 VALUES ('2000-01-31');
```

Parts 11 through 16 are placed in REORG pending status. It is necessary to reorganize these partitions as discussed in Chapter RR. It is not necessary to reorganize the last partition (16) if tablespace is <= 64 GB. Do consider rebinding plans and packages that reference the tablespace to avoid automatic rebinds when they are next executed.

Current and Historical Data

Current and historical data are often placed in a single tablespace. However, they have many different characteristics. Current data is frequently updated, which requires free space to accommodate updates and page or row locking. It is necessary to periodically execute the reorganization, RUNSTATS or inline statistics, image copy or inline copy, and other utilities as discussed in Chapter RR. Rebind of plans and packages are needed periodically as well. The index design for current data frequently differs from that required for historical data.

Historical data is rarely updated. This means that zero free space and a LOCKSIZE of TABLE or TABLESPACE is a good choice. It is not necessary to periodically execute the reorganization, RUNSTATS, image copy, and other utilities. Rebind of plans and packages are needed infrequently. You can also support more indexes with low update activity. This is particularly important in a data warehousing environment.

An alternative is to create a view with UNION ALL of the current and historical data so that tables appear as one table (V7) for select processing provided duplicate rows do not occur or are acceptable. A view can be created to select from the current data, UNION ALL, select from another table, UNION ALL, select from another table, etc. This causes the current data to be searched first. If UNION is required and many rows qualify and must be sorted, an alternative is to have application programs and ad hoc users determine when to process current and/or historical tables. Similarly, developers need to update base tables because an insert, update, and delete cannot be issued on the view. Users and developer can select from a view with UNION ALL or UNION or use a nested table expression.

12 Tables for 12 Months of Data: Another example is useful to show how more than two tables can be used. We will use a view of 12 tables for each of the 12 months of the year. The same principle applies to multiple tables based on ranges of order IDs, customer IDs, account IDs, etc.

```
CREATE VIEW ONE_YEAR (ORDERNO, CUSTNO, ITEMNO,
                      UNIT_PRICE, QTY, ORDER_DATE) as
  SELECT * FROM MONTH1
  WHERE ORDER_DATE BETWEEN '2001-01-01' AND '2001-01-31'
  UNION ALL
  SELECT * FROM MONTH2
  WHERE ORDER_DATE BETWEEN '2001-02-01' AND '2001-02-29'
  UNION ALL
```

```
SELECT * FROM MONTH3
WHERE ORDER_DATE BETWEEN '2001-03-01' AND '2001-03-31';
--Etc. for 12 months of data
```

Do include ranges of values in the view definition to allow access only to the required tables. DB2 accesses only the MONTH2 table to satisfy the following statement.

```
SELECT ORDERNO, CUSTNO, ITEMNO, UNIT_PRICE, QTY, ORDER_DATE
FROM    ONE_YEAR
WHERE   ORDER_DATE BETWEEN '2001-02-05' AND '2001-02-10';
```

CPU and elapsed time is about the same as selecting from less than or equal to 12 tables or one partitioned tablespace with APAR PQ47178 and PQ48588 applied.

Disadvantages: There are some disadvantages of multiple tables. Data may need to be placed in a historical table periodically. Also, a table begins with 0 rows periodically. Chapter CT discusses the updateability of a view and Chapter PL discusses the use of parallelism with UNION and UNION ALL.

Recommendation: If the disadvantages of multiple tables are manageable, do maintain the data in separate tables. This reduces the costs and complexity of maintaining the tablespace and indexes significantly. You can index each table as required rather than indexing a large partitioned tablespace which is used for various purposes. You can have more indexes on tables which are infrequently updated to satisfy usage requirements.

TS.8 DATA COMPRESSION

COMPRESS YES is specified to cause DB2 to compress data in a tablespace. (Compression does not apply to indexes, the catalog and directory.) A dictionary is built containing frequently occurring bytes and a corresponding bit pattern. For example, if John occurs frequently in the tablespace, it is placed in the dictionary along with a bit pattern of say 0110. (12 bits are used rather than the 4 shown in the example.) Each occurrence of John is replaced in the tablespace with the bit pattern, including the occurrence of John in the names Johns, Johnson, Johnsen, Johnston, Johnstone, etc. using enterprise system architecture (ESA) compression. Column boundaries are ignored. This is in contrast to using a compaction algorithm where 40 bytes of blanks are represented by 1 blank preceded by a count of 40, for instance.

Data with repetitive patterns is a good candidate for compression. For example, names and codes for cities, states, countries, departments, divisions, string of blanks, etc. Numeric values that occur frequently like 199.99, 100.00, 1998, identifiers where only the last few digits vary, etc. are also good candidates. Graphic and image data do not compress well.

Savings and Costs of Compression

There are many factors to consider in determining the savings and costs of compression.

DASD space: Significant DASD space savings can be achieved with compression. Between 40 to 70 percent less DASD space is required with compression, depending on the characteristics of the data, with a typical savings of 50 to 60 percent. There are additional savings in terms of I/O, depending on the type of processing. If the data is compressed by 50 percent, twice as many rows can fit on a page and half the number of I/O need to be issued for sequential processing. Random processing has a greater chance that the required row is in the buffer pool since more rows fit in the buffer. This results in a reduction in the number of I/O, I/O time, and CPU time to issue I/O. It reduces the amount of data sent across I/O channels, elapsed time, virtual pool and hiperpool space requirements, and log space required. Compressed data is logged in compressed form. Log records can be decompressed by calling DSNWLI and passing 0306 in the IFCID area.

CPU costs with and without hardware assist: If your computer has the CMPSC instruction, hardware compression will be used to compress and decompress the data. If the computer does not support ESA compression, software compression is used. CPU time is required to compress and decompress the data. You can expect an overall increase in CPU time of from 1 to 5 percent, more toward the 1 percent for hardware compression and more toward the 5 percent for software compression. In general, software compression requires about 3.5 times more CPU time than hardware compression. zSeries computer hardware compression is about 30 to 60 percent faster than earlier computers. In addition, decompression CPU time is reduced 3 to 4 times on zSeries.

Lock Contention: There is an increased potential for lock contention with more rows on a page when using page locking.

Type of processing influences costs: Decompression of all columns in a row is required even if only a few columns are needed. This is particularly costly for long rows because the cost is per byte. Decompression of all rows is required when doing a tablespace scan. It is necessary to decompress rows before applying predicates to determine if the row qualifies. If an index is used to locate qualifying rows, only the identified rows are decompressed. Some of the decompressed rows may not be needed based on additional predicates that are applied after the row is located using an index.

Increases Costs of Logging: If a compressed row is updated, it is necessary to log from first changed byte to end of row.

Utilities that require decompression: Several utilities must decompress all rows in the tablespace including REORG, RUNSTATS, REBUILD INDEX (V6), and DSN1PRNT.

Dictionary Creation and Maintenance: Computer and people resources are required to create, refine, and maintain the compression and decompression dictionary.

Transmission of Data: The data is decompressed before it is transmitted in a distributed environment. This avoids keeping the dictionary synchronized at multiple sites. VTAM can optionally compress data for transmission and decompress it at the receiving site.

How to Use Compression

COMPRESS YES is specified on the CREATE TABLESPACE statement to use compression. COMPRESS NO is the default. Compression can be specified at the partition level to allow for compressing some, but not all partitions. This offers the opportunity to compress partitions that are infrequently updated and not compress partitions that are frequently updated reducing the CPU costs of compression.

The ALTER TABLESPACE statement can be used to turn compression on and off. It is not necessary to drop and recreate the tablespace or unload and reload the data. However, you must reorganize, or unload and reload the data, to gain or eliminate compression.

Some, but not all, rows in a table can be compressed. Only rows that become shorter are stored in compressed form. The first byte of a 6 byte row prefix contains X'00' for a normal row, X'04' for a compressed row, and X'20' for an overflow row.

The ALTER TABLE statement can be used to add a column to a table when using ESA compression, unlike when using EDITPROC compression.

Impact of Compression on the Optimizer and by Program Type

The optimizer factors in compression when choosing an access path and the resources required to process compressed data differ depending on the type of program.

Impact on Access Path: The optimizer includes additional CPU time in its estimate for decompression based on PCTROWCOMP (percentage of rows compressed) in SYSTABLES for compressed tablespaces and SYSTABSTATS for compressed partitions. The row length is also included in the calculations because the CPU cost is per byte. A high PCTROWCOMP results in a higher CPU cost estimate. This means that a matching index scan is more likely and a lower degree of parallelism is also likely. The use of non-compressed indexes to locate the compressed data minimizes the number of rows that need to be decompressed. A tablespace scan requires the decompression of every row before applying predicates to determine if the row qualifies and should be passed to the relational data system (RDS) for further processing. No compression or a low PCTROWCOMP results in a lower CPU estimate per row. This means that a tablespace and non-matching index scan with data reference is more likely and a higher degree of parallelism is likely. Index-only access is not affected by compression because indexes are not compressed.

ESA compression does not use EDITPROC which reduces costs because it is not necessary to do an EDITPROC call and return. Other techniques used for compression use EDITPROC. The optimizer factors in a fixed increase in CPU cost when EDITPROC is used. The estimate is somewhat lower than reality in most cases. The estimate is of limited accuracy because the costs depend on the specific compression and decompression algorithm used with EDITPROC.

Program Types: Among the different program types and processing, batch programs, some utilities, and decision support applications that process many rows will likely experience an increase in CPU time with a decrease in I/O and elapsed time. This is because many rows are typically scanned and decompressed which increases CPU time but decreases I/O and elapsed time because there are more rows per page. Online transactions that process a few rows will probably not have a significant increase in CPU time, I/O usage is unlikely to decrease, and response time is unlikely to increase significantly, typically few rows are processed in online transactions and these rows are usually located using an index which is not compressed.

Capacity Planning Estimates

DB2 Estimator can be used to estimate the changes in CPU, I/O, elapsed time, and DASD space when using compression. You can import descriptions of existing tables and SQL statements into DB2 Estimator. Estimate the costs of frequently executed SQL with and without the compression option, and then compare the estimates.

An alternative is to estimate the CPU costs to compress and decompress the data based on the costs per byte. The CPU time to compress and decompress data is covered in Chapter OP. The CPU and elapsed time for SQL and utility execution tests are reported at the end of this section.

Very Short and Very Long Rows

The length of uncompressed rows impacts the savings and costs of compression.

Very short rows: Very short uncompressed rows will not result in significant saving in most cases. One row is compressed at a time. The 6 byte row prefix and 2 byte page directory entry are not compressed.

Very Long Rows: At least one additional row should fit on a page to realize savings. A very long row may not be compressible such that an additional row will fit on a 4 KB page. If this is the case, consider 8, 16, or 32 KB page which allows for several long compressed or uncompressed rows. This is a good choice if there are frequent sequential scans. Do keep in mind that the I/O time is increased by 8x for a 32 KB page compared to a

4 KB page. This is particularly important if only one or a few rows are frequently processed on a 32 KB page that contains many rows. This can increase elapsed time and require more space in the buffer pool.

Estimating DASD Savings

DSN1COMP can be used to estimate savings for compression. It can be executed against any data set with a DB2 page format. A good choice of input to DSN1COMP is a full or incremental image copy. You probably have an image copy and it does not interfere with the availability of the tablespace to use it for the estimate of DASD savings. If you do not have an available image copy, you can take a copy of the tablespace being considered for compression using DSN1COPY or the image copy utility and use it as input to DSN1COMP. An alternative is to stop the tablespace or partition in a VSAM LDS and use it as input to DSN1COMP.

Here is an example of the parameters that can be specified on the EXEC statement to execute DSN1COMP.

```
DSN1COMP 4K NUMPARTS(24) SIZE(4096)
FREEPAGE(31) PCTFREE(5) FULLCOPY REORG
ROWLIMIT(20000)
```

The first parameter, 4K, is the data set page size used for SYSUT1 and is the default. If the tablespace uses a 8, 16, or 32 KB page size, the appropriate value is specified rather than 4K. NUMPARTS indicates the number of partitions. NUMPARTS(0) is used if the tablespace is not partitioned and is the default. SIZE is the number of entries in the dictionary. You can specify 512, 1024, 2048, or 4096. 4096 is a good choice. If a smaller dictionary size is specified, DSN1COMP requires fewer resources to produce the estimates discussed below. However, the estimates may not be as accurate. The actual compression and decompression dictionary usually has 4,096 nodes of 8 bytes each on 16 pages. The number of bytes is 65,536 calculated as 2 dictionaries * 4,096 nodes * 8 bytes or 16 pages * 4,096 bytes. The default of 16 pages for the dictionary can be changed in DSNZPARM.

The values for FREEPAGE and PCTFREE should be specified as on the CREATE TABLESPACE statement as discussed in Section TS.5. FULLCOPY indicates that the input will be a full image copy of the tablespace. INCRCOPY is an option to indicate that the input will be an incremental copy. REORG means that the estimate should be determined with the sampling algorithm used with REORG. This is in contrast to the method used by LOAD where the dictionary is built based on the first *n* rows as will be discussed in this section. ROWLIMIT(20000) indicates the number of rows that should be evaluated to produce the estimates, 1,000,000 is the maximum. If the number specified is too small, the DSN1941 message is issued indicating that limit should be made larger. The DSSIZE parameter should be specified for tablespaces greater than 64 GB.

Example of DSN1COMP Report

DSN1COMP reports on the number of KB bytes and pages with and without compression along with an estimate of the percentage of bytes that will be saved with compression. It gives the average compressed and uncompressed row length. The report also includes the number of rows scanned to build the dictionary, the number of rows processed to provide the compression estimate, and the number of entries in the dictionary. Figure TS.7 is an example of the report produced by DSN1COMP.

Figure TS.7. Example of DSN1COMP report

```
DSN1940I DSN1COMP COMPRESSION REPORT

      1,289 KB WITHOUT COMPRESSION
        736 KB WITH COMPRESSION
         43 PERCENT OF BYTES WOULD BE SAVED

      2,108 ROWS SCANNED TO BUILD DICTIONARY
     20,000 ROWS SCANNED TO PROVIDE COMPRESSION ESTIMATE
      4,096 DICTIONARY ENTRIES

         81 BYTES FOR AVERAGE UNCOMPRESSED ROW LENGTH
         52 BYTES FOR AVERAGE COMPRESSED ROW LENGTH
         16 DICTIONARY PAGES REQUIRED
        358 PAGES REQUIRED WITHOUT COMPRESSION
        225 PAGES REQUIRED WITH COMPRESSION
         37 PERCENT OF THE DB2 DATA PAGES WOULD BE SAVED

DSN1994I DSN1COMP COMPLETED SUCCESSFULLY, 20,002 PAGES
PROCESSED
```

The data page estimate includes space for the page header, trailer, ID map, and row prefix. However, you do need to add space for the dictionary when estimating the amount of DASD space required for the tablespace or partition.

RUNSTATS Statistics

Statistics collected by RUNSTATS are useful in making decisions regarding data compression. SYSTABLEPART.PAGESAVE is the percentage of pages times 100 saved as a result of compression in a tablespace or partition. For example, assume 30,000 pages without compression, 40 percent savings means that 18,000 pages are required for the compressed data. If PAGESAVE contains a negative number, either the data should not be compressed or the dictionary needs to be rebuilt. For example, -3 means that 30,900 pages are required for the compressed data.

If PAGESAVE decreases over time with update activity, it is likely that the characteristics of the compressed data have changed with insert, update, and delete activity. The dictionary needs to be rebuilt using the reorganization utility to maintain good compression. The average number of bytes per row before and after compression is also useful in determining if the dictionary needs to be rebuilt. These averages are reported by the REORG, LOAD, and DSN1COMP utilities.

RUNSTATS calculates the percentage of rows compressed out of the total number of active rows in the table and places the value in SYSTABLES.PCTROWCOMP. It also places similar percentages for each partition of a partitioned tablespace in SYSTABSTATS.PCTROWCOMP. These statistics are used by the optimizer to estimate the CPU costs of various access paths.

Compression/Decompression Dictionary

Each tablespace and each partition must have a dictionary for compression and decompression. This accounts for the fact that each partition may have different characteristics. A segment in a segmented tablespace is dedicated to the dictionary. For example, SEGSIZE 32 results in 32 pages being dedicated to the dictionary. Of course, savings as a result of compression should be greater than the number of pages required by the dictionary to justify compression. The dictionary is placed after the header and first space map pages and before the data pages. Both the LOAD and REORG utilities can build the dictionary. They validate the dictionary after it has been built and log the build of the dictionary if log of yes is specified.

LOAD build of the dictionary: LOAD builds a tree of 4,096 nodes from which it builds the dictionary based on the first n rows loaded into a tablespace during the RELOAD phase. It processes the number of rows necessary to build the dictionary. The value for n depends on the characteristics of the data. It is usually a small value of a few thousand rows. The first n rows are not compressed to avoid processing the rows twice. Typically, the percentage of uncompressed rows is very small.

If the first n rows of the tablespace are not representative of most rows in the tablespace the dictionary can be less than optimal, resulting in less of a savings due to compression than required. This can be compensated for by taking a sample of the rows that are representative of the data with respect to compression, load a table with the sample which results in building the dictionary, delete the sample rows, and load all of the rows for the table or multiple tables. You can avoid deleting the rows in the table used to build the dictionary by deleting the records in the file used in the sample before loading the table or multiple tables.

An alternative is to reorganize the data and have the REORG utility build a new dictionary. We will see shortly that REORG uses a sampling algorithm to build the dictionary. You must decide whether the sampling algorithm results in a good dictionary for your data. An example of a case where you may want to sample the data yourself is for a telephone directory where common names like Johnson, Jones, and Smith appear toward the end of the table, assuming that the table is loaded in sequence by last name. Consider randomizing the sequence for the dictionary build if this can result in a problem. For example, sort by telephone number, in this example, assuming little or no relationship between telephone number and name. If there are multiple tables in a tablespace and the first n rows of the first table are not representative of all the tables in the tablespace, similar problems are likely to occur.

Another word of caution is that rows inserted by a host program into a tablespace that has never been loaded or reorganized are not compressed until a reorganization.

The KEEPDICTIONARY parameter of LOAD replace and resume avoids the costs of rebuilding the dictionary and replacing a dictionary built and refined by REORG.

REORG build of the dictionary: REORG like LOAD builds the dictionary based on the first *n* rows. REORG uses a sampling algorithm to refine the tree as it unloads the data at intervals:

◆   ½ of   1 thru 1,000 rows
◆   1/4 of 1,001 thru 2,000 rows
◆   1/8 of 2,001 thru 3,000 rows
◆   Etc. up to 1/1,000

You can expect 2 to 10 percent additional savings based on this refinement of the dictionary assuming that the first *n* rows are representative of the entire tablespace with one or multiple tables in the tablespace. REORG reclaims any space not used by the dictionary. A patented "pruning" process is used to reduce the dictionary size. This reduces the costs of traversing the dictionary tree for compression and decompression of the rows processed for SQL statements. Of course, the additional savings and the dictionary size depends on the characteristics of the data.

REORG builds the dictionary during the UNLOAD phase. This applies to UNLOAD CONTINUE (default) and UNLOAD PAUSE. UNLOAD ONLY unloads data in decompressed form and does not build a dictionary.

The KEEPDICTIONARY parameter of REORG as with LOAD reduces the costs of executing the utilities. Perhaps even more important is that KEEPDICTIONARY with REORG avoids recompressing the data. The rows are decompressed as they are unloaded with and without the KEEPDICTIONARY parameter. This is necessary to extract the indexed values, sort them, and rebuild the indexes. The unloaded data contains decompressed indexed values and compressed rows which are reloaded to the tablespace. The default for both utilities is to build the dictionary. (It does not compress the rows LOAD used to build dictionary.)

KEEPDICTIONARY is a good choice in most cases, assuming that the characteristics of the data have not changed with respect to compression between reorganizations. The CPU and elapsed time are reduced significantly based on test results at the end of this section. Do try REORG with and without KEEPDICTIONARY with your data or use DB2 Estimator to get an idea of the differences in costs.

Rule of thumb for when to rebuild the dictionary: Assume that
RUNSTATS has populated SYSTABLEPART_HIST (V7) on a weekly
basis for five weeks resulting in a PAGESAVE values of 73 percent for
week 1, 71 percent for week 2, 69 percent for week 3, 67 percent for week
4, and 64 percent for week 5. If SYSTABLEPART_HIST.PAGESAVE
decreases by > 10 percent, consider rebuilding dictionary. This can be
estimated with:

```
SELECT  TSNAME, MAX(PAGESAVE), MIN(PAGESAVE)
FROM    SYSIBM.SYSTABLEPART_HIST
WHERE   (MAX(PAGESAVE-MIN(PAGESAVE))*100/MAX(PAGESAVE)>10
--                  (73-64)             *100/73            =12
```

SYSTABLEPART_HIST.PAGESAVE decreased by 12 percent in the
example which suggests a reorganization without KEEPDICTIONARY so
that a new dictionary is built.

REORG INDEX does not use compression since the indexes are not
compressed and the utility rebuilds the indexes based on a scan of the leaf
pages. REORG INDEX is a good choice over routine reorganizations of the
tablespace and indexes with an occasional REORG TABLESPACE with
mostly transaction processing as discussed in Chapter RR.

Use of the Dictionary During Execution of SQL

The dictionary is read into database services address space working storage
via a virtual pool when compressed data is first accessed. Data manager
(DM) validates the dictionary after it is placed in working storage. The
dictionary remains in storage while compressed data is being processed (64
KB per open compressed data set). DM interfaces with hardware and
software compression. RDS always receives decompressed data.

Processing an update on a compressed row starts with locating the row to
be updated. If the row is compressed, it is decompressed. Any exit routines
are executed. The columns are changed according to the SET clause. If there
are indexes on the updated columns, they are updated. Any exit routines are
executed again. The changed row is compressed. If the compressed row is
shorter than the row before compression, the compressed row is written to
the tablespace. Otherwise, the decompressed row is written.

Ziv-Lempel-Welch Compression Algorithm

The Ziv-Lempel-Welch algorithm used for hardware and software compression was invented by Ziv and Lempel as published in the article Compression of Individual Sequences via Variable-Rate Coding. Welch explained the algorithm in his article "A Technique for High Performance Data Compression", after which it became popularly used in PKZIP on PCs, Stacker on OS/2, UNIX Compress, and VM and OS/390 Terse.

The dictionary is a tree like structure initialized with all possible values. The tree structure will be explained assuming only three possible values, a, b, and c, assigned the values of 1, 2, and 3 as shown in Figure TS.8.

Figure TS.8. Dictionary tree structure

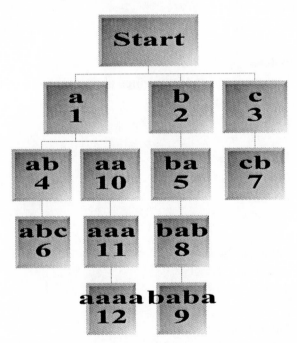

Build of dictionary: We will assume in the example that the dictionary is initially built from an input string of ababcbababaaaaaa. The dictionary is built in steps as detailed below. The underlined characters are those currently being evaluated. The lighter characters represent the node under which a new string is added.

1)   ababcbababaaaaaa

a is present in initialized dictionary
Add next character of b

2)   ababcbababaaaaaa
Assign 4 to ab under node a since a is the prefix of the last character added b.
Add next character of a

3)   ababcbababaaaaaa
Assign 5 to ba under node b since b is the prefix of the last character added of a
Add next character of b

4)   ababcbababaaaaaa
ab is already in dictionary
Add next character of c

5)   ababcbababaaaaaa
Assign 6 to abc under node ab since ab is the prefix of the last character added of c
Add next character of bc

6)   ababcbababaaaaaa
Assign 7 to cb under node c since c is the prefix of the last character added of b
Add next character of a

7)   ababcbababaaaaaa
ba is already in dictionary
Add next character of b

8)   ababcbababaaaaaa
Assign 8 to bab under node ba since ba is the prefix of the last character added of b
Add next character of a

9)   ababcbababaaaaaa
ba is already in dictionary
Add next character of b

10)   ababcbababaaaaaa

bab is already in dictionary
Add next character of a

11)   ababcbab<u>abab</u>aaaaaaa
Assign 9 to baba under node bab since bab is the prefix of the last
character added of a
Add next character of a

12)   ababcbabab<u>aa</u>aaaaa
Assign 10 to aa under node a since a is the prefix of the last
character added of a
Add next character of a

13)   ababcbababa<u>aa</u>aaaa
aa is already in dictionary
Add next character of a

14)   ababcbababa<u>aaa</u>aaa
Assign 11 to aaa under node aa since aa is the prefix of the last
character added of a
Add next character of a

16)   ababcbababaaa<u>aa</u>aa
aa is already in dictionary
Add next character of a

17)   ababcbababaaa<u>aaa</u>a
aaa is already in dictionary
Add next character of a

18)   ababcbababaaa<u>aaaa</u>
Assign 12 to aaaa under node aaa since aaa is the prefix of the last
character added of a

Compression of the data is accomplished by finding the prefix of a string
in the dictionary which is similar to building the dictionary and outputting
the corresponding code. The lighter characters below now represent the
string located in the dictionary. The corresponding code in the dictionary is
output. The final compressed data contains 1 2 4 3 5 8 1 10 11 1. Here is an
example of the steps required to output the compressed data.

1)   ababcbababaaaaaaa
      Add next character of b to produce a prefix of a

2)   ababcbababaaaaaaa
      Locate a prefix and output code of 1
      Add next character of a

3)   ababcbababaaaaaaa
      Locate b prefix and output code of 2
      Add next character of b

4)   ababcbababaaaaaaa
      a prefix has been processed above
      Add next character of c

5)   ababcbababaaaaaaa
      Locate ab prefix and output code of 4
      Add next character of b

6)   ababcbababaaaaaaa
      Locate c prefix and output code of 3
      Add next character of a

7)   ababcbababaaaaaaa
      b prefix has been processed above
      Add next character of b

8)   ababcbababaaaaaaa
      Locate ba prefix and output code of 5
      Add next character of a

9)   ababcbababaaaaaaa
      b prefix has been processed above
      Add next character of b

10)   ababcbababaaaaaaa
      ba prefix has been processed above
      Add next character of a

11)   ababcbababaaaaaaa
      Locate bab prefix and output code of 8
      Add next character of a

12)   ababcbababaaaaaaa
      Locate a prefix and output code of 1
      Add next character of a

13)   ababcbababaaaaaaa
      a prefix has been processed above
      Add next character of a

14)   ababcbababaaaaaaa
      Locate aa prefix and output code of 10
      Add next character of a

16)   ababcbababaaa<u>a</u>aaa
       a prefix has been processed above
       Add next character of a

17)   ababcbababaaa<u>aa</u>aa
       aa prefix has been processed above
       Add next character of a

18)   ababcbababaaa<u>aaaa</u>
       Locate aaa prefix and output code of 11

19)   ababcbababaaaaaaa
       Last character of a, output code of 1

Decompression of the data is simple. It is accomplished by finding the code in the dictionary and outputting the corresponding value to produce the original string: ababcbababaaaaaaa.

CPU and I/O Time Test Results

It is always best to estimate the CPU and I/O times for your data in your environment. An alternative is to use DB2 Estimator. zSeries computers have significant performance improvements for compression and decompression as mentioned at the beginning of this chapter. Figure TS.9 shows the CPU and elapsed time test result to insert 4.4 millions rows from a subselect at end of tablespace with 55 percent compression. The figure gives you the opportunity to get an idea of the CPU and elapsed time for the processing the inserts as well as comparing the processing on zSeries and non-zSeries computers. The elapsed time is reduced with zSeries compression due to fewer pages having to be written. In contrast, the non-zSeries requires more CPU and elapsed time

Figure TS.9. Insert test results on zSeries and non-zSeries

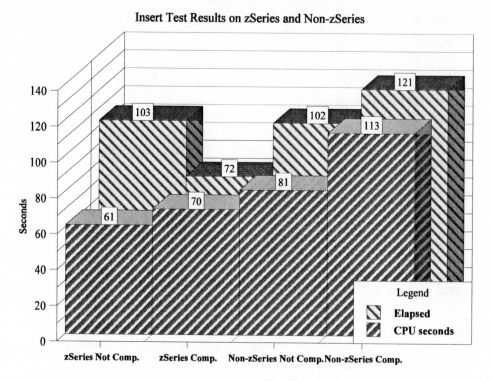

Prior to the availability of zSeries, IBM reported on the average timings of 12 samples of customer data in the manual *DB2 V3 Performance Topics,* GG24-4284. An ES/9000 9121-742 was used for hardware compression and a 3090-300J was used for software compression. Some of the test results of SQL CPU time (class 2) percent increase are summarized in Figure TS.10.

Figure TS.10. SQL CPU Time Percent Increase and Decrease

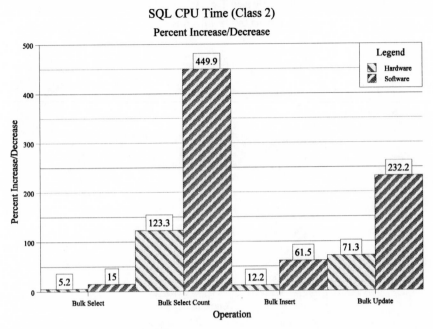

SQL CPU Time (Class 2)

Percent Increase/Decrease

Notice that the hardware compression resulted in significantly less CPU time than software compression. The selection of a large number of rows is the least expensive of the operations. The compression algorithm was optimized for decompression by IBM. The most expensive operation summarized in the figure is a tablespace scan to count the number of rows in the table. Every row must be decompressed before it is processed. The update of a large number of rows is more expensive than INSERTING a large number of rows because the data must be decompressed, updated, and then compressed for updates. This is in comparison to inserts where the rows only need to be compressed. The deletion of rows was not measured because the rows need not be compressed or decompressed in order to be marked as being deleted, assuming that the rows to be deleted are located with an index.

The class 2 elapsed time percent increase and decrease for selecting, counting, inserting, and updating the rows are summarized in Figure TS.11.

Figure TS.11. SQL elapsed time percent increase and decrease

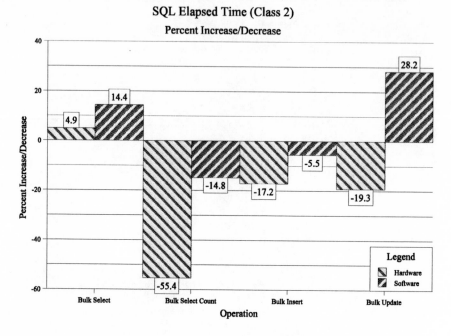

SQL Elapsed Time (Class 2)

Percent Increase/Decrease

Notice that the elapsed time increase in Figure TS.10 to select a large number of rows is a little less than the CPU time in Figure TS.11. The tablespace scan to count the rows decreased significantly because there are fewer pages of compressed data to be scanned than there would be uncompressed data. The insertion and update of a large number of rows using hardware compression also shows a decrease in the elapsed time for similar reasons. The increase in elapsed time for the updates using software compression is surprising.

The effect of compression on frequently executed utilities was tested. The results of the average CPU time increase and decrease from the tests are summarized in Figure TS.12.

Figure TS.12. Utility CPU time percent increase and decrease

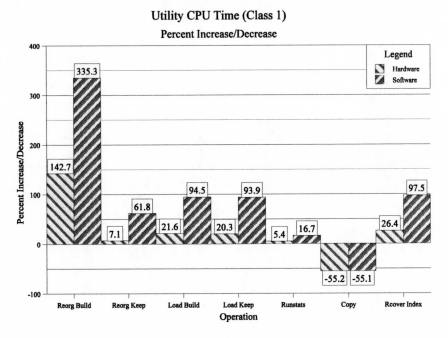

Utility CPU Time (Class 1)

Percent Increase/Decrease

Notice that most of the utilities experienced an increase in CPU time (class 1) using both hardware and software compression. Again we see that the CPU time increased more with software compression, compared to hardware compression. The greatest increase in CPU time was for reorganizations and rebuilding the dictionary. When using KEEPDICTIONARY, the increase in CPU time was dramatically less. This substantiates the recommendation for using KEEPDICTIONARY if there is not a loss in compression efficiency between reorganizations.

There is a good decrease in CPU time when doing an image copy. Compression and decompression are not required when making a copy. The compressed data is copied. Indeed, there is a decrease in the CPU time because less CPU time is necessary to issue fewer I/O on a smaller number of compressed data pages. Both CPU and elapsed time savings will be about the same as the percentage of pages saved. Similarly, recovery (rebuild in V6) savings will be about the same as the copy savings prior to the log apply.

The average utility elapsed time test results are similar to the CPU time test results for the utilities with some notable exceptions as shown in Figure TS.13.

Figure TS.13. Utility elapsed time percent increase and decrease

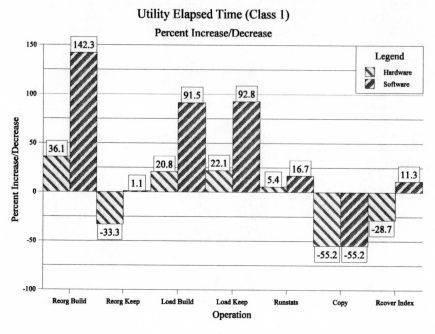

The elapsed time increase was substantially less than the CPU time increase for building the dictionary and compressing the rows with the new dictionary. Again, this is due in large part to the reduced number of I/O required with fewer data pages due to compression. The elapsed time actually decreased with hardware compression and not having to recompress the data because of keeping the dictionary. Again, because fewer data pages are required when using compression, the REBUILD INDEX utility in V6 (the RECOVER INDEX prior to V6) had a reduction in elapsed time when using hardware compression. Overall, compression is a good choice to reduce elapsed time for image copies, recovery, and reorganization with keep dictionary.

TS.9 STRUCTURE OF TABLESPACES

All three types of tablespaces consist of a header page, space map page, compression and decompression dictionary if compression is used, and a number of data pages as shown in Figure TS.14. Space map pages occur throughout the tablespace followed by many data pages. The number of data pages that follow a space map page depend on the type of tablespace and the segment size if segmented tablespaces are used.

Figure TS.14. Header, space map, dictionary and data pages

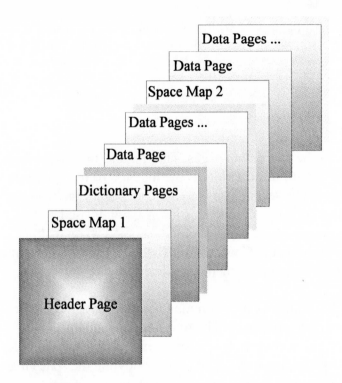

Common Header and Trail Data

All pages begin with a common header consisting of 12 bytes. The first field is a 1 byte flag. The second field is a 6 byte LOGRBA of when the page was last updated and logged. The third field is a 1 byte log ID. The fourth field is a 3 byte page number within the page set. The fifth and last byte contains the page status.

The header page also includes the database ID (DBID), page set ID (PSID), and tablespace ID (OBID). Each of these IDs is 2 bytes in length. Following the IDs is the 6 byte relative byte address (RBA) to which the RECOVER utility has recovered a page set or partition. The HPGRBRBA is the recovery based RBA (RB-RBA) used in logonly recovery. It is updated when the data set is switched to read-only status, the data set is closed, the QUIESCE utility is executed with WRITE YES, the tablespace is stopped, and when DB2 is stopped as discussed in Section TS.6. The level ID follows and is used to detect a down level error as discussed in Chapter CR. The timestamp of when the tablespace was created, the DB2 subsystem name, and additional information are in the header page.

Common trail byte: All pages end with a common trail byte which is used to indicate if the page is broken. The fourth bit must match the fourth bit in the page header.

Space Map Pages

There are three uses of the space map pages. The first use of a space map page is to provide DB2 with information on the location of free space on the data pages that follows. The second use is to indicate pages that have been modified since the last copy by default. This information is used by the COPY utility to determine which pages should be copied when making an incremental copy as discussed in Chapter CR. The third use of a space map page is to identify segments of a segmented tablespace.

A segment header follows the 12 byte common header data on the space map page for a segmented tablespace. The first 2 bytes contains the maximum number of pages covered by the space map page. For example, if the segment size is 4 pages, the number of pages following the space map page is 1,712. If the segment size is 32 pages, the number of pages following the space map page is 4,800. If the segment size is 64 pages, the number of pages following the space map page is 5,504. The second 2 bytes contains the segment size of 4, 8, 16, 32, or 64 pages. The third 2 bytes contain the number of free segments. The fourth 2 bytes contain the lowest free segment number. The fifth field of 4 bytes contains the offset of the last formatted page within the scope of space map pages. The sixth and last field of 4 bytes is reserved for future use.

A 7 byte segment block header follows the segment header of a segmented tablespace. The first 4 bytes contain a pointer to the next segment block on the space map page. The second 2 bytes contain the table object ID (OBID). The third field is a 1 byte flag.

The space map pages of a nonsegmented tablespace contains the header data and the number of pages covered by the space map page in a 4 byte field. A space map page covers 10,760 4 KB pages or 87,216 32 KB pages. The next 4 bytes are the last used entry. The last 6 bytes are reserved for future use.

The space map page segment blocks of a segmented tablespace contain a pointer to a page within the pages of a segment that it describes as indicated in Figure TS.15. Following the pointer is information on the availability of free space within a segment. Four bits are used to describe each page. The meaning of the bit values are:

> 0 - Page is empty and unformatted
>
> 1 - Page is emptied with mass delete
>
> 2 - Page is empty and formatted
>
> 3 - Page has space for longest row
>
> 4-10 Values indicate the difference between the minimum and maximum row size in 12.5 percent increments for placing variable length rows
>
> 11-14 Values reserved for future use
>
> 15 - Page has less than the minimum row space available or is full

Figure TS.15. Segmented space map page and tablespace

Space Map Page

Segment Header	Segment Block 1	Segment Block 2
Segment Block 3	Segment Block 4	Segment Block 5
Segment Block 6	Segment Block 7	Segment Block 8
Segment Block 9	Segment Block 10	. . .

Bit map indicates pages that have been updated since the last image copy (1 bit per page)   Trailer

Tablespace

Seg 1 Table S	Seg 2 Table S	Seg 3 Table S	Seg 4 Table P	Seg 5 Table P	Seg 6 Table P	Seg 7 Table S	Seg 8 Table SPJ	Seg 9 Table SPJ	Seg 10 Table SPJ

DB2 tests the 4 bits to determine if there is space available on a page to insert a row or update a row and make it longer. This minimizes I/O to the data pages to locate free space.

Only 2 bits are used for nonsegmented tablespaces to indicate that space is available for the largest, average, smallest row, or that the page is full. This limited information on the availability of free space is a primary reason that segmented tablespaces have advantages over nonsegmented tablespaces.

Bit Map Describing Updated Pages

There is a bit map at the bottom of each space map page for segmented and nonsegmented tablespaces. The bit map has a bit corresponding to each page within the range of pages covered by the space map page. A bit is turned on when a row is inserted, updated, or deleted after the last image copy was made by default. For example, if a row is inserted on page 10, the tenth bit is turned on. The image copy utility turns off the bits that correspond to the pages that it copies. The utility uses the bit map to determine if it should make an image copy and whether the copy should be a full copy or an incremental copy of only the pages that have changed since the last copy as described in Chapter CR.

The TRACKMOD parameter can be used to control maintenance of the space map page (V6). The default for this parameter is yes. It results in the processing described in the previous paragraph. Maintenance of the space map page can result in contention due to turning on a bit for each row that is inserted, updated, or deleted. The contention is more likely in a sysplex data sharing environment. If you encounter a problem or anticipate a problem due to heavy insert, update, and delete activity, use TRACKMOD NO.

The trade-off of TRACKMOD NO is that incremental copies execute more slowly because the RBA is used to determine which pages should be copied. It is necessary to compare the currently active RBA for a data set with the RBA on the page to determine if the page should be copied. This is in contrast to using the bit map on the space map pages to identify the pages that must be copied when executing the incremental copy utility as discussed in Chapter CR.

You can determine if modification of pages are being tracked from the column TRACKMOD in SYSTABLESPACE. Blank in the column indicates that changed pages are tracked in the bit map on the space map page. *N* indicates that the default has been changed. Changed pages are not tracked in the space map page.

Page Layout

All data pages in all three types of tablespaces have the same layout. The first 12 bytes on each data page contains the common page header described at the beginning of this section. Following the common page header are 2 bytes indicating the total free space on the page, 2 bytes containing the offset to contiguous free space, 2 bytes containing the offset to 1st chained hole, 1 byte containing the number of ID map entries, and the last byte is reserved for future use.

Although the terms row and record are often used interchangeably, there is a difference in DB2. A row in a table consists of all of the columns in the row. A record is the row plus the row prefix (RP) of 6 bytes as indicated in Figure TS.16. The RP begins with a 1 byte row type. It has a value of X'00' for a normal row, X'04' for a compressed row, and X'20' for an overflow row. Next comes a record length of 2 bytes, a 2 byte OBID of the table, and finally a 1 byte map ID for the directory entry at the bottom of the page.

Figure TS.16. Page layout

Page Header		RP 1	Row 1 data
RP 2	Row 2 data		
RP 3	Row 3 data	RP 4	Row 4 data
RP 5	Point to overflow row		Free space
RP 6	Row 6 data		
RP 7	Row 7 data	RP 8	Row 8 data
RP n	Row n data		

Contiguous   free   space

5 (n) Percent   free   left by

LOAD   and   REORG

| Page Directory <=255 entries | Free | Check |

Record = RP (Row Prefix) + Row

The page directory contains up to 255 map IDs, each of which is 2 bytes in length. This maximum number of directory entries corresponds to the maximum number of rows on a page discussed with respect to the MAXROWS parameter in Section TS.5.

The last 2 bytes on the page contain the ID of the first free ID map entry (1 byte) and a common check byte (1 byte).

TS.10 SUMMARY

Segmented tablespaces have significant advantages over simple tablespaces for one or multiple tables per tablespace, managing related tables, and management of free space to maintain clustering and variable length rows.

Do be cautious of mixing tables with different update activity in a single simple or segmented tablespace. A SEGSIZE of 32 is a good choice for all but very small tables.

Do choose a percent free to match the update activity and adjust it to match your reorganization requirements. Free space should be a multiple of the record length. Otherwise, there can be unusable space on every page. If there is random insert, update, and delete activity, FREEPAGE of 31 is a good choice for segmented tablespaces, assuming a SEGSIZE of 32, and 15 is a good choice for nonsegmented tablespaces.

LOCKSIZE of PAGE reduces locking costs and avoids unexpected lock escalations that can occur with LOCKSIZE of ANY. MAXROWS can be used to control the number of rows on a page. Do use CLOSE of NO for frequently processed tablespaces.

Do consider partitioning large tablespaces for improved availability and manageability of the parts. Partitioning provides for spreading I/O across multiple DASD devices, channels and control units. It also provides for DB2 parallelism and limited partition scans. Do specify a larger number of partitions than will ever be used, perhaps the maximum number of partitions allowed, because it is not possible to alter the number of partitions. It is necessary to drop and recreate the tablespace and all related objects. However, the limit key of each partition can be altered which offers a good deal of flexibility if a sufficient number of partitions have been specified.

DSN1COMP provides good information on whether compression will result in significant savings in DASD space and the number of data pages that need to be processed. These savings may well justify the increased CPU time in many cases. The increase in CPU time is frequently not significant for online transactions that process only a few rows. Hardware compression costs substantially less than software compression.

RUNSTATS statistics on compressed data can be used to monitor compression savings, determine when the dictionary should be rebuilt, and collect statistics for use by the optimizer in access path selection. LOAD and REORG can build and refine the dictionary. KEEPDICTIONARY is a good choice once the dictionary is refined and characteristics of the data with respect to compression do not change.

EXERCISES

1. a) If there is insufficient contiguous space on a volume for the PRIQTY allocation, will a resource unavailable message be issued?

b) Why should the SECQTY be specified in multiples of cylinders rather than tracks if the tablespace is expected to occupy multiple cylinders?

c) Why is it important to estimate the PRIQTY carefully and avoid the use of SECQTY allocations?

2. a) How does DB2 use free space?

b) What are the consequences of having insufficient free space when variable length rows are used?

c) What are the consequence of having insufficient free space with respect to maintaining the rows in sequence.

d) What are some considerations that apply to both variable length rows and sequencing of the data?

3. a) Several formula to estimate the amount of free space for tablespaces were presented. What key point should be kept in mind when estimating the free space for a table?

b) What are some characteristics of tables that should have zero free space?

4. a) When will the blank pages left as a result of the FREEPAGE parameter be used?

b) Why is FREEPAGE 31 a good choice when using SEGSIZE of 32?

c) Why is FREEPAGE 15 a good choice when using nonsegmented tablespaces?

5. a) What are the characteristics of tablespaces that can be created with a lock size of table or tablespace?

b) What are the benefits of using lock size of table or tablespace?

6. a) What conditions suggest the need for row locking?

b) What are the costs of row locking?

c) What are some of the conditions that require a page lock even though lock size of row is specified?

d) What are some alternatives to row locking?

7. What are the advantages of a segmented tablespace over a simple tablespace regarding the space map page?

8. a) What are the advantages of multiple tables per segmented tablespace?

b) What are the disadvantage of multiple tables per segmented tablespace?

c) How does the frequency of updates affect the decision to group tables in a tablespace?

9. What are the advantages of a simple tablespace over segmented tablespace?

10. What are the advantages of a partitioned tablespace?

11. a) What are some advantages of using a control table to determine the range of values in a partition?

b) What are some disadvantages of using a control table to determine the range of values in a partition?

ANSWERS

1. a) No. If there is insufficient contiguous space available to satisfy the PRIQTY on a volume, space will be taken on up to and including 5 extents. If more than 5 extents are required, a resource unavailable message will be issued.

b) If the PRIQTY or SECQTY is less than or equal to one cylinder, then track allocation is used, which detracts from performance.

c) One should avoid data going into secondary allocations because excessive seek time can be experienced. The secondary allocation is usually far away from the primary allocation and arm movement is one of the most time consuming aspects of locating data on DASD.

2. a) DB2 uses free space to maintain variable length rows and to maintain the rows in clustering sequence.

b) If there is insufficient free space, variable length rows have to be moved to a near or far page, which requires additional CPU and I/O. A pointer to the new location of the row is left in the original row space on the page. Two I/O to the data pages are required to locate the moved row for future processing.

c) If there is insufficient free space, it will not be possible to insert a row on a page in clustering sequence. Additional CPU and I/O are required to locate space for the row. Performance of transactions and batch programs that rely on the rows being in sequence will degrade as more and more rows are placed out of sequence.

d) The page is dynamically reorganized to gather free space, which adds to the number of instructions that must be executed, and the page is locked during the process. The data will need to be reorganized more frequently if there is insufficient free space to maintain clustering and variable length rows.

3. a) The free space should be a multiple of the row length. For example, the default of 5 percent free will not allow for a row to be inserted if the row is more than 200 bytes in length. The 200 bytes of free space on the data pages will never be used.

b) Read-only tables, those with very low insert/delete activity, and tables where rows are always inserted/deleted at the end of the table do not benefit from free space being available. There is no need to waste space on each page and cause more pages to be used and processed than necessary.

4. a) If a variable length row cannot be increased in length on a page or a row cannot be inserted on the target page to maintain clustering sequence because of insufficient space on a page, space on the blank page will be used.

b) If space is not available on the desired page, the search algorithm for free space in a segmented tablespace begins with trying to place the row within the target segment. FREEPAGE of 31 leaves a blank page within each segment when using SEGSIZE of 32.

c) The search algorithm for free space in a nonsegmented tablespace begins with looking for space within plus or minus 16 pages as indicated on the space map page. FREEPAGE of 15 leaves a blank page within the 16 page range.

5. a) Read-only tables are very good candidates for lock size of table or tablespace. Consideration can be given to using lock size of table or tablespace for tables with very low insert/delete activity (reference tables that rarely change for example). Private tables created by an ad hoc user and used only by that user benefits from a lock size of table or tablespace.

b) There is no need to lock at the row or page level or execute the instructions for lock avoidance (discussed in Chapter CC) for read-only tables and those that are rarely updated.

6. a) Tablespaces that experience high update activity in frequently executed online transactions. Programs that process only a few rows. Very small tables that are frequently updated. Short rows with many rows on a page (compression frequently results in short rows). Rows usually inserted at the end of a table or updates concentrated in any specific areas of the table.

b) If a program typically processes multiple rows on a page, a lock is required for each of the rows processed (rather than a single lock on the page).

c) If a variable length row is increased in length or space on a page is dynamically reorganized to gather free space, a page lock is necessary.

d) Lock avoidance and the UR isolation level reduces costs for read-only processing without row locking. UR must be used cautiously as discussed in Chapter CC.

7. The space map page of a segmented tablespace offers a number of advantages over a simple tablespace. The space map page is used to locate free space more efficiently and to implement the mass delete algorithm. It is used to locate only the pages with active rows for the table being processed

during a tablespace scan and the COPY utility uses the space map page to identify only the pages with active rows. The optimizer has a better estimate of the number of pages that contain rows for a table.

8. a) One advantage of multiple tables in a tablespace is that fewer utilities need to be developed and scheduled in production because most utilities operate at the tablespace level. Recoverability of related tables in a single tablespace is improved. Fewer tablespaces need to be open. Deferred write applies to all tables in the tablespace. These advantages apply to a number of very small reference tables in a single tablespace. In addition, a header and space map page for one or a few pages need not be maintained and a track is not required for each table.

b) The disadvantage of multiple tables in a tablespace is that utilities cannot be scheduled for individual tables as required and all tables are unavailable while a utility is executing in most cases. Pending states apply at the tablespace level. Different tables may need different tablespace parameter values (PCTFREE, SEGSIZE, LOCKSIZE, LOCKMAX, etc.), but only one is definable. If compression is used, the compression dictionary may not be best for all tables in the tablespace.

c) If tables with a different update activity are grouped in a tablespace, the above disadvantages are more intense. It is best not to mix frequently and infrequently updated tables in a tablespace.

Most companies place one table in one tablespace except for small reference tables. Multiple small reference tables are typically placed in one tablespace.

9. There are few advantages of a simple tablespace over a segmented tablespace. The fact that there are more space map pages for segmented tablespaces versus simple tablespaces is not considered a significant increase in space in most cases. (A segmented tablespace with a SEGSIZE of 64 has a space map page every 5,504 pages or 4,800 for a SEGSIZE of 32 versus a simple tablespace with a space map page every 10,760 pages.) The advantage of being able to interleave related rows on a page is overshadowed by the fact there are no automatic facilities to maintain the interleaving of rows on a page.

10. The advantage of a partitioned tablespace is that it provides for dividing a large table into multiple parts for improved availability and ease of management. Utilities can operate on a single partition while other

partitions are available for processing by SQL and other utilities in most cases. Elapsed time for reading a large number of rows can be reduced through the use of parallelism on multiple partitions. Multiple batch jobs can operate on multiple partitions in parallel through application design. Parts of the tablespaces can be placed on multiple DASD devices and channels to reduce I/O contention. Large tables usually have parts that are frequently processed and parts that are rarely processed. The rarely processed parts can be archived using SMS and will be automatically recalled when an SQL statement requires data in the partition. The partitions that are rarely updated can be given 0 percent free to avoid wasting space. In addition, the parts that are rarely accessed can be placed on slower less expensive devices.

11. a) The advantage of using a control table to determine the range of values in a partition is flexibility of adjusting the upper range values of rows to be placed in a partition. This is particularly important for historical data where it is necessary to remove partitions containing data that is no longer needed and add partitions for a new time period.

b) The disadvantage of using a control table is that it must be maintained through application design and development. It must be accessed each time that rows are accessed in the partitioned tablespace. However, if there is not a well defined partitioning index, other alternatives can result in significant performance problems.

FIGURES

Creating Tables and Views

CT.1 INTRODUCTION

The table is DB2's basic unit for data manipulation. A table is sometimes referred to as a base table to distinguish it from a view, which is a virtual table derived from one or more base tables. In a base table, each column holds values for an entity attribute, identified in the column heading. Each row contains a value for each column, with a few exceptions that will be explained later, with all the values in a given column being of the same data type.

CT.2 CREATING TABLES

The table name can be a three part name consisting of LOCATION.AUTHID.NAME. The LOCATION can be used to direct the execution of SQL statements to another relational DBMS. The default is the location where the SQL DML (data manipulation language) or DDL (data definition language) statements are executed. AUTHID (authorization identification) is the current SQLID (SQL identifier) of the person who creates the table. NAME is the name specified when the table is created. Typically, the LOCATION and AUTHID are not specified when creating tables and views and are not specified when using SQL DML statements. Control of the AUTHID for SQL DML is discussed in Chapter PE.

Creation of global temporary and declare temporary tables are discussed in Chapter SP.

Figure CT.1 shows a typical statement for creating a table--in this case for storing information about suppliers. The developer lists within parentheses after the table name, each column name for the table, followed by the data type and length of the column, and whether null values are allowed in the column. (A null indicates that an actual value is either unknown or inapplicable. Nulls hold practical and performance implications to be discussed in a moment.) The maximum length of a column name is 18 and the maximum number of columns in a table or view is 750 except for a dependent table which has a maximum of 749.

Figure CT.1. CREATE TABLE statement

```
CREATE TABLE S
  (SN       CHAR(6)   NOT NULL,
   SNAME   CHAR(20) NOT NULL WITH DEFAULT,
   STATUS SMALLINT WITH DEFAULT NULL
      CONSTRAINT STATUS_C
         CHECK (STATUS BETWEEN 10 AND 200),
   CITY    CHAR(15) WITH DEFAULT 'London'
      CONSTRAINT CITY_C
         CHECK (CITY IN ('Rome', 'Oslo', 'London'),
   AUTHID_OF_INSERTER CHAR(8) WITH DEFAULT USER,
   DATE_RECORDED DATE NOT NULL WITH DEFAULT,
   CONSTRAINT SN_PK PRIMARY KEY (SN))
CCSID EBCDIC
RESTRICT ON DROP
AUDIT NONE
DATA CAPTURE NONE
VALIDPROC CHECKS
   IN DASPJDB.STSP;
```

Column order holds performance implications. When an update changes data, DB2 records the change in a log, which is used to recreate the change if the tablespace must be recovered after a failure. Because DB2 logs only that portion of a row from the first to the last changed byte, placing frequently updated columns next to each other minimizes logging, saving on both processing and storage as discussed in Chapter TS.

Data Types

DB2 offers all the IBM standard data types and some special data types summarized in Figure CT.2. Data type synonyms are available for compatibility with the ANSI (American National Standards Institute) and ISO (International Standards Organization) standards. The synonyms are indicated with an "*" in the figure.

Figure CT.2. Basic data types and lengths

Data Types	N B	COBOL Declaration	PL/1 Declaration	C Declaration
SMALLINT	2	01 V PIC S9(4) COMP-4.	DCL V BIN FIXED(15);	short int id;
INTEGER	4	01 V PIC S9(9) COMP-4.	DCL V BIN FIXED(31);	long int id;
DECIMAL or NUMERIC*	<=16 or <=32	01 V PIC S9(n)V9(m) COMP-3.	DCL V DEC FIXED(S,P);	decimal (x,y)
REAL or FLOAT(n) n <= 21	4	01 V COMP-1.	DCL V BIN FLOAT(21);	float id;
DOUBLE PRECISION, DOUBLE, or FLOAT(n) 22<=n<=53	8	01 V COMP-2.	DCL V BIN FLOAT(53);	double id;
CHAR	255	01 V PIC X(n)	DCL V CHAR(n);	char id [m];
VARCHAR or CHAR VARYING* or CHARACTER VARYING*	4046	01 V. 49 VL PIC S9(4) COMP. 49 VN PIC X(n).	DCL V CHAR(n) VAR;	struct char var id {len & data};
LONG VARCHAR	32714			
GRAPHIC	254	01 V PIC G(n)	DCL V GRAPHIC(n);	wchar_t var id;
VARGRAPHIC	4046	01 V. 49 VL PIC S9(4) COMP. 49 VN PIC G(n) DIS-1.	DCL V GRAPHIC(n) VAR;	struct var id {len & data};
LONG VARGRAPHIC	32714			
DATE	4	01 V PIC X(10)	DCL V CHAR(10)	char id [>=11];
TIME	3	01 V PIC X(8)	DCL V CHAR(8)	char id [>=9];
TIMESTAMP	10	01 V PIC X(26)	DCL V CHAR(26)	char id [>=27];

*SQL92 standard.

"N B" is the number of bytes required by the data type. Do add one byte
  if nulls are allowed.

Numeric Data Types

DB2's data types offer developers a number of choices, some of which affect performance. An INTEGER, for example, requires 4 bytes, which can represent a value of up to 2,147,483,648. If the developer knows that the item's value will never exceed 32,767, however, he or she may use SMALLINT, which can represent values up to that amount but needs only 2 bytes. The shorter representation can save storage and speed processing and I/O operations.

A packed decimal column with a maximum value of 99999.99 can be defined with a data type of DECIMAL(7,2). Seven is the precision of the number and 2 is the scale. This means that 7 is the total number of digits in the number and 2 of the digits are to the right of the decimal point. Four bytes are required to store the value. If the column is defined as DECIMAL(6,2), four bytes are still required to store the value, but the maximum value is 9999.99 because 4 bits are required to represent the sign. This suggests that odd precision should be used to avoid wasting space for each column value and allow for the largest number of digits per byte of storage.

DB2 allows for very large packed decimal values with a maximum value of $10^{31} - 1$ provided that DEC31 is specified in DSNZPARM using DECARTH=DEC31, on the installation panel DSNTIP4 (DEC15 is the default), or setting CURRENT PRECISION special register to DEC31. DEC31 allows for a value of 10 nonillion. A nonillion comes in after a million, billion, trillion, quadrillion, quintillion, sextillion, septillion, and octillion to give you an idea of the magnitude of the number. Section SL.4 discusses alternatives for managing these large values in a host program.

Character Data Types

Most character data types including CHAR, VARCHAR, and LONG VARCHAR use a single byte character set (SBCS). That is, each character requires one byte to represent a character. Graphic data types use a double byte character set (DBCS). This data type uses two bytes to represent non-Asian words in ideograms which is used widely in business with Asia and is referred to as Katakana. Mixed data strings allow for a mixture of SBCS and DBCS with shift codes used to delimit DBCS characters. Data subtypes of SBCS, MIXED, and FOR BIT DATA can be specified for string data types. FOR BIT DATA indicates that the bits need not be associated with a coded character set identifier (CCSID).

VARCHAR with Care

VARCHAR or LONG VARCHAR is required if the character string is more than 255 bytes because the maximum length of the CHAR data type is 255 bytes as can be seen in Figure CT.2. The VARCHAR data type also offers DASD space savings, but there are trade-offs to be considered. The data type has space allocated according to the actual length of each data item, not including trailing blanks, up to the maximum specified in the CREATE TABLE statement. The CHAR data type, on the other hand, allocates the same amount of space--that specified in the statement--regardless of each item's length. If the value is, in fact, shorter than the allocated amount, the remaining bytes are filled with blanks.

It may seem at first that VARCHAR would always use space more efficiently than CHAR. This is not always true, however, because each VARCHAR entry must carry a 2-byte prefix indicating its length. If the values' lengths do not vary significantly, this 2-byte cost on each item can outweigh the gains of space savings on the shorter items. In addition, if the column allows for null, there is a 1-byte null indicator prefix and if there is no value there is a 1-byte place holder. Therefore, a VARCHAR column that allows for null and has no value requires 4 bytes.

Analysis of VARCHAR and CHAR space usage: The following SELECT statement is useful in determining the space used and saved by using a CHAR column compared to a VARCHAR column. You will want to change the name of a table (SYSIBM.SYSCOLUMNS in the example) with a VARCHAR column to the name of the table of interest to you. Also, change NAME to the name of the column defined as VARCHAR and change 18 to the value used to define the VARCHAR column.

```
SELECT 18 * COUNT(*) AS CHAR18,
   SUM(2 + LENGTH(NAME)) AS VARCHAR18,
   18 * COUNT(*) - SUM(2 + LENGTH(NAME))
   AS BYTES_SAVED,
   18 AS AVG_CHAR18,
   AVG(2 + LENGTH(NAME)) AS AVG_VARCHAR18,
   18 - AVG(2 + LENGTH(NAME)) AS COL_B
```

```
          FROM SYSIBM.SYSCOLUMNS;
```

Here is the results of the SELECT statement:

CHAR18	VARCHAR18	BYTES_SAVED	AVG_CHAR18	AVG_VARCHAR18	COL_B
147852	84061	63791	18	10	8

In this case there is a savings of 63,791 bytes if the column is defined as VARCHAR. This suggests that VARCHAR is a good choice. A VARCHAR column is often useful with descriptive text where the user sometimes enters a short description and other times enters a long description.

However, there are some additional factors that should be considered before a final decision is made. The space savings should result in one or more additional rows fitting possibly fitting on a page. Otherwise, there is no real savings in DASD space and I/O. This is because storage and I/O is at the page level. The use of VARCHAR also costs storage space when a VARCHAR column is indexed. The storage space used for each index value does not vary. Instead DB2 inserts blanks to pad each value to its maximum length. In any case, long columns make poor candidates for indexes because they can cause additional levels in the index structure which requires additional I/O to traverse the index structure. The use of a VARCHAR column causes a row to be variable in length as does DB2 data compression.

Index only processing of an index, on a column declared as VARCHAR, is not possible by default. It is necessary to access the data pages to retrieve the length of significant bytes in the column to return to the host program. The length is not stored in the index pages. Index only processing can be enabled by changing RETVLCFK to YES in DSNZPARM DSN6SPRM macro after applying V5 APAR PQ10465. It is necessary to rebind plans and packages that reference VARCHAR columns to take advantage of index only processing. If index only processing is chosen by the optimizer as part of the access path, values returned to host programs are fully padded with blanks and the maximum length of the VARCHAR column is returned in the 2 byte length field. This can require changes to programs that expect only leading significant bytes and the length of the significant bytes in the 2 byte length field. If index only processing is not chosen by the optimizer as part of the access path with the current bind or a future bind, only significant bytes (non-trailing blanks) are returned to the host program. The 2 byte length field contains the length of the significant bytes.

Caution: Programs must be designed to handle an access path with or without index only processing of VARCHAR indexes if index only processing is enabled for the DB2 subsystem.

Compression has advantages over the use of VARCHAR columns, particularly if there are several potential VARCHAR columns in a row. There are a couple of advantages of VARCHAR over compression. Trailing blanks are not passed to relational data system (RDS) and to the host program. Instead, a row is decompressed at the data manager (DM) level and trailing blanks are passed to RDS and the host program. Only if a VARCHAR column is made longer is the row moved to a near or far page if there is not sufficient space on the page. In contrast, an update of any column in a compressed row has a fifty percent chance of causing the rows to be increased in length and moved to a near or far page if there is not sufficient space on the page.

The ALTER TABLE statement can be used to change the maximum length of a VARCHAR column (V5 APAR PQ16674), for example:

```
ALTER TABLE S
ALTER COLUMN SNAME SET DATA TYPE VARCHAR(200);
```

It is not always clear what the new length should be. The following SELECT statement is useful in making this determination. It reports on the column lengths and number of times each length occurs for a given table (SYSIBM.SYSCOLUMNS in the example).

```
SELECT COL_LENGTH, COUNT(*)
FROM (SELECT LENGTH(NAME) AS COL_LENGTH
        FROM SYSIBM.SYSCOLUMNS) AS L
GROUP BY COL_LENGTH
ORDER BY COL_LENGTH;
```

The results of execution of the statement are:

COL_LENGTH	N_OCCUR
2	52
3	111
4	469

COL_LENGTH	N_OCCUR
5	874
6	1,182
7	1,191
8	1,128
9	857
10	613
11	457

The column NAME is defined as VARCHAR(18). Based on the data currently in the column, the column can be declared as VARCHAR(11) which is the maximum length of values in the column. Your data is likely to have a much wider difference in the current definition and the desired definition of the column. Of course, you will want to allow space for values that are not currently in the column.

Altering the length of a VARCHAR column invalidates plans, packages, and dynamic cached statements that reference the column.

It is not necessary to rebuild an index on an altered VARCHAR column immediately. The index is maintained with old and new lengths for up to and including 16 alters. However, REBUILD INDEX, REORG INDEX, or REORG TABLESPACE should be used to rebuild the index as soon as possible to maximize performance.

There are restrictions on VARCHAR columns that can be altered. The column cannot be referenced in a referential integrity structure, view, temporary table, stored procedures, EDITPROC, VALIDPROC, and FIELDPROC.

There are restrictions on the operations that can be performed on a column declared as VARCHAR with a length greater than 255 bytes since it is considered a long string like LONG VARCHAR. It is not possible to place an index on the column, it cannot be used with a predicate other than LIKE, a function other than SUBSTR, a subselect, a UNION without ALL, ORDER BY, GROUP BY, or DISTINCT. (These functions are discussed in

Chapter SL.)

Numerals as Numeric Types

Developers sometimes are tempted to declare variables consisting of numeric identifiers--such as employee identifications or part numbers--as character types. These numbers will not be used in calculations so the developer feels safe in treating them as character variables. The perceived advantage is that the approach avoids the data exceptions that occur after data entry mistakes--the keying in of a character rather than a numeral for a numeric type. A validation procedure would catch such an error, but the lack of thorough validation does occur. Consequently, data exceptions may occur, requiring costly program reruns. If a character type had been declared originally, however, the system would accept the mistake and keep running.

This shortcut can be expensive, however. Putting aside the question of tolerating misinformation, using a character type for numeric data holds tangible disadvantages. One is that it uses unnecessary storage space. SMALLINT, which can handle numbers up to 32,767, and requires only 2 bytes. The five characters needed to represent values that high require 1 byte each--a 3-byte cost per data value. One company saved 3500 cylinders of 3390 DASD by converting a numeric identifier from CHAR(5) to SMALLINT. If the column is indexed, the space cost of this approach more than doubles. In addition, when there are fewer pages in a table and fewer I/O are required to perform a tablespace scan.

Another reason to use the appropriate data type is that occasional users find it confusing to have to enclose some numerals in quotation marks--those that have been declared as characters--in their database requests. Finally, the domain of a column with all numeric data is misrepresented when the column is declared as a character data type. The number of possible values in a column declared as a numeric data type differs from that for a character data type. The optimizer has more accurate information on the number of possible values in a column when the declared data type reflects the data to be placed in the column as discussed in Chapter OP. Clearly all of these potential problems argue strongly in favor of declaring numeric identifiers as numeric types.

Date and Time

Three data types allow for the manipulation of dates and times and for automatic recording of the time that rows are inserted. This capability is useful for keeping track of when orders are entered, for example. The data types are DATE, TIME, and TIMESTAMP. Figure CT.3 summarizes the format of the available DATE and TIME data types.

Figure CT.3. Date and time data types

Format*	Date	Date Example	Time	Time Ex.
ISO (International Standards Organization)	YYYY-MM-DD	1987-05-23	HH.MM.SS	20.10.30
USA (IBM USA Standard)	MM/DD/YYYY	05/23/1987	HH:MM AM	08:10 PM
EUR (European Standard)	DD.MM.YYYY	23.05.1987	HH.MM.SS	20.10.30
JIS (Japanese Industrial Standard Christian Era)	YYYY-MM-DD	1987-05-23	HH:MM:SS	20:10:30

*An exit can be used to define other formats

TIMESTAMP represents both date and time in the ISO format plus six digits of microseconds. It is useful when a large number of sources are entering data into the same table at the same second and the organization wants to differentiate the entries by time. It is almost a million times less likely that two sources will enter data at the same microsecond than at the same second, though it can happen, particularly in a multiprocessor system or across international time zones.

The time and date columns are declared in the CREATE TABLE statement by stating the column name followed by the type name: DATE_RECORDED DATE, for example. As with numeric types, the lengths need not be declared. In fact, DATE requires 4 bytes, TIME 3 bytes, and TIMESTAMP 10 bytes. The internal representation is like a packed decimal representation without the four sign bits. Because the time and date types are very specialized, they do not correspond directly to types provided by host-languages. Host-language variables that receive values from time and date columns must be declared as character types: 10 bytes long for DATE corresponding to the 10 characters in the standard date formats, 8 bytes for TIME, and 26 bytes for TIMESTAMP. When the DATE and TIME variables are used in calculations, a process discussed in Chapter SL, the host-language variable that receives the results must be declared as a decimal type: DECIMAL(8,0) for DATE, DECIMAL(6,0) for TIME, and DECIMAL(14,n) for TIMESTAMP, with n = 0 through 6, depending on the format required.

Specifying the Date and Time Format: The ISO format is the installation default and can be changed in DSNZPARM. (Also, an exit can be used to define other formats.) Do be cautious of setting USA as the default. The unload and reload of a table with a column containing time results in 0 seconds. This can result in duplicate primary keys that have time as part of the key.

Recommendation: The use of the ISO format as the installation default is a good choice. You can specify a different format at precompile time for reporting purposes. For example, specification of USA, EUR, or JIS overrides the installation default. Another alternative is the use of the CHAR scalar function (discussed in Chapter SL) which can be used to specify the format like:

```
SELECT CHAR(ORDER_DATE, USA) FROM ...
```

The CHAR function can be used to override the installation and precompile specifications for specific columns.

Large Object Data Types and Requirements

The term large objects (LOB) is used to refer to the data types of:

♦   Character large object (CLOB)
♦   Binary large object (BLOB)
♦   Double byte character large objects (DBCLOB)

These LOB columns are designed for large character data (a book, for example), photograph, video or audio data, and large double byte character data (a book, for example). The number of bytes in a LOB column value can be 1 to 2,147,483,647 bytes except a DBCLOB is limited to 1,073,741,823 bytes because each symbol requires two bytes. The default for CLOBs and BLOBs is 1,073,741,823 bytes, and for DBCLOBs the default is 524,288 double-byte characters. LOG YES on the tablespace is used by default if the LOB default sizes or smaller are used. If a value larger than the default is specified, LOG NO is required.

A table created with a LOB column must also include a ROWID column. If the CURRENT RULES special register is set to 'STD', DB2 implicitly creates the LOB tablespace, auxiliary table, and an index on the auxiliary table for each LOB column in the base table. The naming convention used by DB2 is described in the *SQL Reference* manual. The utility REPORT TABLESPACESET can be used to identify the LOB tablespaces that DB2 implicitly created. If the special register is set to 'DB2' (default), you need to create these objects using the CREATE TABLESPACE, CREATE AUXILIARY TABLE, and CREATE INDEX statements.

The LOB data is actually stored in an auxiliary table in a LOB tablespace. Each LOB column in a table must be stored in a separate auxiliary LOB tablespace. It is necessary to have one LOB tablespace for each partition if the base table is partitioned.

The ROWID column in the base table is used to locate the LOB in the auxiliary table. The LOB column in the base table is an indicator column defined as VARCHAR(4) that can be used to avoid having to move a LOB column of up to 2,147,483,647 bytes into a host program.

Details on creating and using LOBs can be found in the *Administration Guide, Application Programming and SQL Guide*, and *SQL Reference* manuals.

ROWID Data Type

Direct row access provides for locating a row directly without the I/O and CPU time required to locate a row with an index or tablespace scan (V6). It is useful to locate a row a second time after retrieving the row ID value using an index or tablespace scan. A ROWID column uniquely identifies rows in a table. The following CREATE and ALTER statements are examples of establishing the SPJ_ROWID column as a ROWID data type in the SPJ table.

```
CREATE TABLE SPJ
  (SN   CHAR(6) NOT NULL,
   PN   CHAR(6) NOT NULL,
   JN   CHAR(6) NOT NULL,
   QTY  INTEGER NOT NULL WITH DEFAULT
   SPJ_ROWID ROWID GENERATED ALWAYS NOT NULL);
```

The ALTER TABLE statement can be used to add a column with a data type of ROWID.

```
ALTER TABLE SPJ
ADD SPJ_ROWID ROWID GENERATED ALWAYS NOT NULL;
```

GENERATED clause on CREATE TABLE statement affects how rows can be inserted into a ROWID or identity column discussed later in this section.

GENERATED ALWAYS (default) means that DB2 always generates the value when inserting a row (exceptions will be discussed). This option does not require that an index be created on the column.

GENERATED BY DEFAULT means that you can optionally specify a value when populating the column with the INSERT statement or LOAD utility which is useful for data propagation. This option requires that an index be created on the column (additional columns can be included in the index). If SQLRULES(STD) is used with GENERATED BY DEFAULT, an index is automatically created on the ROWID column. The index name is always 18 characters. The first character is 'I', followed by 10 characters of the column name (if the column name is less than 10 characters, underscore characters are used as padding), and 7 characters of randomly generated characters assigned by DB2. COPY NO is used when the index is created. This means that the index cannot be copied and recovered (it must be rebuilt).

Index only processing can be used to retrieve a row ID value if RETVLCFK is changed to YES in the DSNZPARM DSN6SPRM macro. This allows for index only processing on a variable length column. Be cautious of the implications for the entire DB2 subsystem discussed above in the subsection "VARCHAR with Care".

Inserting and loading rows into a table with a ROWID or identity column is discussed in Chapters PD and LC. The usage of a ROWID column is discussed in the TS, IU, and PD Chapters.

Restrictions on ROWID column: A ROWID column is implicitly defined as NOT NULL. It is advisable to specify NOT NULL in the column definition for clarity. It is not possible to allow for nulls and a default cannot be defined. However, a select of a ROWID column can return null if no rows qualify. Additional restrictions include:

- ROWID column cannot be declared a primary or foreign key. The RID portion of ROWID would differ in a parent and dependent table because the RID identifies the location of a row in a table.
- Only one column in a table can be defined with a ROWID data type.
- Cannot have a ROWID column on a temporary table.
- FIELDPROC and CHECK CONSTRAINT cannot be defined on column.
- EDITPROC cannot be used on a table with a ROWID column.
- Private protocol does not support a ROWID column.
- Column distribution statistics are not collected (all values are unique).

Internal and External ROWID Length: The internal length (space in buffer pool and on DASD, for example) is 19 bytes. The first 2 bytes are a length field and the remaining 17 bytes contain the row ID. The external length is 40 bytes plus a 2 byte length field. A host variable to receive a row ID is declared similar to a VARCHAR declaration like:

```
01   SPJ-ROWID
     49   SPJ-ROWID-LEN PIC 9(4)USAGE COMP.
     49   SPJ-ROWID     PIC X(40).
```

It is also necessary to declare the host variable as a ROWID for processing by precompiler like:

```
EXEC SQL BEGIN DECLARE SECTION END-EXEC.
01   SPJ-ROWID SQL TYPE IS ROWID.
EXEC SQL END DECLARE SECTION END-EXEC.
```

Row ID values are generated by DB2 when a row is inserted into a table. They cannot be changed with an UPDATE statement (-151 SQLCODE). The ROWID column contains a pseudo random number in the first 6 bytes consisting of the low order bytes of the z/OS or OS/390 store clock in reverse order by bit, other identifying information that is proprietary to IBM (may contain object IDs), and RID (changes with a reorganization) in the format of bit data. It can be specified in a WHERE clause and displayed like:

```
X'F0DFD230E3C0D80D81C201AA0A280100000000000203
'
```

Identity Column

Unique, sequential, and recoverable values for each row in a table can be automatically generated by DB2 by defining the column as an identity column as shown in the following example (V6 APAR PQ30652). The use of an identity column has significant performance advantages over the use of a table with the last sequence number as discussed in Chapter PD. IBM compared these two techniques. Their test results show 634 transaction per second using an identity column with CACHE 20 compared to 106 transactions per second using a table with last sequence number. A 2 millisecond delay was experienced for an insert that caused the cache to be refreshed in one case. Details of the tests can be found in the *DB2 UDB Server for OS/390 Version 6 Technical Update* (SG24-6108) manual.

```
CREATE TABLE S_ID
   (SN_ID  INTEGER GENERATED ALWAYS AS IDENTITY
    (START WITH 1, INCREMENT BY 1,
     CACHE 20, NO CYCLE),
   SNAME  CHAR(20) NOT NULL WITH DEFAULT,
   STATUS SMALLINT WITH DEFAULT 99,
   CITY   CHAR(15) NOT NULL WITH DEFAULT,
   CONSTRAINT SN_ID_PK PRIMARY KEY (SN_ID))
      IN DASPJDB.STSP;
```

The data type of an identity column can be INTEGER, SMALLINT, or DECIMAL with a scale of 0. The column can be a distinct type based on one of these data types. Distinct types are discussed later in this section in the subsection Creating and Using Distinct Types. Declaration of an identity column as the primary key is optional. An identity column can be designated on a declare temporary table (not on a create temporary table).

Following is a description of each of the clauses that can be used when defining a column as an identity column.

GENERATED clause has the same meaning as discussed above in the subsection on ROWID columns. Inserting rows into a table with an identity column and ROWID column are discussed in Chapter PD.

AS IDENTITY designates the column as an identity column. The column is implicitly NOT NULL. Only one identity column is allowed for a table.

START WITH provides for generating numbers starting with a number other than 1 which is the default. If you need to override the default, the value specified must be a valid number for the chosen data type. It can be a positive or negative number. If it is a positive number, it is an ascending number. If it is a negative number, it is a descending number.

INCREMENTED BY provides for incrementing the number with a value greater than 1 (1 is the default). The value must be valid for the chosen data type.

CACHE 20 means that 20 (default) preallocated values are kept in memory by DB2. This improves performance as discussed in Chapter PD. A value of between 2 and 2,147,483,648 can be specified.

NO CACHE means preallocated numbers are not kept in memory. This is useful in minimizing gaps in sequence numbers.

Gaps can appear in the generated sequence numbers. If a rollback occurs or if DB2 abends before all numbers in the cache (if used) are assigned, numbers are not reused unless CYCLE is specified. The highest number allocated is used after a recovery to a point-in-time which can result in gaps in the sequence numbers unless the tablespace containing SYSSEQUENCES is recovered to the same point-in-time. Of course, gaps occur when using INCREMENT BY greater than one. Recoverability of the counter value is achieved by reconstructing it from the logs if DB2 abends and there is no cache.

The integrity of an identity column is maintained in a sysplex data sharing environment where multiple processors can be inserting rows at the same time. Each processor is assigned 20 (default) preallocated numbers if the cache is used. Therefore, numbers are not necessarily assigned in the order of row insertion by various processors. Transaction A can be inserting rows at the same time as transaction B on a single processor. Transaction A may not have its rows with strict sequential numbering within a UR.

The MINVALUE and MAXVALUE parameters (optional) provides for specifying the minimum and maximum value of sequential values. If the parameters are not specified, the minimum and maximum values are determined by the data type used.

NO CYCLE (default) means that gaps in sequential values are not reused.

Values are not generated once the MAXVALUE or MINVALUE (for negative sequence numbers) has been reached if specified.

CYCLE provides for the use of gaps within the range of MINVALUE and MAXVALUE. If MAXVALUE is reached (MINVALUE if negative sequence numbers are used), sequential values are generated beginning with the MINVALUE (opposite for negative numbers). It is necessary to create a unique index to avoid duplicates. If a duplicate value is generated, a -803 SQLCODE is returned and the row is not inserted.

Restrictions: EDITPROC cannot be used on the table nor can FIELDPROC be used on the identity column.

CREATE TABLE ... LIKE ... INCLUDING IDENTITY causes the newly created table to inherit the identity column of the old table. This does not apply to creating a table like a view.

The ALTER TABLE statement can be used to add an identity column. If the table is populated when the ALTER is issued, the table is placed in the REORG pending state. Execution of the reorganization utility (discussed in Chapter RR) assigns unique sequential values and removes the pending state. It is not possible to alter the GENERATED clause (may be possible in V7+1).

Identity column catalog tables: SYSSEQUENCES has one row for each identity column including the last assigned value and the definition of the column. SYSSEQUENCEDEP has one row for each identity column including the name of table that has the identity column and the column name.

SYSCOLUMNS.DEFAULT column has the value of I for AS IDENTITY and GENERATED ALWAYS or J for AS IDENTITY and GENERATED BY DEFAULT.

Inserting rows into a table with an identity column and determining the last sequence number inserted are discussed Chapter PD.

Domains

C. J. Date defines a domain as a pool of values from which one or more columns draw their actual values. E. F. Codd suggests that data types should be used to enforce domains. A date data type is a good example of enforcement of a domain through a DB2 data type. A column defined as a date data type must contain a year value between 1 and 9999, a value between 1 and 12, and a day value between 1 and 31. Table check constraints provide for some validation of data and facilities for domain support. Distinct types, table check constraints, and triggers (discussed in Chapters TR) can be used to enforce domains (V6).

Creating and Using Distinct Types

You certainly do not want to compare or do arithmetic operations on US dollars and Euro. They have different values at different times. Similarly, pounds and kilograms are units of weight but should not be compared or used together in arithmetic operations. The same principle applies to temperatures in centigrade and Fahrenheit, distance in miles and kilometers, and many other data types. Errors can be avoided by declaring the appropriate columns as their particular distinct type. Once you define a column with a distinct type, the column can be used only with another column defined with the same distinct type in comparisons, function invocations, stored procedures calls, and assignments. Distinct types are also known as user-defined data types and are considered strong typing.

Built-in data types refer to the basic data types in DB2, including DECIMAL, INTEGER, SMALLINT, CHAR, etc.. Distinct types are represented internally as DB2 built-in data types. They can be used with DRDA (Distributed Relational Database Architecture) (not private protocol distributed processing).

The use of distinct types begins with the CREATE DISTINCT TYPE statement to assign it a name and specify the built-in data type used to store the data. The name of a distinct type has a qualifier which optionally can be the current SQLID or a schema name as discussed in Chapter CO. The following two statements create US_DOLLAR and EURO distinct types both of which are stored as DECIMAL(9,2). You will want to create a distinct type for each country's currency where your company does business.

```
CREATE DISTINCT TYPE US_DOLLAR AS DECIMAL(9,2)
   WITH COMPARISONS;
```

```
CREATE DISTINCT TYPE EURO        AS DECIMAL(9,2)
   WITH COMPARISONS;
```

The WITH COMPARISONS clause means that only like distinct types can be compared. The clause is required for all but large objects (LOB).

Consider the use built-in data types of DECIMAL rather than NUMERIC, and DOUBLE or REAL rather than FLOAT to increase portability across platforms.

The following CREATE TABLE statement uses the US_DOLLAR distinct type for the SALARY column and EURO for the COMM column.

```
CREATE TABLE EMP
  (EMPNO      CHAR(6)              NOT NULL,
   FIRSTNME   VARCHAR(12)          NOT NULL,
   MIDINIT    CHAR(1)              NOT NULL,
   LASTNAME   VARCHAR(15)          NOT NULL,
   WORKDEPT   CHAR(3)                      ,
   PHONENO    CHAR(4)                      ,
   HIREDATE   DATE                         ,
   JOB        CHAR(8)                      ,
   EDLEVEL    SMALLINT                     ,
   SEX        CHAR(1)                      ,
   BIRTHDATE  DATE                         ,
   SALARY     US_DOLLAR                    ,
   BONUS      DECIMAL(9,2)                 ,
   COMM       EURO                         ,
   CONSTRAINT EMPNO_PK PRIMARY KEY (EMPNO));
```

Use of Distinct Types to Avoid Invalid Operations

Let's see how the use of distinct types avoid invalid operations. Here is an incorrect statement to determine employees who have a salary greater than their bonus and their commission.

```
SELECT EMPNO, LASTNAME, SALARY,   BONUS,   COMM
FROM    EMP
WHERE   SALARY > BONUS
AND     SALARY > COMM;
```

The SALARY distinct type of US_DOLLAR avoids the incorrect

operations. It is not valid to compare SALARY in US dollars with BONUS declared as DECIMAL(9,2). Similarly, SALARY cannot be compared to BONUS declared with the distinct type of EURO. The following error message is received.

```
SQLCODE = -401, ERROR: THE OPERANDS OF AN
ARITHMETIC OR COMPARISON
OPERATION ARE NOT COMPARABLE
SQLSTATE   = 42818 SQLSTATE RETURN CODE
```

Another invalid statement shows that arithmetic operations cannot be done on unlike distinct types and built-in data types. Here is an attempt to determine the total income for employee '00200'.

```
SELECT EMPNO,LASTNAME, SALARY + BONUS + COMM
FROM   EMP
WHERE  EMPNO = '00200';
```

The statement does not execute successfully because it is not possible to add columns defined as US_DOLLAR, DECIMAL, and EURO in an SQL statement. The following error results from the attempt.

```
DSNT408I SQLCODE = -440, ERROR:  NO FUNCTION BY THE
NAME + HAVING COMPATIBLE ARGUMENTS WAS FOUND IN THE
CURRENT PATH
DSNT418I SQLSTATE   = 42884 SQLSTATE RETURN CODE
```

It is necessary to take an overt action to allow comparison and arithmetic operations between distinct types and built-in data type data types. DB2 automatically creates functions for this purpose. These cast functions are automatically dropped when the distinct type is dropped. Optionally, you can create sourced functions as discussed in Chapter UD. If you need to perform operations with two or more different distinct types, it is necessary to create functions for this purpose.

Cast To and From Distinct Types

DB2 automatically generates cast functions to allow for operations on a distinct type and built-in data type with the same name and qualifier or schema as the distinct type for which they were created. Two cast functions are created automatically when a distinct type is created. One cast function has the name of the built-in data type, DECIMAL in our example. This cast function provides for casting from the built-in data type (DECIMAL) to the distinct type (US_DOLLAR). Cast functions named US_DOLLAR and EURO are also created automatically by DB2. These cast functions provide for casting literals and host variables from the distinct types of US_DOLLAR and EURO to the built-in data type DECIMAL. The use of cast functions are evaluated at stage 1 and can use a matching index scan (discussed in Chapter PP).

It is not possible to compare SALARY declared as US_DOLLAR with a literal or host variable which uses built-in data types. The following statement to determine employees whose salary is greater than 20,000.00 results in a -401 SQLCODE. DB2 has no way of knowing whether 20,000.00 is in US dollars as is the column.

```
SELECT  EMPNO,  LASTNAME,  SALARY,  BONUS,  COMM
FROM    EMP
WHERE   SALARY > 20000.00;
```

Use of functions to compare a literal or host variable with distinct types: The US_DOLLAR cast function can be used to determine employees whose salary is greater than 20,000.00 like:

```
SELECT  EMPNO,  LASTNAME,  SALARY,  BONUS,  COMM
FROM    EMP
WHERE   SALARY > US_DOLLAR(20000.00);
```

An alternative is to designate salary as decimal and make the comparison.

```
SELECT  EMPNO,  LASTNAME,  SALARY,  BONUS,  COMM
FROM    EMP
WHERE   DECIMAL(SALARY) > 20000.00;
```

An attempt to use the EURO(20000.00) fails with a -401 SQLCODE as it should. It is incorrect to compare salary in US dollars with Euros. They have different values depending upon the current exchange rate.

One should not do arithmetic operations and compare US_DOLLAR, DECIMAL, and EURO values. We will review some additional uses of the cast functions if you find it necessary to do the manipulations in some other situations on other types of data. The real goal is to review various uses of the functions.

If it is required for some reason in another situation with other types of data, that the DECIMAL function be used to designate each distinct type as decimal to allow arithmetic operations and comparisons. The following statement adds salary in US dollars, bonus in decimal, and commission in Euro as well as identifying employees whose salary in US dollars is greater than their bonus in decimal and their salary is greater than their commission in Euro.

```
SELECT  EMPNO,  LASTNAME,  DECIMAL(SALARY)  +
   BONUS  +  DECIMAL(COMM)
FROM    EMP
WHERE   DECIMAL(SALARY)  >  BONUS
AND     DECIMAL(SALARY)  >  DECIMAL(COMM);
```

The CAST function syntax is an alternative to designate each distinct type as decimal to allow the same operations as in the previous statement. However, this formulation is evaluated at stage 2 and cannot use a matching index scan.

```
SELECT  EMPNO,  LASTNAME,
   CAST(SALARY AS DECIMAL)  +
   BONUS  +  DECIMAL(COMM)
FROM    EMP
WHERE   CAST(SALARY AS DECIMAL)  >  BONUS
AND     CAST(SALARY AS DECIMAL)  >
        CAST(COMM AS DECIMAL);
```

These functions do not convert from one unit of measure to another. User-defined functions are required for this purpose as discussed in Chapter UD.

The CAST function can be used to designate COMM (defined as Euro) as decimal in a comparison with a decimal literal or host variable. The developer needs to know that the literal or host variable is in Euro for a valid operation. DB2 has no way to enforce this. Following is a statement to identify employees who have a bonus greater than 100.00. The developer must know that the literal of 100.00 or host variable containing 100.00 is in Euro or is a required comparison in using other data types to achieve accurate results.

```
SELECT   EMPNO, LASTNAME, SALARY, BONUS, COMM
FROM     EMP
AND      CAST(COMM AS DECIMAL) > 100.00;
```

There is no way to cast salary defined as US_DOLLAR and bonus defined as DECIMAL to EURO for performance of arithmetic operations and to do comparisons of different distinct types. Indeed, this is a primary goal of distinct types. The following statement

```
SELECT   EMPNO, LASTNAME, CAST(SALARY AS EURO) +
   CAST(BONUS AS EURO)+COMM--COMM is defined as EURO
FROM     EMP
AND      CAST(SALARY AS EURO) < CAST(BONUS AS EURO)
AND      CAST(SALARY AS EURO) < COMM;
```

results in:

```
DSNT408I SQLCODE = -461, ERROR:  A VALUE WITH DATA
TYPE MKTGXW.US_DOLLAR CANNOT BE CAST TO TYPE EURO
DSNT418I SQLSTATE  = 42846 SQLSTATE RETURN CODE
```

Conversion of salary in US dollars to Euro and bonus in decimal to Euro can be done with an external user-defined function (UDF) written in a host language to do the required calculations as described in Chapter UD.

Uses of US_DOLLAR Cast Function: Recall that DB2 automatically generates a cast function with the name of the distinct type (US_DOLLAR in the examples) in addition to the cast function with the name of the built-in function (DECIMAL in the examples). Thus far we have concentrated mostly on the DECIMAL cast function. A couple more examples using the US_DOLLAR function will further clarify when the cast functions can and cannot be used.

Comparisons can be done between distinct types and built-in data types by designating a column defined with a decimal built-in data type, literal, or host variable as an US_DOLLAR distinct type. The following example uses the US_DOLLAR cast function is designate bonus as US dollars. This provides for identifying employees whose salary in US dollars is greater than their bonus defined with a built-in data type of decimal. Once again, the developer must take care that this is in fact a legitimate comparison.

```
SELECT EMPNO, LASTNAME, SALARY, BONUS, COMM
FROM   EMP
WHERE  SALARY > US_DOLLAR(BONUS);
```

It is not possible to use a function to designate a literal or host variable as a distinct type in an arithmetic operation as in the following example. If you need to add 1,000.00 Euro to employee commissions defined with an EURO distinct type, it is necessary to use a sourced UDF to allow the addition or use any arithmetic operation as discussed in Chapter UD. Also, sourced functions are useful in minimizing the need for casting and avoiding -410 SQLCODEs.

```
SELECT EMPNO, LASTNAME, SALARY, BONUS,
   COMM + EURO(1000.00)
FROM   EMP
AND    SALARY > US_DOLLAR(20000.00);
```

This statement results in:

```
DSNT408I SQLCODE = -440, ERROR:  NO FUNCTION BY THE
NAME + HAVING COMPATIBLE ARGUMENTS WAS FOUND IN THE
CURRENT PATH        DSNT418I SQLSTATE   = 42884 SQLSTATE
RETURN CODE
```

Additional factors that require your consideration are pointed out with examples of SQL statements using distinct types with host variables in Chapter PD.

Privileges for the creation and usage of distinct types are similar to UDF as discussed in Chapter UD except that there is no package involved.. You can grant usage privileges on distinct types and cast functions automatically created by DB2 to others like:

```
GRANT USAGE ON DISTINCT TYPE US_DOLLAR TO
PUBLIC;
```

Dropping Distinct Types: You can drop a distinct type using the required RESTRICT clause as in the following example. This means that there are no tables defined using the distinct type, and no UDF and stored procedures depend on the distinct type. If there is difficulty dropping distinct types, select from SYSROUTINES to determine the dependencies and drop them first.

```
DROP DISTINCT TYPE US_DOLLAR RESTRICT;
```

The drop of a distinct type results in DB2 automatically dropping the cast functions that it created automatically.

Table Check Constraints

The CHECK clause of the CREATE TABLE statement can be used to define rules for having DB2 validate the data when rows are inserted and updated. This eliminates the need for developers to write, test, and maintain host language code to check constraints in many cases. The table check constraint avoids having to repeatedly code for rules in multiple programs. There is no need to be concerned that a constraint may not be properly coded in all programs because of a misunderstanding or a new person joins the team who is not aware of the constraints that must be enforced. The LOAD and CHECK DATA utilities will validate the data according to the constraints defined in the table check constraints.

There is a single source of information about the constraints as recorded in the catalog tables. The constraints can be dynamically added or dropped if the business constraints change without modification to one or more host programs. In addition, constraints are uniformly enforced across all interfaces to DB2 (QMF, for example). This allows for power users to update the data directly and have the data validated according to the constraints defined to DB2.

Definition of Constraints

Most positive conditions that can be specified in a WHERE clause predicate of a SELECT statement, as discussed in Chapter SL, can be used in defining a constraint. The conditions can be joined with AND and OR Boolean operators provided that a constraint definition does not exceed 3800 bytes. The defined constraints will be checked when rows are inserted and updated. If a constraint is violated, a -545 SQLCODE is issued and the row is not inserted or updated.

Figure CT.1 has an example of creating the S table with two constraints named STATUS_C and CITY_C. The STATUS_C constraint does not allow a row to be inserted if the value for the STATUS column is outside of the between 10 and 200 range. Also, a status value cannot be updated to be outside of the range. Null does not violate a constraint. A row can be inserted into the S table without specifying a value for status.

The constraint name is the column name or a variation on the column name being checked followed by '_C ' in the example. The constraint name can be 18 bytes in length. The constraint name is placed in the SQLERRMC field of the SQL Communication Area (SQLCA) when a constraint is violated. It is useful in describing an error to the user as discussed in Chapter PD.

Rules for Defining Constraints

There are some rules for defining constraints. The first operand must be a column name. The second operand can be a literal or column from the row being checked. If the second operand is a literal, basically the column must have equal or greater precision than the literal. For example, one cannot compare a literal with a value greater than 32,767 to a SMALLINT column and a literal of 140.95 with an INTEGER column. If the second operand is a column, it must have matching data type and length with the first operand. The exception is that compatible character strings can have different lengths.

It is necessary to exercise caution when defining constraints. DB2 does not check the semantics of a constraint definition, any more than it will the WHERE clause of a SELECT statement. For example, the following definition of a constraint on status is allowed, but no one can insert any rows with a status value into the table.

```
CONSTRAINT STATUS CHECK (STATUS > 100 AND STATUS <
80)
```

A column cannot be compared to a column function, a special register, host variables, parameter markers, EXISTS and quantified predicates, subselects, and the CHECK clause cannot reference another table.

Referencing Another Table for Validation Purposes

The most restrictive rule is that the CHECK clause *cannot* reference another table. One would prefer to reference a table containing all valid cities rather than having to list them in an IN list as is done for the CITY constraint in Figure CT.1. Another table can be referenced in a trigger definition for validating data. Triggers are available in V6.

You may want to list all valid values in an IN list if the values are static to achieve improved performance over triggers. The values are searched by Data Manager (DM) in central storage which holds significant performance advantage as discussed in Section CT.5. Do list the values that are frequently referenced first in the IN list because the values are searched sequentially. The constraints can be added and dropped with an ALTER statement. For example, a constraint on a STATE column can be defined by listing all of the 50 states in an IN list. An alternative is to use a before trigger as discussed in Chapter TR. However, there are performance and function trade-offs as discussed in the chapter.

Adding Constraints to a Populated Table

The ALTER statement can be used to add constraints to a populated table like:

```
ALTER TABLE S
   ADD CONSTRAINT SN_C
     CHECK (SN BETWEEN 'S1' AND 'S99999');
```

Plans and packages do <u>not</u> require a rebind to take advantage of constraint enforcement. The constraints are checked depending on the CURRENT RULES special register when adding constraints. The CURRENT RULES special register can be set to the SQL standard before executing the ALTER statement like:

```
SET CURRENT RULES = 'STD'
```

The DB2 rule is the default and has advantages. Check pending is turned on and no SQL manipulation statements can be executed until check pending is turned off. After adding a number of constraints, the CHECK DATA utility can be executed to check all of the defined constraints and turn off check pending if there are no violations or if you have specified that violating rows are to be deleted after writing them to an exception table. The DB2 rule has performance advantages when adding more than one constraint.

ALTER TABLE Statement

Many of the parameters specified when creating a table cannot be altered after the table is created. Figure CT.4 is an example of an ALTER TABLE statement that specifies all parameters that can be altered. Special conditions that apply to altering a specific parameter are discussed along with a description of the parameters.

Figure CT.4. ALTER TABLE statement

```
ALTER TABLE S
  ADD COUNTRY CHAR(20) WITH DEFAULT (USA)
  DROP CONSTRAINT STATUS_C;
  ADD CONSTRAINT SN_C
    CHECK (SN BETWEEN 'S1' AND 'S99999')
  FIELDPROC FSN
  VALIDPROC VALIDSN
  AUDIT ALL
  DATA CAPTURE CHANGES
  DROP RESTRICT ON DROP
  DROP UNIQUE SN_PK
  DROP PRIMARY KEY;
```

The ALTER statement in Figure CT.4 has an example of adding a new COUNTRY column to S table in Figure CT.1. When a column is added to a table, it is recommended that the reorganization utility with an inline copy be executed before many values are placed in the new column. This causes space to be allocated for the newly added column and provides a copy of the table with the newly added column. If the reorganization utility is not executed after adding a new column to a table, there is a good chance that most updates to place a value in the new column will cause the row to be moved to a page with free space available for the row that is expanded in length as discussed in Chapter CD.

A table can be renamed with the RENAME statement and authorizations are transferred to the new table name. For example, the S table is renamed to SUPPLIER in the statement:

```
RENAME TABLE S TO SUPPLIER;
```

There are some restrictions on renaming a table. It cannot be renamed if a trigger or view is defined on the table. You can rename a tables acted on by a trigger. If triggers are to apply to newly renamed table, if is necessary to drop the trigger and recreate it to reference the new table name. RENAME does not apply to synonyms and aliases.

To Null or Not Null

Nulls can be used when actual values are unknown or inapplicable. DEFAULT NULL or no null specification clause is the default and tells DB2 to insert or load a row even though there is no value specified for a column.

It is perhaps easiest to understand the concept of nulls by considering the problem that arises when they are unavailable. What value should be placed in the cost column of a product information table for an item whose cost has not yet been set? A value of 0 is inaccurate because the product surely has a cost. A null value solves the problem by showing that the item carries a cost but that it is not known.

The ability to make this distinction takes resources. The use of nulls requires 1 byte of storage for every value in a column that allows nulls and another byte for every value in an index created from a column with nulls. The extra byte provides a prefix for each value that indicates whether it is in fact null. The null prefix is HEX '00' if the value is present and HEX 'FF' if it is not. These extra bytes can add up. A 100,000-row table with 10 columns allowing nulls requires 1 million bytes for the capability. If five of those columns are indexed, another ½ million bytes are needed. Index page splitting will occur for inserting sequential values as discussed in Chapter ID. Application programmers that select data from a column with nulls must know that nulls are allowed in columns and remember to code a null indicator and there is the processing time for testing the null indicators.

Null can also present difficulties for occasional database users and programmers. Null values do not compare as equals in joins, for example. Suppose a database includes one table describing projects and another describing employees who might work on them. A user may request a report requiring an inner join of columns from each table--perhaps a list of the salaries being paid to workers assigned to each project. If some projects have no workers assigned to them, that fact might be indicated with nulls in the project table assignment column because an employee identification would not be applicable as an entry. Those projects with null values for the assignment column will not show up in the report, however, because the inner join ignores them. This may be fine if the report's purpose is to show salaries being paid for active projects. If the report was meant to show how much was being paid in salaries, by project, however, it would be misleading since it would not show the projects for which no salaries were being paid. If the problem is recognized, an outer join can be used as discussed in Chapters JP and ST.

The developer can avoid this and similar problems by using a non-meaningful value in place of null as a code that, in this case, would relate to an "unassigned" row in the employee table. For example, an employee ID of zero in the employee table would carry "unassigned" in the name column, and inactive projects would list zeros for employee IDs in the open slots.

An advantage of using nulls is that they allow for accurate averages in columns that include them. The nulls do not enter into the sum of values or contribute to their count. Consider a column of salaries that must use zeros for employees whose salaries are unknown. If the salaries for 10 employees totaled $300,000, the average is $30,000. If information on a new hire whose salary was unknown were added to the table and the salary was listed as zero, the salary column would still total $300,000, but the count of employees would now be 11. The column average would be $27,272.27. If null was used, the average would not change. One way around this problem if the developer does not wish to use nulls is to specify NOT NULL for the salary column, use zero in place of nulls, and compute the average for values where the salary is not equal to zero. This scheme does not work if the column includes volunteers, and the average should reflect that fact. To avoid this additional problem, the developer might use an impossible salary--perhaps -1--as the null replacement and take the average of salaries not equal to -1.

When null is used in an arithmetic calculation, the result is null unless the SQL statement specifies special handling for nulls. For example, if a statement requests the subtraction of employees' insurance payments from their salaries and the insurance payment value is null, the result is null. The same principle applies to addition and multiplication. Division by null is like division by zero and results in a negative SQLCODE indicating an error. Chapter SL discusses the use of the COALESCE and VALUE functions to substitute values for nulls in SQL expressions. Figure CT.5

summarizes how nulls are treated when manipulated by SQL statements.

Figure CT.5. How nulls are treated by SQL statements

♦   Null is =, >, < no value.
♦   Null does not participate in an inner join.
♦   Addition, subtraction, and multiplication involving null results in null.
♦   Division by null results in a negative SQLCODE.
♦   Concatenation of a null results in a null
♦   All column functions exclude nulls except for COUNT(*) which counts the number of rows.
♦   Outer join produces null for columns in a table with no match on the join columns in the other table as discussed in Chapters JP and ST.
♦   If no rows qualify in a subselect, the result is null.
♦   If no rows qualify with a column function calculation, the result is null and requires a null indicator to avoid a negative SQLCODE.
♦   Existence of a null is tested with WHERE QTY IS (NOT) NULL (not QTY = NULL).
♦   ORDER BY sorts all nulls as higher than non-nulls and GROUP BY groups nulls together.

Programmers must be aware of which columns allow nulls. Whenever they write a program that SELECTS data from a column with nulls, they must declare a null indicator variable and reference it in each SELECT statement for the column. This coding is not difficult. But if it is not done--the programmer does not know or forgets that nulls apply--a negative SQLCODE results. Chapter PD discusses programming for nulls.

Mismatched nullability comparison on joined columns with a test for null and a column function resulting in a null in a subselect compared to a column that does not allow null can be evaluated at stage 1 (stage 1 and 2 predicates are discussed in Chapter PP). Specify OPTNTJP of ON (default is OFF) in DSN6SPRM of DSNZPARM if there will be no adverse effect to existing SQL so that evaluation can be done at stage 1.

WITH DEFAULT NULL is not widely used on column definitions because of exceptions and complexities in managing nulls.

Not Null

DB2 requires that some value be assigned to every row in every column for which NOT NULL is specified. For certain kinds of columns, the developer will almost never allow nulls. A primary key, by definition, must uniquely identify each row. Therefore a unique value should always be inserted into the primary key column. Any column can be declared unique by creating a unique index on it, meaning that DB2 will not allow duplicate values to be inserted in it. In fact, all primary key columns should have a unique index created to guarantee that no values are repeated. In most cases a column that must contain all unique values should be declared NOT NULL and a unique index created. If a column must contain all unique values and multiple null entries can occur in the column, the column must allow for nulls and an index created with the UNIQUE WHERE NOT NULL clause as discussed in Chapter ID. A foreign key column should not contain nulls if there is an absolute dependency of the foreign key table on the primary key table as discussed in Section TS.3. The primary key column, any column that should have only unique values, and frequently the foreign key column should be declared NOT NULL. If a column is added to a table with the ALTER statement, the column cannot be declared as NOT NULL because there are no values initially in a new column.

Not Null with Default

If the developer specifies NOT NULL WITH DEFAULT for a column in the CREATE TABLE statement, DB2 automatically places zeros in empty numeric columns, blanks in empty character columns, and the current date, time, or timestamp in columns with the corresponding date data type.

If a table includes columns for ORDER_DATE and RECIEVED_DATE, the current date is appropriate for the first but not the second when a row is first inserted. An alternative for RECIEVED_DATE is '0001-01-01' or '9999-12-31' (all zeros is not a valid date). The date of '0001-01-01' is used by the reorganization utility after a date column is added to a table with the ALTER statement.

Primary key columns can be declared NOT NULL or NOT NULL WITH DEFAULT. They cannot be assigned a default value. NOT NULL WITH DEFAULT allows a zero or blank as a primary key value, however this is probably not the intended unique identifier. Since NOT NULL WITH DEFAULT makes little sense for a column with a unique index in any case, only one zero or blank is allowed. A possible exception is the use of timestamp as a primary key that would allow for the automatic recording of the timestamp when the row is inserted.

Assignment of a Default Value

A specific value can be specified to be used when an actual value is not available by using the WITH DEFAULT clause on the column definition. For example, if no value is specified for the S.CITY column, the value of London will be used as defined in the WITH DEFAULT 'London' clause in Figure CT.1.

A literal, USER, CURRENT SQLID, and NULL can be specified as the default. USER causes the primary AUTHID of a person who inserts a row to be placed in the column. The column AUTHID_OF_INSERTER will have the primary AUTHID of the person who inserts a row if no value is specified in the Figure CT.1 CREATE TABLE example. CURRENT SQLID causes the current SQLID of a person who inserts a row to be placed in the column. USER and CURRENT SQLID provide some auditing capability. WITH DEFAULT NULL or no parameter value causes the column to be treated as null if no value is provided.

The ALTER statement can be used to add a column specified NOT NULL WITH DEFAULT or WITH DEFAULT. The newly added column will contain the default values after a reorganization. NOT NULL cannot be specified for columns added to a table with the ALTER TABLE statement. A newly added column will obviously contain nulls until its values are inserted. If the developer wants to specify NOT NULL for a new column, he or she must drop the table and re-create it.

Placement of Columns in a Row Effects Logging

Logging of updated rows are affected by the placement of columns that are frequently updated. DB2 logs from the first changed byte to the last changed byte. This suggests that frequently updated columns be placed contiguously to reduce logging. Column C4 should be placed before C3 or after C5 in Figure CT.6, for example. C3 and C5 can be fixed or variable in length (V7). Update of a VARCHAR column does not require logging of the variable length column and all remaining column in the row (V7). If the row length is changed by an update, the length field at the beginning of the row is also logged.

Figure CT.6. Logging of updated rows

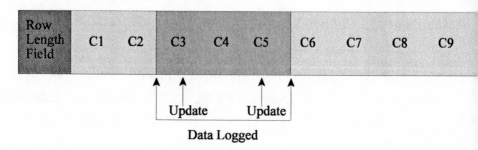

Hardware compressed rows and the rows with an EDITPROC requires more data be logged. Data is logged from first changed byte to the end of the row. Placing frequently updated columns at the end of the row reduces logging. If the row length is changed by an update, the length field at the beginning of the row is also logged as shown in Figure CT.7.

Figure CT.7. Logging with the use of compression and EDITPROC

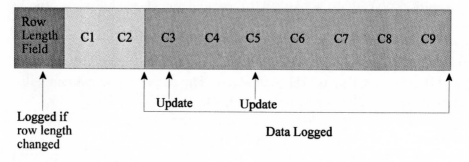

Coded Character Set Identifier

The CCSID can be specified as EBCDIC, UNICODE, or ASCII when creating a table, tablespace, or database as discussed in Chapter CD.

Restrict on Drop

Tables can be dropped by accident. It is very difficult to recover from an accidental drop of an object because the drop results in all information on the object being removed from the catalog tables. The clause WITH RESTRICT ON DROP can be used to minimize the possibility of an accidental drop when a table is created as shown in Figure CT.1. This is not the default. The restriction can be added to an existing tables like:

```
ALTER TABLE P
ADD RESTRICT ON DROP;
```

Once the restriction has been placed on a table, no one can drop the table. In addition, no one (not even SYSADM) can drop the tablespace and database that contains the table. It is necessary to remove the restriction before the table can be dropped. The restriction can be removed like:

```
ALTER TABLE P
DROP RESTRICT ON DROP;
```

Do beware of including the ALTER to remove the restriction in a SPUFI file before the DROP statement. This defeats the purpose of disallowing the drop of an object. Consider placing the ALTER to remove the restriction in a separate SPUFI file that must be executed before the SPUFI file containing the DROP statement. This minimizes accidents that are very difficult to recover from.

Data Capture

The DATA CAPTURE CHANGES parameter causes log records to be written to the log in expanded format rather than logging only part of an updated row as discussed in Chapter TS. A before and after image of the entire row is logged. This increases costs of logging somewhat and the number of log data sets required. If ESA compression is used, the log record will be in compressed form which reduces the space required on the log.

DATA CAPTURE NONE is the default. DATA CAPTURE CHANGES is useful for auditing, replication of data, and disaster recovery. When these functions are required, DATA CAPTURE CHANGES reduces costs compared to application program processing in most cases. The expanded log records can be read by an assembler program using DSNDQJ00 in DSNMACS which contains a mapping macro. There are a number of software products that can read the expanded log records and do processing for auditing, replication of data, and disaster recovery. IBM's program offering for replication of data is DPropD (Data Propagator) and the RRDF (Remote Recovery Data Facility) program offering has a log apply feature for disaster recovery.

The data capture feature can be added to the catalog tables with the ALTER statement (V5 APAR PQ13031). (Utility (DSNUTIL) logged events are not captured by design.) This provides for maintaining shadow catalog tables that can be used by SQL generators and general access to the catalog to reduce lock contention. DPropD (Data Propagator) program offering can be used to propagate changes to the shadow catalog from the catalog at specified intervals of time.

Auditing a Table

DB2 will audit a table's use--keep a record of SQL statements that access it--if the table's creator requests such an audit in the table's CREATE statement and the system administrator specifies that the audit is to occur. With the clause AUDIT CHANGE, the developer requests that records be kept for each insert, update, or delete statement. An AUDIT ALL clause requests records for SELECTS as well. An audit record consists of the SQL statement, the primary AUTHID of the individual issuing the statement, and a timestamp indicating when the statement was issued. AUDIT NONE asks that no auditing be done and is the default.

Before and after images of changed data are not part of the audit record. If a before and after image of the changed data is required, DATA CAPTURE should be considered.

EDITPROC, FIELDPROC, and VALIDPROC

The EDITPROC, FIELDPROC, and VALIDPROC parameters provide for specifying a program that will be executed automatically when a row is processed depending on the specific procedure specified. Figure CT.8 shows how a row is passed through an EDITPROC when the row is inserted, updated, or selected. The same processing is done with a FIELDPROC. A row is passed through a VALIDPROC when it is inserted, updated, or deleted.

Figure CT.8. Processing a row with an EDITPROC

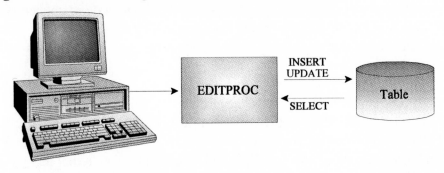

The procedure must be written in assembler, it operates in privileged mode, it can issue no I/O, and SQL statements cannot be issued from a procedure. Procedures are exits from DB2. The sample library, SDSNSAMP, contains sample procedures. Once a procedure has been developed, tested, and its name specified following the keyword of EDITPROC, FIELDPROC, or VALIDPROC on the CREATE TABLE statement, its use is transparent to application programs. Figure CT.1 has an example of specifying a VALIDPROC with the procedure name of CHECKS.

EDITPROC and FIELDPROC can be used to compress, encrypt, or manipulate the data for some other purpose. An EDITPROC can operate on an entire row. FIELDPROC operates on individual columns.

Several software companies offer products for compressing data with the use of EDITPROC. IBM provides a sample procedure DSN8HUFF in the sample library SDSNSAMP. ESA compression is a good alternative for compressing data as discussed in Chapter TS.

FIELDPROC procedures are useful for changing the usual EBCDIC collating sequence. Sorts done on data represented in EBCDIC result in strict alphabetical order, for example, while an organization may want to use exceptions to that order. In an employee list, for example, it may want MacDonald and McDonald next to each other rather than having MacGraw in between. An assembler program invoked using FIELDPROC can account for the special order. Similarly, sorts of EBCDIC represented data does not account for accent marks, sorting words that contain them out of alphabetical order. A FIELDPROC routine can solve the problem of handling accent marks, common in languages other than English.

FIELDPROC can be specified only on a column declared as a character data type (not a numeric data type). It can be used for translating a character code to a name or description when the data is selected. State code is frequently stored in a row rather than the longer state name. The state code of AL can be translated to Alabama automatically for reporting purposes when a row is selected, for example.

FIELDPROC and WITH DEFAULT cannot be used on the same column definition. EDITPROC and FIELDPROC routines affect the way DB2 stores the data. Therefore, they cannot be added to or dropped from a table after it has been created, nor can a column be added to a table that includes an EDITPROC routine. A FIELDPROC routine can be added to a table with a column that is added with an ALTER TABLE statement.

A VALIDPROC routine can be used to check data as they are entered to ensure the values are within permitted ranges. If the routine detects a mistake, it can issue an error message and does not permit the update, insertion, or deletion. It is not invoked when data are retrieved. A VALIDPROC routine provides for centralized validation of data to avoid writing the validation logic into multiple application programs. However, one cannot select from another table from the VALIDPROC routine. This limits the amount of validation that can be done. Check table constraints are a good alternative to the use of a VALIDPROC routine. Check table constraints can be easily defined and altered without having to develop an assembler routine and provide for performance advantages in most cases.

Since VALIDPROC does not affect how the data are stored, an ALTER TABLE statement may add or drop a VALIDPROC routine. A column may also be added to a table that employs a VALIDPROC routine. The routine, unless revised, will not, however, operate on the new column.

IN Clause

The IN clause designates the database and tablespace to house the table. If the IN clause is not specified, the default database DSNDB04 is used and DB2 automatically creates the tablespace using the default storage group SYSDEFLT. In this case, very little space is allocated to the tablespace--12 KB of primary and 12 KB of secondary space. The default tablespace name is the same as the table name if the table name is <= 8 alphanumeric characters, first position is not a number, and name is not currently used for another table or index space. Otherwise, the first 4 characters of table name are used followed by a digit and 3 characters for uniqueness. And if left to DB2 to create the tablespace, DB2 creates a simple tablespace. It was seen in Chapter TS that there are significant advantages of a segmented tablespace even for one table per tablespace. These factors suggest that the developers will, in most cases, want to create their own tablespace and database in which to house the table.

Row Length Considerations

To fit as many rows as possible on each page and avoid wasted space, developers should consider several factors related to row length. DB2 permits a maximum of 255 rows per 4KB data page regardless of their length. This limitation is due to a page's directory, which can list only that many rows. All eight bits of the last byte in the record identifier (RID) are used to locate a slot in the page directory. Thus, $2^8-1 = 255$ rows per page is the maximum.

The developer should avoid row lengths of slightly more than 2037 bytes including overhead. Rows cannot be split across pages. Only one 2038-byte row can fit on a page, leaving almost half the page empty. This requires twice as many I/O operations to access the same number of rows as would be needed if the length were slightly less than 2037 bytes and two rows could fit on each page.

Similarly, a row of more than 4074 bytes including overhead will not fit on a 4 KB page but will need a 32 KB page. Developers should use 32 KB pages only when one or more rows will not fit on a 4 KB page. Contiguous space in an assigned 32 KB page size buffer pools is required for 32 KB pages. The large pages also require eight times the I/O transfer time as 4 KB pages. However, if long textual data is being stored, it is best to use a 32 KB page rather than artificially splitting the row across multiple 4 KB pages.

Creating LIKE Tables

Frequently developers want to create tables exactly like existing ones on the same DB2 subsystem. For example, they may want to create a test table just like an existing production table. A TEST.SPJ table can be created like an existing PROD.SPJ table with the statement:

```
CREATE TABLE TEST.SPJ LIKE PROD.SPJ IN
DATSTDB.DATESTSP;
```

The IN clause is used to designate the database and tablespace that is used for the new table.

COMMENT ON Statements

Developers can use the COMMENT ON statement to enter in the catalog tables, SYSIBM.SYSTABLES and SYSIBM.SYSCOLUMNS, textual descriptions of the tables and columns they have created. These descriptions can be used as part of the documentation for the application system. In effect, the COMMENT ON statement inserts the developer's description in the catalog table REMARKS column in the row describing the table or column the statement specifies. Since the REMARKS column is a 254-character VARCHAR column, the description in the COMMENT ON statement cannot exceed 254 characters.

The COMMENT ON statement for a table identifies the table and, following the keyword IS, gives the description itself within single quotation marks--for example:

```
COMMENT ON TABLE AUTHID.SPJ IS
   'SPJ SHOWS THE RELATIONSHIP BETWEEN
    SN, PN, JN AND HAS THE PN QUANTITY';
```

The COMMENT ON statement for a single column also names the column:

```
COMMENT ON COLUMN AUTHID.SPJ.SN IS
   'SN IS THE SUPPLIER ID';
```

The developer can, however, use a single statement to enter descriptions of several of a table's columns. To do that, he or she names the table in the COMMENT ON statement and, within parentheses, specifies the column names and their associated descriptions--for example:

```
COMMENT ON AUTHID.SPJ
   (SN IS 'SN IS THE SUPPLIER ID',
    PN IS 'PN IS THE PART ID',
    JN IS 'JN IS THE JOB ID');
```

LABEL ON Statements

The LABEL ON statement's purpose is to create labels that substitute for table or column names when interactive reports are generated. For example, a LABEL ON statement may create a label 'SUPPLIER ID' for the SN column in the example SPJ table. Whenever an interactive request generates a report using the column, the values are returned with the label rather than column name as a heading. Labels may be up to 30 characters.

The LABEL ON syntax is similar to that of the COMMENT ON statement. Columns can be labeled individually, or several from the same table can be labeled with a single statement--for example:

```
LABEL ON COLUMN AUTHID.SPJ.SN IS
   'SUPPLIER ID';

LABEL ON AUTHID.SPJ
   (SN IS 'SUPPLIER ID',
    PN IS 'PART ID',
    JN IS 'JOB ID');
```

The COMMENT ON and LABEL ON statements can be used on a table, view, or alias.

CT.3 REFERENTIAL INTEGRITY

Referential integrity means that every foreign key value (not including null) must have a corresponding primary key value to which it refers. (Primary and foreign keys are discussed in Chapter CO.) We will use the supplier/part/job (SPJ) database in Figure CT.9 which consists of four tables to discuss referential integrity (RI). Three of these tables are parent tables-- S, P, and J-- with primary keys of SN, PN, and JN. The dependent table is SPJ which has three foreign keys, SN, PN, and JN. These foreign keys reference the parent tables of S, P, and J. The SPJ table has a composite primary key consisting of the SN, PN, and JN columns. These tables will be used in examples to show the purpose of RI, the rules needed to enforce RI, and how to implement RI using DB2 or application logic. Indeed, the tables are used throughout the book in examples.

Figure CT.9. Suppliers, part, job, and suppliers/part/job tables

S (Supplier Table)

SN	SNAME	STATUS	CITY
S1	Smith	20	London
S2	Jones	10	Paris
S3	Blake	30	Paris
S4	Clark	20	London
S5	Adams	30	Athens

P (Part Table)

PN	PNAME	COLOR	WEIGHT	CITY
P1	Nut	Red	12	Lon.
P2	Bolt	Green	17	Par.
P3	Screw	Blue	17	Rome
P4	Screw	Red	14	Lon.
P5	Cam	Blue	12	Par.

J (Job Table)

JN	JNAME	CITY
J1	Sorter	Paris
J2	Punch	Rome
J3	Reader	Athens
J4	Console	Athens
J5	Collator	London
J6	Terminal	Oslo
J7	Tape	London

SPJ (Sup./Part/Job)

SN	PN	JN	QTY
S1	P1	J1	200
S1	P1	J4	700
S2	P3	J1	400
S2	P3	J2	200
S2	P3	J3	200
S2	P3	J4	500
S2	P3	J5	600
S2	P3	J6	400
S2	P3	J7	800
S2	P5	J2	100
S3	P3	J1	200
S3	P4	J2	500
S4	P6	J3	300
S4	P6	J7	300
S5	P2	J2	200
S5	P2	J4	100
S5	P5	J5	500
S5	P5	J7	100
S5	P6	J2	200
S5	P1	J4	100
S5	P3	J4	200
S5	P4	J4	800
S5	P5	J4	400

Consider the J and SPJ tables shown in Figure CT.9. If the J2 row is deleted from the J table, the SPJ table as it now stands does not make sense. The rows in SPJ referring to J2 are meaningless since there is no longer such a job. The potential for this kind of anomaly exists whenever any changes are made to foreign key columns and whenever primary key columns are updated or deleted. If a foreign key is defined on JN in the SPJ table referencing the J table with a primary key defined, DB2 will not allow the deletion of J2 rows in the SPJ table.

A table with a foreign key is called a dependent table and a table whose primary key is associated with a foreign key is called a parent table. DB2 allows a parent table to exist without associated dependent tables. Such tables are called independent tables. A dependent table can reference multiple parent tables. And, of course, tables can have both primary and foreign keys. However, a parent table can have only one primary key consisting of one or more columns.

Creating the Primary Key

The first step in setting up a new table's RI is to specify the primary key in the CREATE TABLE statement (Figure CT.1). The syntax is straightforward. The constraint name is specified after the key word CONSTRAINT followed by the key words PRIMARY KEY, and the column or columns that comprise the key are listed in parentheses. This is the syntax in V7. It applies to creating foreign keys, unique columns, and table check constraints. Each constraint name must be unique for a table and can be 18 bytes or less in length, except the FK name must be 8 bytes or less. If a constraint name is not specified, it is generated by DB2 based on the column name. Syntax prior to version 7 is acceptable. Constraints are recorded in the catalog tables SYSTABCONST and SYSKEYCOLUSE.

Only one primary key can be defined per table, as the relational model dictates. The SQL standard states that the primary key should be declared on the column definition with the keywords PRIMARY KEY rather than after the column definitions. If the standard is used, the column must be declared as NOT NULL. Another option to comply with the standard is to specify UNIQUE in the column definition which forces the creation of a unique index. This parameter also requires that the column be declared as NOT NULL. PRIMARY KEY and UNIQUE cannot both be specified in a column definition. A FK can be created to reference a column defined as a PK or UNIQUE.

The developer must create a unique index on the column or columns that constitute the primary key or are specified in the UNIQUE clause. A unique index on the primary key provides for an efficient mechanism for DB2 to enforce the requirement that every primary key value be unique—a requirement called entity integrity in relational terms. If there is no unique index on the specified primary key and columns declared as unique, DB2 considers the table definition incomplete. (The STATUS column in SYSIBM.SYSTABLES equals 'I' and the TABLESTATUS column gives the reason for the table being incomplete.) DB2 will not allow SQL data manipulation access to an incomplete table and utilities that require access to the table will fail. An incomplete table can be altered, dropped, and an index can be created.

A unique index is created automatically on a column defined as a PRIMARY KEY or UNIQUE when a table is created using the schema processor which complies with the SQL92 standard.

Recommendation: It is advisable to define a primary key even if there are no dependent tables that reference the primary key table. It clearly documents the primary key in the catalog tables and forces the creation of a unique index on the primary key. There are no rules or performance implications to defining a primary key without having dependent tables. Indeed, the rules that apply to a parent table do not apply to a table with a primary key defined if there are no foreign keys defined referencing the table.

Creating Foreign Keys

The foreign keys are designed with similar syntax as the primary key. The constraint name of the SN foreign key is SN_FK in the SPJ table (Figure CT.10) The constraint name is used in error messages to identify a violated constraint as discussed in Chapter PD. It cannot exceed eight characters and must be unique for a given table. The RI constraint name cannot be the same as a table check constraint name.

Figure CT.10. Creating a foreign key table

```
CREATE TABLE SPJ
    (SN       CHAR(6)   NOT NULL,
     PN       CHAR(6)   NOT NULL,
     JN       CHAR(6)   NOT NULL,
     QTY      INTEGER   NOT NULL WITH DEFAULT,
```

```
      CONSTRAINT SPJ_PK PRIMARY KEY (SN, PN, JN),
      CONSTRAINT SPJ_UNIQUE UNIQUE  (SN, PN, JN),
      CONSTRAINT SN_FK FOREIGN KEY SN) REFERENCES S
         ON DELETE RESTRICT, -- Default
      CONSTRAINT PN_FK FOREIGN KEY (PN) REFERENCES P
         ON DELETE CASCADE,  -- Not Realistic
      CONSTRAINT JN_FK FOREIGN KEY (JN) REFERENCES J
         ON DELETE SET NULL) -- Not Realistic
   IN DASPJDB.SPJTSP;
```

A foreign key column must have the same data type and length as the primary key column. If the foreign key is a composite consisting of more than one column, the columns must be specified in the same order as the composite primary key columns. The primary and foreign keys do not need to match in terms of the null attribute, default values, and column names. The foreign key clause next identifies the single table that the key references. Naming the primary key column is optional. There can be only one primary key for a table; therefore the primary key reference is implicit. DB2 does not allow a foreign key to reference more than one parent table. If you wish to conform to the SQL standard, the column declared as the primary key or declared as being unique can be referenced. Both are not required.

ROWID and LOB columns cannot be defined as primary or foreign keys.

Dropping Constraints and Indexes

It is necessary to drop a constraint before dropping a supporting unique index created with V7, otherwise -669 SQLCODE indicating that the object cannot be explicitly dropped is received. Following is an example of dropping a FK, PK or unique column with dependents, and an index required to enforce uniqueness of the PK or column defined as unique.

```
   ALTER TABLE SPJ DROP FOREIGN KEY SN_FK;

   ALTER TABLE S DROP PRIMARY KEY;

   ALTER TABLE SPJ DROP UNIQUE SN_PK;

   DROP INDEX SN_PK;
```

The constraint and the enforcing index are dropped automatically when the parent or dependent table is dropped. Adding and dropping RI constraints can result in invalidating plans and packages. DB2 does an automatic rebind when plans and packages are next executed. If the automatic rebind fails, the plan or package is marked as inoperative. You can select from the catalog tables to determine invalid and inoperative plans and packages which can be explicitly rebound.

RI Rules

The foreign key clause goes on to identify the type of rule to be enforced when rows are deleted from the primary key table. After the keywords ON DELETE, the developer states whether DB2 should RESTRICT the deletion, CASCADE it to the foreign key table, or set the corresponding values in the foreign key to null (SET NULL). If you wish to conform to the SQL standard, NO ACTION can be specified which is like RESTRICT except as to when enforcement occurs with self-referencing tables as will be discussed. The correct rule defined depends on the business rules and the meaning of the data to the business. Each of the rules are described and examples of when and when not to use each rule is given.

The RESTRICT and NO ACTION rule means that a row cannot be deleted from the parent table if there is a matching foreign key value. In Figure CT.9, for example, because DELETE has been specified on the SNFK referential constraint, which references the S table, if an attempt is made to delete S4 from the S table, a negative SQLCODE will be issued and the S4 row will not be deleted. The RESTRICT rule is a good choice in this relationship. One would not want to delete information about a supplier where parts supplied by that supplier are currently being used on jobs. If information about the supplier is lost and a defective part is discovered, it will be necessary to contact the supplier to order a replacement part.

The CASCADE rule means that when a row is deleted from the parent table, all rows with a matching foreign key value will be deleted in all dependent tables that reference the parent table. For example, if P6 is deleted from the P table, all P6s will be deleted from the SPJ table. This is not a good choice in this case. One would not want to delete information about a part that is currently being used on a job. The RESTRICT rule is a good choice in this relationship.

The CASCADE rule is useful if the foreign key rows have no meaning without a primary key row. For example, if an employee leaves the company and the row describing the employee is deleted from the employee table, there is no reason to keep information about the employee's skills. This example assumes that skills are maintained in a SKILLS table that has been defined with a foreign key that references the employee table.

The SET NULL rule means that when a row is deleted in the primary key table, all rows with a matching foreign key will be set to null in all dependent tables that references the parent table. If J7 is deleted from the J table, all J7s will be set to null in the SPJ table. Of course, this means that JN in the J table must allow for nulls. Again, the RESTRICT rule is a good choice for this relationship. The goal has been to show examples of all three rules with the SPJ database.

Explicit and Implicit RI Rules

An explicit RI rule having to do with the deletion of a primary key and its effect on the matching foreign keys are specified with the ON DELETE clause when a foreign key is designated referencing a primary key as discussed. There are also implicit rules that come into play if a foreign key is designated having to do with the update of a primary key, insertion of a foreign key, and update of a foreign key value.

The update of a primary is not allowed if there is a matching foreign key value. For example, the update of S4 to be S10 would lead to potential problems. If a replacement part supplied by S4 is required for P6 that is used for J3, one should not contact S10 because it was S4 that supplied the part assuming that S10 is a new supplier with no relationship with S4. If S10 is a new supplier who is taking responsibility for parts supplied by S4, it is necessary to delete S4 and insert S10. It will be necessary to develop a procedure to deal with the S4 rows in the SPJ table before the deletion depending on the delete rule defined. The SQL for one possible procedure is:

```
INSERT INTO S (SN) VALUES ('S10');
UPDATE SPJ SET SN = 'S10' WHERE SN = 'S4'
   WITH RR;
DELETE FROM S WHERE SN = 'S4';
```

If the reader is not familiar with basic SQL data manipulation, Chapter SL can be read before reading this chapter.

The insert of a foreign key is allowed only if the value already exists in the parent table. If this implicit rule did not exist, one could insert an orphan row in a dependent table with no matching primary key value.

The update of a foreign key can occur only if the new foreign key value already exists in the parent table. If this implicit rule did not exist, one could update a foreign key such that there would be no matching primary key value. Again this would result in an orphan row in a dependent table.

No Constraint Checking Required

There are two cases where no constraint checking is required.

The insertion of a primary key into a parent table is unrestricted with respect to the dependent tables. For example, one can insert a row describing a new supplier without having already placed an order from the supplier. Of course, a duplicate primary key cannot be inserted into a parent table because of entity integrity.

The deletion of a foreign key from a dependent table is unrestricted. For example, the S4, P6, J3 row can be deleted when J3 is completed with no adverse effect on the parent tables.

Figure CT.11 summarizes the explicit and implicit RI rules.

Figure CT.11. Summary of explicit and implicit RI rules

♦ **Delete of a primary key** depends on the defined foreign key rule:
   ‣ Restrict or no action causes the primary key delete to be rejected if there is a matching foreign key (default).
   ‣ Cascade results in the primary key value and all foreign key values being deleted.
   ‣ Set null results in the primary key value being deleted and all foreign key values set to null.
♦ **Update of a primary key** value can occur only if there is no matching foreign key value.

- **Insert of a foreign key** value only if the value exists as a primary key in the parent table.
- **Update of a foreign key** can occur only if the new foreign key value exists in the parent table.
- **Insert of a primary key** into a parent table is unrestricted with respect to dependent table (duplicate primary keys are not allowed).
- **Delete of a foreign key** from a dependent table is unrestricted.

The ALTER statement can be used to add or drop primary and foreign keys provided that the developer has the appropriate privileges. Adding a foreign key, however, turns on check pending and no SQL data manipulation statements can be issued. This is because values that violate RI may already exist in the foreign key column. The CHECK DATA utility can be used to turn check pending off as discussed in Chapter LC.

Altering a table with respect to RI constraints can invalidate plans and packages. SELECTS from the catalog tables can be used to determine the invalidated plans and packages so that they can be explicitly rebound or DB2 will automatically rebind the plans and packages when next executed.

Foreign Keys and Nulls

Foreign and primary key columns need not have the same null attribute. Whether a foreign key column should allow nulls or not depends on the nature of the data. This can be thought of in terms of whether there is an absolute or conditional dependency of the dependent table on the parent table.

Absolute Dependency: If in the foreign key table a row's information has no business meaning or makes no sense without the associated information in the primary key table, the foreign key column should be declared as NOT NULL. For example, imagine a CUSTOMER_ORDER table with information on product orders that includes a foreign key referencing the CUSTOMER table that describes customers who have placed the orders. If there can be no order without a customer, there must always be a relationship between the description of an order in the CUSTOMER_ORDER table and the description of its customer in the CUSTOMER table. Consequently, there must be a foreign key value in the CUSTOMER_ORDER table referencing a primary key value in the

CUSTOMER table. This is an example of an absolute dependency where the foreign key in the CUSTOMER_ORDER table should be declared NOT NULL.

Conditional Dependency: There need not always be a foreign key value for every row depending on the business rules. Consider an EMPLOYEE table describing employees and including a foreign key referencing a DEPARTMENT table describing the departments to which they are assigned. If the company allows employees to be unassigned, the EMPLOYEE table's foreign key to the DEPARTMENT table should allow for nulls. This is an example of a conditional dependency. If the company had a rule requiring that every employee be assigned to a department, the relationship between the two tables would be absolute and the foreign key should be declared as NOT NULL.

Developers should pay special attention, however, to the null attributes of composite foreign keys. Improper use of nulls in composite foreign keys can lead to violations of RI. In the case of composite keys, DB2 considers the entire key null if any one of its columns is null. This can result in foreign key values without matching primary key values, a violation of RI. If a null appears anywhere in the SN, PN, or JN columns of SPJ, DB2 will allow an insert. (None of the columns should allow for null because the three columns constitute the primary key of SPJ. Assume for a moment that SN, PN, and JN are not the primary key of the SPJ table.) The following insert will be allowed even though there are no matching primary key values in the P and J tables of P99 and J99 because a SN is not specified and the column allows for nulls.

```
INSERT INTO SPJ
VALUES ('P99', 'J99', 200);
```

The problem can be avoided by not allowing for nulls in any columns of a composite index.

CT.4 RELATIONSHIPS THAT REQUIRE SPECIAL HANDLING

There are some relationships that require special handling. There are restrictions on which delete rule can be used with self-referencing tables, cycles, and delete-connected tables through multiple paths. If an attempt is made to define an invalid delete rule for these types of relationships, a negative SQLCODE will be issued. There are two types of SQL data manipulation restrictions that will result in a negative SQLCODE at bind or run time. Most of these restriction are required due to subtle conditions that are best understood through illustrations. Study of the accompanying examples should clarify the potential problems that are avoided by imposing restrictions.

Self-Referencing constraint

A self-referencing table is one that has a foreign key that references the primary key in the same table. In the supplier example, for instance, if each supplier were owned by another, higher-level supplier, those ownerships might be recorded in a new column in the S table. Figure CT.12 shows such a modified S table, S_O table, with the S_OWNER column containing the ownership indications. For example, S2 is owned by S1, S3 by S2, and so on. A nullable foreign key is a good choice for a self-referencing table. Without a nullable foreign key, the fact that S1 has no owner cannot be recorded in a straightforward manner.

Figure CT.12. Self-referencing table

Cascade or No Action

SN	SNAME	STATUS	CITY	S_OWNER
S1	Smith	20	London	null
S2	Jones	10	Paris	S1
S3	Blake	30	Paris	S2
S4	Clark	20	London	S3
S5	Adams	30	Athens	S4

A self-referencing table is useful for a table with information for bill-of-material processing, an organization chart, and budgets allocated by the president of an organization to vice presidents, directors, and managers, for example.

By definition, the foreign key in a self-referencing table must specify the delete rule of NO ACTION or CASCADE. The restrict rule would be of little practical value because its enforcement would be limited to barring deletion of any primary key value that had a dependent foreign key value. This would assure that an existing "ownership" relationship could not be removed from the table, but at the cost of greatly limiting changes to the table. In the example, for instance, only S5 could be deleted because it is the only supplier that does not own another.

The DELETE SET NULL rule is not suitable for a self-referencing constraint because it holds the potential for unpredictable results. For example, this statement would call for deletion of any supplier that does not report to another—in other words, any supplier whose S_OWNER value is null:

```
DELETE FROM S_O WHERE S_OWNER IS NULL;
```

If DELETE SET NULL were in effect, when the SN = S1 row was deleted, S1 in S_OWNER would be set to null. If the rows were processed in order, when the SN = S2 row was deleted, S2 in the S_OWNER column would be set to null. Eventually, all the rows in this table would be deleted—if the rows were processed in order. If the rows were not processed in order or if the values in the S_OWNER column were not in sequence, fewer rows would be deleted.

If the CASCADE rule is used, when any primary key value is deleted, all rows with key values below it in the hierarchy of ownerships are also deleted. If S3 is deleted from the S_O table, for example, the deletions cascade to the SN = S4 row, then to the SN = S5 row. This is the desired result assuming that a decision has been made to stop doing business with S3 and its subsidiaries.

Beware of the CASCADE Rule: Do be cautious when using the CASCADE rule. If the president of an organization is deleted, then all of the employees of the organization will be deleted. The NO ACTION rule can be used where such an accident can occur in order to avoid unintentionally deleting more rows than required.

Cannot Insert Multiple Rows with a Subselect: There must be an existing primary key value for every inserted foreign key value. In the example, an attempt to insert a row with an S_OWNER value of S10 will fail because there is no S10 in the primary key. This problem can surface when a subselect is used to insert values from one table into another self-referencing table. If DB2 detects such a violation during processing, it issues a negative SQLCODE. The rule is that more than one row cannot be inserted into a self-referencing table with a subselect.

A self-referencing constraint must be created with an ALTER TABLE statement. This is because the parent table with the primary key must exist before the related foreign key can be defined. If either the DELETE SET NULL or DELETE RESTRICT rule is specified as the self-referencing constraint, DB2 issues an error message when execution of the ALTER TABLE statement defining the invalid constraint is attempted.

DB2 supports cursor-controlled updates of the primary key and deletions involving self-referencing constraints in version 4 unlike previous versions of DB2. This complies with the SQL standard.

Cycles

A cycle is a situation in which tables are related to each other through both primary and foreign key relationships. In the simplest case, one table is a primary key table to the other; the second table is a primary key table to the first. For example, consider the tables in Figure CT.13. One is a modified J table, or J_S table, that includes a column, SUPERVISOR, showing each job's supervisor. Supervisors are employees of course. The JN column is the primary key. The other table is an employee table, which includes a column, ASSIGNED_JOB, showing the employee's job assignments. The EMPLOYEE column is the primary key. The SUPERVISOR column in the J_S table is defined as a foreign key to the employee table.
ASSIGNED_JOB in the employee table is a foreign key to the J_S table. This is a two-table cycle. Some cycles consist of more than two tables—foreign keys may connect several tables before the loop closes.

Figure CT.13. Relationship with a Cycle

JN	JNAME	CITY	SUPERVISOR
J1	Sorter	Paris	E700
J2	Punch	Rome	E200
J3	Reader	Athens	E500
J4	Console	Athens	E300
J5	Collator	London	E800
J6	Terminal	Oslo	E100
J7	Tape	London	E400

Restrict

~~Cascade~~

EMPLOYEE	...	ASSIGNED_JOB
E100		J6
E200		J2
E300		J4
E400		J7
E500		J3
E600		null
E700		J1
E800		J5

Restrictions: There are restrictions on the type of delete rules that may be used with either two-table or greater than two-table cycles. The CASCADE DELETE rule may not be used in a two-table cycle. In a cycle with more than two tables, at least one of the foreign keys participating in the cycle must employ the RESTRICT or SET NULL rule. DB2 will issue an error message when a CREATE statement with constraint definitions violating these restrictions attempts to execute.

To understand the kind of problem that might occur in cycles, consider what would happen in the example if the foreign key on the SUPERVISOR column were defined with the CASCADE rule and that the ASSIGNED_JOB column were defined with a RESTRICT rule. In that case, every time the row for an employee who is a supervisor is deleted from the EMPLOYEE table, rows in the J_S table showing that employee as a supervisor would also be deleted. Notice what happens when there is an attempt to delete 'E400' from the Employee table. The deletion would cascade to the J7 row in J_S table. That deletion, however, is barred by the restrict rule constraining deletions of JNs that appear in the ASSIGNED_JOB column.

In some cases, even with a valid cycle, some deletions may be impossible. In the example, even if both foreign keys were defined with the restrict rule—a cycle that DB2 would allow—there would be no way to delete most of the rows in both tables. For example, the 'E400' row could not be deleted from the EMPLOYEE table because of the foreign key restriction on the SUPERVISOR column. Neither could the row with 'E400' be deleted from the J_S table because of the ASSIGNED_JOB foreign key's restriction against deleting J7. This kind of difficulty can be avoided in a cycle by defining at least one of the foreign keys with the DELETE SET NULL rule and allowing nulls in the foreign key column.

Delete-Connected Tables

Tables related with a foreign key are called delete connected tables because a deletion in the primary key table can affect or be affected by the contents of the foreign key table. If the delete rule connecting the two tables is cascade, then tables that are delete connected with the foreign key table are also delete-connected on its primary key table. In other words, a table can be delete connected with its grandparent. In Figure CT.14, for example, the J and PJ tables are delete connected by a foreign key on the JN column. Because the JN column's foreign key rule is cascade, the SPJ table, which is delete connected with the PJ table, is also delete connected with the J table.

Figure CT.14. Delete connected tables through multiple paths

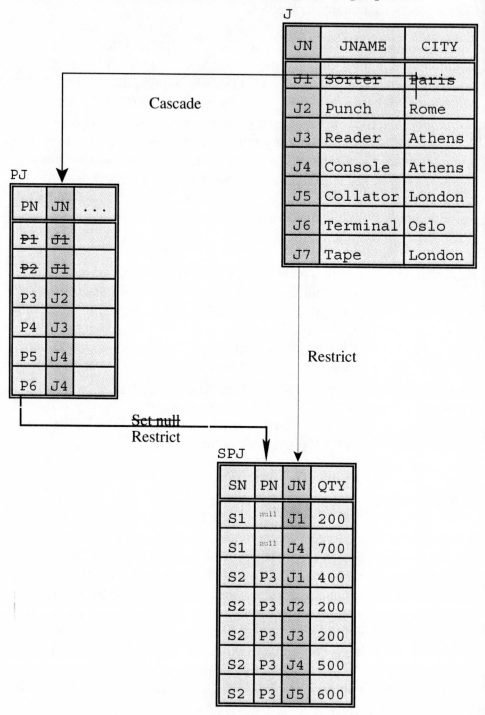

Problems can arise when two tables are delete connected through more than one path. In Figure CT.14, for example, the foreign key relating the J and SPJ tables directly would make those tables delete connected through two paths—the direct connection and the path through the PJ table. Because of the possibility of differing results depending on the order of processing such delete-connected tables through multiple paths, DB2 restricts their definition.

Restrictions: The foreign keys that establish a table's multiple delete connections—in the example, PN and JN in the SPJ table—must all be defined to have the same delete rule, and the rule may not be the SET NULL rule. Both must be defined either by the restrict rule or by the cascade rule. The cascade rule is crossed out in Figure CT.14 to indicate that it is not a valid rule. DB2 will issue an error message whenever a CREATE or ALTER TABLE statement attempts to define keys that violate these restrictions.

Let us look at an example of an inconsistency that can occur if DB2 allowed such multiple path delete connections. If the delete to J1 is first cascaded to PJ, no J1 rows would be deleted. J1 would be deleted if P1 and P2 were not in SPJ. If the delete to J1 is first attempted on SPJ, no J1 rows would be deleted

Invalid Delete with Subselect

When a cascade rule is in effect, DB2 will not allow deletions based on a subselect that references the table from which the deletions are being made. This example illustrates the problem: Consider the two tables in Figure CT.15. One is the familiar S table, with SN as a primary key. The other is the JSUP table, which shows which suppliers supply which jobs. Each job has both a primary and secondary supplier. The PRIMARY_S and SECONDARY_S columns are foreign keys referencing the S table, with both the RI rules specified as delete cascade.

Figure CT.15. Invalid subselect delete

SN	SNAME	STATUS	CITY	S_OWNER
S1	Smith	20	London	null
S2	Jones	10	Paris	S1
S3	Blake	30	Paris	S2

▼ Cascade   ▼ Cascade

JN	PRIMARY_S	SECONDARY_S
J1	S1	S2
J2	S1	S2
J3	S2	S3

The following subselect might be used to delete from the S table all
suppliers who are not used as secondary suppliers on any job.

```
DELETE FROM S SX WHERE SN NOT IN
   (SELECT  SECONDARY_S
    FROM    JSUP
    WHERE   JSUP.SECONDARY_S = SX.SN);
```

The results of this statement, however, will be different depending on the
order in which the rows are processed. If SN = S1 is evaluated in the
subselect first, the NOT IN clause evaluates as true because S1 is not a
secondary supplier. Therefore, S1 is deleted from the S table. Since it is a
primary key value, and the cascade rule is in effect, the S1 rows in JSUP are
also deleted. When SN = S2 is evaluated in the subselect, the NOT IN
clause also returns true, since the previous cascade delete had eliminated the
two jobs in which S2 had been the secondary supplier. S2, therefore, is also
deleted and its deletion cascades to eliminate the J3 row. Now, when SN =

S3 is evaluated in the subselect, the NOT IN clause returns true and S3 is deleted.

Suppose, however, that S3 is the first value from the S table to be evaluated in the subselect. In that case, the NOT IN clause would return false because, at this point in the processing, the J3 row still exists, with S3 as its secondary supplier, and the S3 row will not be deleted. To avoid this kind of anomaly, at bind time, when DB2 encounters a DELETE statement containing this type of subselect combined with a cascade delete rule, instead of binding the statement it issues an error message.

CT.5 DB2 VERSUS APPLICATION ENFORCED INTEGRITY

The advantages of defining RI to DB2 are similar to those of defining table check constraints to DB2. Developers can be relieved of the time and effort to develop, test, and maintain their programs to enforce the constraints. In addition, the SQL that appears to be best for enforcing the RI constraints in applications can result in errors.

SQL Insert that Can Violate RI

The following SQL statements appear to be a reasonable approach to inserting a row with a SN foreign key value of S11 into the SPJ dependent table if there is a matching primary key in the S table.

```
SELECT SN
FROM    S
WHERE   SN = 'S11';

IF SQLCODE = 0
   INSERT INTO SPJ (SN, PN, JN, QTY)
   VALUES ('S11', 'P1', 'J2', 200);
```

The problem is that the S11 can be deleted after the SELECT statement is executed, with a 0 SQLCODE and before the INSERT statement is executed, resulting in an S11 row in the dependent table without a matching S11 in the parent table. There are techniques that can be used to hold a lock on the S11 row in the parent table until the dependent row has been successfully inserted and committed as discussed in Chapter CC. However, a new developer may not be aware that an apparently simple technique can result in violating RI.

SQL Update that Can Violate RI

Another situation is even more subtle and the possibility of an error cannot be avoided with locking techniques. The goal is to update a foreign key value of S2 to S10 in the SPJ table provided there is a matching primary value of S10 in the parent table. The following UPDATE statement with an EXISTS subselect is a possible approach but can result in violating RI.

```
UPDATE SPJ SET SN = 'S10'
   WHERE SN = 'S2' AND EXISTS
   (SELECT SN FROM S WHERE SN = 'S10');
```

An EXISTS subselect returns a true or false to the UPDATE statement as discussed in Chapters SL and ST and locks are released. If a true is returned, the update of SPJ will be successful. The problem is that someone can delete S10 from the parent table after the true condition is determined from the EXISTS subselect and before the update is complete. This will result in S10 being an orphan in the SPJ dependent table. Again, there is the potential for violating RI when using application enforcement of constraints. Indeed, there are few foolproof techniques for implementing RI in application programs without the possibility of introducing erroneous data as discussed in the IBM manual, *DB2 Referential Integrity Usage Guide* (GG24-3312).

Performance of DB2 Enforced and Application Enforced Constraints

The performance considerations for DB2 enforcing RI constraints and table check constraints are similar. Both types of constraints are recorded in the Database Descriptor (DBD). DM checks the constraints in central storage as recorded in the DBD. (The DBD is held in the environmental descriptor (EDM) pool in central storage.) This avoids having a host program execute SQL statements to enforce RI. In the case of check table constraints that are defined with an IN list, SELECTS from a reference table are also avoided.

No code is added to the plan or package for RI and table check constraints when they are defined to DB2. SQL statements need not be executed in application programs to enforce the constraints. SQL statements require execution of code to go through the Application Program Interface (API), RDS, DM, buffer manager, Internal Resource Lock Manager (IRLM) or lock avoidance and back through the layers of code to return the SQLCODE to the host program. Significantly fewer instruction must be executed by DM to check the constraints found in the DBD.

The trade-off is that the DBD will be larger and may require a larger EDM pool. There is always concern about the DBD size because the DBD must be in contiguous space in the EDM pool as discussed in Chapter CD. On the other hand, there may be a savings of space in the EDM pool. It depends on the number of bytes required to store the constraint definitions in the DBD compared to the number of bytes saved in the plan or package as a result of having fewer SQL statements. It is possible that the decreased size of the plan or package will offset the increased size of the DBD in the EDM pool. If more space is required in the EDM pool for a larger DBD, trading more storage for reduced number of instructions that must be executed and reduced number of I/O is usually a very positive trade-off. Very large DB2 installations do need to be concerned with a shortage of space within the 2 GB current architectural limit. The 2 GB limit is due to the 31 bits used for addressability (2 gigabytes = 2^{31} = 2,147,483,648). zSeries computers with z/OS brings 64 bit addressability minus 1 for a parity bit allows for 9 exabytes (9 exabytes= 2^{63} = 9,223,372,036,854,779,000).

The performance trade-offs of having DB2 enforce table check conditions with =, <, <=, >, >=, BETWEEN, IN, LIKE, and NULL comparisons versus having the host program check the condition before attempting to insert or update a row may not be positive. If the host program discovers that the row should not be inserted or updated, the INSERT or UPDATE statement will not be executed at all. Certainly, there is a savings if one can avoid executing a statement.

DB2 verifies that data manipulation adheres to all applicable RI rules as the processing occurs. This is called inflight verification. As processing changes a row's values, DB2 checks for RI violations and takes the specified action if it discovers any. If a restrict rule is in effect, for example, processing stops when a violation occurs. This inflight checking provides improved performance compared with checking in advance or with allowing processing to continue to a commit work point and then rolling back the processing if a violation had occurred. The NO ACTION rule causes enforcement to occur at end of statement processing when deleting more than one row in a self-referencing table.

RI processing does require resources, however, which the installation must take into account. For example, if DB2 were enforcing a restrict rule on the JN foreign key, when a user attempted to delete J2, DB2 would have to first search for J2 in the SPJ table, taking the necessary concurrency control locks, performing the I/O operations, and so on. This processing can be very intensive if the number of changes of key values is high.

In most cases, DB2 integrity enforcement is more efficient than those done by an application. When DB2 enforces the rules, its checking always uses an available index on a primary or foreign key column, whereas for an application's checking, depending on how the checking is coded, the optimizer may not employ an index.

Application Enforced Integrity

There are some situations in which application enforced integrity might make sense. For example, DB2's rules may not match an organization's policy for using the data in question. In some cases, the organization might rather have a primary key update cascade to the foreign key rather than having DB2 bar the change with its implicit restrict rule. Such a cascade is permitted by the relational model.

The application design may be such that referential integrity cannot be violated in most cases. It may be that the PK and FK rows are always inserted, updated, and deleted within the same unit of recovery by an application program. Caution should be exercised in making the decision to use application enforced RI. Although it appears that all cases are covered in programs, they may not be. As additional programs are added to the application system or modifications are made to existing programs, the constraints may not be checked correctly.

RI enforcement by DB2 can add to the costs of INSERTING or updating a large number of rows by a batch program. For example, consider a situation in which there is a foreign key on the SN column of the SPJ table that references the SN in the S table. Suppose that the batch program must insert 100,000 rows into the SPJ table, with each new row indicating the receipt of a part from supplier S1. Before allowing insertion of each new row, DB2 would have to check to see that S1 exists in the S table. The person who writes the program knows, however, that the check can be made only once for the entire batch. It is necessary to hold a lock on S1 in the parent table while INSERTING rows into the dependent table to avoid the parent row being deleted during the inserts.

DB2 does not allow exceptions to integrity rules once they have been defined. In the above example, for instance, the developer may want to have DB2 enforce the rule on the SN foreign key at all times except during batch insertions. The LOAD utility, described in Chapter LC, provides a means for shutting off constraint checking during batch insertions. For batch updates, the only way to shut off that enforcement would be to use an ALTER statement to drop the key from the SPJ table. After the batch update, the key could be added again. In both cases, however, check pending is turned on. Techniques for turning off check pending are discussed in Chapter LC. In addition, there are performance advantages to having a program delete rows from a dependent table before deleting the rows from the parent table.

Checking for Constraint Violations

If DB2 is not used to validate data according to defined table check and RI constraints, SQL statements can be developed and executed to do this. This can be resource intensive, particularly for determining if there are any RI violations. All foreign key values in the JN column of the SPJ table that are not in the primary key JN column of the J table can be identified with either of the following statements.

```
SELECT SN, PN, JN, QTY
FROM    SPJ
WHERE   NOT EXISTS
   (SELECT 1
    FROM    J
    WHERE   J.JN = SPJ.JN);
```

Execution of a NOT EXISTS subselect for each of multiple dependent tables can be resource intensive. If RI is defined to DB2, the CHECK DATA utility can be used to validate the data. This utility will optionally delete violating rows and write an image of the rows to an exception table without logging. Using the utility to check for violations of RI and table check constraints has performance advantages.

Even if DB2 is not used to enforce RI, costs can be reduced compared to executing multiple NOT EXISTS subselects by adding RI constraints with the ALTER statement and executing the CHECK DATA utility. After executing the utility, the ALTER statement can be used to remove the constraints when using application enforced RI.

LOAD with ENFORCE CONSTRAINTS applies to RI and table check constraints. If a row violates a constraint, it will be written to a discard data set by default. This provides for some validation of the data by LOAD and minimizes the need to insert rows with a batch host program if the target tablespace or partition can be made unavailable during a load or load resume.

Another advantage of having DB2 enforce constraints is that the constraints are well documented in the catalog tables. Although application enforced constraints may be well documented initially, additional programs that are written over the years and modifications to existing programs are not always documented. Chapter PD contains SELECT statements from the catalog tables to obtain information about RI and table check constraints defined to DB2 and how the information can be used for error management.

CT.6 VIEWS

The name *view* well describes its object's function: to provide particular views of base tables. Views are virtual tables, made up of columns and rows from base tables and other views, but their data are not stored separately. Instead the developer defines a view in terms of a SELECT statement. DB2 records the defining statement in catalog tables SYSIBM.SYSVTREE and SYSIBM.SYSVLTREE, and resolves it into base table references when an SQL statement using the view is bound. The process is transparent to users, who perceive and deal with views as if they were base tables in most cases.

Views are useful in providing access and update security. Rather than allowing users access to all rows and columns in a base table, developers can grant the use of views that show only columns and rows approved for the users. Views provide for ease of use and have performance advantages without increasing the costs of executing SQL statements significantly.

Security and Views

It is common practice at a company that managers are allowed to see information about employees in their department and no others. Here is an example of how views can be used to enforce such a policy. A MGR_PRIVILEGES table can be created containing the manager's AUTHID in the column USER_ID and the manager's employee number in the column MGRNO like:

```
CREATE TABLE MGR_PRIVILEGES
   (USER_ID CHAR(8) NOT NULL,
    MGRNO   CHAR(8) NOT NULL,
CONSTRAINT USER_PK PRIMARY KEY (USER_ID));
```

Some examples use the EMP (employee) and DEPT (department) tables to make the examples more intuitive. These tables are described in the *Application Programming and SQL Guide* manual. The following MGR_EMP view definition allows managers to see only employees in their departments.

```
CREATE VIEW MGR_EMP AS
   SELECT EMPNO, FIRSTNME, MIDINIT
      WORKDEPT, PHONENO, HIREDATE, JOB,
      EDLEVEL, SEX, BIRTHDATE, SALARY,
      BONUS, COMM
   FROM  EMP, DEPT, MGR_PRIVILEGES
   WHERE MGR_PRIVILEGES.USER_ID =
            USER  -- special register
   AND   MGR_PRIVILEGES.MGRNO  = DEPT.MGRNO
   AND   EMP.WORKDEPT          = DEPT.DEPTNO;
```

Access to the view can be granted to the public while allowing a manager to see only employees in his or her department. USER is a special register that contains the AUTHID of the person using the view. DB2 locates the AUTHID in the MGR_PRIVILEGES table and determines the MGRNO. The MGRNO in turn is used to locate employees who have a manager with the value in the DEPT table by setting the column MGR_PRIVILEGES.MGRNO equal to DEPT.MGRNO in a join. This join processing disallows updates of the view as will be seen shortly. If managers need to update employee rows, a separate view must be created for each manager and privileges granted to each manager to update the view.

Ease of Use and Performance

Views are useful for providing casual users and programmers easy and efficient access to data from several base tables. Managers need not be aware that three tables are accessed to provide the required information about employees in their departments. They simply select from the MGR_EMP view. The manager may need to look at the net salary of employees frequently but does not want to be bothered with keying the calculation of gross salary minus the various deductions. This can also be error prone. A person may forget to subtract some of the deductions on occasion which will give incorrect gross salaries. The term *derived* column is sometimes used to describe the gross salary as calculated in a view definition.

Naming standards frequently result in table and column names that are difficult to remember and are not what the business professional uses when referencing an object. A view can be created that uses the terms that are used by business professionals.

Users are concerned with business processes and cannot be expected to know how to write complex SQL statements and formulate statements that perform well. Developers can create a view of complex operations that do perform well for users.

You can define a view with UNION and UNION ALL in V7. Do not use UNION ALL if duplicate rows can qualify unless the duplicates are acceptable. There is a good deal of flexibility in selecting from a view defined with UNION and UNION ALL. The view can be referenced anywhere that a subselect can be used including within a subselect, in predicates, nested table expression, declare global temporary table, INSERT INTO ... (subselect), and UPDATE ... SET COLUMN1 = (subselect).

It is not possible to insert, update, and delete rows from a view that has UNION or UNION ALL in its definition. Developers usually manipulate multiple tables in programs and are quit capable of can inserting, updating, and deleting rows from multiple tables based on the defined criteria. Both business professionals and developers have the convenience of selecting from view with UNION ALL.

Resolution of Views

The results of a select from a view are not written to a work area in most cases. Rather the optimizer transforms the select from the view to a select from the underlying base tables and determines a good access path for the transformed statement. A manager may want to review the record of all employees in his/her department that were hired before January 1, 1983, and keys the statement:

```
SELECT EMPNO, FIRSTNME, MIDINIT
   WORKDEPT, PHONENO, HIREDATE, JOB,
   EDLEVEL, SEX, BIRTHDATE, SALARY,
   BONUS, COMM
FROM  MGR_EMP
WHERE HIREDATE < '1983-01-01';
```

The transformed statement will look like:

```
SELECT EMPNO, FIRSTNME, MIDINIT
   WORKDEPT, PHONENO, HIREDATE, JOB,
   EDLEVEL, SEX, BIRTHDATE, SALARY,
   BONUS, COMM
FROM  EMP, DEPT, MGR_PRIVILEGES
WHERE MGR_PRIVILEGES.USER_ID= USER
AND   MGR_PRIVILEGES.MGRNO  = DEPT.MGRNO
AND   EMP.WORKDEPT          = DEPT.DEPTNO
AND   HIREDATE < '1983-01-01';
```

Notice that the transformed SELECT statement is the same as the SELECT statement used to define the view with the additional predicate of HIREDATE < '1983-01-01' specified by the manager. Basically the SELECT statement that defines the view is merged with the SELECT from the view.

Cost of Views

In most cases, views cost only a few milliseconds of CPU time when DB2 binds the SQL, a one-time cost for static SQL. For dynamic SQL, using QMF for example, that CPU cost is paid each time a view is used. There are some cases where the use of views can detract from performance.

View Materialization: There are some cases where the rows that qualify according to the SELECT statement that defines the view must be written to a work file. For example, if the SELECT statement has a GROUP BY with a column function, the result of the GROUP BY and column function is written to a work file before the processing is done for the select from the view. This is an example of view materialization that is discussed in Chapter ST.

Retrieving Columns from One Table in a View Join: If a view definition involves a join, you should not select from only one of the tables. Consider the following view involving a join:

```
CREATE VIEW S_SPJ AS
  (SELECT SN, SNAME, STATUS, CITY, QTY
   FROM    S, SPJ
   WHERE   S.SN = SPJ.SN);
```

Here is a select of columns from the S table which is one of the two tables referenced in the view:

```
SELECT SNAME, STATUS, CITY
FROM    S_SPJ;
```

Join processing is done even though only columns from the S table are selected. This is necessary to return the correct results according to the view definition because the view qualifies only suppliers which have parts in the SPJ table. However, the person who SELECTS from the view may not realize that he or she is not seeing all of the suppliers in the S table. In addition, performance will be adversely affected by having to do join processing when only columns from one table are required. It is important to understand the view definition before selecting from a view.

An alternative to minimize the possibility of someone selecting from only one table based on a view of multiple tables is to use a view naming convention with the number of tables referenced in the view as part of the view name. For example, the view name S_SPJ_2 indicates that two tables are referenced in the view definition.

View Restrictions

The developer may use almost any SELECT statement in a view definition. However, DB2 does not allow creation of views with statements including

ORDER BY, UNION ALL, or UNION (the last two operations are allowed in V7). And it does not create a view from a statement including a FOR UPDATE OF clause, a clause used in embedded SQL that indicates the selected data is to be updated.

Updatability of Views: DB2 also does not update certain other views. For example, it makes no sense to update views that include column functions (AVG, SUM, COUNT, MIN, and MAX) because DB2 has no way of knowing what values to assign to the base tables. For example, if the average QTY is increased by 100, should DB2 increase each value by 100? Trying to update views that contain column functions would entail ambiguities and logical inconsistencies between the views and base tables. A view with a scalar function (such as date/time and string functions) in the SELECT clause cannot be updated. DB2 issues an error message when a program or user tries to update a view containing any of the column and scalar functions.

A view definition that contains a GROUP BY or DISTINCT cannot be updated because it can require a sort. If the rows are sorted into a work file, the rows in the base table can change after a copy of the sorted rows are written to the work file. In addition, a view definition of a calculated value or constant cannot be updated although a row can be inserted into such a view.

Nor does DB2 update views created with joins prior to V7. In other words, DB2 does not update a view when it finds more than one table listed in the CREATE VIEW statement's FROM clause. But developers may use subselects to create undatable views from multiple tables. In some cases, DB2 will update a view drawn from multiple tables with a subselect when it will not update the equivalent view created with a join. In recasting a join statement as a subselect, the developer should take care that the statements are, in fact, equivalent and care should be taken that the reformulated statement will perform well. The SELECT and subselect cannot contain same table name.

A read-only view cannot be the object of an INSERT, UPDATE, or DELETE statement.

WITH CHECK OPTION Parameter

The WITH CHECK OPTION parameter is required to avoid an insert or update of a row using a view such that the row is not visible when a select is issued using the view. For example, this view definition allows a user to see only suppliers in London:

```
CREATE VIEW LONDON_S AS
   SELECT SN, SNAME, STATUS, CITY
   FROM   S
   WHERE  CITY = 'London';
```

A user can insert a row using the view for a supplier in Athens with the statement:

```
INSERT INTO LONDON_S VALUES
   ('S20','Thomas',50,'Athens');
```

A user can also update a row that he or she can see through the view even though he or she will not be able to see the row after it is updated like:

```
UPDATE LONDON_S
   SET   CITY = 'Athens'
   WHERE CITY = 'London';
```

The WITH CHECK OPTION parameter must be added to the end of a CREATE VIEW statement to avoid a user being able to insert or update a row such that the row is not visible when selecting from the view. In any case, a user cannot delete and select a row that does not qualify according to the view.

Views created on views including a check option are also checked according to the specified criteria by default. The default parameter is CASCADE. The default can be over-ridden by specifying the LOCAL parameter which means that the WITH CHECK OPTION applies only to the view created with the option and does not apply to views referencing the view created using the WITH CHECK OPTION.

There is a performance concern regarding the WITH CHECK OPTION. An index on columns specified in predicates will not be used to locate a row to be updated unless list prefetch is chosen to access the data pages.

The WITH CHECK OPTION has been used to provide some data validation in releases of DB2 prior to the availability of table check constraints discussed in Section CT.2 of this chapter. The table check constraints and triggers are better suited for validating the data.

Privileges to Create a View

A person needs no special privilege to create a view. The creator of the view will have the same privileges on the view as on the underlying base tables and can grant privileges to others.

Database administration (DBADM) authority allows the person holding the privilege to perform most operations on most objects in a database for which the authority is held. Views are an exception. DBADM of a database which contains tables referenced by a view created by someone else does not have privileges on the view. This prevents a person with DBADM privileges from having access to a table in another database owned by another person. For example, if this restriction did not apply, a person could create a view referencing two tables from two different databases. If the person with DBADM privileges on one database could select from the view, he or she would be able to see information from a table in another database that is not covered by the DBADM authority. There is an exception. A person with DBADM privileges can create a view on tables within their database and manipulate the view provided that it is allowed on installation panel DSNTIPP (V7).

System administration (SYSADM) authority is required to create a view for an AUTHID that is not one of DBADMs composite privileges on tables in various databases.

Levels of Views

Developers can create views on other views and on combinations of views to any number of levels as long as the view references no more than 225 base tables directly or indirectly. As shown in Figure CT.16, for example, VIEW I can be created over some columns and rows in TABLE A; VIEW II can be created on TABLE A and TABLE B; VIEW III can be created on VIEW I and VIEW II; and so on. While this offers a great deal of flexibility, it can also create a great deal of confusion if levels are too deep. The higher-level views depend on those at the lower levels. If a lower-level view or table is dropped, higher-level views depending on it will also be dropped automatically and without a warning. In Figure CT.16, for example, if VIEW I is dropped, VIEW III and VIEW IV are dropped. If TABLE A is dropped, all of the views are dropped.

Figure CT.16. Levels of views

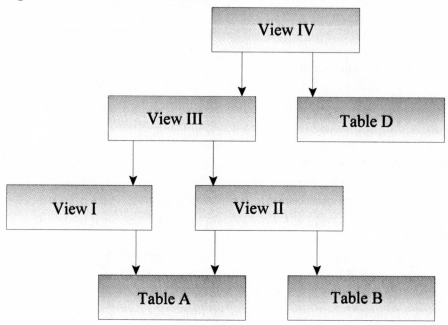

Table Restructuring

Views provide for a layer of data independence when tables must be restructured. Assume that a number of programs have been developed referencing the P table in Figure CT.9. It has been decided to build new automated warehouses and it is necessary to add a new column to the P table containing the size of each part in cubic feet so that robots can move the parts from one bin to another. It is also necessary to create a warehouse table to account for several warehouses in different cities. The CITY column will be removed from the P table and placed in the WAREHOUSE table along with the PN. The P table can be unloaded, dropped, and recreated with the name of P_NEW without the CITY column. A view with the name of the original P table can be created that also references the new WAREHOUSE and P_NEW tables like:

```
CREATE VIEW P AS
    SELECT PN, PNAME, COLOR, WEIGHT, CITY
```

```
FROM    P_NEW, WAREHOUSE
WHERE   P_NEW.PN = WAREHOUSE.PN;
```

Programs that select from the original P table will not need to be revised. This is because the view identifies the same information as the original P table. SQL statements will be automatically rebound when they are next executed after the drop of the original P table or can be explicitly rebound during non-prime time. Notice, however, that the FROM clause includes two tables. DB2 will not update the view, so applications performing updates on the original view will not work with this one.

Views Not Theoretically Undatable

Not all views are undatable in theory. C. J. Date provides an example of a view that utilizes the tables in Figure CT.9 that is not theoretically undatable in his book *An Introduction to Database Systems.*

Consider the view created by this statement:

```
CREATE VIEW CITY_PAIRS (S_CITY, P_CITY) AS
   SELECT S.CITY, P.CITY
   FROM    P, S, SPJ
   WHERE   P.PN   = SPJ.PN
   AND     SPJ.SN = S.SN;
```

This view contains city pairings, each showing a city where a part supplier is located, taken from table S, and a city where the user organization stores the part, taken from table P. P1, for example, is kept in London. It is supplied by S1, also located in London. The row in the CITY_PAIRS table is London-London. P1 is also supplied by S5 in Athens, creating an Athens-London pair. Here is the complete view:

S_CITY	P_CITY
London	London
Paris	Rome
Paris	Paris
Paris	London

S_CITY	P_CITY
London	Paris
Athens	Paris
Athens	London
Athens	Rome

The view is not undatable because the view definition requires a join of the S, P, and SPJ tables. Indeed, this view is not theoretically undatable because it cannot be determined which rows in the underlying base tables should be updated. Some examples will demonstrate the point. Consider this UPDATE statement:

```
UPDATE CITY_PAIRS
   SET   S_CITY = 'Dallas',
         P_CITY = 'New York'
   WHERE S_CITY = 'Paris'
   AND   P_CITY = 'London';
```

Which city should be updated in the S table? Which in the P table? The obvious ambiguity makes the attempted update meaningless. A similar problem occurs with this DELETE statement:

```
DELETE FROM CITY_PAIRS
   WHERE S_CITY = 'London'
   AND   P_CITY = 'Rome';
```

Are all London suppliers and Rome parts to be deleted from the base tables S and P? And consider this INSERT:

```
INSERT INTO CITY_PAIRS
   VALUES ('Dallas','New York');
```

Are NULLS to be inserted in all columns except CITY in the base tables? The INSERT, if allowed, would not provide for a primary key value in the S and P tables.

Whether a view involving a join is undatable is not always obvious. Indeed, the question of theoretically undatable views is a fertile one for researchers. Some views of joins that DB2 does not currently update, however, are theoretically undatable, particularly those joined on the primary and foreign keys. DB2 may provide the ability to update those views in a future release. E. F. Codd discusses view updateability indepth in his book *The Relational Model for Database Management Version 2*.

CT.7 SYNONYMS, ALIASES, AND QUALIFIERS

Synonyms and aliases are useful for creating a more meaningful name for use by a person using a table or view. They are sometimes used by developers to manage the leading qualifier of a table or view. Test and production tables frequently have the same table name with a different qualifier for each set of tables. Developers need to test their programs using the test tables and have a straightforward method for referencing the production tables after their programs are tested successfully. For example, a developer needs to select and update from the TEST.SPJ table in a program that is being developed in a test environment. It is known that when the program is migrated to the production environment, the table will have a different qualifier, such as PROD.SPJ. Developers do not want to reference TEST.SPJ in all FROM clauses because it would be necessary to change the program to reference PROD.SPJ when the program is moved to production.

Use of Synonyms

Synonyms were one of the few methods available for managing references to test and production tables in early releases of DB2. The developer can create a synonym like:

```
CREATE SYNONYM SPJ FOR TEST.SPJ;
```

This allows the developer to simply reference SPJ in all FROM clauses. Then after the move of the program to a production DB2 subsystem, a synonym is created to point to the production table:

```
CREATE SYNONYM SPJ FOR PROD.SPJ;
```

This seems like a straightforward procedure but there are some complicating factors that revolve around the fact that a synonym is specific to the AUTHID that created it. The consequences are that when a table or view is dropped directly or indirectly by dropping a tablespace or database, the synonym is also dropped. It is not uncommon in a development environment to drop and recreate objects. After this occurred, a program that was working fine will no longer execute until the referenced synonym is recreated. Typically a number of developers are writing programs that reference a table. Each developer or a person with the appropriate authority must set his or her current SQLID to that of the developer and recreate the synonym for that developer. This has proven to be quite cumbersome for a number of companies.

Use of an Alias

An alternative to the use of a synonym is to use an alias which is not specific to an AUTHID like synonyms. Aliases are designed for a client/server environment using DRDA (V6) and the private protocol to avoid having to reference the location qualifier of a table or view. They can be used in a local environment as well with or without specifying the location like:

```
CREATE ALIAS SPJ FOR DALLAS.TEST.SPJ
```

The advantage is that the alias is not dropped when the table is dropped. Indeed, the table does not need to exist when the alias is created.

The procedures using synonyms and alias cannot be used in a sysplex data sharing environment because the catalog tables are shared across multiple DB2 subsystem. The procedures require creating two synonyms or aliases with the same name. Creation of the second synonym or alias will fail as being a duplicate of the first in a data sharing environment.

Use of a Qualifier

Another alternative for referencing test tables in test and production tables in production from the same program, perhaps the best of the three, is the use of a qualifier and secondary AUTHIDs. Each person can be assigned up to 245 secondary AUTHIDs and each person on a project team can be assigned the same secondary AUTHID. For example, each person working on the TEST.SPJ table can be assigned the secondary AUTHID of TEST. This allows the developer to set his or her ID to TEST and issue any SQL statement interactively without having to specify the qualifier of TEST. Also, when the developer binds SQL statements into a plan or package, the qualifier parameter can be specified as QUALIFIER(TEST) which causes all unqualified table names to be qualified with TEST. Then the migration to production requires only that the bind statement specify QUALIFIER(PROD). Indeed, the value specified as the qualifier does not have to be a secondary AUTHID. However, secondary AUTHIDs do provide for avoiding qualifying interactive SQL and allows for granting of privileges to a single ID shared by a number of developers.

Synonym, alias, and secondary AUTHID are *not* part of SQL. This means that another technique will be required if the programs are used on a DBMS which does not support these features. The use of an alias is supported by IBM family of relational DBMSs.

CT.8 DROPPING OBJECTS

We have discussed creating objects in the order that they must be created in Chapters CD and TS. A database must be created before a tablespace; a tablespace must be created before a table; a table must be created before creating synonyms, views, and indexes as shown in Figure CT.17.

Figure CT.17. Sequence of creating objects

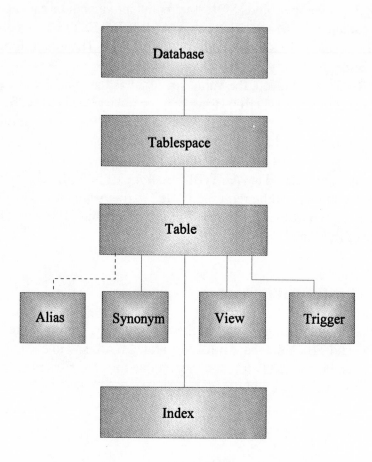

Each object can be dropped with the DROP statement by specifying the type of object and the object name, for example:

```
DROP DATABASE    Name_of_Database;
DROP TABLESPACE  Name_of_Tablespace;
DROP TABLE       Name_of_Table;
DROP SYNONYM     Name_of_Synonym;
DROP ALIAS       Name_of_Alias;
DROP VIEW        Name_of_View;
DROP INDEX       Name_of_Index;
```

Dependent Objects

Dropping an object causes all dependent objects to be dropped. For example, if you drop, a database all objects in the database are dropped and all privileges on the objects are revoked. If you drop an object further down in the hierarchy of objects, the lower objects are dropped. For example, if you drop a table, the synonyms, aliases, views, indexes, and triggers (Chapter TR) on a table are dropped and privileges are revoked. If the data is to be retained, do unload the data before performing a drop that will drop the table.

Recommendation: If the objects are to be recreated, save the CREATE statements in a file, develop CREATE statements based on SELECTS from catalog tables before dropping objects, or use a software product to generate CREATE statements from the catalog tables before dropping the objects.

CT.9 SUMMARY

DB2 offers developers considerable flexibility in designing tables and using views. A number of data types are available to choose from including data types for date and time periods. Also, the ROWID data type can be used to locate a row without index usage or a tablespace scan. This can prove useful in locating a row a second time efficiently after retrieving the row ID value using an index or tablespace scan.

There are a number of options for dealing with unknown or inapplicable values for a row. Not null with default or defining default values avoids complexities of managing nulls. There are advantages in saving development time and costs by defining business rules with the check table constraints and RI constraints. Constraints can be changed as required without modifying programs and the constraints are enforced uniformly regardless of the method used to change rows. There are performance trade-offs that must be considered in defining constraints and the design of tables in general.

RI requires that every foreign key value, other than null, have a corresponding primary key value. If changes to the data were allowed to violate that rule, the tables would likely contain errors after inserting, updating, and deleting rows. Several rules governing data changes will protect against RI violations. Developers define the rules to DB2 when tables are created and can subsequently change the rules with the alter statement. DB2 then enforces the rule whenever changes that affect the key are attempted. Developers should know how to implement all integrity rules and how to use DB2's RI facilities. They should also be aware of limitations on certain data manipulations imposed by DB2's implementation of integrity rules that ensure predictable and repeatable results.

EXERCISES

1. Develop a CREATE statement for an employee table named EMP in the database DAYOURDB and tablespace EMPTSP with the following column names. Specify NOT NULL for the EMPNO, have blank as the default for MIDINIT, and NOT NULL WITH DEFAULT for all of the other columns.

Column name	Data type and length
EMPNO	6 bytes of character data
FIRSTNME	1 to 12 bytes of character data
MIDINIT	1 byte of character data
LASTNAME	1 to 15 bytes of character data
WORKDEPT	3 bytes of character data
PHONENO	4 bytes of character data
HIREDATE	Date data type
JOB	8 bytes of character data
EDLEVEL	Numeric values < 32 K
SEX	1 byte of character data
BIRTHDATE	Date data type
SALARY places	Packed decimal 9 with 2 decimal
BONUS places	Packed decimal 9 with 2 decimal
COMM places	Packed decimal 9 with 2 decimal

2. What is the fully qualified name of the table created in the first exercise?

3. Is VARCHAR(12) for FIRSTNME and VARCHAR(15) for LASTNAME a good choice? Why?

4. The SQL statement SELECT AVG(SALARY) FROM EMP yields incorrect results. What could be the problem and how can the problem to avoided?

5. a) Write a column definition clause to be included in a CREATE TABLE EMP statement such that when the user does not specify a WORKDEPT for

an employee, the value of 'UNK' will be placed in the column.

b) Write a column definition clause such that when a row is inserted into the EMP table, the HIREDATE will be recorded automatically.

c) Write a column definition clause such that a row cannot be inserted into a table unless the EDLEVEL is greater than 12.

6. Create a distinct type of Fahrenheit and one for centigrade. Use the built in data type of integer.

7. Will the following statement execute successfully? Why?

→   Assume that the WEATHER table has a TEMP_F column defined with the distinct type of Fahrenheit and a TEMP_C column with a distinct type of centigrade.

```
SELECT TEMP_F, TEMP_C
FROM    WEATHER
WHERE   TEMP_F > TEMP_C
AND     DATE_W = '2000-01-17';
```

8. Will the following statement execute successfully?

```
SELECT TEMP_F, TEMP_C
FROM    WEATHER
WHERE   INTEGER(TEMP_F) > 70
AND     DATE_W = '2000-01-17';
```

9. Will the following statement execute successfully? Why?

```
SELECT CAST(TEMP_F AS CENTIGRADE) + TEMP_C
FROM    WEATHER
WHERE   CAST(TEMP_F AS CENTIGRADE) > TEMP_C
AND     DATE_W = '2000-01-17';
```

10. If the following DROP statement fails, what might you consider investigating?

```
DROP DISTINCT TYPE FAHRENHEIT RESTRICT;
```

11. Write an ALTER statement to avoid someone accidentally dropping the

EMP table.

12. Will AUDIT and/or DATA CAPTURE write information so that a report of the before and after image of inserted, updated, and deleted rows can be generated?

13. Write a statement to create a BOARD_MEMBER table in the DABMDB database and DABMTSP tablespace with the same definition as the EMP table.

14. What is the primary goal of RI?

15. a) Why is it advisable to define a primary key even if there are no foreign keys in a dependent table referencing the parent table?

b) What are the costs associated with doing this?

16. A table, ORDERS, storing information on orders placed by customers, has the CUSTNO column as a foreign key to the CUSTOMER table. What delete constraint is appropriate?

17. A table, DEPENDENTS, storing information on employees' dependents, has the EMPNO column as a foreign key to the EMPLOYEE table. What delete constraint is appropriate for handling cases when employees leave the company?

18. A table, SUPERVISORS, containing information on which employees are assigned to supervise which jobs, has a foreign key to the employee table. What delete constraint is appropriate for handling cases when employees assigned as supervisors leave the company?

19. Are there any restrictions on the insertion of a foreign key row?

20. Are there any restrictions on the update of a foreign key value?

21. Are there any restrictions on the insertion of a primary key row?

22. Are there any restrictions on the deletion of a foreign key row?

23. What are some advantages of defining RI constraints to DB2?

24. What are some advantages of enforcing RI constraints in application programs?

25. Create a view named WORKDEPT such that the manager of the DBA (department) can see only the employees in the DBA department. Assume that the manager can update information about the employees in the DBA WORKDEPT. Are there any special considerations that apply to the view definition?

26. What are some uses of views?

27. Should the WITH CHECK OPTION be used in the definition of a view where users only select data and do not insert rows and update rows?

28. What functions cannot be specified in the SELECT statement that defines a view?

29. If users are to insert, update, and delete rows, what functions cannot be specified in the view definition?

30. What are the advantages of using the QUALIFIER parameter to specify the qualifier of tables and views when doing a bind and rebind of plans and packages compared to using synonyms and aliases?

ANSWERS

1. Here is a CREATE TABLE statement for the EMP table.

```
CREATE TABLE EMP
  (EMPNO      CHAR(6)        NOT NULL,
   FIRSTNME   VARCHAR(12)    NOT NULL WITH DEFAULT,
   MIDINIT    CHAR(1)        WITH DEFAULT ' ',
   LASTNAME   VARCHAR(15)    NOT NULL WITH DEFAULT,
   WORKDEPT   CHAR(3)        NOT NULL WITH DEFAULT,
   PHONENO    CHAR(4)        NOT NULL WITH DEFAULT,
   HIREDATE   DATE           NOT NULL WITH DEFAULT,
   JOB        CHAR(8)        NOT NULL WITH DEFAULT,
   EDLEVEL    SMALLINT       NOT NULL WITH DEFAULT,
   SEX        CHAR(1)        NOT NULL WITH DEFAULT,
   BIRTHDATE  DATE           NOT NULL WITH DEFAULT,
   SALARY     DECIMAL(9,2)   NOT NULL WITH DEFAULT,
```

```
    BONUS        DECIMAL(9,2) NOT NULL WITH DEFAULT,
    COMM         DECIMAL(9,2) NOT NULL WITH DEFAULT)
 IN DAYOURDB.EMPTSP;
```

2. The fully qualified name of the table created in the first exercise is
LOCATION.AUTHID.EMP where LOCATION is the current location of
the person who enters the statement and AUTHID is the current SQLID of
the person who enters the statement.

3. It is doubtful that the number of letters in a person's first and last name
will vary greatly within the maximum allowed characters of 12 and 15. An
additional 2 bytes are required for the length field for each first and last
name resulting in little DASD space savings if any. If an index is created on
one or both of the columns, the shorter values will be padded with blanks
resulting in no savings in the index pages. Index only processing is not
possible. It is always necessary to get the length value from the data pages
for SELECT statements. In addition, program development time and costs
are increased with the added work for managing VARCHAR columns as
discussed in Chapter PD.

4. The salary column has been specified NOT NULL WITH DEFAULT,
and some rows contain zeros for unknown salaries. The problem can be
avoided by excluding 0 salaries from the average calculation like:

```
    SELECT  AVG(SALARY)
    FROM    EMP
    WHERE   SALARY ¬= 0;
```

An alternative is to have DB2 substitute null for a 0 salary.

```
    SELECT  AVG(NULLIF(SALARY, 0))
    FROM    EMP;
```

If you want to avoid developers having to exclude 0 from the average, the
SALARY column can be defined as allowing for nulls. The SELECT
statement will then ignore null values in taking the average.

5. a) The column definition clause to cause "UNK" to be placed in a column
when the user does not specify a department for an employee is
"WORKDEPT CHAR(3) WITH DEFAULT 'UNK'".

b) The column definition clause to cause the HIREDATE to be recorded automatically when a row is inserted into the EMP table, is "HIREDATE DATE NOT NULL WITH DEFAULT".

c) The column definition clause such that a row cannot be inserted into a table unless the EDLEVEL is greater than 12 is "EDLEVEL SMALLINT NOT NULL CONSTRAINT EDLEVEL_C CHECK (EDLEVEL > 12)".

6. Here are the CREATE statements for two distinct type, one for Fahrenheit and one for centigrade using the built-in data type of integer.

```
CREATE DISTINCT TYPE FAHRENHEIT AS INTEGER
WITH COMPARISONS;

CREATE DISTINCT TYPE CENTIGRADE AS INTEGER
WITH COMPARISONS;
```

7. The following statement will not execute successfully because a comparison cannot be made between a column defined with a distinct type of FAHRENHEIT and a column TEMP_C column defined with a distinct type of CENTIGRADE. An SQLCODE of -401 is returned.

```
SELECT TEMP_F, TEMP_C
FROM    WEATHER
WHERE   TEMP_F > TEMP_C
AND     DATE_W = '2000-01-17';
```

8. The following statement will execute successfully and the correct results received assuming that the value 70 is in Fahrenheit (not centigrade). The statement results in a -401 SQLCODE without the use of the INTEGER cast function. The developer is taking an overt action by using the INTEGER function to make the comparisons. The same principle applies if a host variable is used in place of 70. Host variables are always defined with built in data types. Host languages do not support the definition of a field as a distinct type.

```
SELECT TEMP_F, TEMP_C
FROM    WEATHER
WHERE   INTEGER(TEMP_F) > 70
AND     DATE_W = '2000-01-17';
```

9. The following statement will not execute successfully (-461 SQLCODE).

It is not possible to cast a distinct type TEMP_F (distinct type of FAHRENHEIT) to a different distinct type (CENTIGRADE). One of the primary goals of distinct types is to avoid arithmetic operations and comparison of unlike distinct types. A UDF needs to be developed in a host language with the correct formula to convert Fahrenheit to centigrade.

```
SELECT  CAST(TEMP_F AS CENTIGRADE) + TEMP_C
FROM    WEATHER
WHERE   CAST(TEMP_F AS CENTIGRADE) > TEMP_C
AND     DATE_W = '2000-01-17';
```

10. If the following DROP statement fails, consider determining if there are any UDF and stored procedures dependent on the distinct type by selecting from SYSROUTINES.

```
DROP DISTINCT TYPE FAHRENHEIT RESTRICT;
```

Once the drop is successful, all automatically created cast functions created by DB2 when the distinct type is created are dropped automatically.

11. Here is an ALTER statement to avoid someone accidentally dropping the EMP table.

```
ALTER TABLE EMP
ADD RESTRICT ON DROP;
```

12. DATA CAPTURE (not AUDIT) causes information to be recorded in the log so that a report of before and after images of inserted, updated, and deleted rows can be generated.

13. A statement to create a BOARD_MEMBER table with the same definition as the EMP table in the DABMDB database and DABMTSP tablespace is:

```
CREATE TABLE BOARD_MEMBER LIKE EMP IN
    DABMDB.DABMTSP;
```

14. The primary goal of RI is to insure that every non-null foreign key value in a dependent table has a corresponding primary key value in the parent table. For example, you would not want to have an unpaid bill of $100,000 and not have information on the customer for billing purposes.

15. a) The definition of a primary key, even if there are no foreign keys referencing the parent table, clearly documents the primary key in the catalog tables and requires the creation of a unique index on the primary key columns.

b) There are no costs associated with defining a primary key if there are no foreign keys referencing the parent table. No special processing is required in this case.

16. The restrict delete rule should be defined such that information about a customer cannot be deleted if there is an outstanding order placed by the customer.

17. A cascade delete is a good choice in this case because there is no reason to maintain active information on an individual's dependents when that individual is no longer employed. However, there may be a requirement to archive data on the former employee before deleting information.

18. A SET NULL constraint is a good choice because, although the employee has left the company, the job still exists and the supervisory position needs to be filled.

19. A foreign key row cannot be inserted unless there is a primary key value matching the foreign key value in the row to be inserted. This is an implicit rule.

20. A foreign key value can be updated to only a value that appears in the primary key column of the parent table. This is an implicit rule.

21. The only restriction on the insertion of a primary key row is that the primary key value cannot already exist in the table. There are no other restrictions regardless of whether or not there are foreign keys referencing the parent table.

22. There are no restrictions on the deletion of a foreign key row.

23. There are a number of advantages to defining RI constraints to DB2. You can be sure that RI is enforced uniformly regardless of how the data is updated. It is not necessary to develop SQL and procedural code to maintain RI integrity and be concerned that the constraints may not be understood and enforced in all cases. It is likely that DB2 enforced integrity will

perform better than application enforced integrity because the RI enforcement is done at a lower level and FK indexes are always used to enforce the constraints, assuming that they have been created. There is more flexibility in enforcing constraints. For example, if business rules are changed, the constraints can be changed by dropping existing constraints and adding new constraints without changing any application programs. One can always determine what constraints are enforced by selecting from the catalog tables. The DB2 utilities can be used to enforce the constraints.

24. An advantage of enforcing RI constraints in application programs is if it is believed that RI cannot be violated in some cases and it is not necessary to check the constraints in those cases. One should be very careful with this belief. There may be cases where RI can be violated. Business rules may dictate that constraints should be enforced differently than what is allowed by DB2. Application design may allow checking the existence of a PK and holding a lock so that the PK cannot be updated or deleted while inserting or updating a number of matching FK rows.

25. The following CREATE VIEW statement will allow the manager of the DBA department to see only employees in this department.

```
CREATE VIEW MGR_WORKDEPT AS
   SELECT EMPNO, FIRSTNME, MIDINIT,
          LASTNAME, WORKDEPT,
   PHONENO, HIREDATE, JOB, EDLEVEL, SEX, BIRTHDATE,
   SALARY, BONUS, COMM
   FROM    EMP
   WHERE   WORKDEPT = 'DBA';
```

The SELECT defining the view cannot reference more than one table in the FROM clause when the user plans to update data using a view.

26. Views can be used to enforce column and row level security, provide for automatic calculation of values without the user having to know the correct expression, ease the use of SQL, help ensure good performance of SQL statements, and provide independence in applications from the structure of base tables.

27. There is no need to use the WITH CHECK OPTION in a view definition if users can select data but cannot insert or update rows. The option is useful in not allowing users to insert rows they cannot see, or update rows they can see to be rows they cannot see.

28. ORDER BY and FOR UPDATE OF cannot be specified in a view definition. UNION and UNION ALL can be specified in a view definition in V7.

29. If users are to insert, update, and delete rows, the SELECT statement that defines the view should not include a column or scalar function, derived columns, DISTINCT, GROUP BY, and HAVING clauses, and more than one table in the FROM clause of a view definition.

30. Use of the QUALIFIER parameter avoids having to be concerned with duplicate synonym and alias names on the same DB2 subsystem and when using sysplex data sharing. The QUALIFIER parameter avoids having to recreate synonyms when objects are dropped and recreated.

FIGURES

Index Usage for Performance

IU.1 INTRODUCTION

DB2 can use indexes in a variety of ways to locate required rows efficiently. In the same way that an index in a book is used to quickly locate a particular item of interest, DB2 can use an index to locate a page containing a requested row to avoid scanning the entire tablespace. An index in a book contains keywords that the authors believe are useful to you in locating information. DB2, on the other hand, must be prepared to locate *any* value in the indexed column. Therefore, all unique values that appear in the indexed column are placed in the index.

In this chapter, we describe the basic index structure and how indexes are used to locate data. This is similar for both type 1 and 2 indexes. Type 2 indexes were introduced in V4. Type 1 indexes were removed from DB2 in V6. Index design issues and how the index manager processes pages when rows are inserted, updated, and deleted are described in Chapter ID.

Index Structure

Figure IU.1 is a conceptual representation of a fragment of the index structure used by the index managers to reference data pages containing information on jobs and their names. The last row of boxes represents data pages. If the job table has a million 100-byte rows, there are about 30,000 data pages. Clearly, it is too costly to scan all data pages when only a few rows are required.

Figure IU.1. Index structure

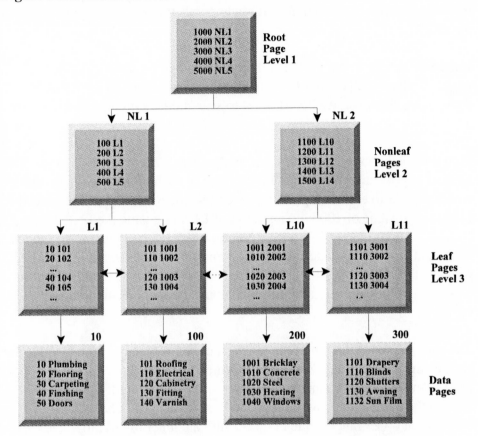

You are likely to need indexes on columns that are frequently searched or joined. In our example, it is the job number (JN) column. At the bottom of the index are the leaf pages represented by the boxes just above the data pages in Figure IU.1. Each leaf page contains indexed values followed by one or more *record identifiers* (RIDs). If the index is on a column with all unique values, the primary key for example, each value has one RID following it. If the index is on a column that contains duplicate values, a CITY column for example, each city in the index has one or more RIDs following it. If there are 200 jobs in Dallas, a leaf page entry has the value of Dallas followed by 200 RIDs.

A RID is four bytes in length (except for partitioned tablespaces greater than 64 GB (gigabyte)) as discussed in Chapter TS. The first three bytes of the RID reference a data page. The fourth byte of the RID points to a slot in the page directory that contains the offset of the row on the page. If the tablespace is greater than 64 GB, the RIDs of indexes on a table in a partitioned tablespace are five bytes in length with the first four bytes referencing a data page and the fifth byte points to a slot in the page directory.

If there is an index on a 10-byte column, there will be about 4,000 leaf pages. Certainly, it is better to scan 4,000 leaf pages than to scan 30,000 data pages. However, we do not want to scan 4,000 leaf pages just to locate a few rows.

Figure IU.1 shows that an index has nonleaf pages above the leaf pages. The nonleaf pages contain the upper range value of each of the leaf pages along with a pointer to each leaf page. For example, the nonleaf page NL1 has the upper range value of 100 with a pointer of L1 referencing the first leaf page, an upper range value of 200 with a pointer of L2 referencing the second leaf page, and so on. Leaf pages between L3 and L9 are not shown, and the leaf pages with a pointer greater than L11 are not shown in the figure. Because of space limitations, only two of the 16 nonleaf pages are shown in the figure.

The *root page* is at the top of the index. It contains the upper range value for each of the nonleaf pages along with pointers to the nonleaf pages. The root page in the example has an upper range value of 1,000 with a pointer of NL1 to the nonleaf page with the values less than 1,000. The root page also contains an upper range value of 2,000 with a pointer of NL2 to the nonleaf page with values less than 2,000 and so on for each nonleaf page in the index.

Clustering Indexes

The clustering index determines how rows are physically ordered in a table. Data manager uses the clustering index to determine where to insert a row. For example, the clustering index on JN causes rows to be maintained in sequence on JN. An insert of JN 105 causes the row to be inserted on the same page as JN 101 and 110, assuming there is free space on the page. Rows are maintained in logical sequence on the column designated as the clustering index. A table can have at most one clustering index.

Cluster Ratio: The *cluster ratio* is the percentage of rows in sequence on the data pages. It is a value computed by the RUNSTATS utility, described in Chapter RR. You can designate only one index as the clustering index on a table. However, several indexes may have a good cluster ratio.

Consider an example of how you can have a high cluster ratio on two columns. Assume that the clustering index is on an employee number and that employee numbers are assigned sequentially as new employees are hired. There is also an index on a timestamp column of when the employee was hired. Both of these indexes will have a very high cluster ratio after they are reorganized using the REORG utility. There are many situations where this can occur that are not so obvious. By selecting the CLUSTERRATIOF column in the SYSINDEXES catalog table, you might be surprised to see a number of your indexes with a good cluster ratio. (CLUSTERRATIOF rather than CLUSTERRATIOF is used by the optimizer once it is populated in V6 as discussed in Chapter RR.) The optimizer considers the cluster ratio for any index with a cluster ratio greater than five percent when determining if and how an index should be used as discussed in Chapter OP.

The terms clustering and non-clustering suggest different index structures. This is not true. Clustering and non-clustering indexes have the same index structure. Clustering refers to how rows are sequenced on the data pages. The cluster ratio is 100 percent in Figure IU.1 because all rows on the data pages are in sequence on the job number.

Well-Clustered Indexes Can Help Avoid Sorts: An index can be used to avoid a sort of data rows. The values on the index leaf pages are maintained in logical sequence. The index manager can follow forward pointers to scan the leaf pages in sequence. The optimizer may choose to scan the leaf pages and follow the RIDs to the rows and retrieve them in sequence. The optimizer is likely to do this if the cluster ratio is 80 percent or more.

The use of an index to avoid a sort of rows is useful for retrieving rows in sequence to satisfy an ORDER BY, GROUP BY, DISTINCT, or to avoid sorts for joins.

If the cluster ratio is low, the use of the index to avoid the sort is too costly. This is because excessive seek time can be required to the data pages to retrieve the rows in sequence. For example:

♦   Atlanta RID references a row on cylinder 100
♦   Chicago RID references a row on cylinder 1
♦   Dallas RID references a row on cylinder 50

- ◆ Houston RID references a row on cylinder 2
- ◆ New York RID references a row on cylinder 75
- ◆ San Jose RID references a row on cylinder 3, etc.

IU.2 BASIC INDEX USAGE

Now that we have described the index structure, let's look at some ways DB2 uses an index. In this section, we describe matching index scans (with and without referencing the data pages), non-matching index scans, and index screening.

Matching Index Scan

DB2 can find a specific row with only a few I/O operations by following a path down through the index structure. For example, a matching index scan can be used to find job 110:

1.   The index manager compares the value 110 to the upper range values in the root page and determines that it is less than 1,000, which indicates that the nonleaf page NL1 should be accessed next.

2.   Job 110 is compared to the upper range values in NL1. Job 110 is greater than 100 but less than 200 indicating that leaf page L2 contains job 110.

3.   Leaf page L2 has the RID 1002 that points to the page 100 containing the row for job 110.

Using a matching index scan with data reference, the job is located with three I/Os to the index pages and one I/O to the data pages. If it is not necessary to access the data pages to satisfy a SELECT statement, the processing is referred to as a matching index scan *without* data reference.

If the index is being used frequently, there is a good chance that the root page, some nonleaf pages, and perhaps some leaf and data pages will be found in the buffer pool from previous searches. This can further reduce the number of I/Os.

Non-matching Index Scan

All of the leaf pages are scanned in a non-matching index scan. Data pages are accessed for each value that qualifies in a leaf page. It is not necessary to start at the top of the index structure to locate each row that is required. There are times when it is not possible or it is not efficient to perform a matching index scan. In these cases a non-matching index is best. A non-matching index scan without data reference is used if it is not necessary to access the data pages to get additional columns that are not in the leaf page to satisfy a SELECT statement.

A matching index scan followed by a scan of the leaf pages can be done to satisfy a range predicate (some form of greater than, less than, BETWEEN, or LIKE). For example, a SELECT statement that requests jobs between 101 and 1030 (WHERE JN BETWEEN 101 AND 1030) is likely to result in a matching index scan to locate job 101 followed by a scan of the leaf pages until all jobs up to and including 1030 have been processed.

IU.3 INDEX LOOKASIDE AND ONE-FETCH ACCESS

Index Lookaside

Index lookaside is a refinement of a matching index scan. Index lookaside begins with a matching index scan. For a leaf page and the next higher nonleaf page, DB2 saves the lowest and highest values, log relative byte address (RBA), and page identifiers. Before doing a second matching index scan, DB2 goes through the following process:

1. It checks to see if the next required value is within the range of saved values for the leaf page. If the value is within the range of values on the leaf page, the value is located on the leaf page.

2. If the value is not within the range of values for the leaf page, DB2 checks to see if the value is within the range of saved values for the next higher nonleaf page. If the value is within the range of values for the nonleaf page, a getpage is issued on the nonleaf page.

3. If the value is not present, a matching index scan is performed. In the context of index lookaside, this is referred to as absolute positioning.

Advantages of Index Lookaside: There are a number of advantages to index lookaside processing. In many cases, a matching index scan is avoided for each value required. Data Manager (DM) issues a release and getpage on a leaf page only after processing all qualifying values on the page.

This is in contrast to issuing a release and getpage for each of 213 values on a leaf page. (The number of indexed values on a leaf is 213 using the example of a 10-byte indexed column and the default of 10 percent free space).

Index lookaside avoids a matching index scan for each required value--all qualifying values are processed before the page is released, and sequential or dynamic prefetch can be used on the leaf pages. These factors result in a significant reduction in the number of getpages, physical I/O, lock requests, and CPU time. This technique is particularly useful for the inner table of nested loop and hybrid joins, correlated subselects, repeated execution of any SQL statement that processes multiple rows, and a singleton select in a programming loop. Index lookaside is not an option of the optimizer. It is a technique coded into DB2 processing. Therefore, the only indication of its use is a reduction in resource consumption as seen in the accounting trace records.

A word of caution is in order. The saved identifiers are reset each time that a commit work is issued when the plan or package is bound with RELEASE(COMMIT). We recommend RELEASE(DEALLOCATE) to maximize the benefits of index lookaside and to gain other performance benefits.

One-Fetch Index Access

The column functions of MIN and MAX can be satisfied by a one-fetch index access using an ascending or descending index (V7). Prior to V7, the MIN function requires an ascending index, and MAX requires a descending index. The one-fetch index access applies to an index on a single column and a composite index on multiple columns. If the minimum or maximum value is requested on the non-leading column of a composite index, it is necessary to specify equal predicates on the leading columns of the index.

Restrictions: A one-fetch index access cannot be used if there is more than one table, more than one column function, and if GROUP BY is used in the select. Also, the leading columns of a composite index must have equal predicates.

Use of one-fetch index access: There are many uses of a one-fetch index access that result in excellent performance. We will use an example to determine the employee who has the highest seniority with the company in each department. There are many similar uses including determining the oldest order placed by a customer, oldest deposit in an account, oldest insurance policy, etc. In this example, assume a composite index and SELECT statement like:

```
CREATE INDEX WKDEPTX ON EMP (WORKDEPT,
  HIREDATE ASC);

SELECT EMPNO, WORKDEPT, HIREDATE
FROM    EMP AS E1
WHERE   HIREDATE =
  (SELECT MIN(HIREDATE)
   FROM    EMP AS E2
   WHERE   E1.WORKDEPT = E2.WORKDEPT);
```

The optimizer is likely to choose a matching index scan on WORKDEPT and an one-fetch index access on HIREDATE.

Similarly, you can use the MAX column function with an index on date to determine the most recently hired employee, the most recent order placed by a customer, the most recent deposit in an account, the most recent insurance policy, etc.

IU.4 LIST PREFETCH AND MULTIPLE INDEX USAGE

List prefetch is a prerequisite of multiple index usage. List prefetch has significant advantages in its own right. We will first look at list prefetch followed by multiple index usage.

List Prefetch

List prefetch is a method for using a single I/O to retrieve up to and including 32 data pages that contain qualifying rows according to one or more predicates. It is necessary to get the RIDs from one or more indexes and place them in the RID pool. The RIDs are sorted, and duplicate page identifiers (first three bytes of the RID) are eliminated using an in-memory sort without work files.

Advantages of List Prefetch: With list prefetch, the seek time to locate pages is minimized by reading pages sequentially as they appear on DASD. There are fewer I/Os to the data pages because the RIDs are sorted and reduced before accessing the data pages. All qualifying rows on a page are processed with list prefetch. This is in contrast to a having to do a matching index scan for each of several rows that might qualify on a page.

Skip-sequential processing is used with list prefetch. That is, unreferenced data pages are skipped. For example, if pages 5, 7, 10, 15, 20, 23, 27, and so on, are required and pages 5, 10, 15, 20, 25 are in the buffer pool, only 7, 23, 27 must be read from DASD. (Buffer manager also avoids rereading pages that are already in the buffer pool for sequential and dynamic prefetch.)

Assuming a buffer pool of 1,000 or more pages, one I/O can be issued to read up to and including 32 pages as identified by RIDs from the leaf pages. This is in contrast with sequential and dynamic prefetch where one I/O is issued to access the next 32 pages in most cases. Sequential and dynamic prefetch have the advantage that they can be used on the index pages in addition to the data pages. They do not require prior access to an index as does list prefetch. Sequential and dynamic prefetch are discussed in more detail in Chapter BP and list prefetch is discussed further in Chapter PP.

Multiple Index Processing

DB2 can use multiple indexes on a table to satisfy multiple predicates joined by AND and OR. The qualifying RIDs are obtained from the indexes for each of the predicates, sorted, and duplicate page identifiers are eliminated--a union process for OR; and an intersection process for AND. Then from the resulting list, DB2 uses list prefetch to retrieve the data from the data pages in sequence as they appear on DASD.

Consider a separate index on SN and PN with the following SELECT statement:

```
SELECT SN, PN, JN, QTY
FROM   SPJ
WHERE  SN = 'S5'
AND    PN = 'P5';
```

A matching index scan can be used to locate S5 in a leaf page. S5 might supply P5 to many jobs and have a number of RIDs following the value of S5. As an example, assume that RIDs 1002, 3003, and 4005 follow S5 as shown in Figure IU.2. These RIDs are written to a temporary work area, which we call work area A in the RID pool. A matching index scan can be used to locate P5 in a leaf page with RIDs 1002 and 2004 following the part number. These RIDs are written to a temporary work area B in the RID pool.

Figure IU.2. Use of multiple indexes

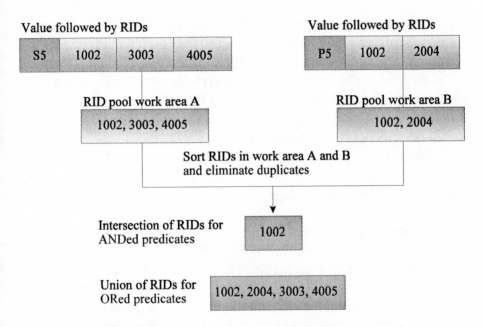

The SELECT statement requires those rows with both S5 *and* P5. To identify the RIDs that have both values, DB2 intersects the RIDs in temporary work areas A and B. RID 1002 is the only RID that appears in both lists of RIDs for S5 and P5. Rather than having to read five pages identified by RIDs 1002, 3003, 4005, 1002 (for the second row on the page referenced by RID 1002), and 2004, only one I/O to the one data page identified by RID 1002 is read with a list prefetch I/O.

Multiple index processing can also be used for ORed predicates like:

```
SELECT  SN,  PN,  JN,  QTY
FROM    SPJ
WHERE   SN  =  'S5'
OR      PN  =  'P5';
```

As for the ANDed predicates, RIDs are located for S5 and P5 and written to temporary work areas in the RID pool. A union of the RIDs is done for the OR condition with the result shown at the bottom of Figure IU.2. That is, the unique RIDs from both lists are required because the OR condition is satisfied if the row has either S5 or P5. I/O is reduced for an ORed condition because duplicate page identifiers are eliminated. In the example, the original list of five RIDs is reduced to four RIDs by eliminating the duplicate 1002 page ID.

Both the intersection and union of the RIDs start by sorting the RIDs and eliminating duplicates on the page identifiers. This is all that is necessary for the union. For the intersection, it is necessary to identify the RIDs that appear in both lists. The sort results in the RIDs being in the same sequence as the pages are on DASD, which minimizes the seek time. List prefetch is used to read up to 32 pages with a single I/O. Multiple-index processing is discussed in more detail in Chapter PP.

Logical Partitioning Index Usage

A nonpartitioned index contains RIDs referencing all partitions of a partitioned tablespace. The first few bits of a RID are used to determine which partition the RID is referencing. The number of bits used depends on the number of partitions. This allows for *logical* partitioning as shown in Figure IU.3. For example, RID R4 indicates that it is referencing a row in partition 2 and RID R3 indicates it is referencing a row in partition 1.

Figure IU.3. Logical partitioning of a nonpartitioned index

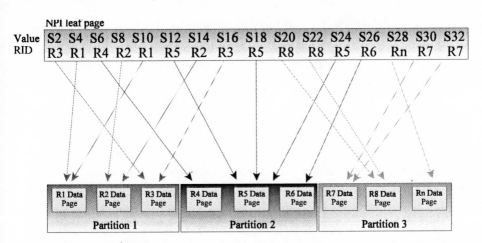

Logical partitioning allows for narrowing the search using a single index. This has performance advantages over using multiple index processing. For example, assume that there is a nonpartitioning index on CITY and a partitioning index on DATE_RECEIVED with 12 monthly partitions and a WHERE clause of:

```
WHERE CITY          = 'Rockwall'
AND   DATE_RECEIVED = '1993-09-16'
```

A matching index scan on CITY can be used to locate the RIDs for rows with Rockwall. The first few bits of the RIDs following Rockwall are used to determine those RIDs that point to rows in partition 9 with September 16, 1993 data. List prefetch is then used to access the rows identified by the RIDs. This has significant performance advantage over using multiple index processing with the CITY and DATE_RECEIVED indexes, particularly if there are few rows for Rockwall and many rows for 1993-09-16.

The same principle applies to ranges of values and noncontiguous partitions in V6. For example, only parts 2, 3, 9, and 10 are scanned for:

```
WHERE CITY          = 'Rockwall'
AND   (DATE_RECEIVED BETWEEN '1994-02-15'
                         AND '1994-03-15'
OR    DATE_RECEIVED BETWEEN '1994-09-27'
                         AND '1994-10-15')
```

IU.5 COMPARING METHODS FOR LOCATING DATA

This chapter has described a number of efficient methods for using indexes to locate data. Let's compare some of these methods using a 10,000 row table on 200 pages. The following SELECT statement is used:

```
SELECT  PN, PNAME
FROM    P
WHERE   CITY = 'Dallas';
```

Tablespace Scan: One approach is to do a tablespace scan to locate all of the parts in Dallas. Initially, one might think that 200 I/Os will be required for each of the 200 pages in the tablespace. The use of sequential prefetch reduces the number of I/O substantially to only 7 (200/32). However, most of your tablespaces contain more than 10,000 rows on 200 pages. Dividing by 32 is not sufficient to give good performance for large tables. You may decide to create an index on the CITY column.

Matching Index Scan: The optimizer computes a *filter factor* to determine if an index is appropriate to locate the rows for Dallas. The filter factor is an estimate of the percentage of rows that will qualify based on a predicate. It is necessary to know the cardinality of a column to compute the filter factor. The *cardinality* of a column is the number of distinct values in the column. If we assume that there are 20 distinct cities in the CITY column, the filter factor formula for an equal predicate is very simple. You want one value with an equal predicate, Dallas, in the example. You want 1 out of the 20 distinct value in the column. That is, 1 divided by 20 or 5 percent of the rows. (The filter factor formulas for other predicates are in Chapter OP.)

The filter factor can be multiplied by the number of rows to give an estimate of the number of I/Os required. In the example, this is 5 percent of 10,000 rows, or 500 I/Os to the data pages plus I/Os to the index. It is rather surprising that the number of I/Os estimated to the data pages using an index is higher than the number of I/Os using a tablespace scan. This is because the index has few distinct values, and we are assuming a zero cluster ratio. The low cardinality of 20 means that typically there will be about 2.5 qualifying rows on each page. That is, a matching index scan without list prefetch must be done for each page 2.5 times. Notice that 2.5 times the number of pages in the tablespace is 500 (2.5 * 200), which is the I/O estimate assuming a zero cluster ratio. Figure IU.4 represents the multiple accesses to the same data page.

Figure IU.4. Use of low cardinality non-clustered index

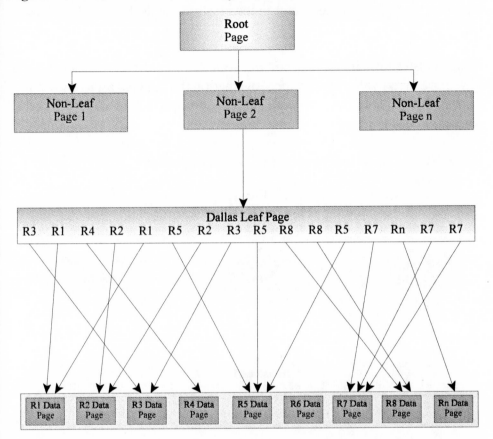

The optimizer recognizes a low cardinality index on the CITY column and considers list prefetch. If list prefetch is chosen, the I/O estimate to the data pages is 7 (200 / 32), which is the same as the tablespace scan. Actually, the number of I/Os is higher than the tablespace scan because I/O is required to the index pages to get the RIDs to use in the list prefetch operation. Also adding to the costs is the fact that RIDs are placed in the RID pool and sorted before issuing the list prefetch I/O.

Matching Index Scan with a Clustering Index: If you have a large table and believe that it is important to avoid a tablespace scan to locate rows for a particular city, consider making the low cardinality index on CITY a clustering index. The I/O estimate using a clustering index is much lower because if the cluster ratio is 100 percent, the optimizer can multiply the filter factor times the number of pages. That gives an I/O estimate of 10 (0.05 * 200 pages). The I/O can be reduced further. If eight or more pages are estimated to contain qualifying rows, prefetch can be used to get the up to and including 32 pages with a single I/O. (This is a simplified example. Actually, the optimizer can factor in the cluster ratio as discussed in Chapter OP.)

A high cluster ratio index on a column with a low cardinality means that the rows for a given value are grouped together on the data pages, as shown in Figure IU.5. Most of the rows for Dallas are grouped together on the data pages.

Figure IU.5. Use of low cardinality clustering index

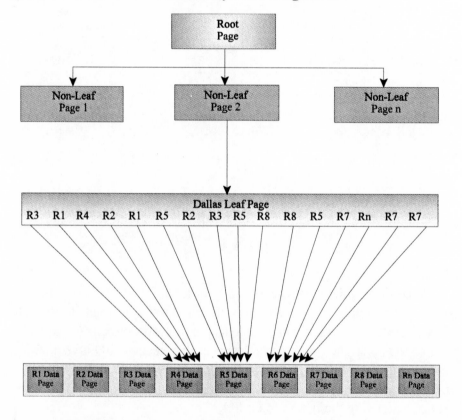

IU.6 USING COMPOSITE INDEXES

A composite index is an index consisting of more than one column. The primary key on the SPJ table consists of the columns SN, PN, and JN and should have a unique composite index on the columns to guarantee unique values. A matching index scan can be done on all columns of a composite index if equal predicates are used as in the WHERE clause:

```
WHERE  SN  =  'S1'
AND    PN  =  'P1'
AND    JN  =  'J4'
```

In order to use a matching index scan with a composite index, it is necessary to specify at least the leading column (first column) of the composite index in the WHERE clause. Without specifying the leading column, it is like trying to find a name in a telephone book without knowing the first few characters of the name. If you wanted to find a name ending in "son", it would be necessary to scan the entire telephone book. The index manager is faced with a similar problem. It must scan the tablespace or all index leaf pages if the leading column of a composite index is not specified in the WHERE clause.

Recall that the root and nonleaf pages have the upper range values that are used to navigate through the index structure to locate the required value on a leaf page and finally the data page. If the leading column of a composite index is not specified, it is not possible to compare the required value with upper range values in the nonleaf pages.

A matching index scan with a composite index on SN, PN, and JN cannot be used to satisfy the following WHERE conditions because there is not a predicate on SN.

```
WHERE  PN  =  'P1'

WHERE  PN  >  'P1'
AND    JN  =  'J4'

WHERE  JN  >  'J4'
```

The optimizer may choose to do a non-matching index scan rather than a tablespace scan because there are usually fewer leaf pages than data pages.

A matching index scan can be done if the first column of the composite index is specified in the WHERE clause. This applies to equal and range predicates as indicated in the examples with comments:

```
WHERE  SN  =  'S1'  -- Match on S1 and process all S1s

WHERE  SN  >  'S1'  -- Match on S1 and scan past S1s
```

The index manager will be able to match on columns, SN and PN, when the following WHERE clause is used:

```
WHERE SN = 'S1' -- Match on S1 and P1, scan past P1s
AND    PN > 'P1'
```

However, a range predicate specified on a column of a composite index breaks the number of columns that can be used in a matching index scan. For example, a range predicate is specified on the second column of the composite index, PN, in the following example. Therefore, the index manager can only do a matching index scan on SN and PN even though there is an equal predicate on JN.

```
WHERE SN = 'S5' -- Match on S5 and P4, scan for J3s
AND    PN >='P4'
AND    JN = 'J3'
```

It is a bit like finding a name in a telephone book that begins with "John" and ends with *n*. If you don't know the characters in between, you can turn to the page with "John", but you will have to scan all of the names beginning with "John" to find those ending with *n* (Johnson, Johnsen, and Johnston, for example).

The index manager is actually doing a bounded search as you would in looking for the names. You won't scan past the names that begin with "John". Here is an example of a WHERE clause that can use a bounded search on the SN, PN, and JN composite index:

```
WHERE SN = 'S5' -- Match on S5 and P4, scan for J3s
AND    PN BETWEEN 'P4' AND 'P8'
AND    JN = 'J3'
```

The index manager can do a matching index scan to locate S5 and P4. It scans the leaf pages looking for J3 until it completes the scan, including the P8s. This is a form of index screening.

Index Screening

Index screening means that a matching index scan is done on the leading columns of a composite index followed by applying additional predicates on the composite index leaf pages. An example will demonstrate the process assuming a composite index on SN, PN, and JN. A matching index scan can

be used to locate S5 followed by a scan of the leaf pages to locate only S5s
that supply parts for JN > 'J4' for the statement:

```
SELECT  SN, PN, JN, QTY
FROM    SPJ
WHERE   SN = 'S5'
AND     JN > 'J4';
```

The goal is to reduce the number of data pages that must be processed by
applying predicates on the index pages. List prefetch processing can be used
on the RIDs identified with index screening. This also applies to a
non-matching index scan.

Non-matching index scan versus a tablespace scan: If a tablespace scan
is chosen by the optimizer because a value for the leading column of a
composite index is not provided by the user, consider encouraging a
non-matching index scan with index screening. This guideline assumes that
a small number of rows qualify according to the predicates on JN and PN,
there are fewer leaf pages than data pages, and the cost of the leaf page
access in addition to data page access is justified.

We will consider two examples of encouraging a non-matching index scan
assuming that a value for SN is not provided by the user. The technique
requires that the lowest possible value in the column is moved to :SN. A
literal will probably result in the optimizer recognizing that a low value does
not narrow the search, particularly with a range predicate.

```
SELECT  SN, PN, JN, QTY
FROM    SPJ
WHERE   SN >  :SN
AND     JN =  :JN
AND     PN =  :PN;
```

If SPJ.SN has a low cardinality which results in a tablespace scan, consider:

```
SELECT  SN, PN, JN, QTY
FROM    SPJ
WHERE   JN =  :JN
AND     PN =  :PN;
AND     SN IN
   (SELECT  SN
    FROM    S);
```

If a non-matching index scan is still not chosen, consider adding OPTIMIZE FOR 1 ROW before the ";" for both statements as discussed in Chapter PP. The IN subselect can be transformed to an IN list as discussed in Chapter ST, and can match on three columns as discussed in Chapter PP.

Index and Column Cardinalities

The index and column cardinalities used by the optimizer depend on whether the index is a composite or single-column index. For a composite index, it also depends on the type of predicate that is specified on the columns in the WHERE clause. Following are the cardinalities used by the optimizer based on the type of index and the predicates used.

FIRSTKEYCARDF column in SYSINDEXES contains the number of distinct values of the first column in an index. It is the value used by the optimizer in calculating the filter factor for a predicate on a single-column index.

FULLKEYCARDF column in SYSINDEXES contains the number of distinct values of all bytes in a composite index. It is the value used by the optimizer in calculating the filter factor if an equal predicate is coded on each column in the composite index.

COLCARDF column in SYSCOLUMNS contains the same value as FIRSTKEYCARDF for the first column of a composite index. The value is used by the optimizer in calculating the filter factor if an equal predicate is not coded on each column in the composite index.

COLCARDF contains a statistical estimate of the number of distinct values in the non-leading columns of a composite index or a non-indexed column. You can get this information into the catalog by executing the RUNSTATS utility using the TABLE and optionally the COLUMN parameters as discussed in Chapter RR. If a matching index scan cannot be used on all columns in a composite index, COLCARDF is used by the optimizer in calculating the filter factor. COLCARDF is also used in calculating the filter factor for predicates on non-indexed columns as discussed in Chapter JP.

If the index is partitioned, FIRSTKEYCARDF and FULLKEYCARDF in SYSINDEXSTATS and COLCARDF in SYSCOLSTATS are used by the optimizer in calculating the filter factor for predicates on the partitioning index of a partitioned tablespace.

Using Index Cardinalities with Composite Indexes

Here are some examples to illustrate how the index cardinalities can be used for a composite index on SN, PN, and JN where equal predicates are not specified on all columns in the index. Assume the following cardinalities and filter factors for equal predicates:

- ♦ SN cardinality of 10 and filter factor of 0.10
- ♦ PN cardinality of 2,000 and filter factor of 0.0005
- ♦ JN cardinality of 500 and filter factor of 0.002

If the 'middle' columns in a composite index are not specified in the WHERE clause, the use of FIRSTKEYCARDF and FULLKEYCARDF do not give a good estimate of the percentage of rows that qualify. The FIRSTKEYCARDF is 10 with a filter factor is 0.10 for an equal predicate on the first column of the composite index. The FULLKEYCARDF is 5,000 with a filter factor of 0.0002 if there are equal predicates specified on all columns in the composite index.

Consider the following SELECT statement on a 10,000 row table on 200 pages:

```
SELECT  SN, PN, JN, QTY
FROM    SPJ
WHERE   SN = 'S4'
AND     JN = 'J7';
```

Based on the FIRSTKEYCARDF of 10 for SN, the optimizer can estimate that 1,000 (0.10 * 10,000) rows qualify by multiplying the filter factor times the number of rows in the table. This suggests that J7 uses about 1,000 parts from S4. Based on the cardinality of all three columns in the composite index (FULLKEYCARDF), the optimizer can estimate that 2 (0.0002 * 10,000) rows qualify. This suggests that J7 uses 2 parts from S4. It is not clear whether 1,000 or 2 rows will qualify based on the FIRSTKEYCARDF or FULLKEYCARDF because not all columns in the composite index are specified with equal predicates.

The optimizer can calculate a better estimate if COLCARDF has been updated for the missing "middle" column (PN). Otherwise, the optimizer interpolates values between the FIRSTKEYCARDF and FULLKEYCARDF filter factors, similar to fitting a line between the two known points and estimating the middle point as the filter factor.

If the leading column but not the trailing columns of the composite index is specified in the WHERE clause, another method must be used to estimate the I/O required and whether the index should be used to efficiently locate the required rows. For example, the trailing JN column is not specified in:

```
SELECT  SN,  PN,  JN,  QTY
FROM    SPJ
WHERE   SN  =  'S4'
AND     PN  =  'P5';
```

The filter factor can be calculated as the filter factor for the predicate on SN based on FIRSTKEYCARDF or COLCARDF times the filter factor for the predicate on PN based on COLCARDF. Multiplication of the filter factors results in a smaller estimate in the percentage of rows that qualify. One would expect a smaller percentage of the rows to qualify if each row must satisfy the two ANDed predicates. The filter factor for the example is 0.00005 (0.10 * 0.0005). It is estimated that the use of the index is a good choice even though the last column of the index is not specified in the WHERE clause. If COLCARDF has not been updated, the default filter factor of 0.04 is used, which makes it rather likely that the index will be chosen by the optimizer for a matching index scan.

Use of an Index with Update

All columns in a composite index must be specified with equal predicates to use an index to locate a row to be updated where the indexed columns are changed unless the optimizer chooses to use list prefetch. A matching index scan on a composite index composed of SN, PN, JN cannot be used to locate the row to be updated for the following statement because PN is not in the WHERE clause.

```
UPDATE  SPJ
SET     PN  =  'P1'
WHERE   SN  =  'S1'
AND     JN  =  'J1';
```

There is an exception. If list prefetch is used to access the data pages after index processing, the index can be used to locate the required rows. This is because DB2 must verify that the values have not changed since the RIDs were located, placed in the RID pool, and list prefetch issued. You can encourage the use of list prefetch by specifying a column that is not in the index if it is not chosen as part of the access path. You might add a predicate on a column that is not in the composite index that does not disqualify rows like:

```
AND QTY >= 0
```

A matching index scan on all three column in the composite index can be used for

```
UPDATE  SPJ
SET     PN = 'P1'
WHERE   SN = 'S1'
AND     PN = 'P4'
AND     JN = 'J1';
```

because equal predicates are specified on all columns in the index.

Of course, a matching index scan can be used on a single column index with an equal predicate to locate a row to be updated like:

```
UPDATE  S
SET     SN = 'S9'
WHERE   SN = 'S8';
```

If an indexed column is to be updated, there are a number of cases where the index cannot be used to locate a row to be updated:

◆   A range predicate is used on the indexed column to be updated except when list prefetch is used.
◆   An arithmetic expression is used on an indexed column in the WHERE or SET clause.
◆   The indexed column is specified in the FOR UPDATE OF clause.
◆   The indexed column is specified in a view definition WHERE clause using the WITH CHECK OPTION (described in Chapter CT).

These restrictions on index usage are necessary to avoid missing rows or going into a looping condition. For example, if an index on STATUS is chosen as the access path, rows will be retrieved in sequence on status for:

```
UPDATE  S
SET     STATUS = :STATUS
WHERE   STATUS > :OLD-STATUS;
```

An update of status from 10 to 50 would cause the cursor position to jump to status 50, skipping the statuses in between.

If an index were used on SN, a looping condition could be caused by:

```
UPDATE  S
SET     SN = SN + 1
WHERE   SN BETWEEN 5 AND 15;
```

SN would be changed from 5 to 6, 6 qualifies for the BETWEEN and would be updated again to a value of 7, 7 qualifies for the BETWEEN and would be updated again to a value of 8, and so on. This is probably not the desired result and would use a considerable amount of CPU time. Therefore, an index is not used to locate the rows to be updated with a range predicate.

In some cases an arithmetic expression can be removed from a SET clause or predicate and placed in the host language code. However, a range predicate cannot be replaced with an equal predicate to achieve the same results.

An index *can* be used to locate rows to be deleted with no restriction. The clustering index *is* always used to determine where to insert a row.

Index-Only Processing

Most DB2 professionals know intuitively that index-only processing is a good thing. An example supports that intuition. A million-row table with 100-byte rows occupies about 28,572 pages (ceiling(1,000,000 / floor(3870/(100 byte row + 8 bytes))). An index on a 10-byte column occupies about 4695 (ceiling(1,000,000 / floor (3634 / (10 byte column + 4 byte RID + 3 bytes)) leaf pages. Obviously, processing all leaf pages is more efficient than processing all data pages. Even if only a few values are required, avoiding I/O to the data pages results in savings.

Consider including frequently-retrieved columns in the index if index-only processing can be achieved. When index-only processing is used, it makes a non-clustered index as efficient as a clustered index because the values are always processed in sequence on the leaf pages.

Following are a few examples of the types of SELECT statements that can be satisfied with index-only processing. Comments are used to indicate how the processing can be accomplished. Assume that all columns referenced are indexed. Assume also that there is a composite index on SN, PN, JN in the SPJ table and a composite index on CITY and SN in the S table. The SN, PN, and JN columns are the primary key (PK) of the SPJ table. The SN column is the PK of the S table. The SN column in the SPJ table is a foreign key (FK) referencing the S table.

```
SELECT  MIN(QTY)  -- One-fetch index access
FROM    SPJ;      -- with an ascending index
                  -- and descending index in V7

SELECT  AVG(QTY)  -- Scan leaf pages
FROM    SPJ;

SELECT  COUNT(*)  -- Index with smallest number of pages
FROM    S;

SELECT  SN        -- Match on CITY, then scan
FROM    S         -- leaf pages for ORDER BY
WHERE   CITY = 'Paris'
ORDER BY SN;

SELECT  S.SN, PN, JN -- Search and join using
FROM    S, SPJ       -- PK & FK indexes only
WHERE   S.SN = SPJ.SN
AND     S.SN > 'S2';

SELECT  SNAME
FROM    S SX
WHERE   EXISTS        -- True/False returned using
    (SELECT SN, PN, JN -- index only processing on SN,
PN, JN
        FROM    SPJ
        WHERE   SN = SX.SN
        AND     PN = 'P5'
        AND     JN = 'J7');
```

Index only processing of an index on a column declared as VARCHAR is not possible by default. The default can be changed as discussed in Chapter

CT along with some words of caution regarding possible program changes to allow for index only processing of VARCHAR columns.

IU.7 DIRECT ROW ACCESS WITHOUT INDEX USAGE OVERVIEW

A column with a data type of ROWID provides for locating a row a second time using direct row access. It is necessary to locate the row with an index or tablespace scan the first time to get the row ID. The second access requires the specification of the ROWID column in the WHERE clause to locate the row directly. The column PLAN_TABLE.PRIMARY_ACCESSTYPE = 'D' (PLAN_TABLE is discussed in Chapter EX) shows the optimizers choice of using a ROWID column for direct row access without index usage or a tablespace scan.

Large Objects (LOBs) require the use of a single ROWID column to identify the location of a large object. A ROWID column is required for a table with a LOB column. It allows for locating the LOB data in an auxiliary tables using an index on the auxiliary table.

A ROWID column can be used to locate a row efficiently the second time to verify that the row has not changed since it was displayed and before it is updated as discussed in Chapter PD.

A ROWID can be used as a partitioning key to spread insert activity throughout the tablespace as discussed in Chapter TS. Caution should be exercised in using this technique. It is not possible to have the clustering index on a column that can be used to efficiently process data for online transactions and batch programs (the partitioning index is the clustering index). In addition, if high insert activity is expected, a large number of random I/O can detract from performance.

IU.8 SUMMARY

In this chapter, we described the various ways that indexes can be used to efficiently locate data. These include matching and non-matching index scans with and without data reference, multiple index processing, index lookaside, list prefetch, one-fetch index access for MIN and MAX with an ascending and descending index, use of composite indexes, and index screening.

EXERCISES

1. a) Under what conditions would you like to see the optimizer choose a matching index scan?

b) Under what conditions is it best not to use a matching index scan?

2. a) If a matching index scan is used, under what conditions will only one leaf page and one data page be processed?

b) Under what conditions will more than one leaf and data page be processed when using a matching index scan?

3. a) What is the meaning of a cluster ratio of 80 percent?

b) Is there a difference between the structure and basic access paths for clustering and non-clustering indexes?

c) What is the difference between clustering and non-clustering indexes?

4. a) Would you like to use an index to retrieve rows in sequence to avoid a sort? Why?

b) Under what conditions would you not want to use an index to retrieve rows in sequence to avoid a sort? Why?

5. a) What are the advantages of list prefetch?

b) How is list prefetch different from sequential and dynamic prefetch?

6. a) What is the filter factor?

b) What is the filter factor formula for an equal predicate?

c) How is the number of I/O estimated?

7. a) What is the purpose of index lookaside?

b) What are the benefits of index lookaside?

8. What is the advantage of multiple index usage?

9. Assume a composite index on SN, PN, and JN.
Which of the following WHERE clauses can use a matching index scan?
Which columns will DB2 be able to match on?

```
WHERE  SN  =  'S5'
AND    PN >='P4'
AND    JN  =  'J3'

WHERE  PN  >  'P4'
AND    JN  =  'J6'

WHERE  SN  >  'S2'

WHERE  SN  =  'S2'
AND    PN  >  'P4'

WHERE  SN  =  'S2'
AND    PN  =  'P4'
AND    JN  =  'J6'
```

10. Assume a composite index on SN, PN, and JN.
Please note on each of the following WHERE clauses whether the optimizer
will use FIRSTKEYCARDF, FULLKEYCARDF, or COLCARDF
(assuming that COLCARDF has been updated by RUNSTATS).

```
WHERE  SN  =  'S2'
AND    PN  =  'P4'

WHERE  SN  =  'S5'
AND    JN  =  'J6'

WHERE  SN  =  'S5'
AND    PN >='P4'
AND    JN  =  'J3'

WHERE  SN  =  'S2'
AND    PN  =  'P4'
AND    JN  =  'J6'
```

11. Assume a composite index on SN, PN, and JN.

a) Can a matching index scan be used for the following WHERE clause on a SELECT statement?

```
WHERE   SN = 'S2'
AND     JN = 'J6'
```

b) Can a matching index scan be used for the following WHERE clause on an UPDATE statement assuming that columns in the composite index are updated?

```
WHERE   SN = 'S2'
AND     JN = 'J6'
```

12. Assume an index on all columns in the WHERE and FOR UPDATE OF clauses. Which of the following statements can or cannot use a matching index scan assuming list prefetch is not chosen as part of the access path? Give the reasons that the statement can or cannot use a matching index scan.

a)
```
UPDATE SPJ SET QTY = :QTY * 1.1
   WHERE QTY > 50;
```

b)
```
QTY = QTY + 10

UPDATE SPJ SET QTY = :QTY
   WHERE QTY = 100;
```

c)
```
EXEC SQL DECLARE SCURSOR CURSOR FOR
           SELECT SN, SNAME, STATUS
           FROM   S
           WHERE  STATUS > :NEW-STATUS
           FOR UPDATE OF STATUS, CITY END-EXEC.
```

d)
```
CREATE VIEW EUROPE AS
    SELECT SN, SNAME, STATUS, CITY
    FROM   S
    WHERE  CITY IN ('London', 'Paris', 'Rome')
WITH CHECK OPTION;

UPDATE EUROPE
   SET CITY = :CITY
   WHERE CITY = 'Paris';
```

13. a) Are there any special conditions for using a matching index scan to locate a row to be deleted?

b) Are there any special conditions for using an index to insert a row?

14. Why might you want to use a matching index scan on a column with a cardinality of 20?

15. Can a one-fetch index scan with index only processing be done for the following statement. Assume a descending composite index on CITY and STATUS prior to V7.

```
SELECT  CITY,  MAX(STATUS)
FROM    S
WHERE   CITY  =  'Copenhagen';
```

16. How can direct row access be used? What are the major prerequisites to using direct row access?

ANSWERS

1. a) A matching index scan is the best choice for an online transaction that displays a few rows to the user.

b) A matching index scan is not a good choice if many rows are to be processed (more than 10-15 percent, for example) in a batch program.

2. a) A matching index scan using a unique index with an equal predicate requires that only one leaf page and one data page be processed.

b) If you are using a range predicate on a unique or nonunique index, it is likely that more than one leaf page and one data page will be processed. Indeed, if you are using an equal or range predicate on an index with a low cardinality, it is likely that more than one leaf page and one data page will be processed.

3. a) A cluster ratio of 80 percent means that 80 percent of the rows are in sequence on the data pages according to the indexed columns.

b) There is no difference between the structure and basic access paths for clustering and non-clustering indexes. A matching index scan, non-matching index scan, list prefetch, index lookaside, one-fetch index access, use of multiple indexes, use of composite indexes, and index-only processing can be used with clustering and non-clustering indexes.

c) The clustering index is used to determine where rows should be inserted to maintain the rows in sequence of the columns in the clustering index.

4. a) The use of an index to avoid a sort has significant advantages if there is a good cluster ratio. It avoids retrieving all qualifying rows and sorting them before the first row can be returned to the program.

b) It is best not to use an index to avoid a sort if many rows will be retrieved and the cluster ratio is low. This is because the seek time to DASD can result in more elapsed time than would be required to retrieve the rows out of sequence and sort them.

5. a) List prefetch results in reading only data pages with qualifying rows based on the predicates evaluated using one or more indexes. The pages are read in sequence as they appear on DASD, which reduces seek time. All qualifying rows on a page can be processed without a getpage and I/O to the same page for each qualifying row on the page. This is in contrast to, say, three matching index scan for three rows on a page.

b) List prefetch requires prior access to one or more indexes to get the RIDs. It reads only the data pages identified by the RIDs in one or more indexes. List prefetch is not to be used on index pages. Sequential and dynamic prefetch can be used on index and data pages. Sequential and dynamic prefetch reads the next 32 pages with one I/O even if all of the pages do not have qualifying rows. List prefetch reads only pages with qualifying rows. It can issue one I/O for less than or equal to 32 pages based on the qualifying RIDs.

6. a) The filter factor is an estimate of the percentage of rows that will qualify according to the coded predicate.

b) The filter factor formula for an equal predicate is one divided by the cardinality of the indexed column.

c) The I/O estimate is based on the filter factor multiplied by the number of rows and pages in the tablespace. If the cluster ratio is high, the number of pages is the stronger factor. If the cluster ratio is low, the number of rows is the stronger factor. How the cluster ratio is factored into the I/O estimate is discussed in Chapter OP.

7. a) The purpose of index lookaside is to minimize the number of matching index scans.

b) The benefits of index lookaside are a reduction in the number of getpages, I/O, and CPU time.

8. Qualifying RIDs from multiple indexes are sorted and duplicates on the page identifier are eliminated to reduce the number of I/Os to the data pages. Taking the intersection of identified RIDs for ANDed predicates can significantly reduce the number of I/Os to the data pages. The intersection of RIDs from two indexes means that only pages referenced by RIDs that qualify from both indexes need to be processed. Taking the union of identified RIDs means that DB2 can access a data page once and retrieve all the qualifying rows. If you have ORed two predicates on two columns, both indexes on the two columns must be used in multiple index processing. Otherwise, a matching index scan is not possible to achieve the correct results with two indexes on the two columns or one composite index on the two columns. List prefetch is used on the manipulated RIDs to achieve the advantages discussed for list prefetch.

9. The columns that DB2 will use in a matching index scan are noted.

```
WHERE SN = 'S5'  -- Match on S5 and P4, scan for J3s
AND    PN >='P4'
AND    JN = 'J3'

WHERE PN > 'P4'  -- Cannot do a matching index scan
AND    JN = 'J6'  -- Must specify the leading column

WHERE SN > 'S2'  -- Match on S2 and scan past

WHERE SN = 'S2'  -- Match on S2 and P4, scan past P4s
AND    PN > 'P4'

WHERE SN = 'S2'  -- Match on S2, P4, J6
AND    PN = 'P4'
AND    JN = 'J6'
```

10. The use of FIRSTKEYCARDF, FULLKEYCARDF, or COLCARDF cardinalities are noted.

```
WHERE  SN = 'S2'  -- FIRSTKEYCARDF
AND    PN = 'P4'  -- COLCARDF on PN

WHERE  SN = 'S5'  -- FIRSTKEYCARDF
AND    JN = 'J6'  -- COLCARDF on JN

WHERE  SN = 'S5'  -- FIRSTKEYCARDF
AND    PN >='P4'  -- COLCARDF on PN
AND    JN = 'J3'

WHERE  SN = 'S2'  -- FULLKEYCARDF
AND    PN = 'P4'
AND    JN = 'J6'
```

11. a) A matching index scan on one column can be used for the WHERE clause on the SELECT statement.

b) A matching index scan cannot be used for the WHERE clause on an UPDATE statement unless list prefetch is chosen by the optimizer. The middle column of the composite index is not specified.

12. a) A matching index scan cannot be used because of the arithmetic expression in the SET clause in the following statement. An arithmetic expression in the WHERE clause will also disallow the use of an index. The range predicate in the WHERE clause also disallows the use of a matching index scan. The reason is that a value can re-occur and cause a loop if an index were used on QTY.

```
UPDATE SPJ SET QTY = :QTY * 1.1
   WHERE QTY > 50;
```

b) A matching index scan can be used with an <u>equal</u> predicate and no arithmetic expression in the WHERE and SET clause for the following statement.

```
QTY = QTY + 10

UPDATE SPJ SET QTY = :QTY
   WHERE QTY = 100;
```

c) A matching index scan cannot be used on STATUS and CITY. If an index were used on a column in a FOR UPDATE OF clause, it could result in missing rows or going into a looping condition.

```
EXEC SQL DECLARE SCURSOR CURSOR FOR
        SELECT SN, SNAME, STATUS
        FROM   S
        WHERE  STATUS > :NEW-STATUS
        FOR UPDATE OF STATUS, CITY END-EXEC.
```

d) A matching index scan cannot be used on CITY because the column is specified in the CREATE VIEW WHERE clause with the WITH CHECK OPTION.

```
CREATE VIEW EUROPE_S AS
   SELECT SN, SNAME, STATUS, CITY
   FROM   S
   WHERE  CITY IN ('London', 'Paris', 'Rome')
     WITH CHECK OPTION;

UPDATE S SET CITY = :CITY
   WHERE CITY = 'Paris';
```

13. a) A matching index scan can be used to locate a row to be deleted like locating a row for a SELECT statement. There are no special conditions regarding DELETE statements.

b) The clustering index is always used to determine where a row should be inserted if the index has been designated with the CLUSTER keyword when the index is created.

14. If there is a skewed distribution of values where some of the 20 distinct values appear very infrequently and others appear very frequently on most pages in the tablespace, you may want to use the index to efficiently locate the infrequently occurring values. This is described in more detail with some alternatives for dealing with the situation in Chapter OP.

15. An one-fetch index scan with index only processing can be used with an descending (or ascending in V7) composite index on CITY and STATUS. This is because there is a matching index scan on the leading column of the composite index.

```
SELECT CITY, MAX(STATUS)
FROM   S
```

```
WHERE   CITY = 'Copenhagen';
```

16. Direct row access can be used to locate a row directly without the use of a tablespace scan or index. The major prerequisites to direct row access are that the table must have a column defined as a ROWID data type, the row ID must be determined before it can be used in a WHERE clause, and a reorganization has not occurred between the time that the row ID was determined and when it is used.

FIGURES

Index Design for Performance

ID.1 INTRODUCTION

It is important for both DBAs and programmer/analysts to understand how to use indexes. DBAs are usually concerned with physical design and maintenance, and programmer/analysts must understand how to write SQL statements that make the best use of indexes. Chapter IU describes the methods used by the index manager to efficiently locate rows.

This chapter describes issues related to designing indexes. It identifies the characteristics of columns that should and should not be indexed, and it describes the characteristics of columns that benefit the most from having a clustering index. Information about designing composite indexes are addressed.

ID.2 INDEX DESIGN GUIDELINES

Indexes can be used in a variety of ways and have a number of advantages. The primary advantage of indexes is the ability to process a small percentage of the rows efficiently with minimal I/O and CPU usage. We would like to see index usage when selecting, updating, deleting, and joining a small percentage (less than 5 to 10 percent) of rows in medium to large tables. A clustering index improves performance for processing a larger percentage of rows (less than 30 to 50 percent), particularly when the rows must be processed in sequence. Indexes can also be used to avoid access to data pages with index only processing. There are many reasons for having many indexes. However, there are costs associated with maintaining indexes that requires minimizing the number of indexes on a table.

Each time a row is inserted or deleted, the corresponding operation must be performed on each index. Each time an indexed column is updated, the record identifier (RID) must be deleted and inserted for the new value. The costs of changing indexes is often more than the costs of changing the data. In addition, there is increased exposure to contention (latches and P-locks when using row locking and sysplex data sharing).

Whenever DB2 loads or reorganizes a table, it must build or rebuild each index to it. Whenever it recovers a tablespace, it must also recover or rebuild the indexes. The index itself may need to be reorganized (rebuilt) more frequently than the tablespace, as a result of index page splitting as discussed in Section ID.5. Finally, indexes require DASD space. Using indexes efficiently is a matter of selecting those whose performance benefits outweigh these costs. The benefits depend on the way the data are to be used and the table size.

Columns That Should Be Indexed

Primary keys and foreign keys are often searched or joined over a small percentage of rows and are good candidates for indexes. Indeed, the primary key must have a unique index to guarantee unique values in the column. If there is no index on the foreign key, an update of a primary key value requires a tablespace scan of each dependent table. This scan is done to verify that the old value does not exist in a dependent table. Similarly, when a row is deleted from a parent table and no index exists on the foreign key, it is necessary to do a tablespace scan on each dependent table to enforce the delete rule, described in Chapter CT. Both DB2 enforced and application enforced referential integrity benefit from having an index on the foreign key.

Joins are often performed on the primary key and foreign key columns; therefore, an index on these columns makes the join much more efficient in most cases.

Figure ID.1 Summarizes the characteristics of columns that benefit from an index.

Figure ID.1. Characteristics of columns that benefit from an index

◆   Primary key and foreign key columns.
◆   Columns which must have unique values to satisfy a business requirement.
◆   Columns that have column functions computed frequently (COUNT, SUM, AVG, MIN, and MAX for example).
◆   Columns used to test for the existence of a value (if the value does not exist, no data pages will be accessed).
◆   Columns which are searched or joined over less than 5 to 10 percent

of the rows when considering a non-clustering index.
- ◆ Columns which are searched or joined over less than 30 to 50 percent of the rows when considering a clustering index.
- ◆ Columns frequently used together in a WHERE clause can benefit from a composite index to avoid maintaining multiple indexes
- ◆ Columns frequently used in an ORDER BY, GROUP BY, or DISTINCT clause to avoid sorts.

Columns That Benefit from Clustering

The choice of the column or columns to be included in the clustering index determines where DB2 inserts rows. The keyword CLUSTER, specified when the index is created, instructs DB2 to maintain the rows on the data pages in sequence according to the indexed column as described in Chapter IU.

The optimizer is likely to use the clustering index to avoid a sort for ORDER BY, GROUP BY, DISTINCT, and join processing. A column where these operations are often performed is a good candidate for the clustering index.

Columns frequently searched or joined over a range of values using the operators BETWEEN, >, <, and LIKE are good candidates for clustering. A clustering index means that values are maintained in sequence on the data pages. A matching index scan can be used followed by a non-matching index scan to satisfy a range predicate. DB2 can use sequential prefetch to scan the data pages and the leaf pages.

A column with few distinct values (a *low cardinality*) is a good candidate for clustering if an index is required on the column at all. Generally it is not a good idea to create an index on a column with a low cardinality because the index does not narrow the search. However, if an index is required, a clustering index on such a column is a good choice because all of the like values are grouped (clustered) together on the data pages.

In earlier releases of DB2, the primary key was often chosen as the clustering index to allow for cursor repositioning operations. The use of the OPTIMIZE FOR *n* ROWS clause makes it unnecessary to use the clustering index for cursor repositioning, as described in Chapter PP. However, if there is batch processing requirements in which the input is in primary key sequence, the primary key is a good choice for the clustering index as described in Chapter BP.

The foreign key is a good candidate for frequent one-to-many joins (where many is large such as greater than 1,000, for example). If all of the foreign key rows are grouped together on the data pages, the join processing is more efficient. An index on the foreign key is also useful for cascading deletes and set nulls of foreign key rows with referential integrity constraint processing. If all of the J7s are grouped together on the data pages of a dependent table, a cascade delete of J7s can efficiently locate and delete all J7s that are grouped together.

Figure ID.2 summarizes the characteristics of columns that benefit from a clustering index. No one column has all of the characteristics listed here. Consider the trade-offs when deciding which column or columns should have the clustering index.

Figure ID.2. Characteristics of columns that benefit from a clustering index

♦　　Column frequently processed in sequence using the operators ORDER BY, GROUP BY, or DISTINCT.
♦　　Column frequently searched or joined over a range of values using predicates such as BETWEEN, >, <, and LIKE.
♦　　Column with a low index cardinality or skewed distribution (if an index is required).
♦　　Primary key column is a good candidate for batch processing.
♦　　Foreign key column is a good candidate for frequent one-to-many joins and enforcement of referential integrity (the many foreign values will be clustered together).

When using a partitioned tablespace, the clustering index must be the partitioning index.

Recommendation: It is very important to specify a clustering index based on your analysis of how the data is processed. If you do not create an index using the parameter CLUSTER, then by default the first index created (or more precisely the first index on the chain of indexes in the database descriptor (DBD)) is used to determine where to insert rows.

One problem with allowing DB2 to default to a clustering index is that when indexes are dropped and recreated, the first index on the chain may not be created first. DB2 starts using the new first index on the chain of indexes in the DBD to determine where to insert rows; what you thought was the clustering index is no longer used as such.

The REORG utility does not resequence rows if a clustering index is not explicitly declared. Further, the parameter SORTDATA on the REORG utility statement is ignored if there is no clustering index declared on a table. This can severely detract from performance. SORTDATA required 74 percent less elapsed time when reorganizing data with a cluster ratio of 80 percent in one case. Another deterrent to good reorganization performance is when SHRLEVEL CHANGE and NOSYSREC is used without an explicitly defined clustering index. With a clustering index defined, the rows are not written to SYSREC during unload and need not be sorted. However, without an explicitly defined cluster index this processing is necessary. The REORG OFFPOSLIMIT threshold applies only to explicitly defined clustering indexes as discussed in Chapter RR.

Consider using the following SELECT statements to verify that all tables created over the years do in fact have a clustering index.

```
SELECT  I.TBCREATOR, I.TBNAME,  I.CREATOR,
         I.NAME,  I.CLUSTERING
FROM     SYSIBM.SYSINDEXES I
WHERE NOT EXISTS
    (SELECT  1
     FROM     SYSIBM.SYSINDEXES X
     WHERE   X.CLUSTERING = 'Y'
     AND     X.CREATOR   = I.CREATOR
     AND     X.NAME      = I.NAME)
ORDER BY I.TBCREATOR,  I.TBNAME;
```

Recommendation: The rows that are returned from the SELECT statement do not have a clustering index defined. It is recommended that all tables have an explicitly declared clustering index.

Exception: If MEMBER CLUSTER is specified when creating a partitioned or simple tablespace as discussed in Chapter TS, rows are not clustered.

When Clustering Is Not Useful: Depending on the type of predicates used on the columns, some columns do not benefit from having a clustering index. If equal predicates are used on a column with a unique index, clustering has no advantages. One matching index scan can be used to locate the one row. With the exception of batch processing, there is generally no advantage to having a clustering index on a primary key with a unique index if equal predicates are used. If few rows are processed (less than 20, for example), the cost of using a non-clustering index can be acceptable. In addition, if the processing is mostly index-only processing, there is no need to access the data pages and the order of rows on the data pages does not matter.

Analyze How Data is Used

To understand the cost vs. benefits of using indexes, you must analyze how the data is used to determine which columns should be indexed. Identify columns that are frequently searched or joined, and estimate the percentage of rows processed by frequently executed SQL statements. Consider creating the clustering index on the column most frequently searched or joined in sequence. Consider non-clustering indexes on searched or joined columns in which less than 5 to 10 percent of the rows are to be selected, updated, deleted, and joined.

Refine this analysis with an estimate of the percentage of the rows that are inserted, updated, and deleted over a given period of time. Minimize the number of indexes when inserting, updating, and deleting more than about 10 percent of the rows on a weekly basis. If heavy update activity is concentrated on a weekly, monthly, quarterly, or annual basis, consider the techniques for avoiding index maintenance described in Chapter BP.

Composite indexes are useful when columns are frequently referenced together. They reduce the number of indexes that must be maintained and increase the chance of index-only retrieval.

These are only general guidelines. The physical design of the tables and indexes requires an analysis of how the data is to be processed. A process analysis matrix sometimes called a CRUD (Create, Retrieve, Update, and Delete) matrix is useful in summarizing how the data will be processed. Figure ID.3 is an example of such a matrix.

Figure ID.3. Process matrix

Transaction/Program*

Table Card/ Column Card	SPJUP	PJASG	SPJSST	PUONJ	ORDP	RECP	FIND	JUSP
S 500K	I1/D1							
SN 500K	P	J1	J1		J1		S1	
SNAME 300K		S1	S1		S10		S1	
STATUS 10	U1	S1			S10		>P	
CITY 20	U1	S1			S10		P	
P 1000K	I1/D1							
PN 1000K	P	J1	J1	J1-P	J1		S1	J1
PNAME 900K		S1	S1	S1	S1		S1	S60
COLOR 30K		S1					S1	S60
WEIGHT 15K		S1					S1	S60
CITY 20	U1	S1			P		P	
J 2000K	I9/D7							
JN 2000K		J1	J1	J1-P			S1	J1-P
JNAME 900K		S1	S1	S1			S1	S1
CITY 20	U1	S1		S1			P	
SPJ 10000K		I1				I10K		
SN 1000K		J1	J1		J1-S9			
PN 2000K		J1	J1	J1-S1	J1-P			J1
JN 3000K		J1	J1	J1-S9				J1
QTY 90K		U1	S1	S9				
Frequency**	10W	3000D	8000D	500D	2000D	2W	1000D	90000D

*Note P (Equal predicate, >P range), Sn (Select column, number of rows), In (Insert), Dn (Delete), Jm (Join, m=x for one of many joins) in each cell
**Frequency of execution: D (Daily), W (Weekly), M(Monthly), A(Annual)

Tables and columns are listed as rows of the matrix. Beside each table is noted the table cardinality (the number of rows in the table) and beside each column is noted the column cardinality (the number of distinct values in the column). Each column of the matrix has the name of a transaction or batch program.

For each cell in the matrix, note S*n* (Select column), I*n* (Insert), and D*n* (Delete) in each cell where *n* represents the number of rows processed. Joins are noted with J*m* where *m* represents one of many joins. If a predicate is specified on the column to narrow the search, note a P for an equal predicate, >P for a greater-than predicate, and so on. The last row in the matrix is for the frequency of execution; D (Daily), W (Weekly), M (Monthly), and A (Annual) are convenient notations. The form of the matrix is not critical. The important thing is to perform a detailed analysis of how the data will be processed and summarize the processing requirements to provide a basis for design of the indexes. The process matrix will also prove useful in tuning the design of the tables.

To make process analysis more manageable, identify the top 10 programs or top 10 percent of the programs for which performance is most critical. The indexes identified will likely be beneficial to most of the programs. You can do more tuning of the index design when the transaction and batch programs are tested.

Index Advisor (V7)

The index advisor is part of DB2 Universal Database (UDB) for Windows 2000, ME, 98, 95, Linux, Unix, AIX, HP-UX, Solaris, UNMA-Q, and OS/2. It is an extension of the optimizer on these platforms. Recommendations and Data Definition Language (DDL) are generated for indexes are based on information downloaded from DB2 for z/OS and OS/390 including:

◆   Subsystem configuration parameters
◆   Table and view definition
◆   Existing indexes
◆   Catalog statistics
◆   SQL workload

Jobs are provided for collecting the SQL workload statistics and downloading it to DB2 including information from IFCID 0316 and 0317. The downloaded information can be adjusted:

◆   Add/remove/change SQL statement text
◆   Change frequency and importance
◆   Specify index space restrictions

♦   Specify analysis time limit

The Control Center and DB2 Connect can be used connect to DB2 for z/OS and OS/390. It accesses the catalog and generates DDL for tables, views, and indexes as well as Data Manipulation Language (DML) for propagating the catalog statistics.

Index advisor can analyze existing indexes and suggest additional index. However, it does not suggest clustering and partitioning indexes. Index design can be similar on most platforms.

ID.3 DESIGNING COMPOSITE INDEXES

A composite index (a single index composed of more than one column) can be used for the following:

♦   To uniquely identify a row for a primary key.
♦   To reduce the total number of indexes and provide for index-only processing.
♦   To narrow a search with ANDed predicates efficiently, as in the following example:

```
SELECT  SN, PN, JN, QTY
FROM    SPJ
WHERE   SN = 'S1'
AND     PN = 'P1'
AND     JN = 'J1';
```

Separate indexes on SN, PN, and JN would require processing RIDs from each of three separate indexes before accessing the data pages. If a large number of RIDs qualify, this can mean unacceptable delays for online transactions.

The three separate indexes can be best, however, if frequent OR conditions are specified in a WHERE clause. A matching composite index scan cannot be used with ORed predicates because rows can be missed (although a non-matching index scan can be used). The following SELECT statement and the SPJ table in Figure ID.4 demonstrate the point.

Figure ID.4. Missed rows with ORed predicates on a composite index

```
SELECT  SN, PN, JN, QTY
FROM    SPJ
WHERE   SN = 'S4'
OR      PN = 'P1'
OR      JN = 'J1';
```

SN	PN	JN	QTY
S1	P1	J1	200
S1	P1	J4	700
S2	P3	J1	400
S2	P3	J2	200
S2	P3	J3	200
S2	P3	J4	500
S2	P3	J5	600
S2	P3	J6	400
S2	P3	J7	800
S2	P5	J2	100
S3	P3	J1	200
S3	P4	J2	500
S4	P6	J3	300
S4	P6	J7	300
S5	P2	J2	200
S5	P2	J4	100
S5	P5	J5	500
S5	P5	J7	100
S5	P6	J2	200
S5	P1	J4	100

If a matching index scan were used to locate the S4 row in the table followed by a scan of the remaining leaf pages, P1s and J1s above S4 would be missed as indicated by the shading in Figure ID.4.

Three separate indexes on the three columns can be used to identify all rows. In addition, multiple indexes have advantages if the WHERE clause does not specify the leading columns of the composite index.

It is possible to use a matching index scan with ORed predicates on the same column. A good way of thinking about it is if the ORed predicates can be transformed to an IN (list), multiple matching index scans can be used. For example, two matching index scans can be used on a composite index on SN, PN, and JN or a single index SN.

```
SELECT  SN, PN, JN, QTY
FROM    SPJ
WHERE   SN = 'S1'
OR      SN = 'P4':
```

ORed predicates are on the same column are equivalent to:

```
SELECT  SN, PN, JN, QTY
FROM    SPJ
WHERE   SN IN ('S1', 'P4');
```

Sequence of Columns in Composite Index Design

Composite index design, like the design of indexes in general, depends on how the data is to be processed. The sequence of columns in a composite index can significantly effect performance.

Design to maximize the number of matching columns: The first column of a composite index must be specified in the WHERE clause to perform a matching index scan. When a range predicate is used on a column, DB2 cannot match on any following columns in the composite index. Columns where equal predicates are usually specified in the WHERE clause should be placed first in the composite index.

Design to avoid sorts: Indexes can be used to avoid sorting rows. This is particularly important if many rows qualify and only a few rows will be fetched, as described in Chapter PD. Consider ordering columns in a composite index to allow for use of the index to avoid sorts for ORDER BY, GROUP BY, DISTINCT, and joins.

Design for index only processing: Index-only processing avoids I/O to the data pages. If only one or two additional columns are required in addition to the columns in a composite index, those columns should be considered for inclusion in the composite index. You will want to avoid adding a column to a primary key index because it can make the composite index non-unique and the column must be carried in dependent tables.

Minimize the number of leaf pages that must be scanned: Avoid placing a low cardinality column first in a composite index. Otherwise, you may find that many leaf pages are scanned even though a matching index scan is the chosen access path. For example, suppose that many online transactions allow the users to scroll forward in the data using a common cursor repositioning technique with a WHERE clause of:

```
      SN  >=  'S2'    AND
   ((SN   =  'S2'    AND
     PN   =  'P3'    AND
     JN   >  'J3')   OR
    (SN   =  'S2'    AND
     PN   >  'P3')   OR
    (SN   >  'S2'))
```

A matching index scan can be used only for the first column in the composite index because of the range predicate on SN. Suppose SN has a cardinality of 20 with a uniform distribution of values, the column is 10 bytes in length, and there are one million rows in the table. That means that there are about 50,000 S2s (one million rows divided by a cardinality of 20) with various PNs and JNs following the S2s that must be scanned and tested for the predicates coded. If the PN or JN columns are placed first in the index, the number of values that must be scanned and tested is reduced significantly assuming that the PN or JN columns have many distinct column values.

Exception: It might be necessary to have a low cardinality column first to avoid frequent sorts. Having a low-cardinality column first is not a problem if most of the SQL statements can specify an equal predicate on the first column and if the second column has a good cardinality and can be specified in the WHERE clause. If the low cardinality column must be placed first, do collect COLCARDF on each non-leading column of the composite index.

Analyzing Existing Indexes

If there are three or more columns in a composite index and the columns are correlated, it is important to have RUNSTATS collect correlation statistics by specifying the KEYCARD parameter as described in Chapter RR. Otherwise, the optimizer can choose a less than optimal access path. Chapter OP describes correlated columns, how to determine if the columns are correlated, and how the optimizer chooses an access path with and without correlation statistics.

Consider investigating composite indexes where non-matching index scans are used for static SQL and dynamic SQL that has been explained. You can easily determine these indexes by selecting from the plan table and the SYSINDEXES catalog table using the following SELECT statement. The PLAN_TABLE is described in Chapter EX. Change the "ABC" in the predicate "I.NAME LIKE 'ABC%'" to take advantage of your naming convention.

```
SELECT DISTINCT I.NAME, I.CLUSTERING, I.UNIQUERULE,
              I.COLCOUNT, P.MATCHCOLS
FROM    SYSIBM.SYSINDEXES I, AUTHID.PLAN_TABLE P
WHERE   P.ACCESSCREATOR = I.CREATOR
```

```
AND      P.ACCESSNAME    = I.NAME
AND      I.CREATOR       = 'Authid'
AND      I.NAME LIKE 'ABC%'
AND      P.MATCHCOLS = 0
AND      I.COLCOUNT  > 1;
```

The P.MATCHCOLS will contain 0 for SQL statements that use a non-matching index scan. If you find composite indexes that are frequently used with non-matching index scans, you may want to investigate reordering columns in the composite index to allow for matching index scans on one or more columns.

You might be able to reorder the columns so that a number of statements that were not using a matching index scan can do so. Don't forget to consider SQL that was doing a matching index scan on the old column order that cannot with the new column order. Request an explain of the access paths with the new ordering of the columns and again execute the select from the PLAN_TABLE and SYSINDEXES to determine if the new order is best overall compared to the old order.

During your analysis, consider using DEFER YES when you create an alternative composite index to avoid building the index until you have evidence that the new order is best. (DEFER YES is described in Section ID.7.) Indeed, you might want to create several composite indexes with various column orderings using DEFER YES and request explain of the access paths chosen by the optimizer for SQL statements that access the table. Based on your analysis, use the column order that maximizes the number of matching columns and minimizes sorts for most SQL statements or those that have critical performance requirements.

No match on all columns: The following SELECT statement identifies static SQL statements and dynamic SQL which has been explained but that do not have a match on all columns in the composite indexes.

```
SELECT DISTINCT I.NAME, I.CLUSTERING,
I.UNIQUERULE,
          I.COLCOUNT, P.MATCHCOLS
FROM     SYSIBM.SYSINDEXES I, AUTHID.PLAN_TABLE P
WHERE    P.ACCESSCREATOR = I.CREATOR
AND      P.ACCESSNAME    = I.NAME
AND      ICREATOR        = 'Authid'
AND      I.NAME LIKE 'ABC%'
AND      P.MATCHCOLS =
         (SELECT MAX(MATCHCOLS)
```

```
          FROM    AUTHID.PLAN_TABLE P
          WHERE   P.ACCESSCREATOR  = I.CREATOR
          AND     P.ACCESSNAME     = I.NAME)
AND       I.COLCOUNT   >
          (SELECT MAX(MATCHCOLS)
          FROM    AUTHID.PLAN_TABLE P
          WHERE   P.ACCESSCREATOR  = I.CREATOR
          AND     P.ACCESSNAME     = I.NAME)
ORDER BY  I.NAME;
```

Index not used by static SQL: The following SELECT statement identifies indexes that are not used in any static SQL statements.

```
SELECT  I.TBNAME, I.NAME, I.CLUSTERING,
        I.UNIQUERULE
FROM    SYSIBM.SYSINDEXES I
WHERE   I.CREATOR = 'Authid'
AND     I.NAME LIKE 'ABC%'
AND     I.NAME NOT IN
        (SELECT PL.BNAME
        FROM    SYSIBM.SYSPLANDEP PL
        WHERE   PL.BCREATOR = 'Authid'
        AND     PL.BNAME LIKE 'ABC%'
        AND     PL.BTYPE    = 'I')
AND     I.NAME NOT IN
        (SELECT PK.BNAME
        FROM    SYSIBM.SYSPACKDEP PK
        WHERE   PK.BQUALIFIER = 'Authid'
        AND     PK.BNAME LIKE 'ABC%'
        AND     PK.BTYPE      = 'I')
ORDER BY I.TBNAME, I.NAME;
```

If it is doubtful that dynamic SQL and future static SQL will use the indexes, drop them to avoid the overhead of index maintenance. There are a couple of cases where you may still need the index. The index may be necessary to guarantee unique values in a column and for enforcing referential integrity constraints. An alternative formulation of the above statement for identifying indexes not used by static SQL is described in Chapter ST row expression subsection.

ID.4 DATA-ONLY LOCKING

Transaction locks are not taken on index pages. *Data-only locking* is done on a row, page, table, or tablespace. It is not necessary to access a data page; DB2 builds a lock name based on object identifiers (object ID, page set ID, RID, etc.).

Index-only processing requires data-only locking for each qualifying value. Predicate evaluation is done before determining if the entry is committed when using a matching or non-matching index scan (not for tablespace scan). This applies to leaf page access to obtain RIDs for list prefetch. A data-only lock must be taken for each qualifying RID if lock avoidance is not successful. The techniques used on data pages for lock avoidance are used on the index pages to avoid data-only locks. (Lock avoidance is discussed in Chapter CC.)

If there is an attempt to access a row identified by a RID found in a leaf page that references a data page that has an X lock, for example, a -911 SQLCODE is issued.

Locks Taken with RR

When using SQL with repeatable read (RR), DB2 ensures that a row is not inserted into a range of values that are locked for RR. It also has to handle the case of insertions after the last value in the index. Srr (rr is an attribute of an IRLM share lock) locks are taken on value/RID pairs for SQL bound with RR. An EOF (End of File) lock is used on the index to manage insertions following the last value in the index. This avoids SQL with RR seeing a new row that it had not seen previously if it rereads the data. RR is discussed in Chapter CC.

Let's consider examples of the use of Srr and EOF locks. If the indexed values of 110 and 120 with RIDs 1002 and 1003 in Chapter IU, Figure IU.1, have an Srr data lock, for example, an insert of 115 waits until the other program issues a commit and releases the Srr locks. An insert takes an X data-only lock on the data referenced by RID 1003 for the indexed value of 120. An insert of 1135 encounters an Srr lock on 1130 and requests an X EOF lock.

Latch Processing

Latches are used on index and data pages when the tablespace is created with a ROW, PAGE, or ANY lock size. They are used to maintain integrity of the index pages similar to data pages as discussed in Chapter CC. They are used to avoid attempts to process data on a page that is being reorganized to reclaim free space and to avoid processing data that is being updated. One would not want to read a partially updated data page or composite index on SN, PN, and JN as a result of the UPDATE statement:

```
UPDATE SPJ
    SET SN = 'S4'  -- Update applied
        PN = 'P4'  -- Update not applied
        JN = 'J4'  -- Update not applied
  WHERE SN = 'S3'
        PN = 'P3'
        JN = 'J3';
```

Latches prevent someone seeing 'S4', 'P3', and 'J3' on the composite index or data page while the values are being changed from 'S3', 'P3', and 'J3' to 'S4', 'P4', and 'J4'. Latch processing is required for each qualifying row with and without index-only processing. Latches are discussed in Chapter CC.

ID.5 INDEX STRUCTURE MODIFICATION

Index structure modification (SMOD) operations are required when index pages are removed from the index structure as a result of all values being deleted from an index page or when an inserted row needs to be referenced on an index page that is full. The index manager maintains a balanced index structure. That is, the number of I/Os to traverse an index structure is always the same regardless of the path taken through the index.

Consider what would happen if the index manager did not maintain a balanced index structure. High insert activity down a particular path of the index structure would cause additional nonleaf page levels to be created. Look at Figure IU.1 in Chapter IU. If two additional index levels were to be added down the job 111 path, the number of index I/Os to locate the job would increase from 3 to 5, resulting in an unbalanced index structure. Users tend to access newly inserted rows frequently. If an unbalanced index structure were used, these users would have additional I/Os down the longer path.

Index Page Splitting

The index manager maintains a balanced index structure by using free space in the index when index entries are inserted or updated. If the free space on an index leaf page is used up, the next insert or update causes the page to split, with half the values remaining on the original page, and half of the values placed on a new page. The nonleaf page above the split page must be updated to point to the new lower-level leaf page. This process can continue up to the root page. If there is no free space in the root page to account for a new nonleaf page, the root page is split, and a new root page is created, resulting in an extra level being added to the index structure. When an additional level is added to the index, an additional getpage and I/O are required for every matching index scan. (An I/O is not required if buffer manager locates the page in the buffer pool.)

Recommendation: Reorganize indexes when additional levels have been added to the index, or if there are many half full pages as a result of page splitting. Chapter RR provides SELECT statements from the catalog tables that can be used to identify these conditions as well as thresholds which can be specified using REORG utility parameters.

Access During Structure Modification

Processing must be serialized during a page split and update of the next higher level page in the index. This is done by turning on the structure modification bit (SM_bit). The SM_bit is used to avoid others having to do latch processing. In addition, a tree lotch is taken. A lotch is a cross between a latch and a lock. It is taken by the index manager (not using the IRLM). SQL statements can traverse the index while the X lotch is held. However, if an SQL statement encounters a page with the SM_bit turned on, it will have to request an S lotch and wait for the X lotch to be released. Again, a lock is not taken for commit duration. These factors mean that the index page will be unavailable for a short period of time.

SQL statements can access any index pages other than the one being split, its parent and dependent pages. For example, assume that an insert of 115 into the index represented in Chapter IU Figure IU.1 results in a page split. Others cannot use the leaf page containing 101 through 130, and they cannot use the next higher page until structure modification (SMOD) processing completes. Others can use all other leaf and nonleaf pages. They can see values 1001 through 6000, for example. If an SQL statement attempts to look at values on the affected pages, they will see that the SM_bit is on and will request an S lotch. The S lotch request must wait for the X lotch to be released. It is not necessary to serialize others until the program causing the SMOD operation issues a commit work. The index manager allows a non-matching index scan, index lookaside, and index screening that is in progress to continue, provided it does not encounter the page being split.

Insertion of Sequential Values

Often, rows are inserted such that they must be referenced in the last leaf page of an index. For example, if there is an index on a timestamp, sequentially assigned IDs for orders, job IDs, employee IDs, etc. reference to the newly inserted row must be placed in the last leaf page. This applies to clustering and non-clustering indexes.

The index manager adds a newly allocated page when the last leaf page becomes full rather than splitting it. This reduces CPU, I/O, serialization contention, and latch wait time. However, if the first column of the index allows for nulls, the index manager cannot do this special processing. A column that allows for nulls has a null indicator of X'FF' as the first byte of the column. This results in nulls always being inserted on the last leaf page rather than the next sequential value.

This special processing applies only to the last leaf page, not the ones at the beginning or middle of the index. It is necessary to reference the new leaf pages in the next higher nonleaf page using the SMOD technique discussed in this section. If there are areas in the index where there is a great deal of insert activity without a corresponding deletion of indexed values in the same pages, consider using 0 percent free in the index pages as discussed in the section on creating indexes. Any requested free space is left by the utilities LOAD, REORG, and REBUILD INDEX in every leaf page and is rarely used on all but the last leaf page.

ID.6 COLUMNS THAT SHOULD NOT BE INDEXED

Columns with a low cardinality, a skewed distribution, or many unknown values make poor candidates for indexing. The use of an index on these types of columns often does not reduce the number of data pages that must be processed, and it costs more to maintain the index.

Low Cardinality Indexes

A non-clustering index on a column with a low cardinality is of limited or no value in satisfying search conditions. This is because it is likely that one or more rows will qualify on each data page. If most pages in a table must be processed, it is best to use a tablespace scan and take advantage of sequential or dynamic prefetch.

You can estimate the average number of occurrences of a value on each data page by multiplying the filter factor times the number of rows and divide by the number of data pages. For example, assume a cardinality of 20 on a city column in a million row table on 30,000 data pages. The filter factor for an equal predicate is one divided by 20--five percent of the rows are required with an equal predicate. Five percent of one million rows (50,000) divided by 30,000 data pages gives an estimate of 1.7 rows on each data page for a given city, assuming a uniform distribution of values on the data pages. If you require all rows for Dallas, it is best to do a tablespace scan because there is typically one or more qualifying rows on each data page with a uniform distribution of values. A screen can be filled with 12 rows using one sequential prefetch I/O to return 54.4 rows for Dallas in the buffer pool or 7 random reads to the data pages returns 11.9 rows to fill a screen. The use of a non-clustering index on city increases the number of I/O (I/O are required to the index pages) and offers no benefits. A general rule of thumb is to avoid creating an index on any column for which, on average, each distinct value appears one or more times on each data page.

In addition, an index on a column with a low cardinality means that many RIDs follow the index value. This chain of RIDs is called a *synonym chain*. In the example, there are typically 50,000 RIDs following a value in the leaf pages.

Look at your existing indexes to see if they can be used to reduce the number of I/Os to data pages. The following SELECT from the catalog tables calculates the number of times a given value appears on a data page on average, assuming a uniform distribution of values. The AVG_PER_PAGE_S is the average occurrences for a single column index and the AVG_PER_PAGE_C is the average for a composite index.

```
SELECT  I.CREATOR, I.TBNAME, I.NAME,
        I.FIRSTKEYCARDF, I.FULLKEYCARDF,
        C.NAME, C.COLCARDF, T.CARDF, T.NPAGESF,
        (T.CARDF*1.0)/T.NPAGESF/I.FIRSTKEYCARDF
           AS AVG_PER_PAGE_S,
        (T.CARDF*1.0)/T.NPAGESF/I.FULLKEYCARDF
           AS AVG_PER_PAGE_C
FROM    SYSIBM.SYSINDEXES  I,
        SYSIBM.SYSTABLES   T,
        SYSIBM.SYSCOLUMNS  C,
        SYSIBM.SYSKEYS     K
WHERE   I.FIRSTKEYCARDF > 0
AND     I.FULLKEYCARDF  > 0
AND     T.CARDF         > 0
AND     T.NPAGESF       > 0
AND     I.UNIQUERULE=  'D'
AND     T.TYPE       =  'T'
AND     I.CREATOR    =  'PAT'
AND     K.IXCREATOR  = I.CREATOR
AND     C.TBCREATOR  = I.CREATOR
AND     T.CREATOR    = I.CREATOR
AND     T.NAME       = C.TBNAME
AND     T.NAME       = I.TBNAME
AND     C.NAME       = K.COLNAME
AND     K.IXNAME     = I.NAME;
```

If you are considering creating a non-clustering index and are concerned that
the index might not minimize the number of data pages to be processed,
evaluate the cardinality before creating the index. Do this by counting the
number of distinct occurrences of a value in a column. For example, if you
are considering an index on SPJ.SN, the following statement gives the
cardinality of the column.

```
SELECT  COUNT (DISTINCT SN)
FROM    SPJ;
```

If there are very few distinct values (less than 20 or less than 5 percent of
the total number of rows, for example), a non-clustering index is of little
value in minimizing I/O to the data pages. It is best to use a tablespace scan
with sequential prefetch because most data pages will have qualifying rows.
Even for an online transaction, there is a good chance that a single prefetch
I/O of 32 pages using a tablespace scan will retrieve the required rows to
display to the user, assuming that rows with like values are spread

throughout the tablespace. There are exceptions. The index may be needed to locate infrequently occurring values in a skewed distribution of values or to avoid sorts.

Skewed Distribution of Values

We have been assuming a uniform distribution of values (also referred to as a flat distribution of values). A uniform distribution of values means that each city occurs the same number of times as every other city in a table. Indeed, this is the assumption made by the optimizer for static SQL using host variables. A column with a skewed distribution of values--some values occur much more frequently that others--has similar problems as one with a low cardinality, at least for the frequently occurring values. Figure ID.5 is an example of a skewed and uniform distribution of values.

Figure ID.5. Skewed and uniform distribution of values

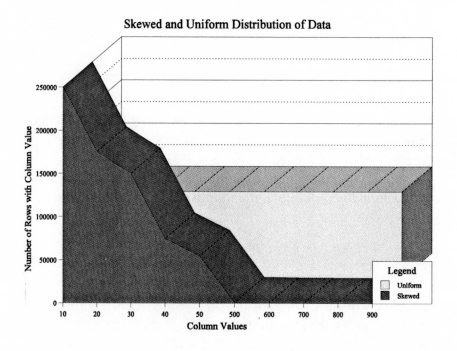

If you are considering indexing a column on STATUS, for example, and suspect that the distribution might be skewed, the following SELECT statement provides information on whether the distribution is skewed.

```
SELECT STATUS, COUNT(*)
FROM    S
GROUP BY STATUS
ORDER BY 2;
```

Figure ID.6 shows an example of the result of the SELECT statement. Using an index to locate the rows with a status of 900 in a million row table is desirable because only 50 rows qualify. It is probably worthwhile to use an index to locate rows with a status of 500 to 900 to avoid a tablespace scan. However, a tablespace scan is best to locate the rows with a status between 10 and 50 because of their frequent occurrences. You certainly do not want to use an index to locate 250,000 rows with a status of 10. A tablespace scan is best for processing one-fourth of the rows.

Figure ID.6. Identifying a skewed distribution of values

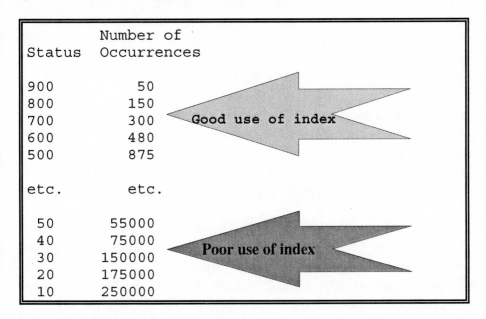

There are several long synonym chains. For example, 250,000 RIDs follow the value of 10, 175,000 RIDs follow the value of 20, 150,000 RIDs follow the value of 30, and so on. Ideally, we would not create an index at all on a column with a skewed distribution of values because of the long synonym chains and the problems of using the index to locate infrequently occurring values as well as not using the index to locate frequently occurring values.

The RUNSTATS utility determines the ten (default) most frequently occurring values in a tablespace and records them in the COLVALUE

column of SYSCOLDIST along with the frequency of occurrence in the
column FREQUENCYF. The FREQUENCYF is the percentage of rows
time 100 that contains the value in the column COLVALUE. Similar
statistics are collected by partition for a partitioned tablespace and are
recorded in SYSCOLDISTSTATS. You can review existing indexes to
determine if there is a skewed distribution of values in the indexes with:

```
SELECT  COLVALUE, FREQUENCY
FROM    SYSIBM.SYSCOLDIST
WHERE   TBCREATOR = 'POSYSTEM'
UNION ALL
SELECT  COLVALUE, FREQUENCY
FROM    SYSIBM.SYSCOLDISTSTATS
WHERE   TBCREATOR = 'POSYSTEM';
```

Developers should avoid indexing columns which have a skewed
distribution of data. Nevertheless, there are times when it is necessary to
retrieve infrequently occurring values in such a column with an index rather
than a tablespace scan to provide good response time. Techniques for
dealing with a skewed distribution are discussed in Chapters PP and OP.

Sparse Index by Application Design: A sparse index references only
specific values rather than all values in a column. DB2 does *not* support
sparse indexes. However, you can design for a pseudo sparse index.
Consider creating a sparse index table, INFREQ_STATUS, containing the
primary key and the infrequently occurring values as shown in Figure ID.7.

**Figure ID.7. INFREQ_STATUS
sparse index table**

SN	CITY
S40	Caplen
S53	Rockwall
S54	Rockwall
S67	Childress
S85	Hollis
Etc.	Etc.

The host language programs can join the target S
table with the sparse index table. Optionally, a
view can be created containing the join so that
developers need not be concerned with coding
the join. If a view is used, the only programs that
must be concerned with the sparse index table
are those that maintain it.

If the user requests an infrequently occurring
status, the following statement will return the
required results from the target S table.

```
SELECT SN, SNAME, STATUS, CITY
```

```
FROM     INFREQ_STATUS, S
WHERE    INFREQ_STATUS.STATUS = :STATUS
AND      INFREQ_STATUS.SN     = S.SN;
```

If the user requests a status that occurs frequently, a 100 SQLCODE will be received for the statement. It is necessary to execute a statement that will do a tablespace scan to get the frequently occurring status.

Advantages of a sparse index table: The advantages are that it is not necessary to maintain a large index on a skewed distribution of values with a long synonym chain of RIDs and the few infrequently occurring values can be processed efficiently.

Disadvantages of a sparse index table: It is necessary to access the INFREQ_STATUS table in addition to the S table in most cases. The INFREQ_STATUS table must be maintained with infrequently occurring values and the corresponding primary key. Programs that change the S table must maintain the sparse index table in addition to the target table. Triggers can be developed to maintain the sparse index table as discussed in Chapter TR. DB2-enforced referential integrity can provide some assistance as well. If you define INFREQ_STATUS.SN as a foreign key referencing the S table using the cascade rule, any time that you delete an SN from the S table, DB2 automatically deletes the corresponding SN from the INFREQ_STATUS table.

Many Unknown Values

A column with many unknown values results in a long synonym chain of RIDs. Consider a customer account table where the customer is asked for their social security number, but it is not required. Many customers do not know their social security numbers when they apply for accounts. The column may be declared as allowing nulls, not null with default, or having a default value assigned automatically when a row is inserted into the table with an unknown social security number. Regardless of the choice for dealing with unknown social security numbers, there will be a long synonym chain of RIDs following the null or unknown value. A column with many unknown values is not a good candidate for an index. However, it may be needed to process the known values.

Management of a Synonym Chain

An indexed column which contains a skewed distribution of values or many unknown values is like a low cardinality index in that columns with this type of data result in long synonym chains of RIDs that are costly to maintain.

Recommendation: Avoid indexing columns with a low cardinality, a skewed distribution of values, or many unknown values. All three of these conditions result in long synonym chains of RIDs.

The index manager stores the highest RID on a leaf page in the next higher nonleaf page as shown in Figure ID.8. This allows for locating the page containing the required RID directly without scanning a large number of leaf pages. Once the required page is located, a binary search of the RIDs on the page speeds the process further.

Figure ID.8. Synonym chain management

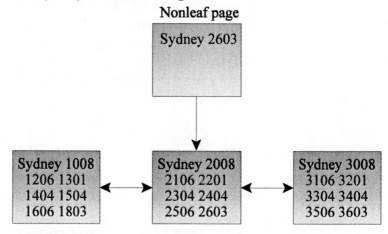

RIDs Maintained in Sequence: The index manager maintains RIDs in sequence. This allows for a binary search to locate the required RID for an update or delete, and to make a slot for an insert with a nonunique index. When a new RID is inserted following an indexed value, it must be inserted in sequence. If the new RID is not the highest RID for the value on the target leaf page, the existing RIDs must be shifted right within a single leaf page to maintain the sequence. If there is not enough space to insert the RID on the target leaf page, the leaf page is split.

Each indexed value in a unique index leaf page is followed by one RID. A nonunique index can have many RIDs following a value on a leaf page. The value occurs only once on a leaf page followed by as many RIDs as fit on the page. The value is repeated on as many leaf pages as necessary to contain all of the RIDs required to reference each row that contains the value.

Additional Columns That Should Not Be Indexed

Figure ID.9 summarizes the cases where you should be careful about indexing columns. The first three items dealing with a column with a low cardinality index, skewed distribution of values, and many unknown values have been described in this chapter.

Figure ID.9. Beware of indexing some types of columns

◆   Avoid indexes on columns with a low cardinality.
◆   Avoid indexes on columns with a skewed distribution.
◆   Avoid indexes on columns that frequently have unknown values.
◆   Minimize indexing columns that are frequently updated because delete and insert processing is required on the index.
◆   Minimize indexing wide columns (more than 30-50 percent of the row length, for example) because the number of index pages will approach the number of data pages. However, the index will be of value for matching index scans where only a few leaf pages need to be scanned.
◆   VARCHAR column are padded to their full length in an index.
◆   Minimize indexes on tables in a tablespace that occupy less than eight pages because the optimizer assumes that less than 8 pages will fit in a buffer pool.

The remaining items in Figure ID.9 are additional guidelines to consider in designing your indexes. The last guideline has significant exceptions. You should always have an index on the primary key, regardless of the number of pages. The optimizer is likely to use the index for the inner table of joins. An index is used for referential integrity constraint checking and to ensure uniqueness for the primary key. List prefetch is considered if two or more pages are estimated to contain qualifying rows. Finally, index only processing can be used.

There is a method for encouraging index usage over a tablespace scan for small tables, small tables that grow rapidly in size, and those where RUNSTATS has not been executed in a test environment, for example (V6 APAR PQ33429). NPGTHRSH in macro DSN6SPRM can be set to:

♦   -1 means that matching index access is favored for all tables including those for which RUNSTATS has not been executed

♦   0 (default) means to select the best access path without any favoritism

♦   n>=1 means to favor index usage if the table has >= SYSTABLES.NPAGESF = n

The subsystem parameter effects all SQL. If it is necessary to encourage index usage consider using OPTIMIZE FOR 1 ROW (discussed in Chapter PP) or optimization hints at the statement level (discussed in Chapter EX) because these techniques are at the statement level.

Of course, a column should not be indexed unless it can be used to narrow the search significantly for frequently executed programs where a tablespace scan would be too costly.

Logically Sequenced Indexed Values

Indexed values are maintained in logical sequence to avoid shifting values down into free space at the bottom of a leaf page. When the LOAD, REORG, or REBUILD INDEX utilities builds the index pages with the values in sequence, it leaves the specified free space at the bottom of a page. For example, assume that the values of 10, 20, 30, and 40 have been loaded into a table. The insertion of the value 25 goes into the free space at the bottom of the page to avoid shifting of the values 30 and 40 into free space as shown in the first box in Figure ID.10.

Figure ID.10. Comparison of insertion of values in index and data pages

```
       Index Leaf                    Data Page 100
          Page
┌───────────────────┐          ┌───────────────────┐
│    10    1001      │          │       PN 10  row  │
│    20    1002      │          │       PN 20  row  │
│    30    1003      │          │       PN 30  row  │
│    40    1004      │          │       PN 40  row  │
│ ---->25  1005      │          │ ---->PN 25  row   │
└───────────────────┘          └───────────────────┘
```

The index manager uses a key map area in leaf and nonleaf pages to retrieve the values in physical sequence to avoid a sort, for example. A two-byte key map entry contains the offset of each value on the page. A new value can be inserted into any available free space on the page without shifting values. It is necessary to shift the key map entries to maintain logically sequenced values. Shifting key map entries into adjacent free space left by utilities requires less processing than shifting values so that the page is unavailable for a shorter period of time. The latch processing provides for the latch being released when the processing is complete. Recall that a latch is not held for commit duration.

The key map is conceptually like the page directory at the bottom of a data page. The row for PN 25 is inserted at the bottom of the page in the free space left by a utility without having to shift rows down to insert 25 in between 20 and 30, assuming that the clustering index is on PN. The page directory is used to locate a row without having to maintain the rows in physical sequence according to the column with the clustering index as indicated in the second box of Figure ID.10.

The key map does not limit the number of values on a page like the page directory limits the number of rows on a page. The index manager attempts to insert a key map entry and value until the page is full.

Reuse of Space From Deleted Values

RIDs are marked as deleted by turning on a bit in a byte preceding each RID. It is not necessary to shift RIDs immediately to fill space from a deleted RID. The space is reusable after a commit. This is important for updates as well because the update of an indexed value uses delete processing followed by insert processing.

When a threshold of pseudo deleted and committed RIDs is reached (thought to be 10 percent), a DELETE statement causes pseudo deleted RIDs to be physically deleted. Physical deletion results in shifting RIDs to fill in the gap of pseudo deleted RIDs while holding a latch. In addition, three or fewer index pages that have all pseudo deleted RIDs within the range of pages addressed by the space map page are deleted. The limit of deleting three index pages at a time is to avoid sporadic poor performance of the SQL statement that causes the deletions. The space map page is used to track pages with only committed pseudo deleted RIDs. This provides for deleting index pages where all RIDs are marked as deleted but the pages are never accessed again for inserts, for example.

SQL using RR results in physical deletions when the percentage threshold is reached within a page. RIDs are physically deleted when the table or tablespace has an X lock. Of course, when an index is rebuilt by a utility, pseudo deleted RIDs are physically removed.

Inserting a RID reuses space from a pseudo deleted RID and the associated value if all RIDs for the indexed value are deleted. For example, Figure ID.11 shows how the RID of 7006 can replace the pseudo deleted RID of 8004 following the indexed value of Sydney. However, if a RID 4003 must be inserted between 3006 and 5001, free space from pseudo deleted RIDs and deleted values must be gathered. An X latch is held on the page during the process.

Figure ID.11. Deletions and reuse of space

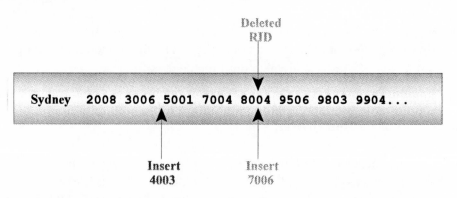

Suffix Truncation in Nonleaf Pages

It is not necessary to store the entire upper range column value in nonleaf pages in order to determine which lower level nonleaf or leaf page to access. Only the leading portion of a value needs to be stored. For example, Gim is sufficient to reference a leaf page containing Giles, Gilford, Gilkey, Gill, and so on. Halc is sufficient to reference a leaf page containing Halbach, Halbert, Halbrook, and so on. These truncated variable length values are sufficient to traverse the index tree. (Gim rather than Gil and Halc rather than Halb is used because the value in the nonleaf page must be strictly greater than the value in the leaf page.) This is called *suffix truncation,* and it is used in the root and nonleaf pages. Suffix truncation reduces the number of trailing blanks that are stored in the nonleaf pages of an index on a VARCHAR column.

Truncated values means that more upper range values and pointers to lower levels in the index tree will fit on a nonleaf page resulting in increased *fanout.* That is, fewer nonleaf pages are required with suffix truncation. Fewer levels result in fewer getpages and I/O to do a matching index scan. Also, less DASD space is required in many cases.

There are no single-level indexes. If all the required indexed values and RIDs fit on a single leaf page, there is a root page with a last page pointer.

ID.7 CREATING AND ALTERING INDEXES

Following is an example of creating a unique ascending index on the PN column in the P table to provide a basis for analyzing the parameters of the CREATE statement.

```
CREATE UNIQUE INDEX PNX
   ON P (PN)
   USING STOGROUP DASPJSTG
      PRIQTY 7200
      SECQTY   720
      ERASE NO
   PCTFREE   10
   FREEPAGE 63
   CLUSTER
   DEFER NO
   PIECESIZE 4 M
    BP0
   CLOSE NO;
```

PCTFREE and FREEPAGE: PCTFREE is the percentage of free space left at the bottom of index pages by utilities that build indexes including LOAD, REORG, and REBUILD INDEX. The default is 10 percent. The PCTFREE value should allow for the insertion of multiples of the indexed value, flag, RID, and key map entry for unique indexes. Less free space is required for nonunique indexes because the indexed value is not repeated for each occurrence of a value. No more than 10 percent free space is left in the nonleaf pages to minimize the number of levels in an index.

If page splitting has resulted in an additional index level or many half-full pages, do reorganize the index. For highly volatile data, it might be necessary to increase the free space value with the ALTER statement to reduce the frequency of reorganizations required in the future.

A FREEPAGE value of 63 as shown in the previous example means that a blank page will be left within every 64 pages. The index manager first analyzes the space map page to determine if there is an available page within plus or minus 64 pages of the page that must be split. If space is found, it is considered a near page. Otherwise a scan of the space map pages is done to locate a free page to accommodate a page split. Use a FREEPAGE of 31 or less if page splits are frequent and occur throughout the leaf pages.

PCTFREE and FREEPAGE of 0 is a good choice if there is low insert and update activity or insert and update activity is concentrated in specific areas of the index, sometimes called "hot spots". This is because the free space is distributed evenly throughout the index and will be quickly used in the hot spots but wasted in most areas of the index. There is no reason to allow for free space in an index on a column where values are almost always inserted in sequence at the end of the index. (The same principle applies to a tablespace where rows are almost always inserted in sequence according the clustering index.) This also applies to a tablespace where the clustering index is on a sequential value. PCTFREE and FREEPAGE should be zero if SYSIBM.INDEXSPACESTATS.Append_Inserts is high. It is necessary to record real-time statistics to make the determination (discussed in Chapter RR, V7).

UNIQUE: This parameter designates a unique index. A negative SQLCODE will be issued if there is an attempt to insert or update a column such that it would result in a duplicate value in the columns designated as a unique index. One null entry is allowed.

UNIQUE WHERE NOT NULL: This parameter is like the UNIQUE parameter except that it allows any number of null entries in the column. As an example of its use, assume there is a business rule where only one employee can be assigned to a job but there can be jobs with no employees assigned. The following table shows that J3 and J4 exist but no employees are currently assigned to the jobs.

J (Job Table)

JN	JNAME	CITY	EMPNO
J1	Sorter	Paris	900
J2	Punch	Rome	400
J3	Reader	Athens	(null)
J4	Console	Athens	(null)
J5	Collator	London	100
J6	Terminal	Oslo	300
J7	Tape	London	200

Be careful about allowing multiple null entries in a unique composite index. If any part of a composite index contains null, duplicates are allowed. For example, two entries of "S4 null J6" are allowed in a composite unique index. This is in conformance with the SQL standard.

CLUSTER: This parameter designates the clustering index. The importance of the clustering index and the characteristics of columns that benefit from clustering are discussed in Section ID.2 and Chapter IU.

ASC or DESC: An ascending (ASC) index is the default. If a descending index is required, DESC must be specified.

PIECESIZE: PIECESIZE provides for separating pieces of a nonpartitioning index on separate DASD devices to achieve multiple I/O paths. The piece size can be between 254 KB and 64 GB with a maximum of 254 pieces (data sets) (V6). The partitioned tablespace must be defined as allowing for more than 64 GB by specifying the DSSIZE parameter with a value of 4 GB or larger as discussed in Chapter TS. The prerequisites to exceeding 4 GB data sets are also discussed in Chapter TS. The PIECESIZE is filled completely by the LOAD, REORG, and REBUILD INDEX utilities. The primary plus secondary quantities should be evenly divisible into PIECESIZE for the best space utilization.

Space allocation, CLOSE, and BUFFERPOOL: The guidelines for index space allocation, CLOSE and BUFFERPOOL are similar to the corresponding parameters specified when creating a tablespace as discussed in Chapter CD.

Index rules: The maximum number of columns in an index is 64 and the maximum number of bytes in the indexed columns is 255. No column can appear more than once in an index. The same column can appear in multiple indexes.

When to Create and Build Indexes

In most cases, indexes should be created after a table is created and before the LOAD utility is used to populate the table. The LOAD utility builds the indexes after extracting the indexed values while inserting rows into the table. The extracted indexed values are sorted and the indexes are built efficiently in parallel or one at a time serially depending on the parameter specified to the LOAD utility as discussed in Chapter LC.

If a table already has rows when an index is created, a tablespace scan is performed to extract the indexed values. There are some significant processing differences between creating an index before or after the table is loaded. When building an index on a populated table, the internal DB2 sort is used to sort the indexed values. It uses logical work files in the work tablespaces in the database DSNDB07. The index build abends if there is not enough space in the work database, which is a real possibility. The work tablespaces are usually sized by the system administrator to accommodate sorts for SQL statements, not the build of indexes on large tables. LOAD, on the other hand, uses an external sort (such as DFSORT), which has performance advantages when sorting a large number of values.

In addition, a lock is held on the DBD while the index is being built, preventing the execution of all data definition statements and binds of SQL referencing objects in the database. If multiple indexes are created on a populated table, the processing is repeated serially for each index created.

Defer Building of Indexes

When creating indexes on a populated table, consider using DEFER YES on the CREATE INDEX statement. This results in minimal processing. The underlying VSAM data set to receive the index is created, rows are inserted into the catalog tables describing the index, the DBD is updated with information on the new index, recover pending is set for the index, and a +610 SQLCODE is issued to indicate that the index is not usable.

The REBUILD INDEX or REORG TABLESPACE utilities can be used to build the indexes at a time which is good for other activity in the system. The build uses processing similar to the LOAD utility. This has significant performance advantages. In one case there was a 37 percent savings in elapsed time and a 23 percent savings in CPU time using DEFER YES followed by building an index on a 394,785 row table. It required 572 elapsed and 59 CPU seconds with DEFER NO compared to 359 elapsed and 45 CPU seconds with DEFER YES and building the index.

Caution must be exercised in the timing of creating the indexes and building them. The optimizer can choose to use the index before it is built. Even if no plans or packages are bound between the time that the index is created and the time that it is built, a -904 SQLCODE indicating that a resource is unavailable can be received. This is because insert and delete statements must update all indexes. DB2 will see the newly created but unbuilt index in the DBD and attempt to insert a reference to a new row or delete a reference to a row when a delete is attempted.

Recommendation on when to use DEFER YES: Perhaps the most important case when you will want to use DEFER YES is when you believe it is necessary to use INSERT statements to populate a new table rather than the LOAD utility as suggested in Chapter BP. INSERT statements issued in a host language program results in excessive index page splitting and the same leaf page is updated repeatedly. These inefficiencies can be avoided by inserting rows that have been sorted in clustering sequence into a new table before creating indexes. Consider using the sort utility to check for duplicates on a column that will have a unique index to avoid errors when the index is built. After inserting the rows, create the indexes with DEFER YES, and then use REBUILD INDEX or REORG TABLESPACE.

DEFER YES is useful for testing the usefulness of additional indexes without the cost of building them. It is best to update the index statistics in the catalog tables with an estimate of the statistics that will be collected when RUNSTATS is executed after the index is built. If this is not possible, the optimizer will use default statistics to determine an access path. SQL that may benefit from the additional indexes can be explained to determine if the resources required to build and maintain the indexes are worthwhile.

If it is necessary to drop indexes before executing a batch job to avoid the costs of index maintenance as discussed in Chapter BP, DEFER YES is a good choice when re-creating the indexes.

Altering Indexes

Most index parameters can be altered. The CLUSTER, UNIQUE, UNIQUE WHERE NOT NULL, and DEFER parameters cannot. An alter of parameters that affects how the index is stored on DASD requires the index to be rebuilt before the new parameter value can be utilized for the index. These parameters are PCTFREE, FREEPAGE, and PIECESIZE. Here is an example of altering an index.

```
ALTER INDEX PNX
   USING STOGROUP DATOMSTG
      PRIQTY 14400
      SECQTY    720
      ERASE NO
   PCTFREE   25
   FREEPAGE 15
   PIECESIZE 8 M
   BUFFERPOOL BP1
   CLOSE YES;
```


ID.10 Creating Additional Indexes on the Catalog Tables

If you frequently select from the catalog tables with predicates on the indicated columns in Figure ID.12, creation of indexes on the columns avoids a tablespace scan in most cases. Based on your usage of the catalog tables, you may not require all of the indexes and perhaps there are additional indexes that can be created for your frequent accesses to the catalog tables.

Figure ID.12. Create additional indexes on the catalog tables

Catalog Table	Columns	Used to Determine
SYSCOLUMNS	NAME, TBNAME, TBCREATOR	Table layout without TBNAME and TBCREATOR (there is an index on TBCREATOR, TBNAME, NAME)
SYSDBRM	NAME	Information about program from which DBRM was created
SYSDBRM	PLNAME	Name of the application plan of which this DBRM is a part
SYSFOREIGN-KEYS	CREATOR, TBNAME, RENAME, COLSEQ	Referential integrity relationships
SYSPACKDEP	DNAME	Objects dependent on a package
SYSPLANDEP	DNAME	Objects dependent on a plan
SYSRELS	CREATOR, TBNAME, RELNAME	Referential integrity relationships
SYSSYNONYMS	TBCREATOR, TBNAME	Synonyms on a table
SYSSTMT	PLCREATOR, PLNAME, NAME, STMTNO	SQL statements used by a plan. Can be a very large index.
SYSVIEWDEP	DCREATOR, DNAME	Tables and views that have a view defined on them

Catalog Table	Columns	Used to Determine
SYSVOLUMES	SGCREATOR, SGNAME	Volume ID of volumes in a given storage group if not managed by SMS

ID.8 SUMMARY

Index design and usage affects application performance more than any other single factor in the design and development of application systems. DB2 provides a multitude of indexing options. It is difficult to predict how tables will be accessed. However, it is essential to carefully analyze how SQL will be used in online transactions, batch programs, and data warehousing applications to determine which columns should be indexed. A process matrix is a good tool for doing this.

The choice of which column should have the clustering index is very important. The characteristics of columns that benefit most from having a clustering index are where the index can be used to retrieve data in sequence without a sort, to facilitate efficient join processing, to satisfy range and string searches, and for batch processing. For columns with a low cardinality or skewed distribution a clustering index is best if an index is required at all. No single column will have all of these characteristics, and you must consider the many trade-offs when deciding which column should have the clustering index.

EXERCISES

1. a) Why should you limit the number of indexes on a table?

b) Are there types of tables that can have more indexes than others?

2. In general, how should you determine which columns should be indexed?

3. a) How does the index created with the CLUSTER parameter affect the data and index?

b) Does the clustering index structure and maintenance differ from a non-clustering index structure and maintenance?

4. a) If an index is not created with the keyword CLUSTER, how does DB2 determine where to insert a row in a table?

b) How is a reorganization affected by the lack of an index created with the keyword CLUSTER?

5. a) Why is the clustering index or any index with a good cluster ratio important?

b) What are some of the various ways that an index with a good cluster ratio can be used?

6. a) What are the advantages of having the clustering index on the PK?

b) What type of processing results in little benefit to having the clustering index on the PK?

7. a) What are the advantages of having the clustering index on the FK?

b) What are the characteristics of a FK that results in less benefit from having a clustering index?

8. a) Is the clustering index a good choice on a column with a low cardinality, skewed distribution of values, or many unknown values, if an index is required? Why?

b) What are the disadvantages of having an index on a column with a low cardinality, skewed distribution or many unknown values?

9. What are some guidelines for composite index design?

10. a) Can index only processing be done with data only locking?

b) Is it necessary to access a data page to take a data-only lock for index processing?

11. a) Is lock avoidance used on indexes?

b) How can one get a -911 SQLCODE when accessing an index page?

ANSWERS

1. a) It is more costly to insert/update/delete index pages than data pages. Even if there is only one index on a table, the costs are higher because of the possibility of page splitting for inserts and maintenance of RIDs when rows are deleted. The update of a row results in changing the row on a page (a variable length row that has been increased in length may need to be moved if there is insufficient space). The update of an index requires that the indexed value and/or RID be removed from an index page and inserted in another index page in most cases. The more indexes that are on a table, the higher the cost of maintenance. It costs about 3 times as much to maintain 3 indexes. There is also the additional costs for each index when executing the load, reorg, and recover utilities.

b) More indexes can be created on tables that have very low insert/update/delete activity. Be cautious about too many indexes on tables that contain extracted data. Even though the data is not updated in the table, the extracted data must be refreshed periodically -- frequently with a load replace.

2. It is necessary to do a process analysis to determine which columns should be indexed. You should identify columns which are frequently searched or joined and estimate the percentage of rows that will be processed. If the percentage is small and the table is large, consider indexes on those columns. Certainly an index is required on the PK, and indexes should be seriously considered on FKs.

3. a) DB2 attempts to maintain the rows in sequence on the column with the clustering index as long as there is free space. There is no affect on the index itself.

b) No, the clustering index has exactly the same structure and is maintained like non-clustering indexes through page splitting. Issues specific to the clustering index will be discussed in subsequent exercises.

4. a) DB2 uses the first index on the DBD index chain to determine where a row should be inserted. If indexes are dropped and recreated, the first index created may be different when the indexes are recreated.

b) Data is _not_ reclustered by the reorganization utility. The SORTDATA parameter on the REORG statement is ignored. SORTDATA significantly improves reorganization performance in the majority of cases. For example, the reorganization of a tablespace with an 80 percent cluster ratio required 74 percent less elapsed time when SORTDATA was used in one case. An exception is when the cluster ratio is 100 percent, in which case the elapsed time was increased by 4 percent. In addition, it is not possible to avoid writing data to SYSREC when using REORG with SHRLEVEL CHANGE during the unload and sort which detracts from performance.

5. a) An index with a good cluster ratio provides an efficient access path for selecting, updating, and deleting rows.

b) An index with a good cluster ratio is useful in retrieving rows in sequence without the delay, I/O, and CPU time that is required to retrieve all qualifying rows and sort them before the first row can be returned to the user. All 3 join methods have performance advantage when a clustering index can be used.

6. a) If there is a good deal of batch processing in sequence on the PK, the clustering index offers significant advantages. The clustering index is also important for cursor repositioning in a batch program for restart and when a -911 or -913 is received.

b) Cursor repositioning in an online transaction that requires the processing of only a few rows to be displayed to the user does not require a clustering index when OPTIMIZE FOR n ROWS (where n is small) is used in most cases. (This clause is discussed in Chapters PD and PP.) An index with almost any cluster ratio can be used to retrieve a few rows in sequence. In addition, many online transactions use equal predicates on the PK in which case clustering of the data has little or no benefit.

7. a) A one-to-many join (1 PK and many FK values) where the many matching FKs are clustered on the data pages can result in enhanced join performance. In addition, DM can enforce the cascade or set null constraint efficiently with the FK values clustered on the data pages. For example, the deletion of S4 from the S table requires that all S4s be located and deleted from the SPJ table when the cascade delete constraint is defined. A matching index scan can be used to locate S4 in the FK index. The S4 value has all RIDs pointing to the S4 FK rows following the value of S4 in the leaf pages. Also, most of the pages identified by the RIDs are in sequence on DASD, making the deletion of all S4 rows quite efficient.

b) If the FK column has a high cardinality, there will be few duplicate FK values in most cases and the benefits of a) will not apply. For example, a one-to-one relationship between the PK and FK would result in little or no benefit in having the clustering index on the FK.

8. a) Yes, the duplicate values are grouped together on the data pages so that a single matching index scan can be done followed by scanning the leaf pages and dipping down to retrieve the rows that are grouped together on the data pages.

b) The index is of very little value in processing a large percentage of rows which frequently qualify when there is a low cardinality, skewed distribution of values, or many unknown values. Indeed, I/O to the index adds to the processing costs. A tablespace scan with asynchronous prefetch is the best access path when processing a large percentage of the rows. If the cardinality is <= 3, it is very doubtful that the optimizer will choose to use a matching index scan. There is a good probability that the required values to display to the user will be on the first 32 pages prefetched with 1 I/O for a tablespace scan when there is a low cardinality. An index with a low cardinality, skewed distribution, or many unknown values results in a long synonym chain of RIDs which are costly to maintain when deleting, updating, and inserting rows.

9. It is best to place columns used with equal predicates first in a composite index. Try to order columns to minimize sorts. Consider adding columns to the index to allow for index only access. (Avoid adding a column to a PK index if the column must be carried in the dependent tables.) Avoid placing a low cardinality column first in a composite index unless it is necessary to avoid frequent sorts or the first column can be specified with an equal predicate and the second column with a good cardinality can be specified in most WHERE clauses.

10. a) The index manager can do index only processing without access to data pages.

b) It is not necessary to access a data page to take a data-only lock. The lock name is based on data page identifiers including the object ID, page set ID, RID, etc.

11. a) Yes, if the RBA of when the index page was last updated and logged

is < RBA for the index space, no data-only lock is required. The techniques used on data pages for lock avoidance are used on index pages to avoid data-only locks.

b) The index manager attempts to get a data-only lock when an index page is accessed if lock avoidance is not successful. If the data page is already locked, a -911 SQLCODE will be received. The lock name for the data-only lock is the same as the lock name for the data page lock. This is necessary to ensure data integrity.

FIGURES

The Basics of SQL Data Manipulation

SL.1 INTRODUCTION

The label *structured query language* is a misnomer in that the language it refers to provides much more than query capabilities. It also provides data definition and data control facilities and, as this chapter describes, rich data-manipulation capabilities. The name is misleading in another sense. Although the language serves well for interactive queries and updates, it can also be embedded within host-language programs for database access. With only a few minor additions to the syntax, embedded SQL works exactly the same as interactive SQL.

The primary data-manipulation functions provided by SQL are SELECT, UPDATE, INSERT, and DELETE. The SELECT capabilities provide a powerful, flexible collection of methods for finding desired data within a database. UPDATE, INSERT, and DELETE allow for the changing, addition, and removal of rows, respectively. We will examine all of these capabilities in detail by looking at examples of statements that employ them. The examples refer to the tables presented in Figure CT.6. By working through the example statements manually—referring to the tables and identifying selected rows, for example—one can easily grasp each statement's meaning.

SL.2 SELECT STATEMENTS

All SELECT statements take this basic form:

```
SELECT SNAME, CITY
FROM   S
WHERE  SN = 'S4';
```

In general, the SELECT clause indicates the column or columns that are to provide the information; the FROM clause indicates the table or tables that contain those columns; the WHERE clause, contains the conditions by which the information is to be selected. Each condition is referred to as a predicate. A SELECT list may contain up to 750 columns and a FROM clause up to 15 tables.

The WHERE clause contains one or more conditions that must be met before a row is included in the returned set. A condition may be that a row's value must relate to some other value in a particular way. SQL allows the standard comparison operators: the "equal to" (=), "not equal to" (!=, ¬=, or <>), "greater than" (>), "greater than or equal to" (>=), "less than" (<), and "less than or equal to" (<=) operators. The > and < operators can be preceded by ! or ¬ to represent negation. The operators are referred to as simple operators and apply to alphanumeric as well as numeric values.

In the statement above, for example, the WHERE clause stipulates a search for information related to a supplier with a supplier number (SN) equal to S4. The WHERE clause can stipulate multiple search criteria through the use of the AND and OR Boolean operators. In addition, another kind of SELECT statement, called a subselect, may serve as a search criterion. Section SL.10 introduces this facility and the performance implications are discussed in Chapter ST.

SELECT *

An asterisk (*) after SELECT indicates that all columns in the selected rows are to be returned. The asterisk avoids the need to specify all the column names or even to know what they are. SELECT * should not be used in host-language programs, however. Such use would detract from data independence in this way: When an SQL statement SELECTS data for use by a program, the program must have a host variable to receive a value from each column selected. If a column were added to the table, the embedded SELECT * would automatically pass its value to the program. If there is no host variable, DB2 has no place to store the returned value for access by the program. Similarly, if a column were deleted, SELECT * would not return the correct values to the program. If the columns to be selected had been listed, however, the added columns would not have affected the program and the deleted column would affect only the programs referencing the column. In addition, SELECT * detracts from good performance as discussed in Chapter PP.

This example illustrates the use of SELECT * and the operation of a simple WHERE clause. The problem is to determine from the example tables the jobs that use part number P6 supplied by supplier S5 and the number of parts (QTY) assigned to each of those jobs. The Supplier/Part/Job (SPJ) table in Figure CT.6 contains all of that information. This statement SELECTS it:

```
SELECT  *
FROM    SPJ
WHERE   SN = 'S5'
AND     PN = 'P6';
```

The SELECT * clause indicates that all column values from the appropriate rows are to be returned. The FROM clause indicates the rows are to be found in the SPJ table. And the WHERE clause stipulates that only rows in which SN equals S5 and PN equals P6 are to be returned. Single quotation marks in the statement identify character string values. Before reading the report returned by this SELECT statement, presented below, try locating in the SPJ table the rows that satisfy the WHERE criteria. Here is the report with the needed information:

SN	PN	JN	QTY
S5	P6	J2	200
S5	P6	J4	500

Notice that SELECT * returns the columns in the order in which they were defined in the CREATE TABLE statement, and the column names are returned as headings.

Naming a Result with AS

A SELECT statement produces a report when executed interactively using QMF or SPUFI, for example. The column headings of the report are the same as the column names in a table as was seen in the previous examples. You may want the report headings to be different than the column names. This can be accomplished with the AS clause. Here we want the QTY column to have a report heading of NUMBER_OF_PARTS:

```
SELECT SN, PN, JN, QTY AS NUMBER_OF_PARTS
FROM    SPJ
WHERE   SN = 'S5'
AND     PN = 'P6';
```

The report produced with the AS clause looks like:

SN	PN	JN	NUMBER_OF_PARTS
S5	P6	J2	200
S5	P6	J4	500

The AS clause is particularly useful in naming a calculated expression as we will see in this section.

Selecting Nulls

SQL statements that test for the presence of nulls hold the potential for a programming difficulty. It may seem natural for programmers to test for nulls in the same way they test for any other value. A typical SQL statement to locate suppliers with a status of 30 would be:

```
SELECT SN, SNAME, STATUS
FROM    S
WHERE   STATUS = 30;
```

The equals sign would not be correct syntax, however, for a statement that seeks null salaries. As DB2 sees it, a null does not equal—or compare in any way with—anything. SQL therefore provides a special predicate using the verb IS to test for nulls. In this case, the proper statement would be: WHERE STATUS IS NULL.

SELECT Using OR or IN

A user or programmer can limit a search to rows containing any one of a number of values by using a series of OR operators in the WHERE clause or by using the IN (list). Consider a request for information about suppliers S1, S3, and S4. We would like to know the parts supplied by each, how many of each part is supplied, and the jobs in which they are used. All of that information is contained in the SPJ table. Using the OR operator, this statement returns the necessary rows:

```
SELECT SN, PN, JN, QTY
FROM    SPJ
```

```
WHERE   SN = 'S1'
OR      SN = 'S3'
OR      SN = 'S4';
```

The SELECT returns all columns from the SPJ table for rows having a supplier number of S1, S3, or S4. The equivalent statement using the IN operator is:

```
SELECT SN, PN, JN, QTY
FROM   SPJ
WHERE  SN IN ('S1', 'S3', 'S4');
```

The statement can be read as "Return all column values from the SPJ table for rows with supplier numbers included in the set of numbers consisting of S1, S3, and S4." The responses to the statements are the same:

SN	PN	JN	QTY
S1	P1	J1	200
S1	P1	J4	700
S3	P3	J1	200
S3	P4	J2	500
S4	P6	J3	300
S4	P6	J7	300

If the user requires the selection of a varying list of values, consider the use of an IN subselect from a temporary table as discussed in Chapters ST and SP.

Range SELECTS

SQL also allows users to retrieve rows associated with ranges of search values—for example, all rows from the Part (P) table containing weight values greater than or equal to 12 and less than or equal to 14. The language provides two equivalent ways of formulating these requests. One way uses the symbolic relationship operators. Those operators would be used to report on parts with weights included within the range just stated in the following way:

```
SELECT  PN, WEIGHT
FROM    P
WHERE   WEIGHT >= 12
AND     WEIGHT <= 14;
```

The alternative uses the BETWEEN operator:

```
SELECT  PN, WEIGHT
FROM    P
WHERE   WEIGHT BETWEEN 12 AND 14;
```

Besides being easier to type and perhaps a bit easier to grasp, this second statement holds performance benefits—explained in Chapter PP—over the one using the symbolic operators. One must remember, however, that the BETWEEN operator includes within its range the numbers used in the statement. A way to remember is to understand that the range defined by the BETWEEN operator is equivalent to that created by the *less than or equal to* and *greater than or equal to* operators. (NOT BETWEEN does not include the end points.)

The report returned by either statement is:

PN	WEIGHT
P1	12
P4	14
P5	12

String Searches

The LIKE predicate specifies searches for values that contain any character or string of characters. The operator allows the user to specify the location of the target character or string within a longer string by using underscores and the percent (%) sign. Each underscore represents a character position of any value. The % sign is a wild card standing for any number of alphanumeric values. Examples will illuminate the points.

The following statement requests a search for the name of any supplier in the Supplier (S) table whose name includes a K:

```
SELECT  SN,  SNAME
FROM    S
WHERE   SNAME LIKE '%K%';
```

The % signs indicate that any combination of characters can precede or follow the K or only the value of K exists in the SNAME. A scan of the S Table's SNAME column reveals that two values fit the criteria: Blake and Clark.

If a string search is being done within a host-language program, the host-language variable used to provide the value to be found must match the length of the column being searched. If that variable is short, it must be padded with underscores or the % sign. In the example above if the column being searched is CHAR(5), the host variable must contain %K%%%. The additional % signs, not needed with interactive SQL, pad the variable to the required five character length. Such padding is not necessary for a column declared as VARCHAR. Chapter PD discusses host-language variables more fully.

A request for suppliers with a K in the fourth position of their names demonstrates the use of the underscore with the LIKE operator:

```
SELECT  SN,  SNAME
FROM    S
WHERE   SNAME LIKE '_ _ _K%';
```

The one value satisfying this request is Blake.

Negating a Predicate

The NOT operator in the WHERE clause allows the SELECT to search for rows that do not meet the stated criteria. The word NOT preceding another operator causes this negation. The symbol ¬= placed before a comparison operator negates it. For example, these statements return suppliers not located in London or Athens:

```
SELECT  SN,  SNAME,  CITY
FROM    S
WHERE   CITY NOT IN ('London',  'Athens');
```

or

```
SELECT  SN, SNAME, CITY
FROM    S
WHERE   CITY ¬= 'London'
AND     CITY ¬= 'Athens';
```

SL.3 COLUMN FUNCTIONS AND ARITHMETIC CALCULATIONS

SQL offers a number of built-in mathematical functions called column functions for use in the SELECT clause that allow users to request data on the basis of simple mathematical operations or according to several numeric properties. It returns, for example, the sum or average of the values that meet the search criteria, and it identifies the minimum or maximum value found. In addition, SQL allows users to request computations—addition, subtraction, multiplication, division, and combinations of those operations—on the selected data. The operators are AVG, SUM, MIN, MAX, COUNT, and DISTINCT and the familiar arithmetic symbols +, -, *, and /. The built-in functions, except for COUNT, ignore nulls in their calculations. Examples best explain the functions' use.

MIN, MAX, and AVG

The SPJ table (Figure CT.6) contains the quantity of each part each supplier supplies for each job. To find the minimum, maximum, and average number of parts supplied by supplier S2, the SELECT statement must identify the quantities in rows where supplier number is S2 and apply the MIN, MAX, and AVG operators to those amounts:

```
SELECT  MIN(QTY), AVG(QTY), MAX(QTY)
FROM    SPJ
WHERE   SN = 'S2';
```

Eight rows satisfy the WHERE clause. In those rows, the minimum QTY value is 100, and the maximum is 800. The average QTY for those rows is 400. The statement returns:

MIN(QTY)	AVG(QTY)	MAX(QTY)
100	400	800

Headings above the resulting values may or may not be returned depending on the interactive tool that is being used and whether the AS clause is used. The AS clause can be used to assign a name to the result of a column function or to a calculated expression. The AS name appears as the column heading when using QMF or SPUFI as will be seen in the following example.

Math in the SELECT Clause

Suppose we want to know the difference between the maximum quantity and the average for parts supplied by S2. A simple adjustment of the SELECT clause, inclusion of a minus sign, provides the answer:

```
SELECT MAX(QTY)  -  AVG(QTY)
    AS DIFFERENCE
FROM    SPJ
WHERE   SN = 'S2';
```

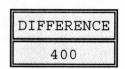

DIFFERENCE
400

The SELECT clause can handle more complex calculations. When functions are used in combination in SELECT equations, SQL follows the standard order of operations. It first computes expressions within parentheses, beginning with the innermost set if parentheses are nested. Then it performs multiplication and division before addition and subtraction. For example, to calculate the difference between the maximum quantity and average quantity that we have just found as a percentage of the average, we must divide the difference by the average and multiply by 100. Here is that computation in the SELECT clause:

```
SELECT  (MAX(QTY)  -  AVG(QTY)) / AVG(QTY)  *  100
```

The parentheses enclosing the subtraction are necessary to ensure the operation is performed first, as the computation demands. The answer in this case is 100. Suppose the parentheses were forgotten. The clause would be:

```
SELECT MAX(QTY)  -  AVG(QTY) / AVG(QTY)  *  100
```

SQL would perform the division and multiplication first (400/400*100 = 100) and then the subtraction (800 - 100 = 700), not the intended computation.

COUNT Column Function

The COUNT column function can be used to count the number of rows in a table or the number of rows that meet a specified condition. When COUNT is followed by an asterisk in parentheses and there is no WHERE clause, the number of rows in the table is returned.

```
SELECT  COUNT(*)  AS  NROWS
FROM    SPJ;
```

NROWS
24

If a WHERE clause is specified, the COUNT function counts all rows that satisfy the condition.

```
SELECT  COUNT(*)  AS  NROWSP3
FROM    SPJ
WHERE   PN  =  'P3';
```

NROWSP3
9

DISTINCT Function

Although the DISTINCT function is not a column function per se, it can be used with column functions. It filters out all redundant column values in the rows satisfying the WHERE clause or, if no WHERE clause is used, of the entire table. For example, the following statement would be used to find the unique supplier number and part number pairs that appear in the SPJ table. Notice that DISTINCT applies to all the columns in the SELECT clause even though commas separate the columns.

```
SELECT  DISTINCT  SN,  PN
FROM    SPJ;
```

SN	PN
S1	P1
S2	P3
S2	P5
S3	P3
S3	P4
S4	P6
S5	P1
S5	P2
S5	P3
S5	P4
S5	P5
S5	P6

DISTINCT can work with column functions, removing the repeated values before performing the specified function. For that use, DISTINCT is specified within parentheses, along with the name of the column being acted upon. Here we want to determine the number of unique PNs in the SPJ table:

```
SELECT  COUNT  (DISTINCT  PN)  AS  UNIQUE
FROM    SPJ;
```

UNIQUEPN
6

SL.4 DATA TYPE CONVERSIONS

DB2 offers a number of scalar functions that can be used in the SELECT or WHERE clause for converting the data types of values from columns, host-language variables, and calculations. Scalar functions act on a single value in contrast to a column function which usually acts on multiple values in a column. We will discuss many of the basic scalar functions in this chapter. There are many user defined function and you can develop more as discussed with Chapter UD. The performance implications of scalar and column functions are discussed in Chapter PP.

The scalar function DIGITS converts a numeric value to a character string with leading zeros and without a sign or decimal point. If the value is a SMALLINT type, the result is a 5-byte string; if it is an INTEGER type, the result is a 10-byte string; and if it is a DECIMAL, the result has the same number of digits as the original value.

The function CHAR can be used to convert a decimal data type to a character string. This can be useful for converting very large numbers to a character representation for reporting purposes. Most host languages support a decimal value no greater than the equivalent of DECIMAL(15). DB2 supports numbers up to and including DECIMAL(31) if DEC31 is specified in DSNZPARM or the special register CURRENT PRECISION is set to 'DEC31' as discussed below. The IBM COBOL V2R2 compiler does support the equivalent of DEC31. If your compiler does not support very large numbers, the following statement is an example of converting a very large DEBT column value to a character string for reporting with a sign and decimal point assuming that :DEBT is declared as PIC X(33) in a COBOL program. EXEC SQL and END-EXEC are discussed in Chapter PD.

```
EXEC SQL SELECT CHAR(DEBT)
         INTO   :DEBT
         FROM   BUDGET
         WHERE  ID = :ID END-EXEC.
```

If you need to override the DEC15 default for the DB2 subsystem when using dynamic SQL (discussed in Chapter PD), the CURRENT PRECISION special register can be set like:

```
SET CURRENT PRECISION = 'DEC31'
```

You can determine the current precision like:

```
SET :HVDEC = CURRENT PRECISION
```

The function DECIMAL can be used to convert a numeric value in a character data type to a decimal data type. For example, assume NUMERICID = '123456 ', DECIMAL (NUMERICID, 6,0) results in a decimal value of 123456. Notice that the trailing blanks are truncated.

The function DECIMAL can also be used to convert any numeric data type into a packed decimal data type. If the numeric value to be converted is called BALANCE, the function DECIMAL (BALANCE, 6,2) changes it to a packed decimal with a precision of six and two decimal places. A typical conversion of a calculation would be DECIMAL (AVG(BALANCE, 6,2)), which computes the average of BALANCE and returns it with a precision of six and two decimal places. FLOAT(BALANCE) converts a numeric BALANCE to a double precision floating point number.

The INTEGER function works in a similar fashion to convert any numeric type to an integer. It is particularly useful for rounding off numerals. For example, INTEGER (AMOUNT + 0.5) rounds up and truncates to an integer any numeric AMOUNT with a fractional part of 0.5 or more and rounds down to an integer any decimal amount with a fractional part less than 0.5. The result is a 4-byte binary number. The ROUND user-defined function discussed in Chapter UD is a good alternative and offers a good deal of flexibility. When INTEGER is used with a mathematical function such as SUM, the order of the functions in a statement is important. For example, the clause INTEGER (SUM (AMOUNT + 0.5)) sums the AMOUNT values and round off the result. The column function SUM

(INTEGER (AMOUNT + 0.5)) rounds off the AMOUNT values before summing.

The HEX function converts any data type other than LONG VARCHAR to hexadecimal representation. The results are presented as a VARCHAR type with twice as many bytes as the original value. The HEX function is useful for converting values in the START_RBA column of the catalog table SYSIBM.SYSCOPY. This column presents the relative byte address (RBA) to which the RECOVER utility should recover in a log. The utility requires that the RBA be presented in hexadecimal representation.

Finally the VARGRAPHIC function converts a character string of 254 bytes or fewer to a double-byte DBCS representation, which is used for Asian Katakana ideograms.

SL.5 STRING MANIPULATION FUNCTIONS

DB2 provides several scalar functions for manipulating character strings.

Substring Function

The substring function (SUBSTR) extracts a portion of a character string, with numbers presented with the string value's name indicating which alphanumeric value begins the extract and the number of characters to be included. For example, SUBSTR (SNAME, 1,3) instructs DB2 to begin with the first character in the SNAME value and include three bytes. If the SNAME value were JACKSON, the function's result would be JAC. If there are not enough characters to fill the receiving host variable or column, the result is padded with trailing blanks.

One interesting use for SUBSTR in conjunction with DIGITS is to break apart intelligent identification numbers (those including codes). For example, the seventh digit of a part identification number of INTEGER type might indicate the city in which it is stored. An SQL statement like this might be used to select according to that digit:

```
SELECT  CITY, QTY
FROM    INVENTORY
WHERE   SUBSTR (DIGITS (PARTID), 7,1) = '4';
```

In the WHERE clause, DIGITS converts PARTID to a character string, and SUBSTR extracts the seventh character. If that character is '4', the search criterion is satisfied.

Concatenation Function

The concatenation function is in a way the reverse of the substring function. Rather than taking strings apart, as SUBSTR does, concatenation puts them together. The function can be used to combine any combination of character variables and literals. Concatenation is used in the SELECT clause to format results or in a WHERE clause to put data in the desired format for processing and is invoked with the CONCAT operator. In the statement's results, the character string coming before CONCAT is joined with that after the CONCAT operator. Literals are enclosed in single quotes.

For example, the following statement finds the names and colors of parts stored in London, and returns them, separated by a comma and a space:

```
SELECT  PNAME CONCAT ','
    CONCAT COLOR
FROM    P
WHERE   CITY = 'London';
```

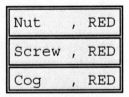

Notice that these results assume that PNAME has been declared as CHAR(5). For CHAR columns, the concatenation takes place after the trailing blanks that pad a value to the column's length. For VARCHAR columns, concatenation takes place immediately after each value's final character.

If PNAME is declared VARCHAR, the results is:

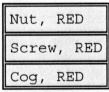

Another string manipulation function, LENGTH, counts the number of bytes, or characters, in a CHAR or VARCHAR value, excluding bytes used as null and VARCHAR indicators. LENGTH includes a count of trailing blanks for CHAR columns. VARCHAR columns have no trailing blanks. The result is an integer.

STRIP Function

The STRIP function can be used to remove a specified character (blank is the default) from leading, trailing, or both the leading and trailing (default) positions of a character data type column or field. If the CITY column has the value of ' Copenhagen ', the function STRIP(CITY, BOTH, ' ') results in 'Copenhagen'. Actually all that is needed in this case is STRIP(CITY) to give the result of 'Copenhagen'. This is because the second operand of BOTH is the default and the default for the third operand is blank (' ').

You can indicate that only the leading or trailing specified characters are to be removed. For example, if the AMOUNT host variable contains '0014.950' and the function STRIP(AMOUNT, LEADING, '0') is applied the result is 14.950 with the leading zeros stripped off. Similarly, the function STRIP(AMOUNT, TRAILING, '0') results in 0014.95 with the trailing zeros stripped off.

COALESCE and VALUE Functions

COALESCE and VALUE are synonyms. COALESCE conforms to the SQL standard. These scalar functions provide flexibility for handling nulls and zeros in computations. Without the use of one of these functions, for example, division by null or zero would result in a negative SQLCODE, which indicates an error. If the COALESCE function is applied to the division by zero or null, the result is a null. The calculation COALESCE (AMOUNT/PERCENT) returns null whenever PERCENT is zero or null.

COALESCE can also be used to substitute a numeric value for any nulls used in computations. That function is used by identifying the value to be substituted for nulls after the name of the data item used in the computation. For example, in the calculation NET_SALARY - COALESCE (INSURANCE, 0), zero is subtracted from NET_SALARY whenever INSURANCE is a null. Otherwise if the null was subtracted, the result would also be null. Similarly, adding a null or multiplying by null results in null.

NULLIF Function

The NULLIF function is useful for dealing with a value used to represent that no valid value exists. Chapter CT discusses alternatives for representing unknown values. One alternative is to define a column such that a specified value will be placed in the column when a row is inserted into the table without giving a value for the column. For example, the WEIGHT column can be defined as WEIGHT INTEGER WITH DEFAULT -1. This results in a -1 being placed in the WEIGHT column if the user does not know the weight of a part when information about a new part is inserted into the table.

If the user requests the total weight of parts in London for shipment to Edinburgh, the -1 value should not be included in the sum. This can be accomplished like:

```
SELECT  SUM(NULLIF(WEIGHT,  -1))
FROM    P
WHERE   CITY = 'London';
```

The NULLIF function avoids inclusion of any -1 values in the summation. If the first and second operands are equal, a null is returned, and as we saw in Section SL.5, null is not included in the calculation of a column function. In the example, if WEIGHT = -1, a null is returned and is not included in the summation. If the first and second operands are not equal, the first operand value is returned and in this case included in the summation which is the desired result. Although, the user should be notified if the total weight does not include some parts to be shipped to Edinburgh, particularly if the user is estimating the costs to ship the parts and the costs are based on weight.

SL.6 DATE AND TIME FUNCTIONS AND CALCULATIONS

DB2 offers a number of functions for working with its three date and time data types—DATE, TIME, and TIMESTAMP—and a number of calculations that may be used with the data types. The flexibility of the DATE and TIME data types begins with the formats of the dates and times they represent, which include international, U.S., European, and Japanese standards. Examples of the formats are given in Figure CT.3. The International Standard Organization's (ISO) formats are the defaults, but the system's installer can change these defaults. The default values are used unless the SQL statement using DATE or TIME specifies otherwise. The format can also be chosen for an application program at precompile time.

The CHAR function is used in SQL statements to specify a format for a DATE or TIME value other than the default. For example, if the default is the ISO standard but the programmer wants to use the USA standard, the CHAR function used with the column name makes the conversion. The syntax is CHAR(DATE_COL, USA), where DATE_COL is the column name and USA is the desired format. The conversion returns the date as a character string with USA punctuation, 06/23/1987, for example. If the punctuation is not desired, the HEX function can be used like: HEX(DATE_COL). The CHAR function can also be used to convert the results of date or time calculations to character strings rather than the decimal representation that would otherwise result. For example, CHAR(DATE_COL - 60 DAYS) would subtract 60 days from the value in the DATE_COL column and return the result as a character string. CHAR includes the delimiters—the dashes or slashes—that are part of the DATE representation.

DB2 offers a number of scalar functions for extracting only part of a DATE, TIME, or TIMESTAMP. For example, MONTH(DATE_COL) returns only the month. If DATE_COL held 12/15/1989, 12 would be returned. The DAY and YEAR functions work similarly for the day or year portion of a DATE value. And the HOUR, MINUTE, and SECOND functions return those portions of TIME values. The MICROSECOND function returns the microsecond portion of a TIMESTAMP column.

DATE and TIME values may participate in several types of calculations. One type involves the addition or subtraction of labeled durations. For example, any number of years, months, or days may be added to or subtracted from a DATE value. The syntax simply identifies the date column, followed by a plus or minus sign, followed by the number of units and the unit's name—YEARS, MONTHS, or DAYS. But the result of the addition or subtraction is not so straightforward.

YEAR and MONTH Calculations

In most cases, the YEARS or MONTHS calculation results in the same date as the original DATE value, plus or minus the number of units indicated, regardless of the number of days in the interval covered by the addition or subtraction. Consider the calculation DATE_COL + 1 MONTHS, for example, when the DATE value is '09/30/1989'. Although the following month, October, has 31 days, DB2 does not add that many days. Instead it returns '10/30/1989', the same date plus one month. Some dates, however, exist in some months or years, but not others. For example, the calculation '08/31/1989' + 1 MONTH could not result in '09/31/1989', since September has only 30 days. In these cases, DB2 returns the last day of the appropriate month; in the example, '9/30/1989'. The same principle applies to a labeled duration calculation that would result in February 29 of a non-leap year.

Use of the DAYS units provides more precise results, with the result date being exactly the number of days added or removed from the original date as the number indicates in the calculation—for example, '09/30/1989' + 31 days = '10/31/1989'.

Last Day of Month Calculations

Often a program may have to know the last day of the current month—so that bills can be sent out on that date, for example. But the last date of a month might be the twenty-eighth, twenty-ninth, thirtieth, or the thirty-first. The following clause using a combination of DATE and string functions can determine the current month's last date, no matter the month or year. Imagine a PARTS_ORDERED table that includes a column, SCHED _DATE, showing the scheduled delivery date for all ordered parts. For accounting purposes, we want to know which parts are scheduled to be delivered after the last day of the current month. This statement finds that information:

```
SELECT  PN
FROM    PARTS_ORDERED
WHERE   SCHED_DATE
        DATE(SUBSTR(CHAR(CURRENT DATE, ISO), 1,8)
        CONCAT '01')
        + 1 MONTH - 1 DAY;
```

The clause beginning "DATE" determines the current month's last date. Assuming a current date of February 15, 1989, the following list presents the results of each element in the clause, beginning with the innermost parentheses:

```
1.  CHAR(CURRENT DATE, ISO)   = 1989-02-15
2.  SUBSTR(..., 1,8)          = 1989-02-
3.  (...CONCAT '01')          = 1989-02-01
4.  (...) + 1 MONTH           = 1989-03-01
5.  (...) - 1 DAY             = 1989-02-28
```

In the first step, the CHAR function puts the current date into a character string in the ISO format. The second step uses the substring function to truncate that date to just the year and month. Step three's concatenation sets the date to the first of the month. Step four's addition of a month sets the date at the first day of the next month. The final step subtracts a day, resulting in the final day of the current month. DATE at the beginning converts the date to the DATE data type for DB2's use in the comparison.

TIME Calculations

Addition or subtraction of time units to a TIME value is similar to date calculations but without some of the complications. The labeled units are HOURS, MINUTES, and SECONDS. The time calculations take into account the 24-hour representation for the ISO, European, and Japanese formats and the 12-hour representation for the USA format. For example, if 12 hours were added to a non-USA format TIME value of '16.30.00', the result would be '04.30.00'. If 12 hours were added to a USA format TIME value of '04:30 AM', the result would be '04:30 PM'. All of the labeled durations available for TIME and DATE values may also be used in TIMESTAMP calculations. In addition, MICROSECOND can be used in TIMESTAMP calculations.

Subtracting DATE and TIME Values

DATE values may be subtracted from one another but not added, and TIME values may be subtracted from one another but not added. In addition, DATE or TIME values may be subtracted, respectively, from special registers called CURRENT DATE and CURRENT TIME, which represent exactly what their names say. DB2 also provides CURRENT TIMESTAMP and CURRENT TIMEZONE, the latter of which provides the time duration of the local time zone from GMT (Greenwich Mean Time). (GMT is now known as the universal time coordinate). When subtraction of these values occurs, the results take the special form YYYYMMDD, which is a packed decimal type representing the number of years, months, and days that the subtraction yields. For example, if the CURRENT DATE is '06/20/1989', subtracting a DATE value of '03/30/1987' yields 00020221, for 2 years, 2 months, and 21 days.

DB2 performs subtractions on dates with differing formats. For instance, using the PARTS_ORDERED table from the above example and assuming SCHED_DATE is in ISO format, DB2 can handle this statement to determine which parts are due to arrive at least two years after December 31, 1989:

```
SELECT  PN
FROM    PARTS_ORDERED
WHERE   YEAR(SCHED_DATE - '12/31/1989') > 2;
```

Notice that SCHED_DATE is in the ISO format but '12/31/1989' is in USA date format. Notice also that '12/31/1989' is not even identified as a date. It is merely a character string. DB2 recognizes the string's format as a date and treats it as such.

The DAYS Function

The DAYS function provides a way to calculate the number of days between two DATE values. DAYS determines the number of days between a given date and 12/31/0000. That number by itself is rarely useful; however, by determining the DAYS values for two dates and subtracting one from the other, DB2 finds the number of days separating the two dates. For example, for a DATE_COL1 value of '02/28/1989' and a DATE_COL2 value of '01/31/1989', the calculation DAYS(DATE_COL1) — DAYS(DATE_COL2) returns 28.

Day of the Week: The DAYS function is useful in determining the day of the week of a given date in a column or host variable of DATEREC prior to V6, for example.

```
SELECT DAYS(DATEREC) - (DAYS(DATEREC) -1) / 7 * 7
FROM    PARTS_ORDERED;
```

The values returned are 1, 2, 3, 4, 5, 6, or 7 representing Monday, Tuesday, Wednesday, Thursday, Friday, Saturday, or Sunday.

DAYOFWEEK user-defined function can be used to retrieve the day of the week (1 represents Sunday) as discussed in the UD Chapter in V6.

A similar calculation can be used to determine the Monday on or before DATEREC:

```
SELECT  DATE((DAYS(DATEREC)  -  1)  /  7  *  7  +  1)
FROM    PARTS_ORDERED;
```

If the Monday after DATEREC is required, the following calculation provides the date:

```
SELECT  DATE((DAYS(DATEREC)  -  1)  /  7  *  7  +  1  +  7)
FROM    PARTS_ORDERED;
```

If Tuesday is required, -2, +2 rather than -1, +1 should be used in the calculation. If Wednesday is required, -3, +3 rather than -1, +1 should be used. For Thursday and the remaining days of the week increment by -1 or +1 for each of days.

Converting to the DATE Data Type

If dates are stored as character or numeric types in a format DB2 does not accept, the DATE function and string manipulations in an SQL statement can convert them to the proper type and format. Suppose ORDER_DATE is stored as a CHAR(6) type in the form YYMMDD. This statement converts ORDER_DATE values to a DATE type in the ISO format:

```
SELECT  DATE  ('19'
        CONCAT  SUBSTR(ORDER_DATE,1,2,)  CONCAT  '-'
        CONCAT  SUBSTR(ORDER_DATE,3,2)   CONCAT  '-'
        CONCAT  SUBSTR(ORDER_DATE,5,2))
FROM    PARTS_ORDERED
WHERE   SN  =  'S4';
```

Looking at an example date helps one understand how the statement works. Suppose ORDER_DATE has the value of 880131. The statement in the parentheses begins with '19'. Concatenated with that is the substring of ORDER_DATE, beginning with the first position and including two characters—'88'. That yields '1988'. The next concatenation adds the hyphen, '1988', and the next adds a two-character substring from ORDER_DATE beginning at position 3—'01'. So far, we have '1988-01'. The next concatenation adds another hyphen and the final one adds the final two characters from the string—'1988-01-31'. The DATE function then converts that character string to the DATE data type.

If ORDER_DATE were stored as a DECIMAL or INTEGER, the conversion statement would be only slightly different, having to account first for the conversion from the numeric to character type before the substring function can be used. The following statement handles the conversion of either DECIMAL or INTEGER types:

```
SELECT  DATE('19'
        CONCAT SUBSTR(DIGITS(ORDER_DATE),1,2) CONCAT '-'
        CONCAT SUBSTR(DIGITS(ORDER_DATE),3,2) CONCAT '-'
        CONCAT SUBSTR(DIGITS(ORDER_DATE),5,2))
FROM    PARTS_ORDERED
WHERE   SN = 'S4';
```

The DATE function is also useful in counting the number of orders placed since the first of last month including this month regardless of today's date.

```
SELECT  COUNT(*)
FROM    PARTS_ORDERED
WHERE   ORDER_DATE >
        DATE(SUBSTR(CHAR(CURRENT DATE,
ISO),1,8)
        CONCAT '01') - 1 MONTH;
```

Use of Scalar Functions without Selecting from a One Row Table

Most host languages do not support all of the scalar function available in DB2. The SET or VALUE statement provide for the use of the scalar functions within a host program. For example, you can determine the month portion of ORDER_DATE like:

```
EXEC SQL SET :MO = MONTH(ORDER_DATE) END-EXEC.
```

or

```
EXEC SQL VALUES(MONTH(ORDER_DATE)
         INTO  :MO END-EXEC.
```

Use of functions interactively require selecting from a one row table as in the following example. The catalog table SYSIBM.SYSDUMMY1 is designed for this purpose.

```
SELECT  MONTH(ORDER_DATE)
FROM    SYSIBM.SYSDUMMY1;
```

Recommendation: The SET and VALUES statements have performance advantage over selecting from a one row table. Therefore, do consider the use of these statements in a host language program as discussed in Chapters BP, TR, and UD.

SL.7 SELECTING BY GROUPS

The GROUP BY clause may be used in SELECT statements for searches designed to return a single value—a sum or minimum, for example. But rather than performing the search and returning the value for an entire column, GROUP BY separates the rows into groups according to duplicate values in the named column and then operates on each group. In other words, the GROUP BY operator creates a separate group for each distinct value in the named column. Then it performs the column function on each group and returns a single row for each group. Grouped by CITY, for example, the Supplier table has three groups: for London, Paris, and Athens. This statement, then, finds the maximum supplier status in each city:

```
SELECT  CITY, MAX(STATUS)
FROM    S
GROUP   BY CITY;
```

CITY	MAX(STATUS)
London	20
Paris	30
Athens	30

A HAVING clause works like a WHERE clause to qualify a search, but the HAVING clause criteria applies to each groups created with a GROUP BY clause rather than to individual rows:

```
SELECT  CITY, MAX(STATUS)
FROM    S
GROUP   BY CITY
HAVING  COUNT(*) > 1;
```

CITY	MAX(STATUS)
London	20
Paris	30

SQL applies the HAVING clause criteria to each group. In this case, it counts the values in each group, eliminates any group having fewer than two, and returns the maximum value for those remaining. Basically it eliminates unwanted groups. A way of thinking about the HAVING clause is to pretend that the GROUP BY results are written to a work file (this is true only if a sort is required) like:

CITY	COUNT (*)
London	2
Paris	2
Athens	1

The conditions specified in the HAVING clause (HAVING COUNT(*) > 1 in the example) is applied to the pretend work file. Athens is not included in the result as indicated by the being crossed out in the table. This is because there is only one supplier in the city. The unwanted group is eliminated.

GROUP BY can establish groups according to the values in more than one column, creating a separate group for each unique combination of values in the columns specified. A select from the SPJ table might group according to supplier number and part number (GROUP BY SN, PN). In that case, the S1-P1 combination represents a group, consisting of two rows, the S2-P3 combination forms a group with seven rows, and so on. The number of columns that may be used in a GROUP BY clause is limited by the total number of bytes in their columns. Theoretically DB2 allows columns totaling 4,000 bytes to make up a GROUP BY clause, which should allow enough columns to satisfy almost any request.

Notice that any column included in the SELECT clause of a statement that contains a GROUP BY clause must either have an associated column function or appear in the GROUP BY clause. The function returns a single value based on the information in the indicated column for the grouped rows. But which of the group's values would the select return if no function was specified? For example, suppose that in the above statement, the SELECT clause had included the SNAME column. Which supplier name would SQL return with the London row?

SL.8 SEQUENCING THE QUALIFYING ROWS

An ORDER BY clause, placed at the end of a select, tells SQL the sequence in which to present the results. The user can specify sequencing by one or more of the columns. It is not necessary to select columns specified in

ORDER BY clause (V5 APAR PQ23778). SQL
sequences first according to the first column indicated.
Then within each group created by the first sequence,
it sequences according to the second column
indicated, and so on—for example:

JN	PN	QTY
J1	P3	400
J2	P4	500
J4	P1	700
J4	P3	500
J4	P4	800
J4	P5	400
J4	P6	500
J5	P3	600
J5	P5	500
J6	P3	400
J7	P3	800

```
SELECT  JN, PN, QTY
FROM    SPJ
WHERE   QTY >= 400
ORDER BY JN, PN;
```

The rows are sequenced by job numbers—J1, J2, J4,
J5, J6, J7. Then within groups of rows having
duplicate job numbers, the rows are sequenced by part
number—J4-P1, J4-P3, J4-P4, and so on. As with the
GROUP BY statement, the maximum number of
columns that may be used with an ORDER BY
depends on the total length of the column values, with
4,000 bytes being the limit.

The ORDER BY clause need not identify the returned column or columns to
be used in the sequence by name. Instead it can identify them by their
position in the SELECT clause. An equivalent ORDER BY clause for the
above statement would be ORDER BY 1, 2. This facility is useful for
substituting for long column names.

The position must be specified if the ORDER BY is on a calculated
expression or an AS name can be assigned. For example, it is necessary to
ORDER BY 4 or the AS name of INCREASE in the statement:

```
SELECT  JN, PN, QTY, QTY * 1.10 AS  INCREASE
FROM    SPJ
ORDER   BY INCREASE;
```

DB2 sequences null values as being higher than any other value. It will
sequence in ascending or descending order. Ascending is the default. A user
specifies descending order by placing the word DESC after the column in
the ORDER BY clause—for example, ORDER BY PN DESC.

SL.9 CASE EXPRESSIONS

CASE expressions can reduce the number of SQL statements that must be developed, tested, and maintained. They offer performance benefits, particularly when multiple tablespace scans for each of several SELECT statements can be avoided with the use of a CASE expression.

A CASE expression yields a constant or computed value based on finding which of several conditions are true. CASE can be used in a SELECT statement in SET, or the WHERE clause of an UPDATE statement. The expression in a CASE clause is similar to SELECT and WHERE clause expressions.

One use of a CASE expression is to report on text rather than a code that appears in a column of a table. A column name tested for equality can be in the CASE or WHEN clause. Here is an example of testing the SEX column for a value of 'M' and 'F' and returning the value of 'Male' and 'Female' for the corresponding code.

```
SELECT EMPNO, LASTNAME,
CASE SEX
     WHEN 'M'  THEN 'Male'
     WHEN 'F'  THEN 'Female'
     ELSE 'UNKNOWN'
END AS GENDER
FROM    EMP
WHERE   WORKDEPT = 'D4';
```

If the ELSE clause is not used, null is the result for a row that does not match the WHEN condition. The AS name following the END delimiter is optional. In the example, GENDER is the column heading for a report generated using an interactive tool.

A good way to read a CASE expression is to say in case an 'M' is found in the SEX column, then return 'Male'. In case an 'F' is found in the SEX column, then return 'Female'. If neither value tested in the WHEN clauses is found, then return 'UNKNOWN'.

Additional details on CASE expressions is in Chapter PP.

SL.10 SUBSELECTS

Subselects are SELECTS that work in conjunction with other SELECTS, providing values that determine part of the search criteria. In simple as opposed to correlated subselects, DB2 usually first performs the subselect, or inner select, presented within parentheses below the primary, or outer, select. The value or values returned for the subselect provide values for the search criteria for the primary select.

In correlated subselects, the subselect's search criteria depend on values from the table identified in the outer select. SQL evaluates the outer select first and passes a value to the subselect, which returns values one at a time to be used in completion of the outer select. Both types of subselects can best be explained through examples.

To understand a simple subselect, consider a search for parts that exceed the average weight of all the parts kept in London. A subselect can determine the average weight and pass that value to a primary select that locates the heavier parts:

```
SELECT  PNAME, WEIGHT
FROM    P
WHERE   WEIGHT >
  (SELECT  AVG(WEIGHT)
   FROM    P
   WHERE   CITY = 'London');
```

PNAME	WEIGHT
Screw	17
Bolt	17
Cog	19

Subselect Returning Multiple Values

Subselects can also pass multiple values to the primary select, most frequently done by using the an IN subselect in the primary select to address a set of values returned by the subselect. To determine the part number and name of parts supplied by supplier S2, for example, a subselect can locate S2's part numbers in the SPJ table and pass that set to a select that finds those parts' names in the P table. The statement for this select is:

```
SELECT  PN, PNAME
FROM    P
WHERE   PN IN
  (SELECT  PN
   FROM    SPJ
   WHERE   SN = 'S2');
```

PN	PNAME
P3	Screw
P5	Cam

The primary select can also use three other operators—ALL, ANY, and SOME—to address sets of values returned by the subselect. Used in the select's WHERE clause, ALL, ANY, or SOME instructs the select to find rows based on their comparison to the values in the returned set. For ALL, each returned row satisfies the comparison against all values in the set. For ANY and SOME, which are equivalent, each satisfies the comparison against at least one value in the set. For example, the following statement determines all parts that weigh more than each and every part stored in Paris:

```
SELECT PNAME, WEIGHT, CITY
FROM    P
WHERE   WEIGHT > ALL
  (SELECT WEIGHT
   FROM    P
   WHERE   CITY = 'Paris');
```

The words ANY and ALL are somewhat ambiguous and do not naturally carry to some users the operators' precise meanings. Moreover, SQL's handling of unknown values with respect to these operators can be misleading. Since searches provided by the ANY, ALL, and SOME operators can be performed with equivalent statements using more straightforward terminology, users may be wise to avoid these operators entirely rather than having to deal with their somewhat confusing distinctions. For example, selecting parts that weigh more than each and every part stored in Paris is the same as selecting parts that weigh more than the heaviest part stored in Paris. The MAX operator can identify those rows.

```
SELECT PNAME, WEIGHT, CITY
FROM    P
WHERE   WEIGHT >
  (SELECT MAX(WEIGHT)
   FROM    P
   WHERE   CITY = 'Paris');
```

If COALESCE(MAX(WEIGHT), 0) is used, all parts > 0 are returned.

The MIN operator can perform the function of ANY or SOME. To say that a given value is greater than any or some of the values in a set is the same as saying that it is greater than the least value in the set and that the different formulation returns the same results.

Care must be exercised if there is a possibility that no rows will qualify for the subselect when using ALL and MAX interchangeably since the result can differ. If there are no parts in Paris, all weights are greater than an empty set, but no weights are greater than a null from MAX. If there are parts in Paris, MAX returns the same results as does ALL. MIN and ANY or SOME return the same results regardless of whether rows qualify in the subselect. No weights are greater than an empty set, and no weights are greater than a null MIN.

Nulls are also troublesome if they appear in rows in a table processed in a subselect. Assume for a moment that the PN column contains a null in the SPJ table and that there is a P99 in the P table. It is necessary to determine information on parts in P that are not used on jobs in SPJ, and the statement used is:

```
SELECT PN, PNAME, COLOR, WEIGHT, CITY
FROM    P
WHERE   PN NOT IN
   (SELECT PN
    FROM    SPJ);
```

The P99 in the P table is not identified. The rational is that the unknown value in the SPJ might be P99. Either of the following two formulations of the request identifies the P99 that is not currently being used on any job.

```
SELECT PN, PNAME, COLOR, WEIGHT, CITY
FROM    P
WHERE   PN NOT IN
   (SELECT PN
    FROM    SPJ
    WHERE   SPJ.PN IS NOT NULL);
```

The subselect excludes any nulls with the predicate WHERE SPJ.PN IS NOT NULL. These are just a few of the potential problems when dealing with nulls and the reason that most developers do not allow for nulls in most columns.

Nested Subselects

A subselect can pass an intermediate answer set to a subselect that uses it in defining the search criteria that allow it to pass an intermediate answer to another subselect, and so on for up to 15 subselects in a single SQL statement. Each subselect can reference up to 15 tables in the FROM clause. A single SQL statement including its subselects cannot exceed 32,767 bytes.

In most cases, SQL executes the innermost subselect first and works its way up. This is a noncorrelated subselect (correlated subselects are discussed in the Correlated Subselects subsection that follows). For example, a search to locate the part number and name for parts supplied by supplier Jones would be similar to the search presented above in which we found the part numbers and names for parts supplied by S2. In this case, however, an additional subselect is needed to find Jones's supplier number. The necessary statement is:

```
SELECT  PN,  PNAME
FROM    P
WHERE   PN IN
   (SELECT  PN
    FROM    SPJ
    WHERE   SN =
       (SELECT  SN
        FROM    S
        WHERE   SNAME = 'Jones'));
```

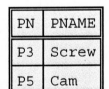

PN	PNAME
P3	Screw
P5	Cam

Correlated Subselects

In a correlated subselect, the outer select identifies a table from which SQL draws values for use in the subselect. The outer select passes one value from a row at a time from the identified table to the subselect, which uses the column specified in the subselect to perform the subselect. For example, to determine the names of parts used on job 1, the search can check each part listed in the P table against all the parts listed in the SPJ table. When the part number (PN) from P matches the PN from SPJ, and the job number equals J1, the select returns that part's name. The correlation name of PX as specified with the AS clause in the outer select (first select) is used in the inner select (second select) to refer back to the outer select. An alternative to specifying the AS name in the FROM clause is to separate the table name form the correlation name with a space (FROM P PX, for example). This statement satisfies the search:

```
SELECT  PNAME
FROM    P AS PX
```

```
WHERE   'J1' IN
  (SELECT JN
   FROM   SPJ
   WHERE  SPJ.SN = PX.PN);
```

To perform this search, SQL first passes the first part number from the P table to the subselect. The subselect uses the part number, P1 for example, from that row in its search. This search finds P1 used in two jobs—J1 and J4—which make up the set returned to the outer select for evaluation with the IN subselect. Since J1 is the first value returned, the outer select returns PNAME from the P1 row in the P table—Nut. SQL continues the process by passing to the subselect each subsequent part number from the P table in turn. Try continuing the search using the remaining values from the P table.

Chapter ST discusses the performance implications of subselects.

SL.11 INTERSECTION AND DIFFERENCE

In set operations, *intersection* represents the values common to both original sets. *Difference* represents the values of one set that do not also belong to the second set. EXISTS and NOT EXISTS subselects can be used to determine the intersection and difference. The subselect (second select in parentheses) returns a true or false to the outer select (first select) depending on the subselect evaluation. For EXISTS, if there is a value satisfying the subselect, the operator returns true. For NOT EXISTS, if there is no value satisfying the subselect, the operator returns true. The outer select includes a row whenever the subselect returns a true evaluation.

Intersection: A select to determine the cities that have both suppliers and part stocks represents the intersection of the two sets of city values from S and P tables.

This statement can be used to determine that intersection (SELECT CITY rather than SELECT 1 in the subselect can be specified as discussed in Chapter ST):

```
SELECT DISTINCT CITY
FROM    S AS SX
WHERE   EXISTS
  (SELECT 1
```

CITY
London
Paris

```
FROM    P
WHERE   P.CITY = SX.CITY);
```

DB2 performs the search by passing the first city from S to the subselect, which finds a match for London and therefore returns a true evaluation. The outer select therefore includes the row, returning London. Then it continues the process for each subsequent row. The shaded area in Figure SL.1 represents the intersection. Notice that the only cities that appear in both S and P are London and Paris.

Figure SL.1. Intersection

S cities	Intersection	P cities
Athens	London	Paris
London	Paris	London
London		Paris
Paris		London
Paris		Rome

Difference: Similarly a search to determine whether there are any cities with parts but no suppliers, found by subtracting the cities in S from those in P, would represent a difference. The statement to determine this difference is:

```
SELECT DISTINCT CITY
FROM    P AS PX
WHERE   NOT EXISTS
   (SELECT 1
    FROM    S
    WHERE   CITY = PX.CITY);
```

CITY
Rome

If the CITY value from a row in P does not match any CITY value in S, the subselect returns a true value for the NOT EXISTS operator, causing the outer select to return that CITY. In this case, the difference between PART cities and SUPPLIER cities is Rome. The shaded area in Figure SL.2 represents the difference. Notice that Rome is the only remaining P city after subtracting the S cities.

Figure SL.2. Difference

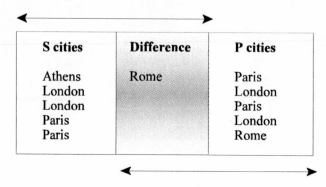

SL.12 NESTED TABLE EXPRESSIONS

A nested table expression looks a bit like a subselect in that it is a SELECT statement enclosed in parentheses. However, a nested table expression appears in the FROM clause and a subselect appears in the WHERE clause. Here is an example of using a nested table expression to determine the suppliers who supply > 1,000 parts to jobs.

```
SELECT SN, TOTAL_PARTS
FROM
   (SELECT SN, SUM(QTY)
      AS TOTAL_PARTS
   FROM    SPJ
   GROUP BY SN) AS SUMQTYBYSN
WHERE   TOTAL_PARTS > 1000;
```

SN	TOTAL_PARTS
S1	900
S2	3200
S3	700
S4	600
S5	3100

The result of the nested table expression is given a name. In the example, the name is SUMQTYBYSN. The result of column functions can also be given a name, the sum of QTYs in the SPJ table is named TOTAL_PARTS. This name can be referenced in the outer select. The following table shows the results of only the nested table expression in parentheses. Typically, the results of a nested table expression with GROUP BY, DISTINCT, and column function are written to a work file. There are many types of nested table expressions which are not written to a work file as described in Chapter ST.

The results of the nested table expression can be tested in the outer select. That is, the SN qualifies in the outer select if the TOTAL_PARTS calculated in the nested table expression are greater than 1,000. Here is the result of the SELECT statement with the nested table expression:

SN	TOTAL_PARTS
S2	3200
S5	3100

SL.13 JOINS

In general, joins combine information from two or more tables by comparing all the values that meet the search criteria in the designated column or columns of one table with all the values in corresponding columns of the other table or tables. When the values meet the comparison criteria, the rows containing them are joined and used for the select. This kind of join is called an *inner join*. *Outer joins*, discussed in Chapter JP, do not require a match in both columns to be joined.

A simple example illustrates the join concept. To find all suppliers of part P4, their names, cities, and amounts they supply, columns must be drawn from tables S and SPJ. The first step can be to find the P4 suppliers, identified by supplier number, in the SPJ table. Those rows, shaded in Figure SL.3, provide the quantities supplied.

Figure SL.3. A join

SPJ

SN	PN	JN	QTY
S1	P1	J1	200
S1	P1	J4	700
S2	P3	J1	400
S2	P3	J2	200
S2	P3	J3	200
S2	P3	J4	500
S2	P3	J5	600
S2	P3	J6	400
S2	P3	J7	800
S2	P5	J2	100
S3	P3	J1	200
S3	P4	J2	500
S4	P6	J3	300
S4	P6	J7	300
S5	P2	J2	200
S5	P2	J4	100
S5	P5	J5	500
S5	P5	J7	100
S5	P6	J2	200
S5	P1	J4	100
S5	P3	J4	200
S5	P4	J4	800
S5	P5	J4	400
S5	P6	J4	500

S (Supplier Table)

SN	SNAME	STATUS	CITY
S1	Smith	20	London
S2	Jones	10	Paris
S3	Blake	30	Paris
S4	Clark	20	London
S5	Adams	30	Athens

Result of Join

SNAME	CITY
Blake	Paris
Adams	Athens

The next step is to find the suppliers' names and cities by matching the SN values associated with P4 in the SPJ table with the SN values in the S table—that is, by comparing the values for equality. When a match is found, the combined row provides the information for the select.

The FROM clause of the SELECT statement for the join must include the tables that participate. The WHERE clause identifies the columns to be compared and the type of comparison. Although most joins involve a match of values—called a *natural join* or *equi-join*—any of the comparison operators may be used. The statement needed for this join is:

```
SELECT SNAME, CITY, QTY
FROM   S, SPJ
WHERE  S.SN = SPJ.SN
AND    PN   = 'P4';
```

Although not a requirement, in most cases, the columns on which the tables are joined have the same name, data type, and length. When they have the same name, it must be qualified by the table name—SPJ.SN, for example.

Three-way Joins

A SELECT statement may join up to 15 tables, but joins of many tables are not common. The additional joins are simply added to the WHERE clause. Suppose, for example, that we wish to find the name of P4 along with the other information requested in the above search. Part names are included in the P table, so including that table in the join is one way to expand the search. In this case, we join the P and SPJ tables on the PN column. The necessary statement is:

```
SELECT SNAME, S.CITY, PNAME,
   QTY
FROM   S, SPJ, P
WHERE  S.SN   = SPJ.SN
AND    SPJ.PN = P.PN
AND    P.PN   = 'P4';
```

SNAME	CITY	PNAME	QTY
Blake	Paris	Screw	500
Adams	Athens	Screw	800

Notice that the CITY column in the SELECT clause is modified by the S table name to distinguish it from the CITY column in the P table, also part of the joined tables.

Joins Using Comparisons Other Than Equality

Any of SQL's comparison operators may be used as the basis on which tables are joined. The following example search, while perhaps of limited utility except to a port authority, demonstrates such a join. In the example, we want DB2 to compare the ship length in the ship table to the dock length in the dock table to determine which docks are long enough to accommodate a ship pulling into port. The SELECT returns the dock ID that can be communicated to the ship. The necessary statement is:

```
SELECT  SHIP_LENGTH,  DOCK_ID
FROM    SHIP, DOCKS
WHERE   SHIP_LENGTH < DOCK_LENGTH;
```

Joining a Table with Itself

SQL can join a table with itself, treating the table as if it were two identical copies of itself. A request to find the combined quantity of parts P2 and P6 for each supplier that supplies both parts for the same job demonstrates a join of a table with itself. To grasp how this join works, imagine that there are actually two SPJ tables, as shown in Figure SL.4. The statement is:

```
SELECT I.SN,  I.JN,  I.PN,  I.QTY,  II.QTY,
       I.QTY + II.QTY
FROM   SPJ I,  SPJ II
WHERE  I.SN  = II.SN
AND    I.PN  = 'P2'
AND    II.PN = 'P6'
ORDER BY 7;
```

I.SN	I.JN	I.PN	I.QTY	II.PN	II.QTY	I.QTY+II.QTY
S5	J2	P2	200	P6	200	400
S5	J4	P2	100	P6	500	600

To evaluate the statement, consider that each row of SPJ I is compared against each row of SPJ II. I.SN must equal II.SN because the request deals with the activity of individual suppliers. I.JN must equal II.JN because the activity relates to one job. Joining rows that meet those criteria and include parts P2 and P6 provides the answer. Those rows are shaded in Figure SL.4. In practice the search would probably be narrowed to P2 and P6 before the join.

Figure SL.4. Joining a table to itself

SPJ I

SN	PN	JN	QTY
S1	P1	J1	200
S1	P1	J4	700
S2	P3	J1	400
S2	P3	J2	200
S2	P3	J3	200
S2	P3	J4	500
S2	P3	J5	600
S2	P3	J6	400
S2	P3	J7	800
S2	P5	J2	100
S3	P3	J1	200
S3	P4	J2	500
S4	P6	J3	300
S4	P6	J7	300
S5	P2	J2	200
S5	P2	J4	100
S5	P5	J5	500
S5	P5	J7	100
S5	P6	J2	200
S5	P1	J4	100
S5	P3	J4	200
S5	P4	J4	800
S5	P5	J4	400
S5	P6	J4	500

SPJ II

SN	PN	JN	QTY
S1	P1	J1	200
S1	P1	J4	700
S2	P3	J1	400
S2	P3	J2	200
S2	P3	J3	200
S2	P3	J4	500
S2	P3	J5	600
S2	P3	J6	400
S2	P3	J7	800
S2	P5	J2	100
S3	P3	J1	200
S3	P4	J2	500
S4	P6	J3	300
S4	P6	J7	300
S5	P2	J2	200
S5	P2	J4	100
S5	P5	J5	500
S5	P5	J7	100
S5	P6	J2	200
S5	P1	J4	100
S5	P3	J4	200
S5	P4	J4	800
S5	P5	J4	400
S5	P6	J4	500

Chapter JP discusses the three types of join processing used by DB2 and the performance implications of joins.

SL.14 UNION

In set operations, a union includes values that appear in either or both of the original sets, with duplicate values excluded from the results. Columns participating in a union must be of compatible data type—broadly defined, a numeric type can be unioned with another numeric type and a character type can be unioned with another character type.

In general, a union consists of multiple SELECT statements combined with UNION operators. Each SELECT identifies the column or columns on which the union is to be performed. The participating SELECTS must specify the same number of columns or literals, and literals can be specified instead of columns. The SELECT statements also identify the columns to be included from each table in the union operation. For example, this statement determines the suppliers included in either or both the S and SPJ tables:

```
SELECT  SN
FROM    S
UNION
SELECT  SN
FROM    SPJ;
```

SN
S1
S2
S3
S4
S5

In many cases, rows or column values will be selected from each table in a union for different reasons. In those cases, literals printed out with each returned value allow users to keep track of the reason it was selected. A SELECT clause's literals, which are enclosed in single quotation marks, print out along with the values returned by the select.

Consider, for example, a search for parts that weigh more than 16 pounds and parts that are supplied by S2. The first set of parts can be found in the P table and the second set in the SPJ table. A union of the two sets returns all the parts requested. Literals used with each SELECT identifies in the report the reason each part is included. Since each SELECT associates a different literal with each returned value, duplicate part numbers selected from the two tables may be included. The necessary statement is:

```
SELECT PN, 'WEIGHT > 16'
   AS CRITERIA
FROM    P
WHERE   WEIGHT > 16
UNION
SELECT PN,'SUPPLIED BY S2'
   AS CRITERIA
FROM    SPJ
WHERE   SN = 'S2'
ORDER BY CRITERIA, PN;
```

PN	CRITERIA
P3	SUPPLIED BY S2
P5	SUPPLIED BY S2
P2	WEIGHT > 16
P3	WEIGHT > 16
P6	WEIGHT > 16

If the output is to be sorted, the ORDER BY clause must appear after the final SELECT and must specify the columns to be sorted by the AS name. An alternative to the AS name is to specify the numeric position of the column and literal in the statement like: ORDER BY 2,1 . UNION automatically eliminates duplicate rows returned by the participating SELECT statements. The UNION ALL instructs DB2 to leave duplicates in the union's results.

Performance implications of UNION and UNION ALL are discussed in Chapter PP.

SL.15 INSERTING, UPDATING, AND DELETING DATA

SQL allows users to change the values of stored data. The statements required for inserts, updates, and deletes are straightforward.

Inserts

All INSERT statements begin with the words "INSERT INTO" followed by the name of the table to receive the inserts and, in parentheses, the columns to receive the data. The data to be inserted can be specified within parentheses in a VALUES clause, or can be selected from another table. If all of a table's columns are to receive data, their names need not be specified in the INSERT INTO clause. The following statement, for example, inserts the specified values into all the columns in the S table:

```
INSERT INTO S
   VALUES ('S10', 'JOHNSON', 50, 'DALLAS');
```

If the column names are not specified in the INSERT INTO clause, the values must be listed in the order that the columns were specified in the CREATE TABLE statement. Each inserted value must have a compatible data type and length specified for the column that receives it.

When SQL is embedded in a program, even if all of a table's columns are to be included in an insert, it is good practice to specify them anyway; that way, if a new column is added to the table, the insert program will not have to be changed to account for it. If the columns are named in the INSERT statement, the values to be inserted must be in the order of the named columns. If the user does not specify a column name and a value for a column, a third column named STATUS in the following example, DB2 inserts the row provided that the missing column is declared as NOT NULL WITH DEFAULT, WITH DEFAULT value, or WITH DEFAULT NULL. If the column is defined as NOT NULL, the row is not inserted and a negative SQLCODE is received.

```
INSERT INTO S (SN, SNAME, CITY)
   VALUES ('S10', 'JOHNSON', 'DALLAS');
```

Flexibility of VALUES clause: You can include expressions discussed throughout the book like special-registers, labeled durations, case expressions, cast specifications, arithmetic expressions, scalar functions, constants, host variables, and non-table user-defined functions in the VALUES clause (V6). Following is an example of using the scalar function CONCAT to insert 'Smith John' in the SNAME column. The statement also shows how to use the DEFAULT key word to indicate that the value specified as the default when the table is created should be inserted into the STATUS column. You can also use NULL to indicate that null is to be inserted into the column. These keywords allow for specifying the column name and indicating that the default or null is to be inserted into a column.

```
INSERT INTO S (SN,   SNAME,   STATUS, CITY)
   VALUES ('S99', 'Smith ' CONCAT 'John',
   DEFAULT, 'Dallas');
```

When a SELECT statement is used with an INSERT, the select copies the data it retrieves into the specified table rather than returning it to the user or program. Developers find the method useful for building a small test table from a subset of a production table, as demonstrated by this example:

```
INSERT INTO S_TEST
   SELECT SN, SNAME, STATUS, CITY
   FROM   S
   WHERE  SN  < 'S4';
```

You can insert into a table with a subselect from the same table (V6). Do be cautious of a -803 SQLCODE indicating duplicate primary key values.

If a medium to large number of rows are to be inserted into a table, the LOAD utility has significant performance advantage as discussed in Chapter LC.

If table reference in the subselect is empty (S table in example), a +100 SQLCODE and '02000' SQLSTATE is returned. If the receiving table is self-referencing (referential integrity discussed in RI section), the subselect must not return more than one row unless NO ACTION is used when defining the FK.

Updates

An update, which changes values already stored, includes an UPDATE clause, which indicates the table containing the information to be changed, and a SET clause, which indicates the columns to be changed and their new values. It also uses a WHERE clause to identify specific rows to be changed. Suppose supplier S1 has moved to Dallas and increased its status by 10. Its new name is not known. The necessary update of the S table would require this statement:

```
UPDATE S
SET CITY   = 'DALLAS',
    STATUS = STATUS + 10,
    SNAME  = NULL
WHERE SN   = 'S1';
```

Notice that DB2 updates numeric columns based on arithmetic calculations as in the STATUS column. Notice also that an equal sign is used to assign a null to a column, in contrast to the test for a null with a SELECT statement, which requires the special IS operator.

An update can also use a subselect. For example, Supplier Blake has sent an additional 10 of each parts it supplies to jobs recorded in the SPJ table, but the person wanting to update QTY does not know Blake's supplier number. This UPDATE statement with a subselect handles the change:

```
UPDATE SPJ
SET QTY = QTY + 10
WHERE SN IN
   (SELECT SN
    FROM   S
    WHERE  SNAME = 'Blake');
```

Deletes

DELETE statements identify the table from which rows are to be removed and, through a WHERE clause, the specific rows. For example, this statement to delete from the J table jobs performed in Rome removes the only row that satisfies the WHERE criterion—that for job J2:

```
DELETE FROM J
   WHERE CITY = 'Rome';
```

Searched Update and Delete Based on Results of Subselect

You can set a column equal to the result of a subselect that returns only one set of values. If more than one row qualifies in the subselect, a -811 SQLCODE is returned (V6 APAR PQ30383). Following is an example of updating the SPJ.PN to P.PN for bolt if SPJ.SN contains S4.

```
UPDATE SPJ
SET PN =
   (SELECT PN
    FROM   P
    WHERE  PNAME = 'Bolt')
WHERE SN = 'S4';
```

The following statement is an extension of the previous statement which shows that multiple columns in a table can be set to multiple columns resulting from a subselect and that an expression can be used in the subselect.

```
UPDATE SPJ
SET (PN, QTY) =
  (SELECT PN, :QTY * 1.1
   FROM    P
   WHERE   PNAME = 'Bolt');
```

A GROUP BY in a statement usually results in more than one row
qualifying. Therefore, it is not allowed when updating columns according to
the result of a subselect, rather a -815 SQLCODE is returned. The subselect
in the SET clause can include an expression, NULL provided that the
column being updated allows for nulls, or the keyword DEFAULT
(meaning the default established when creating a table as discussed in
Chapter CT).

If no rows qualify in the subselect, null is returned. The column is assigned
null if it allows for null based on the creation of the table. If the column
does not allow for null, an error of -407 SQLCODE is received.

Explanation of Update and Delete Based on Results of Inner Select: The
SET clause of an UPDATE statement can contain an inner select. If it is
noncorrelated subselect, a searched or positioned update using FOR
UPDATE OF and WHERE CURRENT OF can be used. If it is a correlated
subselect, a searched UPDATE statement can be used. The WHERE clause
of a searched DELETE statement can contain an inner select. In addition,
the statement can be self-referencing. That is you can update or delete a
table referenced in the inner select.

You can use a correlated subselect as a condition. For example, the
STATUS column can be set to the number of times a supplier is used on a
job:

```
UPDATE S AS S1
SET STATUS =
  (SELECT COUNT(*)
   FROM    SPJ AS SPJ1
   WHERE   S1.SN = SPJ1.SN);
```

It is also possible to update a table referenced in the inner select provided
that the column in the inner select is not the same column in the outer
portion of the statement (V7). However, if more than one row qualifies in a
noncorrelated subselect, -811 SQLCODE is returned. If more than one row
qualifies in a correlated subselect using IN, =ANY, =SOME, and EXISTS,

RIDs of qualifying rows and the column value for updates are written to a work file. Rows are reread using RIDs in the work file and the updates are applied.

The same principles apply to deleting rows as updating rows based on the results of a subselect. That is you can delete rows from a table based on the results of a subselect. Following is an example of a self-referencing DELETE statement that deletes the supplier with the minimum status. The same principle applies to an UPDATE statement.

```
DELETE FROM S S1
WHERE S1.STATUS =
   (SELECT MIN(S2.STATUS)
    FROM S S2);
```

You can delete or update a table referenced in an inner select. An exception is that it cannot be a column in the inner SELECT. For example, STATUS cannot be in the WHERE clause and inner SELECT.

```
DELETE FROM S S1
WHERE S1.STATUS =
   (SELECT S2.STATUS
    FROM S S2);
```

Two Step Processing for Correlated UPDATE and DELETE Statements: Step one consists of writing the RIDs of qualifying rows and the column value for updates to a work file. Step two consists of rereading the rows using the RIDs from the work file and the updates or deletes are applied. This two step processing is required if more than one row qualifies in a correlated subselect using IN, =ANY, =SOME, and EXISTS. Another case is if the column being updated is also referenced in the WHERE clause of the UPDATE or is used in the correlation predicate of the inner select. The two step process is always required for a correlated DELETE statement. If more than one row qualifies in a noncorrelated subselect, -811 SQLCODE is returned and there is no further processing.

SL.16 SUMMARY

SQL provides rich data access and manipulation capabilities. This chapter provides a grounding in those capabilities including information on SQL syntax and on how to employ the SQL operators. Mastering this information is only the first step in learning to use SQL with DB2, however. One must also understand how to use it within programs and understand DB2's implementation of SQL to be able to formulate the most efficient statements. Chapters PD through EX discuss how to develop programs for DB2 and efficient use of SQL.

EXERCISES

Most of the exercises are based on the tables found in Figure CT.6. Please refer to the figure when writing the needed SQL statements and to verify the results of the statements.

1. There is frequently more than one way to write a statement to obtain results. Write two SELECT statements to determine the PN, PNAME, and WEIGHT of parts that weight 15 pounds or more and 20 pounds or less.

2. Write a SELECT statement to determine the suppliers in Athens assuming that most people key the first three letters of the city correctly but may have misspelled the remaining portion. Give the results of the statements including the SN, SNAME, and CITY.

3. Write a statement to determine the minimum weight of parts in London. Give the results of the statement including the PN and PNAME.

4. Write a statement to compute the average status for suppliers by city from the S table and have the rows sequenced by CITY. Use AVGSTATUS as the heading of the report column for the averages. Give the results of the statement.

5. Use the GROUP BY operator to find how many P5s are available, on average, from each supplier that supplies it. The SELECT should provide each SN that supplies P5 on a job in the SPJ table and the average. Further, report on only the SN that provide P5 with an average quantity greater than 300. Have the column heading of AVGQTY appear in the report for the averages and show the results.

6. Write a statement to identify all rows and the number of rows that have more than one occurrence of a pair of SN and PN in a row. This type of statement is useful for identifying rows that have duplicate values in one or more columns.

7. Write a statement to identify the SNs in the SPJ table that have 3 in the second position of the SN column and show the results.

8. Write the SELECT clause to determine the microsecond portion of a column ORDER_TIMESTAMP that has been declared as a timestamp data type.

9. Write a SELECT clause to add one month to the date 8/31/1987 and give the result.

10. Write a SELECT clause to add 30 days to a column DATEREC containing '01/31/1987' and give the result (1987 is not a leap year).

11. Write a SELECT clause to subtract 1/31/1987 from 3/31/2001 and give the results.

12. Write a statement to determine the jobs using parts from supplier Blake and give the results. Include the SN, SNAME, PN, JN, and QTY.

13. Write a statement to determine the names of all jobs using part numbers P1 or P6 and the quantities used. Sequence the results by JNAME and QTY; include the PN with each returned row. Give the results.

14. The requirement is to determine the PN, PNAME, COLOR, WEIGHT, and CITY from the P and SPJ tables. The following statement satisfies the requirement but returns duplicate rows. Modify the statement to eliminate the duplicate rows.

```
SELECT P.PN, PNAME, COLOR, WEIGHT, CITY
FROM   P, SPJ
WHERE  P.PN = SPJ.PN
AND    QTY  = 200;
```

15. Write a SELECT statement to report SN, SNAME, STATUS, and a description of each suppliers status. The description is poor, average, or excellent based on a status of 10, 20, or 30, respectively.

16. Write a statement to report PN, PNAME, WEIGHT, and whether the part is considered heavy or light. A part is considered heavy if it weighs greater than or equal 15 and light if it weighs less than 15. Give the results.

17. Develop a SELECT statement with a CASE expression to calculate the total sales by month during the first 3 months of the year for DIVISION = 'CENTRAL'. Assume that the SALES table has one row per month. Each row has 1 for January, 2 for February, and 3 for March in a MONTH column. The sales amount is in the SALES_AMOUNT column.

18. Reformulate the following statement without using a nested table expression.

```
SELECT S.SN, SNAME, CITY, TOTAL_PARTS
FROM    S,
        (SELECT SN, SUM(QTY) AS TOTAL_PARTS
         FROM    SPJ
         GROUP BY SN) AS SUMQTYBYSN
WHERE S.SN = SUMQTYBYSN.SN;
```

SN	SNAME	CITY	TOTAL_PARTS
S1	Smith	London	900
S2	Jones	Paris	3200
S3	Blake	Paris	700
S4	Clark	London	600
S5	Adams	Athens	3100

19. Write two formulations of a statement to determine PNs in the SPJ table that are not in the P table.

20. Write two formulations of a statement that identifies all of the suppliers in Dallas or that have a status of 30 and give the results including the SN, SNAME, CITY, and STATUS. Assume that there are no duplicate rows or that duplicate rows are acceptable.

21. Write a statement to insert a row into the S table with a SN of S6, SNAME of Flora, STATUS of 40, and CITY of Rome.

22. A new packing requirement increases the weight of parts by 10 percent. Write an update statement to increase the weight of all parts by 10 percent.

23. The warehouse in Paris has been closed. Delete all of the rows from the P table for Paris.

ANSWERS

1. The parts that weigh between 15 and 20 pounds can be determined with the BETWEEN predicate or the >= and <= predicates like:

```
SELECT  PN,  PNAME,  WEIGHT
FROM    P
WHERE   WEIGHT BETWEEN 15
AND 20;

SELECT  PN,  PNAME,  WEIGHT
FROM    P
WHERE   WEIGHT >= 15
AND     WEIGHT <= 20;
```

PN	PNAME	WEIGHT
P2	Bolt	17
P3	Screw	17
P6	Cog	19

2. All of the suppliers in a city beginning with ATH are identified with:

```
SELECT  SN,  SNAME,  CITY
FROM    S
WHERE   CITY LIKE 'ATH%';
```

SN	SNAME	CITY
S5	Adams	Athens

3. The following statement determines the minimum weight of parts in London and the results follow.

```
SELECT  PN,  PNAME,  MIN(WEIGHT)
FROM    P
WHERE   CITY = 'London'
GROUP BY PN,  PNAME;
```

PN	PNAME	
P1	Nut	12
P4	Screw	14
P6	Cog	19

Notice that the minimum weight does not have a column heading in the report because the AS clause is not used.

4. The following statement computes the average status for all suppliers in each city of the S table and sequences the results by CITY. The averages have the column heading of AVGSTATUS.

```
SELECT CITY, AVG(STATUS)
AS AVGSTATUS
FROM    S
GROUP BY CITY
ORDER BY CITY;
```

CITY	AVGSTATUS
Athens	30
London	20
Paris	20

ORDER BY in addition to GROUP BY is required to insure that the rows are returned in sequence.

5. The following statement gets each of the SNs from SPJ into a group and computes the average quantity for those SNs that supply P5 to a job and have an average quantity greater than 300. The averages have a column heading of AVGQTY.

```
SELECT SN, AVG(QTY) AS AVGQTY
FROM    SPJ
WHERE   PN = 'P5'
GROUP BY SN
HAVING AVGQTY > 300;
```

SN	AVGQTY
S5	333

6. The following statement identifies all rows and the number of rows that have more than one occurrence of a pair of SN and PN in a row.

```
SELECT SN, PN, COUNT(*)
FROM SPJ
GROUP BY SN, PN
HAVING COUNT(*) > 1;
```

7. The substring scalar function can be used to identify the SNs with 3 in the second position of the identifier.

```
SELECT SN
FROM    SPJ
WHERE   SUBSTR(SN,2,1) = '3';
```

SN
S3
S3

8. The SELECT clause to determine the microsecond portion of the column ORDER_TIMESTAMP is:

```
SELECT MICROSECOND(ORDER_TIMESTAMP)
```

9. The SELECT clause to add one month to the date 8/31/1987 is:

```
SELECT '08/31/1987' + 1 MONTH
```

The result is '09/30/1987' because there are 30 days in September.

10. The SELECT clause to add 30 days to a column DATEREC is:

```
SELECT DATEREC + 30 days
```

The result is '03/02/1987'.

11. The SELECT clause to subtract 1/31/1987 from 3/31/2001 is:

```
SELECT '03/31/2001' - '01/31/1987'
```

The result is 00140200 which means 14 years and 2 months are between the two dates.

12. The following join gets information about the supplier Blake from the S table and the PN, JN, and QTY of parts from the SPJ table.

```
SELECT SPJ.SN, SNAME,
       PN, JN, QTY
FROM   SPJ, S
WHERE  SPJ.SN = S.SN
AND    SNAME  = 'Blake';
```

SN	SNAME	PN	JN	QTY
S3	Blake	P3	J1	200
S3	Blake	P4	J2	500

13. It is necessary to select from the SPJ and J table to get all of the jobs using PNs P1 or P6 with the quantity of parts used on the jobs. The ORDER BY clause results in the required sequence.

```
SELECT JNAME, QTY, PN
FROM   SPJ, J
WHERE  SPJ.JN = J.JN
AND    PN IN ('P1', 'P6')
ORDER BY JNAME, QTY;
```

JNAME	QTY	PN
Console	100	P1
Console	500	P6
Console	700	P1
Punch	200	P6
Reader	300	P6
Sorter	200	P1
Tape	300	P6

14. The DISTINCT function can be used to eliminate the duplicate rows like:

```
SELECT DISTINCT P.PN, PNAME, COLOR, WEIGHT,
CITY
FROM    P, SPJ
WHERE   P.PN = SPJ.PN
AND     QTY = 200;
```

15. The following SELECT statement reports on poor, average, and excellent suppliers with only one tablespace scan. The results follow the statement.

```
SELECT SN, SNAME, STATUS,
CASE STATUS
        WHEN 10 THEN 'Poor'
        WHEN 20 THEN 'Average'
        WHEN 30 THEN 'Excellent'
        ELSE 'Invalid'
END AS STATUS_DESC
FROM    S;
```

SN	SNAME	STATUS	STATUS_DESC
S1	Smith	20	Average
S2	Jones	10	Poor
S3	Blake	30	Excellent
S4	Clark	20	Average
S5	Adams	30	Excellent

16. The following statement reports on PN, PNAME, WEIGHT, and whether the part is considered heavy or light. Notice that the column WEIGHT must be in the WHEN clauses because a comparison other than equal is done.

```
SELECT PN, PNAME, WEIGHT,
CASE
WHEN WEIGHT <  15 THEN 'Light'
WHEN WEIGHT >= 15 THEN 'Heavy'
        ELSE 'No weight'
```

```
END AS WEIGHT_DESC
FROM    P;
```

PN	PNAME	WEIGHT	WEIGHT_DESC
P1	Nut	12	Light
P2	Bolt	17	Heavy
P3	Screw	17	Heavy
P4	Screw	14	Light
P5	Cam	12	Light
P6	Cog	19	Heavy

17. Here is a SELECT statement with a CASE expression to calculate the total sales by month for the central division during the first 3 months of the year.

```
SELECT SUM(CASE WHEN MONTH = 1
            THEN SALES_AMOUNT ELSE NULL END)
            AS JAN_SUM,
       SUM(CASE WHEN MONTH = 2
            THEN SALES_AMOUNT ELSE NULL END)
            AS FEB_SUM,
       SUM(CASE WHEN MONTH = 3
            THEN SALES_AMOUNT ELSE NULL END)
            AS MAR_SUM
FROM    SALES
WHERE   DIVISION = 'CENTRAL';
```

18. The nested table expression

```
SELECT S.SN, SNAME, CITY, TOTAL_PARTS
FROM    S,
        (SELECT SN, SUM(QTY) AS TOTAL_PARTS
         FROM    SPJ
         GROUP BY SN) AS SUMQTYBYSN
WHERE S.SN = SUMQTYBYSN.SN;
```

can be reformulated as a join. Both give the same results.

```
SELECT S.SN, SNAME, CITY, SUM(QTY)
   AS TOTAL_PARTS
FROM    S, SPJ
WHERE   S.SN = SPJ.SN
GROUP   BY S.SN, SNAME, CITY;
```

The nested table expression has performance advantages. In the nested table expression, each unique SN with the sum of QTYs is written to a work file and only those unique SN must be joined with the S table. In contrast, the join requires joining each SN, including duplicates, in SPJ with each SN in the S table, then sorting the rows for the GROUP BY and calculating the sum of the QTYs. Performance implications of CASE expressions are discussed in Chapter PP.

19. The PNs in SPJ but not in the P table can be identified using a NOT EXISTS or NOT IN subselect like:

```
SELECT PN
FROM    SPJ AS SPJX
WHERE   NOT EXISTS
   (SELECT 1
    FROM    P
    WHERE   PN = SPJX.PN);

SELECT PN
FROM    SPJ
WHERE   PN NOT IN
   (SELECT PN
    FROM    P);
```

No rows qualify from the statements. There is no PN in the dependent SPJ table that is not in the parent P table.

20. Two predicates on CITY and STATUS can be ORed or a UNION ALL can be used to identify any suppliers in Dallas or that have a STATUS of 30 because we are assuming that no duplicate rows qualify or duplicate rows are acceptable.

```
SELECT SN, SNAME, CITY, STATUS
FROM    S
WHERE   CITY = 'Dallas'
OR      STATUS = 30;
```

```
SELECT  SN, SNAME, CITY, STATUS
FROM    S
WHERE   CITY = 'Dallas'
UNION ALL
SELECT  SN, SNAME, CITY, STATUS
FROM    S
WHERE   STATUS = 30;
```

SN	SNAME	CITY	STATUS
S3	Blake	Paris	30
S5	Adams	Athens	30

There are no suppliers in Dallas.

21. Here is a statement to insert the row into the S table:

```
INSERT INTO S (SN, SNAME, STATUS, CITY)
    VALUES ('S6', 'Flora', 40, 'Rome');
```

22. The following statement increases the weight of all parts by 10 percent. Do be cautious when you do not specify a WHERE clause for UPDATE and DELETE statements. Keep in mind that all rows in the table are affected.

```
UPDATE P
SET WEIGHT = WEIGHT * 1.10;
```

23. The following statement deletes all of the rows from the part table for Paris.

```
DELETE FROM P
WHERE   CITY = 'Paris';
```

FIGURES

Concurrency Control

CC.1 INTRODUCTION

Concurrency is the process of allowing multiple users or applications to use the same data. However, we also want to ensure that one user or program does not change data while another is in the process of using or changing that data, a situation that can lead to errors or inconsistencies in the data. DB2 manages concurrency with several types of locks that restrict access to data while the data are being used. Generally, DB2 SELECTS the appropriate lock type based on concurrency requirements inherent in the transaction. These are called *implicit locks*. However, it is also possible for programmers to use *explicit locks* in their programs to lock a table for specific periods. The IRLM (Internal Resource Lock Manager) controls all locks. A hashing algorithm based on the data set identifier and page number is used to locate a hash table entry point to a chain of hashing synonyms to determine if the required lock is available. About 250 bytes per lock are required in most cases.

If locks are not available to control concurrency, serious errors can occur. Assume the Johnson's have a $1,000 checking account balance. Mrs. Johnson withdraws $200 at 10:01:01.001 A.M. At precisely that instant plus a millisecond, before her transaction completes and the new $800 balance is entered, Mr. Johnson withdraws $300. His deduction is taken from the still-intact $1,000, and a new balance of $700 is written to the account, overwriting Mrs. Johnson's work. Mrs. Johnson received her $200, but the transaction was lost. Since the final balance should have been $500, the bank also lost. A lock on the account during Mrs. Johnson's transaction would have held Mr. Johnson's transaction at bay. A number of other errors are possible when more than one transaction accesses the same data at the same time.

The specific points in a transaction when DB2 acquires or releases locks and the amount of data covered by any particular lock depends on decisions the designer makes during tablespace creation and when issuing a bind command. Locks involve important performance trade-offs. Locking large units of data can result in poor response times because users and programs must wait their turns at the data. Locking smaller units of data can allow better access to the data (better concurrency) but can require considerable CPU time and virtual storage for managing the locks. To use locks most efficiently and to insure data integrity, you must understand the options for controlling locks, how DB2 reacts to your choices, and the application traffic. Figure CC.1 summarizes the lock size and type determinants.

Figure CC.1. Lock size and type determinants

♦   The lock sizes and lock limits declared on the tablespaces in the SQL CREATE statements defining them.
♦   The installation limits for the number of locks per tablespace (NUMLKTS) and number of locks per user (NUMLKUS).
♦   The isolation level, current data, and acquire/release options you choose.
♦   Type of SQL statements--whether SELECT or UPDATE, for example--within a commit scope.
♦   Clauses that can be specified on SELECT statements.
♦   The access path chosen by the optimizer.
♦   The presence of explicit LOCK TABLE statements.

Protecting the Transaction's Work

Locks protect data while DB2 performs the logical units of recovery necessary to complete a database transaction, such as the withdrawal of funds from a savings account or the addition of a part to an inventory. Typically, such transactions require a series of updates, insertions, and deletions as well as internal operations such as fetching and summing data. The total of these steps represents the transaction's unit of recovery (UR). (A UR is also known as a unit of work (abbreviated as UOW)). For the savings withdrawal, for example, the transaction must make an entry in the account, adjust and enter the new balance, and adjust and enter the bank's new cash position. To maintain consistency, for a transaction to be successfully completed and recorded, all of its steps must be completed. Otherwise, none of the work should be recorded.

Generally DB2 begins acquiring locks on a transaction's affected data when the first SQL statement in a program is executed and holds them until the UR is complete or the program terminates. When the work is complete,

DB2 commits it, records it in an active log data set, and can write the changed data to the tablespace at the commit point or later along with other changed pages to make the process more efficient. Although these logical units of recovery are obviously of importance to the logic of the program, there are also recovery and concurrency considerations tied to the UR.

Of relevance to concurrency, once the change is safely recorded in the log, any locks on the data can be released and the pages can be used by others without requiring additional physical I/O. Use the COMMIT or COMMIT WORK statement within TSO, CAF, and RRSAF programs to indicate the end of a UR. The statements and processes used to commit a UR with CICS and IMS are discussed in Chapter PD. You can also COMMIT to establish shorter units of recovery within a larger application logical unit of recovery if this is permitted by business rules. This provides for releasing locks so that others can get at the data. In addition, it creates smaller units of recovery and can reduce the time it takes to restart a program in the event that it fails in the middle of a UR. This may or may not be acceptable to the business process. In some cases, all of the changes must be made to the data or none of the changes are to be made to the data.

In the event of a failure, DB2 uses the information in the log to roll back values changed by the failing transaction since the last commit point. If no commit was issued, then all database changes since the transaction started will be rolled back. After the rollback, DB2 releases the locks and issues an error message. Locks themselves can in certain circumstances prevent transactions from completing as a result of a deadlock or timeout.

Latches: Latches are similar to locks in that they are used to maintain the integrity of the data. However, internal latches require about one-tenth the number of instructions as locks. Latch processing is at the page level and is required for each qualifying row to avoid processing data that is in the process of being updated. This is particularly important when using lock avoidance and uncommited read as will be discussed in Sections CC.5 and CC.6. For example, you would not want to see the new supplier name of Jones before the new status of 50 is applied as a result of the statement:

```
UPDATE  S
    SET  SNAME   = 'Jones',  -- Update applied
        STATUS   =  50       -- Update not applied
    WHERE  SN    = 'S4';
```

Latches are maintained by DB2, not by IRLM. Latches have advantages over locks. Deadlocks cannot occur with latches, not between each other or with other locks. DB2 avoids deadlocks (or dead latches, if you prefer) involving latches by requesting only conditional locks while holding a latch, or by requesting latches in a specific order. Latches are not held until a commit is issued as are locks. Rather they are released once the data manager work involving the latched page has been completed. This is known as manual duration in contrast to commit duration.

Latch processing is required for each qualifying row. However, if no rows qualify on a page at stage 1 for a SELECT, UPDATE, and DELETE statement, no page or row is locked if using CS or RS. This applies to CURRENTDATA of YES and NO. However, a page or row lock is taken when the row is passed to RDS even if no rows qualify according to stage 2 predicates (except when using UR).

Although IBM considers detailed information on latches as proprietary, you can monitor their activity using accounting or monitor class 3, IFCIDs 0226 and 0227.

CC.2 DEADLOCKS AND TIMEOUTS

Certain transactions executing at the same time can lock each other out of data that they need to complete their logical units of recovery. Since neither can complete its work and commit, neither can release its locks. Nevertheless, each waits for the other in a situation called a deadlock or, by some, a deadly embrace.

We refer to the Johnson's again for a simple example to illustrate deadlocks. Assume that their checking account balance is again $1,000 and that they also have a $2,000 savings account balance. Assume also that the system is programmed to consider that a transfer from one account to the other is a single transaction, made up of a withdrawal and deposit. Mrs. Johnson attempts to withdraw $200 from the savings account and deposit it in the checking account. At the same time, Mr. Johnson tries to transfer $300 from checking to savings. Mrs. Johnson's transaction begins by locking the savings account so the deduction can be made without threat of a concurrent change. Mr. Johnson's work begins with a lock on the checking account for the same reason. Mrs. Johnson's transaction tries to continue with an update of the checking account but cannot gain access because of Mr. Johnson's lock. His transaction cannot complete because it encounters his wife's lock on the savings account. Neither transaction can release its lock until it completes and its work is committed. Neither transaction can complete. Mr. and Mrs. Johnson, or at least their transactions, are in deadly embrace (Figure CC.2).

Figure CC.2. Deadlock

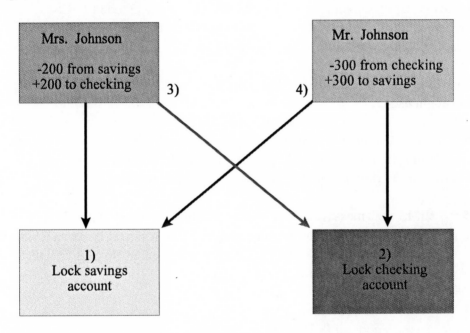

DB2 resolves a deadlock by rolling back any action already taken by the transaction in the deadlock that has the fewest log records or most current lock if IMS is the transaction manager. This rollback releases that transaction's locks and allows the other transaction to continue. In this example, DB2 releases Mr. Johnson's lock on the checking account, which allows Mrs. Johnson to complete her business. Then Mr. Johnson's transaction can try again.

Detecting Deadlocks: The IRLM checks for deadlocks every 5 seconds unless the system administrator has changed this default value on the DSNTIPJ installation panel. When a deadlock occurs, a -911 or -913 SQLCODE is returned to the application program and console message DSNT376I or DSNT375I is written for a timeout and deadlock.

In most cases you will see a -911, which means that a rollback of all changes during a current unit of recovery has occurred. If you are using CICS and ROLBE=YES is specified in the RCT (Resource Control Table), the transaction can be restarted by specifying the task in the PCT (Program Control Table). If you are using CICS and ROLBE=NO, a -913 is received, the locks for the SQL statement which caused the -913 are released, and the other locks are held until the program rolls back or commits the unit of recovery. Open cursors are closed. A -913 can occur in a non-CICS environment. CICS provides a transaction restart facility for handling deadlocks that works with DB2 transactions.

Deadlock and timeout using IMS/DC are managed depending on the type of region used.

♦   IMS message driven BMP, MPP, IFP deadlock and timeout results in rollback, abend code of 0777, and IMS reschedules the transaction. No SQLCODE is returned to program.

♦   IMS non-message driven region results in rollback with -911 SQLCODE if rollback is successful. If the rollback is not successful, IMS issues a code of 0777 and program abends. No SQLCODE is returned to program.

♦   DL/1 batch results in abend with a completion code of 04E and reason code of 00D44033.

♦   Deadlock between DB2 and DL/1 results in a timeout. The last lock requestor is rolled back. The other UR continues processing.

Programming Recommendation: Typically a program should call a subroutine or module to process SQLCODEs. Depending on the error code and the error routine, the program might automatically reissue Mr. Johnson's transaction or send him a message asking him to reenter the request. Chapter PD discusses error handling in more detail.

To avoid deadlocks, it is best that all concurrently executing programs access the tables in the same order. For example, processing tables in alphabetic order of table names can prevent deadlocks on data pages. Any predetermined order followed by all programs will accomplish the same goal. However, the user doesn't control the order of table access within a statement.

Timeouts

The IRLM services requests for locks on a first-in, first-out basis. If a lock required by a program is unavailable because it is being used by another program, that program is suspended until the lock becomes available. If the locked resource is not available within an installation-specified time, a timeout occurs. By default, IRLM tries for 60 seconds to get the lock.

Specifying the Timeout Interval: Installation panel DSNTIPI has a RESOURCE TIMEOUT field that allows the systems administrator to specify the minimum number of seconds before a timeout can occur. DB2 uses the timeout period and a multiplier to determine if a timeout has occurred. Different types of programs use different multipliers. Most transactions use a multiplier of 1. However, IMS DL/I batch and IMS Fast Path non-message processing use a multiplier of 6, the BIND command uses 3, and IMS batch message programs use 4. Utilities use a multiplier of 6. The STOP DATABASE command tries 15 times before a timeout.

If IRLM cannot get a lock within the time limit, a -911 or -913 is issued, similar to a deadlock. The reason code indicates whether the negative SQLCODE is a result of a deadlock or timeout and console message DSNT376I or DSNT375I is written.

Changing the Timeout Factor: The system administrator can change certain timeout multipliers, as shown here:

Type of Process	How to Change Timeout Multiplier
Utilities	UTILITY TIMEOUT field of DSNTIPI
IMS BMP	BMPTOUT subsystem parameter
DL/I Batch	DLITOUT subsystem parameter

Deadlocks and Timeouts in a Distributed Environment

If two processes are running on separate DB2 subsystems at different locations, a deadlock is reported as a timeout. DB2 provides the option at the subsystem level to timeout a distributed thread (user) which is inactive, holding a lock, and has not committed. The condition is checked every three minutes. Once the condition is detected, a rollback occurs and all resources are released. The requester thread is canceled if timed out. DB2 effectively issues a CANCEL DDF THREAD command. This avoids using resources to derive results which cannot be transmitted to the requester. If a thread is to be canceled, the systems administrator must specify the timeout period in seconds on IDLE THREAD TIMEOUT of DSNTIPR installation panel or the IDTHTOIN of DSNZPARM (not the default). The timeout does not apply to an inactive thread that is not holding a lock and to indoubt threads.

CC.3 LOCK SIZES AND TYPES

DB2 determines its locking strategy for each transaction during the bind process in most cases. DB2 locks data in units of differing sizes: row, page, table, or tablespace. DB2 does not take transaction locks on indexes at all, but uses data-only locking. A variety of lock types can be used with these locks, offering different concurrency levels.

Determining the Lock Size

When creating or altering the tablespace, you can specify a lock size (ROW, PAGE, TABLE or TABLESPACE) or choose ANY, indicating that DB2 should choose the lock size whenever the table is accessed. In that case, DB2 usually chooses a lock size of PAGE.

Decisions about lock sizes depend on how the particular table and indexes will be used, with the general trade-off between response times and CPU and virtual storage usage in effect. Smaller lock sizes, such as row locks, can offer greater concurrency, but because they are usually more numerous than page, table or tablespace locks, they can require considerable CPU resources.

Advantages and Costs of Row Locking

Even with row locking, it is necessary to serialize processing at the page level to gather free space for such things as expanding a variable-length row. A page latch is taken to serialize processing while gathering free space on a page, but the latch is not held until commit.

There are some situations that might benefit from row locking:

♦ A high transaction rate is required with high update activity. Row locking allows multiple programs to update different rows on the same page at the same time (although not at the same instant because of page latching for each qualifying row).

♦ If a program processes only a few rows and there are lock contention problems, row locking can help by locking only those few rows rather than locking all the rows on a page, which might be locking out another program that is trying to process different rows on that page.

♦ There are small tables that are frequently updated. Row locking can allow more access to needed rows on a page.

♦ There are short rows with many rows on a page. If you are using data compression, this is often the case. With page locking, more data is unavailable to other applications. Row locking means that only the needed rows are locked.

♦ Updates and deletes concentrated in specific areas of a table are considered "hot spots". Lock contention in these hot spots is minimized with row locking.

♦ Row locking is used on catalog tables that do not use link.. These catalog tables can be identified in the manual *Diagnosis Guide and Reference.*

Row locking is *not* required to reduce lock contention when inserting rows at the end of a table. Data pages at the end of the tablespace are filled and written with deferred write (no I/O to read the pages is required). If the page is locked when attempting to insert rows not at the end of the table, the row is inserted in a near or far page using the algorithm as if there is no free space on the page. The trade-off is that clustering is lost more quickly. There is also the additional I/O required to search for a page to insert the row in many cases. In balance, however, it is usually worth these trade-offs to avoid lock contention.

Costs: There are costs associated with locking at the row level versus the page level. More locks means more lock overhead. For example, if a transaction processes two rows on a page, you've doubled the costs to take locks. However, the cost to release locks is not doubled because only one call is required to release the locks. If your batch process processes most rows on the page, you could increase locking cost many times. A worst case scenario is if the batch program processes all rows on each page. If there are 40 rows on a page, row locking can require up to 40 times the number of locks as that required for page locking.

IBM tested updating 23,826 rows with a single dynamic UPDATE statement using V4 on a 50 MIPS processor as reported in the manual *Locking in DB2 for MVS/ESA Environment,* SG24-4725. The elapsed time when using a page locksize was almost half that required when using a row locksize as shown in Figure CC.3. The CPU time was increased about 50 percent when using row locking. Using these test results, we can estimate the CPU time required to take a lock at about 51 microseconds ((3.27 - 2.08) / (23,983 - 660). The number of lock requests was dramatically higher with row locking at 23,983 compared to 660 for page locking.

Figure CC.3. Comparison of elapsed and CPU class 2 time using page and row locking

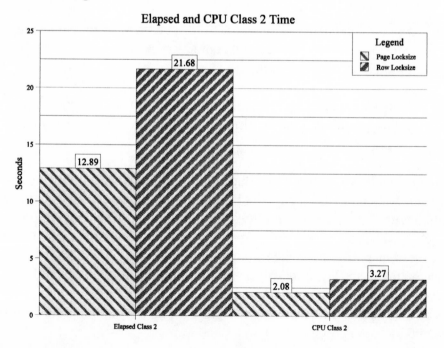

Recommendation: If lock contention is not a problem now, do not use row locks.

Use of page locks provides the best performance in most cases (assuming that the table or tablespace locksize is not appropriate for the processing). If lock contention continues to be a problem, consider altering to a row lock size. Use a monitor to determine if lock contention has been reduced with a row lock size and if the cost increase is acceptable.

If row locking is necessary for online transactions during the day, but the table undergoes batch processing at night, consider altering the table to a lock size of page before executing the batch program. Alter it back to row locking after it executes. Plans and packages do not require a rebind when the locksize is altered. The use of LOCK TABLE statement as an alternative is discussed in Section CC.10.

Share, Update, and Exclusive Locks

Locks can be taken in share (S), exclusive (X), or update (U) mode. *Share* locks allow two or more programs to read simultaneously but not change the locked unit, with each taking a share lock. DB2 uses share locks when it responds to SELECT statements. An *exclusive* lock bars all other users from the locked unit while an update takes place. After a program has taken an exclusive lock, no other transaction can read the data or take any kind of lock against it. (Uncommitted read is an exception to be discussed.) It is necessary for DB2 to read a row before it can be updated or deleted, and during this read a less restrictive *update* lock can be taken.

Before changing a value, DB2 can take an S or U lock against the page or row and then *promote* that to an X to make the change. It could take an X lock initially, but that would limit concurrency unnecessarily, since there would be many cases in which a program can read data in anticipation of changing it but then not make the change at all. By using lock promotion, concurrent users can read the data until the last possible moment before the change--if the change is made at all.

However, this approach also increases the possibility for deadlocks. Between the time the update transaction takes the S lock and promotes it to an X lock, a second update transaction is also entitled to take an S lock against the same page. Each share lock would hold, waiting for the other to be released so it could take an exclusive lock and make its change. Neither will be released, of course because each is preventing the other from taking the X lock it needs to complete.

The U lock avoids these deadlocks in certain cases while still affording a high level of concurrency. A U lock is compatible with S locks but not with other U locks or X locks. Chapter PD discusses how to select rows and declare an intent to update or delete rows. This processing results in a U lock being taken while looking for a page to change. Before the change is actually made, the lock is promoted to an X lock after existing S locks held by other programs are released. (The matrix in Figure CC.4 shows compatibility among the different modes of page- or row-level locks.)

Figure CC.4. Page and row lock compatibility

Program A has lock

Program B
can take lock

Lk	X	U	S
X	-	-	-
U	-	-	Y
S	-	Y	Y

If and when the program wants to make the change, it waits for preceding S locks to be released and promotes the U to an X lock. The S locks are likely to be released because none of them represents an update transaction vainly waiting its turn for an X lock. If one of the concurrent transactions were for an update, it would have had a U lock, barring the second update transaction and avoiding a deadlock. Between the time a transaction acquires a U lock and promotes it, other transactions can acquire share locks, enabling them to read the data. The update transaction must wait for all previous S locks taken by other transactions to be released before promoting to an X lock for the change if the change is needed. If a change is not made, the U lock is released depending on the isolation level used and always when a commit work is issued.

Update locks are available at the page level and are used when searching for a row to be updated or deleted. They are usually used when a cursor is used to fetch the data and the user has specified an isolation level of cursor stability. The DECLARE {name} CURSOR statement with the FOR UPDATE OF clause invokes the use of U locks. (Cursors and the FOR UPDATE OF clause are discussed in PD.) DB2 also uses U locks while searching for data to be updated without a cursor, particularly for updates that affect multiple rows.

CC.4 LOCK LIMITS AND ESCALATIONS

DB2 provides administrators with the ability to limit the number of locks that can be taken by any one program or interactive user for a particular tablespace and within the entire DB2 subsystem.

Control at the Tablespace Level

Use the LOCKMAX parameter of the CREATE TABLESPACE to limit the number of locks that an application can take on that tablespace. You can specify an integer from 1 to 2,147,483,647. A zero (0) means that lock escalation is disabled. The value SYSTEM means that the value specified in the NUMLKTS subsystem parameter is used. The system administrator can change the default maximum value of 1,000 on the DSNTIPJ installation panel or by specifying NUMLKTS in DSNZPARM. If you do not specify LOCKMAX when creating a tablespace with a lock size of ANY, the system value of 1,000 is used. If you do not specify LOCKMAX when creating a tablespace with a lock size of ROW or PAGE, the default of zero is used.

The value specified for LOCKMAX applies to tablespaces defined with LOCKSIZE ANY, PAGE, or ROW. DB2 counts all page and row locks against this value. The count includes locks required for triggered SQL statements that are invoked and those taken for the enforcement of referential integrity when it is defined to DB2. Although the tables may not be explicitly referenced in SQL statements, a count of the locks are included and checked against the NUMLKTS and NUMLKUS limits. This can result in exceeding the limits, even though an analysis of the SQL statements might not lead to that conclusion.

When a program reaches the NUMLKTS limit, the intent lock of the tablespace is escalated to an S or X lock. If the tablespace is segmented, then escalation occurs to a table lock. If LOCKPART of YES is specified when the tablespace is created, only the accessed partitions are locked. The individual page or row locks are released after the escalation.

Recommendation: No positive or negative SQLCODE is issued when locks are escalated as a result of meeting the lock limit for the tablespace. In most cases, it is best to disable lock escalation. Do this by specifying 0 for

LOCKMAX and NUMLKTS. Use lock controls on the thread level to control the total number of locks taken by a single transaction or batch program.

This recommendation is less critical in V6. This is because message DSNI031I is written to the operator along with database and tablespace name, partition number, lock state (escalated to S or X lock), plan or package name, statement number, etc.

Control on the Thread Level

The NUMLKUS parameter in DSNZPARM and the DSNTIPJ installation panel is the maximum number of page or row locks that a single thread can hold at any one time. This value applies for objects created with a lock size of ROW, PAGE, or ANY. The default value is 10,000.

If a user or program exceeds the value in NUMLKUS, a -904 SQLCODE is returned to the program. The cursor is automatically closed. The program's error module can then choose to commit or rollback to release the locks. If a fetch or close cursor is attempted, a -501 indicates that cursor is not open for a fetch or close and a -507 indicates the curser is not open for an update or delete.

Recommendation: Do not choose zero for NUMLKUS. A zero means that the thread can hold an unlimited number of locks; unlimited, that is, until IRLM runs out of storage.

If a program attempts to get a lock and the IRLM has no space available, the program abends. The IRLM does not abend, rather it writes a message to console when it does not have enough space to take additional locks (V5 APAR PQ07327).

```
DXR175E irlmnm IRLM IS UNABLE TO OBTAIN STORAGE -
storage_type
```

The IRLM address space needs to be increased in size or programs that accumulate a large number of locks need be identified and revised to commit more frequently.

Avoiding Lock Limits

To avoid exceeding lock limits, commit work frequently, which causes the locks to be released. (Commit frequency is discussed in Chapter PD.) Use of the cursor stability or uncommited read isolation levels for fetching data, as discussed in Section CC.6, further reduces the chances that a program will exceed the lock limits.

If you can tolerate the possible loss of concurrency, issuing a LOCK TABLE statement in the program reduces the number of locks taken dramatically. The explicit lock means that data and index page locks are not taken against the tablespace, and any previous locks are released.

CC.5 LOCK AVOIDANCE

Lock avoidance is a technique used by DB2 to reduce the number of locks that must be taken during read-only SELECT processing. If lock avoidance is successful, a qualifying row is returned to the program without taking a lock. (Lock avoidance also applies to checking dependents for a primary key update or for delete with a restrict constraint as discussed in Chapter CT.)

If no rows qualify on a page, it is not necessary to lock a page or row when lock avoidance is successful. This applies to read-only SELECT statements as well as to UPDATE and DELETE statements which are bound with the isolation level of cursor stability or read stability. Isolation levels are discussed in Section CC.6.

Lock avoidance applies to read-only SELECT statements and ambiguous SELECT statements bound with CURRENTDATA(NO) (YES is the default). No lock is taken for a singleton select with CURRENTDATA(NO) unless the isolation level of RR or RS is used in which case a lock is taken.

The clause FOR FETCH ONLY explicitly declares a SELECT statement as read-only. (FOR READ ONLY syntax complies with the SQL standard and has the same meaning as FOR FETCH ONLY.) If a row will not be updated and can change after it is fetched, use FOR FETCH ONLY in the cursor declaration like:

```
EXEC SQL DECLARE SCURSOR CURSOR FOR
         SELECT SN, SNAME, STATUS
```

```
FROM S
WHERE STATUS > :NEW-STATUS
FOR FETCH ONLY END-EXEC.
```

It is advisable to add the FOR FETCH ONLY clause to all new SELECT statements to clearly indicate that the SELECT statements are used to only read rows and the rows will not be updated or deleted after they are read. You should also consider adding the clause to SELECT statements in programs that are being revised. The FOR FETCH ONLY clause clearly designates the statement as read-only. It is clear to the developer, to someone revising the program, and to DB2.

An ambiguous cursor means that DB2 cannot determine if the cursor is read only because it is in a plan or package that contains PREPARE or EXECUTE IMMEDIATE (fetched row could be modified by a dynamic SQL statement), it does not have a FOR FETCH ONLY, FOR READ ONLY or FOR UPDATE OF clause, if the cursor is not the target of WHERE CURRENT OF clause on an UPDATE or DELETE statement, or a work file is not required, it is considered ambiguous. You can allow lock avoidance for ambiguous cursors by specifying CURRENTDATA(NO) at bind time.

Why Read-Only Data?

Why is lock avoidance used only for read-only data? Data can change after it is read because no locks are taken. An obvious consequence can be illustrated using the Johnson's bank account once again. Assume that Mr. and Mrs. Johnson have a balance of 1,000 dollars in their checking account. If Mrs. Johnson withdraws 1,000 dollars and, before the balance of 0 is committed, Mr. Johnson withdraws the same amount. A bank will not stay in business very long if this is allowed to happen.

A more subtle example shows how a read-only SELECT statement can result in erroneous processing. Assume the program reads a row and an SQLCODE of 0 is returned. An UPDATE or DELETE statement is executed but the program does not check the SQLCODE again. The developer assumes that the update or delete was executed successfully because the required row was read successfully. Processing continues as if the row was successfully updated or deleted. However, it is possible that the row was not updated or deleted because it was changed after it was read and before the update or delete was issued. To avoid this problem, use the FOR UPDATE OF clause on the SELECT statement if a returned row might be updated or deleted. Do be cautious with the use of the FOR UPDATE OF clause. It disallows some efficient techniques for processing the data as discussed in Chapter PD.

How DB2 Lock Avoidance Works

To avoid locks, DB2 must first determine if the data has been committed. If it has, it does not need to take a lock on it. It compares the log relative byte address (RBA) of the oldest active UR for a particular tablespace or partition against the RBA in the page header that indicates when the page was last updated. Typically, many URs are active at any one time as represented in Figure CC.5. The arrows indicate the beginning and end of a UR. Notice that URs F and H have not ended their URs. DB2 tracks the oldest active UR for each page set--this is called the *commit log sequence number* (CLSN). The CLSN is 10 in the example. This means that all data on a page with an RBA less than 10 has been committed.

Figure CC.5. CLSN used in lock avoidance

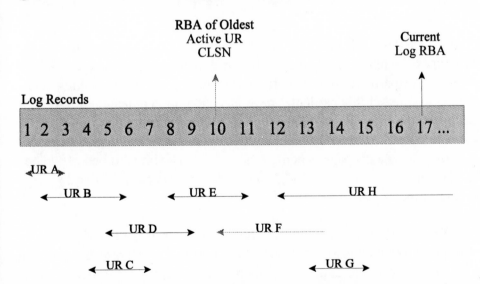

Assume that someone selects a row from a page that was last updated with an RBA of 3 as recorded in the page header (Figure CC.6). Because 3 is earlier than the CLSN of 10, it is safe to assume that everything on the page has been committed. DB2 can avoid taking a lock on that page. A latch is taken at the time the page is read.

Figure CC.6. Lock avoidance implementation

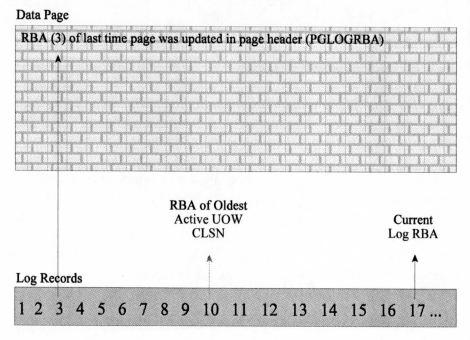

Data Page

RBA (3) of last time page was updated in page header (PGLOGRBA)

RBA of Oldest
Active UOW
CLSN

Current
Log RBA

Log Records

1 2 3 4 5 6 7 8 9 10 11 12 13 14 15 16 17 ...

If the page RBA is 12, however, it is still possible that data on that particular page has been committed because the CLSN is for the entire tablespace or partition, not the particular page or row DB2 is looking at. To determine whether this particular page has uncommited data on it, DB2 checks the possibly uncommitted (PUNC) bit that is maintained for each row in the row prefix. The PUNC bit is turned on by insert and update activity on a row and when a page is being reorganized. The bit is turned off when the page or row is locked or CLSN processing is successful and > 25 percent of the bits are on.

If the PUNC bit is on, a lock is attempted. However, if the PUNC bit is off, the page or row lock is avoided, the row is returned to the program, and the row can be selected or updated by others. For example, if Program A has a U or X lock on a page and is processing row 10 on that page, Program B can read row 15 on that same page.

Recommendations: Use lock avoidance whenever possible by fulfilling the prerequisites in Figure CC.7. The use of lock avoidance improves concurrency and performance.

Figure CC.7. Prerequisites for using lock avoidance

- The LOCKSIZE must be ROW, PAGE, or ANY
- Cursor stability must be specified at bind time
- Applies to read-only and ambiguous SELECT statements bound with CURRENTDATA(NO) (YES is the default)
- Applies to pages with no qualifying rows for SELECT, UPDATE, and DELETE statements bound with cursor stability and read stability and with CURRENTDATA of YES and NO

Monitoring Lock Avoidance: Performance class 7, IFCID 0223, and performance class 6 or accounting class 1, IFCID 0218, contain information on lock avoidance.

CC.6 ISOLATION LEVELS

If an SQL statement embedded in a host-language program might return multiple rows, you must declare in the program a cursor that presents them to the host program one at a time, usually within a repeatedly executed block. DB2 handles locking for these cursor reads in different ways. The choices, called *isolation levels*, are uncommited read (UR), cursor stability (CS), read stability (RS), and repeatable read (RR). RR is the default. The levels apply to data covered by ROW, PAGE, and ANY lock sizes.

How to Specify an Isolation Level: Specify the isolation level at bind time for all statements in a plan or package, or on individual statements using the WITH clause of the SELECT statement. The isolation level specified on a WITH clause, as shown below, overrides the bind isolation level. This capability can give you more flexibility in designing your applications for concurrency.

```
SELECT  SN, SNAME, STATUS, CITY
FROM    S
WHERE   CITY = 'Vancouver'
WITH UR;
```

If the WITH clause is not specified, the package bind isolation level is used if specified. If the package isolation level is not specified, the plan isolation level is used.

Uncommitted Read (UR)

UR means that a program can read data that has not yet been committed by another program. No locks are taken except for the special S mass delete lock used to serialize UR readers and mass deleters, which requires an X mass delete lock. In addition, an IX lock on any tablespace in the work file database (DSNDB07, usually) is taken to avoid a drop for the tablespace that is being processed. UR, like all of the isolation levels, causes SQL to be serialized with most utilities, depending on the phase of processing, by using claim and drain processing as discussed in Chapter LC.

If using UR, your program can be reading data that is in the process of being changed. It provides a high level of concurrency, but do not use UR if seeing uncommited data could affect a business decision.

When Not to Use UR

There are many cases where errors can result from reading uncommited data. You do not want to read data with a read-only SELECT statement and then update the row just fetched--the row could have changed after it was fetched. Do not use UR when balancing financial accounts or when balancing the number of parts received and sold.

Here is a more subtle example. One should not schedule the manufacture of an item if all of the materials are not available. This can result in idle time in a plant. It can also result in defective merchandise in an automated manufacturing environment. For example, chemicals may be added automatically at a point in the manufacturing process. There may not be enough chemicals in a container because a previously manufactured item used the last of the chemical. A program may not see the shortage because it read a row while there was an X lock to subtract the amount used by the last item.

A dramatic example is the possibility of scheduling train usage of railroad tracks where two trains are on a collision course. While reserving a room at a hotel for a person when a room is not available is not catastrophic, it can result in a person not having a place to sleep for the night and is likely to result in the permanent loss of a guest for the hotel.

Restrictions: UR can only be specified for read-only SELECT statements for similar reasons as given for the use of lock avoidance.

If the WITH UR clause is not specified and UR is used as the bind isolation level, UR will be used for read-only SELECT statements and cursor stability will be used for non-read-only SELECT statements.

When to Consider Using UR

If business professionals are willing to see the data even if it is currently being updated, UR may be considered. Consider a case where a newly inserted row is displayed to the user but is subsequently rolled back. Did the data exist? Yes, it did exist for a moment in time. It is reminiscent of the philosophical questions regarding existence addressed in the early 1600s. Descartes is credited with ending the debate with his statement: "I think, therefore I am."

Your users may not have a philosophical bend. It is best to ask them some questions in terms of their application system. Formulate some worse case scenario and ask them if UR is acceptable. Figure CC.8 contains some questions to stimulate thinking. The important point is for you and your business professionals to decide when it is appropriate to use UR. Even after users understand and accept the consequences of using UR, consider including a timestamp on screens and reports to indicate the time to six digits of microseconds when the data existed as presented.

Figure CC.8. Questions for considering the use of UR

Ask users the following types of questions, modified for the particular application under discussion:

♦ Is it acceptable to see a row that was inserted or updated but for which a rollback occurred rather than a commit?
♦ Is it acceptable for a passenger to reserve an airline seat even though the last seat is being sold to someone else? Some airlines do allow tickets to be over-sold.

♦ Is it acceptable for a customer to order an item even though the last item is being sold to someone else? This is a policy used by some catalog companies. The customer is notified that the item is on back order with a follow-up letter.

♦ Is it acceptable to see the total number of Fords in Perth while the last car is being purchased for scheduling the manufacture of Fords in Australia, scheduling shipments of Fords to Perth, or a potential buyer in Perth?

♦ Is it acceptable to see the total number of Fords sold at 10:30.20 on September 27, 1994 since the beginning of the month while a car is being sold at 10:30.19 and committed at 10:30.21?

Tables that are always updated in a single-threaded batch program without other programs executing are good candidates for UR. It is appropriate to use UR when accessing data extracted for a data warehousing application and for historical data that is never updated. It may be appropriate to use UR when computing a column function where the results do not have to be exact. For example, the average price of an item since the beginning of the year may be acceptable even though the price of the item is being updated but has not been committed or rolled back. There are probably some reference tables that are rarely updated (a state code table, for example) where UR is justified. The use of UR when selecting from the catalog tables is a good choice in most cases. You can read locked pages and avoid locking others out. A SPUFI plan bound with UR is not provided with DB2. If it is acceptable to use UR with SPUFI in a test environment, consider rebinding the RR SPUFI plan with UR, assuming that the RR SPUFI plan is not used. An alternative is to add the clause WITH UR to your read-only SELECT statements.

Determining Where UR Is Being Used

If there is a possibility that someone might use UR without realizing the full consequences of reading uncommited data, the SELECT statements in Figure CC.9 will prove useful. The SELECT statements from the catalog tables can be used to identify plans and packages that were bound with UR or that have WITH UR on a SELECT statement. In addition, IFCIDs 0060, 0061, 0065, 0108, 0112, 0113, 0177, and 0124 from performance trace classes 3, 10, and 11, or monitor trace class 1 shows the isolation level used at execution time, which is useful for programs using dynamic SQL.

Figure CC.9. SELECT statements to identify the use of UR

```
SELECT DISTINCT Y.PLNAME
FROM    SYSIBM.SYSPLAN X,
        SYSIBM.SYSSTMT Y
WHERE (X.NAME = Y.PLNAME
AND     X.ISOLATION = 'U')
    OR Y.ISOLATION = 'U'
ORDER BY Y.PLNAME;

SELECT DISTINCT Y.COLLID, Y.NAME,
        Y.VERSION
FROM    SYSIBM.SYSPACKAGE   X,
        SYSIBM.SYSPACKSTMT Y
WHERE (X.LOCATION  = Y.LOCATION
AND     X.LOCATION  = ' '
AND     X.COLLID    = Y.COLLID
AND     X.NAME      = Y.NAME
AND     X.VERSION   = Y.VERSION
AND     X.ISOLATION = 'U')
    OR Y.ISOLATION = 'U'
ORDER BY Y.COLLID, Y.NAME, Y.VERSION;
```

Cursor Stability (CS)

Under CS, if a lock is taken at all on a particular page or row, that lock is released after the cursor moves to another page or row. However, if a row is inserted, updated, or deleted with or without the FOR UPDATE OF clause, locks continue to be accumulated for pages and rows that are changed. In most cases, the lock on the last page or row accessed is released when a COMMIT is issued, when an SQLCODE of +100 is issued, and when the cursor is closed. The lock is also released if a row or page is returned to an intermediate work file.

Recommendation: To prevent holding a lock on the last row or page, close the cursor when it is no longer needed.

Caution: Compared to RR and RS, CS provides more concurrency; however, because it allows other users to access the pages or rows a given program has already read in the midst of a process, this isolation level may allow the data to be changed by another program without the knowledge of the original program. For example, consider a program that reads through a table of plumbing parts to be sure all those needed for a particular job are in stock before submitting an order for any of them. If CS is used, another program might scoop up the last number 5 elbow pipe between the time the original program saw it was available and the time when the order including it was placed.

CS also opens the possibility--though usually only a slight one--that rows can be mistakenly processed twice or not at all. Consider an application, SREPORT, that selects suppliers from the Supplier table in SN order. At the same time, an update program, SCHANGE, is changing supplier numbers. If SCHANGE increases the SN of a row that SREPORT has processed into a range that it is yet to be processed, SREPORT might very well select that row twice. In Figure CC.10, for example, SREPORT has processed rows S1, S2, and S3. While it is processing rows S4 and S5, SCHANGE changes S3 to S6. SREPORT will almost surely process the row again if the search has been using an index. The update will have added a pointer from the index for value S6 to the row. Even if the search is using a tablespace scan that does not return to the page that held the changed value, it might still encounter the row again if the update had caused it to be moved. The reverse problem occurs--SREPORT misses a row--when SCHANGE lowers the row's SN into a range SREPORT has already processed.

Figure CC.10. Double processing under CS

```
UPDATE  S
SET     SN = 'S6'
WHERE   SN = 'S3';
```

SN	SNAME	STATUS	CITY
S1	Smith	20	London
S2	Jones	10	Paris
S3	Blake	30	Paris
S4	Clark	20	London
S5	Adams	30	Athens
S6	Blake	30	Paris

An isolation level of RR or RS, under which SREPORT holds locks on pages or rows until all processing is complete, would avoid most of these problems. (LOCK TABLE may be required in some cases.) But whether RR or RS should be used depends on the application and the processing schedule. Running batch update and reporting programs in sequence rather than concurrently avoids these double or missed processing problems. Also, the seriousness of these problems varies. If the only difficulty that arises from rare processing anomalies is that a plumbing parts inventory might say there are 1,020 $0.02 bolts available when there are only 1,000, the inconsistency may be tolerable. (The data in the table is correct. It is a matter of what the program saw while it was processing the data.) If, on the other hand, the application might say a banking customer has $2 million rather than $1 million, there is considerable risk.

CURRENTDATA Option

We introduced the CURRENTDATA option in the discussion on lock avoidance. It is important to understand, though, that the CURRENTDATA option can affect results in those cases where a cursor is not accessing data through a work file. CURRENTDATA(YES) tells DB2 that the data on which your cursor is positioned must remain "current" with the data in the base table. In most cases, use CURRENTDATA(NO) to take advantage of lock avoidance. CURRENTDATA(YES) is the default in Version 4. (CURRENTDATA(NO) was the default prior to Version 4.) You must explicitly specify CURRENTDATA(NO) to take advantage of lock avoidance in Version 4.

Read Stability (RS)

Under RS, DB2 takes a lock on the page or row the cursor is accessing and holds the lock only for rows that satisfy predicates. Locks on qualifying rows or pages are held until the program issues a COMMIT. If no rows qualify on a page, a lock is not taken unlike when using RR. Lock avoidance can be used for stage 1 processing but is not used if the row passes stage 1 processing and is rejected at stage 2. (Stage 1 and 2 predicates are discussed in Chapter PP.)

No other program can update or delete a row that is part of the answer set returned to the application. However, it is possible that additional rows can be inserted (or a non-qualifying row updated) that can satisfy the predicate the second time around.

RS and NC (No Commit) conforms to the SQL standard. DB2 does not accept NC as an isolation level. If the SQL is bound with NC on a server that supports NC and the SQL is executed on DB2, it is treated as UR.

Repeatable Read (RR)

Under RR, all page and row locks are held as the cursor moves through the rows. Locks are held even for non-qualifying rows, and are not released until the next commit point. This effectively locks out all other application processes from accessing those pages or rows.

If RR is specified and at bind time the optimizer does not find a usable index for a matching index scan, the optimizer chooses a table or tablespace lock and issues a message, DSNX103I, alerting you that a table or tablespace lock will be used to avoid accumulating a lock on every page or row for a tablespace scan or non-matching index scan.

S or U Locks with RR or RS: By default, DB2 takes S locks on rows or pages when using RS or RR. This has performance advantages if FOR UPDATE OF is used and updates are infrequent. You can use the RRULOCK DSNZPARM value YES to have DB2 take U locks directly rather than initially taking S locks and then changing them to a U when a row is located for update or delete. This can provide some performance advantage if you use RR or RS isolation with frequent updates.

KEEP UPDATE LOCKS: The KEEP UPDATE LOCKS clause causes X locks to be taken immediately rather than taking S and U locks initially on rows or pages that have qualifying rows. The clause applies when using FOR UPDATE OF and WITH RS or WITH RR. If WITH RS is specified, locks are held even though the row does not qualify at stage 2 and is not returned to the program. If WITH RR is specified, locks are taken on all rows or pages including rows that fall within the range of the selection expression (predicates and CASE expressions, for example). The locks are released with a commit. The KEEP UPDATE LOCKS clause avoids some types of deadlocks. The clause is specified like:

```
EXEC SQL DECLARE SCURSOR CURSOR FOR
         SELECT SN, SNAME, STATUS
         FROM    S
         WHERE   STATUS > :NEW-STATUS
         FOR UPDATE OF SNAME
         WITH RS KEEP UPDATE LOCKS END-EXEC.
```

Recommendations for Isolation Levels

If a program can tolerate reading "dirty data", UR offers the best concurrency and performance. However, most programs do require some sort of concurrency control. CS with CURRENTDATA(NO) is a good choice to take advantage of lock avoidance in most cases.

If a program requires greater control than that offered by CS, consider RS. It offers greater control over the data but does not lock non-qualifying rows and pages as does RR. In most cases, it holds fewer locks than RR. Both RS and RR have the additional risk of having the page or row locks promoted to a table or tablespace lock if the maximum number of locks per tablespace is exceeded. If a cursor's SQL statement requires DB2 to create and process an intermediate work file--as it would for sorts and for processing several types of subselects, for example--RR or RS holds its locks during the processing, which could be a long time. It also risks an error code if the NUMLKUS limit is exceeded.

CC.7 INTENT LOCKS

When an SQL statement in a transaction first accesses a tablespace with a page or row level lock, DB2 first takes a particular type of lock, called an intent lock, at the table and tablespace level for a segmented tablespace or tablespace level for a nonsegmented tablespace. It later takes an S, U, or X lock against the page or row on which the data reside as SQL is executed. In a sense, the intent locks act as traffic signals that regulate the use of page and row level locks, and signal to concurrent transactions the type of access the pages or rows are undergoing.

Intent locking reduces the processing needed to manage the locks, while allowing a high degree of compatibility among concurrent locks. For example, if a given transaction needs the data it is about to read to remain unchanged, DB2 can take a share lock against the table or tablespace, which allows subsequent transactions to read but not change the data. The transaction must also be sure, however, that no changes are underway before it takes the S lock. That is where the intent lock comes in. For any X lock on a page or row in the tablespace, which would indicate an imminent change, DB2 will have taken an intent lock on the table or tablespace.

Instead of having to search all page or row locks to find those applying to a specific page, DB2 can look for the one tablespace intent lock, in this case a share with intent exclusive (SIX) lock. If it finds it, the transaction knows it must wait for the current changes to be completed before it proceeds with an update.

Types of Intent Locks

There are three types of intent locks: Intent share (IS), intent exclusive (IX), and share with intent exclusive (SIX).

Intent share: The transaction intends to read but not update data pages and, therefore, takes S locks on them; it tolerates concurrent transactions taking S, IS, SIX, IX, or U locks.

Intent exclusive: The transaction intends to read or change data and therefore take an X lock against the data pages; it tolerates concurrent transactions taking IX or IS locks.

Shared with intent exclusive: The transaction intends to read or change data; it tolerates other transactions taking an IS lock on the tablespace, which allows them to read data by taking S page locks. They cannot change the data.

A primary purpose of intent locks is to cause a program to wait for a required S, U, or X lock at the table and tablespace level until the necessary locks have been released from the rows and pages and there is a compatible intent lock.

Allowable Combinations of Table and Tablespace Locks

The matrix in Figure CC.11 shows the allowable combinations of table and tablespace lock. Locks are at the partition level when using a partition scan as discussed in Chapter PL. The last two rows in the matrix indicate when row or page locks can be taken depending on the current tablespace lock. The matrix shows the type of activity each lock will allow in the data pages or rows beneath it. Note, for example, that if transaction A holds an IX lock, it allows subsequent transactions to take IX or IS locks, permitting those transactions eventually to take exclusive or share locks, which allow them to nchange or read a page or row. IS and IX intent locks are the most common when using a lock size of row and page.

Figure CC.11. Table and tablespace lock compatibility

Program A has lock

Lock	X	U	SIX	IX	S	IS
X	-	-	-	-	-	-
U	-	-	-	-	Y	Y
SIX	-	-	-	-	-	Y
IX	-	-	-	Y	-	Y
S	-	Y	-	-	Y	Y
IS	-	Y	Y	Y	Y	Y
ROW	-	-	S	S/X	-	S/X
PAGE	-	-	S	S/X	-	S/X

Program B

can take lock

CC.8 ACQUIRING AND RELEASING LOCKS

Page or row locks are always taken when required during a program's execution and they are always released when the program executes a COMMIT or ROLLBACK statement. To a certain extent, however, you can control at which points DB2 acquires or releases locks against table and tablespaces, including intent locks. Use the BIND parameters ACQUIRE and RELEASE to indicate this.

Acquiring Locks

There are two options for acquiring table and tablespace locks: USE and ALLOCATE.

ACQUIRE(USE) causes DB2 to obtain a table or tablespace lock only when it executes an SQL statement that references a table in the tablespace. DB2 uses ACQUIRE(USE) when checking referential integrity constraints, regardless of the ACQUIRE parameter you specify at bind time. ACQUIRE(USE) is the default for plans and is effectively used for packages which do not allow for an ACQUIRE parameter.

ACQUIRE(ALLOCATE) gets locks on all tables and tablespaces referenced directly and indirectly by a program when it allocates the program's thread-- just before it executes the first SQL statement in the program. If a SELECT statement appears in the same program as an INSERT, UPDATE, or DELETE statement, a more restrictive IX lock is taken, even if those particular statements are never executed. This has certain advantages in that it is not necessary to first take an IS lock on a tablespace and then change it to an IX lock for an INSERT, UPDATE, or DELETE statement executed on the same tablespace.

A program for which ALLOCATE is specified must wait for all referenced tables and tablespaces to be available for the required locks before it can execute. This may delay that program's execution, but it minimizes the chance for deadlocks that exist when a number of programs execute concurrently against the same tables and tablespaces. However, this is not usually a problem anyway because the tablespace IS and IX locks are compatible. A program can have an IX lock at the table or tablespace level when executing an INSERT, UPDATE, or DELETE statement. Another program can be holding an IX or IS lock and be updating data or selecting data on another page.

Benefit of ACQUIRE(USE): ACQUIRE(USE) provides greater concurrency because the tablespace locks are not taken until they are actually needed. It allows for selective partition locking which is discussed in Chapter CD.

Releasing Locks

There are two options for releasing table and tablespace locks: COMMIT and DEALLOCATE. RELEASE(COMMIT) releases table and tablespace locks at commit or rollback points. RELEASE(DEALLOCATE) holds these locks until the thread is deallocated and the program terminates. DB2 follows a plan or package's RELEASE parameter for referential integrity checking.

RELEASE(DEALLOCATE) only serializes access to pages and rows when using S, U, and X locks at the table or tablespace level as a result of one of the following conditions: a LOCKSIZE of table or tablespace is used, the LOCK TABLE statement is executed, or lock escalation has occurred.

Benefits of RELEASE(DEALLOCATE): RELEASE(DEALLOCATE) has performance benefits. Counter and control information is not reset for sequential detection, index lookaside, and dynamically-generated compiled assignment procedures. It is not necessary to re-initialize processing including (IPROC, UPROC, and SPROC) after each commit as discussed in Chapter CO. RELEASE(DEALLOCATE) avoids taking and releasing the same locks repeatedly when using thread reuse in CICS and WFI (Wait for Input) in IMS, and in a data sharing environment. Figure CC.12 summarizes when lock sizes are acquired and released.

Figure CC.12. When locks are acquired and released

♦ Page and row locks are taken when required during execution of the program.
♦ Page and row locks are released depending on the use CS, RR, and RS but always with a commit or rollback
♦ Table and tablespace locks are acquired and released depending on the acquire and release parameter specified at bind time.
♦ IS and IX are usually taken at the table and tablespace levels when using page and row locking. This can be verified with EXPLAIN as discussed in Chapter EX.
♦ S, U, and X locks can be taken on individual rows and pages when IS and IX locks are in effect at the table and tablespace levels.

All combinations of ACQUIRE and RELEASE parameter values are valid except for ACQUIRE(ALLOCATE) with RELEASE(COMMIT) (Figure CC.13). The ACQUIRE option is not available for packages because DB2 always uses ACQUIRE(USE). These choices affect the amount of processing required for managing the locks and whether and when users and programs can access the data.

Figure CC.13. ACQUIRE and RELEASE sequences for tablespace locks

```
        unlock              lock table/tablespace              unlock
PLAN A ——————— ACQUIRE(USE) ————————————————————————— RELEASE(COMMIT) ———


        unlock              lock table/tablespace              unlock
PLAN B ——————— ACQUIRE(USE) ————————————————————————— RELEASE(DEALLOCATE) ——


                            lock table/tablespace              unlock
PLAN C  ACQUIRE(ALLOCATE)  ————————————————————————— RELEASE(DEALLOCATE) ——
```

Recommendation: ACQUIRE(USE) and RELEASE(DEALLOCATE) provide good concurrency when using page or row locking and maximize performance.

To hold exclusive locks as short a time as possible, it is advisable to group INSERT, UPDATE, and DELETE statements together in a host language program followed by a COMMIT. If these SQL statements are interspersed with host language code, the locks are held while executing the host language code.

CC.9 EXPLICIT LOCK TABLE STATEMENT

The LOCK TABLE statement within a program overrides and releases all lock sizes and types that otherwise would be in effect for the accessed tables except for an intent lock held at the tablespace level. The explicit table lock allows use of the table lock size for specific programs that update heavily even though a LOCKSIZE of row, page, or any was specified when the tablespace was created. Use the LOCK TABLE statement to avoid having a program take a large number of row or page locks. It is a good alternative to RR and RS when a large percentage of a table's rows or pages are to be updated.

The statement takes the form LOCK TABLE {name} IN SHARE MODE or LOCK TABLE {name} IN EXCLUSIVE MODE. While the statement requires the table's name, in nonsegmented tablespaces, DB2 takes the lock against the tablespace containing the referenced table. The LOCK TABLE statement locks only the specified table if it is in a segmented tablespace with an intent lock at the tablespace level. A PART parameter can be used to specify a specified partition that is be locked along with the name of a table in a partitioned tablespace, for example LOCK TABLE {name} PART 5 IN EXCLUSIVE MODE. The lock does not take effect until the statement executes, even if ACQUIRE(ALLOCATE) had been specified at bind time. If an IX lock is already held, an SIX is acquired. If SIX, U, or X lock is already held, locking the table in share mode has no effect. The explicit lock releases according to the RELEASE parameter specified at bind time.

Do issue LOCK TABLE after each commit if RELEASE(COMMIT) is used. The table lock is released with a commit. Page or row locking is used if LOCK TABLE is not issued again.

The LOCK TABLE statement does not operate on views or on tables located on another DBMS, including another DB2 subsystem. If a LOCK TABLE statement is used on a view, DB2 returns a negative SQLCODE (-156). An error may be issued at bind time depending on the precompiler being used to avoid the execution time error condition. To use the LOCK TABLE statement for a view, you must specify the underlying base table. Installations can use this feature to control use of LOCK TABLE statements. When developers are authorized to use only views, access to base tables is barred, thus enforcing the prohibition against LOCK TABLE statements except in special cases.

If you can afford to lock out all access to a table, locking the table has performance advantages. Figure CC.14 summarizes the elapsed and CPU minutes used by one program with and without LOCK TABLE. Notice that there is a savings of about 30 percent in elapsed and CPU time by using LOCK TABLE in this one case. An alternative is to start the tablespace in read-only mode in which case no locks are taken.

Figure CC.14. Effect of LOCK TABLE on performance

	Elapsed Minutes	CPU Minutes
No Lock Table	110	28
Lock Table Exclusive	78	20

An alternative to using the LOCK TABLE statement is to start the tablespace in read-only mode in which case no locks are taken. This avoids modifying the program and going through program preparation. It also allows for placing the tablespace in read-only mode when a batch read-only window is available and allowing for updates by other programs when the window is not available. The DASPJTSP can be started in read-only mode like:

```
-START DATABASE(DASPJDB) SPACENAM(DASPJTSP)
    ACCESS(RO)
```

CC.10 MONITORING LOCKS

There are a number of tools within DB2 that can be used to monitor locks. If lock contention becomes a problem, these tools can be quite useful in determining the lock size and type of locks so that corrective action can be taken. The EXPLAIN statement gives the lock mode in the PLAN_TABLE column TSLOCKMODE. (The use of EXPLAIN is discussed in Chapter EX.) If you see a value other than IS, IX, or N, investigate to see if your program is locking out other programs from reading or updating data when it executes.

Chapter PD discusses the SQLCA data structure used to communicate information between DB2 and a program. The field SQLERRMC contains a message indicating the database, tablespace or index space, and page number involved in the lock contention. The message is positional, beginning with the DB2 error code and describing the object involved in the lock contention as indicated in Figure CC.15.

Figure CC.15. Lock contention message

```
----|----1----|----2----|----3----|----4----|----5

00C9008E 00000301 PROTO    .ICLOSE2 .X'0003B6'.X'01'

        Position 01-08  =  DB2 error code
        Position 10-17  =  Resource type
        Position 19-26  =  Database name
        Position 28-35  =  Tablespace or index space
        Position 37-45  =  Page number (hex)
        Position 47-51  =  Index sub-page number (hex)
```

Typically the system or database administrator has authority to issue the DISPLAY DATABASE command. This command gives current table and tablespace locks held and lists resources that are waiting for locks when the LOCKS parameter is specified.

If an UR is active across up to and including 255 checkpoints (default is 0, no limit), the message DSNR035I is written to the operator along with AUTHID, plan name, and etc. The UR continues. You can specify the number of checkpoints as UR CHECK FREQ on DSNTIPN installation panel or DSNZPARM URCHKTH.

Recommendation: Do modify the program to commit more frequently if the number of checkpoints within a UR is high.

Any of three traces can be turned on for general monitoring and accounting. The *statistics* trace records gives the total number of times a condition occurred for all SQL executed in the DB2 subsystem (class 1 and 3). The conditions specifically related to locking are suspensions, deadlocks, timeouts, and lock escalations. The *accounting* trace records give similar information but can be for specific authorization IDs, plans, and packages (class 1, 3, and 8). These records also give the maximum number of page locks held by a plan, which is useful for tuning lock limits and to determine if the program needs to issue a COMMIT more often to stay within those limits. The *performance* trace records show the progression of locks in detail but are very costly to have turned on for all plans and packages. Up to three times the usual number of DB2 instructions are executed while the full trace is turned on. Also, the result of the performance trace is very lengthy and difficult to read. It is a last resort in problem determination.

You will want to use a performance monitor to analyze the results of the trace data. IBM's DB2PM product provides good information on locking through the locking, accounting, and statistics reports. A number of software companies sell performance monitors for analysis of the statistics collected by DB2.

CC.11 LOCKS ON THE CATALOG TABLES AND DIRECTORY

Pages in the catalog tables and the directory are locked whenever an object is created or dropped. A lock against catalog table pages or the directory from a given developer, user, or program may bar others from creating objects, binding SQL, or even executing SQL. It is advisable to issue a COMMIT after each CREATE, ALTER, or DROP statement to avoid holding locks any longer than necessary. All access to the catalog table pages by an internal plan for data definition language (DDL) statements and binds use RS regardless of the isolation level of the program executing the statements (including SPUFI). Drain processing is used for DDL to avoid X tablespace locks. An exception is the creation of an index on a table in a segmented tablespace. This is because no claim/drain processing is done at the table level when using segmented tablespaces. Catalog tables are subject to lock escalation just as are application tables when using a locksize of ANY after accumulating more than 1,000 locks (default). These factors suggest frequent commits when using DDL. Locks are taken on the database descriptor (DBD) in the directory for a number of operations (including an X lock during object creation, alteration, and deletion, during index build, and an S lock during plan or package bind).

Locks are acquired at bind time on the catalog tables, and directory. An IX lock is taken on most catalog tablespaces, X lock on the SKCT and SKPT in directory (also locked for DROP and REVOKE statements), and S lock on the DBD. At execution time an IS lock is taken on the SYSPLANAUTH and SYSPACKAUTH catalog tables to check execution authority, S lock on SKCT and SKPT in the directory, and no locks are required on the DBD except for dynamic SQL, in which case an S lock is taken. The operations and locks are summarized in Figure CC.16 from the *IBM Locking in DB2 for MVS/ESA Environment* manual

Figure CC.16. Locks taken on the catalog and directory

Object of Locking	Static SQL	Dynamic SQL	Bind	Create Table	Alter Table	Drop Table Space	Grant	Revoke
Catalog Table Space	IS (a)	IS (b)	IX	IX	IX	IX	IX	IX
SKCT or SKPT	S	S	X	-	X (c)	X (d)	-	X
DBD	- (e)	S (f)	S	X	X	X	-	-

(a) IS locks on the catalog tablespaces are held only for a short time to check execute authority if the plan or package is not public or the authorization list is not cached in the EDM pool.

(b) Except when checking EXECUTE authority (see Note a), IS locks on the catalog tablespaces are held until the COMMIT point. Cannot execute DDL.

(c) SKCT or SKPT is marked invalid if a referential constraint (such as a new primary key or foreign key) is added or changed, or the AUTHID attribute is changed in the table.

(d) SKCT or SKPT is marked invalid as a result of a drop tablespace operation.

(e) If the DBD is not in the EDM pool, S-locks are acquired on the DBD tablespace, which efficiently locks the DBD.

(f) Share lock is not taken on the DBD if the package or plan is cached (APAR PQ24634)

Several DB2 subsystem plans are used in bind operations, to validate user's authority, to perform service tasks, and for utilities as summarized in Figure CC.17. These locks can cause processing to be serialized.

Figure CC.17. DB2 subsystem plans that are locked

Plan	Description
DSNBIND	Used for all binds. Is a major contributor to the length of time required to complete a bind.

Plan	Description
ACT	Used to validate a user's authority to access a specified plan. Is executed each time a thread is created with a lock of short duration.
BCT	Used to perform service tasks and handle requests from DB2 resource managers with lock usually of short duration.
DSNUTIL	Used by utility control program DSNUTILB. The lock duration varies with specific utility function.

CC.12 SUMMARY

It is difficult to point to typical transactions as guides for concurrency control decisions. Two extreme cases, however, summarize the trade-offs available between resource usage and concurrency levels.

To allow many concurrent programs to change data at the cost of CPU time and virtual storage usage, consider:

◆   Use a page locksize. Use row locking only if your performance monitor indicates that lock contention is occurring on data pages.
◆   Have DB2 hold locks for as short a time as possible by employing ACQUIRE(USE) and RELEASE(DEALLOCATE) and by setting isolation level at CS with CURRENTDATA(NO) to take advantage of lock avoidance for ambiguous SELECT statements in most cases. Consider using UR when appropriate.
◆   Use FOR FETCH ONLY (or FOR READ ONLY) when writing new SELECT statements and when revising old ones.
◆   In programs, issue frequent commits, hold off updates to as near a commit point as possible, and commit before waiting for terminal input.

To accommodate mostly read-only programs and batch programs that can afford to limit other program access while using a minimum amount of resources:

♦   Use a lock size of table or tablespace. The isolation level has no
     effect when using a lock size of table or tablespace.
♦   Use ACQUIRE(ALLOCATE) and RELEASE(DEALLOCATE).
♦   Commit work infrequently.

These guidelines minimize the demand for resources, but there can be no
concurrent updates by multiple programs.

These are the extremes. Each application has a unique mix of transactions
with differing performance characteristics and needs that determine your
concurrency control choices.

If acceptable, use CURRENTDATA(NO) to allow lock avoidance for
ambiguous SELECT statements and UR to eliminate locking.

EXERCISES

1. What LOCKSIZE is best if there will be no concurrent update activity?

2. What LOCKSIZE should be used when concurrent update activity is
expected?

3. Assume a LOCKSIZE of page. A very small sample of data (2-3 pages)
has been loaded into tables for testing of programs under development.
Developers are frequently experiencing lock contention. What is the
problem and possible solution to the problem?

4. Is a lock size of row required to minimize lock contention when there is
heavy insert activity at the end of the table or in any concentrated area of the
table? If this type of heavy insert activity is expected, what value should be
specified for PCTFREE and FREEPAGE?

5. How can you avoid lock escalation when using a lock size of row, page,
or any? How can the lock escalation be isolated to a particular program or
SQL statement?

6. If your program holds an S, U, or X lock on a page and it is using an
isolation level of cursor stability (CS), repeatable read (RR), or read stability
(RS), which SQL statements can another program execute successfully that

act on the page? If the other programs are using the UR isolation level, which SQL statements can they execute successfully?

7. How do CS, RS, and RR differ with respect to how long page locks are held? How long are locks held with CS on a SELECT statement with the FOR UPDATE OF clause?

8. What are the primary requirements to take advantage of lock avoidance?

9. If no rows qualify on a page for a SELECT, UPDATE, or DELETE statement, will a lock be taken on the page or row if the CS or RS isolation level is used with the CURRENTDATA parameter of YES or NO.

10. Besides lock avoidance, what are the other benefits of read-only SELECT statements?

11. Assume that you select a row and display it to a user with a CICS pseudo-conversational or an IMS online transaction. Page locking is used, the plan is bound with CURRENTDATA(YES), and an isolation level of CS, RR, or RS is used. You issue an UPDATE statement based on information keyed by the user. Can you be certain that no one has changed the row after the row was displayed to the user and before the UPDATE statement was executed? What is an alternative for dealing with the situation?

12. What effect do the BIND and REBIND parameters ACQUIRE and RELEASE have on when row and page locks are acquired and released?

13. Under what conditions can RELEASE(DEALLOCATE) reduce concurrency, assuming the use of row or page locking and the CS isolation level?

14. What are the advantages of RELEASE(DEALLOCATE)?

15. Bonnie Baker, an outstanding consultant and speaker, encountered the following locking procedure during an assignment. You will find her resolution in the answer. What are the problems with the procedure?

a. Use "LOCK TABLE tablename IN EXCLUSIVE MODE" to lock the table that will be updated and to override the page-level locking normally used for the table. (Bypass the LOCK TABLE statement if a parameter so indicates.)

b. Read two million records from a transaction file.

c. As each transaction record is read, perform an update to a DB2 table.

d. Commit after every five updates (commit frequency chosen for restartability because of the fear of long-running rollbacks, and in anticipation of the eventual need to run concurrently with online programs).

5. Bind with RELEASE COMMIT.

ANSWERS

1. A LOCKSIZE value of table or tablespace is best if no concurrent update activity will take place.

2. In most cases, a LOCKSIZE of page is best when concurrent update activity is expected.

3. Locks are taken at the page level. One-half to one-third of the rows in the very small tables of 2-3 pages are being locked each time a change is made to the tables. Consider using row locking, a larger PCTFREE value, or cause each row to occupy a separate page by adding dummy columns to the table. If the table is large in production, consider using page locking.

4. Row locking is *not* required to reduce lock contention when INSERTING rows at the end of a table or in any concentrated area of the table. If the page is locked when an insert of a row is attempted, the row is inserted in a near or far page as if there is no free space on the page. PCTFREE and FREEPAGE should be zero when heavy insert activity is expected in concentrated areas of the table. There is no reason to waste space on each page by specifying a value for PCTFREE and it is not useful to leave a blank page every 63 pages or less. The free space and blank pages are used in the concentrated areas but wasted in most areas of the tablespace. Indeed, PCTFREE and FREEPAGE of 0 is the best choice, particularly for inserts at the end of the table. This causes DB2 to simply add additional pages for the new rows, rather than using its search algorithm to find free space somewhere in the tablespace.

5. Use LOCKMAX of 0, which is the default when using LOCKSIZE of ROW or PAGE, to avoid lock escalation. When using LOCKSIZE ANY, specify a LOCKMAX of 0, or set the NUMLKTS to 0 in DSNZPARM. To determine which program or SQL statement is causing lock escalation, it is necessary to turn on a performance trace.

6. If your program is using an isolation level of CS, RR, or RS and holds an S or U lock on a page, other programs can read the page but not insert, update, or delete rows on the page. If your program holds an X lock on a page, other programs cannot select, insert, update, or delete rows on the page. If other programs are using UR, they can select rows on the page that has an S or X lock while your program is executing select, insert, update, or delete statements that act on the page.

7. With CS isolation, a page lock is released when you fetch a row on another page. With RS isolation, locks are held on pages processed with qualifying rows. With RR isolation, locks are held on pages processed with qualifying and non-qualifying rows. A commit or rollback causes all page locks to be released with all three isolation levels. When using a SELECT statement with the FOR UPDATE OF clause and CS, locks on updated pages are held until a commit or rollback occurs.

8. Lock avoidance applies to read-only SELECT statements and ambiguous SELECTS bound with CS or RS and CURRENTDATA(NO), and when row or page locking is used. These options must be specified explicitly because RR and CURRENTDATA(YES) are the defaults.

9. If no rows qualify on a page for a SELECT, UPDATE, or DELETE statement, the page or row is not locked if CS or RS and CURRENTDATA of YES or NO.

10. Read-only SELECT statements allow for the use of the UR isolation level and the blocking of data for transmission. It also increases the likelihood that parallel processing can be used for the SQL statement.

11. The row can change after it is displayed to the user and before the UPDATE statement is executed because locks are released when a screen is displayed. One of the several alternatives presented to deal with the situation is to save the primary key and all columns displayed before displaying the screen. Use a fully qualified UPDATE statement on all of the

saved columns. The UPDATE statement is successful only if the row has not changed since it was displayed to the user. If the row has changed, the program receives an SQLCODE of +100 indicating that the row was not found to be updated. This means that the row has changed or was deleted after it was displayed and before the UPDATE statement was executed.

12. The ACQUIRE and RELEASE parameters do not affect when row and page locks are acquired and released.

13. RELEASE(DEALLOCATE) can reduce concurrency when using row and page locking if lock escalation has occurred to an S or X lock at the table or tablespace level or if a program issues the LOCK TABLE statement. Once an S table or tablespace lock is in effect, no other program can execute an INSERT, UPDATE or DELETE statement on the table. Once an X table or tablespace lock is in effect, no other program can execute a SELECT, INSERT, UPDATE or DELETE statement on the table.

14. RELEASE(DEALLOCATE) has performance advantages. This is because counter and control information is not reset for sequential detection, index lookaside, and dynamically-generated compiled assignment procedures. It is not necessary to re-initialize processing after each commit. Thread reuse in CICS and WFI (Wait for Input) in IMS benefit when RELEASE(DEALLOCATE) is used.

15. Bonnie Baker gives the following analysis.

First, the initial LOCK TABLE statement did indeed eliminate page-level locking -- but only for one unit of recovery. At the first commit, the X table lock and IX tablespace lock were released (because that's what RELEASE COMMIT does). When the second unit of work began, the locks acquired by the LOCK TABLE statement had been released. So the table resumed its normal page-level locking -- an IX lock on the tablespace, an IX lock on the table, and X locks on every single page updated. Each commit then released any page locks. (Page locks are always released at commit, regardless of the RELEASE parameter.) But each and every commit also released the table and tablespace intent locks. At the beginning of each new unit of work the intent locks on the tablespace and table had to be reacquired. Not good. Especially for a program that intended to acquire no page locks, just two big locks, one on the tablespace and one on the table, and keep them for the duration of the program run.

Second, because the commits were done after every five updates, the UPROC (discussed in Chapter CO) was barely built when it was destroyed by the commit (because that's what RELEASE COMMIT does). This job paid for building of 400,000 UPROCs without enjoying the benefits of a single one. The premature demise of the UPROC was very expensive. Again, not good.

FIGURES

Program Development

PD.1 INTRODUCTION

Programs written in a number of host languages--COBOL, PL/1, C, FORTRAN, Assembler, APL2, BASIC, Ada, Prolog, REXX, and Java--can contain SQL statements that access DB2 data. That is, SQL statements embedded in a host language can update a DB2 database or return selected values from the database to a program. When you develop a program to use DB2 data, you must develop the host-language source code and the embedded SQL. The maximum number of table that can be referenced in a SELECT, INSERT, UPDATE, and DELETE statement is 225 (not including joins as discussed in Chapter JP).

Static and Dynamic SQL

SQL works within host-language programs in two ways--statically and dynamically. With static SQL, you know the SQL statement to be used and can therefore code it in the program. This allows the statements to be bound before executing the program, and that bound SQL remains static during execution. (All of the host languages that support SQL can use static SQL except for BASIC and APL2, which, because they are interpretive languages, bind SQL statements each time they are executed.) Static SQL, although less flexible than dynamic SQL, usually offers the best performance for online transactions with a high transaction rate.

With dynamic SQL, the program can formulate statements based on choices made and entered by the user as the program runs. In this case, the program must have code that allows the program to construct the statement, submit it to the bind process, execute it, and deal with its results. An alternative is to dynamically execute an SQL statement so that the optimizer can use the content of host variables in its access path selection process. (We will discuss dynamic SQL in more detail later in this chapter.)

With a few additions, embedded SQL uses the same syntax that interactive SQL uses. You must indicate where an SQL statement begins and ends in order to set it apart from the host language code. The beginning delimiter is always EXEC SQL, which immediately precedes the statement. In COBOL, END-EXEC. signifies the statement conclusion; in PL/1, a semicolon performs that function. FORTRAN recognizes the end of a line as the statement end. Each SQL statement must have a beginning and ending delimiter.

Figure PD.1 is a fragment of a COBOL program showing the four data manipulation statements. It contains minimal COBOL code to show the SQL and does not show complete COBOL logic. For example, logically it is impossible to reach the DELETE statement.

Figure PD.1. Embedded SQL in a COBOL fragment

```
EXEC SQL SELECT SN, SNAME, STATUS, CITY
         INTO   :SN,:SNAME,:STATUS,:CITY
         FROM   S
         WHERE  SN = :SN-IN END-EXEC.

IF SQLCODE = 0
   MOVE 'YES' TO SN-PRESENT.

IF SN-PRESENT = 'NO '
   EXEC SQL INSERT INTO S
                 (SN, SNAME, STATUS, CITY)
         VALUES(:SN,:SNAME,:STATUS,:CITY)
   END-EXEC.

IF SN-PRESENT = 'YES'
   EXEC SQL UPDATE S SET STATUS = :STATUS
            WHERE  SN = :SN-IN END-EXEC.

GO TO ACCEPT-NEXT-S.

EXEC SQL DELETE FROM S
         WHERE SN = :SN-IN END-EXEC.
```

IBM-Provided Sample Programs

DB2 provides a number of sample programs that include code that might be useful for building your own programs. Most developers keep model or skeleton programs in their source libraries to use in developing new programs. DB2's library of sample programs can provide starting points for these skeletons. They are in the SDSNSAMP library, and the load modules are in the SDSNLOAD library. There are sample programs for batch, CICS, IMS, and ISPF. Here are a few member names of the SDSNSAMP library of sample programs that you may find useful:

- ◆ DSN8BC3 contains a sample COBOL program
- ◆ DSN8BP3 contains a sample PL/1 program
- ◆ DSN8BD3 contains a sample C program
- ◆ DSN8BF3 contains a sample FORTRAN program

The sample programs are described in the *Application Programming and SQL Guide* manual.

PD.2 USING HOST LANGUAGE VARIABLES

When a SELECT statement returns values to a program rather than to a user's terminal, the program must have host-language variables to receive them, and the SELECT statement must include information indicating those variables. Host variables in embedded SQL are identified by a colon preceding the variable names. If a host variable name is split for readability, in COBOL a hyphen must join the two parts (:SN-IN, for example); in PL/1 an underscore joins the two (:SN_IN). DB2 column names must be split with an underscore. These seemingly trivial points are the source of frustration at precompile time for COBOL developers. It is easy to remember the distinction but difficult to key the hyphen or underscore, depending on whether it is a host variable or column name.

An INTO clause in an embedded SELECT statement identifies the host variables that are to receive the selected values. Here is a typical SELECT statement embedded in COBOL:

```
EXEC SQL SELECT SN, S_NAME, S_ADDRESS
         INTO :SN, :S-NAME, :S-ADDRESS
         FROM  S_DETAIL
         WHERE SN = :SN-IN END-EXEC.
```

Values from the columns SN, S_NAME, and S_ADDRESS are received by the host variables :SN, :S-NAME, and :S-ADDRESS, respectively.

A single host language data structure cited once in an SQL SELECT ...
INTO statement can receive values from multiple columns. Consider the
following definition of a COBOL data structure S-DETAIL:

```
01   S-DETAIL.
     05   SN          PIC X(2).
     05   S-NAME      PIC X(30).
     05   S-ADDRESS   PIC X(60).
```

S-DETAIL can receive values from three columns. The values are assigned
to the lower-level variables in the order in which the columns are listed in
the SELECT statement. In this example:

```
EXEC SQL SELECT SN, S_NAME, S_ADDRESS
             INTO :S-DETAIL
             FROM  S_DETAIL
             WHERE SN = :SN-IN END-EXEC.
```

SN, S_NAME, and S_ADDRESS are received by the variables SN, S-
NAME, and S-ADDRESS, respectively.

Programming Recommendation: As the above examples demonstrate,
there can be equivalent SELECT ... INTO statements using several
individual host variables or a single multilevel variable. It is usually better,
however, to avoid using multilevel variables. For one thing, if lower-level
variables are added or deleted from the multilevel variable, the SQL
statement referencing it will no longer work--the columns cited will no
longer match the lower-level variables. For another, in order for column
values to match the lower-level variables, the statement may have to select
more columns than are actually needed for the application, a waste of
processing resources, as discussed in Chapter PP.

Varying-length Variables

The COBOL language deals with variable length character data through the
use of 49-level variables. Here is an example of defining the 49-level host
variables to receive a VARCHAR column value.

```
01   SNAME.
     49   SNAME-LENGTH PIC S9(4) COMP.
     49   SNAME-TEXT   PIC X(100).
```

:SNAME-LENGTH contains the number of bytes in :SNAME-TEXT when selecting SNAME. SNAME-TEXT should be the same length as defined for the column (VARCHAR(100)). It is advisable to move space to SNAME-TEXT before selecting a column value into the host variable. Otherwise, unexpected characters can appear after the column value. For example, if the SNAME column contains Blake, the SNAME-LENGTH field will contains 5, the first five bytes of SNAME-TEXT will contain Blake, and the remaining 95 bytes will contain whatever was there before the move of data from the column to the host variable.

For UPDATE and INSERT statements, the program must calculate SNAME-LENGTH if it is unknown. Otherwise, trailing blanks are stored in the VARCHAR column. There are three alternatives for determining the number of characters before trailing blanks.

1)   Assign each character of the value to an array, count the number of trailing blanks, and subtract the value from the total length of the string.

2)   Use the following COBOL statement:

```
UNSTRING SNAME-TEXT DELIMITED BY ' ' COUNT IN
SNAME-LENGTH.
```

3)   POSSTR scalar function can be used to determined the position in a string of another string:

```
EXEC SQL SET :SNAME-LENGTH =
   POSSTR('ERIC CLARK        ', ' ') - 1
END-EXEC.
```

:SNAME-LENGTH contains 10 (there are 10 bytes in ERIC CLARK before training blanks) with the use of UNSTRING and POSSTR. Be careful of the use of these two techniques. It assumes that two blanks are not embedded in a character string. For example, if the string is 'EricbbClark', 'Clark' will be lost.

Qualifying a Variable by Table Name

When the same column name appears in more than one table, a host-language variable for each column's values must indicate to which table it refers. In a COBOL program, outside of SQL statements, the usual syntax for qualifying a variable applies. Inside SQL statements, however, DB2 requires a different format. For example, if the S_NAME column is included in both the Supplier table and the S_DETAIL table, each reference to an S-NAME host-language variable must identify the appropriate table. Outside of SQL statements, the COBOL references might be S-NAME OF S-DETAIL or S-NAME IN S-DETAIL. Inside SQL statements, however, the qualification format joins the table name and column name with a period. For example, S-DETAIL.S-NAME indicates that the variable refers to the S_NAME COBOL 05 level in the S_DETAIL 01 level. Used in an SQL statement, that format looks like this:

```
EXEC SQL SELECT  S_NAME
            INTO :S-DETAIL.S-NAME
            FROM  S_DETAIL
            WHERE SN = :SN-IN END-EXEC.
```

Programming for Nulls

If a host program is to receive a value from a column that allows nulls, the program requires variables for both the value and its associated null indicator. A null indicator variable is declared in the program as any other variable. For simplicity, programmers usually name the null indicator variable with a variation on the name of its associated variable. For example, a variable to receive values from the SNAME column, which allows nulls, might be called :SNAME. The associated null indicator variable might be called :SNAME-INDNULL. You can use the DCLGEN option of DB2I to generate an array of null indicator variables as discussed in Chapter PE.

The null indicator variable must be included in the SELECT ... INTO statement, as shown in this example:

```
EXEC SQL SELECT SNAME
            INTO :SNAME:SNAME-INDNULL
            FROM  S
            WHERE SN = :SN-IN END-EXEC.
```

Notice that no comma or space separates the variable and associated null indicator variable in the statement.

If SNAME has a value, SNAME-INDNULL contains a value of 0. If SNAME is null, SNAME-INDNULL contains a -2 and a +305 SQLCODE is returned.

If a column contains nulls and you don't include a null indicator, the program receives a -305 SQLCODE.

Even if no columns allow for nulls, it may be necessary to use a null indicator to avoid a -305 SQLCODE. For example, if the average salary of employees in department X is computed and there are no employees in the department, the result is null and a null indicator must be coded on the SQL statement to avoid a negative SQLCODE.

Recommendation: If a null indicator is needed, you should test the null indicator as well as the SQLCODE.

For example, if an SQL statement moves a null from a nullable integer column into a small integer host variable, it sets the null indicator at -2 and issues a +304 SQLCODE. The host variable will have the same value as before the SQL statement was executed.

Inserting a null also requires special handling. Outside of the SQL INSERT statement, the program must move a negative number to the null indicator for the column receiving the null value. For example, if the user does not provide a value for STATUS, a -1 can be moved to the null indicator associated with the STATUS column like:

```
MOVE -1 TO STATUS-INDNULL.

EXEC SQL INSERT INTO S
    (SN, SNAME, STATUS, CITY ) VALUE
    (:SN,:SNAME,:STATUS:STATUS-INDNULL,  :CITY)
END-EXEC.
```

Additional techniques for managing nulls and defaults used to represent unknown or not applicable values are discussed in Chapter SL Section 15.

Data Type Compatibility

Although host variable names need not match the names of the columns that provide their values, the data types must be compatible, and the lengths should match. When DB2 generates the data structures, it creates host-language structures that match the columns' definitions in the catalog tables. Mismatch errors can occur in working storage variables defined by programmers. Mismatches can also occur when a SELECT clause's calculation produces a value too large for its variable or when a user enters a value with the wrong type or length.

Some mismatches are not allowed. DB2 issues a negative SQLCODE when a mismatch occurs. For example, a statement is not allowed to execute if it attempts to move a number into a numeric data type with insufficient precision to handle it--a value over 32,767 into a small integer, for example. And if a SELECT clause's calculation results in a value too large for its host variable or is an impossible value, a number divided by zero, DB2 simply leaves the variable set at its previous value and issues a negative SQLCODE.

However, DB2 automatically corrects for some mismatches, allowing processing to continue. For example, it removes the fractional part of a column's decimal or float value when moving it into an integer or small integer host variable. For example, 430.90 is truncated to 430. DB2 also truncates the trailing characters of a character column's value when moving it to a host variable that is not long enough to hold it.

These corrections can lead to incorrect or unanticipated results if the program does not account for them. To describe the data corrections it has made, DB2 uses SQLCODEs and null indicator values. For example, if a statement moves a value from a nullable integer column into a small integer host variable, it sets the null indicator at -2 and issues a +304 SQLCODE.

Recommendation: To determine if any of these data conversion situations have occurred, test for the null indicator's value in host-language code following the SQL statement. It is always best to avoid the problem by ensuring that column and host variable data types match. Not only does that avoid anomalous results, but also saves on the processing DB2 must otherwise perform to correct mismatches and improve its performance.

Data Type Conversion Functions

DB2 has many functions, called scalar functions, which can be used to convert from one data type to another. This can be handy when data has to be moved into a host variable of another type. For example, assume you have a DEBT column defined as DECIMAL(31). This means that the column can contain 31 digits. However, most host languages (except the IBM COBOL V2R2 compiler) only support the equivalent of DECIMAL(15). The CHAR scalar function can be used to convert the column DEBT to a character string, which can then be moved to a host variable defined as CHAR(33) or PIC X(33) as shown here:

```
EXEC SQL SELECT CHAR(DEBT)
             INTO :DEBT
             FROM  BUDGET END-EXEC.
```

A number of additional functions are discussed in Chapter SL.

Affect on Access Path: In most cases, when you use a scalar function on a column in a WHERE clause, a matching index scan cannot be used.

Use of Distinct Types

Distinct types provide for ensuring that designated columns can only be compared and arithmetic operation performed on columns defined with the same distinct type. For example, it should not be possible to compare a column containing distance measured in miles with another column containing distance in kilometers. Nor should it be possible to perform arithmetic on the two column. One should not add miles and kilometers, for example, the result is not accurate. Chapter CT describes how to create distinct types for each of the two columns and how DB2 automatically generates cast functions to designate miles as a built-in data type and the opposite. Additional operations can be done on distinct types with user-defined functions as described in Chapter UD.

Use of Host Variables and Literals with Distinct Types: Host variables defined with built-in data types and literals can be used to receive and assign distinct type values in SELECT, INSERT, UPDATE, and DELETE statements. DCLGEN generates fields with the built-in data types for the distinct types of US_DOLLAR for SALARY, EURO for COMM, and

DECIMAL built-in data type for COMM. Indeed, all three columns are stored using the built-in data types specified when the distinct types are created as discussed in Chapter CT.

```
10  SALARY   PIC  S9(7)V9(2)  USAGE  COMP-3.
10  BONUS    PIC  S9(7)V9(2)  USAGE  COMP-3.
10  COMM     PIC  S9(7)V9(2)  USAGE  COMP-3.
```

Host variables cannot be defined as distinct types. This is the reason that cast functions are automatically generated when distinct types are created. Cast functions provide for comparisons in a WHERE clause and arithmetic operations on distinct types as discussed in Chapter CT. However, assignment of the distinct type column values to host variables do not require cast functions. Here is an example of the use of the DECIMAL cast function to allow for the comparison of a column salary with a distinct type of US dollars with a host variable defined with a built-in data type of decimal.

```
EXEC SQL
SELECT EMPNO, LASTNAME, SALARY, BONUS, COMM
 INTO  :EMPNO,:LASTNAME,:SALARY,:BONUS,:COMM
FROM    EMP
WHERE   EMPNO             = :EMPNO
AND    *DECIMAL(SALARY)  > :SALARY END-EXEC.
```

A cast function is not required to assign literals to distinct type columns as shown in the following INSERT statement. The last line of the statement assigns 50000.00, 2000.00, and 20000.00 to the columns SALARY, BONUS, and COMM which are defined with the distinct types of US_DOLLAR, DECIMAL (is a built in data type), and EURO.

```
EXEC SQL
INSERT INTO EMP
(EMPNO, FIRSTNME, MIDINIT, LASTNAME,
 WORKDEPT, PHONENO, HIREDATE,
 JOB, EDLEVEL, SEX, BIRTHDATE,
 SALARY, BONUS, COMM)
VALUES
('00201','FLEUR','A' ,'JOHNSON',
 'D11','4501', '1974-03-03',
 'DESIGNER', 16, 'M', '1941-05-29',
 50000.00,  2000.00, 20000.00) END-EXEC.
```

Similarly, host variables defined as built-in data types can be used to assign values to distinct type columns with the SET clause of an UPDATE statement. The data types of each column in the SET clause are preceded with '--'.

```
EXEC SQL
UPDATE EMP
   SET SALARY  = :SALARY, --US_DOLLAR
       BONUS   = :BONUS,   --DECIMAL
       COMM    = :COMM     --EURO
   WHERE EMPNO = :EMPNO END-EXEC.
```

A DELETE statement is like a SELECT statement in that the cast function of DECIMAL is used to designate a column defined with a distinct type of US_DOLLAR to allow the comparison with a host variable defined with a built in data type of decimal in the WHERE clause.

```
EXEC SQL
DELETE FROM EMP
   WHERE DECIMAL(SALARY) > :SALARY END-EXEC.
```

PD.3 INSERTING ROWS INTO A TABLE WITH AN IDENTITY OR ROWID COLUMN

The SN_ID columns of the S_ID table is defined as an identity column (described in Chapter CT subsection Identity Column). The definition causes DB2 to generate sequence numbers according to the parameters specified when the column is defined. You can insert a row into the S_ID table with or without specifying the identity column as in the following examples. This applies if the column is declared as GENERATED ALWAYS or GENERATED BY DEFAULT.

```
       INSERT INTO S_ID
       (SN_ID, SNAME, STATUS, CITY) VALUES
       (DEFAULT, 'Johnson',  20, 'Childress');
or
       INSERT INTO S_ID
       (SNAME, STATUS, CITY) VALUES
       ('Johnson',  20, 'Childress');
```

If SN_ID is defined as GENERATED BY DEFAULT, a specific value can be inserted into the column. If the value would result in a duplicate, a -803 SQLCODE is issued based on a unique index on the column which is required when using GENERATED BY DEFAULT.

```
INSERT INTO S_ID
(SN_ID, SNAME, STATUS, CITY) VALUES
(4000, 'Johnson',  20, 'Childress');
```

The OVERRIDING USER VALUE clause is required for an insert with a subselect if the identify column is declared as GENERATED ALWAYS. DB2 generates values for INSERT INTO table and ignores values in SELECT table. This is useful for data propagation.

```
INSERT INTO S_ID_TEST (SN_ID, SNAME, STATUS,
CITY)
    OVERRIDING USER VALUE
      SELECT SN_ID, SNAME, STATUS, CITY
      FROM   S_ID
      WHERE STATUS < 40;
```

If you plan to load production data into a test table or want to propagate data to another table, and want the same identity and ROWID column values in the table, consider defining the production table column with GENERATED ALWAYS and the test table column with GENERATED BY DEFAULT. This provides for loading production identity column values into other tables. It is not possible to alter the GENERATED clause. An alternative is to use DSN1COPY to copy production tables and indexes to other tables and indexes.V8 may have techniques for retaining sequential values when placing the data in another table.

The rules that apply to inserting values into an identity column applies to inserting values into a ROWID column.

Determine value inserted: You can determine the last sequence number that you inserted into a table with the SET statement like:

```
EXEC SQL SET :CURSEQNO = IDENTITY_VAL_LOCAL()
END-EXEC.
```

The :CURSEQNO host variable contains the value that you most recently inserted value after a successful singleton insert (V6 APAR PQ36328). This applies to sequence numbers generated by DB2 or assigned by the program if GENERATED BY DEFAULT is used. The value can be useful in determining the generated primary key to be used to insert corresponding foreign key rows. The LOAD utility generates the sequential values when loading a table. If you are using the sequence number as the primary key, an alternative is to use the natural primary key to assign sequence numbers to foreign key rows. GENERATED BY DEFAULT can be used on the foreign key tables.

If a value has not been generated since a commit (not savepoint), null is returned. Only the SET statement is supported (SELECT, VALUE, etc. statements give unpredictable results particularly if a parallel access path is used). The host variable to receive the sequence number can be defined as DECIMAL(31,0) regardless of the definition of the column. If you need to override the DEC15 default for the DB2 subsystem, the CURRENT PRECISION special register can be set like:

```
SET CURRENT PRECISION = 'DEC31'
```

The value of the special register can be determined like:

```
SET :HVDEC = CURRENT PRECISION
```

PD.4 COMMIT AND ROLLBACK WORK

To ensure that updates will be applied to the database, the program must make sure the changes are committed. A commit turns responsibility over to DB2 to make sure that all changes are applied to the database. The changes are seen by subsequent SQL statements on that data, even though the data is not usually written immediately to the table. DB2 tries to keep pages in the buffer pool so that others can select and update them without having to do a read or write from DASD. There are a number of thresholds and operations that cause buffer manager to write pages to the table as discussed in Chapter CD.

Commit and rollback processing closes all the cursors and releases locks. For more information about how commit processing affects the concurrency of an application, see Chapter CC.

Changes can also be rolled back, ensuring that those changes will not be reflected in the database.

When Is Work Committed or Rolled Back?

Work is committed when a program ends normally. Work is rolled back when a program abends. It is best to explicitly request a commit or rollback. How this is done depends on the transaction manager that is used.

TSO, CAF (Call Attached Facility), and RRSAF (Recoverable Resource Services Attachment Facility) commit and rollback points are:

♦   EXEC COMMIT or EXEC COMMIT WORK
♦   EXEC ROLLBACK

CICS commit and rollback points are:

♦   EXEC CICS SYNCPOINT
♦   EXEC CICS RETURN (to CICS)
♦   TERMINATE (DL/1)
♦   EXEC CICS ROLLBACK

IMS commit and rollback points are:

♦   GU call to I/O PCB (MODE=SNGL)
♦   CHKP or XRST calls
♦   ROLL or ROLB

When using CICS and IMS online transactions, most programs display a screen and issue a statement that results in a commit. The commit processing applies to DB2 and DL/1 data.

How Often to Commit Work

The recommendation is often given, and rightly so, that to achieve the best concurrency, and to shorten restart times, programs should commit frequently. Because commit processing has costs of its own, particularly with respect to logging, it can be a challenge to decide how often to commit.

IBM tested this effect on DB2 V4 with a 50 MIPS processor as reported in the manual *Locking in DB2 for MVS/ESA Environment*, SG24-4725. The test consisted of updating 8,664 rows in a 90,972 row table on 2,178 pages using a matching index scan. Figure PD.2 summarizes the test results.

Figure PD.2. Commit frequency

Commit Freq.	Elapsed Seconds Class 2	CPU Seconds Class 2	Commits	Updates per Commit	Get-page	Max. Lock Held	STS
8664	3.13	1.46	1	8664	242	242	1
1000	5.19	1.86	9	963	247	28	2
500	8.82	1.91	18	482	254	15	6
100	17.79	1.98	86	101	321	4	13
50	31.58	2	170	51	406	3	28
10	90.21	2.37	867	10	998	2	81
1	686.2	6.92	8664	1	8678	1	670

Notes:
Commit Frequency   Commit every *n* updates
Elapsed Class 2   Elapsed time executing DB2 calls
CPU Class 2   CPU time executing DB2 calls
Commits   Number of commits (close to number of rows
                         updated, 8664, divided by commit frequency)
Updates per Commit   Number of rows updated, 8664, divided by commits
Getpages   Number of getpage requests
Maximum Locks Held   High-water-mark for the number of locks held by
                         the program
STS   Service task switch suspensions (in this example,
                         corresponds to synchronous log writes).

*Logs on 3380 DASD, 3390 DASD with fast write will reduce elapsed time

Consider these test results as relative numbers. That is, a commit every 10 updates compared to commit after each update required about one-seventh of the elapsed time. The elapsed time goes down further with a commit every 100 and 1,000 updates and still further if a LOCK TABLE is issued. As always, your results will vary depending on your specific CPU model, DASD hardware, workload, and other variables in your environment. It is always best to test the effect of a commit frequency in your environment and base your decision on your results.

Recommendation: The results in Figure PD.2 suggest that, for best performance, avoid committing after every update. If business requirements permit, a good commit frequency for an online transaction is about every 10 updates to minimize CPU time and I/O. A good target for batch processing is to commit every 1,000 updates. (Batch processing is discussed in Chapter

BP.) Use a LOCK TABLE statement to reduce resource consumption further if others do not need access to the table during the execution of the program.

PD.5 EMBEDDED UPDATES AND DELETES

Embedded SQL allows you to update and delete rows with or without a cursor.

Without a Cursor

An embedded UPDATE or DELETE statement can act on all of the rows meeting its WHERE clause criteria in response to a single execution of the statement. Multiple rows therefore may be updated or deleted in a program with the same statement as an interactive user would employ for that action. For example, if all parts above a given weight in a particular city were to be reassigned to another city, an application for managing the change might prompt the user to enter the cutoff weight, the city where the parts are to be found, and the city to which they are to be reassigned. If those values were read into variables :WEIGHT-LIMIT, :OLD-CITY, and :NEW-CITY, this embedded statement would update all qualifying parts:

```
EXEC SQL UPDATE P SET CITY = :NEW-CITY,
         WHERE WEIGHT > :WEIGHT-LIMIT
         AND   CITY   = :OLD-CITY END-EXEC.
```

Notice that it is not necessary to first select the rows and then delete them. This improves performance and saves development time.

With a Cursor

In some cases, however, the updates or deletions are done in conjunction with other processing that requires a cursor. If the rows returned with a cursor are to be updated or deleted, the cursor definition must indicate that fact. A FOR UPDATE OF clause alerts DB2 that the update or delete is coming so that the a fetched row cannot be changed before an update or delete. DB2 keeps the rows stable by holding locks. Locks are accumulated on each page or row that is updated after being fetched until a commit or rollback point with or without the FOR UPDATE OF clause. Locks are accumulated on each page or row accessed even if no rows qualify with RR.

If the program to reassign parts over a certain weight from one city to another employed a cursor, its declaration would look something like this:

```
EXEC SQL DECLARE PCURSOR CURSOR FOR
    SELECT PN, WEIGHT
    FROM    P
    WHERE   WEIGHT > :WEIGHT-LIMIT
    FOR UPDATE OF CITY END-EXEC.
```

Notice that the column being updated need not appear in the SELECT clause, although it usually does. FOR UPDATE OF without naming any columns (V7) detracts from performance.

When a cursor is used for updates, the UPDATE statement must use a WHERE CURRENT OF CURSOR clause to indicate the row to be processed--for example:

```
EXEC SQL
    UPDATE P
    SET CITY = :NEW-CITY
    WHERE CURRENT OF PCURSOR END-EXEC.
```

The WHERE CURRENT OF clause causes the row at which the cursor points to be updated. The update does not advance the cursor, however. A FETCH ... INTO statement is necessary for that.

Restrictions on Update: Certain SELECT statements return values that are not undatable. For example, what values in a column should be changed to "update" the column's average? Because DB2 has no way of answering that question, it disallows use of the FOR UPDATE OF clause in cursor declarations that include the AVG function, the SUM, COUNT, MIN, MAX, and DISTINCT functions, or the GROUP BY operator. The FOR UPDATE OF clause does not work with an ORDER BY, thus it cannot be used with cursor repositioning logic. Finally, unions, joins, and most subselects create temporary work files, as do a number of the other operations, that cannot be updated since the underlying base tables may be changed independently, creating inconsistencies in the data. Basically, FOR

UPDATE OF cannot be used on a read-only cursor. Read-only SELECT statements are discussed in Chapter CC.

FOR UPDATE OF disallows the use of some efficient processing that requires read-only SELECT statements including lock avoidance, and uncommited read as discussed in Chapter CC and block fetch as discussed later in this chapter.

DB2 does not use index access on columns specified in the FOR UPDATE OF clause unless list prefetch is used. If it were to use an index on a column being updated, some updates would not be applied after the initial update since the index itself would be changed by the update. For example, if an index on the STATUS column were used to retrieve rows, those rows would be returned in STATUS order. An update of STATUS from 10 to 50 would cause the cursor position to skip to a STATUS of 50, missing 20, 30, and 40. If equal predicates are used on the updated column and all preceding columns, an index can be used to locate the row to be updated. An index cannot be used on a column with an arithmetic expression in the WHERE or SET clause. The restriction also applies to columns in predicates when the WITH CHECK OPTION is used in defining a view.

Recommendation: Updating with a cursor, with its need for a cursor declaration, FETCH ... INTO statement, and UPDATE ... WHERE ... CURRENT statement, requires considerably more coding than the simple embedded update statement. A primary purpose of the FOR UPDATE OF clause is to hold locks on all pages or rows updated to avoid others updating the data. But displaying a screen using CICS pseudo-conversational and IMS results in a commit, which releases all locks. Since the cursor update also precludes the use of indexes on columns specified in the FOR UPDATE OF clause, it also carries a performance deficit. For these reasons, and because in most cases an update without a cursor can carry out the same updates as an update with a cursor, it makes sense to avoid cursor updates except for some batch processing.

PD.6 MAINTAIN DATA INTEGRITY AFTER DISPLAYING A SCREEN

DB2 automatically issues the equivalent of a commit work when a program displays a screen using CICS pseudo-conversational or IMS, depending on the mode of operation. (To be precise, locks are released when control is returned to CICS when using pseudo-conversational. Displaying a screen is one of the operations that causes control to be returned to CICS.) A commit (or its equivalent depending on the transaction manager used as discussed in this chapter) should be issued before a program asks for terminal input when using CICS conversational, TSO, CAF, and RRSAF where a commit is not issued automatically to release locks. If locks are not released until after the input is provided, the person entering the information ends up determining how long those locks will be in effect. If he or she leaves for a coffee break or answers the telephone before remembering to provide the required input, those locks can block others from the data for a considerable amount of time.

Consider a potential data integrity problem. Assume that Eric requests information about P4, the information is displayed to the screen, and commit processing occurs. Eric is interrupted by a telephone call or goes on a break. Meanwhile, Fleur requests information on P4 as well. She updates information about the part and it is committed. Eric returns to his screen, updates the now old data and his update is written over Fleur's update. Fleur's update is lost. Certainly, this is not acceptable. There are several alternatives and variations on the alternatives to avoid having one persons update written on top of another persons update.

The information on P4 can be saved before displaying the screen like:

```
PN-OLD      =  'P4'
PNAME-OLD   =  'Screw'
COLOR-OLD   =  'Red'
WEIGHT-OLD  =  14
CITY-OLD    =  'London'
```

Eric can change any of the values and the transaction issues:

```
UPDATE  P
    SET  PN      =  :PN
         PNAME   =  :PNAME
         COLOR   =  :COLOR
         WEIGHT  =  :WEIGHT
         CITY    =  :CITY
  WHERE  PN      =  :PN-OLD
    AND  PNAME   =  :PNAME-OLD
    AND  COLOR   =  :COLOR-OLD
    AND  WEIGHT  =  :WEIGHT-OLD
```

```
AND    CITY   =   :CITY-OLD;
```

If no one has made a change to P4 since the row was displayed, the update is successful and returns an SQLCODE of 0. If DB2 returns SQLCODE of 100, it indicates that the row no longer exists as it did when originally displayed, or it indicates that the row was deleted since it was displayed and the user should be informed.

The technique performs well because DB2 changes only the required information. If an indexed value has not been changed, DB2 does not update the index. If the user did not change any value, the data page is not written to DASD, and it is not logged. Lock and latch processing is done in all cases.

If there is a timestamp column in the row, an alternative that can minimize the number of columns that must be saved and used in the WHERE clause is to save only the primary key and timestamp when the row was displayed. Update the row with the new data and new timestamp when the row is changed. If there is not already a timestamp column on the row and you do not want to add 10 bytes to the row length, include a two- or four-byte counter. Have all programs that update the column update the counter column and use it in the WHERE clause to qualify the update.

Another technique for handling this kind of problem is to have the program reread the row with the FOR UPDATE OF clause after the user enters the new data. Compare it with the values saved before the screen was displayed. The update is issued if the data has not changed between the time that the row was displayed and the changed data was read by the program. The disadvantage of this technique is that the row must be reread before it is updated. There are some additional concerns with the FOR UPDATE OF which are discussed in this chapter. This requires more programming effort, and the additional read of the data detracts from performance.

If the table has a column declared as a ROWID data type (P_ROWID column in the example), it can be used to provide for direct row access without the use of an index or tablespace scan. A ROWID column does add 19 bytes to the row length. (Declaration of a ROWID column is discussed in Chapter CT, its basic usage in Chapter IU, and more on its usage in the next section including the reason for specifying the primary key in the WHERE clause as a fallback access path.) The UPDATE statement can be issued as:

```
UPDATE  P
   SET  PN        =   :PN
        PNAME     =   :PNAME
        COLOR     =   :COLOR
        WEIGHT    =   :WEIGHT
        CITY      =   :CITY
 WHERE  PN        =   :PN-OLD
   AND  P_ROWID   =   :P-ROWID
   AND  PNAME     =   :PNAME-OLD
   AND  COLOR     =   :COLOR-OLD
   AND  WEIGHT    =   :WEIGHT-OLD
   AND  CITY      =   :CITY-OLD;
```

(to the right of the shaded block:) **Can verify that row has not changed with any techniques discussed**

PD.7 USAGE OF DIRECT ROW ACCESS

Direct row access provides for locating a row directly without the I/O and CPU time required to locate a row with an index or tablespace scan (V6). It is necessary to retrieve the ROWID value through the use of an index or tablespace scan before it can be used in an SQL statement for direct row access.

Direct Row Access Requirements

Direct row access applies only to stage 1 predicates. Simple Boolean term predicates qualify for direct row access:

```
WHERE  C1 = :HV
```

The C1 column must be declared with a ROWID data type. The :HV host variable represents a non-column defined as described in Chapter CT.

An index must exist on C1 to allow:

```
WHERE  C1 IN (:HV1, :HV2, :HV3)
```

This is equivalent to:

```
WHERE  C1 =  :HV1
OR     C1 =  :HV2
OR     C1 =  :HV3
```

Direct row access cannot be used for ORed predicates on different columns:

```
WHERE  C1  =  :HV1
OR     C2  =  :HV2
```

Direct row access can be used to satisfy ANDed predicates where one predicate is on a ROWID column:

```
WHERE  C1  =  :HV1
AND    C2  =  :HV2
```

If there are multiple predicates and a ROWID column in the WHERE clause, the optimizer is likely to choose direct row access on the ROWID column if the above criteria are met.

Parallelism and list prefetch are not used with direct row access either as a primary or fallback access path. If an SQL statement qualifies for both direct row access and parallelism or list prefetch (multiple index processing and hybrid join require list prefetch), direct row access is chosen.

Changing from Direct Row Access to ACCESSTYPE at Run Time

A second access path is chosen when direct row access is chosen by the optimizer. The PLAN_TABLE.PRIMARY_ACCESSTYPE = 'D' indicates direct row access. The PLAN_TABLE.ACCESSTYPE indicates index usage or a tablespace scan. The second access path allows for an alternative access path if direct row access cannot be used at run time.

A saved row ID value before a reorganization cannot be used to locate a row after a reorganization. This is because a row ID value gives the location of a row and the location of a row changes with a reorganization. Therefore, do not save a row ID column value before a reorganization and expect to locate the same row after a reorganization. A subtle situation must be avoided. Reorganization (including online reorganization) can be executed while a program is executing after the program commits and before it completes processing. If a reorganization after a commit can be performed, retrieve the row ID again after the commit. Do not save row IDs in a table or file and use them after a commit. If an index exists on the row ID column, the beginning portion of the row ID is used to locate the row. If the RID in the index does not match the RID in a row ID column, the fallback access path is used.

Do take the necessary steps to avoid a tablespace scan when direct row access is expected. Certainly, the I/O and CPU time will be much more costly with a tablespace scan compared to direct row access in the great majority of cases. Users quickly become accustom to very good response time with direct row access and will even more quickly complain when a tablespace scan occurs. The same principle applies to a batch program that performs well most of the time but poorly when DB2 cannot use direct row access at run time.

Do provide for a good fallback access path: A good choice is to specify the primary key in the WHERE clause assuming an index on the primary key. An alternative is to specify a predicate on a column with a usable index.

PD.8 USING CURSORS

When executing a SELECT statement interactively, all qualifying rows are returned as the user pages through the results. A host language program must declare and manage a cursor to receive more than one row from a SELECT statement. A cursor allows the SELECT to qualify a set of rows and return them one at a time. Imagine the set of rows being returned to a screen display. A screen cursor can point to one row at a time. A host language program must use a DB2 cursor to process one row at a time.

Declaring and Opening Cursors

A declarative SELECT statement is used to establish a cursor. (Because it is a declarative rather than an executable statement, it can be placed in the data or procedure division of a COBOL program, but must physically come before the OPEN.) The declaration takes the form DECLARE {name} CURSOR FOR, in which the cursor's name follows the word DECLARE. Here is a complete example declaration:

```
EXEC SQL DECLARE SCURSOR CURSOR FOR
    SELECT SN, SNAME, STATUS, CITY
    FROM    S
    WHERE   STATUS > :OLD-STATUS
    AND     SN     > :OLD-SN
    FOR FETCH ONLY END-EXEC.
```

The FOR FETCH ONLY clause is optional but highly advisable if you are not going to update or delete a row that is fetched. It informs DB2 that the SELECT statement is read-only. There are a number of processes in DB2 that require read-only SELECT statements or an ambiguous SELECT bound with CURRENTDATA(NO) including lock avoidance, some forms of parallel processing, and blocking of data for transmission. Most of these processes significantly improve performance and concurrency. An alternative form of the clause is FOR READ ONLY, which complies with the SQL standard.

The program calls on the cursor for processing through two statements: one for opening the cursor and the other for fetching its rows. The OPEN statement readies the SELECT for execution. DB2 attempts to process one qualifying row at a time to pass to the program--unless all rows are required by a sort, for example. The OPEN statement simply uses the key word OPEN followed by the cursor's name:

```
EXEC SQL OPEN SCURSOR END-EXEC.
```

Fetching from the Cursor

The FETCH statement identifies the cursor to be used and employs an INTO clause to indicate the host variables that are to receive the values from each row:

```
EXEC SQL
   FETCH FROM SCURSOR INTO
      :SN,  :SNAME,  :STATUS,  :CITY END-EXEC.
```

As with the SELECT ... INTO statement used when a single row is returned, the variables used in a FETCH ... INTO statement must be of compatible data type with the columns that supply their values. The FROM clause of the FETCH statement is optional according to DB2 and is required by the SQL standard. A number of cursors can be opened at one time, on a single table or on multiple tables.

Typically a FETCH statement is coded within a program loop, which returns after processing a row to receive the next row. DB2 does not have to return all rows requested by a cursor's statement when the cursor is opened or at the first fetch unless one of the following is true:

- The statement requires a sort or an intermediate work file in which case all rows must be processed. Use of an index, which allows rows to be retrieved in order, avoids sorts. Some types of subselects require an intermediate work file as discussed in Chapter ST.

- Sensitive and insensitive scrollable cursors (V7) result in qualifying rows being written to a work file when the cursor is opened.

- If materialization is required, rows identified by a view definition or nested table expression are written to a work area not including rows disqualified by predicates. (Materialization is discussed in Chapter ST).

- If list prefetch is used, all RIDs must be retrieved and sorted in most cases before the first row can be returned to the program. (List prefetch is discussed in Chapter PP.)

A fetch causes the cursor to advance to the next row. Because the program usually has to process a number of the qualifying rows, a test for the existence of rows usually controls the loop. DB2 communicates with programs about the processing status through SQLCODEs. The +100 SQLCODE indicates that the fetch found no rows or no more rows. The program can test for a +100 SQLCODE and move out of the loop when it is encountered. The 0 SQLCODE means one or more rows were found.

Singleton Select Versus a Cursor

A cursor is *not* needed when you retrieve a single row with an equal condition on a primary key for example. Indeed, a singleton select outperforms a cursor select if only one row is required because it requires only one trip between the host program and DB2. DB2 does manage an internal cursor used to fetch the one row. A second internal fetch is executed to return a 0 SQLCODE if a qualifying row is found or a -811 SQLCODE if more than one row qualifies.

Recommendation: Do avoid executing a singleton select many times to retrieve many rows for improved performance.

A cursor select requires three trips between the host program and DB2 - first for the open cursor, second for a fetch (can have multiple fetches), and third for the close cursor. A combination of a singleton select and a cursor is a good choice if more than 40 to 50 percent of the time, zero or one row qualifies. In this case, issue a singleton select and if -811 SQLCODE is received, open a cursor and fetch the required rows. The *DB2 for OS/390 Application Design Guidelines for High Performance,* SG24-2233, manual offers test results that suggest this guideline.

Exception: A cursor may be needed to influence the access path with OPTIMIZE FOR *n* ROWS as discussed in Chapter PP.

Closing and Reopening Cursors

A CLOSE statement--EXEC SQL CLOSE SCURSOR END-EXEC.--closes the cursor. A Commit statement also closes all open cursors except those declared using the CURSOR WITH HOLD clause discussed later in this section. After a cursor has been closed, it can be reopened without having to be declared again.

Conceptually, when a cursor is reopened, its SELECT statement is executed again. If the values that set the SELECT's criteria have not changed, the SELECT returns the same set of rows depending on the locking choices made as discussed in Chapter CC. This becomes a problem if a program closes a cursor in the midst of processing the set and then reopens the cursor to resume processing. If the program does not change the value that determines the search criteria to reflect the fact that some rows have been processed, the reopened cursor returns the original set (exceptions are discussed in Chapter CC). The program then begins processing rows that have already been processed rather than resuming at the next row after where the cursor was closed. One way to solve this problem is to track the cursor's position.

Tracking the Cursor's Position

To track the cursor's position as it works through the qualifying rows, use the last row processed to reset the search criteria. This technique works only if the search returns unique column values in an order that the program can follow. This is the case if the search criteria include a primary key column, which by definition includes only unique values, and the results are ordered by that column. DB2 can use an index to return the ordered rows, or it will get the qualifying rows and sort them. To allow for this cursor tracking technique, you should include a primary key in the predicate of a cursor declaration, and order the results by that column even when the search does not require it.

For example, the SCURSOR declared above might be used in an application to credit bonuses to suppliers with greater than a certain status. That status can be determined by the application's user, entered in response to a prompt and read into variable :OLD-STATUS. That variable is all that is needed to set the original search criteria to identify the suppliers to be credited. However, you may want to be able to commit in the midst of this processing or display a screen and resume processing at the proper row when the cursor is reopened. Because SN is a primary key, if the SELECT returned the rows in order by SN, the program can track the cursor's movement precisely through the set. Set the original :OLD-SN value at "blank." If the user enters 10 for :OLD-STATUS, SCURSOR's SELECT statement returns:

SN	SNAME	STATUS	CITY
S1	Smith	20	London
S3	Blake	30	Paris
S4	Clark	20	London
S5	Adams	30	Athens

The cursor initially points to the first row. Then as the rows process according to the FETCH ... INTO statement, the program saves the current SN in :OLD-SN. If the cursor closes after the program completes its second loop through the statement, :OLD-SN will equal S3. When the cursor reopens, its SELECT statement using that value returns:

SN	SNAME	STATUS	CITY
S4	Clark	20	London
S5	Adams	30	Athens

Processing can complete in order.

If the rows are not returned in supplier number order, which is likely in a tablespace scan without an ORDER BY clause, this technique would skip rows for processing. Consider the effect, for example, if the cursor's SELECT statement returns rows in this order:

SN	SNAME	STATUS	CITY
S1	Smith	20	London
S3	Blake	30	Paris
S2	Jones	10	Paris
S4	CLARK	20	London
S5	Adams	30	Athens

After the second fetch loop :OLD-SN equals S3. When the cursor is closed and reopened after this fetch, the cursor's SELECT statement does not return the S2 row.

Recommendation: Do not assume that rows will always be returned in the correct sequence, even if they are now. The access path can change in the future as a result of a new index added to the table, changes made to the optimizer, or any number of changes that can occur in the future. The only way to ensure that the rows are returned in the required sequence is to use the ORDER BY clause.

Optimizing for a limited number of rows: If the number of qualifying rows is large, performing a sort to satisfy the ORDER BY every time the cursor is opened is likely to be prohibitively expensive. Frequently, only 15 rows or the number that will fit on a screen to be displayed to a user is all that is required for online transactions. The OPTIMIZE FOR n ROWS ($n = 15$ in this example) clause informs the optimizer that only a small number of rows is required, and it is likely that it will choose to use an index to locate the rows in sequence and avoid a sort. (Chapter PP discusses this clause in more detail, FETCH FIRST n ROWS ONLY, and how DB2 can use indexes to avoid a sort.)

```
SELECT  SN, SNAME, STATUS, CITY
FROM    S
WHERE   SN > :OLD-SN
ORDER BY SN
```

```
FOR FETCH ONLY
OPTIMIZE FOR 15 ROWS
```

Care should be exercised in using OPTIMIZE FOR n ROWS. You can fetch beyond the number that you specify for n for any number of qualifying rows. However, a good access path for n rows is probably not a good access path for 10,000 rows. It is best to give your best estimate of the number of rows to be fetched. Avoid using OPTIMIZE FOR 1 ROW if you plan to fetch more than one row. This is a special case that the optimizer recognizes, and it will not use sequential prefetch, list prefetch, and multiple index processing for a select from a single table.

Cursor Repositioning with a Composite Primary Key

When a cursor is controlled by a composite primary key, reopening in sequence can be complex. Consider a composite primary key on the SN, PN, and JN columns of the SPJ table (Figure PD.3). Assume that the last row fetched contains the values of S2, P3, J3, and 200 before a screen is displayed, a commit is issued, or the cursor is closed.

Figure PD.3. Reopening a cursor with a composite primary key

SN	PN	JN	QTY
S1	P1	J1	200
S1	P1	J4	700
S2	P3	J1	400
S2	P3	J2	200
S2	P3	J3	200
S2	P3	J4	500
S2	P3	J5	600
S2	P3	J6	400
S2	P3	J7	800
S2	P5	J2	100
S3	P3	J1	200
S3	P4	J2	500
S4	P6	J3	300
S4	P6	J7	300
S5	P2	J2	200
S5	P2	J4	100
S5	P5	J5	500
S5	P5	J7	100
S5	P6	J2	200
S5	P1	J4	100
S5	P3	J4	200
S5	P4	J4	800
S5	P5	J4	400
S5	P6	J4	500

Left-hand selection criteria:

```
      SN >= 'S2' AND
((SN   = 'S2' AND
 PN    = 'P3' AND
 JN    > 'J3') OR

 (SN   = 'S2' AND
 PN    > 'P3') OR

 (SN   > 'S2'))
ORDER BY SN, PN, JN
OPTIMIZE FOR 12 ROWS
```

Right-hand selection criteria:

```
NOT (SN  = 'S2' ANI
     PN  = 'P3' ANI
     JN <= 'J3') ANI

NOT (SN  = 'S2' ANI
     PN  < 'P3') ANI

    (SN >= 'S2')
ORDER BY SN, PN, JN
OPTIMIZE FOR 12 ROWS
```

Alternative 1: The basic approach to finding the next row using a composite primary key is the same as that described above for when a single-column primary key is used. The last key values processed are saved in host language variables, in this case, :OLD-SN, :OLD-PN, and :OLD-JN. Then this series of selection criteria in the cursor's SELECT statement will reopen it at the next row:

```
WHERE (SN = :OLD-SN AND
```

```
        PN  =  :OLD-PN  AND
        JN  >  :OLD-JN)  OR
      (SN  =  :OLD-SN  AND
       PN  >  :OLD-PN)  OR
      (SN  >  :OLD-SN)
ORDER BY SN,  PN,  JN
OPTIMIZE FOR 12 ROWS
```

In this case, OLD-SN = 'S2', OLD-PN = 'P3', and OLD-JN = 'J3'. The first portion of the criteria returns the next row, which holds the values 'S2', 'P3', and 'J4' as shown in Figure PD.3. The predicates on the left and right side of the figure show the rows that qualify for each group of predicates. Notice that no matter what values the host variables hold, the results always include the next row, and the ORDER BY clause assures it will be the next one processed. As explained in Chapter IU, however, DB2 does not use a matching index scan when satisfying an SQL statement that uses the 'OR' operator on multiple columns of a composite index. A non-matching index scan or multiple index processing on the one composite index can be used, but this can result in poor performance if the table is medium to large in size with many leaf pages to scan.

Alternative 2: All of the predicates in the previous example are surrounded by parentheses and an additional ANDed predicate is added to allow for a matching index scan on the first column of the composite index like:

```
WHERE    SN >=  :OLD-SN  AND
      ( (SN  =  :OLD-SN  AND
        PN  =  :OLD-PN  AND
        JN  >  :OLD-JN)  OR
       (SN  =  :OLD-SN  AND
        PN  >  :OLD-PN)  OR
       (SN  >  :OLD-SN) )
ORDER BY SN,  PN,  JN
OPTIMIZE FOR 12 ROWS
```

This formulation does have the advantage that it allows for a matching index scan on the first column. If the first column has a low cardinality (a small number of distinct values), this can require the scan of many leaf pages which can negatively affect performance.

Alternative 3: A third alternative, similar to the first alternative uses negative logic to eliminate the ORed conditions like:

```
WHERE NOT (SN  =  :OLD-SN   AND
           PN  =  :OLD-PN   AND
           JN <=  :OLD-JN)  AND
      NOT (SN  =  :OLD-SN   AND
           PN  <  •:OLD-PN) AND
           (SN >= :OLD-SN)
ORDER BY SN, PN, JN
```

This alternative can use a matching index scan on the first column of the composite index. However, the negative logic makes the formulation confusing. A good way to ease the understanding of the formulation is to think "but not" where you see "AND NOT".

Alternative 4: Compare a concatenation of the three columns in the composite index with a concatenation of the three host variables containing the last values processed. This is very similar to coding the repositioning statement for a single column primary key.

```
SELECT SN, JN, PN
FROM   SPJ
WHERE  SN BETWEEN 'S2' AND :HIGH-VALUES
AND    SN CONCAT PN CONCAT JN >
       :OLD-SN CONCAT :OLD-PN CONCAT :OLD-JN
ORDER  BY SN, PN, JN
OPTIMIZE FOR 12 ROWS
```

Unfortunately, this straightforward concatenation technique cannot use an index because the concatenation is evaluated at stage 2. In order to use a matching index scan, the predicate must be evaluated at stage 1. (Stage 1 and 2 processing is discussed in Chapter PP) The BETWEEN predicate allows for a matching index scan on the first column of the composite index and a scan on the remaining leaf pages. However, each occurrence of SN, PN, JN beyond S2 and including S2 must be passed to stage 2 for concatenation and evaluation, which increases the costs substantially.

Alternative 5: An easy alternative is not to commit or close the cursor until the leading column changes. In the example, process all S2 and then reposition on S3. This can be a usable technique for batch processing where the cardinality of the first column is suitable for commit processing.

Alternative 6: If the table being accessed is small, processing resources are plentiful, and run time is unimportant either of the above five approaches work fine. A sixth approach maximizes the number of columns that can be used in a matching index scan. This technique requires several cursors and more programming logic, as indicated in the following pseudo code. The number of cursors that must be coded and managed can be minimized by using separate cursors only for the leading columns with a low cardinality followed by alternative 2.

```
SELECT SN, PN, JN, QTY
FROM   SPJ
WHERE  SN = :OLD-SN
AND    PN = :OLD-PN
AND    JN > :OLD-JN
ORDER BY SN, PN, JN
OPTIMIZE FOR 12 ROWS

IF SQLCODE = 100
    More rows needed to fill screen,
    process cursor for next SELECT

SELECT SN, PN, JN, QTY
FROM   SPJ
WHERE  SN = :OLD-SN
AND    PN > :OLD-PN
ORDER BY SN, PN, JN
OPTIMIZE FOR 12 ROWS

IF SQLCODE = 100
    More rows needed to fill screen,
    process cursor for next SELECT

SELECT SN, PN, JN, QTY
FROM   SPJ
WHERE  SN > :OLD-SN
ORDER BY SN, PN, JN
OPTIMIZE FOR 12 ROWS

IF SQLCODE = 100
    All qualifying rows have been fetched
```

The first SELECT statement can use a matching index scan on all three columns of the composite index and will probably return enough rows to be displayed to the user. If not, the second SELECT can use a matching index scan on two of the columns in the composite index and will probably return enough rows to be displayed to the user. If not, the third SELECT can use a matching index scan on one of the columns in the composite index. If not enough rows are fetched to fill a screen before receiving a 100 SQLCODE, there are not enough qualifying rows to be displayed.

Scrolling Backward

Users sometimes want to take second looks at rows that were previously displayed. They would like to be able to press a key that redisplays those rows.

A technique for scrolling backward is to save the first primary key of each displayed panel as far back as the user is permitted to scroll, and refetch the data. The user may agree that they do not plan to scroll backward more than ten pages, for example. Assume that the first row on the first panel has a primary key of S1, P1, and J1 which is hidden on the panel or saved in a work area. The first row of the second panel has a primary key of S2, P3, and J4. The first row of the third panel has a primary key of S3, P3, and J1. Figure PD.4 shows an example of a technique for scrolling backward three panels.

Figure PD.4. Example of technique for scrolling backward

	SN	PN	JN	QTY	
Display panel 1	S1	P1	J1	200	If user scrolls back
Save S1, P1, J1	S1	P1	J4	700	3 panels,
	S2	P3	J1	400	Display message that
	S2	P3	J2	200	cannot scroll back
	S2	P3	J3	200	further
Display panel 2	S2	P3	J4	500	If user scrolls back
Save S2, P3, J4	S2	P3	J5	600	2 panels,
	S2	P3	J6	400	Reposition using
	S2	P3	J7	800	S1, P1, J1
	S2	P5	J2	100	Display panel 1
Display panel 3	S3	P3	J1	200	If user scrolls back
Save S3, P3, J1	S3	P4	J2	500	1 panel,
	S4	P6	J3	300	Reposition using
	S4	P6	J7	300	S2, P3, J4
	S5	P2	J2	200	Display panel 2

If the user scrolls back one panel after displaying three panels, use the primary key of S3, P3, and J1 as hidden on the panel or saved in a work area to refetch the rows that were displayed using the forward repositioning technique discussed above. If the user scrolls back two panels, use the primary key of S2, P3, and J4 to refetch the rows required to fill the displayed panel and if the user scrolls back three panels, use the primary key of S1, P1, and J1 to reposition and refetch the rows required to fill the displayed panel.

Use of ROWID to Allow for Scrolling Forward and Backward with One Index: You can select required rows in ascending sequence using an ascending index to avoid a sort (opposite is true for a descending index) or DB2 can sort the rows. Save the row ID values in an array or work area as the rows are fetched. Select the rows a second time with the ROWID column in WHERE clause and process the row IDs in reverse sequence from an array or work area. This avoids creating an ascending and descending index on the same column.

The technique may not perform well if many rows are fetched because all row ID values must be fetched, saved, and the rows retrieved a second time in reverse sequence. In addition, seek time can be high depending on the location of the rows. An alternative to reduce costs is to limit the number of rows that the user can scroll backward which is a fairly common practice. If few rows qualify and must be sorted, consider sorting the rows in the required sequence if an index cannot be used to avoid the sort. However, the technique can be useful for a medium number of rows as an interim solution.

A drawback to the previous two techniques is that other processing may change the data between when the original rows were displayed and the cursor is opened a second time. If rows are inserted, the second series of fetches will return rows that were not seen the first time. If rows were deleted, some rows seen the first time will not be seen the second time the screen is displayed. Actually this can be considered an advantage in that the user sees the data as it currently exists. However, some users prefer to see exactly what they saw the first time even though that it not what exists on the table at the moment.

The problems of more or less rows displayed the second time can be avoided by saving the rows returned by the cursor in a temporary table or some other temporary storage available to the program. Depending on the transaction manager being used, the data can be saved in an array in the program, ISPF internal table, CICS temporary storage, or IMS/DC SPA. An alternative is to use CICS BMS paging or IMS MFS logical paging.

The disadvantage of saving the data to be displayed a second time is that although the user requires the ability to scroll backward through the data, they in fact seldom do scroll backward. Yet, the data is always saved which increases the cost of the transaction substantially. In addition, depending on the locking used, the data may have changed since the data was placed in the temporary area. This is an advantage in that the user sees the same data when scrolling backward. However, complications are introduced when the user also requires the ability to update the data, which may have changed since it was saved. The update transaction must avoid updating a row that has been deleted or writing an update over an updated row that the user did not see. Techniques for accomplishing this are discussed in Chapter CC.

PD.9 SCROLLABLE CURSORS (V7)

A scrollable cursor relieves the developer from managing cursor repositioning to a large extent with a great deal more flexibility than the use of the CURSOR WITH HOLD clause as discussed at the end of this section. Both scrollable cursors and CURSOR WITH HOLD are useful for batch processing and can be used with TSO, CAF, RRSAF, DL/1 batch, a background CICS task, and IMS BMP. However, they cannot be used to avoid cursor repositioning with CICS pseudo-conversational or IMS/DC interactive processing. When a screen is displayed a commit is effectively issued, all cursors are closed, and the thread is deallocated. Indeed, it is not desirable to hold resources while a user is looking at the data or answering a telephone call.

Scrollable cursors require that all requested rows be written to a declare temporary result table which is lost when a screen is displayed (except when using CICS conversational). A database named TEMP and tablespaces must be created in the database to hold temporary result tables.

Scrollable cursors and CURSOR WITH HOLD have the advantage that cursor repositioning logic need not be executed after each commit. This has performance advantages for batch programs. You will need to develop cursor repositioning logic for application program restart processing. If a program abends, obviously CURSOR WITH HOLD cannot hold position. Also cursor repositioning logic may need to be executed depending on how locks are managed and the use of claims.

Scrollable cursors are supported in host languages, REXX, ODBC, and JDBC. They are supported using Distributed Relational Data Access (DRDA) (not private protocol).

The following DECLARE, OPEN, and FETCH statements are used as an example in discussing scrollable cursors. The SELECT statement determines parts and their suppliers for a given job.

```
EXEC SQL DECLARE SPJSC CURSOR
    SENSITIVE STATIC SCROLL FOR
    SELECT SN, PN, JN, QTY
    FROM    SPJ
    WHERE   JN = :JN
```

```
         ORDER BY SN, PN, JN END-EXEC.

    EXEC SQL OPEN SPJSC END-EXEC.

    EXEC SQL FETCH SPJSC INTO :SN, :PN, :JN, :QTY
    END-EXEC.
```

The OPEN statement causes all requested rows to be saved in a temporary result table. The RID is saved along with the selected columns. CURRENTDATA (NO) is a good choice in most cases. No locks are held after the temporary result table is populated assuming the use of CS or UR isolation level. Locks are held after the temporary result table is populated with RR or RS (assuming that rows qualifies at stage 1 for RS).

A claim is held on the base tablespace with a SENSITIVE cursor (discussed in the next subsection). This means that online reorganization cannot complete until it can complete draining claims. The requirement is due to the fact that the RIDs in the temporary result table do not point to the correct rows after a reorganization.

Column functions are computed when the cursor is opened and the results are not changed when the data is changed, for example:

```
    WHERE QTY > AVG(QTY)
```

The average QTY is computed when the cursor is opened. It is not changed as rows are inserted, updated, and deleted while processing a scrollable cursor.

The CLOSE statement frees space for the temporary result table.

Sensitivity of Scrollable Declare Cursor Statement

SENSITIVE STATIC means that rows in the base table are always seen even if they differ from the temporary result table rows due to updates and deletes on the base table. Inserted rows are *not* seen. This is accomplished by DB2 reevaluating a fetched row against predicates of the cursor. The row is refreshed from the base table by locating the row using the RID placed in the temporary result table. An updated row is not seen if it no longer matches the predicate and a deleted row is not seen at all.

SENSITIVE DYNAMIC may be seen in V7+1 to indicate that a temporary result table is not used. Scrollable cursors can be implemented using bidirectional indexes that provide for the use of an ascending index to avoid a descending sort. The opposite is true for access to the base table without the use of a temporary result table. Forward dynamic prefetch is used to read data and index pages in a forward direction. Backward dynamic prefetch provides for reading data and index pages in a backward direction (V7), but is not used for scrollable cursors at present.

INSENSITIVE STATIC means that only rows in the temporary result table are seen when rows are fetched again. New values in the base table as a result of an update and insert are not seen. Deleted rows in the base table rows are seen.

The DB2 implementation of scrollable cursors is a subset of SQL99 standard which includes DYNAMIC and ASENSITIVE.

Sensitivity of Fetch Statement

The sensitivity of a FETCH statement is the same as its declare cursor statement by default. If the declare cursor is defined with SENSITIVE, you can specify FETCH INSENSITIVE. If the declare cursor is defined with INSENSITIVE, you cannot specify FETCH SENSITIVE.

If the executing program changes data using the cursor (positioned update or delete, for example), the change is visible to the executing program before and after a commit. This is accomplished by applying the change to the temporary result table.

If the executing program or another program changes the data outside of the cursor, changes are seen only when using FETCH SENSITIVE. This includes before and after commit of the executing program. Another program must issue a commit for its change to be seen. Only the fetched row is refreshed.

The SQLCA fields provides a good deal of information on scrollable cursors as summarized in Figure PD.5.

Figure PD.5. Explanation of SQLCA fields on scrollable cursors

Field	Value	Meaning
SQLWARN1	N	Non-scrollable
SQLWARN1	S	Scrollable
SQLWARN4	I	Insensitive
SQLWARN4	S	Sensitive static
SQLWARN5	1	Read-only implicitly or explicitly
SQLWARN5	2	Select and delete allowed on result table
SQLWARN5	3	Select, delete, and update allowed on result table

Fetching from a Scrollable Cursor

The FETCH statement provides for requesting:

◆   NEXT row from current position (always used with non-scrollable cursors).
◆   PRIOR row from current position.
◆   FIRST/LAST row of the temporary result table.
◆   ABSOLUTE n positions the cursor at the n row from the top of the result table (bottom of table if n is negative).
◆   RELATIVE n positions the cursor n rows after the current position. A negative n means to position before the current position.

The n in ABSOLUTE and RELATIVE can be a literal or host variable defined as INTEGER or DECIMAL(n,0).

Assume that five sets of four rows each have been processed by the program as shown in Figure PD.6 with a '1' in an arrow pointing to the current position. This example provides for demonstrating how one can scroll forward and backward.

Figure PD.6. Scrolling forward and backward

	RID	SN	PN	JN	QTY
	101	S1	P1	J1	200
	102	S1	P1	J4	700
	103	S2	P3	J1	400
	104	S2	P3	J2	200
	105	S2	P3	J3	200
	106	S2	P3	J4	500
	107	S2	P3	J5	600
2 ⟹	108	S2	P3	J6	400
	109	S2	P3	J7	800
	110	S2	P5	J2	100
	111	S3	P3	J1	200
	112	S3	P4	J2	500
	113	S4	P6	J3	300
	114	S4	P6	J7	300
	115	S5	P2	J2	200
3 ⟹	116	S5	P2	J4	100
	117	S5	P5	J5	500
	118	S5	P5	J7	100
	119	S5	P6	J2	200
1 ⟹	120	S5	P1	J4	100
	121	S5	P3	J4	200
	122	S5	P4	J4	800
	123	S5	P5	J4	400
	124	S5	P6	J4	500

Assume that the program scrolls backward three sets of 4 rows. This puts us at '2' in an arrow pointing to the current position with the following fetch.

```
EXEC SQL FETCH RELATIVE -12 SPJSC
        INTO :SN, :PN, :JN, :QTY END-EXEC.
```

Four FETCH NEXT statements can be executed to process the rows like:

```
EXEC SQL FETCH NEXT SPJSC
          INTO :SN, :PN, :JN, :QTY END-EXEC.
```

The program now scrolls forward one set of 4 rows. This puts us at '3' in an arrow pointing to the current position with the following fetch.

```
EXEC SQL FETCH RELATIVE 4 SPJSC
          INTO :SN, :PN, :JN, :QTY END-EXEC.
```

Issue three more FETCH NEXT statements to process the rows.

Holes in a STATIC SCROLL Cursor

The number of rows in the temporary result table is fixed with a STATIC SCROLL cursor. There can be delete and update holes which are detected with SENSITIVE FETCH and +222 SQLCODE is returned to inform the developer. A delete hole results when a row in the base table is deleted. An update hole results when a selected row in the base table is changed. A SENSITIVE FETCH causes reevaluation of predicates against the base table. If a row no longer qualifies according to conditions in the WHERE clause, the row in the temporary result table is marked as an update hole. If the row is updated again to its original value according the WHERE clause, the update hole is unmarked in the temporary result table. The row in the temporary result table is visible and is returned with a fetch.

Updating with Scrollable Cursors

A sensitive scrollable cursor can be defined with the WITH FOR UPDATE OF clause and can be updated using WHERE CURRENT OF CURSOR. DB2 accomplishes this by locating the row in base table and takes a lock. It verifies that the row qualifies according to the WHERE clause. It also verifies that selected columns have not changed.

An update is applied to the base table and temporary result table if the row in base table qualifies. Changes can be seen by executing program. If the row no longer qualifies according to the WHERE clause, the row is marked as a hole. The processing for the deletion of a row is similar except that the row is never seen on a subsequent fetch.

Starting and Resulting Cursor Position

Kalpana Shyam of IBM Silicon Valley Lab provided the table in Figure PD.7 in her presentation "Scrollable Cursors: Fetching Opportunities for DB2 for OS/390" at the DB2 and Business Intelligence Technical Conference, October 16-20, 2000 (cut/paste of table).

Figure PD.7. Starting and resulting cursor position

Fetch Orientation	Current Position before first row	Current Position on first row	Current Postion on last row	Current Position After Last row	Resulting Position on Delete Hole	Resulting Position on Update hole	Resulting Postion on normal Row	Resulting Position Before First row	Resulting Position After Last Row
NEXT	OK	OK	+100	+100	+222	+222	IF OK	IF +100 FROM FIRST ROW	IF +100 FROM LAST ROW
PRIOR	+100	+100	OK	OK	+222	+222	IF OK	IF +100 FROM LAST ROW	IF +100 FROM FIRST ROW
FIRST	OK	OK	OK	OK	+222	+222	IF OK	N/A	N/A
LAST	OK	OK	OK	OK	N/A	N/A	IF OK	N/A	N/A
BEFORE,	OK	OK	OK	OK	N/A	N/A	N/A	IF OK	N/A
AFTER	OK	OK	OK	OK	+222	+222	N/A	N/A	IF OK
CURRENT RELATIVE 0	+231	OK	OK	+231	+222	+222	IF OK	N/A	N/A
ABSOLUTE +N	OK	OK	OK	OK	+222	+222	IF OK	N/A	IF +100 AND N OUT OF RANGE
ABSOLUTE -N	OK	OK	OK	OK	+222	+222	IF OK	IF +100 AND N OUT OF RANGE	N/A
RELATIVE +N	OK	OK	+100	+100	+222	+222	IF OK	N/A	IF +100 AND N OUT OF RANGE
RELATIVE -N	+100	+100	OK	OK	+222	+222	IF OK	IF +100 AND N OUT OF RANGE	N/A

If a fetch encounters an update or delete hole, a +222 SQLCODE is returned to the program.

Performance Considerations

If too many rows qualify and must be placed in a temporary result table when the cursor is opened or you only need to scroll forward one row at a time, do consider other alternatives for scrolling. It is important to limit the size of the temporary result table whenever possible. For example, apply as many predicates as possible and use FETCH FIRST *n* ROWS ONLY where *n* is the maximum number of rows through which the program can scroll. However, keep in mind that if rows must be written to a work file to satisfy an ORDER BY, for example, they will be written to a work file when using FETCH FIRST *n* ROWS ONLY.

The temporary result table is discarded when a screen is displayed (except with CICS conversational). If you need to continue scrolling, it is necessary to rebuild the temporary result table when the cursor it opened with cursor repositioning logic after displaying a screen.

Scrollable cursors can include CURSOR WITH HOLD and WITH RETURN. CURSOR WITH HOLD can be used in batch programs to avoid closing the cursor and discarding the temporary result table. WITH RETURN (discussed in Chapter SP) results in blocks of data having to be retransmitted if sensitive data is required.

INSENSITIVE cursors and fetches have performance advantage because it is not necessary to access the base table to determine if the row has changed.

If some rows must be sensitive and others can be insensitive, consider declaring the cursor as SENSITIVE. Use FETCH SENSITIVE only for required processing and use FETCH INSENSITIVE where it is not necessary to see data changed after the cursor is opened.

Using CURSOR WITH HOLD

The CURSOR WITH HOLD clause in a cursor declaration statement avoids closing the cursor and repositioning it to the last row processed when the cursor is reopened. CURSOR WITH HOLD like scrollable cursors are useful for batch processing and can be used with TSO, CAF, RRSAF, DL/1 batch, a background CICS task, and IMS BMP. CURSOR WITH HOLD can be coded but will be ignored when used with CICS pseudo-conversational or IMS interactive processing because DB2 repositions by saving the last primary key value in a way much like what was discussed for manual cursor repositioning. The saved values are maintained with the thread. When a screen is displayed using CICS pseudo-conversational and IMS, a commit is effectively issued, all cursors are closed, the thread is deallocated, and the last primary key value is lost.

The declaration looks like this:

```
EXEC SQL DECLARE SCURSOR CURSOR WITH HOLD FOR
    SELECT SN, SNAME, STATUS, CITY
    INTO   :SN,:SNAME,:STATUS,:CITY
    FROM   S
    WHERE  STATUS > :NEW-STATUS
    FOR FETCH ONLY END-EXEC.
```

A FETCH must be the first statement after a commit is issued when using CURSOR WITH HOLD. Locks are released with a commit assuming RELEASE LOCKS of YES (default) on installation panel DSNTIP4 or in DSNZPARM DSN6SPRM RELCURHL (V6). Recall from Chapter CC that locks can be released as a result of a -911 or -913 SQLCODE from a deadlock or timeout if RELEASE LOCKS of NO is specified. The cursor position is released when the locks are released. (The LOCK TABLE statements can be issued at the beginning of the program to avoid deadlocks and timeouts in the batch program. However, other programs trying to process the data can get deadlocks and timeouts.) A claim is held on the tablespace which means that an online reorganization cannot complete until it can complete draining claims.

Dynamically prepared SQL is kept in the Environmental Descriptor Manager (EDM) pool past a commit point without using the dynamic cache as discussed in this chapter when using CURSOR WITH HOLD.

Restrictions: CURSOR WITH HOLD disallows parallelism and is ignored in stored procedures when using the DB2 established stored procedure address space.

PD.10 TESTING FOR EXISTENCE

A frequent requirement is to determine whether a particular value exists one or more times in a table. Further processing is based on the results of the existence test. We will review several alternatives for existence tests with an analysis of the performance implications of the alternatives.

A commonly used technique to determine if a value exists in a table (S4 in the sample) follows. Notice that It is not necessary to actually select a column value to determine if a value exists in a table. Indeed, you can select a literal (1, 2, 'ABC', etc.) and determine if the value exists based on the SQLCODE. This is a good technique if an index can be used to locate the value and following issues are addressed. Do be cautious of a tablespace scan. If zero or one row qualifies, it is necessary to scan the entire tablespace to determine the SQLCODE to return as described below.

```
SELECT 1
FROM    SPJ
WHERE   SN = 'S4';
```

Two cases need to be tested if a cursor on the SELECT statement is defined.

a) If the SQLCODE is 0, S4 does exist.

b) If the SQLCODE is 100, S4 does not exist in the table.

If a singleton SELECT statement is used, a third case needs to be tested.

c) If the SQLCODE is -811, more than one occurrence of S4 exists in the table when a cursor has not been defined. It is not advisable to depend on the values returned in host variables when a negative SQLCODE is received. Even if you receive values from the first row found today, you may not receive comparable results in the future with a change to DB2. The is particular important for the second row fetched by DB2 to determine which SQLCODE to return. If a subselect is used and no rows qualify in the subselect, the outer table is accessed at all because a -811 is seen by DB2 indicating that no rows quality in the subselect. There are some cases where you will not receive any values at all as shown in the following example.

```
SELECT SN, PN, JN, QTY
FROM    SPJ
WHERE   SN =
   (SELECT SN
    FROM    S
    WHERE   CITY = 'Stockholm');
```

If there are multiple suppliers in Stockholm, the subselect returns a -811 SQLCODE. DB2 does not access the SPJ table at all and therefore no values are returned from the SPJ table. An alternative is to use an IN subselect as discussed in Chapter ST.

The FETCH FIRST 1 ROW ONLY clause without a cursor is useful in testing if one row qualifies (V7) like:

```
SELECT 1
FROM   SPJ
WHERE  SN = 'S4'
FETCH FIRST 1 ROW ONLY;
```

The clause avoids a -811 SQLCODE if more than one row qualifies without a cursor and avoids an additional internal fetch to determine the SQLCODE which needs to be returned. It increases the likelihood of using an index to locate the value. If a tablespace scan is required, it is not necessary to continue the scan once a S4 is found to determine which SQLCODE should be returned. It is not necessary to declare a cursor, open, fetch, and close the cursor which can save up to 30 percent in CPU time. If a cursor is used, it is closed automatically when the first row is fetched and held locks are released. This reduces the overhead of having cursors open that are no longer needed and holding unnecessary locks. Another advantage is the reduction in message traffic in a client/server environment. The FETCH FIRST *n* ROWS ONLY clause is discussed in Chapter PP.

EXISTS subselect is a good choice if the required action can be taken based on the results of an inner select. Here is an example of determining information on suppliers who supply part P5 where the part is being used on J7:

```
SELECT SN, SNAME, STATUS, CITY
FROM   S AS SX
WHERE  EXISTS
  (SELECT 1
   FROM   SPJ
   WHERE  SN = SX.SN
   AND    PN = 'P5'
   AND    JN = 'J7');
```

If the values tested in the inner select exists, true is returned to the outer select and rows are returned from the S table.

The same principle applies to UPDATE and DELETE statements with a correlated subselect (V7). You can update a table based on the results of an inner select as well as test for the existence of a value in another inner select.

```
UPDATE SPJ SPJX
SET (PN, QTY) =
   (SELECT PN, 10
    FROM    P
    WHERE   PNAME = 'Bolt')
WHERE  EXISTS
   (SELECT 1
    FROM    P
    WHERE   P.PN = 'P4'
    AND     P.PN = SPJX.PN);
```

Here is an example of deleting rows from a table based on the existence of a value in another table referenced in the inner select.

```
DELETE FROM SPJ SPJX
   WHERE  EXISTS
      (SELECT 1
       FROM    S
       WHERE   S.SN = 'S4'
       AND     S.SN = SPJX.SN);
```

The use of subselects have performance advantages in that one rather than two or more statements need to be executed which reduces the path length (the number of instructions that must be executed). The statements can be transformed to a join including the UPDATE and DELETE statements (V7) which improves performance if the criteria described in Chapter ST are met. Indeed, the previous three statements were transformed to a join when tested.

Count number of occurrences: If it necessary to know the number of occurrences of a value, the COUNT column function can be used:

```
SELECT COUNT(SN)
FROM    SPJ
WHERE   SN = 'S4';
```

This statement performs poorly if the index or table is large. It is necessary to locate each S4 by scanning all of the leaf or data pages and count each occurrence. Certainly, you do not want to use this formulation if the question is simply whether the value exists one or more times.

Attempts to get DB2 to stop processing when it finds a value: Two technique are often used to try to get DB2 to stop processing when it finds the first occurrence of a value. Unfortunately, DB2 locates all S95 rows and returns a value of one with the following formulation.

```
SELECT  COUNT(DISTINCT SN)
FROM    SPJ
WHERE   SN = 'S95';
```

The following formulation is an attempt to get DB2 to find S95 for the inner select and return a true value. Unfortunately, the statement is not a correlated subselect and DB2 will locate all S95 rows.

```
SELECT 1
FROM    SYSIBM.SYSDUMMY1
WHERE   EXISTS
   (SELECT 1
    FROM    S
    WHERE   SN = 'S95');
```

Unsatisfactory alternatives are reviewed to avoid someone thinking of one of them and testing it only to determine that it performs poorly.

PD.11 GENERATING SEQUENCE NUMBERS

It is sometimes necessary to generate sequence numbers for orders, invoices, or perhaps employee identification numbers. Four alternatives are presented for generating sequence numbers along with the associated pros and cons. The first alternative has performance advantages over using an application table to track the last used sequence number.

Alternative 1: An identity column can be defined to DB2 as described in Chapter CT (V6 APAR PQ30652). The insertion of rows with an identity column is discussed in this chapter.

In the following alternatives, we will use the variable SEQNO to represent the required sequence number to be inserted into the target table and next the next sequence number (NEXTSEQNO) which is stored in a one row table.

Alternative 2: The NEXTSEQNO is selected with a cursor including the clauses of FOR UPDATE OF, WITH RS (or RR), or KEEP UPDATE LOCKS. These clauses are used to hold an X lock on the one row table containing NEXTSEQNO until a commit is issued. This avoids someone else getting the sequence number and producing a duplicate. An UPDATE statement with the WHERE CURRENT OF clause is used to increment the NEXTSEQNO. The SEQNO is set to the NEXTSEQNO plus one using host language code. A row is then inserted into the target table with the generated SEQNO.

Alternative 3: In this alternative the NEXTSEQNO is incremented immediately in the one row table with an UPDATE statement. This causes an X lock to be held until a commit is issued so that no one else can get the same sequence number. The NEXTSEQNO is decremented by one in a SELECT statement that puts the result in the host variable SEQNO. The row is then inserted into the target table as in alternative 2.

Alternative 4: The maximum sequence number is selected from the target table with the MAX(SEQNO) function. The SEQNO is incremented by one and inserted into the target table. If a -803 SQLCODE is returned, someone else has gotten the same MAX(SEQNO) incremented it by one and successful inserted it into the target table. A unique index on the SEQNO column is required to avoid duplicate sequence numbers being inserted into the target table. It should be a descending index (can be an ascending or descending index in V7) to maximize performance by allowing for one-fetch index access. If the -803 SQLCODE is received, the program must select another MAX(SEQNO) and attempt its insert again repeatedly until a 0 SQLCODE is received indicating a successful insert.

Pros and cons of alternatives: Alternatives 1 (assuming the use of GENERATED ALWAYS), 2, and 3 do not require a unique index on the sequence number column in the target table to avoid duplicates nor is it necessary to manage the -803 SQLCODE. This avoids index maintenance if an index is not required on the column for other purposes. Alternative 2 requires three SQL statements one of which requires a declare cursor, open, and fetch. Alternative 4 requires two SQL statements in most cases and has performance advantages if an index can be used to achieve one-fetch index access. This alternative does not require a one row control table to track NEXTSEQNO with potential lock contention on the control table.

It is likely that there will be lock contention on the control table about 10 percent of the time if one transaction per second is executed and the transaction requires 0.1 seconds to execute.

The average wait time for a lock can be calculated with the formula

```
AVG wait time = (P(PL) / (1 - P(PL)) * AVG
lock duration
```

where P(PL) is the probability of the page being locked. The following sample calculation assumes that the page will be locked 10 percent of the time and the average lock duration is 0.1 seconds.

```
0.11 seconds  = (0.10  / (1 - 0.10)) * 1
second
```

It is estimated that the average wait time for a lock is about 0.11 seconds. The formula is covered in detail in the manual *Locking in DB2 for MVS/ESA Environment*, SG24-4725.

PD.12 ERROR HANDLING

It is possible to handle error conditions in a variety of ways. Although you can handle error conditions by writing code immediately after the statement that causes the error, most organizations find it more efficient to place all of the error handling within a separate common module that can be used by all programs. Using a common module can avoid redundancy in coding and ease maintenance.

The SQL Communications Area

The SQL Communications Area (SQLCA) is a data structure that must be included in any host-language program using SQL. The SQLCA provides a way for DB2 to pass feedback about its operations to the program. As a program runs, after each SQL statement executes, DB2 returns, via the SQLCA, codes indicating that the execution was successful or identifying errors or special conditions. The program can then test for these codes and handle them appropriately.

The SQLCA is included in a COBOL program by the precompiler as a result of the statement:

```
EXEC SQL INCLUDE SQLCA END-EXEC
```

Each host language has somewhat different syntax for including the SQLCA in the program. The INCLUDE syntax and the details on the fields in the SQLCA is described in the *Application Programming and SQL Guide* manual. We describe some of the key fields in the SQLCA.

The SQLCODE field in the SQLCA should be checked after each SQL statement that is executed. If the value is 0, the statement executed successfully. If the value is 100, no rows or no more rows qualify for the statement. If the SQLCODE is any other positive number, it is a warning or informative message. If the SQLCODE is a negative number, there is an error condition.

The SQLSTATE is for compliance with the SQL standard. Its error descriptions are more general in nature than the SQLCODE descriptions. This is because the description must be applicable to any DBMS that complies with the standard. If there is a possibility that your program may execute on a relational DBMS other than DB2 for z/OS or OS/390, it is a good idea to process the SQLSTATE as well as the SQLCODE to minimize the changes needed to a program when it is executed on another DBMS, such as DB2 Universal Database (UDB) has this support on a number of platforms including OS/390, z/OS, Windows 2000, ME, 98, 95, Linux, Unix, AIX, HP-UX, Solaris, UNMA-Q, OS/2, and OS/400. Most of the SQLCODEs used by these DBMSs are not the same as those used by DB2 UDB for z/OS or OS/390.

The SQLCODE has more precise description of a condition. The SQLSTATE is more general for multiple DBMSs. It is advisable to check the SQLCODE and/or SQLSTATE after each statement or command is executed.

The SQLSTATE is 5 bytes of character data with a class and subclass. The first 2 bytes are the class and the last 3 bytes are the subclass. You can define an SQLSTATE with triggers and user-defined functions as discussed in Chapters TR and UD. Do avoid conflicts with SQL92 SQLSTATE values by using the first character of the letters between I and Z or the digits 7, 8, or 9. Details on the SQL92 SQLSTATE rules for defining values can be found in the *SQL Reference* manual.

The third element in the SQLERRD array is an integer containing the number of rows inserted, updated, or deleted. It is best to use this field to determined the number of rows changed with an SQL statement that processes more than one row. The alternative of counting the number of rows is more costly. Do keep in mind that the field does not include a count of foreign key rows deleted as a result of the use of a cascade delete constraint or updated due to the use of the set null rule. In addition, it does not include the number of rows deleted using the mass delete algorithm (discussed in Chapter BP.)

Error Message Text

The SQLERRMC field in the SQLCA contains up to 70 bytes of descriptive information about the error or special condition identified by the SQLCODE. A program can display this text during program testing and use the information to write a friendly message to the user describing the error.

Example: Here is an example of using information in the SQLERRMC to inform users about referential constraint violations. If an UPDATE statement violates a referential integrity constraint, it is necessary to know the constraint name that was violated. Recall from Chapter CT that a constraint name is given when defining the foreign key. This name can be found in SQLERRMC when a negative SQLCODE is received, usually beginning with a -53. For example, if a -530 is received indicating that an insert or update would have resulted in an orphan dependent row, the SQLERRMC can be moved to a host language structure like:

```
IF SQLCODE = -530
    MOVE SQLERRMC TO CONSTRAINTS.
```

CONSTRAINTS can be defined in working storage like:

```
01   CONSTRAINTS.
     03   PARM-LENGTH      PIC S9(4) COMP.
     03   REF-CONSTRAINT   PIC X(08).
```

```
    03  FILLER           PIC X(62).
```

The host variable REF-CONSTRAINT contains the constraint name given when the foreign key is defined.

The violation of a table check constraint is managed similar to referential integrity constraints. (Table check constraints are discussed in Chapter CT.) If you receive a -545, the constraint name is found in the SQLERRMC field.

After you have the constraint name, more information is needed to notify the user. You can extract information about the constraints from the catalog tables, and place the information in an application table for retrieval and analysis in a production environment. The referential integrity constraint name is in the column SYSIBM.SYSFOREIGNKEYS.RELNAME, and the table check constraint name is in the column SYSIBM.SYSCHECKS.CHECKNAME. The following SELECT statements identify the information needed to notify the user about the constraint that was violated for objects created with the authorization ID of POSYSTEM.

```
    SELECT F.RELNAME,  F.COLNAME,
           F.CREATOR,  F.TBNAME,
           R.REFTBCREATOR,  R.REFTBNAME,
           C.NAME,  C.KEYSEQ,  C.COLTYPE,
           C.LENGTH,C.SCALE
    FROM   SYSIBM.SYSFOREIGNKEYS F,
           SYSIBM.SYSRELS         R,
           SYSIBM.SYSCOLUMNS      C
    WHERE  F.CREATOR      = 'POSYSTEM'
    AND    F.CREATOR      = R.CREATOR
    AND    F.TBNAME       = R.TBNAME
    AND    F.RELNAME      = R.RELNAME
    AND    R.REFTBCREATOR = C.TBCREATOR
    AND    R.REFTBNAME    = C.TBNAME
    AND    F.COLSEQ       = C.KEYSEQ
    ORDER BY F.RELNAME,  F.COLNAME,
             F.CREATOR,  F.TBNAME,
             C.NAME,  C.KEYSEQ
    SELECT C.CHECKNAME,  CDEP.COLNAME,
           C.CREATOR,  C.TBNAME,
           C.CHECKCONDITION
    FROM   SYSIBM.SYSCHECKS    AS C,
           SYSIBM.SYSCHECKDEP AS CDEP
```

```
WHERE   C.CREATOR      = 'POSYSTEM'
AND     C.TBOWNER      = CDEP.TBOWNER
AND     C.TBNAME       = CDEP.TBNAME
AND     C.CHECKNAME    = CDEP.CHECKNAME
ORDER BY C.CHECKNAME,  CDEP.COLNAME,
         C.CREATOR,  C.TBNAME;
```

By using an application table that contains SQLCODEs, constraint information, and descriptive text, a program that receives an SQLCODE can select from the table and retrieve the text to display to the user.

Wherever possible, suggest how the user should proceed to resolve the problem. For example, if the user attempts to insert a row into a dependent table that does not have a corresponding parent row, the user needs to be informed and told how to proceed to resolve the problem. Simply displaying the SQLCODE of -530 is of little value to the user. If the SQLCODE of -551 is received, the user needs to be notified that they do not have the required privilege and who they should contact to get the privilege. If the SQLCODE of -911 is received because of a timeout or deadlock, the user needs to be informed that someone else is currently processing the data. Consider developing retry logic for these situations. Perhaps the program can try to get the data three times and each time inform the user that the data is locked by someone else before giving a message that the user must re-execute the transaction later. A rollback of all INSERT, UPDATE, AND DELETE statements within a UR occurs with an SQLCODE of -911 and must be executed again. In addition, cursor repositioning logic is required.

Detailed Error Descriptions: Some error conditions require a technical person to resolve the problem. If the SQLCODE of -818, -805, or -812 is received, an administrator must investigate and resolve the fact that DB2 cannot find a valid plan or package to execute. Similarly, an SQLCODE of -904 indicating that a resource is unavailable requires that someone find out why that resource is unavailable. Some companies also write a log of error messages to identify error patterns for resolution and to provide information for further analysis. The person resolving the problem requires a detailed description of the error which can be made available in the error log.

Detailed message information can be retrieved using a sample program provided in object form in the SDSNLOAD library. The assembler program DSNTIAR can be called, passing it the SQLCA ,and it can return up to 960 bytes of text describing the error. It is necessary to define a data structure to receive the message text like:

```
01    ERROR-MESSAGE.
      02    ERROR-L       PIC S9(4) COMP VALUE +960.
      02    ERROR-TEXT    PIC X(120) OCCURS 8 TIMES
                          INDEXED BY ERROR-INDEX.
77    ERROR-TEXT-L        PIC S9(9) COMP VALUE +120.
```

Here is an example of calling DSNTIAR from a program:

```
CALL 'DSNTIAR' USING SQLCA
     ERROR-MESSAGE, ERROR-TEXT-L.
```

DSNTIAR issues z/OS or OS/390 GETMAINs to allocate storage. If you are using CICS, it is best to call DSNTIAC which issues CICS GETMAINs. This will reduce the amount of CPU time required.

PD.13 CONNECTING TO REMOTE SITES

You can connect to multiple remote sites and update data at various sites within a unit of recovery. When you issue a commit, DB2 takes responsibility for insuring that all updates issued at all sites will be completed or none of the updates will take place with its two-phase commit protocol.

Type 2 Connection

The type 2 CONNECT statement applies to application directed distributed facilities. You can connect to multiple DBMS that conform to DRDA architecture. A host variable or literal can be specified in the CONNECT statement to indicate the location where the following SQL statements are to be executed. The first CONNECT statement in Figure PD.8 establishes a connection to the content of the host variable :ROME. A row is inserted into the SPJ table in Rome. (The host variable has the same name as the content of the host variable in the example.)

Figure PD.8. Connecting to multiple sites

```
EXEC SQL CONNECT TO :ROME END-EXEC.
```

```
        EXEC SQL INSERT INTO SPJ (SN, PN, JN, QTY)
                  VALUES ('S10', 'P40', 'J7', 400)
        END-EXEC.

        EXEC SQL CONNECT TO :SYDNEY END-EXEC.
        EXEC SQL UPDATE P SET CITY = 'Perth'
                  WHERE PN = 'P4' END-EXEC.

--      If DELETE is to occur in :Rome,
--          CONNECT TO :ROME if SQLRULE(DB2) (default)
--          SET CONNECTION :ROME if SQLRULE(STD)

        EXEC SQL DELETE FROM J
                  WHERE   JNAME = 'Electrical'
                  AND     CITY  = 'Sydney' END-EXEC.

        EXEC SQL RELEASE :SYDNEY END-EXEC.
--      Next SELECT will execute in :SYDNEY

        EXEC SQL SELECT SN, SNAME, STATUS, CITY
                  FROM    S
                  WHERE   SN = 'S4'
                  FOR FETCH ONLY END-EXEC.

        EXEC SQL COMMIT END-EXEC.

--      Connection to :ROME still exists (default)

        EXEC SQL CONNECT RESET END-EXEC.
--      Return to local site
```

The second CONNECT statement in Figure PD.8 establishes a connection
to Sydney. Now two connections exists but only one is active at any one
time. That is, all SQL statement after the CONNECT statement will be
executed at the location specified in that statement. If further processing is
to be done in Rome, it is necessary to re-activate the connection to Rome.
This is done with either a CONNECT TO :ROME or SET CONNECT TO
:ROME if you wish to comply with the SQL standard. The statements
preceded by "--" are comments in the example. The DELETE statement is
executed in Sydney.

When all processing is complete at a site, it is advisable to release the
connection to minimize the resources required by the program and allow

others to use the resources. This can be done with the RELEASE statement followed by a COMMIT statement. The connection is not physically broken until the COMMIT statement is executed. The SELECT statement will be executed in Sydney even though the connection has been released. You will want to release connections immediately before a commit to avoid confusion, unlike the example, with a comment to emphasize the fact that the connection is not physically broken until the commit. It is necessary to hold connections until a commit to ensure a two-phase commit where all updates within the unit of recovery are made at all locations. The connection to Rome still exists after the commit because it was not released prior to the commit. You can return to the program's location with the CONNECT RESET statement. Any SQL statements executed after the reset will be against tables at the program's location. The currently active site can be determined with the following statement.

```
SET :CURRENT = CURRENT SERVER
```

The current location is in the host variable :CURRENT. The SQLERRP field in the SQLCA data structure contains a server ID indicating the IBM DB2 product, version, release, and modification level.

Methods for Specifying the Location

Use of the CONNECT TO statement detracts from location independence because the location must be known to move into the :ROME host variable for successful execution of:

```
EXEC SQL CONNECT TO :ROME END-EXEC.
EXEC SQL INSERT INTO SPJ (SN, PN, JN, QTY)
          VALUES ('S10', 'P40', 'J7', 400)
END-EXEC.
```

A good alternative is to use an alias when using DRDA (V6) and the private protocol. Prior to executing an SQL statement at a location, create an alias with the location as the first node of the table name like:

```
CREATE ALIAS SPJ FOR ROME.POSYS.SPJ;

EXEC SQL INSERT INTO SPJ (SN, PN, JN, QTY)
          VALUES ('S10', 'P40', 'J7', 400)
END-EXEC.
```

The alias (SPJ in the above example) can be specified in SQL statements. This requires the use of the DBPROTOCOL(DRDA) bind parameter which is the default unless changed on DSNTIP5 installation panel or DSNZPARM DSN6SYSP DBPROTCL. The DBPROTOCOL(PRIVATE) parameter is not advisable as will be seen in the next section.

An alternative that detracts from location independence is to use fully qualified table or view name like:

```
EXEC SQL
INSERT INTO ROME.POSYS.SPJ (SN, PN, JN, QTY)
    VALUES ('S10', 'P40', 'J7', 400) END-EXEC.
```

Type 1 and 2 Connections

A type 1 connection can be specified to override the default of a type 2 connection with the precompiler parameter of CONNECT(1). Also a type 1 connection is used if the CURRENTSERVER bind parameter is used to designate the initial connection. Type 1 connection results in using the private protocol (also known as system directed distributed facilities). There are several disadvantages of this older protocol. It is possible to connect only to another DB2 subsystem using the DB2 private protocol. It is necessary to commit and break the current connection before establishing another connection. Significantly more bytes must be transmitted compared to the use of the DRDA protocol. Finally, the private protocol is expected to be eliminated in the future.

Type 2 connections use the more current DRDA (also known as application directed distributed facilities) protocol. These connections allow for connection to multiple DBMS that conform to the DRDA architecture. The CONNECT(2) parameter is the precompiler default.

You must make a decision to use type a 1 or type 2 connection in all packages executed by a transaction. Otherwise, a -808 SQLCODE is received if PROGA has a type 1 connection and PROGB attempts a type 2 connection.

Recommendation: Type 2 connections with the use of the DRDA protocol are recommended rather than type 1 connections which means the use of the private protocol. The advantages of DRDA over the private protocol are discussed in Chapter CO.

Releasing a Connection

The description of the RELEASE statement in Figure PD.8 assumes the default of EXPLICIT. The action to take when a commit is executed is determined by the bind parameter DISCONNECT.

DISCONNECT(EXPLICIT) means that all released connections are destroyed. DISCONNECT(AUTOMATIC) means that all remote connections will be destroyed even if they have not been explicitly released. In both cases, open cursors are implicitly closed.

DISCONNECT(CONDITIONAL) means that all remote connections will be destroyed except for those with CURSOR WITH HOLD when a commit is executed.

Continuous Blocking of Data for Transmission

If a SELECT statement is read only, non-scrollable cursor, or scrollable insensitive cursor, 32 KB of data and control information is blocked and transmitted in one message continuously with a maximum of 100 blocks. This has significant performance advantages over formatting and transmitting one row at a time. There is an exception, if a scrollable cursor is used and the fetch orientation is reversed, FETCH SENSITIVE is used, or a subsequent FETCH target is far apart (not within the fetched blocks), the blocks are discarded.

The OPTIMIZE FOR n ROWS clause effects the number of rows blocked and transmitted.

♦   If OPTIMIZE FOR 1 ROW is used, DB2 blocks and transmits MIN(16 rows, 32 KB of data).

♦   If OPTIMIZE FOR n ROWS is used where n results in <= 32 KB of data and control information, DB2 blocks and transmits n rows at a time with a maximum of 32 KB.

♦   If OPTIMIZE FOR *n* ROWS is used where *n* results in >= 32 KB of data and control information, DB2 blocks and transmits <= 100 blocks 32 KB of data based on the limit specified on installation panel DSNTIP5. The default is EXTRA BLOCKS REQ = 100 and EXTRA BLOCKS SRV = 100 which can be changed to a value between 0 to 100.

The FETCH FIRST *n* ROWS ONLY clause controls the number of rows blocked and transmitted. The cursor is closed when limit is exceeded which has performance advantages.

Fast implicit close is used in a distributed environment to reduce network traffic if the following conditions are true (V7). Limited block fetch must be used. The cursor is not a scrollable. If FETCH FIRST *n* ROWS ONLY, the cursor is closed when *n* rows are fetched or no more rows qualify. If CURSOR WITH HOLD is not used or it is used along with the KEEPDYNAMIC(YES) bind parameter. It does not apply when LOBs are retrieved.

PD.14 ORGANIZATION CHART PROCESSING (OR BILL OF MATERIALS)

Organization chart structures are not uncommon in application system design. Most companies have an organization chart similar to the one in Figure PD.9. Information is frequently stored according to the reporting structure of employees and cost center allocation of budgets and expenses. This type of structure occurs in manufacturing, commonly called bill-of-material processing, where it is necessary to know the components needed to build a product and the subcomponents of each component. For example, a bill-of-material for an airplane would have at the top level the end product airplane analogous to the president's level shown in the organization chart. At the next level down would be the wings of the airplane rather than the vice presidents, the next level might be the engines rather than the assistant vice presidents, the next level might be the fan of the engine rather than the director, etc. until all components necessary to build the airplane are accounted for.

Figure PD.9. Organization chart

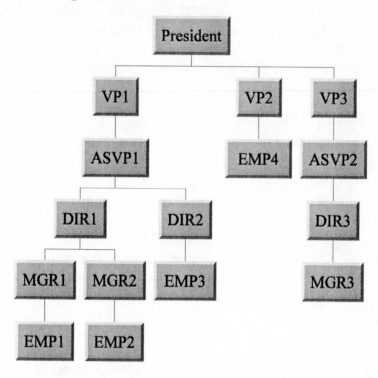

An organizational chart or bill-of-materials can be "flattened" into a table as shown in Figure PD.10. The top level, the president, appears as the parent and each position that reports to the president is listed as a dependent, in the example vice presidents VP1, VP2, and VP3. Each vice president is also listed in the parent column, with the associated reporting employees listed as dependents. Each dependent appears as a parent if he or she has a reporting employee. EMP1, EMP2, EMP3, and EMP4 do not appear in the parent column since they have no one reporting to them. The PL column is a numeric indicator of the level of reporting for the parent and the DL column indicates the level of reporting for the dependent. The PL and DL columns are optional but can be useful for reporting purposes.

Figure PD.10. Organization chart table

PARENT	DEPENDENT	PL	DL
President	VP1	1	2
President	VP2	1	2

PARENT	DEPENDENT	PL	DL
President	VP3	1	2
VP1	ASVP1	2	3
VP2	EMP4	2	6
VP3	ASVP2	2	3
ASVP1	DIR2	3	4
ASVP1	DIR1	3	4
ASVP2	DIR3	3	4
DIR1	MGR1	4	5
DIR1	MGR2	4	5
DIR2	EMP3	4	6
DIR3	MGR3	4	5
MGR1	EMP1	5	6
MGR2	EMP2	5	6

The SQL code to perform an explosion to determine all employees who report directly or indirectly to VP1 is shown along with comments as to the result of each statement:

```
SELECT  DEPENDENT     -- ASVP1 is returned
FROM    ORG_CHART
WHERE   PARENT = &VP1;

SELECT  DEPENDENT     -- DIR1, DIR2 is returned
FROM    ORG_CHART     --  one at a time when fetched
WHERE   PARENT = &ASVP1;

SELECT  DEPENDENT     -- MGR1, MGR2, EMP3 is returned
FROM    ORG_CHART     --  one at a time when fetched
WHERE   PARENT =&DIR1;--  using DIR1, DIR2

SELECT  DEPENDENT     -- EMP1, EMP2 is returned
FROM    ORG_CHART     --  one at a time when fetched
```

```
WHERE   PARENT =&MGR1;--   using MGR1, MGR2, EMP3
```

The positions are indicated with QMF parameters for ease of understanding.
Each parameter would be replaced by a host variable in a program. The first
SELECT determines that ASVP1 reports directly to VP1. The second select
determines those employees who report directly to ASVP1, DIR1 and DIR2.
The third select determines that MRG1, MGR2, and EMP3 report directly to
DIR1. The last select shown determines that EMP1 and EMP2 report to
MRG1. Using this approach, a select is needed for each level in the
organization chart, and a cursor is necessary for each of the SELECTS. Also
needed is logic to save the intermediate values used to determine the next
level of reporting, and logic coded in the host language to determine which
statement to execute until all reporting levels have been located.

Using Subselects to Reduce Host Language Code

The amount of host language code that needs to be developed can be
reduced significantly by having DB2 save the intermediate results using
subselects:

```
SELECT PARENT, DEPENDENT, PL, DL
FROM    ORG_CHART
WHERE   PARENT = &VP1 OR PARENT IN
(SELECT DEPENDENT FROM ORG_CHART WHERE PARENT =
&VP1 OR PARENT IN
(SELECT DEPENDENT FROM ORG_CHART WHERE PARENT =
&VP1 OR PARENT IN
(SELECT DEPENDENT FROM ORG_CHART WHERE PARENT =
&VP1 OR PARENT IN
(SELECT DEPENDENT FROM ORG_CHART WHERE PARENT =
&VP1 OR PARENT IN
(SELECT DEPENDENT FROM ORG_CHART WHERE PARENT =
&VP1 OR PARENT IN
(SELECT DEPENDENT FROM ORG_CHART WHERE PARENT =
&VP1 OR PARENT IN
(SELECT DEPENDENT FROM ORG_CHART WHERE PARENT =
&VP1 OR PARENT IN
(SELECT DEPENDENT FROM ORG_CHART WHERE PARENT =
&VP1 OR PARENT IN
(SELECT DEPENDENT FROM ORG_CHART WHERE PARENT =
&VP1 OR PARENT IN
```

```
(SELECT DEPENDENT FROM ORG_CHART WHERE PARENT =
&VP1 OR PARENT IN
  -- EMP1, EMP2
(SELECT DEPENDENT FROM ORG_CHART WHERE PARENT =
&VP1 OR PARENT IN
  -- MGR1, MGR2, EMP3
(SELECT DEPENDENT FROM ORG_CHART WHERE PARENT =
&VP1 OR PARENT IN
  -- DIR2, DIR1
(SELECT DEPENDENT FROM ORG_CHART WHERE PARENT =
&VP1 OR PARENT IN
  -- ASVP1
(SELECT DEPENDENT FROM ORG_CHART WHERE PARENT =
&VP1))))))))))))))
ORDER BY 3,1,4,2;
```

There is a limit of 15 levels using the subselect technique because a maximum of 15 tables can be referenced in an SQL statement. This limit applies even if it is the same table name referenced 15 times as is the case for the table ORG_CHART. Also it will be seen in Chapter ST that an IN subselect results in a tablespace scan which will significantly detract from performance with the 14 subselects in the statement.

Either of the techniques described above for explosions can be used for implosions. For example, an implosion would be used to determine who employee EMP1 reports to directly or indirectly. Each occurrence of the DEPENDENT column would be replaced by the PARENT column and each occurrence of the PARENT column would be replaced by the DEPENDENT column.

Designing Indexes for Performance: Good index design enhances performance for both techniques. A composite index on the parent and dependent columns in that order allows index-only processing to accomplish an explosion. If implosions are frequently required, the composite index would be on the dependent and parent columns in that order.

Simple SQL with Increased Table Costs: The SQL can be simplified significantly by storing the explosion in the table. Figure PD.11 shows a table design where the parent is repeated for each direct and indirect reporting level in the dependent column. The president is not included in the table since only a SELECT * is needed to determine all those that report directly and indirectly to the president.

Figure PD.11. Expanded organization chart table

PARENT	DEPENDENT	PL	DL
VP1	ASVP1	1	2
VP1	DIR1	1	3
VP1	MGR1	1	4
VP1	EMP1	1	5
VP1	MGR2	1	4
VP1	EMP2	1	5
VP1	DIR2	1	3
VP1	EMP3	1	5
ASVP1	DIR1	2	3
ASVP1	MGR1	2	4
ASVP1	EMP1	2	5
ASVP1	MGR2	2	4
ASVP1	EMP2	2	5
ASVP1	DIR2	2	3
ASVP1	EMP3	2	5
Etc.			

All employees who report directly or indirectly to VP1 can be determined very simply:

```
SELECT DEPENDENT
FROM    EXP_ORG_CHART
WHERE   PARENT = &VP1
FOR FETCH ONLY;
```

The expanded organization chart may be acceptable for a small number of rows (say 10,000) and where business professionals need direct ad hoc access. The expanded version would be unacceptable for a large organizational or bill-of-material structure because of the amount of DASD space that would be required and the complexity of updating the data.

PD.15 EMBEDDED DYNAMIC SQL

Embedded, dynamic SQL is a powerful but costly feature. In many cases, it is too costly for use in high transaction rate applications. Dynamically generated SQL statements are prepared--that is, optimized and bound--just as static SQL--except the plan is not stored in the directory. There are SQL statements that must be used within the host-language program to accomplish that preparation. In addition, if the dynamic statement is a SELECT, the program must be able to determine the data structures needed to receive the selected values and be able to generate those structures, just as the programmer includes the necessary data structures in a host-language program for static SQL as generated by DCLGEN as discussed in Chapter PE. With dynamic SQL, however, a program must dynamically allocate memory to receive the values for them.

Dynamic Statements Other than Select

The host program must first include a variable to receive the SQL statement, which should be a varying-length character variable for COBOL and Assembler, or a varying or fixed-length string variable in PL/1. Make the variable long enough to accommodate the longest statement a user is likely to require. We will call that variable SQLSTATEMENT. It is declared as any other host variable would be. Set the variable equal to an SQL statement in this way:

```
MOVE 'UPDATE SPJ SET QTY = QTY + 10
      WHERE SN = 'S3'
      AND   PN = 'P3'' TO SQLSTATEMENT
```

If the dynamic SQL statement, as here, uses constants instead of host-language variables, DB2 binds and executes it at once in response to a single statement, the EXECUTE IMMEDIATE statement, which looks like this:

```
EXEC SQL EXECUTE IMMEDIATE :SQLSTATEMENT
    END-EXEC.
```

If a dynamic statement is to be executed again, however, the EXECUTE IMMEDIATE statement is an inefficient way of doing it because it requires that the statement be rebound for each execution. The more efficient approach, and the one needed if the statement uses host-language variables or is a SELECT statement, binds the statement once in response to a PREPARE statement and executes it any number of times in response to EXECUTE statements. (In either case, the optimizer returns its relative cost estimate for a dynamic bind from a host-language program as SQLERRD(4) in the SQLCA.)

For a dynamic SQL statement to be executed repeatedly, a host-language variable is needed to reference the bound SQL statement. We will call the variable SQLBOUND. The embedded SQL statement that orders preparation of the code structure is PREPARE, followed by the name of the variable to reference it, followed by the keyword FROM, and followed by the name of the source code variable that provides the statement. The PREPARE statement for the example is:

```
EXEC SQL
    PREPARE SQLBOUND FROM :SQLSTATEMENT
    END-EXEC.
```

Because the bind process locks the DBD of all databases containing tables being referenced by the SQL statement, be sure to test the SQLCODE for an unsuccessful PREPARE. If a prepare is unsuccessful, branch to a rollback to release the locks.

The statement is now ready for execution, which is invoked by an embedded EXECUTE statement like:

```
EXEC SQL EXECUTE SQLBOUND END-EXEC.
```

Arguments and Parameters

A dynamic SQL statement cannot include a host variable. It can, however, use question marks to indicate variables to which values are assigned and passed to the EXECUTE statement. These question marks are called parameter markers. For example:

```
SQLSTATEMENT = 'UPDATE SPJ SET QTY = QTY + 10
                WHERE SN = ?
                AND   PN = ?'
```

A USING clause in the EXECUTE statement indicates the variables that are to take the places of the question marks. After the statement has been prepared as above, its EXECUTE statement would look like this:

```
EXEC SQL EXECUTE SQLBOUND USING :SN, :PN
END-EXEC.
```

The USING clause assigns its variables to the parameters in the order listed. The dynamic statement can execute any number of times with differing values for SN and PN without rebinding.

Dynamic SELECT Statements

There are two types of dynamic SELECT statements: fixed list and variable list. The first is used when you know when the program is written the number, types, and lengths of variables that are needed to receive returned values. This somewhat limits the usefulness of dynamic SQL. In that case, a COBOL programmer can declare INTO variables in the data division. Most of the other SQL statements, such as INSERT, UPDATE, and DELETE, which return only SQLCA feedback, not data, work quite well dynamically within COBOL or FORTRAN because there is no uncertainty about the data type and length of returned columns. SQL data definition and data control statements also work well within COBOL and other host languages.

If the information about the variables will be developed only as the program executes, a variable-list SELECT is needed. In this case, the program must be able to allocate storage for those variables dynamically. This is possible only with PL/1, Assembler C, and with COBOL programs calling subroutines in these languages. COBOL pointer and set constructs can be used. The IBM sample COBOL program DSN8BCU1 is a good example of how to allocate storage and DSN8BCU2 is the called program that does pointer manipulation. These programs are documented in the *Application Programming and SQL Guide* manual.

The SQL Descriptor Area

For the variable-list SELECT, DB2 provides the program the information it needs to allocate storage through the SQL descriptor area (SQLDA), a data structure similar to the SQLCA in that both communicate information between DB2 and host-language programs. The SQLDA receives a description of the value to be returned from the SELECT statement in the program. DB2 interrogates the catalog tables for the information describing the columns returned by the SELECT and passes that information back to the program. A number of statements are needed to carry out those functions.

The variables for the dynamic SELECT statement are declared just as they would be for non-SELECT statements. The PREPARE statement that invokes the bind process is the same. (The statement to be prepared is restricted, however, in that even if a single value might be returned, the select must use a cursor rather than a SELECT ... INTO clause. Consequently the PREPARE statement does not work with a dynamic SELECT statement that includes INTO.)

An INCLUDE statement, INCLUDE SQLDA, which is similar in syntax to INCLUDE SQLCA, is required to bring the SQLDA structure into the program. The DESCRIBE statement, is needed to bring the descriptions of the variables the SELECT will return into the SQLDA. A PL/1 DESCRIBE statement looks like this:

```
EXEC SQL DESCRIBE SQLBOUND INTO SQLDA;
```

DESCRIBE INPUT provides for having a DB2 server to describe the input parameter data into an SQLDA (V5 APAR PQ24584). This improves performance for DRDA and Open Database Connectivity (ODBC) applications by avoiding the expense of additional catalog queries and network messages.

Declaring the Cursor

The dynamic SELECT statement also requires a cursor. Instead of including the actual SELECT statement in the cursor declaration as would be done with static SQL, the declaration here refers to the variable referencing the statement's plan--for example:

```
EXEC SQL DECLARE SCURSOR FOR SQLBOUND;
```

It also requires OPEN and FETCH statements. The OPEN statement is the same as in static SQL, but the FETCH statement is slightly different. Instead of using an INTO clause to fetch values into specified host-language variables, FETCH here employs a USING DESCRIPTOR clause, which indicates the values are to be returned to variables identified in the SQLDA--for example:

```
EXEC SQL OPEN SCURSOR;
      DO WHILE ...
            EXEC SQL FETCH SCURSOR USING
DESCRIPTOR SQLDA;
      END;
EXEC SQL CLOSE SCURSOR;
```

Costs of Dynamic SQL

Dynamic SQL is a sophisticated feature of DB2 and can be valuable when required. When performance is an issue, however, use dynamic SQL with care. EXECUTE IMMEDIATE requires that DB2 bind a plan each time it executes a statement dynamically. A prepared statement can be executed repeatedly with only one PREPARE. Indeed, we will see how a prepared statement can be cached to avoid repeated prepares. However, if a dynamic SQL is prepared frequently, I/O to the catalog and CPU costs for access path selection are increased. These costs can be significant and are not likely to be acceptable if a high transaction rate is required. A method for reducing I/O to the catalog tables is discussed in Chapter OP regarding reoptimization which like dynamic SQL requires that the access path be chosen at run time.

Caching of Dynamic SQL

The frequency of PREPARE executions can be reduced by caching the dynamic statements in the EDM pool. Statements cached in the EDM pool can be shared among different threads, plans, and packages. The plans and packages are retained past a commit point. They are not shared with other members of a data sharing group because each member has its own EDM pool.

The caching of dynamic SQL is a good choice if the exact same dynamic statement is executed repeatedly. This is particularly useful for client/server applications and tools that use dynamic SQL. It applies to DRDA, not the private protocol.

If an SQL statement is executed repeatedly, a prepare need not be executed for each execution of the statement. A statement can be prepared, executed, and a commit work can be issued. The statement can be executed again repeatedly without doing another prepare if the statement is found in the cache. The second execution of a dynamic statement costs only about 1.2 percent more in CPU time compared to static SQL. The details of the tests results are in *DB2 for OS/390 Version 5 Performance Topics,* SG24-2213.

The prepared statement and the statement string are saved. If a statement with literals is prepared again, it must be identical to the initially prepared statement to take advantage of the cache. An exception is that leading and trailing blanks are ignored. The following two SELECT statements are not identical. Notice that the second statement has two blanks after "SELECT SN," rather than one blank as in the first statement.

```
'SELECT SN, SNAME FROM S WHERE STATUS = 30';

'SELECT SN,  SNAME FROM S WHERE STATUS = 40';
```

Caching of prepared statements is of no values when using QMF, SPUFI, DSNTEP2, or any interactive tool where users do not execute exactly the same statement with the same literals repeatedly.

The sharing of cached statements requires the same bind authority, bind parameter values for DYNAMICRULES, CURRENTDATA, ISOLATION, SQLRULES, QUALIFIER, and special register values for CURRENT DEGREE and CURRENT RULES.

The execution of the RUNSTATS utility (with all UPDATE options including NONE) causes all cached statements referencing tables and indexes for which statistics were collected to be reprepared when next executed (V5 APAR PQ17905). This allows for access path selection based on new statistics and newly created indexes when the statement is next executed.

Caching of dynamic SQL requires that it be enabled on the DSNTIP4 installation panel by specifying CACHE DYNAMIC SQL of YES. This is not the default. You must make a choice between caching dynamic SQL and reoptimization. The default of NOREOPT(VARS) is required when caching dynamic SQL. This is because the value of parameter markers and special registers used in the WHERE clause are not available when the PREPARE is executed. Therefore, reoptimization and the use of the cache are mutually exclusive. The purpose of the cache is to avoid bind processing including access path selection. The purpose of reoptimization is to determine a good access path for values requested by users.

If you want to reoptimize dynamic SQL that uses parameter markers and special registers at run time and not use the cache, it is necessary to specify the bind parameters REOPT(VARS) and DEFER(PREPARE). REOPT(VARS) does not increase the costs of binding dynamic SQL. DEFER(PREPARE) means that prepare processing is postponed until OPEN, EXECUTE, or DESCRIBE. This allows the optimizer to see the content of parameter markers and special registers for access path selection. Do check the SQLCODE after an OPEN as would be checked after a PREPARE. DEFER(PREPARE) also has the advantage that it reduces network traffic in a client/server environment.

KEEPDYNAMIC(YES): The use of the bind and rebind parameter KEEPDYNAMIC(YES) (not the default) means that a PREPARE need not be issued after a commit, reduces network traffic, and avoids the possibility that a dynamic statement might have to be reprepared because its space was reused by others in the EDM pool when using the cache. Figure PD.12 summarizes the processing with and without use of the cache. Notice that without the cache DB2 must issue an implicit prepare after a commit and with the cache DB2 uses the prepared statement in memory.

Figure PD.12. Processing with and without the cache

Processing	Without Cache	With Cache
PREPARE S1 FROM ... EXECUTE S1 COMMIT	Statement prepared and put in memory	Same
EXECUTE S1 COMMIT	No PREPARE issued. DB2 issues an implicit prepare. Do check SQLCODE for an unsuccessful prepare.	No PREPARE issued. DB2 uses the prepared statement in memory
EXECUTE S1 COMMIT	No PREPARE needed	Same

If a PREPARE is issued, the statement is prepared with and without the use of the cache. This means that you should not code more than one PREPARE for the same SQL statement. Indeed, it is necessary to remove multiple PREPARE statements from existing programs to avoid multiple prepares. If CURSOR WITH HOLD is used, the prepared statement is retained past a commit with and without use of the cache and KEEPDYNAMIC(YES).

KEEPDYNAMIC(YES) results in local and global copies of statements with and without the use of the cache.

Local copies of the prepared statement and statement string are retained in DBSA address space working storage with and without the cache. A global copy of a prepared statement is retained in the EDM pool when using the cache.

If the cache is used, local copies and the global copy are retained after a commit (local copy of prepared statement is made as in use). An OPEN, EXECUTE, or DESCRIBE causes the local copy of the prepared statement to be used after validity checking. DROP, ALTER, or REVOKE statements executed on a dependent object make the local statement invalid. PREPARE causes the local prepared statement to be replaced. The local copy of a prepared statement is discarded when a PREPARE is issued for the same statement, application process ends, rollback, or a statement is marked invalid. The space is reused on a LRU basis.

If the cache is not used, the prepared statement is discarded after a commit, rollback, or PREPARE of an identical statement. OPEN, EXECUTE, DESCRIBE or PREPARE causes a prepare of the saved statement string which is referred to as an implicit prepare.

Cost of Using the Cache

Costs are increased somewhat when using the cache. It is necessary to locate the statement in the cache and, if it is not present because the space has been reused by another plan or package, prepare processing is required. Additional space is required in the EDM pool for the cache. One skeleton copy of a prepared statement is retained in EDM pool. It is advisable to size the EDM pool to avoid having to reread static plans and packages from the directory and to avoid having to repeatedly prepare dynamic statements. Data spaces can be used for the EDM pool similar to the use of data spaces for buffer pools discussed in Chapter CD when using the dynamic cache.

A hit ratio for cached dynamic SQL can be calculated similar to calculating a hit ratio for buffer pools. The required fields are in the IFCID (Instrumentation Facility Component ID) records 0002, 0003, and 0148 when using the statistics trace. The field QISEDSC contains the number of pages used for the cache, QISEDSG contains the number of cache search requests, and QISEDSI contains the number of times that a statement was placed in the cache because it was not found there. The hit ratio is calculated like:

```
Hit ratio = (QISEDSG - QISEDSI) / QISEDSG
```

If the hit ratio is low and identical dynamic statements are executed repeatedly, do increase EDM size to avoid rereading static statements from the directory and repreparing dynamic statements. If you are using KEEPDYNAMIC(YES), do increase the MAX KEPT DYN STMTS of 5000 (default if cache used) on the DSNTIPE panel. This results in a 9 MB cache (5000 * 1.8 KB (average prepared statement size)). If space for a cached statement is reused, a dependent object no longer exists, or privileges are revoked, an implicit PREPARE occurs.

User Privileges Required for Dynamic SQL

You will want to use the bind parameter DYNAMICRULES(BIND) (not the default) if the user is allowed to select and update data only through specific programs rather than through any interactive tool. If this parameter is used, the plan or package owner AUTHID privileges are used for all objects referenced in SQL as with static SQL. Also like static SQL, the QUALIFIER value is used for unqualified object names. You cannot use SET CURRENT SQLID and you cannot use dynamic GRANT, REVOKE, ALTER, CREATE, or DROP in a plan/package bound with DYNAMICRULES(BIND).

The default is DYNAMICRULES(RUN) which requires that you grant select privileges on tables to users who will execute the dynamic SQL. INSERT, UPDATE, and DELETE privileges must also be granted if the user is allowed to perform these operations on the data. If the privileges are granted, the users can perform the operations on data directly from tables using QMF, for example, which may violate your security policies. Unqualified object names are qualified by the value in the special register CURRENT SQLID.

Use of Dynamic SQL for Generalized Reporting

Dynamic SQL can be quite useful when used in the proper circumstances. For example, consider using dynamic SQL for generalized reporting programs. If users cannot narrow down the search conditions they use, there can be an excessive number of static SQL statements to code. For example, if there are 20 search conditions, the use of static SQL would require that over a million SELECT statements be developed! (The million estimate is calculated as $1,048,576 = 2^{20}$ possibilities.)

Some organizations take the "no dynamic SQL" rule as hard and fast. These organizations have fulfilled the generalized reporting tool requirement in many cases by using the BETWEEN predicate for the various search conditions as shown here:

```
SELECT SN, SNAME, STATUS, CITY
FROM   S
WHERE  SN      BETWEEN :SN-LOW    AND :SN-HIGH
```

```
AND     SNAME   BETWEEN : SNAME-LOW   AND : SNAME-HIGH
AND     STATUS  BETWEEN : STATUS-LOW  AND : STATUS-HIGH
AND     CITY    BETWEEN : CITY-LOW    AND : CITY-HIGH
FOR FETCH ONLY;
```

All variables are initialized with the lowest or highest values for the column. You should consider using 'AAA' and 'ZZZ' or the lowest and highest possible values for the column when using literals. Do avoid initializing the low and high values with X'00' and X'FF' when using reoptimization. The values will be treated as if they are the same value by the optimizer because they are outside the range of A-Z, 0-9, and blank considered in filter factor calculations. This makes the use of indexes likely even though the use of indexes may not give the best access path.

The user is asked which values are required. If a user requests all suppliers in Dallas with a status >= 20, then 20 is moved to :STATUS-LOW and 32,767 is moved to STATUS-HIGH. Dallas is moved to both :CITY-LOW and :CITY-HIGH.

Disadvantage of the Approach: With a statically bound plan, the optimizer might choose multiples index access for the four BETWEENs or some other access path that is less than optimal. Indexes on SN and SNAME should not be used because all values qualify with the host variables initialized to low and high values. We do not want 25 percent of the SN and SNAME RIDs to be placed in the RID pool only to be discarded as discussed in Chapter PP.

If dynamic SQL is used, the developer can build a statement with only the needed predicates on columns specified by the user using the literals requested like:

```
SELECT SN, SNAME, STATUS, CITY
FROM    S
WHERE   STATUS >= 20
AND     CITY   = 'Dallas'
FOR FETCH ONLY;
```

The PREPARE of a simple dynamic SELECT requires about the same CPU time as applying one unnecessary predicate 10,000 times or two unnecessary predicates 5,000 times. In our example, if the S table contains 5,000 rows and the predicates on SN and SNAME are not specified, we can justify the CPU cost of dynamic SQL.

Programming Recommendation: Use static SQL for the few search conditions that are frequently required, such as those needed to fulfill weekly or daily report requests. Embedded dynamic SQL can be used to handle those conditions that are required infrequently. An alternative is the use of reoptimization.

Use of Reoptimization for Generalized Reporting

Reoptimization is an alternative for having the optimizer choose the access path at run as discussed in Chapter OP. It applies to static SQL as well as embedded dynamic SQL with parameter markers.

In one case, a company found that the following SELECT statement required 20 minute with multiple index processing. A much better access path was chosen when the bind parameter REOPT(VARS) was used resulting in only 10 seconds required to achieve the required results.

```
SELECT A.DOCUMENT_NO, A.PROCESS_DATE, B.DOCUMENT_SEQ_NO,
        B.RECORD_TYPE, A.BILL_TO_CD, A.SHIP_TO_CD, A.SORG_CD,
        A.PAYEE_NAME, B.PROGRAM_NO, B.PAY_AMT
FROM    TDNFDBA.SLDL_TPC_HEADER_T2 A, TDNFDBA.SLDL_TPC_DETAIL_T3 B
WHERE A.DOCUMENT_NO = B.DOCUMENT_NO
AND A.RECORD_TYPE    = B.RECORD_TYPE
AND A.PROCESS_DATE   = B.PROCESS_DATE
AND A.DOCUMENT_NO   BETWEEN :WS-DOC-NO-MIN AND :WS-DOC-NO-MAX
AND B.RECORD_TYPE   BETWEEN :WS-PMT-TYPE-MIN AND :WS-PMT-TYPE-MAX
AND A.SORG_CD       BETWEEN :WS-SORG-MIN AND :WS-SORG-MAX
AND A.BILL_TO_CD    BETWEEN :WS-BILL-TO-MIN AND :WS-BILL-TO-MAX
AND A.SHIP_TO_CD    BETWEEN :WS-SHIP-TO-MIN AND :WS-SHIP-TO-MAX
AND A.PAYEE_NAME    BETWEEN :WS-NAME-MIN AND :WS-NAME-MAX
AND A.SLS_REGION    BETWEEN :WS-REG-MIN AND :WS-REG-MAX
AND A.SLS_DISTRICT  BETWEEN :WS-DIS-MIN AND :WS-DIS-MAX
AND A.SLS_TERRITORY BETWEEN :WS-TER-MIN AND :WS-TER-MAX
AND B.PROGRAM_NO    BETWEEN :WS-PROG-MIN AND :WS-PROG-MAX
AND B.GRP_CD        BETWEEN :WS-GRP-MIN AND :WS-GRP-MAX
AND B.SUBGRP_CD     BETWEEN :WS-SUB-MIN AND :WS-SUB-MAX
AND A.PROCESS_DATE  BETWEEN :WS-PROC-DT1-MIN AND :WS-PROC-DT1-MAX
AND A.REFERENCE_NO  BETWEEN :WS-REF-NO-MIN AND :WS-REF-NO-MAX
AND B.INVOICE_NO    BETWEEN :WS-INV-NO-MIN AND :WS-INV-NO-MAX
AND B.SHIP_DATE     BETWEEN :WS-SHIP-DT1-MIN AND :WS-SHIP-DT1-MAX
AND A.SLSREP_CD     BETWEEN :WS-SREP-MIN AND :WS-SREP-MAX
AND A.PAY_AMT       BETWEEN :WS-PMT-AMT-MIN AND :WS-PMT-AMT-MAX
ORDER BY A.DOCUMENT_NO,A.PROCESS_DATE,B.RECORD_TYPE,
B.DOCUMENT_SEQ_NO;
```

PD.16 SUMMARY

DB2 provides for a number of ways to use SQL with a number of programming languages. The syntax for embedded SQL is virtually the same as the standard interactive SQL with the exception of CURSOR manipulation. Cursor repositioning can be a challenge particularly with a composite primary key. Several techniques for cursor management and testing for the existence of a value were discussed. Many factors need to be analyzed to determine which formulation of a request will give the best performance, thus the saying that "". The goal in this book is to give you information on what it depends upon.

EXERCISES

1. Assume that TEMP_F (temperature in Fahrenheit), TEMP_C (temperature in centigrade) are declared as distinct types. Will the following INSERT statement execute successfully? Why?

```
EXEC SQL
INSERT INTO WEATHER (DATE_W, TEMP_F, TEMP_C)
            VALUES (:DATE-W,:TEMP-F,:TEMP-C)
END-EXEC.
```

2. Under what conditions are all rows processed by DB2 when a cursor is opened or when the first row is fetched?

3. What guidelines should be used to determine the value for n in OPTIMIZE FOR n ROWS? Why?

4. What value should be used for n to inform the optimizer not to use list prefetch and sequential prefetch? What other types of processing are discouraged as well?

5. A program for reviewing the number of parts assigned to a given job periodically repeats rows the user has already seen. What is the problem? Provide a possible solution.

6. If n is specified as the number of rows in a table, will it encourage a tablespace scan?

7. What are the disadvantages of the each of the following techniques for cursor repositioning when using a composite index?

```
a)  SELECT  SN, PN, JN
    FROM    SPJ
    WHERE   SN >= 'S2' AND
            PN >= 'P3' AND
            JN >  'J3'
    ORDER BY SN, PN, JN
    OPTIMIZE FOR 12 ROWS;


b)  SELECT  SN, PN, JN
    FROM    SPJ
    WHERE  (SN  = 'S2' AND
            PN  = 'P3' AND
            JN  > 'J3') OR
           (SN  = 'S2' AND
            PN  > 'P3') OR
           (SN  > 'S2')
    ORDER BY SN, PN, JN
    OPTIMIZE FOR 12 ROWS;


c)  SELECT  SN, PN, JN
    FROM    SPJ
    WHERE NOT (SN  = 'S2'  AND
               PN  = 'P3'  AND
               JN <= 'J3') AND
          NOT (SN  = 'S2'  AND
               PN  < 'P3') AND
              (SN >= 'S2')
    ORDER BY SN, PN, JN
    OPTIMIZE FOR 12 ROWS;


d)  SELECT  SN, PN, JN, QTY
    FROM    SPJ
    WHERE   SN = :OLD-SN
    AND     PN = :OLD-PN
    AND     JN > :OLD-JN
    ORDER BY SN, PN, JN
    OPTIMIZE FOR 12 ROWS;
```

IF SQLCODE = 100, more rows needed to fill screen,
process cursor for next SELECT statement

```
    SELECT  SN, PN, JN, QTY
    FROM    SPJ
```

```
WHERE   SN = :OLD-SN
AND     PN > :OLD-PN
ORDER BY SN, PN, JN
OPTIMIZE FOR 12 ROWS;
```

IF SQLCODE = 100, more rows needed to fill screen,
  process cursor for next SELECT statement

```
SELECT SN, PN, JN, QTY
FROM    SPJ
WHERE   SN > :OLD-SN
ORDER BY SN, PN, JN
OPTIMIZE FOR 12 ROWS;
```

IF SQLCODE = 100,
  all qualifying rows have been fetched

```
e) SELECT SN, PN, JN
   FROM    SPJ
   WHERE   SN BETWEEN 'S2' AND :HIGH-VALUES
   AND     SN CONCAT PN CONCAT JN >
           :OLD-SN CONCAT :OLD-PN CONCAT :OLD-JN
   ORDER  BY SN, PN, JN
   OPTIMIZE FOR 12 ROWS;
```

8. Which of the cursor repositioning techniques in the previous question performs the best? Modify one of the statements so that it has the best performance and is easy to understand assuming a high cardinality on the first column of a composite index.

9. Develop a DECLARE, OPEN, FETCH, and pseudo code to retrieve the last five transactions from Fleur's checking account using a SENSITIVE STATIC cursor and INSENSITIVE fetch. Here is a sample SELECT statement:

```
SELECT TRANS_DATE, AMOUNT
FROM    CHECKING
WHERE   CUST_NAME = 'Fleur'
ORDER BY TRANS_DATE
```

10. Why does the FOR UPDATE OF clause increase the likelihood of lock contention?

11. How can the columns specified in the FOR UPDATE OF clause affect performance?

12. a) A CICS pseudo conversational transaction is to be written to add parts to jobs as requested by the user. The program has been written to display a screen requesting the information required including the SN, PN, JN, and the additional QTY of parts required. Is it advisable to use the following partial SQL?

b) Is the SQL useful for a batch program?

```
EXEC SQL DECLARE SPJCUR CURSOR FOR
         SELECT SN, PN, JN, QTY
         FROM    SPJ
         WHERE   SN = :SN
         AND     PN = :PN
         AND     JN = :JN
         FOR UPDATE OF QTY END-EXEC.


EXEC SQL UPDATE SPJ
         SET   QTY = :QTY
         WHERE CURRENT OF SPJCUR END-EXEC.
```

13. What are the disadvantages of selecting all columns defined into a 01 group level generated by DCLGEN, like:

```
EXEC SQL SELECT SN, S_SNAME, S_ADDRESS
         INTO   :S-DETAIL
         FROM    S_DETAIL
         WHERE  SN = :SN-IN END-EXEC.
```

14. Under what conditions is an index not used to locate a row to be updated or deleted?

15. Users require the ability to scroll backwards through returned data. a) What questions should you ask users to clarify the requirement?

b) How do answers to those questions affect your decision about how to accomplish the task?

16. a) What is a user requirement that suggests the use of embedded dynamic SQL? b) What are two reasons for using embedded dynamic SQL

to satisfy the user requirement? c) How can the costs of using embedded dynamic SQL be reduced? d) Will the use of the dynamic cache be useful in reducing the costs to satisfy this user requirement?

ANSWERS

1. The following INSERT statement will execute successfully. The assignment of a host variables to distinct type columns with and INSERT and UPDATE statement does not require the use of a cast function.

```
EXEC SQL
INSERT INTO WEATHER (DATE_W, TEMP_F, TEMP_C)
            VALUES (:DATE-W,:TEMP-F,:TEMP-C)
END-EXEC.
```

2. If a sort is required, all rows must be processed and sorted when the cursor is opened. (An index can be used to avoid processing and sorting all rows when the cursor is opened.) All qualifying rows for an inner select (second or later SELECT) of a subselect must be retrieved before the outer select (first SELECT) can be processed. Materialization may be required for some views and nested table expressions when the first FETCH statement is executed. Materialization is discussed in the ST Chapter.

3. It is best to estimate the number of rows to be fetched and use the value for n in OPTIMIZE FOR n ROWS. For an online transaction, this is usually the number of rows necessary to fill a screen. The optimizer has been enhanced in every release of DB2 and will probably be enhanced in subsequent releases of DB2. If n is specified as your best estimate of the number of rows to be fetched, the optimizer is able to estimate the best access path in the current release and in future releases of DB2.

4. OPTIMIZE FOR 1 ROW informs the optimizer not to use list prefetch and sequential prefetch when selecting from a single table. This also discourages prefetch with multiple table access, multiple index access, merge and hybrid join, and parallel processing. OPTIMIZE FOR 1 ROW should be used only if the required performance is not achieved by estimating the actual number of rows to be fetched.

5. The application is using a cursor to present the rows. When a COMMIT executes, the cursor is closed. When it reopens, it SELECTS the original set

of rows and resumes processing at the beginning. The program can track the cursor's progress through the set and adjust the cursor statement to accommodate it when the cursor is reopened.

6. If *n* is specified as the number of rows in a table, it will <u>not</u> encourage a tablespace scan. The optimizer estimates the number of rows that will qualify. If *n* is greater than the number estimated by the optimizer, the value is ignored.

7. a) Rows that should be processed can be missed. For example, a row with J1 or P1 will be missed further down in the table.

b) The technique cannot use a matching index scan because of the OR predicates on multiple columns in a composite index. Rows can be missed if a matching index scan is used.

c) If there is a low cardinality on the first column of the composite index, many index pages will be scanned. The technique can use a matching index scan on only the first column.

d) This technique requires that more host language code be developed and tested.

e) A matching index scan cannot be used since concatenation is evaluated at stage 2. The BETWEEN predicate allows for a matching index scan on 1 column. However, like technique c) if there is a low cardinality on the first column of the composite index, many index pages will be scanned. In addition, each value must be passed to RDS (Relational Data System) for stage 2 processing.

8. The technique that performs the best is d), in which there are the same number of SELECT statements as there are columns in the composite index. (You need only develop a SELECT statement for each of the leading columns in the composite index that have a low cardinality.) It provides for a matching index scan on the maximum number of columns possible.

Statement b) can be modified so that a matching index scan can be done on the first column of the composite index like the following statement. It is easier to understand than the NOT formulation which can also use a matching index scan on the first column.

```
SELECT  SN,  PN,  JN
FROM    SPJ
WHERE   SN >=  'S2'  AND
        ((SN  =  'S2'  AND
         PN   =  'P3'  AND
         JN   >  'J3')  OR
        (SN   =  'S2'  AND
         PN   >  'P3')  OR
        (SN   >  'S2'))
```

9. Following is a DECLARE, OPEN, FETCH, and pseudo code to retrieve the last five transactions from Fleur's checking account using a SENSITIVE STATIC cursor and INSENSITIVE fetch. Here is a sample SELECT statement:

```
EXEC SQL
        DECLARE CHECKACC CURSOR
        SENSITIVE STATIC SCROLL FOR
        SELECT TRANS_DATE, AMOUNT
        FROM    CHECKING
        WHERE   CUST_NAME = 'Fleur'
        ORDER BY TRANS_DATE END-EXEC.

EXEC SQL OPEN CHECKACC END-EXEC.

EXEC SQL
        FETCH INSENSITIVE ABSOLUTE-6
        FROM    CHECKACC INTO :TRANS_DATE,  :AMOUNT
END-EXEC.

        DO I = 1 TO 5
           FETCH NEXT FROM CHECKACC INTO :TRANS_DATE,
:AMOUNT
              --Required processing
        END

EXEC SQL CLOSE CHECKACC END-EXEC.
```

10. Locks are held on each row or page updated until the cursor is closed. This holds true even if the package or plan is bound with cursor stability.

11. An index on columns specified in the FOR UPDATE OF clause that is specified in the SET clause of the UPDATE statement is not used to locate rows depending on the predicate and if list prefetch is used. This is because rows can be missed or a looping condition can occur.

12. a) It is not necessary to select the row before an update is issued. In addition, locks taken for the FOR UPDATE OF clause are not held after the screen is displayed.

b) The FOR UPDATE OF clause on the SELECT statement and WHERE CURRENT OF avoids a separate getpage or physical I/O for the SELECT and UPDATE statement for a batch program.

13. Often, all columns are not required. More CPU time is required for selecting more columns than are required. The likelihood of having to modify a program is increased if a column data type or length needs to be changed, a column is added, or a column is deleted. Performance and data independence are improved by selecting only the columns required by the program. Performance is improved by reducing the number of columns to be passed from DM to RDS and to the host program by selecting only the required columns. This reduces CPU time since the path length is reduced. A sort requires more resources to sort a longer row than necessary.

14. An index cannot be used to locate a row to be updated if there is a range predicate specified on the column to be updated and list prefetch is not chosen as part of the access path. An index cannot be used on a column in a predicate specified in a view that includes a WITH CHECK OPTION clause. An index cannot be used on a column with an arithmetic expression in the WHERE or SET clause of an UPDATE statement. An index can be used to locate a row to be deleted without any restrictions. The clustering index is used to determine where to insert a row.

15. a) Consider asking the user how many screens they will look back at, how often they tend to scroll backward, and whether they plan to update the rows when they scroll backward.

b) The number of screens that the user will look at a second time will determine the number of primary keys (one for each screen) that must be saved for reposition processing. If you decide to use a temporary work area, it will allow you to determine the number of rows that will be placed in the temporary work area and to calculate the amount of space required. If they seldom plan to scroll backward, it is very costly to fetch and save all rows for all screens compared to saving only one primary key for each screen. If the user plans to update rows on the screen when they scroll backward, it is necessary to use one of the alternatives discussed to insure that a row has not changed since it was displayed and before the update is issued.

16. a) A user requirement that suggests the use of embedded dynamic SQL is where the user needs to request information based on a large number of conditions.

b) One reason is that it is impractical to develop static SQL for each combination of conditions. The second reason is that the multiple BETWEEN conditions required to use static SQL are likely to result in a poor access path.

c) The costs of using embedded dynamic SQL can be reduced by developing static SQL for the frequent combination of conditions requested by most users and use dynamic SQL for the infrequently requested combination of conditions.

d) The dynamic cache is not useful in reducing costs to satisfy this user requirement. This is because it is unlikely that the user will request exactly the same combination of conditions with the same value frequently enough for the dynamic statement to be reused in the cache.

FIGURES

Batch Processing

BP.1 INTRODUCTION

The task of applying hundreds of thousands of updates, inserts, and deletes to a multimillion row table represents a challenging, though not uncommon, programming problem. Seductively easy, and apparently reasonable, approaches can be extremely expensive. We will use a real-world case, altered to use the SPJ example tables, to explore some mass update techniques and their implications.

BP.2 ALTERNATIVES FOR BATCH PROCESSING

The production table, SPJ_PROD, has 6 million rows. Periodically it receives about 500,000 updates from the identically structured SPJ_UPDATE table. Typically, the updates would be in a sequential file. The alternatives apply when the updates are in a sequential file in most cases. If there is a match on the two tables' primary key columns, the SN, PN, and JN, QTY in the SPJ_PROD table's row is updated with the QTY value from the SPJ_UPDATE row. If there is no match, the SPJ_UPDATE row is inserted into SPJ_PROD.

Alternative 1: Matching Index Scan

One approach is to use a cursor statement without a predicate to select the entire SPJ_UPDATE table. Using a programming loop, each primary key value fetched from that cursor is then used in a SELECT statement to search for a match in the SPJ_PROD table.

♦   If a match is found, a separate statement updates the row.

♦   If there is no match--which is indicated when the select from SPJ_PROD returns an SQLCODE of 100--another statement inserts the row into the SPJ_PROD table.

This approach seems reasonable, but when it was tried, processing lasted more than *24 hours* before the developer gave up and canceled the job.

This approach can be improved upon slightly by using a cursor and a FOR UPDATE OF clause with the SELECT statement searching the SPJ_PROD table. That would avoid having to find each row being updated twice--once to look for the match and once for the update. But, in light of the more than 24-hour processing for the initial approach, saving one search, even if it cut the work in half, would not be savings enough. Another approach is needed.

Alternative 2: Matching Index Scan Variation

This is similar to the first alternative in that it fetches each row from SPJ_UPDATE with a tablespace scan as was done in the previous example. However, it eliminates the initial SELECT from the SPJ_PROD and the use of the UPDATE with cursor. Instead this approach goes directly to an UPDATE statement on SPJ_PROD without a cursor. In this UPDATE statement, the search criteria specifies equalities on the primary key columns and the values from SPJ_UPDATE are presented by a cursor and programming loop:

```
EXEC SQL UPDATE SPJ_PROD
         SET QTY = :SPJ_UPDATE.QTY
         WHERE SPJ_PROD.SN = :SPJ-UPDATE.SN
         AND    SPJ_PROD.PN = :SPJ-UPDATE.PN
         AND    SPJ_PROD.JN = :SPJ-UPDATE.JN
END-EXEC.
```

If the statement returns an SQLCODE of +100, indicating no row with that primary key was found, the program inserts the row in SPJ_PROD. If inserts are in the majority, attempt the insert first rather than the update. If the program receives a -803 SQLCODE indicating a duplicate on the primary key, then issue the UPDATE.

DB2 can use an index on the primary key in SPJ_PROD to look for the update matches. But, even so, searches of the 6 million row table, with perhaps as many as 500,000 searches of a 3-level index, plus I/O to the data pages, could require considerable processing. This alternative might be appropriate if a small percent of rows would be updated.

Alternative 3: Dropping and Recreating Indexes

This approach deletes rows from the SPJ_PROD table that have primary key values matching those in SPJ_UPDATE. Then, all rows from the SPJ_UPDATE table are inserted into SPJ_PROD.

To make this process efficient, it was decided to first drop the unique and clustering indexes on SPJ_PROD. This forces a tablespace scan and avoids having to delete and insert values into the index. Then, create a unique index on the primary key in SPJ_UPDATE. By doing this, index-only access can be used to satisfy the delete subselect. The SQL statements are:

```
DELETE FROM SPJ_PROD
WHERE   SN CONCAT PN CONCAT JN IN
   (SELECT  SN CONCAT PN CONCAT JN
    FROM    SPJ_UPDATE);
```

and

```
INSERT INTO SPJ_PROD
   SELECT SN, PN, JN, QTY
   FROM    SPJ_UPDATE;
```

One of several drawbacks to this approach is that it is not possible to commit work periodically. If there is a failure, the processing must be started again at the beginning.

Because there was no index on the production table, rows were not inserted in clustering sequence. You must recreate the indexes and then reorganize the table. Another way is to do the following steps:

♦   Unload the table
♦   Sort the data set in clustering sequence
♦   Recreate the indexes
♦   Reload the table

Whichever approach you use, the plans and packages that were invalidated when the indexes were dropped must be rebound.

This approach to batch processing allowed the installation to process the mass update in 3 hours, as opposed to the more than 24 hours required using the initial method. It is possible to come up with dramatically better solutions if the clustering index can be placed on the primary key. (The application developers believed that the clustering index had to be on another column.)

Alternative 4: Match-Merge Processing

The idea behind match-merge processing is to use two cursor SELECT statements: one selecting from the table providing the update values, the other from the production table. The host language program compares the selected values and uses the matching values in an UPDATE statement. Because the rows can be returned by the two SELECTS in order, each table need be read only once using an index with a high cluster ratio (80 percent or better in most cases) to avoid a sort for the ORDER BY.

In the example, the cursors' two SELECT statements are:

```
SELECT  SN,  PN,  JN,  QTY
FROM    SPJ_PROD
ORDER BY SN,  PN,  JN;
```

and

```
SELECT  SN,  PN,  JN,  QTY
FROM    SPJ_UPDATE
ORDER BY SN,  PN,  JN;
```

The returned values are fetched into host language variables. Each set of values from the production table is compared against corresponding values from the update file. (The original case study had the input to the batch program in a table. Most often the input will be in a sequential file.) The first row from the production table is compared with the first record from the update file. If there is no match, the program inserts the row. If there is a match, it updates the row. The program continues processing each compared set of rows and records in this fashion. This approach is illustrated in Figure BP.1.

Figure BP.1. Match-merge processing

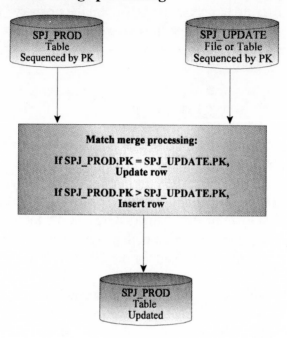

This approach does allow for periodic commit work statements, which avoids lengthy restart processing should the program fail.

Designing for Performance: Although this approach does require that all rows in the production be processed, it can be very efficient if more than 10-20 percent of the rows are to be processed. (We will see in Section BP.5 that the percentage may be even lower based on some I/O time estimates.) The key to obtaining the best performance from match-merge processing is to make it so that DB2 will be able to fetch pages in a sequential fashion. This allows DB2 to present the rows without having to do a costly sort, and it also means that it is likely to use *sequential prefetch* for I/O on the index and data pages, in which case it can bring 32 pages at a time into the buffer, rather than one page at a time. (One I/O is used to read 32 pages, assuming a buffer pool of 1,000 or more pages.)

To accomplish this goal, put a clustering index on the primary key in the production table and sort the update file in sequence on the primary key. Then, be sure to specify the primary key columns in the predicate. The ORDER BY clause in the SELECT statement insures that the rows are returned in order and increases the likelihood that the optimizer will choose to use the index to avoid a sort, assuming that there is a good cluster ratio on the primary key index.

To avoid processing a long series of rows in the production table that do not have a match in the update file, consider counting the number of rows with no match. If the count is greater than some number, 10,000 perhaps, close the cursor and reopen it when the primary key in the production table is greater than or equal to the primary key in the update file.

Alternative 5: Match-merge Variation Using Load

The match-merge processing described above is efficient, but it does require maintenance of the indexes on the table. Insert, update, and delete processing of indexes is almost always more costly than doing the same processing on the data. Figure BP.2 illustrates a process in which this index maintenance can be avoided.

Figure BP.2. Match-merge processing with updates and deletes

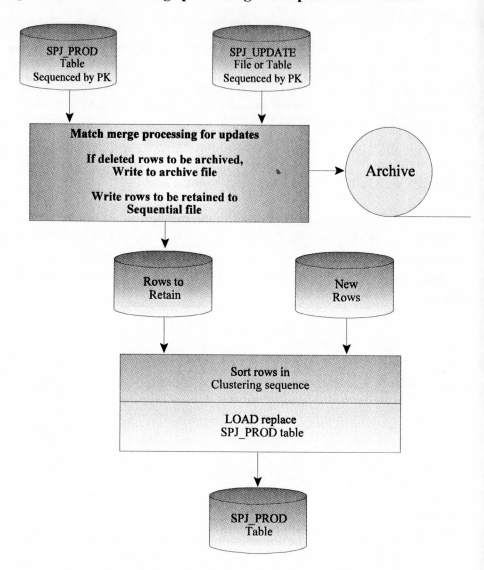

Here is an explanation of the processing in Figure BP.2.

1.   Have the production table and the update file sequenced by primary key, the same as described already for match-merge processing.

2.   Do match-merge processing similar to that described above, except use host-language code to update the required rows (not an SQL UPDATE statement) and write the changed rows, rows to be retained, and rows to be inserted from the SPJ_UPDATE file into a

sequential file (shown as "Rows to Retain" in Figure BP.2). If you are deleting rows and want to keep archives, either use SQL to write deleted rows to an archive table, or use host-language code to write to an archive sequential file. Do not insert, update, and delete the rows on the production table using SQL INSERT, UPDATE, and DELETE statements. This avoids index maintenance without having to drop the indexes and invalidate plans and packages that use the indexes.

3.   If the rows in "Rows to Retain" are not in sequence from the extract and update processing or the new rows to be inserted arrive in a separate file ("New Rows" in Figure BP.2), sort the rows in preparation for the load process.

4.   Use the LOAD utility to load and replace the data in the production table. If the production table is in a segmented tablespace you can use the mass delete algorithm to delete all rows from the production table and use LOAD RESUME. (The mass delete algorithm is discussed in Section BP.6.)

5.   Do not log the data as you load it. Instead, create a recovery point by making an image copy of the tablespace after it is loaded. If you are replacing the data, an inline copy can be made as the data is replaced in the tablespace.

Data is unavailable to other applications during the LOAD processing. However, if the table is in a partitioned tablespace, only the partition currently being loaded is unavailable.

BP.3 BENEFITS OF SEQUENTIAL PREFETCH

A tablespace scan is best at times due primarily to the efficiencies of sequential prefetch. Prefetch means that up to 32 pages can be read with a single I/O instruction. The average I/O time for each page read is 1.7 ms (milliseconds) compared to reading each page individually, which requires about 16 ms on a 3390 DASD device.

Sequential prefetch can be used for a tablespace scan and for a non-matching index scan when processing eight or more data or leaf pages. It can be used on the data and index pages after finding a starting position with a matching index scan if the cluster ratio is greater than 80 percent. Prefetch can be used for an update and delete when a cursor is not used. DB2 uses prefetch for its work tablespaces and the utilities use prefetch.

Sequential Detection

The benefits of sequential prefetch are so significant that it may be initiated during execution even if not requested by the optimizer. Sequential detection is used to initiate sequential prefetch at execution time if a number of data or index pages are being accessed in sequence. The thresholds for when prefetch can be activated and deactivated can change from one release to another. Currently, if 5 pages of the last 8 pages contain required values, forward prefetch is activated. If 5 pages of the last 8 pages do not contain required values, prefetch is deactivated. The algorithm is reversed for backward dynamic prefetch (V7). Dynamic prefetch can be repeatedly activated and deactivated for any cursor or non-cursor SQL statement. It can be of significant benefit in processing the inner table in joins and the use of EXISTS and NOT EXISTS subselects.

There are a few cases where sequential detection will not be used. It is not used for referential integrity processing of tables and indexes not explicitly named in the SQL statement. This suggests having an index on the foreign key that can be used in a matching index scan. Sequential detection can be used for update and delete processing if index only processing is shown in the plan table.

EXPLAIN provides information on the access path chosen by the optimizer by causing rows to be inserted into the PLAN_TABLE as discussed in Chapter EX. EXPLAIN does not show the use of prefetch as a result of sequential detection since it occurs at execution time. The developer can encourage the use of prefetch at bind time, which is shown when using EXPLAIN. The simplest technique for encouraging the use of prefetch is to not use a predicate. Obviously if a predicate is not coded, a tablespace scan is required and the optimizer will almost certainly specify the use of sequential prefetch. However, it is always best to narrow the search with predicates to minimize the number of rows that must be returned to the program. You can code a predicate and inform the optimizer not to use an index to satisfy the predicate by using "OR 0 = 1" in parenthesis with the predicate. For example, if you do not want to use an index on S.SN, code: (WHERE S.SN > 'S4' OR 0 = 1).

The use of ORDER BY on a column with a high cluster ratio index will encourage the use of sequential prefetch on the data and leaf pages as will the use of range predicates like BETWEEN, less than, and greater than. It is best to avoid repeated execution of a singleton select; rather use a cursor when retrieving more than one row in a program. Issue global update and delete statements without first selecting the rows. As was seen in the batch case study, it is best to process the rows in sequence, which means that the updates to be applied to a table should be sorted in the sequence of retrieval of the table.

Deferred Write

Deferred write is like sequential prefetch in that 32 pages are processed with a single I/O. As the name indicates, deferred write is used to write 32 changed pages to a tablespace or index with a single I/O. In addition, the page addresses are sorted so that pages can be written serially across DASD which minimizes seek time to write the pages. It is necessary to have sufficient space in the buffer pool and not exceed certain thresholds to take advantage of this efficient processing as discussed in Chapter CD. If you believe that deferred write is not being used because a batch job varies in elapsed time depending on the DB2 workload when the job is executed, for example, check with the system administrator or use a performance monitor to determine if your program is taking advantage of deferred write.

BP.4 I/O TIME ESTIMATES FOR INDEX USAGE VERSUS PREFETCH

To illustrate the possibly great reduction in elapsed time when using sequential prefetch over a matching index scan, we can use a formula to estimate how much I/O time is used in each case. Assume the following:

- 100,000 rows must be located at random in a one million row table with a three-level B-tree index
- 30,000 data pages with row lengths of 100 bytes
- 4,000 leaf pages for a 6-byte indexed column
- 16 ms per page for random read on 3390 DASD
- 1.7 ms per page for sequential prefetch on 3390 DASD

I/O Estimate for Matching Index Scan: We can assume 400,000 I/O operations (100,000 rows x (3-level B-tree +1 for data page)). The time can vary depending on whether any index pages remain in the buffer. Let's take the worst case first, and assume that no pages remain in the buffer pool. The I/O time is 1.78 hours, calculated as:

400,000 I/O x 16 ms / 1,000 for seconds / 60 for minutes / 60 for hours = 1.78 hours of I/O time.

If the root and nonleaf pages remain in the buffer, we can cut the number of I/O operations in half and come up with an estimate of 0.89 hours of I/O time. Index lookaside on leaf pages and sequential detection on index and data pages can reduce I/O time further, depending on the success of these techniques at run time.

Sequential Prefetch I/O Time Estimate: The estimates for this depend greatly on how well the data is clustered. Let's take two extreme cases:

Case 1: Assume that the data is clustered and processed in sequence. The 100,000 required rows are on 3,000 data pages and are referenced on 400 leaf pages. In other words, a fairly limited range of index leaf pages must be referenced. Perhaps only a range of supplier numbers between 20,000 and 80,000 must be updated. In this case, a matching index scan is used to position in the leaf and data pages. Then, sequential prefetch is used to scan across the required pages. In this scenario, we come up with an estimate of 0.10 *minutes* of I/O time (3,400 I/O x 1.7 ms / 1,000 for seconds / 60 for minutes).

Case 2: Assume that the data is not well-clustered; the rows to be processed are scattered on most data pages. In this case, DB2 must scan all leaf and data pages. In this scenario, we come up with an estimate of 0.96 minutes of I/O time (34,000 I/O x 1.7 ms / 1,000 for seconds / 60 for minutes).

Figure BP.3 is a handy table that uses the above formula to calculate I/O time for the matching index scans, guided tablespace scan (scan of required leaf and data pages), and a tablespace scan based on the percentage of rows read.

Figure BP.3. I/O time estimates for matching index scan vs. prefetch

Percent of Rows Read	Hours for MIS* Root & Non leaf Pages Remain in Buffer	Minutes for Sequential Prefetch	Minutes for Scan of All Leaf & Data Pages with Prefetch
0.01	0.0888888889	0.0096333	0.963333333
0.05	0.44444444444	0.04816667	0.963333333
0.10	0.88888888889	0.09633333	0.963333333
0.15	1.33333333333	0.1445	0.963333333
0.20	1.77777777778	0.192666667	0.963333333
0.25	2.22222222222	0.240833333	0.963333333
0.30	2.66666666667	0.289	0.963333333
0.35	3.11111111111	0.337166667	0.963333333
0.40	3.55555555556	0.385333333	0.963333333
0.45	4	0.4335	0.963333333
0.5	4.44444444444	0.481666667	0.963333333

*MIS = Matching Index Scan

The graphic representation of the I/O time estimate in Figure BP.4 shows the dramatic differences using the three methods. Indeed, the difference is even more dramatic than illustrated because the matching index scan processing is in hours while the two columns showing the prefetch I/O time are in minutes. The line representing the matching index scan goes up very quickly with the percentage of data processed. The line representing the prefetch I/O time for the various percentages of data and index pages processed goes up very slowly. The line representing the prefetch I/O time for processing all of the data is flat. It shows that a tablespace scan requires less I/O time than processing less than 10 percent of the data with a matching index scan and scanning a higher percentage of the data and index pages.

Figure BP.4. Graphic of I/O time estimates

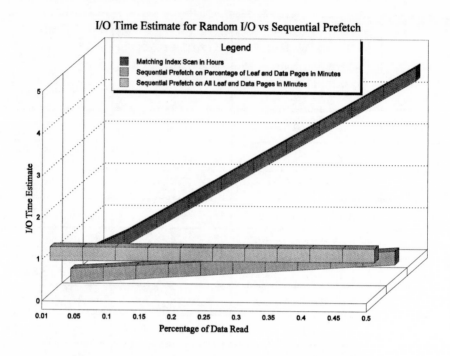

I/O Time Estimate for Random I/O vs Sequential Prefetch

Legend
- Matching Index Scan in Hours
- Sequential Prefetch on Percentage of Leaf and Data Pages in Minutes
- Sequential Prefetch on All Leaf and Data Pages in Minutes

Percentage of Data Read

BP.5 LOAD UTILITY VERSUS INSERT STATEMENTS

When large amounts of data must be inserted, the LOAD utility has advantages over application program INSERT statements. In one situation it saved 35 percent in CPU time and ran nine times faster. LOAD has significant advantages for improved performance and in other areas as well.

Logging: All data for inserts are written to the log. With the LOAD utility, you should specify LOG NO and have the utility take an inline copy as discussed in Chapter LC.

Preformatting: For insert processing, DB2 has to preformat ahead by writing out hex zeroes either 2 cylinders or tracks ahead. Preformatting is done asynchronously when 16 pages have been filled with rows (half of the deferred write threshold if the buffer pool has 1,000 or more pages) in V7. This avoids wait time when the last row within the preformatted pages is inserted. However, LOAD resume without SHRLEVEL CHANGE does not have to do this preformatting; free space at the bottom of the page is part of the deferred write processing. An alternative is the use of the PREFORMAT parameter discussed in Chapter LC.

Free Space for Future INSERTS: LOAD leaves the specified percent free for data and index pages, leaving room for future updates. INSERT does not.

Path length: The LOAD communicates directly with the data manager component of DB2. Insert processing must go through the application program interface and the relational data system before going to data manager. Also, LOAD does not have to check for broken pages as do INSERT and DELETE statements.

Compression: If you use data compression, LOAD builds the compression dictionary and compresses the data. Rows inserted into a newly created table that has never had rows is not compressed until a reorganization. This is because there is no dictionary. The LOAD and REORG utilities can create and refine the compression/decompression dictionary.

Index Builds: Perhaps the biggest contributor to application program elapsed time for INSERT statements are index values being inserted at random in most cases. As we recommended earlier, the data should be sorted in clustering index order before processing. (LOAD does not sort the data.) The data cannot also be sorted in sequence according to the non-clustering indexes. This means that non-clustering index leaf pages will be updated somewhat at random and the same leaf pages will have to be updated repeatedly to point to the rows.

Figure BP.5 is an example of how leaf pages for a non-clustering index must be processed repeatedly and somewhat at random. For example, assume we have an index on supplier city, which is not the clustering index. Record 1 is a row for Dallas and must be referenced on leaf page L3, record 2 is a row for Abilene and must be referenced on leaf page L1, record 3 is a row for Houston and must be referenced on leaf page L4, record 4 is a row for Chicago and must be referenced on leaf page L2, record 5 is a row for Atlanta and must be referenced on leaf page L1, etc. Notice that the leaf pages are not referenced in sequence. This can result in excessive DASD seek time. In addition, a leaf page must be processed multiple times.

Figure BP.5. Updates to leaf pages of a non-clustering index

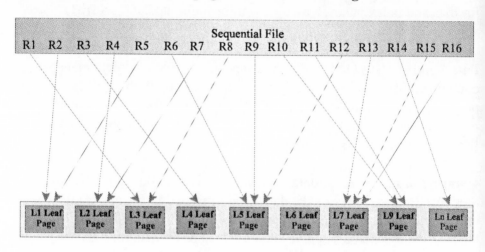

LOAD extracts the index values into a work file as it loads the data. It can then use an external sort facility such as DFSORT to sort non-clustering indexed values. By doing this, it can avoid skipping around the leaf pages, thus significantly reducing seek time. In addition, LOAD does not need to traverse the clustering index to determine where to insert each row.

If INSERT statements must be used, do sort the input rows in sequence on the clustering index. This avoids page splitting on the last leaf page of the clustering index provided nulls are not allowed on the indexed column. If PCTFREE and FREEPAGE are set to 0 as discussed in Chapter TS, data pages at the end of the tablespace are filled and written with deferred write. Deferred write requires only 0.4 to 2 ms per page depending on the DASD device used as discussed in Chapter OP. In addition, no I/O is required to read pages upon which to insert rows, getpages, synchronous I/O, and lock requests to search for free space to insert rows are avoided. This type of processing is used by the LOAD utility as well.

Adding rows to a table: If you were asked to write a program to insert about 2,000 rows into a quarter of a million row table, you would probably do so without concern for performance. Let's consider a test where one percent of 262,000 rows were added to a table with 2 indexes. LOAD RESUME with SHRLEVEL NONE required 43 elapsed seconds. INSERT statements required almost twice as long at 78 elapsed seconds. The test was repeated for adding five percent of 262,000 rows to the table. When adding about 13,000 rows, the difference is even greater with LOAD RESUME with SHRLEVEL NONE requiring 91 elapsed seconds and INSERT statements required 377 elapsed seconds. LOAD RESUME with SHRLEVEL NONE was over four times faster in this case. You will find that the larger the percentage of rows to be added to a table, the greater the savings with LOAD RESUME with SHRLEVEL NONE.

Consider using DB2 Estimator to estimate the costs of loading a large number of rows compared to using the INSERT statement for the same rows. Figure BP.6 summarizes estimates calculated by DB2 Estimator for DB2 V5. The first is an estimate for loading one million rows into a table with two indexes using an inline copy and the SORTKEYS parameter (discussed in Chapter LC). Use of the INSERT statement with the million rows using a subselect requires 10 times more CPU time than loading the rows and even more I/O and elapsed time. The last estimate is based on the costs of using the INSERT statement to insert one row multiplied by one million which is even more costly than using the subselect.

Figure BP.6. Comparison of LOAD and INSERT using DB2 Estimator V5

Description	CPU Min:Sec	I/O Min:Sec	Elapsed Min:Sec
LOAD with inline copy & SORTKEYS	2:26.06	1:25.77	2:26.06
INSERT with subselect of 1 million rows	22:46.40	44:32.24	57:35.74
1 INSERT * 1 million rows	33:33.00	133:33.00	133:33.00

Online Load Resume and Insert Comparison: RESUME YES with SHRLEVEL CHANGE causes the LOAD utility to add new rows using processing similar to an INSERT statement and activates triggers (V7). Chapter LC has details on how LOAD processing the data with the parameters. There are performance advantages over the use of INSERT statements because the utilities work directly with data manager. Figure BP.7 shows the savings in CPU and elapsed time using RESUME YES with SHRLEVEL CHANGE compared to INSERT statements.

Figure BP.7. Online load resume and insert comparison

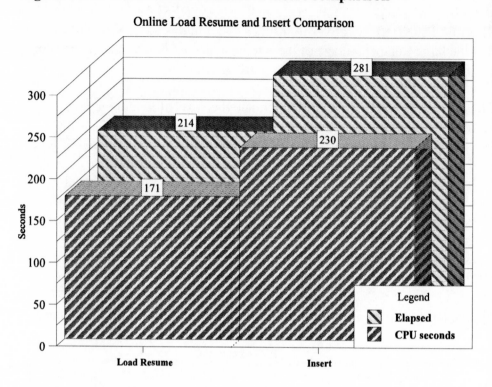

Why INSERT Statements Are Used Rather Than LOAD

Considering all the advantages of the LOAD utility, why consider using INSERT statements at all? One simple reality is that not everyone has the authority to use LOAD. Another reason is data availability. During LOAD processing, data is unavailable to other application programs except when using RESUME YES with SHRLEVEL CHANGE. If a tablespace is partitioned, it is possible to load only one partition at a time, thereby reducing the scope of the outage at any given time when using . When using INSERT, only the pages where rows are inserted are unavailable due to locks taken by DB2 until commit processing, assuming page level locking.

Another reason some people balk at using the LOAD utility is because the data must be validated. For example, perhaps only certain ranges or types of data can be loaded into the table. Consider validating the data and doing any updates or deletes that are required. Write the validated data into a separate file, sort it in clustering sequence and then use LOAD. Another option is to define table check constraints on the table. Those constraints can be enforced by the LOAD utility. Chapter CT has detailed information about check constraints. If triggers reference the table, a major disadvantage of using LOAD RESUME with SHRLEVEL NONE rather than INSERT is that triggers are not activated by the LOAD utility. This can be overcome by using LOAD RESUME with SHRLEVEL CHANGE (V7) in which case most of the advantages of LOAD are lost since the processing is very much like INSERT statements as discussed in Chapter LC. If seeing some but not all rows inserted within a business unit of recovery is not acceptable, do be cautious of using LOAD RESUME YES with SHRLEVEL CHANGE. This is because another program can see some but not all items ordered, for example.

Rows are inserted according to clustering index provided free space is available, a claim (no drain processing) is used. It is necessary to use LOG YES. However, performance is better than the use of INSERT statements.

If the table has an identity column, there are plans to use LOAD REPLACE, and the original sequential values are to be retained, consider defining the column with the GENERATED BY DEFAULT clause. If the table is defined with an identity column using GENERATED ALWAYS and existing values are to be retained, it is necessary to unload the data, drop the table, recreate the table with GENERATED BY DEFAULT (cannot change back to GENERATED ALWAYS), recreate indexes, and load the table.

Managing Repeated Access to Reference Tables

Many batch programs must access small reference tables to determine such things as whether a valid state has been keyed by a user or to determine if a city is serviced by a particular division. It can be quite costly to use SELECT statements to access these tables repeatedly. A SELECT statement must go through several layers of software through DB2 and back to the program with a cost of from about 20,000 to 40,000 instructions, depending on the specific statement executed.

One way to avoid this cost is to read each reference table into an array in the program. The program can search the array to validate data for each row processed. If you are using COBOL, a SEARCH ALL statement does a binary search of the array, or a SEARCH can be used for a sequential search. Although this technique requires development time and effort, it is well worth the savings that will result when the batch program is repeatedly executed.

BP.6 DELETING A LARGE NUMBER OF ROWS

The deletion of a large number of rows, whether it is a large percentage of the rows in a table or all rows in table, is a costly process. The primary cost is in the deletion of values from the indexes, particularly if there are several indexes on the table. Some alternatives for reducing the cost of index maintenance are discussed.

Deletion of a Large Percentage of Rows in a Table

The reorganization utility can be used to efficiently delete rows that meet specified conditions during the reorganization process (V5 APAR PQ19897). This is done by specifying the DISCARD parameter, the table from which to delete the rows, and conditions under which to delete them. Optionally, discarded rows can be written to a discard data set in an external format that can be read by an application program or loaded into an archival table, for example, if SHRLEVEL NONE OR REFERENCE (not CHANGE) is used. Details on this processing is in Chapter RR.

Advantages: REORG ... DISCARD has significant performance advantages over using the DELETE statement followed by a reorganization. It avoids having to delete reference to the discarded rows from one or more indexes. There is little or no increase in the cost of a reorganization when using the DISCARD parameter, particularly if the discarded rows are not written to a discard data set. Indeed, the costs of the reorganization may be reduced because fewer rows must be reorganized and referenced in one or more indexes that are rebuilt with a reorganization of a tablespace. Delete processing can be done with a scheduled reorganization. If reorganizations need to be scheduled more frequently to accommodate the delete processing, most SQL processing benefits from more frequent reorganizations.

The costs of logging the deleted rows is saved in comparison with using DELETE statements. This assumes that log of no is used with an inline copy or followed by an image copy with the reorganization. Also X and most S locks if using lock avoidance and latch processing are avoided when using the REORG utility.

Disadvantage: The use of REORG means that others cannot update data in the tablespace or partition during most of the reorganization processing which detracts from 24 hour availability of the data

If it is necessary to delete rows from only some partitions of a partitioned tablespace, then only those partitions are unavailable. Application programs can be designed for a limited partition scan or use of DB2 parallelism discussed in Chapter PL to allow processing of other partitions that are not being loaded.

Delete Many Rows without REORG ... DISCARD: If REORG ... DISCARD is not appropriate for the application, an alterative is available to reduce costs. The cost of index maintenance can be avoided when deleting a large percent of the rows in a table by selecting all the rows using a tablespace scan and writing the rows to be retained to a sequential file (not including the rows to be deleted). If the deleted rows need to be archived, they can be written to a separate file. Sort the rows to be retained in clustering sequence and use the LOAD utility with an inline copy to replace the data if there is one table in the tablespace. If there is more than one table in the tablespace, use the mass delete algorithm followed by a LOAD RESUME with SHRLEVEL NONE where possible.

There are a number of advantages to the procedure. It avoids index maintenance, logging of deleted rows, X locks on pages, most S locks if lock avoidance is used, and latch processing. In one case the technique reduced a 26 hour job to 15 minutes of CPU time when index maintenance on seven indexes was eliminated. It is not necessary to follow the procedure with a reorganization because the data is well organized after the processing described. This is an added cost savings because a batch update program frequently needs to be followed by a reorganization. The disadvantage of the procedure is that no one can update the data during most of the processing, which detracts from 24 hour availability of the data. If it is necessary to delete rows from only some partitions of a partitioned tablespace, then only those partitions are unavailable. Application programs can be designed for a limited partition scan or use of DB2 parallelism discussed in Chapter PL to allow processing of other partitions that are not being loaded.

Deletion of All Rows in a Table

Mass Delete Algorithm: The mass delete algorithm is very efficient in deleting all of the rows in a table. It accesses, updates, and logs only the space map pages of the data and indexes. It does not read and write the data and index pages to mark the rows and indexed values as being deleted as is necessary without using the mass delete algorithm. There are restrictions on when the mass delete algorithm can be used:

♦   The tablespace must be segmented.
♦   The table cannot be a parent table with dependent tables defined.
♦   The table cannot be created with a VALIDPROC and DATA CAPTURE CHANGES.
♦   The DELETE statement cannot reference a cursor and cannot have a WHERE clause.

If these restrictions are met, the following DELETE statement uses the mass delete algorithm to effectively and efficiently delete all of the rows and index entries in the SPJ table.

```
DELETE FROM SPJ;
```

There are a couple of disadvantages of the mass delete algorithm. If there are multiple tables in a tablespace, the space is not reusable for tables other than the one from which all the rows were deleted. The DROP TABLE statement is necessary to free space for use by other tables. The number of rows deleted is not recorded in the SQL communications area (SQLCA) discussed in Chapter PD. This means that the number of rows deleted cannot be reported by SPUFI, QMF, and other interactive tools.

If LOAD RESUME with SHRLEVEL NONE is used to place rows in the table after deleting the existing rows, there is a performance benefit. The LOAD utility does not have to format the existing pages.

Load Replace: An alternative is to LOAD REPLACE the table with a dummy or empty input file. It is particularly useful for a nonsegmented tablespaces and a parent table for which the mass delete algorithm does not work. However, it does place the parent table in check pending state if there are any dependent tables defined. Do be cautious about using LOAD REPLACE if there is more than one table in a tablespace. It will result in losing all tables in the tablespace since LOAD REPLACE deletes and defines the underlying VSAM data sets.

Optionally, the REUSE parameter can be added to the LOAD statement. It causes a logical reset of the data sets (V5 APAR PQ19077) which keeps the data sets at the same location on DASD. This eases the maintenance of data set placement on DASD and improves performance over deleting and redefining the data sets.

BP.7 RUNNING BATCH AND ONLINE CONCURRENTLY

When running batch programs concurrently with online transactions, it is important to take steps to ensure that online transaction performance does not suffer from the batch processing.

Adjusting Priorities

An obvious way to keep batch programs from taking resources from online transactions is to give the batch programs a lower priority. One caveat is to be careful to avoid lock contention; a low-priority batch program can hold onto its locks for a long time, locking out higher-priority transactions.

With z/OS or OS/390, it is possible to assign priority relative to a set of goals. A set of goals is a particular service class. Workload manager dynamically dispatches work relative to the service class of a particular application type, a particular application, and several other specifications.

If you do not have workload manager, or if you are not using goal mode yet, realize that the I/O of all programs has the dispatching priority of the database services address space. However, it is possible to adjust I/O priority separately for synchronous reads and writes and prefetch reads. Consider speaking to your system programmer about using z/OS or OS/390 I/O priority scheduling to set the I/O priority of the application's address space. For example, you can set the I/O priority of the CICS address space higher than that of batch. Chapter CD has an example of setting the I/O priority of the database services address space.

Commit Frequency

To avoid having a long-running batch job hold locks on data for long periods of time, the batch program must issue COMMIT statements periodically. Adjust the commit frequency to meet the required response time goals and to minimize lock contention. To determine how often to commit, you must know the maximum amount of time that is acceptable for an online transaction to wait for a lock to be released. We will use the test results discussed in Chapter CC and summarized in Figure BP.8 to analyze the number of pages locked and for what period of time depending on the commit frequency. If the commit frequency is every 10 updates, two pages are locked for about 0.10 seconds (90 seconds of elapsed time executing DB2 calls / 867 commits while updating 8,664 rows). The user will have to wait more than 0.10 seconds to access the two pages if other programs are attempting to process the locked pages and are queued to get locks, a long running SQL statement is executing, or the programs are doing other work while locks are held. If the user can wait more than 0.10 seconds plus the other factors for access to the data being processed by the batch program, consider a commit every 100 or 1,000 updates. If the user can wait 0.58 seconds plus the other factors, the batch program can commit every 1,000 updates and complete updating 8,664 rows in 5.19 seconds compared to committing after every update and requiring 686.20 seconds (Figure BP.8). Committing based on a specified time has the advantage that you know that the locks taken by the program are held no longer than the specified time. In general, consider committing every 0.5 to 1 second. These are only general guidelines based on one test. As always it is best to test a scenario that you are considering in your environment.

Figure BP.8. User wait time and commit frequency

Time User Can Wait for Locked Pages*	Number of Pages Locked	Commit Frequency	Time to Update 8664 rows*
0.08+	1	1	686.20
0.10+	2-10	10	90.21
0.22+	4-100	100	17.79
0.58+	28-1000	1000	5.19

*Elapsed time in seconds executing DB2 calls

A DB2 professional attending a course covering this material had a long running batch job that typically required 5.5 hours. He modified the program to commit every 20 seconds rather than after each unit of recovery before going home for the day. The next morning he reported to the class that the job ran for only 57 minutes. (He did not know how many update statements were in a unit of recovery.)

You would like to commit frequently to release locks and you would like to reduce the costs of executing batch programs. During heavy transaction usage, you will need to commit more frequently and during low activity you can commit less frequently to gain the performance benefits. Figure BP.9 is an example of an application table that can be used to specify time periods with heavy and low transaction usage and an appropriate commit frequency.

Figure BP.9. Commit frequency based on time of day

COMMIT_FREQUENCY

Start_Time	End_Time	Frequency
08.00.00	09.00.00	100
09.00.01	11.00.00	10
11.00.01	13.00.00	100
13.00.01	17.00.00	10
17.00.01	07.59.59	1000

Application programs can use the SET statement to determine the time that their batch program is executing by setting a host variable equal to the special register CURRENT_TIMESTAMP and optional do calculations (V6) as in the following example.

```
SET :CURRENT_TIMESTAMP = CURRENT_TIMESTAMP +
30 DAYS END-EXEC.
```

The SET statement can also be used to execute functions as in the following statement. The use of the VALUE ... INTO statement is an alternative for executing functions as discussed in Chapter UD.

Transaction rates are usually low on weekends. If this is the case in your environment and you want to lower the costs of your batch program execution, consider determining whether your program is executing on a weekend like (V6):

```
EXEC SQL SET :DAY-WEEK =
```

```
DAYOFWEEK(CURRENT DATE) END-EXEC.
```

DAYOFWEEK returns an integer in the range of 1 to 7, where the values of 1, 2, 3, 4, 5, 6, 7 represent Sunday, Monday, Tuesday, Wednesday, Thursday, Friday, Saturday.

It is necessary to use DAYOFWEEK in a SELECT statement from a one row table interactively as in the following example without the use of the formula.

A formula is needed prior to V6 for a host program as well as interactively.

```
SELECT DAYS(CURRENT DATE) -
   (DAYS(CURRENT DATE) -1) / 7 * 7
FROM    SYSIBM.SYSDUMMY1;
```

If the result is 1, it is Monday, if 2 it is Tuesday, if 3 it is Wednesday, and so forth. On weekends, consider committing after 1,000 updates.

You may also want to consider committing less often on holidays when your transaction rate is low. Figure BP.10 is an example holiday table that can be read to determine the commit frequency.

Figure BP.10. Commit frequency for holidays

COMMIT_FREQ_HOLIDAYS

Date	Holiday	Frequency
1992-01-01	New Years	1000
1992-04-19	Easter	1000
1992-12-25	Christmas	1000
Etc.		

Partition Processing to Fit in a Batch Window

If you have a small batch window where some of the data can be unavailable to transactions for a short period of time, consider partitioning the tablespace such that the batch processing can be done on a partition within the available time period. For example, if a batch job requires one hour and there is a five minute batch window available, consider twenty partitions such that each partition can be processed in three minutes. The additional two minutes that are available allow for overall variation in the workload of the computer. The time also allows for submitting multiple batch jobs, each of which operates on one partition and for the contention expected when multiple batch jobs execute concurrently. The batch program must be designed to process one partition. You may be able to take advantage of a limited partition scan and DB2 parallelism discussed in Chapter PL. Optionally, several jobs, each of which is designed to operate on one partition, can be submitted and executed in parallel.

Partitioning allows for executing most utilities on a single partition with other partitions available for select, insert, update, and delete processing. Partition independence is discussed in Chapter LC.

BP.8 DESIGNING RESTARTABLE BATCH PROGRAMS

Restarting a long-running batch update program presents challenges. A simple approach is to issue no commits during the processing. All updates are rolled back automatically if a failure occurs. However, this approach is generally not recommended. Even for a 15-minute run, it can take 15 minutes to apply the updates, 30 minutes to roll back, and another 15 minutes to apply the updates a second time. Even worse, during most of this time some, perhaps many, of the pages would have exclusive locks, excluding all other access. Consequently, to avoid the possibility of lengthy rollbacks and holding locks, the batch program should commit work periodically.

We will describe three techniques to allow for commits, one in which restart logic is coded in the program and two in which data is simply copied before processing begins. Note that if a program relies on copies of the data, it must issue a LOCK TABLE statement before it can begin processing. This locks out other updaters, whose updates would be lost if the image copies were restored.

Alternative 1: Restart Logic

When commit works are issued, the program must be able to determine where to resume processing after a failure. The technique for coding this logic is similar to that for reopening a cursor described in Chapter CC. The primary key value of the last row processed before the commit is saved and is used to reestablish position when processing resumes. It is not enough for that key value to be saved in the program because it will be lost in the failure when the program abends. However, if that key value is saved in another table, a control table, with the update of that table committed along with the processing on the primary data tables, the value is always available to the program when it restarts. This control table contains the last primary key value, control information, intermediate results, and perhaps the commit frequency for future modification if commits need to be more or less frequent.

The restarted program must read the control table to reestablish position and continue processing. (CURSOR WITH HOLD does not hold position after a program has abended.) Recall that ORDER BY is required to avoid missing rows, and an index can be used to avoid a sort as discussed in Chapter PD. If the input to the update program is on a GSAM file and IMS extended restart is available, it can be used on the input and output files but cannot be used on the DB2 table to re-establish position when the program is restarted.

The development of a generalized application restart program is non-trivial. There are several software companies that sell restart packages. Consider estimating the time it would take to develop a generalized restart program and compare that to the cost of buying one.

Alternative 2: Image Copy

A technique used to avoid developing complex restart logic in a program and to allow for periodic commits is to take an image copy of the tablespaces before submitting the batch job. If the job fails, recover the tablespaces, recover or rebuild indexes, to the image copies and re-run the batch job.

Disadvantage: When using referential integrity, dependent tablespaces will have check pending set on. This can be avoided by quiescing all the related tables to an RBA (relative byte address) point and recovering to the RBA as will be discussed in Chapter CR. Both techniques require that all indexes on all tables must be rebuilt.

Alternative 3: DSN1COPY

Use DSN1COPY, a standalone utility discussed in Chapter CR, to copy all the tablespaces to be updated along with all indexes to sequential files. Then, if a failure occurs, use DSN1COPY again to copy the sequential files back to the tablespaces and indexes and rerun the batch job. This alternative avoids having to rebuild the indexes.

BP.9 EXECUTING BATCH PROGRAMS

Three alternatives are described here: the DSNTEP2 sample program shipped with DB2, TSO TMP, and the call attachment facility.

DSNTEP2 Sample Program

DSNTEP2 is a sample PL/1 program that reads SQL statements and executes them dynamically. It is provided in source form only prior to V6, so you need a PL/1 compiler and run-time library or Language Environment to use it. It is provided in object form in member DSNTEP2L with a DBRM member of DSN@EP2l (V6). DSNTIAD is similar to DSNTEP2, except it is written in Assembler and cannot execute SELECT statements.

DSNTEP2 allows up to 10 errors (MAXERRORS) after which it terminates with a return code of 8. It does not issue a rollback; unlike SPUFI which issues a rollback to the last commit point in such a situation.

Figure BP.11 contains example JCL for executing DSNTEP2. It contains the SQL embedded in the JCL. Usually you will want the SYSIN DD statement to reference a file or PDS member that contains the SQL. It is often referred to as batch SPUFI because people frequently test interactively with SPUFI and use DSNTEP2 to execute the SQL in batch.

Figure BP.11. JCL to execute DSNTEP2

```
//SUPDATE    JOB ... USER=AUTHID
//TERM       EXEC PGM=IKJEFT1B,DYNAMNBR=30
//SYSIN      DD
SELECT * FROM S;
SELECT * FROM P;
/*
//SYSTSIN    DD   *
TIME
DSN SYSTEM(DSN)
RUN PROGRAM(DSNTEP2) PLAN(DSNTEP2)  -
    LIBRARY('PROJ.AUTHID.LOAD')      -
END
TIME
/*
//
```

Functional comments can be provided in SYSIN (V6 APAR PQ24360). You can specify the maximum number of rows to return for each subsequent SELECT statement (-1 indicates that all rows are fetched).

```
--#SET ROWS_FETCH 250
```

You can specify the maximum number of rows to output for each subsequent SELECT statement (-1 indicates that all rows are output).

```
--#SET ROWS_OUT 250
```

You can change to/from different terminator characters. This is particularly useful when creating complex triggers as discussed in Chapter TR. The following functional comments sets the statement terminator to '#'.

```
--#SET TERMINATOR #
```

TSO Terminal Monitor Program

The TSO terminal monitor program (TMP) executes statements as if they were keyed from TSO. It is frequently used to execute batch programs. Figure BP.12 contains sample JCL to execute the TMP which has the name IKJEFT01. The TMP executes statements as if they were keyed interactively using TSO. The DSN710.SDSNLOAD library is the default and is frequently changed to, for example, SYS1.DSN710.SDSNLOAD when the DB2 subsystem is installed. You will need to determine the name given at your installation. All commands like RUN can be executed from the DSN processor. Do change DSN SYSTEM(DSN) to the name given to the DB2 subsystem when it is installed, for example, DSN SYSTEM(DB2T) or DSN SYSTEM(DB2P).

Figure BP.12. JCL to execute a batch program using TSO TMP

```
//SUPDATE    JOB ... USER=AUTHID
//*
//STEP1      EXEC PGM=IKJEFT01,DYNAMNBR=30
//STEPLIB    DD   DSN=DSN710.SDSNLOAD,DISP=SHR
//SYSPRINT   DD   SYSOUT=A
//SYSTSPRT   DD   SYSOUT=A
//SYSUDUMP   DD   SYSOUT=A
//SYSOUT     DD   SYSOUT=A
//REPORT     DD   SYSOUT=A
//PARMIN     DD   DSN=PARMIN.FILE
//*
//SYSTSIN    DD   *
TIME
DSN SYSTEM(DSN)
RUN PROGRAM(SUPDATE) PLAN(SUPDATE)  -
    LIBRARY('PROJ.AUTHID.LOAD')      -
    PARMS ('/VALUE1 VALUE2 VALUE3')
END
TIME
/*
```

The TSO TIME command is executed before and after the SUPDATE program in the example. The purpose is to get a rough estimate of the CPU and elapsed times required by the batch program by subtracting the time values.

Alternate TSO Entry Points: TSO provides two alternate entry points, IKJEFT1A and IKJEFT1B, which have some advantages over IKJEFT01. When using either of these entry points, TSO does not intercept errors from a program abend. They also allow the JCL return codes (CODE= parameter) to be passed to the next job step. They act more like a standard z/OS or

OS/390 batch program in the disposition of data sets after a program abend and in the content of a dump after a system or application-initiated abend.

Disposition of Data Sets: You specify the disposition of a data set after a program has abended by coding the DISP parameter on a DD statement. If the disposition parameter is coded as DISP=(NEW,CATLG,DELETE), the data set is deleted if the program abended in a standard z/OS or OS/390 batch. However, if IKJEFT01 is used to execute a batch program, the data set is cataloged--the middle parameter is used. If IKJEFT1A is used, the data set is cataloged if there is an application abend--a COBOL call to ILBOABN0, a PL/I call to PLIDUMP with the S option, or an assembler ABEND macro is executed. The use of the IKJEFT1B entry point results in the same disposition of the data set as standard z/OS or OS/390 (Figure BP.13). If there is a system abend as a result, of say, a data exception (0C7), the data set will be deleted as indicated in the third parameter. The dump content and abend code passed to the next step in the job vary, depending upon the entry point used as summarized in Figure BP.14. Again IKJEFT1B more closely resembles standard z/OS or OS/390 batch. In addition, parameters cannot be passed on a JOB or STEP statement to a program using TMP. It is necessary to pass them through the use of a CLIST. For these reasons, CAF or RRSAF is some times used to execute batch programs. A sample CAF assembler program is in SDSNSAMP(DSN8CA).

Figure BP.13. Data set disposition, depending upon the environment

Assume DISP=(NEW,CATLG,DELETE) on DD statement

Program abend	z/OS or OS/390	IKJEFT1B	IKJEFT1A	IKJEFT01
System abend	DELETE	DELETE	DELETE	CATLG
Appl. abend	DELETE	DELETE	CATLG	CATLG

Figure BP.14. Dump content and abend code, depending upon the environment

Program abend	z/OS or OS/390	IKJEFT1B	IKJEFT1A	IKJEFT01
System abend	Appl.	Appl.	Appl.	TSO
Abend code	As is	04C	04C	Not pass
Appl. abend	Appl.	Appl.	TSO	TSO
Abend code	As is	As is	Not pass	Not pass

Passing Parameters Using TSO TMP: Job step PARM values cannot be passed using DSN. You can use a CLIST to do this, however. Figure BP.15 is an example of a CLIST, AUTHID.TSO.CLIST(EXPARM).

Figure BP.15. CLIST used to pass parameters

```
PROC 0 SUBSYS(DB2P)  PARM(DEFAULT)
DSN SYSTEM(&SUBSYS)
RUN PROGRAM(UPDATE)  PLAN(SUPDATE)  PARM('&PARM') -
    LIBRARY('PROJ.AUTHID.LOAD')
SET &SAVECC = &LASTCC
DATA
END
ENDDATA
/*
```

When you execute the batch program, use JCL like that shown in Figure BP.16. It shows the batch program passing a parameter value and a new subsystem identifier to the CLIST. The alternative to this approach is to pass parameters on the RUN statement, which might not conform to batch standards.

Figure BP.16. JCL using CLIST to pass parameters

```
//STEP2      EXEC  PGM=IKJEFT1B,
//                 PARM='%EXPARM SUBSYS(DB2T) PARM(value)'
//SYSTSPRT   DD    SYSOUT=*
//SYSPROC    DD    DISP=SHARE,DSN=AUTHID.TSO.CLIST
//SYSTSIN    DD    *
additional TSO commands as needed
/*
```

Call Attachment Facility (CAF)

If you are looking for an attachment that acts more like a standard z/OS or OS/390 batch program, consider the CAF or RRSAF. Although it has no performance advantage over TSO TMP once the batch program starts executing in its own address space, the return codes, parameter values, and disposition handling are as with any batch job.

CAF and RRSAF provides for direct control over connections to DB2 without the other standard attachments, and it can be used to issue instrumentation facility interface (IFI) calls. It can be used in the following environments:

◆   z/OS or OS/390 batch and z/OS or OS/390 started task
◆   IMS batch
◆   TSO background and foreground

The *Application Programming and SQL Guide* manual contains information on how to use the CAF and RRSAF.

RRSAF (discussed in Chapter SP) has no performance advantage over CAF. Indeed, RRSAF is CAF extended to allow for two phase commit.

BP.10 SUMMARY

The design techniques used for batch programs and online transactions are quite different. Batch techniques should be used for batch processing. Matching index scans, while a good choice for online transactions, are usually not a good choice for batch programs when processing more than 10 to 20 percent of the rows.

It is important to minimize index maintenance for batch update programs. We saw several techniques for doing this, including using LOAD RESUME rather than inserting a large number of rows with a host language program.

EXERCISES

1. Why is a tablespace scan often best for batch processing?

2. If a matching index scan is chosen for the predicate WHERE JN > 'J3', what can you do to disallow the use of the index and encourage a tablespace scan?

3. → Assume that you need to write a batch program to update 10 to 20 percent of the rows in a large production table and the input to the program is in a sequential file. Is it important to have the production table and sequential file in sequence on the primary key? Why?

4. What strategy would you suggest for a batch program to process about 50,000 rows to be updated in a million row table named SPJ? The information to be used to update the rows is in a sequential file named UPDATES. About 150,000 rows are to be deleted and archived as indicated by a date range that is input to the program. About 200,000 rows are to be inserted into the table and are currently in a sequential file called INSERTS.

5. What is a major disadvantage to the strategy suggested in the above exercise?

6. How can you minimize the time that the data is unavailable during the batch process?

7. If you have a batch window when all of the data can be made unavailable but the table is too large to be processed within the time frame, what is an approach to consider?

8 What is an advantage of using the mass delete algorithm followed by LOAD RESUME compared to LOAD REPLACE?

9. What are the performance benefits of CURSOR WITH HOLD for a batch program?

10. Should a batch program provide for cursor repositioning logic when CURSOR WITH HOLD is used? Why?

11. Is it advisable to use OPTIMIZE FOR 12 ROWS when repositioning a cursor in a batch program?

12. If prefetch is not chosen as part of the access path by the optimizer, is it possible that prefetch may be used at execution time?

13. Under what condition might the optimizer not choose sequential prefetch for a batch program?

14. Usually a batch job executes in a couple of minutes of elapsed time. Assume that the problem is within DB2, not due to the workload of other software on the computer.

a) Occasionally, the batch job takes several minutes of elapsed time. Why?

b) Occasionally, the batch job takes over 30 minutes of elapsed time. Why?

c) What action can you take?

ANSWERS

1. Sequential prefetch is usually chosen by the optimizer for a tablespace scan. Sequential prefetch results in reading 32 pages with a single I/O, assuming a buffer pool of 1,000 pages or more. The average I/O time for a prefetched page is 1.7 ms using 3390 DASD. This is compared to the I/O time for a page read at random, which is 16 ms. In addition, a page read at random means the use of an index, which requires processing a three level index in most cases.

2. Add "OR 0 = 1" to the predicate to disallow the use of a matching index scan. For example, WHERE (JN > 'J3' OR 0 = 1) disallows the use of a matching index scan on JN and encourages a tablespace scan.

3. Yes, it is important to have the production table and sequential file in sequence on the primary key. This allows for match-merge processing with sequential prefetch used on the leaf and data pages with no sort.

4. It is advisable to have the sequence of the table to be updated and the sequence of the UPDATES file match. If the clustering index is on the primary key, a sort can be avoided for an ORDER BY clause. The UPDATES file can be sorted in sequence on the primary key.

A good strategy is to design for a guided tablespace scan with sequential prefetch on the million row tablespace and clustering index. Read the table and UPDATES file until there is a match using match-merge logic in the program. Modify the row and write it to a sequential file named EXTRACTS, for example. The row is not updated in the table to avoid updating indexes. While doing the match-merge processing, test if the row has a date within the range of dates to be deleted. If the row is to be deleted, write it to an archive file and not to the EXTRACTS file if the deleted rows need to be archived.

Sort the EXTRACTS and INSERTS files into a file named COMPLETE. The files can simply be concatenated and a sort is not necessary if the rows are to be added to the end of the table and are in sequence. As one of the last statements in the batch program, use the mass delete algorithm to delete all rows in the table if it is not a parent table and it is in a segmented tablespace. For example, DELETE FROM SPJ with no predicate. Use LOAD RESUME to repopulate the SPJ table with the records in the COMPLETE file and rebuild the indexes. If the table is in a tablespace with no other tables, LOAD REPLACE can be used.

5. A major disadvantage to the technique is that the table is unavailable during the batch processing.

6. Consider using a partitioned tablespace. Design the batch process to update data in one partition at a time. All other partitions are available for reading and updating while the batch program is processing a partition. If one partition can be unavailable for three minutes, for example, size the partitions such that the batch program can process the data in one partition in three minutes.

7. Consider partitioning the tablespace such that a separate batch job can be submitted for each partition (or set of partitions) and can be executed in parallel. For example, assume that the batch job usually requires one hour of elapsed time but you have only 15 minutes available for the job in your batch window. Consider, dividing the tablespace into 10 parts where each part can be processed in about 6 to 10 minutes. Submit 10 batch jobs to

process data in each of the 10 parts that will be executed in parallel. Notice that some additional time is allowed in the example. Ideally, the longest running batch job working on one partition will require 10 minutes and we assumed a 15 minute batch window.

8. The mass delete algorithm does not delete/define the data sets as does LOAD REPLACE. This means that LOAD RESUME does not have to reformat existing data and index pages as is necessary when using LOAD REPLACE.

9. CURSOR WITH HOLD avoids the cost of repositioning the cursor after each COMMIT. Another performance benefit is that any temporary work areas are held after a COMMIT and need not be regenerated.

10. A batch program should provide for cursor repositioning when CURSOR WITH HOLD is used. If a rollback occurs because of a deadlock, it is necessary to reposition and redo the processing that was rolled back. In addition, cursor repositioning is necessary for application program restart processing.

11. No, it is not advisable to use OPTIMIZE FOR 12 ROWS, as discussed in Chapter PP, when repositioning a cursor in a batch program if a large number of rows are to be processed before a commit. (CURSOR WITH HOLD is a good choice to avoid the need to execute cursor repositioning logic in most cases.) When it is necessary to reposition after rollback or program restart, it is likely that a large number of rows will be processed. OPTIMIZE FOR 12 ROWS encourages a good access path for processing 12 rows which is probably not a good access path for processing thousands or tens of thousands of rows.

12. Sequential detection may result in dynamic prefetch being used at execution time even though the optimizer did not choose to use prefetch.

13. A singleton SELECT statement that returns one row may be performed in a paragraph repeatedly. The optimizer will choose a good access path to process one row which does not include prefetch. However, at execution time dynamic prefetch may be activated if rows are being retrieved on consecutive pages.

14. a) It may be that DB2 is not able to take advantage of deferred write a good deal of the time because < 50 % of the pages are stealable. DB2 must

frequently write updated pages one at a time rather than using the more efficient deferred write and write 32 pages with a single I/O.

b) It may be that > 95 percent of the pages in the buffer pool are marked as in use and DB2 is writing a page for every row that is updated. A one minute batch job required over 30 minutes of elapsed time before it was canceled at a company when the 95 % threshold was exceeded.

c) It is advisable to check with the system administrator to determine if the buffer pool is sized correctly for the workload.

FIGURES

Triggering Actions in DB2

TR.1 INTRODUCTION

Triggers give you the opportunity to turn responsibility for some actions over to DB2. You can define and implement business rules and actions using triggers. Complex validation of data can be done through the use of triggers. Values can be automatically generated each time an INSERT statement is executed. Exception conditions can be checked and the appropriate action taken as defined in a trigger. These actions can be based on a comparison of values before and after an update. You can execute additional INSERT, UPDATE, and DELETE statements after an event based on a trigger definition. Triggers can be used to update summary information after an event, and maintain audit or mirror data.

Order processing tables are used to demonstrate how triggers are created and used. One of the primary tables used in examples is the ORDER table created like:

```
CREATE TABLE ORDER
    (ORDERNO     INTEGER       NOT NULL WITH DEFAULT,
     CUSTNO      INTEGER       NOT NULL WITH DEFAULT,
     ITEMNO      INTEGER       NOT NULL WITH DEFAULT,
     UNIT_PRICE  DECIMAL(9,2)  NOT NULL WITH DEFAULT,
     QTY         INTEGER       NOT NULL WITH DEFAULT,
     WEIGHT      INTEGER       NOT NULL WITH DEFAULT,
     COUNTRY     CHAR(6)       NOT NULL WITH DEFAULT,
     SHIP_COSTS  DECIMAL(9,2)  NOT NULL WITH DEFAULT,
     TAXES       DECIMAL(9,2)  NOT NULL WITH DEFAULT,
     DUTY        DECIMAL(9,2)  NOT NULL WITH DEFAULT,
     ORDER_DATE  DATE          NOT NULL WITH DEFAULT,
     SHIP_DATE   DATE          WITH DEFAULT '9999-12-31',
     CONSTRAINT ORDER_PK PRIMARY KEY (ORDERNO));
```

TR.2 COMPONENTS OF TRIGGERS

Triggers provide for defining actions to DB2 that are to be taken before or after an event on a table.

Before triggers are activated before any action is taken on a table by DB2. These triggers do not activate other triggers. After triggers are activated after actions are taken on a table by DB2. These triggers can result in the activation of other triggers. An event can be an INSERT, UPDATE, or DELETE statement on one table. Triggers do not apply to utilities except for LOAD RESUME YES with SHRLEVEL CHANGE as discussed in Chapter LC.

An action can be to execute one or more SQL statements on local tables depending on the conditions defined and type of trigger. An action can occur for each row processed or statement executed. Triggers cannot be used to take an action outside of DB2. However, user-defined functions (UDF) and stored procedures can be invoked from within a trigger definition that takes an action outside of DB2. A program that causes the trigger to be activated cannot access the result of a stored procedure. UDF and stored procedures are discussed in Chapters UD and SP.

The maximum size of a trigger is 32 KB in V7 and below.

BEFORE Trigger to Validate Data

A BEFORE trigger is useful to validate data. For example, a row should not be inserted into a CUSTOMER table if the customer is not in a city where the company does business. Assume that the VALID_CITY table contains all cities where the company does business. The following BEFORE INSERT on the CUSTOMER table trigger ensures that a row can never be inserted unless the company does business in the city.

```
CREATE TRIGGER BCUS10
  NO CASCADE BEFORE INSERT ON CUSTOMER
  REFERENCING NEW AS N
  FOR EACH ROW MODE DB2SQL
  WHEN (N.CITY <>
    (SELECT CITY
     FROM    VALID_CITIES
     WHERE   CITY = N.CITY))
  BEGIN ATOMIC
     SIGNAL SQLSTATE 'IBC10'
        ('Not a valid city');
  END#
```

Each component of the CREATE TRIGGER statement is described in this chapter.

Triggers cannot be created on a view, temporary table, auxiliary table, alias, synonym, or catalog table. However, triggers defined on a table referenced in a view are activated when manipulating the view.

Multiple SQL Statements Can be Executed in a Trigger Body

If there is more than one SQL statement in the trigger body, the statements must be preceded by BEGIN ATOMIC and ended with an END statement. These constructs are optional if there is only one SQL statement in the trigger body. If there are more than one statement in a trigger body, each statement must be terminated by a ";".

SPUFI and DSNTEP2 use ";" as a terminator for a complete SQL statement by default. This can result in DB2 seeing only part of the trigger definition. It is necessary to use a different statement terminator when more than one SQL statement appears in a trigger body.

The SPUFI SQL terminator can be changed using the CURRENT SPUFI DEFAULTS panel. The first entry on the panel is SQL TERMINATOR with a default of ";". Key over the ";" terminator with "#" if this is your desired terminator character. The default ";" can be replaced with another character but it cannot be blank (" "), comma (","), underscore (_), double quote ("), single quote ('), left parenthesis "(", and right parenthesis ")". The "#" terminator is used in example CREATE TRIGGER statements in this chapter where there are one or more statements in a SPUFI input file. If ";" must be used to terminate multiple SQL statements in the trigger body, "#" or the designated terminator must be used for all other statements in the file.

The DSNTEP2 terminator can be set with a functional comment embedded in the input file containing the SQL to be executed as read from SYSIN provided the V6 APAR PQ24360 has been installed. If you wish to change the terminator character to "#", the following statement must proceed the use of the terminator.

```
--#SET TERMINATOR #
```

The terminator can be changed again within the file so that subsequent SQL statements use the newly defined terminator.

Activation Time

The activation time of a trigger can be BEFORE or AFTER an event as indicated by these keywords in the CREATE TRIGGER statement. The previous CREATE TRIGGER statement applies to the insertion of rows as indicated by "BEFORE INSERT" in the statement. If you also want to ensure that a city value cannot be updated to a city where the company does not do business, a BEFORE UPDATE trigger is required like:

```
CREATE TRIGGER BCUS20
   NO CASCADE BEFORE UPDATE OF CITY ON CUSTOMER
   REFERENCING NEW AS N
   FOR EACH ROW MODE DB2SQL
   WHEN (N.CITY <>
      (SELECT CITY
       FROM    VALID_CITIES
       WHERE   CITY = N.CITY))
         SIGNAL SQLSTATE 'IBC20'
            ('Not a valid city');
```

NO CASCADE is required for all BEFORE triggers. This is because a BEFORE trigger cannot activate another trigger.

Triggering Event

The event that causes the trigger to be activated can be an INSERT, UPDATE, or DELETE statement executed on the named table in the ON clause. The trigger applies only to the specified statement type. You can name one or more columns in an UPDATE trigger which is advisable. Otherwise, the trigger applies to the update of any columns in the row. It detracts from performance to execute a trigger if it does not apply to the column updated.

Referential Integrity: An action taken as a result of enforcement of referential integrity (RI) can invoke a trigger. For example, if a primary key (PK) row is deleted with dependent tables defined to DB2 with the constraints of DELETE CASCADE or DELETE SET NULL, all corresponding foreign key (FK) rows are deleted or the FK is updated to be null. This results in invoking triggers defined on the affected FK tables. This part of the cascading effect is discussed in Section TR.6.

Granularity

The trigger can apply to each row processed in the table or each statement executed. This is known as the granularity of the statement and is specified with the FOR EACH ROW or FOR EACH STATEMENT clause.

FOR EACH ROW results in the trigger being activated for each row processed in the table. Multiple rows can be processed by an SQL statement as a result of the set oriented nature of SQL. Costs increase as the number of rows processed increases. The trigger does not apply if no rows qualify. It is referred to as a row trigger.

FOR EACH STATEMENT results in the trigger being activated for each UPDATE or DELETE statement executed on the named table. The trigger is activated once even if no rows qualify as a result of the triggering statement. FOR EACH STATEMENT applies to AFTER triggers (not BEFORE triggers). It is referred to as a statement trigger.

Mode

DB2SQL mode is currently implemented in DB2. Additional modes may be available in the future. The SQL92 standard has immediate and deferred modes defined. The clause MODE DB2SQL results in processing like the immediate mode.

TR.3 TRANSITION VARIABLES

Transition variables provide for referencing a row or table before (OLD) and after (NEW) a triggering event. The REFERENCING clause is used to assign transition variables. A correlation name is assigned using an AS clause. Figure TR.1 summarizes the types of transition variables available, gives a brief description, and indicates the type of trigger where the variables can be used. Of course, you can choose your own correlation names rather than those used in the examples.

Figure TR.1. Transition variables

Transition Variables	Description
REFERENCING OLD AS O	O can be used to reference columns <u>before</u> modification. Applies to update and delete triggers.
REFERENCING NEW AS N	N can be used to reference columns <u>after</u> modification. Applies to update and insert triggers.
REFERENCING OLD_TABLE AS OT	OT can be used in a FROM clause and as a correlation name to reference a table <u>before</u> modification. Can count the number of rows in Oslo before a triggering event, for example. Applies to update and delete triggers.
REFERENCING NEW_TABLE AS NT	NT can be used in a FROM clause and as a correlation name to reference a table <u>after</u> modification. Can count the number of rows in Oslo after a triggering event, for example. Applies to update and insert triggers.

The REFERENCING keyword appears only once for multiple transition variables, for example:

```
REFERENCING OLD AS O NEW AS N OLD_TABLE AS OT
NEW_TABLE AS NT
```

The following formulation results in an error:

```
REFERENCING OLD AS O
REFERENCING NEW AS N
```

The use of OLD_TABLE and NEW_TABLE correlation names in the FROM clause, can be used to evaluate a column function (MIN, MAX, AVG, SUM, COUNT) for more than one row in a table before or after a

triggering event. You might want to think of the OLD_TABLE and
NEW_TABLE as being before and after read-only images of the table.
Indeed, the referenced tables cannot be modified.

When Transition Variables Can Be Used

Use of transition variables depends on the activation time, triggering event,
and granularity as summarized in Figure TR.2. None of the transition
variables are required in a CREATE TRIGGER statement. If used, old row
and old table refers to the data before the triggering action. New row and
new table refers to data after the triggering action.

Figure TR.2. Rules for the use of transition variables

Activation & Triggering Event	FOR EACH ROW Granularity	FOR EACH STATEMENT Granularity
BEFORE INSERT	New row	Not applicable
BEFORE UPDATE	Old row, new row	Not applicable
BEFORE DELETE	Old row	Not applicable
AFTER INSERT	New row, new table	New table
AFTER UPDATE	Old row, new row Old table, new table	Old table, new table
AFTER DELETE	Old row, old table	Old table

The rules for use of transition variable are logical. For example, it is not
possible to reference an old row when executing a BEFORE and AFTER
INSERT trigger because one does not exist. In addition, there is no new row
when executing a BEFORE and AFTER DELETE trigger. All combinations
of old and new rows and tables can be referenced only for AFTER
UPDATE triggers.

Transition Variables and Performance

Values for AFTER trigger transition variables and transition tables are
saved in a DSNDB07 work tablespace until a commit is issued. This can
require more space in the work tablespaces. (If a small number of rows

qualify, they may be stored in memory in future. The transition variables are stored in a format similar to the base table. That is the entire row is stored (not just the columns referenced). VARCHAR columns are padded with blanks to their full length.

A work file contains the full set of updated or inserted rows for row and statement triggers. The entire work file is scanned (no index is created) for each row processed for a row trigger and once for a statement trigger when processing transition variables. This detract from performance for large transition tables.

There are costs of work file processing including:

◆   24 pages are allocated for each work file initially (more space is allocated as required)
◆   Creation, use, and deletion of work files
◆   I/O and/or GETPAGE requests to work files
◆   Potential contention with work files used for other processing (sorts, data for global temporary tables, materialization of nested table expression and views, some joins, most subselects, etc.)

If NEW and OLD transition variables are used, two work files are created. There is some savings in using work files in that no logging is done.

Use transition variables only when required to avoid work file processing and maximize performance. Also consider the use BEFORE triggers where possible (work files are not used).

Additional performance considerations: The initialization cost of executing a trigger is about the same as a fetch (about 3,500 to 9,000 instructions) except when work files are required. If trigger is not executed (update of a column that does not have trigger defined on it but there is a trigger defined on another column of the table, for example), the cost is negligible. The is no overhead for an SQL statement that does not activate a trigger. If an INSERT trigger is defined on a table, there is no overhead for UPDATE and DELETE statements, for example.

An index can be used on column in "subselect" of WHEN condition. An index can be used on VALID_CITIES.CITY in the BCUS10 trigger introduced in Section TR.2.

The Database Descriptor (DBD) is increased in size. The object descriptor (OBD) of a trigger is associated with the table description. This can require more space in the EDM (Environmental Descriptor Manager) pool. Data Manager determines if a trigger should be activated.

TR.4 TRIGGER BODY AND WHEN CONDITIONS

The trigger body contains actions to be taken based on the results of the WHEN condition (optional). A BEFORE and AFTER trigger body can contain only certain statements.

A BEFORE trigger body can have the following types of statements:

♦   SELECT
♦   SIGNAL SQLSTATE
♦   VALUES
♦   CALL a stored procedure and invoke a UDF that does not contain an INSERT, UPDATE, or DELETE statement that modifies the triggering table.
♦   SET transition variable. It is not possible to set a transition variable to the result of a SELECT statement.

You can perform most of the functions of a BEFORE trigger in an AFTER triggers. In addition, can modify a table with INSERT, UPDATE, and DELETE statements as summarized:

♦   SELECT
♦   SIGNAL SQLSTATE
♦   VALUES
♦   CALL of a stored procedure and invoke a UDF
♦   INSERT
♦   UPDATE (without cursor to locate row to be updated)
♦   DELETE (without cursor to locate row to be deleted)

The SELECT, INSERT, UPDATE, and DELETE statements are discussed throughout the book with an introduction in Chapter SL. Calling a stored procedure is discussed in Chapter SP. The use of UDF is discussed in Chapter UD. The remaining statements -- SIGNAL SQLSTATE, VALUES, and SET are discussed in this chapter.

Host variables and parameter markers cannot be used in a trigger body. It is not possible to reference tables and views at a client site nor use dynamic SQL in a trigger. However, you can CALL a stored procedure, and use a function that references objects at a client site, and use dynamic SQL. CALL parameters can be literals, transition variables, table locators, or expressions (not host variables).

WHEN condition controls when the trigger body is executed. If there is no WHEN condition, the trigger body is executed when the trigger is activated. A WHEN condition is similar to a simple WHERE condition. It can include transition variables and subselects. If a row trigger is used, the condition is evaluated once for each modified row. If a statement trigger is used, the condition is evaluated once for each execution of the triggering statement. AND and OR can be used to join multiple conditions within a WHEN condition. All conditions for WHEN clause must be in parenthesis. The result of a WHEN condition can be true, false, or unknown. The trigger body is executed only if the WHEN condition is true.

Recommendation: Use good programming practices when writing the logic of WHEN conditions for good performance.

SIGNAL SQLSTATE

The SIGNAL SQLSTATE statement provides for disallowing successful execution of the triggering statement, statements that would have been invoked by the trigger, and any RI enforcement. For example, an order cannot be deleted before the item is shipped. Assume that the SHIP_DATE column is defined WITH DEFAULT '9999-12-31' for the following CREATE TRIGGER statement.

```
CREATE TRIGGER BORDER40
   NO CASCADE BEFORE DELETE ON ORDER
   REFERENCING OLD AS O
   FOR EACH ROW MODE DB2SQL
   WHEN (O.SHIP_DATE >= CURRENT DATE)
   BEGIN ATOMIC
      SIGNAL SQLSTATE 'IBR40' ('Item has not
been shipped');
   END#
```

The error code 'IBR40', in the example, is returned in the SQLSTATE field of the SQLCA (discussed in Chapter PD). The error code must be defined in the program as a 5 character literal consisting of upper case letters and digits. You can avoid conflicts with SQL92 SQLSTATE values by using a first character of the letters between I and Z or the digits 7, 8, or 9.

The error message ('Item has not been shipped'), in the example is returned in the SQLERRMC field of the SQLCA. It must be less than or equal to 70 characters.

All actions under the control of DB2 and Resource Recovery Services (RRS) are rolled back and a -438 SQLCODE is returned in addition to the SQLSTATE and message. The rollback does not include sending an email message, for example.

Figure TR.3 summarizes several SQLCODEs issued by DB2 as a result of a severe error encountered in the trigger that results in a rollback. The rollback affects the trigger statement (not the other SQL statements in the program). It applies to the SQL statement that activated the trigger, all triggers, and cascading actions involved (a trigger can be activated by another trigger). The rollback also applies to cascading RI relationships including DELETE CASCADE and DELETE SET NULL.

Figure TR.3. Errors resulting from execution of a trigger

SQLCODE	Description from *Messages and Codes* Manual
-901	Unsuccessful execution caused by a system error that does not preclude the successful execution of subsequent SQL statements.
-906	The SQL statement cannot be executed because this function is disabled due to a prior error.
-911	The current unit of recovery has been rolled back due to deadlock or timeout. REASON reason-code, TYPE OF RESOURCE resource-type, and RESOURCE NAME resource-name.

SQLCODE	Description from *Messages and Codes* Manual
-913	Unsuccessful execution caused by a deadlock or timeout. REASON CODE reason-code, TYPE OF RESOURCE resource-type, and RESOURCE NAME resource-name.

A -723 SQLCODE ('09000' SQLSTATE) indicates that a statement within the trigger body abended. All statements within the trigger body (not within program) are rolled back. Information is placed in the SQLCA. Warnings are not returned to the program.

TR.5 SET, VALUE, AND CASE IN BEFORE TRIGGERS

The SET, VALUE, and CASE clauses are explained through the use of a number of create trigger examples. The CREATE TRIGGER statements are analyzed to show how to use these clauses as well as the clauses described in previous sections of this chapter.

Use of the SET Statement to Modify a Row

BEFORE triggers can be used to modify data before inserting, updating, or deleting a row. For example, shipping costs are 10 percent higher in cities outside of the USA when the item weight is greater than 25. The following statement is used to increase the shipping costs by 10 percent if the country is not the USA and the weight is greater than 25 before the order is inserted into the ORDER table. Also, the trigger sets the SHIP_DATE to the current date because international orders are shipped on the date of the order.

```
CREATE TRIGGER BORDER10
    NO CASCADE BEFORE INSERT ON ORDER
    REFERENCING NEW AS N
    FOR EACH ROW MODE DB2SQL
    WHEN (N.COUNTRY <> 'USA'
        AND N.WEIGHT    > 25)
            SET N.SHIP_COSTS = N.SHIP_COSTS * 1.1,
                N.SHIP_DATE  = CURRENT DATE;
```

The REFERENCING NEW clause is required for BEFORE INSERT triggers. Other referencing clauses do not apply to the BEFORE INSERT trigger. However, the column qualification is optional for BEFORE INSERT triggers. For example, COUNTRY or N.COUNTRY can be used in the WHEN clause. Similarly SHIP_COSTS or N.SHIP_COSTS can be used in the SET statement.

The WHEN clause is used to test the required conditions. Notice that the two conditions joined by AND are enclosed in parenthesis.

SET Transition Variable Explanation

The SET statement is used to assign values to columns when using BEFORE triggers. One or more columns can be set to:

- Expressions (arithmetic operators, DB2 or UDFs, special registers, etc.)
- Default (default value specified for the column when the table was created)
- Null

A SET statement begins with the keyword SET followed by setting one or more columns to a value, each of which is separated by a comma. In the previous example, the use of the SET statement can be seen with reference to the N.SHIP_COSTS and N.SHIP_DATE.

Overriding the Triggering Statement

Here is an example of overriding the triggering statement. Assume that there is a business rule that does not allow the increase in unit price to be greater than 50 percent. This is specified in the WHEN clause. Signal the invoking SQL statement that an adjustment cannot be made to the original requested increase in the unit price.

```
CREATE TRIGGER BINV10
   NO CASCADE BEFORE UPDATE OF UNIT_PRICE
      ON INVENTORY
   REFERENCING OLD AS O NEW AS N
   FOR EACH ROW MODE DB2SQL
```

```
      WHEN (N.UNIT_PRICE > 1.5 * O.UNIT_PRICE)
      BEGIN ATOMIC
        SIGNAL SQLSTATE 'IBI10'
          ('Unit price cannot be increased by > 50
%');       END#
```

OLD and NEW transition variables can be defined with UPDATE triggers. Columns on both sides of the SET equal must be qualified with the correlation name. Columns on the left side of the equal must be qualified with the NEW row correlation name (N in the example).

VALUES Statement

The VALUES statement can be used to execute a UDF or stored procedure unconditionally -- once for each row in a row trigger or once for each statement trigger. The previous example is expanded to invoke a UDF.

The ADJINC UDF logs attempts to adjust unit price by more than 50 percent.

```
CREATE TRIGGER BINV10
  NO CASCADE BEFORE UPDATE OF UNIT_PRICE ON INVENTORY
  REFERENCING OLD AS O
             NEW AS N
  FOR EACH ROW MODE DB2SQL
  WHEN (N.UNIT_PRICE > 1.5 * O.UNIT_PRICE)
  BEGIN ATOMIC
      VALUES (ADJINC(O.ITEMNO, N.UNIT_PRICE,
                     O.UNIT_PRICE));
      SIGNAL SQLSTATE 'IBI10'
        ('Unit price cannot be increased by  > 50 %');
  END#
```

ADJINC can be a stored procedure and invoked like:

```
BEGIN ATOMIC
  SET   N.UNIT_PRICE = 1.5 * O.UNIT_PRICE;
  CALL  ADJINC(O.ITEMNO, N.UNIT_PRICE, O.UNIT_PRICE);
  SIGNAL SQLSTATE 'IBI10'
     ('Unit price cannot be increased by  > 50 %');
END#
```

VALUES and CASE

VALUES and CASE can be used to test multiple WHEN conditions. For example, if an item is shipped more than 7 or 14 days after the order is placed, DISCOUNT UDF is executed for discount processing.

```
CREATE TRIGGER BSHIP10
  NO CASCADE BEFORE INSERT ON SHIPMENT
  REFERENCING NEW AS N
  FOR EACH ROW MODE DB2SQL
 BEGIN ATOMIC
    VALUES CASE
      WHEN DAYS
        (N.SHIP_DATE) - DAYS(CURRENT DATE)
          BETWEEN 8 AND 14
            THEN DISCOUNT
              ('USH10', 'Between  8 & 14 days')
      WHEN DAYS(N.SHIP_DATE) -
        DAYS(CURRENT DATE) > 14
          THEN DISCOUNT ('USH20', '>14 days')
      ELSE ' '
   END;
   END#
```

TR.6 AFTER TRIGGERS

An AFTER trigger is executed after its triggering SQL statement and all of its constraints are successful. They can insert, update, and delete rows from tables and views not associated with the trigger. AFTER triggers see the results of BEFORE triggers executed before them.

Cascading Triggers

An AFTER trigger can activate other triggers as a result of its action. This is referred to as cascading triggers. The limit to cascading is 16 levels of nesting including triggers, UDF, and stored procedures. If there is an attempt to execute a 17th trigger, UDF, or stored procedure, a rollback occurs with -724 SQLCODE and '54038' SQLSTATE including all SQL in triggers, UDFs, and stored procedures in the cascade. If trigger A is activated after trigger B and completes after trigger B completes, it is not considered a cascading trigger, for example:

```
Trigger B activated
Trigger A activated
Trigger B completes
Trigger A completes
```

Restrictions: It is not possible to modify a table that has been modified at a higher level of nesting (-746 SQLCODE). A trigger cannot reference a remote table in the trigger definition. However, the trigger can invoke a UDF and stored procedure that acts on local and remote data.

Referential Integrity: If a parent row is deleted by an AFTER trigger and it has dependents with DB2 enforced RI, constraints are enforced. For example, cascade delete causes all foreign key rows matching the primary key to be deleted. This results in delete triggers defined on the dependent table being activated. The set null RI constraint causes all foreign keys matching the primary key to be set to null. This results in activation of update triggers defined on the dependent tables.

Beware of too complex of cascading actions. It can be difficult to manage and debug. There is no significant performance difference between invoking a single trigger compared to invoking the trigger within other nested operations.

AFTER UPDATE of Columns Trigger

It is advisable to name columns for which the trigger is to be executed. This avoids updating a column added with the ALTER statement which invokes the trigger. This is probably not the intent.

Consider an example of inserting a before and after image of information into CUSTOMER_MOD table when the customer name or credit limit of a customer is changed.

```
CREATE TRIGGER ACUS10
  AFTER UPDATE OF CNAME, CREDIT_LIMIT ON CUSTOMER
  REFERENCING OLD AS O
              NEW AS N
  FOR EACH ROW MODE DB2SQL
    WHEN (O.CNAME        <> N.CNAME
      OR  O.CREDIT_LIMIT <> N.CREDIT_LIMIT)
    BEGIN ATOMIC
      INSERT INTO CUSTOMER_MOD
```

```
                       (  CUSTNO,   CNAME,   CREDIT_LIMIT)
          VALUES  (O.CUSTNO,O.CNAME,O.CREDIT_LIMIT);
       INSERT INTO CUSTOMER_MOD
                       (  CUSTNO,   CNAME,   CREDIT_LIMIT)
          VALUES  (N.CUSTNO,N.CNAME,N.CREDIT_LIMIT);
     END#
```

Explanation of AFTER UPDATE of columns trigger: Notice that one or
more columns can be referenced in the AFTER UPDATE OF clause. You
can reference old and new rows in an AFTER trigger. The WHEN clause
can contain multiple conditions using OR and AND. One or more SQL
statements can be executed in the trigger body. Each statement is terminated
with ";" These statements must be preceded with BEGIN ATOMIC and
terminated with END followed by the defined terminator character, "#" in
the example.

Additional effects of inserting rows into the CUSTOMER_MOD table:
Columns not named in the INSERT statement can be changed
automatically. Assume that the CUSTOMER_MOD table has an
UPDATER column defined with WITH DEFAULT USER and a
CHANGE_TIMESTAMP column defined as NOT NULL WITH
DEFAULT. After the trigger executes successfully, the UPDATER column
contains the primary AUTHID of the person who executed the program and
the CHANGE_TIMESTAMP contains the current timestamp of when the
change was made.

Cascade Update with a Trigger

Cascade update means that if a PK value is updated, the corresponding FK
value in all dependent tables should be updated automatically. DB2 RI does
not support cascade update. However, it can be implemented with a trigger
like:

```
CREATE TRIGGER ACUS20
  AFTER UPDATE OF CUSTNO ON CUSTOMER
  REFERENCING OLD AS O
               NEW AS N
  FOR EACH ROW MODE DB2SQL
  BEGIN ATOMIC
    UPDATE  ORDER
       SET   CUSTNO = N.CUSTNO
```

```
              WHERE  CUSTNO  =  O.CUSTNO;
        UPDATE   SHIPMENT
           SET    CUSTNO  =  N.CUSTNO
           WHERE  CUSTNO  =  O.CUSTNO;
     END#
```

The trigger definition results in updating the FK CUSTNO in the dependent ORDER and SHIPMENT table when an UPDATE statement is issued on the CUSTNO in the CUSTOMER table. If the FK appears in multiple dependent tables and cascade update is to occur on each table, it is your responsibility to update each dependent table.

Creation of a trigger of enforce any form of RI or other constraints does not check for any existing violation of constraints in the table. In contrast, creation of RI or table check constraints causes check pending to be turned on. The CHECK DATA utility should then be executed to deal with the violations as discussed in Chapter LC.

Pass Trigger Transition Table to Stored Procedure or UDF

You can pass trigger transition tables to a stored procedure or UDF. For example, after the ORDER table is updated, the results are to be passed to the PROCORD stored procedure.

```
     CREATE  TRIGGER  AORDER20
        AFTER  UPDATE  ON  ORDER
        REFERENCING  NEW_TABLE  AS  NT
        FOR  EACH  STATEMENT  MODE  DB2SQL
        BEGIN  ATOMIC
           CALL  (PROCORD(TABLE  NT));
        END#
```

The REFERENCING NEW_TABLE AS NT clause identifies the updated rows. The CALL statement references the NT correlation name as a parameter when calling the stored procedure.

The stored procedure must declare table locator field PROCORD-LOCATOR in working-storage like:

```
     01 PROCORD-LOCATOR SQL TYPE IS TABLE LIKE
           ORDER AS LOCATOR.
```

```
01 ORDERNO PIC S9(9) COMP-4.
```

It is necessary to declare a cursor, open, fetch and close the cursor for the
transition table in the stored procedure like the following fragment of code:

```
EXEC SQL DECLARE CORDER CURSOR FOR
SELECT ORDERNO
FROM    TABLE(:PROCORD-LOCATOR LIKE ORDER)
WHERE   UNIT_PRICE > 10000 END-EXEC.

EXEC SQL OPEN   CORDER END-EXEC.
EXEC SQL FETCH CORDER INTO :ORDERNO END-EXEC.

EXEC SQL CLOSE CORDER END-EXEC.
```

Example of NEW_TABLE and Column Function

NEW_TABLE and OLD_TABLE with correlation names are useful for
evaluating column functions (MIN, MAX, AVG, SUM, COUNT) on one or
more rows before or after executing an AFTER trigger. For example, after
inserting a row for an ordered item, the user needs to be notified if the total
cost (sum of unit price * quantity) of an item (not including shipping costs)
exceeds a 10,000 limit.

```
CREATE TRIGGER AORDER10
  AFTER INSERT ON ORDER
  REFERENCING NEW_TABLE AS NT
  FOR EACH ROW MODE DB2SQL
  WHEN (10000.00 >
        (SELECT SUM(NT.UNIT_PRICE * NT.QTY)
         FROM    NT
         WHERE   CUSTNO  = NT.CUSTNO
         AND     ORDERNO = NT.ORDERNO))
  BEGIN ATOMIC
    SIGNAL SQLSTATE 'IAR10'
      ('10,000 limit exceeded');
  END#
```

If the limit is exceeded, the error code 'IAR10' is returned in the
SQLSTATE field and the error message ('10,000 limit exceeded') is
returned in the SQLERRMC field of the SQLCA and a rollback occurs.

The use of REFERENCING NEW_TABLE AS NT provides for the results of the SET statement to be seen when referencing NT in a FROM clause.

Caution: It is assumed that a customer usually orders only a few items and that they seldom exceed their credit limit. If the customer usually orders many items, the trigger must be invoked for each item ordered which detracts from performance. In addition, if a customer frequently exceeds their credit limit, a long rollback can occur. A rollback is costly as discussed in Chapter BP. Indeed, it can cost twice as much as doing the work initially. Do be cautious of developing triggers that can result in costly rollbacks. If this is a possibility, consider doing the work through program design. For example, sum the cost of line items as they are placed in an array in the program, compare subtotals to the credit limit, and notify the customer when the credit limit is exceeded. If the credit limit is not exceed at the end of the order, insert the rows from the array into the ORDER table.

AFTER DELETE Trigger

Assume that there is a business rule that if a customer is deleted from the CUSTOMER table that all rows for the customer are to be deleted from the ORDER table. The following trigger can be used to implement the business rule.

```
CREATE TRIGGER ACUS20
   AFTER DELETE ON CUSTOMER
   REFERENCING OLD AS O
   FOR EACH ROW MODE DB2SQL
   DELETE FROM ORDER
      WHERE CUSTNO = O.CUSTNO;
```

An alternative is to use DB2 enforced RI as discussed in Chapter RI. A cascade delete can be defined on the dependent ORDER table such that if a row is deleted from the parent CUSTOMER table, DB2 will automatically delete the matching FK rows in the ORDER table. We will see in Section TR.10 that DB2 enforced RI can have performance advantages over implementing RI through triggers.

TR.7 ORDER OF PROCESSING TRIGGERS AND CONSTRAINTS

The order of processing a trigger can affect the results and performance. Figure TR.4 summarizes this order. It can be seen that the order of processing is quite involved. Do consider a naming convention to indicate whether it is a BEFORE or AFTER trigger, the table associated with the trigger, and a sequence number to indicate the order of creation and execution. A naming convention is helpful but not sufficient. The catalog tables are required for an analysis of the processing order of triggers and constraints as discussed in Section TR.9.

Figure TR.4. Order of processing triggers and constraints

◆   OLD transition variables are bound.

◆   BEFORE triggers are executed in the order created for each qualifying row based on the timestamp in SYSTRIGGERS.CREATEDTS.

◆   NEW transition variables are applied for BEFORE triggers.

◆   RI constraints with DELETE CASCADE or DELETE SET NULL rules are applied before delete triggers or before update triggers on dependent tables.

◆   Actual insertion, deletion, or update is applied to the table.

◆   Unique index, RI, and table check constraints are checked. A rollback occurs when the first row violates any constraint checked.

◆   Insertion of a row into the PLAN_TABLE, DSN_STATEMNT_TABLE, and DSN_FUNCTION_TABLE by DB2 does not activate an INSERT trigger on those tables. A trigger defined on these tables is activated when SQL is executed on the tables.

◆   NEW transition variables are bound before AFTER triggers are executed.

◆   AFTER triggers are executed after BEFORE triggers based on timestamp of creation. The BEFORE trigger rules above are applied.

◆   AFTER triggers are executed in the order created for each row modified by the triggering statement and enforcement of RI based on the timestamp in SYSTRIGGERS.CREATEDTS. An AFTER trigger is executed once even if no rows qualify when using the FOR EACH STATEMENT clause.

◆   SQL statements within the AFTER trigger body are executed in the order written. An executed statement can activate another trigger (or the same trigger) which follows the execution order described.

◆   An AFTER trigger sees the effect of previously executed AFTER triggers as well as before triggers.

Triggers and Special Registers

Special registers are saved before a trigger is activated and restored after the trigger completes. During the execution of a trigger, special registers inherit their value from the triggering SQL operation (insert, update, delete) including:

♦   CURRENT DATE
♦   CURRENT TIME
♦   CURRENT TIMESTAMP
♦   CURRENT DEGREE
♦   CURRENT LOCALE LC_CTYPE
♦   CURRENT OPTIMIZATION HINT
♦   CURRENT PATH
♦   CURRENT PRECISION
♦   CURRENT RULES
♦   CURRENT SERVER
♦   CURRENT SQLID
♦   CURRENT USER

The CURRENT PACKAGESET special register is set to the qualifier or schema name of the trigger (schema are discussed in Chapter CO. The CURRENT TIMEZONE is set to the z/OS or OS/390 TIMEZONE parameter.

TR.8 TRIGGER MANAGEMENT

Triggers like most objects in DB2 have a qualifier and an owner as well as privileges to create a trigger. The creation of a trigger results in DB2 automatically creating a package for the trigger. These issues are discussed in this section.

Trigger Naming Convention and Ownership

A trigger name has a qualifier (similar to the qualifier of a table name). The name must be unique for triggers assigned to a table and within an AUTHID or schema. It cannot exceed eight bytes. You can use a qualifier rather than a schema. If a qualifier is not explicitly specified when creating a trigger, the current SQLID of the creator of the trigger is the qualifier when it is created dynamically. If the trigger is created from a host program, the AUTHID used in the REBIND QUALIFIER parameter is the qualifier of the trigger. If a QUALIFIER is not specified when binding a package or plan, the owner of the package or plan is the trigger qualifier.

A schema can be used to logically group triggers, UDF, distinct types (also known as user-defined data types), stored procedures, and other objects (somewhat like a database is a grouping of physical objects). If a schema is used, the qualifier of objects created within a schema is the schema name. Schema creation is done using a batch program (not SPUFI) according to the SQL92 standard as discussed in Chapter CO. The PATH parameter of bind and rebind provides for specifying the schema name for static SQL. The CURRENT PATH special register provides the schema name for dynamic SQL.

The owner of the trigger is the qualifier or schema name. SYSTRIGGERS.SCHEMA contains the qualifier or schema name in the SCHEMA column.

Authority Required for Triggers

SYSADM or SYSCTRL can create and drop triggers. CREATEIN privilege can be granted on an AUTHID or schema to allow for creating and managing triggers. One or more of the following privileges are required without SYSADM, SYSCTRL, or CREATEIN:

♦ TRIGGER privilege on the table upon which the trigger is defined, for example

```
GRANT TRIGGER ON AUTHID.ORDER TO FLEUR;
    -- or PUBLIC
```

♦ DBADM on the database that contains the table

♦ ALTER privilege on the table to which the trigger is attached

If transition variables are used, SELECT privileges are required on the table to which the trigger is attached. SELECT privileges are also required on all tables and views referenced in the WHEN condition. Privileges are required on the objects manipulated by SQL in the trigger body as with a host program. If the trigger invokes a UDF or stored procedures, EXECUTE privilege is required on the object. DYNAMICRULES(RUN) is required to execute CREATE TRIGGER as an embedded dynamic SQL statement. The owner of the package or plan must have the required privileges to create a trigger.

The trigger body is executed under the authority of the creator (not the executor). This is similar to static and dynamic SQL with the bind parameter DYNAMICRULES(BIND) for plans and packages.

Trigger Package

A package is created automatically for SQL in the trigger body when a trigger is created and has the same name as the trigger. The collection name is the name of the qualifier or schema. The version ID is an empty string which means that multiple versions of a trigger cannot exist. It is not necessary to grant privileges on a trigger package to executors. Triggers are not specified in a package list for the plan containing SQL that invokes the trigger.

It is not possible to drop a trigger package. It is dropped automatically when the trigger or triggering table (table named in ON clause) is dropped. You can rebind a trigger package. This is useful if the trigger package has been marked invalid or inoperative due to dropping a referenced table, alias (not synonym), index, adding a column to the trigger table, or revoking a privilege that the trigger package depends upon. Rebind of a trigger package provides for choosing an improved access path based on new indexes or statistics. There is an example of rebinding a trigger package:.

```
REBIND TRIGGER PACKAGE (DACUSID.ACUS20);
```

Figure TR.5 lists the bind parameters used when creating a trigger and thus a trigger package. Only the parameter marked with "*" can be changed with a rebind.

Figure TR.5. Trigger Package Bind Parameters

```
ACTION(ADD)
CURRENTDATA(YES)*
ISOLATION(CS)*
RELEASE(COMMIT)*
EXPLAIN(NO)*
FLAG(I)*
IMMEDWRITE(NO)*
OWNER(AUTHID)
QUALIFIER(AUTHID)
PATH(PATH)
QUERYOPT(1)
DBPROTOCOL(DRDA)
DEGREE(1)
DYNAMICRULES(BIND)
ENABLE(*)
NOREOPT(VARS)
NODEFER(PREPARE)
SQLERROR(NOPACKAGE)
VALIDATE(BIND)
```

*Parameter that can be changed with a rebind of the trigger package

A package cannot be created based on the trigger package with the BIND COPY command. Optionally, you can specify the location as part of trigger package name. However, it must be the current server location where the package resides. It is not possible to do a remote rebind.

Recommendation: Do a REBIND with EXPLAIN(YES) to determine the access path chosen for the trigger. Do consider the use of overriding the default and using RELEASE(DEALLOCATE) as discussed in Chapter CC.

Dropped and Invalid Triggers

The DROP statement can be used to delete a trigger like:

```
DROP TRIGGER BCUS10 RESTRICT;
```

Dropping a trigger automatically drops the trigger package. It is not possible to drop or free a trigger package directly. Drop of a trigger does not cascade and drop other objects. If a triggering table is dropped, the associated trigger and trigger package are also dropped.

Trigger packages like all packages are marked as invalid when an object (referenced table, index, view, etc.) that it depends on is dropped or required privileges are revoked. DB2 attempts an automatic rebind with the next attempt to invoke the trigger. Do consider executing an explicit rebind after re-establishing the dependencies. This avoids automatic rebind during prime time. It also avoids the user getting an error message if the trigger package is marked as inoperative which means that it must be explicitly bound. Fortunately, a trigger package is unlikely to be marked inoperative because if a table is dropped, the trigger is dropped. If an index is dropped, there is always an alternative access path. Invalid and inoperative trigger packages can be identified like:

```
SELECT  COLLID, NAME
FROM    SYSIBM.SYSPACKAGE
WHERE   TYPE  = 'T'
AND     (VALID = 'N' OR OPERATIVE = 'N');
```

TR.9 TRIGGERS IN THE CATALOG TABLES

You may well want to know the triggering actions that are taken when you manipulate a table. This can be determined by selecting from the catalog tables. Here is a statement to determine information on all triggers created on the CUSTOMER table with a specified owner.

```
SELECT DISTINCT SCHEMA, NAME, TRIGTIME,
               TRIGEVENT, GRANULARITY, CREATEDTS
FROM    SYSIBM.SYSTRIGGERS
WHERE   TBNAME  = 'CUSTOMER'
AND     TBOWNER = 'AUTHID';
```

The SCHEMA column contains the name of the schema or qualifier for the trigger.

The NAME column contains the name of the trigger.

The TRIGTIME indicates when the trigger is activated. "B" means that it is activated before an event. "A" means that it is activated after an event.

The TRIGEVENT indicates the event that causes the trigger to be activated. "I" means that the trigger is activated for an insert, "D" for a delete, and "U" for an update.

The GRANULARITY indicates that the trigger is executed once for each statement with a "S" in the column or for each row with a "R" in the column.

The CREATEDTS column contains the timestamp of when the trigger was created. The timestamp is used to determine the order of execution of multiple triggers.

The text (<=3460 bytes) of a trigger with the schema or qualifier of DACUSJDB and name of ACUS20 can be determined using the following statement. The maximum size of a trigger at present is 32 KB represented in multiple rows as indicated by SEQNO. Each row contains a maximum of 3460 bytes.

```
SELECT TEXT, SEQNO
FROM    SYSIBM.SYSTRIGGERS
WHERE   SCHEMA = 'DACUSJDB'
AND     NAME   = 'ACUS20'
ORDER BY SEQNO;
```

The COMMENT ON statement can be used to describe the trigger in SYSTRIGGERS.REMARKS like:

```
COMMENT ON TRIGGER ACUS20 IS
  'Delete all rows from ORDER table when
  a customer row is deleted';
```

TR.10 TRIGGERS AND CONSTRAINTS

Triggers have a number of valuable usages. However, there are alternatives for some types of triggers and some of these alternatives have performance advantages as discussed in this section.

Trigger and Constraint Similarities

Both triggers and constraints provide for having DB2 enforce rules and actions. Constraints can be RI and table check constraints. They both provide for global enforcement of rules and actions which are uniformly enforced across all interfaces including QMF, for example. They reduce program development time and costs by avoiding having to repeatedly code actions in multiple programs. Further, there are reductions in program maintenance time and costs. Certainly, dropping and recreating triggers and constraints requires less time than modifying programs. Triggers and constraints are automatically recorded in the catalog without concern for maintaining documentation on the actions implemented application programs. These advantages are discussed in more detail in Chapters CT and RI.

Constraints Contrasted with Triggers

RI and table check constraints have performance advantages over triggers in that they are enforced by Data Manager which reduces the path length. Triggers are implemented by the Relational Data Systems through the use of packages which results in more instructions being executed.

Constraints can only test simple predicates without subselects compared to the complex processing that can be defined in triggers. Constraints are good for declarative comparisons. They can be enforced when created. In contrast, the creation of a trigger does not check existing rows nor turn check pending on. Constraints can be enforced with the LOAD and CHECK DATA utilities. There is no utility support for triggers except for load resume with SHRLEVEL CHANGE (V7) which performs similar to INSERT statements as discussed in Chapter LC. Unfortunately, validation triggers are not activated when loading data despite the many performance advantages of using the LOAD utility to populate a table for the first time or add rows to a table compared to INSERT statements as discussed in Chapter BP. Constraints apply to INSERT, UPDATE, and DELETE statements. In contrast, a trigger must be created for each required operation.

A major advantage of triggers is that they provide for complex processing and validation of data.

Alternatives to Triggers

Do use the following techniques rather than triggers if they accomplish the goal due to their performance advantages.

- ♦ RI constraints when creating tables
- ♦ Table check constraints when creating a table
- ♦ User defined defaults when creating a table
- ♦ Distinct types
- ♦ If complex logic is required, consider placing most of the processing in a stored procedure and call the stored procedure from the trigger
- ♦ Data replication or propagation to maintain a copy of the data

If application enforced RI is used only where required (not for all cases), do consider the use of triggers.

TR.11 SUMMARY

Triggers provide for having DB2 enforce rules and actions. They can be activated before or after an event.

BEFORE triggers are useful for validation of data before inserting, updating, and deleting data. They can reference other tables in the WHEN clause. Triggers can be used to automatically generate values for newly inserted rows. They can modify row values for which the trigger was activated. However, they cannot modify other rows in the same or other tables.

AFTER triggers can be used to insert, update, delete, and select from a table. It is necessary to define a separate trigger for each operation if the action is to occur for more than one operations. You can compare values before and after an update as well as test a condition and execute one or more statements if the condition is true.

BEFORE triggers are executed followed by AFTER triggers in the order created.

Do be cautious of too complex of cascading triggers, UDFs, and stored procedures.

EXERCISES

The exercises that require the creation of triggers are on the sample EMP and DEPT tables to allow you to test your answers on DB2 for z/OS or OS/390 without having to create tables.

1. a) What is a logical reason that REFERENCING OLD AS O does not apply to insert triggers?

b) What is a logical reason that REFERENCING NEW AS N does not apply to delete triggers?

2. a) Is it necessary to proceed more than one statement (SQL or trigger statement) in the body of a trigger with BEGIN ATOMIC and end it with END?

b) What terminator must be used following each statement between BEGIN ATOMIC and END?

c) What terminator must be used following the END of BEGIN ATOMIC section?

3. Develop a trigger to validate that an employee to be inserted into the EMP table was born more than 18 years ago. Return an SQLSTATE of 'IBE10' and a message of 'Employee is less than 18 years' in the SQLCA. Rollback the INSERT statement that activated the trigger.

4. Attempt to execute the following statement and review the results.

```
INSERT INTO EMP
(EMPNO, FIRSTNME, MIDINIT, LASTNAME,
 WORKDEPT, PHONENO, HIREDATE, JOB, EDLEVEL,
 SEX, BIRTHDATE, SALARY, BONUS, COMM)
VALUES
('000099','MICHAEL',' ','HANNAN',
'A00','3978','2000-01-01','PRES',18,
 'M','1999-07-04',52750.00,1000.00,4220.00);
```

5. Develop a trigger such that MGRNO in the DEPT table cannot be updated to a value not in the EMPNO column of the EMP table.

6. Why can ";" be used as the terminator for the previously created BDEP10 trigger?

7. Attempt to execute the following statement. Why does the update fail.

```
UPDATE DEPT
   SET MGRNO     = '12345'
   WHERE DEPTNO = 'D12';
```

8. Develop a trigger to disallow the deletion of employees whose COMM is greater than their SALARY without further investigation.

9. What program logic can be developed to allow deletion of an employee whose COMM > SALARY despite implementation of the previous trigger?

10. Develop a trigger so that insertion of a new employee into WORKDEPT 'A00' is not allowed if it causes the sum of the salaries for the department to exceed 10,000.00.

11. Assume that updating the MGRNO column in the DEPT table means that a new manager has been assigned to a department and the person is given a 10 percent increase in salary. Develop an AFTER trigger to accomplish this.

12. After a department is deleted, send an email with information on the deleted department to the director. Assume that an EMAILD UDF has been created for this purpose. The function requires input parameters of DEPTNO, DEPTNAME, and MGRNO.

13. Is it possible to alter a trigger?

14. How is a trigger package created?

15. How can you determine the access path chosen for a trigger package.

ANSWERS

1. a) REFERENCING OLD AS O refers to the state of a row before the trigger processing. There is no row prior to inserting a row.

b) REFERENCING NEW AS N refers to the state of a row after trigger processing. There is no row after deleting a row.

2. a) It is necessary to proceed more than one statement (SQL or trigger statement) in the body of a trigger with BEGIN ATOMIC and end it with END.

b) The ";" terminator must be used following each statement between BEGIN ATOMIC and END.

c) You must define the terminator that follows the END of the BEGIN ATOMIC section according to the rules discussed in this chapter. The terminator "#" has been used in examples.

3. Here is a trigger to validate that an employee to be inserted into the EMP table was born more than 18 years ago. The SIGNAL statement is used to return an SQLSTATE of 'IBE10' and a message of 'Employee is less than 18 years old' in the SQLCA. A rollback of the INSERT statement that activated the trigger occurs if the SIGNAL statement is activated.

```
CREATE TRIGGER BEMP10
NO CASCADE BEFORE INSERT ON EMP
REFERENCING NEW AS N
FOR EACH ROW MODE DB2SQL
WHEN (CURRENT DATE - 18 YEARS < N.BIRTHDATE)
BEGIN ATOMIC
   SIGNAL SQLSTATE 'IBE10'
     ('Employee is less than 18 years');
END#
```

4. The result of executing:

```
INSERT INTO EMP
(EMPNO, FIRSTNME, MIDINIT, LASTNAME, WORKDEPT,
 PHONENO, HIREDATE, JOB, EDLEVEL, SEX,
 BIRTHDATE, SALARY, BONUS, COMM)
VALUES
('000099','MICHAEL',' ','HANNAN', 'A00',
 '3978', '2000-01-01', 'PRES', 18, 'M',
 '1999-07-04',52750.00,1000.00,4220.00);
```

is:

```
DSNT408I SQLCODE = -438, ERROR:  APPLICATION RAISED ERROR WITH DIAGNOSTIC
TEXT:
         Employee is less than 18 years
DSNT418I SQLSTATE   = IBE10 SQLSTATE RETURN CODE
DSNT415I SQLERRP    = DSNXRTYP SQL PROCEDURE DETECTING ERROR
```

```
DSNT416I SQLERRD   = 1  0  0  -1  0  0 SQL DIAGNOSTIC INFORMATION
DSNT416I SQLERRD   = X'00000001'  X'00000000'  X'00000000'  X'FFFFFFFF'
         X'00000000'  X'00000000' SQL DIAGNOSTIC INFORMATION
---------+---------+---------+---------+---------+---------+---------+-----
DSNE618I ROLLBACK PERFORMED, SQLCODE IS 0
DSNE616I STATEMENT EXECUTION WAS SUCCESSFUL, SQLCODE IS 0
```

Notice that -438 SQLCODE was received along with a rollback and the specified SQLSTATE and message. Do be cautious of the terminator used. The question and answer used a terminator of ";". If you executed the CREATE TRIGGER and INSERT statement in the same file, it is necessary to use "#" as the terminator for the INSERT statement assuming that you used "#" as the terminator for the CREATE TRIGGER statement.

5. Here is a trigger such that a MGRNO in the DEPT table cannot be updated to a value not in the EMPNO column of the EMP table.

```
CREATE TRIGGER BDEP10
  NO CASCADE BEFORE UPDATE OF MGRNO ON DEPT
  REFERENCING NEW AS N
  FOR EACH ROW MODE DB2SQL
  WHEN (N.MGRNO NOT IN
    (SELECT EMPNO
      FROM   EMP))
        SIGNAL SQLSTATE 'IBD10'
            ('Manager is not in the EMP table');
```

6. The ";" can be used as the terminator for the previously created BDEP10 trigger because there is only one statement to be executed and there is no BEGIN ATOMIC and END clause.

7. The update failed because EMPNO '12345' is not in the EMP table which is required by the BDEP10 trigger.

8. The following trigger disallows the deletion of employees whose COMM is greater than their SALARY without further investigation.

```
CREATE TRIGGER BEMP20
NO CASCADE BEFORE DELETE ON EMP
REFERENCING OLD AS O
FOR EACH ROW MODE DB2SQL
WHEN (O.COMM > O.SALARY)
BEGIN ATOMIC
  SIGNAL SQLSTATE 'IBD10'
    ('Good sales person');
```

```
          END#
```

9. One possibility is to set the COMM for the employee to zero before deleting the employee row.

10. Following is a trigger that does not allow the insertion of a new employee into WORKDEPT 'A00' if it causes the sum of the salaries for the department to exceed 10,000.00.

```
          CREATE TRIGGER AEMP10
          AFTER INSERT ON EMP
          REFERENCING NEW_TABLE AS NT NEW AS N
          FOR EACH ROW MODE DB2SQL
          WHEN (10000.00 >
            (SELECT SUM(SALARY)
             FROM    NT
             WHERE   WORKDEPT = 'A00'))
               BEGIN ATOMIC
                 SIGNAL SQLSTATE 'IAR10'
                     ('A00 salary budget exceeded');
          END#
```

The trigger can be tested with the following INSERT statement.

```
          INSERT INTO EMP
          (EMPNO, FIRSTNME, MIDINIT, LASTNAME,
           WORKDEPT, PHONENO, HIREDATE, JOB, EDLEVEL,
           SEX, BIRTHDATE, SALARY, BONUS, COMM)
          VALUES ('000333', 'Michael',' ','Hannan',
           'A00','3978','1965-01-01', 'PRES', 18,
           'M', '1933-08-14',6000.00,1000.00,8000.00)#
```

11. The following trigger will increase the salary of the EMPNO by 10 percent in the EMP table after updating the corresponding MGRNO column in the DEPT table.

```
          CREATE TRIGGER ADEP20
          AFTER UPDATE OF MGRNO ON DEPT
          REFERENCING OLD AS O
                      NEW AS N
          FOR EACH ROW MODE DB2SQL
          BEGIN ATOMIC
            UPDATE EMP
            SET SALARY  = SALARY * 1.1
```

```
        WHERE EMPNO = N.MGRNO;
    END#
```

12. Send an email to the director when a department has been deleted using the EMAILD UDF.

```
    CREATE TRIGGER ADEP30
        AFTER DELETE ON DEPT
        REFERENCING OLD AS O
        FOR EACH ROW MODE DB2SQL
        BEGIN ATOMIC
            VALUES (EMAILD (O.DEPTNO, O.DEPTNAME,
                    O.MGRNO));
        END#
```

13. It is not possible to alter a trigger. It is necessary to drop the trigger and recreate it to make any changes.

14. A trigger package is created automatically when the trigger is created.

15. Rebind the trigger package with the parameter EXPLAIN(YES)

FIGURES

Stored Procedures

SP.1 INTRODUCTION

Stored procedures can be subroutines, modules, or main programs. They are developed and executed much like any subroutine except that they are called using SQL CALL rather than CALL. Stored procedures are managed by DB2 after the developer executes the CREATE PROCEDURE statement which updates the SYSROUTINES and SYSPARMS (V6) catalog tables. The calling program can call multiple stored procedures at the local site and multiple remote sites with two phase commit processing.

Stored procedures can be written in COBOL, PL/1, C, JAVA, COMPJAVA, REXX (V7, V6 APAR PQ30219, V5 APAR PQ29706), assembler, and the SQL procedure language. The SQL procedure language consists of BASIC like procedural code (from SQL99 and ISO standards, also known as Persistent Stored Module (PSM)) and SQL. Stored procedures can contain multiple static and dynamic SQL statements. They can be called from any programming language that allows for an SQL CALL statement including Microsoft Visual Basic and Studio, IBM VisualAge for JAVA, PowerBuilder, etc. The stored procedure and calling program need not be written in the same language nor run on the same platform. A stored procedure can be written in COBOL, and be called from a C program on the client, for example. It is necessary to use the Language Environment (LE) regardless of the programming language. LE establishes a common run-time environment, provides storage management and condition handling to host programs. LE run-time library and any language specific libraries are specified in the link-edit step. Details can be found in the *OS/390 Language Environment for OS/390 & VM Programming Reference* manual. The platform for developing and calling procedures can be DB2 Universal Database (UDB) DB2 has this support on a number of platforms including OS/390, z/OS, Windows 2000, ME, 98, 95, Linux, Unix, AIX, HP-UX, Solaris, UNMA-Q, OS/2, and OS/400.

Advantages of Stored Procedures

A primary advantage of stored procedures is to reduce the costs of formatting and transmitting messages in a client/server environment. These significant costs are reduced by formatting and transmitting a message to execute a stored procedure which can contain any number of SQL and procedural statements. These statements are executed at the remote site and the results transmitted to the caller. Also, lock contention is reduced because most locks are not held while messages are sent and received. In one test, IBM found that the use of stored procedures resulted in 85 percent more transactions per second. Using the client/server workload, the transaction rate was 30.3 transactions per second without the use of stored procedures compared to 56.7 transactions per second with the use of stored procedures.

Stored procedures can be used to manage client processes centrally. Their use avoids having to modify many client programs if the data or processing changes. You can modify stored procedures without affecting the calling program if call parameters are not changed. Stored procedures provide for encapsulating portions of an application program so that the caller need not have knowledge of sensitive data and processing. Procedures can be developed on one platform and deploy on another platform.

Procedures Can Call Procedures (V6)

A procedure can call a procedure. There is a limit of 16 levels of nesting including procedures, triggers, and user defined functions at local and remote sites.

Restrictions: Qualifying rows are returned only to the previous nesting level. It is not possible to nest procedures between DB2 managed and WLM (Workload Manager) managed procedures. The use of COMMIT ON RETURN YES is not allowed.

External Stored Procedures and SQL Procedures

DB2 offers two types of stored procedures both of which are invoked with EXEC SQL CALL. The costs of executing SQL is the same with and without the use of stored procedures. The term *procedure* is used to refers to both external stored procedure and SQL procedure when the description applies to both. Any differences are noted. This subsection introduces the two types of procedures with subsequent detailed coverage throughout the chapter.

An External stored procedure can be written in a host language as a subroutine or main program. They must be defined to DB2 using the CREATE PROCEDURE statement.

An SQL procedure is developed using the CREATE PROCEDURE statement. The statement also defines the procedure to DB2 as with external stored procedure. The difference is that the SQL procedure is developed within the CREATE PROCEDURE statement using SQL statements and SQL stored procedure language. The language provides for ease of use but limited functionality compared to a full function host language.

The DB2 Stored Procedure Builder (SPB) with a Graphical User Interface (GUI) front end can be used to build SQL procedures. You can be prompted to build a procedure resulting in SQL procedure language and SQL statements. You can build, modify, run, and manage procedures. You can use the SQL procedure language, JAVA, or REXX. The SPB generates a C program and package which can run on the DB2 Universal Database (UDB) has this support on a number of platforms including OS/390, z/OS, Windows 2000, ME, 98, 95, Linux, Unix, AIX, HP-UX, Solaris, UNMA-Q, OS/2, and OS/400. A debugger option is available.

SP.2 CALLING A PROCEDURE

EXEC SQL CALL is required to call a procedure. The procedure name is a three part name consisting of the location, server name, and procedure name; each part has a maximum of 18 bytes. The location portion of the name is the name of the DBMS where the procedure is stored. If it is not specified in the SQL CALL, the content of the current server special register is used. This special register can be set using the CONNECT statement. Location independence is supported using DRDA (V6), therefore the CONNECT statement is not required. The second part of the name, server name, should be SYSPROC when using DB2 for z/OS or OS/390 as the server. The third component of the name is the procedure name. The three part name can be called using a literal or host variable preceded by a ":" as in the following statement. If a host variable is used to contain the procedure name, an incremental bind is required on the first call. Subsequent calls use an executable form of the bound CALL statement to reduce costs (V6).

```
EXEC SQL CALL :INORUP (:SN-IN, :SN, :SNAME,
      :STATUS, :CITY, :OPERATION, :SCODE)
END-EXEC.
```

Each parameter of the SQL CALL can be a host variable (not a data structure) or literal as defined as in the CREATE PROCEDURE statement.

The call parameters can be defined in the linkage section and using clause of the procedure division of the procedure. An example of this in COBOL for the above SQL CALL is in Figure SP.1.

Figure SP.1. Defining a parameter list in COBOL

```
IDENTIFICATION DIVISION.
. . .
DATA DIVISION.
. . .
LINKAGE SECTION.
01  SN-IN      PIC X(2).
01  SN         PIC X(2).
01  SNAME      PIC X(20).
01  STATUS     PIC S9(4) USAGE COMP.
01  CITY       PIC X(15).
01  OPERATION  PIC X(6).
01  SCODE      PIC S9(4) COMP.
```

The fragment of code in Figure SP.2 requires the transmission of a message for each SQL statement and for each test of the SQLCODE. If the code is part of an external stored procedure, it is necessary only to format and transmit the call statement:

```
EXEC SQL CALL :INORUP (:SN-IN, :SN, :SNAME,
      :STATUS, :CITY, :OPERATION, :SCODE)
END-EXEC.
```

Arguments can contain expressions including Operators (+, -, *, /), functions, CASE, user-defined data types, anc CAST.

Figure SP.2. Fragment of code for an external stored procedure

```
EXEC SQL SELECT SN, SNAME, STATUS, CITY
         INTO  :SN,:SNAME,:STATUS,:CITY
         FROM  S
```

```
            WHERE   SN = :SN-IN END-EXEC.

  IF SQLCODE = 0
     EXEC SQL UPDATE S SET STATUS = :STATUS
               WHERE   SN = :SN-IN END-EXEC.
     MOVE 'UPDATE' TO OPERATION.
     MOVE SQLCODE TO SCODE.
     Return to client

  IF SQLCODE = 100
     EXEC SQL INSERT INTO
               S(SN, SNAME, STATUS, CITY)
         VALUES(:SN,:SNAME,:STATUS,:CITY)
     END-EXEC.
     MOVE 'INSERT' TO OPERATION.
     MOVE SQLCODE TO SCODE.
     Return to client
```

You will find the red manual *Cross-Platform DB2 Stored Procedures: Building and Debugging*, SG24-5485-01 to be useful.

SP.3 RETURNING DATA TO THE CALLING PROGRAM

Result sets can be returned to the calling program. The calling program can fetch from the cursors declared and opened in the procedure as if the cursor had been established in the calling program. An alternative is to have the procedure return a single message to the calling program. We will first look at returning a result set.

Return a Result Set to the Caller

The WITH RETURN clause on the cursor declaration and a declare locator host variables provide for the calling program to fetch rows from a cursor declared in a procedure (can be on a temporary table). The WITH HOLD clause is required for result set to be usable after a commit. In addition, COMMIT ON RETURN YES is required in the CREATE PROCEDURE statement as discussed in Section SP.4. The cursor must be declared and opened in the procedure like:

```
    EXEC SQL DECLARE SCURSOR CURSOR
        WITH HOLD WITH RETURN FOR
```

```
        SELECT  SN, SNAME, STATUS, CITY
        FROM    S
        WHERE   STATUS > :NEW-STATUS END-EXEC.

EXEC SQL OPEN SCURSOR END-EXEC.
```

The calling program must declare, associate, and allocate a locator host variable as shown in a fragment of a program written in COBOL (Figure SP.3). L1 is declared as a RESULT-SET-LOCATOR in a 01 level data structure and must be variable in length. The L1 result set locator is associated with the procedure :INORUP in an EXEC SQL ASSOCIATE RESULT SET LOCATOR statement after calling the :INORUP procedure. It is also necessary to allocate the cursor name as specified in the procedure DECLARE CURSOR statement with the :L1 locator variable using the EXEC SQL ALLOCATE statement. ALLOCATE cursor does not open the cursor; it must be opened in the procedure. The calling program can then fetch from the SCURSOR cursor declared in the procedure as if it had declared and opened the cursor. The calling program or procedure can close the cursor. The cursor is not closed in the procedure when it ends unless it is explicitly closed.

Figure SP.3. Declare, associate, and allocate a locator host variable

```
EXEC SQL BEGIN DECLARE SECTION END-EXEC.
01  L1 SQL TYPE IS RESULT-SET-LOCATOR VARYING.
EXEC SQL END DECLARE SECTION END-EXEC.
...
EXEC SQL CALL :INORUP (:SN-IN, :SN, :SNAME,
     :STATUS, :CITY, :OPERATION, :SCODE)
END-EXEC.

EXEC SQL ASSOCIATE RESULT SET LOCATOR (:L1)
        WITH PROCEDURE :INORUP END-EXEC.

EXEC SQL ALLOCATE SCURSOR CURSOR FOR RESULT
SET :L1 END-EXEC.

EXEC SQL FETCH SCURSOR INTO
        :SN-IN, :SN, :SNAME, :STATUS, :CITY,
        :OPERATION, :SCODE END-EXEC.
```

Multiple locator variables can be declared, associated, and allocated for each of multiple cursors. The calling client program can fetch from the cursors in any order independent of the order returned from the procedure provided that DRDA level 3 is supported.

The members of DSN8ED1 and DSN8ED2 in the SDSNSAMP library are sample programs calling procedures.

ODBC and CLI: When using Open Database Connectivity (ODBC) and Call Level Interface (CLI), the calling program must fetch from the result sets in the order returned by the server to comply with the ODBC rules. A procedure can be called from ODBC and CLI calls can be issued from within a procedure. ODBC and X/OPEN CLI can be used by z/OS or OS/390 application programs which is useful when porting work station server applications to z/OS or OS/390.

Returning a Single Message

An output parameter can be defined for each row fetched or each column in each row to be returned to the client. This can be cumbersome if the procedure must return a number of columns and rows to be displayed on a screen at the client site.

An alternative is to have the procedure build a character string of 1920 bytes to fill a 24x80 screen based on multiple rows processed and transmitted it to the caller. It is necessary for the client and server programs to establish conventions for the exchange of data. Another possibility is to define an output parameter for each row fetched or each column to return to the client. The second alternative can result in a very long parameter list.

There are generous limit on the number of bytes that can be returned in a single parameter and for the entire procedure. The maximum number of bytes that can be passed in a single parameter of an SQL CALL statement is 32,765. The maximum number of bytes that can be passed to or from a procedure is 5.4 MB.

SP.4 CREATE PROCEDURE STATEMENT

The CREATE PROCEDURE statement is used to describe a procedure to DB2 (V6). This determines how the procedure is to be executed. The statement populates two catalog tables. SYSROUTINES contains a row for every routine including a procedure, user-defined function, and cast function. SYSPARMS table contains a row for each parameter of a routine or multiple rows for table parameters (one for each column of the table). The first example contains only the basic parameters.

```
CREATE PROCEDURE INORUP(IN SN_IN CHAR(2),
   OUT SN CHAR(2), OUT SNAME CHAR(20),
   OUT STATUS SMALLINT, OUT CITY CHAR(15),
   INOUT OPERATION CHAR(6), OUT SCODE SMALLINT)
DYNAMIC RESULT SETS 4
EXTERNAL  NAME INORUP
LANGUAGE  COBOL
PARAMETER STYLE DB2SQL
RUN OPTIONS 'HEAP(,,ANY),BELOW(4K,,),
   ALL31(ON), STACK(,,ANY,)';
```

INORUP is the name used to call the procedure. The parameters following INORUP in parenthesis must begin with IN, OUT, or INOUT (input, output, or input and output parameter), optionally the name of name of a host variable can be specified or a literal can be used, the last description of the input/output field must designate the data type and length of field.

DYNAMIC RESULT SETS 4 indicate that rows can be fetched from 4 cursors, for example.

EXTERNAL NAME is the name of the load module (need not be the same name as the procedure).

LANGUAGE COBOL means that the procedure is written in COBOL. It can be COBOL, PLI, C, ASSEMBLE, REXX, COMPJAVA (can specify a jar name), or SQL for SQL procedures.

Create Parameters in Detail

A few of the basic parameters have been discussed in this chapter. Most parameters apply to external and SQL procedures. The parameters that apply only to external procedures (not SQL procedures) are EXTERNAL, LANGUAGE, PARAMETER STYLE, NO SQL, DBINFO, and CALLED ON NULL INPUT. The parameters used in the following statement are similar to those used when creating a user-defined function (UDF) in the next Chapter UD. There are some additional parameters that apply only to

UDF which are described in that chapter. Please see Chapter UD Section 9 for a summary of the similarities and differences between procedures and UDF.

```
CREATE PROCEDURE INORUP(IN SN_IN CHAR(2),
   OUT SN CHAR(2), OUT SNAME CHAR(20),
   OUT STATUS SMALLINT, OUT CITY CHAR(15),
INOUT OPERATION CHAR(6),
   OUT SCODE SMALLINT)
DYNAMIC RESULT SETS 4
EXTERNAL  NAME INORUP
LANGUAGE  COBOL
PARAMETER CCSID EBCDIC
PARAMETER STYLE DB2SQL
COMMIT ON RETURN YES
WLM ENVIRONMENT WLMENVCU
PROGRAM TYPE SUB
STAY RESIDENT NO
CALLED ON NULL INPUT
MODIFIES SQL DATA
NO DBINFO
DETERMINISTIC
FENCED
ASUTIME LIMIT 80000
NO COLLID
SECURITY DB2
INHERIT SPECIAL REGISTERS
RUN OPTIONS 'HEAP(,,ANY), BELOW(4K,,),
   ALL31(ON), STACK(,,ANY,)';
```

EXTERNAL NAME identifies the name of the load module resulting from program preparation of a stored procedure or UDF. 'INORUP' is the external name of the INORUP function. This is the name used in the SQL CALL statement for procedures or in an SQL statement for invocation of a UDF. 'TOTALAMT' is the external name of the TOTAL_AMOUNT UDF in Chapter UD. Optionally, the external name can be enclosed in single quotes for all languages except JAVA and COMPJAVA which require the single quotes.

LANGUAGE COBOL gives the name of the host program language used to develop the procedure or UDF. It can be COBOL, PLI, C, REXX, JAVA, COMPJAVA, or ASSEMBLE for external stored procedures. An SQL procedure requires LANGUAGE SQL.

PARAMETER CCSID EBCDIC (default) for all parameters if CCSID is not specified for a data type definition using CCSID EBCDIC, UNICODE or ASCII which supports multilingual data. The default can be changed on installation panel DSNTIPF to CCSID UNICODE or ASCII. All CALL parameters must be of the same encoding scheme. An SQL statement must reference data of the same encoding scheme.

PARAMETER STYLE DB2SQL (default) indicates the linkage convention that the procedure or UDF uses to receive input parameters from and return values to the invoking SQL statement. It has similar meaning when used with procedures and UDF. The CALL parameters (input and output parameters for UDF), null indicator for each parameter on the CALL statement, SQLSTATE to be returned to DB2, qualified and specific name, SQL diagnostic string to be returned to DB2, etc. It cannot be used with LANGUAGE REXX.

The following PARAMETER STYLE clauses apply only to procedures (not UDF). They can be used with REXX.

PARAMETER STYLE GENERAL indicates that only the parameters on the CALL statement are passed to the stored procedure. The parameters cannot be null.

PARAMETER STYLE GENERAL WITH NULL is like GENERAL except that a vector of null indicators for each CALL parameter are also passed to the procedure that allows the procedure to accept or return null parameter values.

PARAMETER STYLE JAVA must be used with LANGUAGE JAVA and COMPJAVA. It indicates parameters are passed to conform to JAVA and SQLJ specifications. INOUT and OUT parameters are passed as single-entry arrays. The DBINFO structure is not passed.

COMMIT ON RETURN NO (default) means that the UR is not to be committed upon successful return (non-negative SQLCODE) from the procedure or invocation of UDF. This parameter value is required when nesting procedures.

COMMIT ON RETURN YES means that the UR is to be committed upon successful return (non-negative SQLCODE) from the procedure or UDF. Commit applies to calling program and the procedure. It avoids the possibility that the procedure or UDF does not commit in a timely fashion, ensures that locks are released in a timely fashion, and reduces message traffic. If the cursor is to be usable after the return, it must be defined with CURSOR WITH HOLD. COMMIT ON RETURN YES cannot be used in a procedure definition if called by a UDF, trigger, or another procedure.

WLM ENVIRONMENT without a name following the parameter means that the procedure or UDF runs in the work load manager (WLM) established stored procedure address space that is specified at installation time. If the parameter is followed by a name, this means that the procedure or UDF runs in the named WLM environment.

WLM ENVIRONMENT followed by (name,*) means that when an SQL application program directly invokes a procedures or UDF, the WLM environment in which the procedure or UDF runs is used. If a procedure or UDF invokes another procedure or UDF, it runs in the same environment that the invoking routine uses.

NO WLM ENVIRONMENT means that the procedure is to run in the DB2-established stored procedure address space (does not apply to UDF). This parameter cannot be used with PROGRAM TYPE SUB, SECURITY USER, SECURITY DEFINER, LANGUAGE JAVA or COMPJAVA, and parameters with a LOB data type or distinct type based on a LOB data type. This parameter cannot be used with REXX.

The users of a procedure or UDF must have the appropriate authorization to execute functions in the specified WLM environment. RACF can be used to provide the required authority.

PROGRAM TYPE MAIN (default when using DB2 rather STD) means that the UDF is written and executed as a main program. This option gives you full language capabilities and guaranteed resources are freed (storage, for example).

PROGRAM TYPE SUB means that the procedure or UDF is written and executed as a subroutine. It cannot be used with NO WLM ENVIRONMENT. Reduces CPU cost for call processing and cleanup (30 K instructions) compared to a MAIN program. However, some languages have restrictions (no I/O for Pl/1, for example). The program must be dynamically loadable (fetchable). It is the developers responsibility to free resources (storage and files, for example). SUB is always in effect when using LANGUAGE REXX.

STAY RESIDENT NO (default) means that the load module of the procedure or UDF does not remain resident in memory. The load module is deleted from memory at end of its processing. This is a good choice for non-reentrant procedures and UDF.

STAY RESIDENT YES means that load module remains resident in memory at the end of its processing. This is a good choice for reentrant load modules that are used frequently.

RETURNS NULL ON NULL INPUT means that UDF is not invoked if any of the input arguments are null. The result returned to the invoking program is null. NOT NULL CALL is a synonym for RETURNS NULL ON NULL INPUT.

CALLED ON NULL INPUT (default) means that the procedure or UDF is invoked regardless of whether the input argument is null or non-null. The developer is responsible for testing for nulls. The result can be null or a non-null value. The procedure or UDF should check for null to determine the required processing. NULL CALL is a synonym for CALLED ON NULL INPUT

MODIFIES SQL DATA (default) means that you can execute most SQL DML, DDL, and DCL statements in the procedure or UDF. ROLLBACK and RELEASE statement (without the TO SAVEPOINT clause) cannot be used in UDF or a procedure if the procedure is in the calling chain of a UDF or trigger. DISALLOW PARALLEL is a good choice to avoid unexpected results if different results can occur when a parallel path is or is not chosen. This is the default when MODIFIES SQL DATA is used.

READS SQL DATA means that you cannot execute SQL statements that modifies data. It is possible to use statements to read data including SELECT and cursor management statements. Also some statements including DECLARE and related statements, statements for preparation and execution of dynamic SQL, most SET statements, and etc. can be processed.

CONTAINS SQL means that no SQL statements that read or modify data can be executed. It is possible to invoke some statements including

DECLARE and related statements, statements for preparation and execution of dynamic SQL, most SET statements, and etc.

NO SQL means that no SQL statements can be executed in the procedure or UDF. However, most DECLARE statements can be used in procedures.

Details on each statement allowed and disallowed in a procedure and UDF based on the chosen parameter is given in the *SQL Reference* manual.

NO DBINFO (default) means that no additional information is passed to the procedure or UDF when it is invoked.

DBINFO means that additional arguments can be passed when the procedure or UDF is invoked, for example the run-time AUTHID, schema name, name of the table or column that the object might be inserting into or updating, and the database server ID that invoked the procedure or UDF. The *Application Programming and SQL Guide* manual contains additional details.

NOT DETERMINISTIC (default) means that the procedure or UDF might not return the same result for identical input arguments. A random number returned from a procedure or UDF that generates values based on the range of input parameters is not the same in most cases, for example. Scrollable cursors can result in fetching the same row multiple times yielding varying results. If a parallel path is chosen, different results can be returned. This can be avoided by specifying DISALLOW PARALLEL which is the default when using this parameter. VARIANT is a synonym for NOT DETERMINISTIC.

DETERMINISTIC means that a procedure or UDF always returns the same result for identical input arguments. DAYOFWEEK always returns an integer in the range of 1 to 7, where 1 represents Sunday, for example. NOT VARIANT is a synonym for DETERMINISTIC.

FENCED (default) means that the procedure or UDF runs in an external address space to prevent the function from corrupting DB2 storage. If fenced is not used, the procedure or UDF can cause DB2 to abend since it runs within a DB2 address space. If the object is thoroughly tested, performance is improved.

ASUTIME NO LIMIT (default) means that there is no processor time limit for the procedure or UDF.

ASUTIME LIMIT with a value provides for specifying the total amount of processor time, in CPU service units, that a single invocation of a procedure or UDF can use. ASU is the amount of CPU time in service units depending on the computer model used. The value can be up to and including 2 GB. The *OS/390 MVS Initialization and Tuning Guide* manual in the section SRM (System Resource Manager) gives the details. The ASU equals the CPU seconds * service units per second. For example, if you wish to have a limit of 10 CPU seconds and the service units per second for your computer is 800, 8000 would be specified as the ASUTIME LIMIT. The procedure or UDF is cancelled when the limit is exceeded. The value specified here is not related to the ASUTIME column of the resource limit specification table.

NO COLLID (default) means that the package collection for the procedure or UDF is the same as the package collection of the object that invokes the procedure or UDF. If a trigger invokes the procedure or UDF, the collection of the trigger package is used. If the invoking program does not use a package, the package collection is the value of the CURRENT PACKAGESET special register.

COLLID followed by the name of a collection is the package collection that is used when the procedure or UDF is executed.

SECURITY DB2 (default) means that the AUTHID that is associated with the WLM-established stored procedure address space is used if the object accesses resources that an external security product protects. Procedures and UDFs do not require an external security environment.

SECURITY USER means that the primary AUTHID of the process that invoked the object is used to determine if the function can access resources protected by an external security product. An external security environment should be established for the procedure or UDF if this parameter value is chosen.

SECURITY DEFINER means that the AUTHID of the invoked object owner is used to determine if the procedure or UDF can access resources protected by an external security product. In this case an external security environment should be established for the object and NO WLM ENVIRONMENT cannot be specified as with SECURITY USER

Special Register values are passed to procedures and UDF depending on the parameters INHERIT SPECIAL REGISTERS (default) and DEFAULT SPECIAL REGISTERS. INHERIT SPECIAL REGISTERS means that special register values from the invoker are used. DEFAULT SPECIAL REGISTERS means that occasionally, values specified at installation are used. The rules for passing each of over 20 special registers are summarized in the *SQL Reference* manual table "Characteristics of special registers in a user-defined function or a stored procedure". The table also indicates whether each special register can be set in a procedure or UDF.

RUN OPTIONS provides for passing 254 or fewer bytes of options to the LE to be used for the procedure or UDF. The parameter cannot be specified with LANGUAGE JAVA or COMPJAVA. If the parameter is not specified, an empty string is passed and the installation defaults are used. The parameters H(,,ANY),STAC(,,ANY,),STO(,,,4K), BE(4K,,),LIBS(4K,,),ALL31(ON) limits storage that is required by LE. The *OS/390 Language Environment for OS/390 & VM Programming Reference* manual contains details.

SYSADM or SYSCTRL can create and manage procedures. Optionally CREATEIN privilege for the AUTHID, schema or all schemas can be granted like:

```
GRANT CREATEIN ON SCHEMA MKTGXW TO PUBLIC;
```

ALTER and DROP Procedures

The ALTER PROCEDURE statement can be used to change most parameters. Except the input and output parameters, CALLED ON NULL INPUT, and FENCED parameters cannot be altered. The procedure package is invalidated.

A procedure can be dropped like:

```
DROP PROCEDURE INORUP RESTRICT;
```

The parameter RESTRICT is required. It avoids dropping a procedure used by a trigger. The procedure package is dropped.

Packages and plans calling the procedure are invalidated.

SP.5 SAVEPOINT MANAGEMENT

The SAVEPOINT statement provides for establishing a point to which you can rollback or you can release the savepoint (V6 APAR PQ30439). A savepoint with the name of REDO can be established like:

```
EXEC SQL SAVEPOINT REDO UNIQUE
    ON ROLLBACK RETAIN CURSORS END-EXEC.
```

You can rollback work to the named savepoint like:

```
EXEC SQL ROLLBACK TO REDO END-EXEC.
```

Optionally, you can release a savepoint like:

```
EXEC SQL RELEASE SAVEPOINT REDO END-EXEC.
```

A savepoint applies to the DBMS where it is set (not other DBMSs). It is possible to connect to another location within the scope of a savepoint when using the DRDA CONNECT statement. This does not apply when using the private protocol. For example, a savepoint set in Los Angeles is unknown to SQL statements executed in San Francisco and vice versa. It is not possible to use an alias or three-part name to access a remote DBMS within the scope of a savepoint using DRDA and private protocol. This is because developers need not be aware of remote sites involved.

Savepoints can be used in a host program including stored procedures and external user-defined functions defined with MODIFIES SQLDATA. They cannot be used in triggers nested within user-defined functions. Savepoints can be executed statically or dynamically. If they are executed dynamically, it is necessary to bind with DYNAMICRULES of RUN.

Establishing a SAVEPOINT

A savepoint must be given a name of 128 bytes or less. REDO is the name given to the savepoint established in previous and following examples. The are three additional clauses that can be used when defining a SAVEPOINT, two of which are shown in the statement:

```
EXEC SQL SAVEPOINT REDO UNIQUE
```

```
            ON ROLLBACK RETAIN CURSORS END-EXEC.
```

UNIQUE means that the savepoint name must be unique within a unit of recovery (UR). If you do not use UNIQUE and establish a savepoint with a duplicate name, the first savepoint is destroyed and a new savepoint is established (release rules discussed later in this section do not apply). It is advisable to avoid using the same name for multiple savepoints. Indeed, UNIQUE cannot be used when manipulating savepoints within a loop.

ON ROLLBACK RETAIN CURSORS means not to close cursors opened after establishing a savepoint and issuing a rollback. Cursors are not tracked. However, the cursor may not be useable. For example, if an inserted row is rolled back, an error results from an attempt to update or delete the row.

ON ROLLBACK RETAIN LOCKS means that any locks acquired after establishing the savepoint are not released upon a rollback to a savepoint. Locks are not tracked.

The cost of establishing a savepoint is about the same as fetching a row.

Rollback to a Savepoint

Rollback work to where the REDO savepoint was established can be accomplished with or without the keyword 'WORK'.

```
      EXEC SQL ROLLBACK      TO REDO END-EXEC. or
      EXEC SQL ROLLBACK WORK TO REDO END-EXEC.
```

If the savepoint name is not specified, a rollback of all savepoints set within a UR occurs.

```
      EXEC SQL ROLLBACK TO REDO END-EXEC.
```

If there is not an active savepoint when the rollback is issued, an error is received.

Savepoints set after the one rolled back are also rolled back. For example, assume that REDO1, REDO2, and REDO3 savepoints are established in the order specified. The rollback to REDO2 rolls back REDO2 and REDO3.

A rollback applies to changes made to the data, schema, and declared global temporary tables (not created global temporary tables). Some work is not rolled back including:

♦ Results of SQL issued on a created temporary table (warning is issued)
♦ Open or close of cursors
♦ Changes to cursor positioning
♦ Acquisition and release of locks
♦ Caching of rolled back dynamic statements

Release Savepoint

It is not possible to rollback to a savepoint or savepoints established after the named saved point once it is released. A savepoint can be released with either of the statements:

```
EXEC SQL RELEASE    REDO END-EXEC. or
EXEC SQL RELEASE TO REDO END-EXEC.
```

This applies to savepoints established in a main program and subroutines called by the main program. For example, assume that a main program establishes REDO1 savepoint, subroutine A establishes REDO2 savepoint, and subroutine B establishes REDO3 savepoint. If the main program releases REDO1 after it executes and the two subroutines are executed, savepoints REDO1, REDO2, and REDO3 are released.

COMMIT releases all savepoints within the current UR.

COMMIT and ROLLBACK

A COMMIT or ROLLBACK statement issued in a procedure results in a commit or rollback of all changes within the UR including work in the procedure and work in the calling program (V7). All cursors in the procedure and calling program are closed except those defined with CURSOR WITH HOLD.

A procedure that executes a COMMIT or ROLLBACK must be defined with CONTAINS SQL, READS SQL DATA, or MODIFIES SQL DATA.

The COMMIT ON RETURN has no effect on execution of COMMIT and ROLLBACK statements.

A procedure cannot successfully execute a COMMIT or ROLLBACK if the procedure:

♦   Is nested within a trigger or UDF (user-defined function).
♦   Is called by a client that uses 2 phase commit processing.
♦   Client program uses connects to the remote server that has the procedure.
♦   Cannot include ROLLBACK in a procedure if DB2 is not the commit coordinator.

If any of the above conditions apply, the procedure and caller are put in a must-rollback state and both are given a -751 SQLCODE. The caller must issue an explicit rollback or terminate execution which results in an implicit rollback. This is effectively a work-around to allow the procedure to force the calling program to rollback.

Prior to V7, -751 SQLCODE is received by the calling program if a COMMIT or ROLLBACK is issued in the procedure.

SP.6 FUNCTIONS NOT SUPPORTED IN A PROCEDURE

Most functions performed in a DB2 application program can be performed in a procedure with some exceptions prior to V7.

Calling a procedure from a procedure (V5): Statements that result in a -751 SQLCODE which forces the calling program to issue a rollback are:

♦   SQL CALL to another procedure
♦   CONNECT
♦   RELEASE
♦   SET CONNECTION
♦   SET CURRENT SQLID

These restrictions are a result of the inability to call a procedure from another procedure (V5).

Use of CAF: If the call attach facility (CAF) is used by DB2 to manage procedures, it cannot be used by the procedure.

DRDA and the private protocol: A program cannot mix the Distributed Relational Database Architecture (DRDA) with private protocol within a UR. The protocols are also known as application directed (DRDA) and system directed (private protocol) processing.

Access to Non-DB2 Resources

DL/1 databases, message queue series (MQSeries), VSAM, and flat files can be accessed from a procedure in addition to tables. It is necessary to define DD statements for the files in JCL for a procedure address space.

A procedure can change DB2 tables, DL/1 databases, recoverable VSAM files, and MQSeries messages. A COMMIT or ROLLBACK applies to all of these resources. That is, all updates within a UR are committed or rolled back. z/OS or OS/390 WLM-established procedure address spaces must be used for this two phase commit processing. Procedure address spaces are discussed in Section SP.10.

DB2 notifies z/OS or OS/390 RRS (Resource Recovery Services) about commit and rollback decisions and RRS passes the decision to other resources. The path length is increased when updating non-DB2 data. It is necessary to use the recoverable resource manager services attachment facility (RRSAF). This is done by specifying the ATTACH(RRSAF) parameter to the precompiler. DSNRLI must be linkedited with the procedure and AMODE(31) is needed to run above the 16 MB line. Thread reuse can be used with RRSAF. This is particularly useful for any program that requires that a UR span multiple data sources.

Any program can use RRSAF rather than CAF or TSO TMP (Terminal Monitor Program). Basically, a copy of CAF was enhanced to span multiple data sources through the use of z/OS or OS/390 RRS within a commit scope. It is doubtful that there would be a significant performance difference when using RRSAF or CAF if the commit scope does not space multiple data sources.

A procedures can access the external CICS interface (EXCI) for synchronous execution of CICS transactions. The CICS MQI (Message

Queue Interface) product can be used for asynchronous execution of CICS transactions.

IMS DL/1 calls cannot be executed from a procedure. However, IMS transactions can be invoked asynchronously using MQI. The CICS EXCI can be used from a procedure synchronously to run a CICS transaction that has DL/1 calls.

SP.7 TEMPORARY TABLES

There are two types of temporary tables that can be created and manipulated much like base tables in any host program including procedures with some exceptions. There are a number of uses for temporary tables. Rows can be inserted into a temporary table as read from tables, DL/1 databases, VSAM, flat files, and other resources. Here is an example of inserting rows into a temporary table that will be created in a moment from another table.

```
INSERT INTO MIAMI_S (SN, STATUS)
   SELECT SN, STATUS
   FROM   S
   WHERE CITY = 'Miami';
```

The rows from the various sources can then be manipulated with SELECT statements. If it is necessary to select the same rows from a table more than once, consider placing the rows in a temporary table to avoid having to select the rows a second time. This is particularly important if the SELECT statement is costly to execute. If you need a varying number of values in an IN (list), consider placing values in temporary table and use an IN subselect referencing the temporary table.

Manipulation of temporary tables: You can use the INSERT and SELECT statements on temporary tables just like on base tables including joining temporary and base tables. WITH RETURN can be used when selecting from temporary tables. How UPDATE and DELETE statements can be used depends on the type of temporary table as will be discussed.

We will describe and analyze the differences between the two types of temporary tables to determine which best suites your requirements:

◆   CREATE GLOBAL TEMPORARY table

♦   DECLARE GLOBAL TEMPORARY table

Creation and Declaration of Global Temporary Tables

A global temporary table can be created like (V5):

```
CREATE GLOBAL TEMPORARY
  TABLE MIAMI_S
    (SN      CHAR(6),
     SNAME   CHAR(20),
     STATUS  SMALLINT,
     CITY    CHAR(15));
```

A declare global temporary table can be created like (V6 APAR PQ32670):

```
DECLARE GLOBAL TEMPORARY
  TABLE SESSION.NEWYORK_S
    (SN      CHAR(6),
     SNAME   CHAR(20),
     STATUS  SMALLINT,
     CITY    CHAR(15))
      ON COMMIT PRESERVE ROWS;
```

You can declare a global temporary table based on a subselect like in the following example. This does not populate the table as indicated by the clause DEFINITION ONLY.

```
DECLARE GLOBAL TEMPORARY SESSION.NEWYORK_S AS
  (SELECT SN, STATUS
   FROM   S) DEFINITION ONLY;
```

Both global and declare temporary tables can be created using the LIKE parameter:

```
CREATE GLOBAL TEMPORARY TABLE MIAMI_S
  LIKE S;

DECLARE GLOBAL TEMPORARY TABLE SESSION.NEWYORK_S
  LIKE S;
```

INCLUDING IDENTITY clause can be used with DECLARE GLOBAL TEMPORARY, not CREATE GLOBAL TEMPORARY TABLE.

Comparison of Declare & Create Global Temporary Tables

The syntax of declare and create temporary tables are similar. In general, DECLARE GLOBAL TEMPORARY is useful if heavy reuse of a subset of rows and CREATE GLOBAL TEMPORARY is useful if there is light reuse of all rows. There are some major differences in the implementation of the objects that will influence your decision as to which is appropriate for your requirements as summarized in Figure SP.4. Do pay special attention to the notes indicated in parenthesis following the Y and N.

Figure SP.4. Comparison of declare and create global temporary tables

Description	DECLARE GLOBAL TEMPORARY	CREATE GLOBAL TEMPORARY
Create database and segmented tablespace	Y (1)	N
Storage of rows	User created tablespace	DSNDB07 work tablespaces
Same table name can be used in multiple programs	N	Y (2)
Table qualifier	SESSION (3)	Like a base table
Authorization required	N (4)	Y (5)
Recorded in catalog tables	N	Y (6)
When instance of table created	Execution of DECLARE GLOBAL TEMPORARY	Open, insert, select into, or delete is issued
Can insert rows into temporary table from another table	Y	N

Description	DECLARE GLOBAL TEMPORARY	CREATE GLOBAL TEMPORARY
Create index on table	Y	N
Incremental bind at run time	Y	N
Searched DELETE and UPDATE	Y	N (7)
Retain rows in table across commit point	Y if PRESERVE N if DELETE	N (8)
Can rollback changes to last commit or savepoint (UNDO log records used)	Y (except for INSERT statements)	N

Here is a explanation of the notes on the comparison of declare and create global temporary tables:

(1) It is necessary to **CREATE DATABASE ... AS TEMP** and a segmented tablespace within the database before executing the DECLARE GLOBAL TEMPORARY statement. The size is limited by PRIQTY and SECQTY specified when the tablespace is created. Only one TEMP database can exist on a DB2 subsystem. Each member of a sysplex data sharing group must have a TEMP database if DECLARE GLOBAL TEMPORARY is used on that member. It is recommended that the FOR MEMBER clause be used to designate the member. Otherwise, the member that executes the statement is the designated member and only that member can accept DECLARE statements for the database.

(2) Each program has an instance of a create global temporary table as defined in the catalog tables (see note (6)). Various programs and executions of the same program do not have access to the same rows for both types of temporary tables.

(3) SESSION can be specified on DECLARE statement as the qualifier. If no qualifier is specified, SESSION is used. It is recommended that you reference SESSION.table_name in your SQL statements. Optionally, you can bind with QUALIFIER(SESSION). However, the qualifier applies to all

tables in the package or plan. It is likely to result in errors because most base tables do not have a qualifier of SESSION. Incremental bind processing is done for SQL referencing a declare global temporary table at run time. Processing is like using dynamic SQL except that the dynamic cache cannot be used. This is because the table does not exist at bind time. This is in contrast to create global temporary tables which can be referenced by static SQL because the temporary tables are defined in catalog tables.

(4) No, except must have select privileges on table referenced in LIKE clause if used.

(5) Yes, privileges required are similar to a base table or you can GRANT CREATETMTAB TO AUTHID.

(6) A row is inserted into SYSTABLES with TYPE = 'G' as a result of the CREATE GLOBAL TEMPORARY TABLE statement. However, each of many programs can have an instance of the table. The rows are deleted when the temporary table is dropped. You can manually update catalog statistics, otherwise default statistics are used. Statistics are useful to the optimizer in determining the table join sequence, for example. Do be cautious of the fact that the statistics apply to all instances of global temporary tables some of which can be large and others small. Regardless of whether you choose to update the statistics, the number of rows and pages are accumulated and kept in memory for use with dynamic SQL without use of the cache.

(7) There are data manipulation restrictions for global temporary tables. It is not possible to UPDATE specific rows in a create global temporary table. However, you can reference the temporary table in the WHERE clause of UPDATE of a base table. It is not possible to DELETE from a create global temporary table with a WHERE clause or WHERE CURRENT OF. However, you can DELETE FROM table with no WHERE clause. That is delete all rows in the create global temporary table.

(8) Create global temporary table rows are deleted and space freed with COMMIT (except when using CURSOR WITH HOLD), ROLLBACK, thread deallocation, and DROP TABLE. Declare global temporary tables are dropped when the thread that created the table is deallocated.

Items that apply to both types of temporary tables: Rows in a temporary table cannot be shared across multiple programs or multiple executions of the same program. There is no locking, logging, and recovery of temporary tables. Except share locks are taken on the tablespace and database used for DECLARED GLOBAL TEMPORARY TABLES. An exception regarding logging is that UNDO (not REDO) log records are used for DECLARE GLOBAL TEMPORARY TABLE. Do drop both types of temporary tables when they are no longer required to free space. There are restrictions on temporary tables in addition to those noted in Figure SP.4:

♦   Cannot define referential integrity
♦   Cannot specify a default for a column
♦   Cannot create a column declared as a ROWID or LOB (V6)
♦   Cannot create a table LIKE a declare global temporary table
♦   Cannot issue a LOCK TABLE statement on a temporary table
♦   DB2 parallelism cannot be used (true for any data in a work tablespace)
♦   DBPROTOCOL(PRIVATE) cannot be specified when binding SQL referencing temporary tables

SP.8 PREPARATION OF EXTERNAL PROCEDURES

A external stored procedure is prepared very much like any host program with a precompile, compile, linkedit into an z/OS or OS/390 load library, and bind. It is necessary to linkedit with DSNRLI when using multiple procedure address spaces established by WLM or, or DSNALI (for a static link) or DSNHLI2 (for a dynamic link) language interface module for CAF connection to ssnmSPAS when using a DB2-established procedure address space. A package (not a plan) must be used for the SQL in a procedure. A procedure must be created and recorded in the catalog before binding the package.

Reentrant procedures have advantages in that the operating system need not load a package each time it is called. Multiple tasks in a WLM-established procedures address space can share a single copy of a package which decreases the amount of virtual storage needed for code in the address space. There are also performance advantages if for example two address spaces and perhaps to two processors can work on the calling program and procedure. It is recommended that the RENT linkage editor option be used as well as the CREATE PROCEDURE ... STAY RESIDENT parameter.

A client in Dallas can develop a procedure and bind the associated DBRM into a package at the server in Rome, for example:

```
BIND PACKAGE (ROME.SPCOLLID) MEMBER (INORUP)
```

The collection (SPCOLLID in the example) can be specified in the CREATE PROCEDURE statement.. The collection of the caller is used if the column contains blank. A procedure does not require a plan when called from a client. The DDF (Distributed Data Facility) thread of a caller is used to call a procedure. The SQL CALL can be issued from a plan or package. The caller of the procedure needs to be granted privileges to execute the procedure package like:

```
GRANT EXECUTE ON PACKAGE SPCOLLID.INORUP TO
FLEUR;
```

Optionally, the privilege can be granted to the public.

Calling a Non-procedure: A module or subroutine (not a procedure) that has a package can be called from a procedure using a CALL statement (not SQL CALL). The procedure and module or subroutine packages can be in the same collection. An alternative is to use the SET CURRENT PACKAGESET to reference a collection that contains the module or subroutine before calling it. If SQL is executed from the calling procedure after calling the module or subroutine, the SET CURRENT PACKAGESET statement must be used to set the collection back to the procedure collection. If a local plan or package calls a local procedure, the PKLIST of the local plan must include the procedure package.

SP.9 SQL PROCEDURES

LANGUAGE SQL designates an SQL procedure as contrasted with an SQL external procedure developed in a host language (LANGUAGE COBOL, for example). Procedural logic can be specified within CREATE PROCEDURE statement using Basic like statements (examples will be given). SQL procedures avoid developers having to know a host language, how to embed SQL in the program, and program preparation can be done using SPB. There are two alternatives for developing an SQL procedure. The CREATE PROCEDURE statement can be developed with SQL and some procedural code. The SPB tool on DB2 Universal Database (UDB) has this support on a number of platforms including Windows 2000, ME, 98, 95, Linux, Unix, AIX, HP-UX, Solaris, UNMA-Q, OS/2, and OS/400. These stored procedures can be executed from the platform where they were developed or OS/390 and z/OS. The SQL procedure language is complied into a C procedure.

SQL Procedure Example

Following is an example of an SQL procedure that performs functions similar to the external stored procedure in Section SP.4.

```
CREATE PROCEDURE INORUP
   (IN     SN_IN       CHAR(2),
    OUT    SN          CHAR(2),
    OUT    SNAME       CHAR(20),
    OUT    STATUS      SMALLINT,
    OUT    CITY        CHAR(15),
    INOUT  OPERATION   CHAR(6),
    OUT    SQLCODEOUT  INTEGER)
LANGUAGE SQL
PINORUP: BEGIN
   DECLARE SN_IN_SP   CHAR(2);
   DECLARE SN_SP      CHAR(2);
   DECLARE SNAME_SP   CHAR(20);
   DECLARE STATUS_SP  SMALLINT;
   DECLARE CITY_SP    CHAR(15);
   DECLARE SQLCODE    INTEGER;
   DECLARE SQLSTATE   CHAR(5);

DECLARE SCURSOR CURSOR FOR
   SELECT SN, SNAME, STATUS, CITY
   FROM    S
   WHERE   SN = SN_IN;
OPEN SCURSOR;

S_LOOP: LOOP
   FETCH SCURSOR INTO SN_SP, SNAME_SP,
                  STATUS_SP, CITY_SP;
   IF SQLCODE = 0 THEN
     UPDATE S SET STATUS = STATUS_SP
     WHERE   SN = SN_IN;
     SET OPERATION   = 'UPDATE';
     SET STATUS      = STATUS_SP;
```

```
      SET SQLCODEOUT = SQLCODE;
      LEAVE S_LOOP;
   END IF;

   IF SQLCODE = 100 THEN
      INSERT INTO S(SN, SNAME, STATUS, CITY)
             VALUES(SN, SNAME, STATUS, CITY);
      SET OPERATION  = 'INSERT';
      SET SNAME      = SNAME_SP;
      SET STATUS     = STATUS_SP;
      SET CITY       = CITY_SP;
      SET SQLCODEOUT = SQLCODE;
      LEAVE S_LOOP;
   END IF;
 END LOOP;
 CLOSE SCURSOR;
 END INORUP
```

The first section in parenthesis define input and output variables for the
SQL procedure. The DECLARE statements following PINORUP: BEGIN
declares SQL variables for use within the SQL procedure. This
accomplishes the same goal as defining input and output variables for
external stored procedures discussed in Section SP.7. Notice that the
receiving variables (host variables) in the SQL are not preceded by a colon
as in a host program.

Compound Statement

A compound statement consists of one or more SQL and procedure
statements between BEGIN and END. The statements must follow the
order:

1.   SQL variable and condition declarations
2.   Cursor declarations
3.   Handler declarations
4.   Procedure body statements (CALL, CASE, IF, LOOP, REPEAT,
      WHILE, SQL, for example

BEGIN and BEGIN NOT ATOMIC does not require that all statements
before the END statement must execute successfully or all are rolled back

BEGIN ATOMIC means that all statements before the END must execute successfully or all are rolled back. This option is not supported on DB2 for z/OS or OS/390 at present.

Terminating character: The procedure body has no terminating character. If a statement is nested within other statements in the procedure body, the statement must end with a semicolon (;). If the statement is the only statement in the procedure body, the statement does not need a terminating character.

Procedural Statements for Use in SQL Procedures

Figure SP.5 summarizes procedural statements for use in SQL procedures, most of which were used in the previous example of an SQL procedure. The remaining statements will be used later in this section.

Figure SP.5. Summary of procedural statements for use in SQL procedures

Statement	Description
SET	Assigns a value to an output parameter or to an SQL variable, which is a variable that is defined and used only within a procedure body. The right side of an assignment statement can include SQL built-in functions.
IF	Selects an execution path based on the evaluation of a condition.
CASE	Selects an execution path based on the evaluation of one or more conditions. Similar to usual CASE statement.
LOOP	Executes a statement or group of statements multiple times.
REPEAT	Executes a statement or group of statements until a search condition is true.

Statement	Description
SET	Assigns a value to an output parameter or to an SQL variable, which is a variable that is defined and used only within a procedure body. The right side of an assignment statement can include SQL built-in functions.
WHILE	Repeats the execution of a statement or group of statements while a specified condition is true.
LEAVE	Transfers program control out of a loop or a block of code including a LOOP, REPEAT, and WHILE which determine where to continue processing.
GOTO	Transfers program control to a labeled statement.
GET DIAGNOSTICS	Obtains information about the previous SQL statement that was executed.

Some statements are not supported in DB2 for z/OS and OS/390 at Present. These statements are supported on other platform as summarized in Figure SP.6.

Figure SP.6. Summary of procedural statements supported on other platform than OS/390 and z/OS

Statement	Description
FOR	Method for executing a group of statements repeatedly.
SIGNAL	Method for invoking a handler or returning an SQLSTATE to invoker.
RESIGNAL	Method for repeating a signal with the same or different condition.
RETURN	For SQL functions or methods, it returns the result of the function or method. For an SQL procedure, it optionally returns an integer status value.
ITERATE	Repeat a labeled set of statements while a specified condition is true.

UPDATE with CASE Expression

A CASE expression can be used in an SQL procedure. It is particularly useful with updates to avoid having to select rows, test conditions in a host program, and execute multiple UPDATE statements for multiple conditions each of which can require a tablespace scan. Following is an example of increasing a given EMPNO (IN EMPNOIN parameter) salary. If the employee is in D1, the salary is increased by 10 percent and if they are in D2, the increase is 20 percent provided their bonus plus commission is greater than their salary.

```
CREATE PROCEDURE INCSALARY
   (IN EMPNOIN    CHAR(6))
    LANGUAGE SQL
    MODIFIES SQL DATA
    CASE WORKDEPT
       WHEN 'D1' THEN
          UPDATE EMP
          SET    SALARY = SALARY * 1.1
          WHERE  EMPNO  = EMPNOIN
```

```
            AND     BONUS + COMM > SALARY;
      WHEN 'D2' THEN
            UPDATE EMP
            SET     SALARY = SALARY * 1.2
            WHERE   EMPNO  = EMPNOIN
            AND     BONUS + COMM > SALARY;
      ELSE
            UPDATE EMP
            SET     SALARY = SALARY
            WHERE   EMPNO  = EMPNOIN;
   END CASE
END INCSALARY
```

Figure SP.7. Statements that can be used in an SQL procedure

```
DECLARE CURSOR        CALL
OPEN                  ALLOCATE*
FETCH                 ASSOCIATE*
CLOSE                 RELEASE
SELECT INTO
INSERT                CREATE
UPDATE                DROP
DELETE                RENAME
VALUES INTO*          DECLARE GLOBAL TEMPORARY TABLE
                      COMMENT ON
EXECUTE               LABEL ON
EXECUTE IMMEDIATE
PREPARE FROM          GRANT
                      REVOKE

ROLLBACK (V7)
SAVEPOINT
RELEASE SAVEPOINT
ROLLBACK TO
SAVEPOINT
LOCK TABLE

*Not supported in DB2 for OS/390 & z/OS at present
```

DECLARE Handlers

DECLARE handlers indicate the action to take if a condition is met. They
are useful in managing SQLSTATEs and SQLCODEs. It is advisable to test

the SQLSTATE in addition to the SQLCODE other than 0 and 100 for compatibility across platforms. The handles are designed to manage SQLSTATEs with a class code of '00', '01', or '02' in the first two bytes of the SQLSTATE.

Here is an example using the not_found condition handler with a fragment of previous SQL procedure definition as highlighted in bold.

```
DECLARE not_found CONDITION FOR '02000';
DECLARE SQLCODE    INTEGER;
DECLARE SQLSTATE   CHAR(5);
DECLARE SCURSOR CURSOR FOR
   SELECT SN, SNAME, STATUS, CITY
   FROM    S
   WHERE   SN = SN_IN;
DECLARE CONTINUE HANDLER FOR
   not_found SET NOROWS = 1;
OPEN SCURSOR;
   FETCH SCURSOR INTO SN_SP, SNAME_SP,
      STATUS_SP, CITY_SP;
CLOSE SCURSOR;
```

All variable names are folded to upper case (not_found becomes NOT_FOUND for example). That is names, variables, labels, etc. are not case sensitive. If you refer to an SQL procedure parameter in the procedure body, do not declare an SQL variable with a name that is the same as that parameter name.

EXIT handler can be used to end a compound statement as in the following example. Assume that RETURN_MESSAGE has been declared as an output parameter.

```
DECLARE SQLCODE    INTEGER;
DECLARE SQLSTATE   CHAR(5);
DECLARE RESOURCE_UNAVAILABLE
   CONDITION FOR '57011';
DECLARE EXIT HANDLER FOR RESOURCE_UNAVAILABLE
   SET RETURN_MESSAGE = 'Resource unavailable';
DECLARE SCURSOR CURSOR FOR
   SELECT SN, SNAME, STATUS, CITY
   FROM    S
   WHERE   SN = SN_IN;
OPEN SCURSOR;
```

```
FETCH SCURSOR INTO SN_SP, SNAME_SP,
                    STATUS_SP, CITY_SP;
CLOSE SCURSOR;
```

SQLEXCEPTION handler receives control if any SQL statement in the procedure body receives a negative SQLCODE and the execution of the procedure ends. Assume that SQLSTATEOUT has been declared as an output parameter.

```
DECLARE SQLCODE    INTEGER;
DECLARE SQLSTATE   CHAR(5);
DECLARE EXIT HANDLER FOR SQLEXCEPTION
  SET SQLSTATEOUT = SQLSTATE;
DECLARE SCURSOR CURSOR FOR
  SELECT SN, SNAME, STATUS, CITY
  FROM    S
  WHERE   SN = SN_IN;
OPEN SCURSOR;
  FETCH SCURSOR INTO SN_SP, SNAME_SP,
                    STATUS_SP, CITY_SP;
CLOSE SCURSOR;
```

DECLARE CONTINUE HANDLER FOR SQLEXCEPTION can be used to continue processing and does not end the procedure. This can be appropriate for character truncation that returns an SQLSTATE = ' 22001' and SQLCODE = -302 or numeric truncation that returns an SQLSTATE = ' 22003' and SQLCODE = -304.

DECLARE ... FOR SQLWARNING is similar to SQLEXCEPTION except it applies only to the '01' class in the first two bytes of the SQLSTATEs. If an error occurs without a defined handler, execution of compound statement is terminated. If NOT ATOMIC (not the default) is specified within a compound statement, rollback does not occur for an error within the compound statement.

WHILE Statement Used with Handler: This example shows the use of the WHILE statement in addition to a handler.

```
DECLARE at_end INT DEFAULT 0;
DECLARE SQLCODE    INTEGER;
DECLARE SQLSTATE   CHAR(5);
DECLARE SCURSOR CURSOR FOR
  SELECT SN, SNAME, STATUS, CITY
```

```
      FROM    S
      WHERE   SN = SN_IN;
OPEN SCURSOR;
WHILE at_end = 0 DO
   FETCH SCURSOR INTO SN_SP, SNAME_SP,
                         STATUS_SP, CITY_SP;
   IF SQLCODE = 100 THEN SET at_end = 1;
      END IF;
END WHILE
```

WHILE causes one or more statements to be executed until a specified condition is true. The example uses WHILE statement to fetch rows until no rows or no more rows are found in which case at_end = 1 and END WHILE is executed.

The REPEAT statement is the last SQL procedural statement for which an example has not been shown.

```
      fetch_s_loop:
►──►REPEAT
│        FETCH SCURSOR INTO SN_SP, SNAME_SP,
│                             STATUS_SP, CITY_SP;
│     UNTIL
│        SQLCODE <> 0
└──────END REPEAT fetch_s_loop
```

REPEAT can be used to execute one or more statements until a search condition is true. Condition (SQLCODE <> 0, in the example, is tested after execution of each SQL statement (FETCH SCURSOR INTO in the example). If the condition is true, the SQL procedure statement is not executed again.

The GET DIAGNOSTICS statement determines the number of rows effected by the previous INSERT, UPDATE, or DELETE statement. (It is retrieved from the third element of the array SQLERRD in the SQLCA.)

Increase the quantity of parts being used on 'J4' by 20 % as an example of the statement:

```
BEGIN
DECLARE nrows INTEGER;
UPDATE SPJ
SET QTY = QTY * 1.2
```

```
WHERE JN = 'J4';
GET DIAGNOSTICS nrows = ROW_COUNT;
END
```

The variable "nrows" contains the number of rows updated.

Stored Procedures Provided with DB2

A number of stored procedure are provided with DB2 as summarized in Figure SP.8. These procedures can be invoked with an EXEC CALL statement like any external stored procedure. Most of the procedures are used by the Control Center except as noted in the description. SDSNSAMP with procedure name as the member name gives parameters required to invoke the procedure.

Figure SP.8. Stored procedures provided with DB2

Name	Description
DSNTPSMP*	Does program preparation and populates the catalog table describing SQL procedures.
DSNACCMG*	Can format SQLCA similar to DSNTIAR
DSNACCQC	Provides statistics to aid in determining when utilities should be executed including statistics can be obtained with SELECT statements in RR.
DSNACCAV	Similar to above DSNACCQC except provides statistics on partitioned tablespaces.
DSNUTILS	Can invoke utilities from a local or remote client program.
DSNACCMD	Can execute DB2 commands.
DSNWZP	Can return normal and hidden DSNZPARMs and V6 DSNHDECP values. Used by Visual Explain and WLM_REFRESH.

DSNWSPM	Can retrieve performance statistics such as SQL CPU time.
DSNACCDE	Can determine if a data set exists.
DSNACCDL	Can list data sets.
DSNACCDR	Can rename data sets.
DSNACCDD	Can delete data sets.
DSNACCDS	Can create, append to, or replace LRECL=80, RECFM=FB PDSE data set members or PS data sets.
WLM_ REFRESH	Can refresh a WLM environment from a remote workstation and recycle the environment in which it runs, as well as any other WLM environment.
INSTALL_ JAR	Can install a set of Java classes into the current SQL catalog and schema.
REPLACE_ JAR	Can replace a previously installed jar.
REMOVE_ JAR	Can remove a Java jar file and its classes from a specified catalog.

*Not used by Control Center

Preparation of SQL Procedures

There are two basic tasks in the preparation of SQL procedures. You must create a load module and package. This is done by preprocessing the CREATE PROCEDURE statement which generates a C language source program. The CREATE PROCEDURE cannot be executed dynamically using SPUFI or QMF, for example. This applies to SQL procedures (not external procedures). JCL or the SPB is required. The C program is precompiled which generates the DBRM member with the coded SQL and the modified C program (discussed in Chapter PE). The DBRM member must be bound into a package.

The second task is to the define the procedure to DB2 which is done through the execution of the CREATE PROCEDURE statement in V6. If you are

SP 695

using the SPB, the statement is generated and executed automatically for you. In V5, it is necessary to insert a row into the SYSPROCEDURES catalog describing the procedure as described in Section SP.9.

JCL for Preparation of SQL Procedures without the SPB is in the SDSNSAMP library. The member DSNHPSM preprocesses the CREATE PROCEDURE statement. It reads only one statement from a partitioned data set member. It proceeds the C language source program The name of the program is the first 8 bytes of SQL procedure name by default. The name of the program, DBRM, and C load module must be the same. Do exercise caution if you override the defaults. The JCL produces an INSERT statement for defining the procedure in SYSPROCEDURES when using V5.

The SDSNSAMP library contains a number of useful members:

DSNHSQL contains JCL which preprocesses, precompiles, compiles, prelink-edits, and link-edits an SQL procedure.

DSNTEJ63 contains JCL to invoke the JCL procedure and DSNHSQL to prepare the SQL procedure DSN8ES1 for execution.

DSN8ES1 contains an SQL procedure that accepts a department number as input and returns a result set that contains salary information for each employee in that department.

DSNTEJ64 contains JCL which prepare the client program DSN8ED3 for execution.

DSN8ED3 contains a C program that calls SQL procedure DSN8ES1. It precompiles the C program generated by DSNHPSM which produces the DBRM containing SQL and the modified C language program. It is then necessary to compile and link-edit the modified C program which produces an executable C language program. The DBRM must be bound into a package (not a plan).

The INSERT INTO SYSPROCEDURES statement produced by DSNHPSM must be executed (V5). But before you execute the statement, do modify the statement if required. For example, change the LOADMOD name if it was changed from the default.

Stored Procedure Builder

The SPB is useful in creating and managing procedures using the SQL procedure language, JAVA, or REXX. The GUI interface provides for being prompted to build procedures as well as viewing and edit generated procedure code. A sample SPB screen is shown in Figure SP.9. You can copy and paste stored procedures across connections. Procedures can be run from the SPB with or without customizing settings to enable remote debugging of installed stored procedures. It generates a C program and package through program preparation managed by the SPB. It can run on Windows 2000, ME, NT, 98, 95, AIX, Solaris, OS/2, AS/400, and other platforms in the future.

Figure SP.9. Sample SPB screen

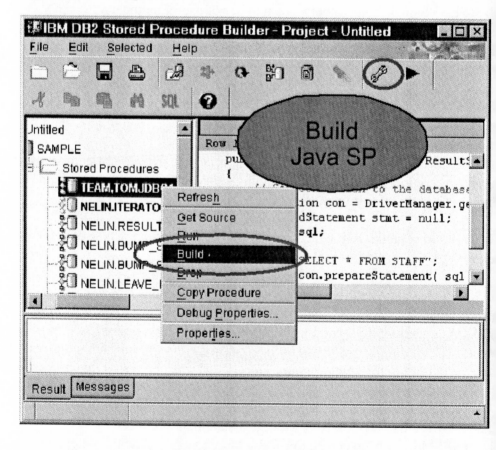

The SPB invokes DSNTPSMP (REXX procedure) using the TSO attach which performs similar steps as described in the previous subsection. DSNTPSMP requires a dedicated WLM-established procedure address

pace. Do not attempt to run multiple copies of DSNTPSMP concurrently.
Optionally, you can use RRSAF (V6 APAR PQ24199).

Optionally, you can use call the DSNTPSMP procedure directly from a
program after setting up the environment as described in V6 APAR
PQ30492.

SP.10 UPDATING SYSPROCEDURES V5

Rows must be inserted into SYSPROCEDURES describing each procedure
to be called prior to V6. DB2 only reads this catalog table, it does not
maintain it in any way. You can use the INSERT, UPDATE, DELETE
statements on the table or LOAD rows as with an application table. Figure
SP.10 is a sample INSERT statement to describe the INORUP procedure.

Figure SP.10. Describe a procedure in SYSPROCEDURES

```
INSERT INTO SYSIBM.SYSPROCEDURES
    (PROCEDURE, AUTHID, LUNAME, LOADMOD,
    LINKAGE, COLLID, LANGUAGE, ASUTIME,
    STAYRESIDENT, IBMREQD, RUNOPTS, PARMLIST)
VALUES
    ('INORUP', ' ', ' ', 'INORUP', ' ',
    'SPCOLLID', 'COBOL', 0, ' ', 'N', ' ',
    'SN-IN CHAR(2)   IN,   SN CHAR(2) OUT,
    SNAME CHAR(20) OUT, STATUS SMALLINT OUT,
    CITY   CHAR(15) OUT,
    OPERATION CHAR(6) INOUT,
    SCODE SMALLINT OUT');
```

The columns of SYSPROCEDURES are descriptive of their meaning. The
first column, PROCEDURE, must contain the name of the procedure. The
AUTHID column can contain the authorization identifier of the caller of the
procedure. The example in Figure SP.10 shows the insertion of a blank in
the column which indicates that any AUTHID can call the procedure. The
LUNAME column is also blank in the example, indicating that the
procedure can be called from any location. Multiple rows can be inserted
describing a procedure, one for each of many AUTHIDs and LUNAMEs
that can call a procedure. The columns PROCEDURE, AUTHID, and
LUNAME uniquely identify the rows and make up the primary key of
SYSPROCEDURES.

LOADMOD must contain the name of the load module for the procedure. The column can be updated to reflect the version to be used when the procedure is called. LINKAGE of blank means that output parameters can be null but input parameters cannot be null. COLLID contains the name of the collection (SPCOLLID in the example) where the procedure package can be found on the server. LANGUAGE indicates that the procedure is written in COBOL.

The ASUTIME is useful in controlling the amount of CPU time that can be used by host language code plus that used by static SQL and dynamic SQL. The maximum resources that can be used before the procedure is cancelled are given in service units like those specified in the resource limit table (Chapter PP).

STAYRESIDENT of yes is a good choice if the procedure will be executed frequently rather than using the default of blank shown in the example. You will probably want the procedure to run above the 16 MB line and can specify this by using the RUNOPTS of HEAP(,,ANY),STACK(,,ANY,),STORAGE(,,,4K), BELOWHEAP(4K,,), LIBSTACK(4K,,),ALL31(ON), linkedit with AMODE(31), RMODE(ANY), and compile a COBOL procedure with RES and DATA(31).

The last column in SP.10, PARMLIST, provides for specifying the names, data types, and lengths of parameters, and whether they are input, output, or both input and output to the procedure such as:

♦   IN (input only to the procedure)
♦   OUT (output only from the procedure)
♦   INOUT (input and output to the procedure)

Most data types and lengths can be specified similar to when creating a table (Chapter CT) with some exceptions. DATE, TIME, and TIMESTAMP are *not* valid data type declarations prior to V6. These data types must be declared as CHAR data similar to the data type used for host variables that receive columns from a table. The date and time must have a valid format if the parameter is to be used in an SQL statement. For example, a valid International Standards Organization (ISO) date format is '1999-04-02'.

More columns can be specified than are shown in the Figure SP.10 example. The RESULT_SETS column allows for specifying the maximum number of result sets that can be returned from the procedure. Procedures are run in a DB2-established procedures address space by default. The WLM_ENV column provides for naming the application environment to be used by the WLM to manage the procedure in one of multiple address spaces. PGM_TYPE provides for specifying that the procedure consists of a subroutine rather the a main program. Development of a procedure as a subroutine or module has performance advantages over developing it as a main program.

EXTERNAL_SECURITY of yes means that a RACF environment will be automatically created by DB2 each time the procedure is invoked so that RACF can manage access to non-SQL resources. The default of no has performance advantages and is a good choice if access to non-SQL resources is not required.

COMMIT_ON_RETURN of yes means that the unit of recovery is automatically committed when control is returned successfully to the calling program. This has performance advantages in that it reduces message traffic and ensures that locks are released in a timely fashion. It reduced the transaction rate from 76.7 to 64.7 transactions per second in one case.

A summary of the column definitions in SYSPROCEDURES are shown in Figure SP.11.

Figure SP.11. Definition of columns in SYSIBM.SYSPROCEDURES

Column/Data Type	Description
PROCEDURE* CHAR(18) NOT NULL	Name of procedure used in SQL CALL statement.
AUTHID* CHAR(8) NOT NULL WITH DEFAULT	AUTHID of user running the program issuing the SQL CALL. AUTHID after any outbound or inbound translation. blank = Row applies to all AUTHIDs.

Column/Data Type	Description
LUNAME* CHAR(8) NOT NULL WITH DEFAULT	blank = Row applies to all callers of the procedure (default). Can specify LUNAME of remote or local LUNAME for which this row applies.
LOADMOD** CHAR(8) NOT NULL	Member name of procedure load module.
LINKAGE CHAR(1) NOT NULL WITH DEFAULT	blank = SIMPLE linkage convention is used where input parameters cannot be null. Output parameter can be null. N = SIMPLE WITH NULL, caller can supply null values for any of the parameters defined in PARMLIST (required by SQL procedures).
COLLID CHAR(18) NOT NULL	Name of package collection containing SQL for the procedure. blank = Uses the same collection name as the calling package or SET CURRENT PACKAGESET collection is used.
LANGUAGE CHAR(8) NOT NULL	'COBOL', 'PLI', 'C', or 'ASSEMBLE' describes the host language used in the procedure.

Column/Data Type	Description
ASUTIME INTEGER NOT NULL WITH DEFAULT	Maximum number of service units that can be used before the procedure is canceled. Includes CPU time used for host language code, static, and dynamic SQL. 0 = No limit.
STAYRESIDENT CHAR(1) NOT NULL WITH DEFAULT	blank = Load module is deleted from memory after the procedure ends if LE Release 3 is available. 'Y' = Load module remains resident in memory after the procedure ends. Should be reentrant.
IBMREQD CHAR(1) NOT NULL	'Y' = Row came from basic machine readable material (MRM) tape. 'N' = Did not come from MRM.
RUNOPTS*** VARCHAR(254) NOT NULL	blank = Default LE runtime options. 'MSGFILE(OUTFILE), RPTSTG(ON), RPTOPTS(ON)' is an example of LE runtime options.
PARMLIST VARCHAR(3000) NOT NULL	Parameter list expected by the procedure.
RESULT_SETS SMALLINT NOT NULL WITH DEFAULT	Maximum number of result sets that can be returned by this procedure. Default is 0, no results sets will be returned (DB2 and WLM owns).

Column/Data Type	Description
WLM_ENV CHAR(18) NOT NULL WITH DEFAULT	Blank = Procedure is run in the DB2-established procedures address space (default). Can name application environment with associated JCL to be used for procedure (WLM owns).
PGM_TYPE CHAR(1) WITH DEFAULT 'M'	M = Procedure is a main program (default) and is required for DB2-established address space. S = Procedure is a subroutine and can be used with WLM-established address space (WLM owns).
EXTERNAL_SECURITY CHAR(1) NOT NULL WITH DEFAULT 'N'	N (default) - RACF access to non-SQL resources is not required. Good choice if procedure only accesses SQL objects. Y - RACF environment should be automatically created by DB2 each time the procedure is invoked so that RACF can manage access to non-SQL resources (WLM owns).

Column/Data Type	Description
COMMIT_ON_RETURN CHAR(1) WITH DEFAULT 'N'	N = UR is not to be committed upon successful return (non-negative SQLCODE) from the procedure (default). Y = UR is to be committed upon successful return (non-negative SQLCODE) from the procedure. Reduces message traffic and ensures that locks are released in a timely fashion (DB2 and WLM owns).

*   PROCEDURE, AUTHID, and LUNAME uniquely identify the row. Multiple rows can be inserted, allowing multiple AUTHIDs and LUNAMEs to call the procedure.

** Procedure version is associated with the load module name. SYSPROCEDURES.LOADMOD can be updated to reflect the version to be used when the procedure is called.

*** If program can run above the 16 MB line, use RUNOPTS:
   ▸   HEAP(,,ANY),STACK(,,ANY,),STORAGE(,,,4K), BELOWHEAP(4K,,),LIBSTACK(4K,,),ALL31(ON)
   ▸   Linkedit with AMODE(31), RMODE(ANY)
   ▸   Compile COBOL with RES and DATA(31)

SP.11 PROCEDURE ADDRESS SPACES

In this section we will look at how procedures can run in a single address space established by DB2 or multiple address spaces managed by z/OS or OS/390 WLM, and how priorities can be assigned. We will also look at the interaction of the caller of a procedure, the DB2 subsystem, and a procedure address space.

DB2-Established Address Space

The DB2-established procedure address space is an allied address space with the name of ssnmSPAS where "ssn" is the DB2 subsystem name, "m" is a subsystem identifier, and "SPAS" represents procedure address space. In this environment, procedures are executed in a FIFO (First-In-First-Out) sequence as they are called under the priority assigned to the ssnmSPAS address space. The systems administrator can start/stop the address space without restarting DB2. If the address space is not explicitly started, DB2 issues an z/OS or OS/390 START command to activate ssnmSPAS when the first procedure is executed. DB2 START, STOP, and DISPLAY commands can be used to manage procedures and the ssnmSPAS address space. JCL generated during installation can be customized, to include other program libraries, additional DD statements required by procedures, and the region size which can be increased from the default of 2,048 KB.

Multiple procedures can be run concurrently in the ssnmSPAS address space. If a procedure is to be called from multiple programs, it should be reentrant. (The RENT linkage editor option should be used.) If a procedure is *not* reentrant and STAYRESIDENT = ' ', the load module is loaded for each SQL CALL. This can require an excessive amount of space in the address space.

Eight concurrent task control blocks (TCB) can run procedures by default and a maximum of 1,000 can be specified on the installation panel DSNTIPB. You probably want less than 50 procedures running in the address space. Each procedure requires 100 KB of storage below the 16 MB line for each concurrently executing TCB when using LE V3.

Address Spaces Managed by Work Load Manager

Multiple procedure address spaces established and managed by z/OS or OS/390 WLM have advantages. Multiple address spaces provide for dedicating high priority procedures to an address space with a high priority. A single procedure or group of procedures can be assigned to specific address spaces with the appropriate priority. The assigned priority applies to the execution of host language and SQL code. Procedures can also be isolated so that one procedure does not abend and cause another to abend.

Priority of Procedure Threads

An z/OS or OS/390 enclave provides for assigning individual dispatching priorities to a single thread or group of threads used by procedures and DDF. (An enclave is a special kind of z/OS or OS/390 service request block (SRB) that behaves like a TCB.) WLM can be used to assign priorities using goal or compatibility mode. Goal mode provides for defining priorities in terms of the required response time for a given percentage of the time. For example, PROGA should execute in less than two seconds 80 percent of the time. WLM can be used to generate and shut down procedure address spaces based on assigned priorities, the work load, and service classes. When using compatibility mode, the priority is defined in SYS1.PARMLIB using a service class (SRVCLASS) and the systems administrator must manage the address spaces with z/OS or OS/390 commands. A locally called procedure inherits the priority of the caller (CICS, TSO, etc. for example).

Threads can be classified into different service classes by plan, package, AUTHID and LUNAME, and performance periods can be used. Period aging enables short running work to run at a high priority and long running work drops to a lower priority after using a designated number of service units. For example, assume that the following periods have been assigned the indicated service units:

◆   Period 1:   100000 service units
◆   Period 2: 1000000 service units
◆   Period 3: to end of transaction

Once a task uses 100000 service units, its priority will be dropped until it uses 1000000 services units after which its priority will be dropped again and remain there until the end of the transaction. Do be cautious of continuously active threads, they can go to a higher period and remain there even though there is a good deal of think time on behalf of the user.

Managing WLM Address Spaces

WLM panels are used to associate the application environment name specified in the WLM ENVIRONMENT parameter of the CREATE PROCEDURE statement. z/OS or OS/390 WLM commands are used to start, stop, and display information on the WLM application environment when using goal mode. z/OS or OS/390 commands are used to manage the address spaces when compatibility mode is used. DB2 commands are used to start, stop, and display information on procedures within the environment.

It is advisable to avoid having WLM create too many procedure address spaces by minimizing the number of WLM environments and z/OS or OS/390 service classes. WLM creates an address space for each combination of WLM environment name and service class when a procedure is executed unless a particular environment or service class is not used for a long period of time. For example, if there are seven environment names and each one has four possible service classes, and all of the combinations are used, it is possible to have 28 procedure address spaces.

Interaction of Address Spaces

There are a number of steps required to execute a procedure as summarized in Figure SP.12. Each of these steps is described assuming a DB2-established procedure address space.

Figure SP.12. Interaction of address spaces

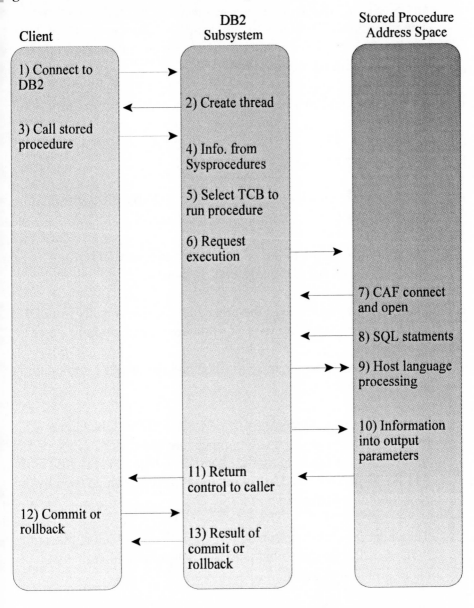

1)   A connection between the caller at the client site and the DB2
       subsystem is established.

2)   A thread is created for the execution of the procedure.

3)   A request to run the procedure is made to DB2 based on the SQL
       CALL issued by the client.

4)   DB2 gets information about the procedure from the SYSROUTINES and SYSPARMS catalog tables as placed there by the developer. The information is cached to avoid further access to the table. DB2 verifies that the client is authorized to execute the package associated with the procedure.

5)   An z/OS or OS/390 TCB is selected under which to run the procedure.

6)   DB2 requests execution of the procedure.

7)   The procedure attach code issues a CAF CONNECT to the DB2 subsystem and opens (allocates) the package.

8)   The SQL statements in the procedure are executed in DB2 alternating with host language code in step 9).

9)   The host language code in the procedure receives results from DB2 and executes alternating with SQL statement execution in step 8).

10)   The SQL CALL parameters are filled and the results returned to the client program.

11)   Control is returned from the procedure to DB2 and the client program. All cursors opened by procedure are closed. (Cursors can be left open for fetching by the client when using WITH RETURN and WLM procedure address spaces.) Working storage used by the procedure is reclaimed.

12)   The client program issues a commit or rollback which applies to SQL issued in the procedure and any SQL issued directly by the client program as a UR.

13)   The result of the commit or rollback is returned to client program. This last message can be eliminated when using WLM address spaces and COMMIT ON RETURN YES on the CREATE PROCEDURE statement.

If the procedure abends, a -935 SQLCODE is returned to the client and the client's UR is rolled back.

Data is returned to the client program using block fetch. Block fetch means that up to 32 KB of data is accumulated, formatted, and transmitted to the client. In order to use block fetch, the cursor must be read-only or ambiguous with CURRENTDATA of NO specified with a bind. The effect of OPTIMIZE FOR *n* ROWS is discussed in Chapter PD and PP.

Timeout of a Client

A distributed user (thread) which is inactive, holding a lock, and has not committed can be timed out by specifying a timeout period in seconds on the installation panel DSNTIPR (no timeout is the default). If the specified time limit is exceeded, a rollback occurs and all resources are released. This does not apply to an inactive thread that is not holding a lock and indoubt threads. If a requester thread is terminated, DB2 effectively issues a CANCEL DDF THREAD command. This avoids using resources to derive results that cannot be transmitted to the requester.

SP.12 COMMANDS FOR CONTROLLING PROCEDURES

DB2 START, STOP, and DISPLAY commands are used to manage procedures. These commands are also used to manage the DB2-established procedure address space. z/OS or OS/390 WLM commands are used to manage WLM procedure address spaces with goal mode. z/OS or OS/390 commands are used with compatibility mode. In this section we will describe the DB2 commands used to manage procedures in any address space and in the DB2-established procedure address space.

START Command

A START command can be used to start a procedure like:

```
-START PROCEDURE (INORUP, SPJ*)
```

Specific procedures can be listed, or leading characters of procedures (SPJ*, for example) can be used, or '*.*' can be used to indicate that all procedures are to be started. Optionally, you can specify the schema or qualifier (GKWADM.INORUP, for example).

It is not necessary to start a procedure. A procedure is started automatically when it is called regardless of whether it is a newly defined procedure or one that has existed for some time.

The START command is not necessary in V6 to refresh the cache because the ALTER and DROP commands do this. You may also want to start frequently executed procedures after starting DB2 to avoid the overhead of caching the information from the catalog tables when the procedures are first called. Another reason for using the START command is to activate a stopped procedure.

The START command does not refresh LE when using WLM-established address spaces. The use of the following command refreshes the LE environment and load module. This applies to UDF as well.

```
MVS VARY WLM,APPLENV=applenv,REFRESH
```

Additional commands for managing WLM-established address spaces are described in the *Administration Guide* manual.

STOP Command

Procedures can be stopped using a format similar to the START command -- specific procedures can be named or "*.*" can be used. Any currently running, queued, and scheduled procedures will complete execution. Here is an example of stopping the INORUP procedure.

```
-STOP PROCEDURE(INORUP) ACTION(QUEUE)
```

The ACTION(QUEUE) parameter means that all requests to execute the procedure will be queued for 180 seconds by default. If this does not give adequate time to make required changes, the timeout value can be made more generous -- up to 1800 seconds or no limit can be specified on the installation panel DSNTIPX or DSNZPARM STORMXAB. The START command can be used to start the procedure at any time.

If it is necessary to stop the procedure without queuing requests, the ACTION(REJECT) parameter can be used to reject all requests for the procedure.

It may be necessary to stop a procedure that is not running correctly, to add or replace a procedure load module, or to allow for compression of the load library.

If a procedure exceeds the abend count specified on the installation panel DSNTIPX, calls to the procedure will be rejected. The abend count is 0 by default with a maximum of 225. The first abend of a procedure results in additional calls being rejected until the procedure is explicitly started. This may be appropriate in a production environment but is rather severe in a test environment. Some one will receive a good many calls to start a procedure that has abended during initial testing. Do consider increasing the count, particularly in a test environment.

Permanently Stopping a Procedure: The STOP command does not permanently stop a procedure. If DB2 is stopped and started, a procedure that has been stopped can be executed. Permanently stopping a procedure can be accomplished by dropping the procedure, altering the EXTERNAL NAME (name of load module), or renaming or deleting the load module from load library.

DISPLAY Command

Information about procedures can be determined by using the DISPLAY command like:

```
-DISPLAY PROCEDURE (*)
```

One can name specific procedures or use "*.*" as with the START and STOP command. The commands can be used with user-defined functions provided that the specific name is used (discussed in Chapter UD).

Figure SP.13 is an example of the results of the DISPLAY commands. Optionally you can display information about user-defined functions by keying -DISPLAY FUNCTION SPECIFIC (specific name).

Figure SP.13. Example Result of -DISPLAY PROCEDURE (*)

```
DSNX940I csect - DISPLAY PROCEDURE REPORT FOLLOWS -
PROCEDURE  MODULE    STATUS   ACTIVE    MAXACT   QUEUED   MAXQUE  TIMEOU
SPJSP01    SPJMOD01  STARTED    0          1        0        1
SPJSP02    SPJMOD02  STOPQUE    0          2        5        5
SPJSP03    SPJMOD03  STARTED    2          2        0        6
SPJSP04    SPJMOD04  STOPREJ    0          1        0        1
PROCEDURES A THROUGH Z9999999999999999 HAVE BEEN STOPPED WITH
   ACTION(QUEUE)
DISPLAY PROCEDURE REPORT COMPLETE

Brief description of each column in the report:

  PROCEDURE = Name of procedure
  MODULE  = Name of load module
  STATUS  = Started, stopped and queued, stopped and rejected
  ACTIVE  = Number of threads currently running the load module
  MAXACT  = Maximum number of threads that have run the load
            module concurrently since DB2 was started
  QUEUED  = Number of threads that are waiting for the
            procedure to be scheduled
  MAXQUE  = Maximum number of threads that have waited
            concurrently for the procedure to be scheduled
            since DB2 was started
  TIMEOUT = Number of times an SQL CALL statement timed out
            while waiting for a request for the procedure
            to be scheduled
```

The DISPLAY THREAD command also provides information on procedures. SW means that the thread is waiting for a procedure to be scheduled. SP means that the thread is executing within a procedure.

SP.13 SUMMARY

A primary advantage of a procedure is to reduce the number of messages transmitted in a client/server environment. Another significant advantage of procedures is the ability of manage client processes centrally and minimize maintenance at client sites.

Procedures are straightforward to develop because the same host languages can be used as in developing any host program with embedded SQL statements. Cursors can be defined and opened in a procedure, and fetched from the calling program in any order after a locator host variable is declared, associated, and allocated for each cursor.

The SPB is a good choice for those not versed in host languages and for quickly developing a procedure and getting it in production.

Multiple address spaces can be managed by WLM or a DB2-established address space can be used.

START, STOP, and DISPLAY commands provide for managing procedures. Commands used for managing the procedure address spaces depends on the environment.

EXERCISES

1. What are two primary advantages of procedures?

2. What are the differences in developing a procedure and preparing it compared to a subroutine or module?

3. What are the differences in calling a procedure compared to calling a subroutine or module?

4. What is a primary prerequisite to ensure that all changes to DB2 tables, DL/1 databases, recoverable VSAM files, and MQSeries messages are made or no changes are made when a COMMIT statement is executed?

5. Are there any restrictions on selecting and changing rows in a global temporary table compared to a base table?

6. Why should null indicator variables be used in the parameter list of an SQL CALL statement?

7. How does one specify that a procedure is to be executed in a WLM procedure address space?

8. ASUTIME in SYSROUTINES provides for limiting the number of service units used for what type of processing in a procedure?

9. If a procedure abends, how is the client program notified?

10. The START, STOP, and DISPLAY DB2 commands are used to manage which resources?

ANSWERS

1. The two primary advantages of procedures are to reduce network traffic and provide for managing client processes centrally.

2. There are very few differences in developing a procedure and preparing it compared to a subroutine or module. The differences are that a cursor should not be closed before the procedure ends when using WITH RETURN. It is necessary to describe the procedure to DB2 using the CREATE PROCEDURE statement, and it is necessary to bind the SQL into a package (not a plan).

3. There are basically no differences between calling a procedure compared to calling a subroutine or module with the exceptions that it is necessary to use an EXEC SQL CALL rather than a CALL statement and the procedure name is a three part name (location, server name, and procedure name).

4. A primary prerequisite to ensure that all changes to DB2 tables, DL/1 databases, recoverable VSAM files, and MQSeries messages are made or no changes are made is the use of WLM procedure address spaces.

5. There are no restrictions on selecting rows in a global temporary table compared to a base table. Rows can be inserted into a temporary table. Specific rows identified in a WHERE clause cannot be deleted from a temporary table although all rows can be deleted without a WHERE clause. Rows cannot be updated in a temporary table although a temporary table can be referenced in the WHERE clause of an UPDATE statement on a base table.

6. Message traffic can be reduced by specifying a null indicator variable when values are frequently not specified for a parameter in the SQL CALL statement. If the null indicator variable is a negative value, DB2 does not transmit the content of the parameter.

7. The fact that a procedure is to be executed in a WLM procedure address space is specified by naming the application environment using the WLM ENVIRONMENT parameter of the CREATE PROCEDURE statement.

8. ASUTIME in SYSROUTINES provides for limiting the total number of service units used for host language code, static SQL, and dynamic SQL.

9. If a procedure abends, the client program is notified with a negative SQLCODE (-935).

10. The START, STOP, and DISPLAY DB2 commands are used to manage procedures in any address space.

FIGURES

Printed in the United States
5601